The Wrong Guys

The Wrong Guys

MURDER, FALSE CONFESSIONS, AND THE NORFOLK FOUR

TOM WELLS AND RICHARD A. LEO

THE NEW PRESS

NEW YORK
LONDON

Requests for permission to reproduce selections from this book should be mailed to:
Permissions Department, The New Press, 38 Greene Street, New York, NY 10013.

Published in the United States by The New Press, New York, 2008
Distributed by W. W. Norton & Company, Inc., New York

LIBRARY OF CONGRESS CATALOGING-IN-PUBLICATION DATA

Wells, Tom, 1955–
The wrong guys : murder, false confessions, and the Norfolk Four /
Tom Wells and Richard A. Leo.
p. cm.
Includes bibliographical references and index.
ISBN 978-1-59558-401-4 (hc.)
1. Bosko, Michelle, d. 1997. 2. Murder—Virginia—Norfolk—Case studies.
3. Rape—Virginia—Norfolk—Case studies. 4. Murder—Investigation—
Virginia—Norfolk. I. Leo, Richard A., 1963– II. Title.
HV6534.N878W45 2008
364.152'3092—dc22
2008014401

The New Press was established in 1990 as a not-for-profit alternative to the large,
commercial publishing houses currently dominating the book publishing industry.
The New Press operates in the public interest rather than for private gain, and is
committed to publishing, in innovative ways, works of educational, cultural,
and community value that are often deemed insufficiently profitable.

www.thenewpress.com

Composition by NK Graphics
This book was set in Minion

Printed in the United States of America

2   4   6   8   10   9   7   5   3   1

To my wife, Lisa Bryant, and my son, Willie Wells

—Tom Wells

To Kate Germond, Jim McCloskey, Peter Neufeld,
and Barry Scheck for their efforts to free the innocent

—Richard A. Leo

Contents

Foreword

DONALD S. CONNERY

The story you are about to read is true.

That's a shame. A national shame.

It would be comforting to think that *The Wrong Guys* is fiction. Surely this saga of serial injustices is too implausible to have actually occurred.

Think again. And fasten your seat belts. The story told by Tom Wells and Richard A. Leo is all too real. They are meticulous in setting down the facts and reporting the fate of ordinary people caught up in one of the most bizarre and complex miscarriages of justice in history.

What happened to the seven men wrongly accused of rape and murder in Norfolk, Virginia—especially the four who went to prison—is the present-day equivalent of such insanities as the Salem "witch trials" of the 1690s, the ordeal of Alabama's Scottsboro Boys in the 1930s, and the epidemic of false sex abuse accusations that broke out in Wenatchee, Washington, in the 1990s.

In my previous life, I was a Cold War foreign correspondent. Living in the Soviet Union and reporting from other places where the rule of force always trumped the rule of law, I was accustomed to the reality of bewildered good citizens suddenly snatched from their homes, soon to disappear into a merciless system of injustice.

In 1973, having returned to the United States and its civil rights protections, I made a sharp career turn because of the Peter Reilly case, a nationally publicized false-confession drama played out close to my home in Connecticut. I was shaken by my sudden immersion in a topsy-turvy world where self-deluded authorities, abandoning common sense as well as any sense of decency, were all too willing to destroy a blameless teenager while giving a killer a free pass. The powerful interrogation-room psychological pressures on eighteen-year-old Reilly led him to believe that he had "blacked out" his memory of murdering his mother. His "confession" was composed of detailed fantasies. He was later exonerated.

In the decades since then, I have tracked wrongful conviction cases all across the country, most of them involving coerced false confessions, yet I have found none so reeking with absurdities committed by those sworn to uphold the law as the catastrophe described in this work.

Given the privilege of reading the manuscript before it went to press, my mind ignited with a host of images: The blind leading the blind. A pile-up of vehicles on a highway shrouded by fog. The slow fall of the Japanese train at the end of *The Bridge on the River Kwai* and the bewildered British colonel asking, "What have I done?"

I thought too of Joseph Conrad's *Heart of Darkness* and the perils of venturing into the unknown. It seems to me that readers of this book are being asked to journey upriver to the deepest malignancy of our justice system: the all-too-common failure of the responsible legal authorities to put things right when they are so clearly wrong and must realize they are wrong.

Until the beginning of the DNA revolution in the mid-1980s, it was both the pretense of the justice system and a common assumption that wrongful imprisonments were rare and false confessions rarer still. These days we know better. With DNA exonerations of the innocent multiplying (along with DNA convictions of the guilty), and with Innocence Projects sprouting like dandelions all across the land, we have learned that mistakes by the system are of a magnitude far greater than anyone imagined. The wrongly convicted in America's prisons number not in the hundreds or thousands but in the many tens of thousands.

There is now, at last, a widespread awareness of the reasons why this is so: everything from the frequent police rush to judgment with the most convenient suspect and the zealotry of ego-driven prosecutors to flawed eyewitness testimony, coerced false confessions, "junk science," incompetent defense lawyers, uncaring judges, political pressures, and more.

What is valuable about the Norfolk case is that it incorporates, as a perfect storm, so many of these elements. To know what happened to the accused in this story is to understand what occurs all too often in every state to falsely accused men and women whose despair never makes the headlines or the evening news.

They are America's "disappeared." Most of them are doomed because they are invisible.

They have no hope of rescue.

In that sense, then, ridiculous as the thought may seem, "the wrong guys" in this story are the lucky ones. This book puts them in plain sight for the whole nation to see.

The Wrong Guys

1
Discovery

When the USS *Simpson* pulled up at the pier in Norfolk, Billy Bosko had expected to see his wife waiting for him. She was usually there to greet him when he returned from a cruise. Before he'd left this time, she'd promised to be there unless she had to start her new job. Michelle had been hired at McDonalds, where she'd worked earlier in Pittsburgh, her hometown. "She didn't know for sure" when she was going to start, Bosko recounted later, "but if possible she was going to meet me on the pier."[1]

Bosko, an attractive nineteen-year-old with jet-black hair, long eyelashes, and a well-proportioned frame, had been gone for almost a week. His eighteen-year-old wife had spent much of a day cooking a big dinner for him the night before he'd left. He was on duty, so she'd brought it to him on board his ship. "Don't worry, toots," he'd told her. He'd be back soon: "Be ready for when I get home." She'd smiled at that.[2]

But, at the pier, Michelle was not to be seen. She must have started work, Bosko tried to persuade himself. He and his shipmates had to shore up, but after they had knocked off over an hour later, he grabbed his bags, hailed a cab, and headed for his apartment right outside gate four of the Norfolk Naval Air Station. Neither Billy nor Michelle had a car; Michelle didn't even have a driver's license.[3]

They had moved into the apartment only five and a half weeks earlier. It was a low-rent one bedroom: apartment F-111 at 254 West Bay Avenue in the two-story, redbrick Bayshore Gardens complex. The apartment was all of about seven hundred square feet. Lots of other young navy people lived in the complex. Country and western music could often be heard outside, coming from one of the units. "I was primarily looking for a safe place for her because I knew I was going to be out to sea a lot," Billy later testified. Before signing the lease, he had asked about crime and been told the neighborhood was relatively safe, with hardly any violent crime. "It wasn't a bad area," confirms one longtime Norfolk civic activist. "Not a hot spot for drug activity."[4]

Billy and Michelle's apartment was on the first floor of their building. There were three other units on their floor—two on each side of a common hallway—and four more on the second floor. A few linoleum tiles were missing in the common hallway; the stairway up to the second floor was run-down. When they first moved in, they found a dirty toilet and a dirty bathroom sink; tiles were missing around the bathtub, and the bathroom towel rack was broken. That first week in the apartment, the oven broke. But they'd wed only weeks earlier and "we were so proud of ourselves because we were making it; we were doing it by ourselves, and no one was helping us," Bosko recalled. "And you look at our apartment—we don't have a whole lot, but we were proud of what we had because we both worked to get it." "It was their first apartment, so it was the greatest thing," Michelle's close friend Erin Litle remembers.[5]

Michelle's parents were not as pleased. Pretty and petite, with a pleasant and caring nature, Michelle was an innocent and sheltered girl who'd been raised fairly strictly. She was living away from home for the first time, and her parents were not happy that she had followed Billy to Virginia. "We just cried and cried," Michelle's mother, Carol Moore, would later testify. "She wasn't ready." And they had reservations about Billy, who did not always treat Michelle well, and who had fashioned himself as a bad boy from the wrong side of the tracks in school. But Michelle's main goal in life had been to marry him. "That's all she really ever wanted," Billy's younger sister, Sarah, recalls. Billy and Michelle had kept their marriage a secret from Michelle's parents, who were planning for a fall wedding.[6]

Bosko arrived in the cab at their apartment at around 5 P.M. He opened one of the two outside doors that led into the common hallway on the first floor of their building and walked inside. At the front door of their apartment, he noticed nothing unusual. The door was locked, which was to be expected if Michelle had started work. After opening the door with his key, he stepped into their living room and called out her name. There was no response. Usually, when he came in the front door, Michelle would come charging to greet him and jump into his arms. "So I figured she was probably working," he remembered. The window blinds were closed; the apartment was dim.[7]

In the living room, Bosko again noticed nothing unusual. The room was clean and neat, pristine even. Everything seemed to be in its proper place. The brown parquet floor gleamed. The apartment looked as if a cleaning service had just come through, one attorney would observe. And no wonder: Michelle and a new friend, Tamika Taylor, a single mother of twin infants whom she had met at the apartment complex's pool a month earlier, had cleaned the place the previous evening in preparation for Billy's return. Michelle liked to play homemaker and did "a lot of cleaning," Taylor, who looked older than her eighteen years, would testify. "She was like a busy woman." Before Michelle had cleaned the apartment that evening, "it wasn't even dirty," Taylor recalled. Taylor had planned to drive Michelle in her mother's car to meet Billy at the pier.[8]

Taylor, who lived on the second floor of a building next to Michelle's in the apartment complex, had spent most of the previous day with Michelle. They had spent many days together since becoming friends. "We saw each other all day every day from the day we met," Taylor later testified, with typical exaggeration. They'd look for jobs, go to the beach, play with Taylor's kids, perhaps see a movie. Or maybe they'd party a bit.[9]

Sometimes they'd hang out with a longtime friend of Taylor's named Omar Ballard. Michelle had become friends with Ballard too. They'd gotten to know each other after Taylor had brought Ballard with her over to Billy and Michelle's apartment one day two weeks before Billy returned from his cruise. They'd sat around talking, smoking cigarettes, watching television. Chilling, Taylor might put it. Their visit had been interrupted by loud banging on the patio door of Billy and Michelle's apartment. When Billy had answered, he had seen more than two dozen people out there. Some were yelling and cursing. Did he have a "nigger" in the apartment? Send him out, the mob had demanded, because they were going to lynch him. Why? Bosko had asked. Because he'd beaten this girl. Bosko didn't believe it, so when the mob had threatened to rush in and grab Ballard, he'd threatened to kill the first one through the door. Eventually the crowd had dispersed.[10]

On the day before Billy returned from his cruise, a warm and typically humid one, Michelle and Taylor had taken Taylor's kids to Ocean View beach and out to eat. At about 8 P.M., according to Taylor (though Michelle's phone record would indicate that it had to have been at least two hours earlier), they had returned to Taylor's apartment, then walked over to Michelle's, where they had done their cleaning, watched TV and a movie, and played Nintendo.[11]

Taylor often spent the night at Michelle's when Billy was at sea. "Every time he left, I was there," Taylor remembered. "She would always ask me to come spend the night with her." Michelle didn't like to be alone at home. "She got nervous being alone," Bosko recalled. "And, quite frankly, I didn't feel real safe about her staying there either."[12]

Michelle had recently become wary of one of her neighbors. Danial J. Williams, a twenty-five-year-old steam-propulsion maintenance supervisor in the navy on the USS *Saipan*, lived catty-corner across the hallway of their building. The other two apartments on their floor were empty. Williams was a newlywed like Billy and Michelle. He and his wife, Nicole, had wed only ten days earlier. Nicole was dying of ovarian cancer. The cancer had seemed to come on quickly. She had returned home from a hospital stay for surgery two days before Billy returned from his cruise. Danial and Nicole shared their apartment with Joseph J. Dick Jr., a twenty-year-old sailor also on the *Saipan*.[13]

According to Tamika Taylor's later testimony, Williams would "constantly" come by Michelle's apartment late at night when Billy was away, ostensibly to use her phone. Williams would appear at her door around 2 A.M. or even later "every time Bill was gone," Taylor recounted. After using her phone, Williams would then sit there "for the longest time" and try to "conversate" with Michelle, Taylor stated. Williams would bring his black CD case and CDs with him "every time he came," according to Taylor. Taylor, who didn't like Williams, would eventually tell him to leave. Taylor also testified that Williams "constantly" peered out his window blinds and ran to his door to say hello to Michelle as she exited and entered her apartment. If Michelle came in and out of their building ten times in one day, Taylor said, Williams would emerge to say hello ten times.[14]

On the eve of Billy's return from his cruise, July 7, 1997, Taylor did not spend the night at Michelle's apartment. She had received a phone call at Michelle's place (Taylor didn't have a phone herself) that night from her sister-in-law relating that her brother had been jailed in New Jersey. So, at around 10:30, she and Michelle had walked over to Taylor's apartment, where Taylor's mother was tending to her two kids. Tamika had told her mother about her brother's jailing. "She was all upset and everything, so what happened was I told Michelle to come spend the night with us," Taylor testified. But Michelle had responded, "No, Bill is coming home, so I'm going to go clean and get ready for him to come home." She still had lots to do before he returned, Michelle had told Taylor. According to Taylor, Michelle appeared frightened. "You okay?" Taylor asked her. "I'm all right," Michelle replied. After Michelle had reached the entryway to her building, which was about twenty-five paces from the entryway to Taylor's building, the two continued to talk for about five minutes. It was now around 11 P.M., Taylor testified. "Are you sure you're not scared?" Taylor had asked Michelle. "No, I'm fine," Michelle had responded. "Go up there with your mom. I'm just going to go get the stuff together for Bill to come home." Taylor watched as Michelle entered her building.[15]

The next morning, at around 8 o'clock, Taylor walked over to Michelle's apartment and knocked on her door. Michelle didn't answer. Taylor thought she was probably sleeping. At around 10, after falling back asleep herself, Taylor returned to Michelle's door, but still there was no response. Taylor found that weird. She went back to Michelle's at 11:30. Again there was no answer. The whole thing was strange, Taylor thought.[16]

In his living room, Billy Bosko dropped his bags just inside the front door, next to a black-and-white striped couch to his left. As he scanned the room, his eyes would have taken in his overstuffed black-and-white striped chair to his right. Behind the chair, a long black-and-white cow decoration hung from the wall. There were cows all over the apartment. Stuffed cows, models of cows, pictures of cows, cow art, cow magnets, a cow notepad, you name it. Michelle "collected anything that had to do with cows," her friend Erin Litle recalls. She loved them. "She just had some fascination with them," Joel Vanucci, her high school guidance counselor, remembers. On her lower right leg was a tattoo of the head of a cow with a rose in its mouth.[17]

On the floor to Bosko's right was a black CD case. Some CDs were scattered nearby. Taylor would say later it looked like Michelle's CD case. But Joe Dick, Danial Williams's roommate, who would be shown the case at a trial and recognized some of the CDs in it as his own, says it was Williams's. Prosecutors never determined its ownership.[18]

Bosko walked into his dining room. Michelle would usually leave a note for him if she were out, so he looked for one on the red-and-white-checkered tablecloth on the dining room table. He found one, face up, but it didn't put his mind at ease. Dated the day before, it said "how happy she was to be with me and how happy she was that everything was going great, and she'd never been happier, and how I was the greatest thing since sliced bread, and how she and her friend Tamika were going on a diet and wanted me to be their coach," and some "little wifey stuff," Bosko recalled. But it didn't say anything about where she was. That and the date were unsettling to Bosko. The table itself appeared normal to him, with the usual clutter on it. "Pier 5 2:30" read one piece of notepaper—probably where and when Michelle was supposed to have met him at the pier.[19]

Bosko did not notice that Michelle's purse was spread out on the table, with some of its contents spilled out. But he wondered why the overhead light in the small kitchen to his left was on. "We were always real careful to make sure the lights were out to save money on the electricity," he said later. "Just starting out, we didn't have a whole lot of money." Perhaps Michelle had been in a hurry and simply forgot to turn the light off, he mused. Save for the light and some eggshells on the floor, the kitchen also appeared normal to him.[20]

Bosko walked down a narrow hallway a few feet to their bedroom on the right. He planned to take off his naval uniform, hop into the shower, shave, put on some nice clothes, and surprise Michelle at McDonalds. On some open shelves between the hallway and the kitchen to his left rested knickknacks and papers, including mail, articles, and bills. Some of these papers were protruding off the shelves into the hallway; material under a mail organizer was jutting out substantially. But that, too, was normal.[21]

Upon entering his bedroom, Bosko encountered a gruesome sight. On the parquet floor, near a small black-and-white stuffed cow, around two feet from the bed and parallel to it, his wife's pale body lay spread-eagled in a pool of blood. She was clad only in a black Crown Royal concert-series T-shirt. The shirt, which she usually wore to bed, was pulled up around her neck. It bore red stains and puncture holes. Blood soiled her face; some of it appeared to have come from her nose, though in all likelihood it emanated mainly from her mouth. Some had collected around her right eye. Blood was also spattered on her arms, which were pointing up and away from her shoulders, as though they had been pinned down, and on the floor around her. Her eyes were open. A pair of panties, two bras, and three towels lay nearby. "Appears to have been raped," a police report subsequently recorded. An autopsy would confirm that.[22]

Her 5'5", 110-pound body lying face up, head tilted slightly leftward, Michelle Moore-Bosko had been stabbed four times in her left upper chest. The stabs had been inflicted within a small 2" by 2¾" area. Three of the stab wounds were deep; each was 5" long. Their angles of entry were also essentially the same. They had penetrated all the way to the back of her chest wall. Any one of them could have been fatal. Her left lung had collapsed. The fourth stab wound was superficial, at ½" deep. Among these wounds there were also five knifepoint abrasions, or superficial scratches, probably inflicted by the tip of a knife. "Hesitation marks," the prosecutors D.J. Hansen and Valerie Bowen would both call them, although Hansen would later argue that they were evidence of a "sick ritual"—a Druid ritual, another prosecutor suggested. "Wimpy stab marks," Bowen also deemed them. Another possibility was that someone had tried to torture Michelle into submitting to sex and used the knife pricks to help subdue her, or tormented her for other reasons. In addition to being stabbed, Michelle had been strangled, indicated by bruising and hemorrhaging on her neck. Either the stab wounds or the strangulation could have killed her. She had died during the attack or shortly thereafter, Dr. Elizabeth Kinnison, the forensic pathologist who performed the autopsy, would testify.[23]

Michelle's body bore no defensive injuries, such as fresh chips or tears to her fingernails or bruises on her forearms. But there was blood under her fingernails, and it wasn't hers. She had no restraint injuries, such as bruises on her wrists or ankles, or blunt-force trauma to her face. And there were no signs of a struggle in the bedroom. A nightstand and the many objects on it were still in place, though a mainly blue patterned comforter on the bed would appear to one police investigator to be a bit disheveled, and a makeup container and brush lay on the floor. The bathroom was undisturbed; the sink, toilet, and bathtub were "extremely clean," the investigator testified.[24]

Partially underneath a chest of drawers near Michelle's head, a bent serrated steak knife with a wooden handle and red stains rested on the floor. Its blade was around 4½" long.

Upon seeing his wife's body, Bosko lost it. "I went crazy," he recounted. In shock, and unsure of what to do next, he bolted out of the bedroom and searched for his cordless phone, which he and Michelle usually kept in its base on the kitchen floor. He could not locate it, because, it turned out, it was buried underneath a pillow in his chair in the living room. He raced out of his apartment and began pounding on the front door of the apartment directly across the hall. He'd forgotten that no one lived there. In a frenzy, he then began banging on the front door of the apartment next to it.[25]

Rhea and Norman Williams, of Owosso, Michigan, were then visiting their son Danial inside. They had driven up to Virginia three days earlier from Tennessee, where their other son, Chris, was in diesel mechanic school. Rhea, a homemaker, and Norman, a longtime assembly-line worker for General Motors, had been staying in their trailer at the Jamestown campground about forty-five minutes out of Norfolk. Danial had visited them at the campground when his wife, Nicole, was in the hospital. He had told them about Nicole's cancer and his marriage to her. The next day, when Nicole had come home from the hospital, Danial's parents had spent most of the afternoon with her and Danial at their apartment. Danial and Nicole had then visited his parents again at the campground the following day, a Monday. They had stayed until it was almost dark, then driven back to their apartment, stopping for dinner at a Cracker Barrel restaurant. Danial had been exhausted from tending to the ill Nicole. He had "totally crashed out" on both Sunday and Monday nights, he remembers.[26] Michelle had been murdered on Monday night.

That Tuesday morning, before Rhea and Norman Williams had driven down from the campground, Nicole had informed Danial that she had heard someone arguing in the common hallway outside their front door during the night. One of the two voices was male, the other was female, she said. She had tried to rouse Danial, but couldn't. She had then gone to the door to see what was going on. But by then the fighting was over. Danial hadn't heard anything.[27]

After having breakfast that morning, Danial and Nicole had spent several hours running errands, including one to the Social Security office to change Nicole's records because they had gotten married. Danial's parents had been waiting for them in the parking lot of their apartment building when they had returned in the midafternoon. Rhea and Norman Williams had brought them some wedding presents, including a coffeemaker and a microwave oven; Norman and Danial had then assembled a cart for the microwave as Nicole made a pot of coffee. Danial and Nicole had seemed happy, according to Danial's parents.[28]

Danial, Nicole, and Rhea had been sitting around drinking coffee and getting ready to go out for dinner when Bosko came upon his wife's body across the hall. Norman had been walking the family dog. Rhea remembers hearing a "loud shriek" from inside Bosko's apartment, followed by seemingly indiscriminate banging on the walls in the common hallway and on front doors of apartments. "What is *that*?" she asked the others. Maybe someone was partying or horsing around, she thought, fleetingly. Then came the pounding on their own door.[29]

Danial opened it. Obviously frantic, Bosko exclaimed "that his wife was dead on the floor and she wasn't moving, and he needed to use the phone," Williams recounts. "So I called 911." As soon as Williams punched the last number on his phone, Bosko ran back to his apartment. Williams trailed close behind, still on the phone, followed by Nicole, Rhea, and later Norman. "She's dead, she's dead!" Bosko kept wailing. To Bosko's consternation, Williams followed him into the bedroom. "I kept trying to stop him, telling him, 'No, I don't want you in here,'" Bosko recalled. "I didn't want him to see Michelle like that. And he wouldn't listen, and I was really in no position to stop him at that point." Williams helped Bosko cover up Michelle's lower body with a white blanket that was on the bedroom floor next to her. "He grabbed the corner of it, I grabbed the corner of it, and he helped me cover her up," Bosko testified. Williams remembers going into Bosko's apartment to see whether Michelle was actually dead and to help her if she wasn't. "At the time I was certified in CPR" through the navy, he would recall in a boyish-sounding southern voice. "And I didn't know how long she had been laying there. . . . It was just like, 'Is there anything I can do for her?' But once I felt for a pulse and I couldn't find one, and realized that her body temperature was too far down, [I knew] there was no way that she could be revived—that she's been dead for a while."[30]

Bosko also felt for a pulse. Her body was cold.

Rhea, Norman, and Nicole Williams had meanwhile gathered in Bosko's living room. Rhea and Norman noticed how clean and tidy the room was. Nicole then walked down to the bedroom herself. Bosko saw her in the hallway. Enraged over the whole situation, he punched a hole in the wall across from the bedroom, to the left of a photo collage, knocking a ceramic figurine off a shelf; he then kneed the wall by the kitchen. "I was just out of my mind," he later remembered. He grabbed the note from Michelle that he had found on the dining room table. "Look, this was yesterday," he pleaded. "How could this happen?" The Williamses urged him to calm down and wait for the police. He then sat slumped in his living room chair. Bosko later vomited in the bushes outside.[31]

After Norman and Rhea directed Danial and Nicole not to touch anything in Bosko's apartment and to leave, the Williamses assembled in Danial and Nicole's living room and waited for the police themselves. They had no idea what was in store for them.

2

The Neighbor

The cops arrived minutes later. First came the patrol cars, then the detectives. When Maureen Evans and Scott Halverson pulled up at the apartment complex, they spoke to the first officers and other detectives on the scene, who had already gone into Michelle Moore-Bosko's apartment. They were "giving me and Halverson a brief," Evans remembers. As Halverson continued to gather information outside, Evans went in.[1]

Mo Evans had been on the Norfolk police force for eight years, two in homicide. Thirty-one years old, she'd been raised in the area. Her father was a retired navy officer; two other relatives were cops. An athletic woman, she'd played basketball in college and softball all her life; she was addicted to golf. She was a strong-willed, outgoing, and talkative person, good with people, though she could be blunt. "I'm just not a bullshitter," she says. She tended to speak fast. She was the only woman on the Norfolk homicide squad, which wasn't easy. "There was a lot of trust issues," she recalls.[2]

When Evans approached the front door of the apartment, a uniformed officer was stationed there to prevent unauthorized people from entering. Evans noticed no signs of forced entry. The victim, she inferred, probably knew her killer. Inside, Evans did a brief walk-through, taking notes on conditions (lights, objects, anything that looked odd or otherwise significant), trying to get a sense of the state of the apartment without disturbing the scene. She knew that the conditions would be documented in police photographs and videotape, but it was important to keep little things like that in her head. And she knew that the scene would begin to erode as other officers walked through it—she only had one shot at it. As she proceeded down the short hallway to the bedroom, she noticed the hole in the wall. What was that all about? she wondered.[3]

At the doorway to the bedroom, Evans saw Michelle's body on the floor. She had handled about eighteen murders by this time (mostly domestics and drug shootings), and not many crime scenes affected her, but this one did. It looked like something out of a horror movie. "It really took my breath away," she would recall. "I said to myself, 'What the *hell* happened here?'" She could tell that it had been a very violent death, and that this girl had died suffering.[4]

Evans crouched down, staying away from the body. "I was just taking notes like there was no tomorrow, because I wanted to make sure that I had everything," she recounts. "And I was just shaking my head." She noticed the bent knife with blood on it above Michelle's head, all the blood on Michelle's shirt, and what she thought was probably aspirated blood on her face. "But I still didn't know really how she died," Evans recounts. "I just assumed seeing the knife that she must have been stabbed." The cause of death wasn't her call anyway.[5]

After exiting the apartment, Evans met up with Detective Halverson to discuss their game plan. They spoke to Billy Bosko in their car. The detectives at first found him in no shape to talk, but they were ultimately able to get his account of events: when he'd left on the cruise, when he'd returned, what he'd done upon getting home, and so on. He was "very distraught, very in disbelief," Evans remembers. "He was definitely in shock—there was no doubt in my mind." Her gut feeling, which she felt was pretty good, told Evans that Billy was not her guy. And she knew she could easily verify whether he'd been out to sea or not. Meanwhile, other detectives were knocking on apartment doors, asking neighbors whether they'd seen or heard anything. One of those neighbors, they knew, could be Michelle's killer.[6]

Investigator Wayne Bryan, who specialized in fingerprint examination, arrived at the apartment a little after 6 P.M. Other forensic investigators were already there, and the crime scene had been taped off. Groups of apartment residents were milling around nearby, wondering what had happened. Bryan videotaped the scene to preserve it, starting with the outside of the apartment, where he focused on the doors, then scanning the common hallway inside the building before going back outside. After training his camera on Michelle's front door, Bryan moved inside, videotaping the living room, the hallway, those knickknacks and papers on the open shelves, and Michelle's rifled purse and other material on the dining room table. Then he moved into the tiny kitchen, where he zeroed in on a block of knives. Bryan next moved down the hallway into the bedroom, where he methodically recorded the grisly scene there. Bryan and Investigator J.L. Butcher, the lead forensic man, also snapped photographs. They sprinkled black fingerprint powder in all the rooms and on the front door. "We printed the entire apartment," Bryan testified later. Its polished parquet floor was excellent for lifting prints. In the bedroom, which they also searched, they dusted the floor around Michelle's body and other hard surfaces. Going the extra mile, Bryan also built a small plastic tent over Michelle's body, heated superglue (creating a vapor), and powdered her body to try to extract prints off it. He was unsuccessful, but he was able to lift a dozen prints from the scene and to later identify seven of them.[7]

The seven were around Michelle's body. But they were all Michelle's and Billy's.[8]

From around 9 P.M. until 2:30 A.M., in that stuffy little apartment, Bryan and Butcher collected items that appeared to have some evidentiary value, including the white blanket on Michelle, the comforter on the bed, the knife, a screwdriver, the panties, bras, and three towels on the bedroom floor, the black CD case and CDs, the contents of three ashtrays, Michelle's purse, and hairs and fibers from the floor around Michelle. Those hairs and fibers would never be analyzed. Bryan also took swabbing samples of three deposits of what he would describe as a clear white substance around Michelle; none of the samples, it would turn out, contained semen. He departed the scene around 3 A.M.[9]

Meanwhile, police had approached Danial Williams, Michelle and Billy's neighbor, outside the apartment. Williams had indicated to an Investigator Graupmann that he was the person who had called 911 about Michelle's murder. "They just really wanted to know if I knew anything about it," Williams remembers. How well had he known the victim? Where had he been last night? They had not seemed particularly suspicious of him; they had no reason to think that he had been involved, and his wife and parents were right there with him. During his conversation with police, Williams had gone back inside his apartment to fetch his wife's medication because she had had a "dizzy spell," he recounts. "And then I took her inside after she was feeling a little bit better. And the detective asked me to step back outside to talk to me a little bit more."[10]

Police had begun to hear from Michelle's friend Tamika Taylor that Williams might have had "a thing" for Michelle. "I need you to help me," Evans had told Taylor. "Because we don't know who did this." But, Evans had indicated, Michelle had known her attacker. "I said, 'In your gut feeling, who would have done this to her?'" Evans recounts. "And she said, 'You see that guy over there?'" Taylor nodded toward Williams, who was standing a short distance away. "I think he did it," Taylor offered. Why? Evans asked. "Well, he's kind of obsessed with her," Taylor replied. And in a creepy sexual way.[11]

Only three or four nights earlier, Taylor, Michelle, another friend of Michelle's named Missy, Taylor's mother, and Taylor's friend Omar Ballard had been partying at Michelle's place. Williams had come over "real late" with his little CD case as usual and not departed until around 4 A.M., Taylor would later testify. After seemingly using the phone, he had asked to join the party and begun dancing in a sexual manner. "He was like pumping walls and pumping the floor," Taylor testified. He seemed to be leering at Michelle at one point.[12]

But Taylor wasn't sure that Williams had done it. It was, of course, only a hunch. She'd been reluctant at first to venture an opinion to Evans. She'd asked "a hundred million questions" of her own about the crime. She realized there were plenty of crazy people out there, and she knew some criminals herself. Taylor, who talked to police for several hours that evening, would even ask them to check out her friend Omar Ballard, who she was aware sometimes visited Michelle. But the police declined to speak to Ballard or to pursue other leads from their conversations around the apartment complex. "Within an hour of arriving at the crime scene, and with no evidence tying him to the crime, police convinced themselves that Danial was the sole culprit," some attorneys who would become involved in this case later observed.[13]

Such tunnel vision is often the first blunder in a long process that leads to a wrongful conviction. Police latch onto a suspect for one reason or another (a tip, a witness's identification, a hunch, suspicious behavior), convince themselves that he's their guy, play up supportive evidence, and discount conflicting information and other suspects. If their man confesses, their tunnel vision calcifies. They may fail to collect relevant physical evidence or pursue other leads. If exculpatory evidence surfaces after their suspect is convicted, police frequently refuse to admit their mistake. Indeed, they often continue to believe in his guilt long after their case has collapsed. Tunnel vision, which is more a response to pressure on police to clear cases and secure convictions than a product of maliciousness or indifference, affects all phases of criminal cases—investigations, interrogations, prosecutions, trials, plea bargaining, even appeals. It was a factor in the wrongful convictions of almost all of the more than two hundred people who have been exonerated through DNA evidence in the last two decades, and surely a factor in countless other miscarriages of justice that have not been corrected.[14]

In a 2005 report on wrongful convictions in Virginia, the Innocence Commission for Virginia found that police tunnel vision—especially in high-profile cases—was one of the most common causes of those convictions. The commission recommended that police be trained to document all exculpatory evidence about a suspect and include it in their official reports. To the detriment of defendants, most police reports deliberately exclude exculpatory evidence, and police training rarely considers the dangers of tunnel vision. The commission also urged that police be taught to pursue all reasonable lines of investigation even if they point away from their suspect. "In most cases, if the police do not conduct an objective, neutral, and thorough investigation, no one will," the law professor Stanley Fisher points out.[15]

After finishing up at the scene, Evans nonchalantly approached Williams, who was getting ready to leave for dinner with his wife, Nicole, and his parents. "Hey, you know, you called 911. You've been in the scene. I need to get a sworn statement from you," she told him. "You mind if you come down to the Police Operations Center and talk with myself and Detective Halverson?" "No, not at all," Williams replied. He could even drive his truck and follow them down, Evans said. Williams appeared overly cooperative to her. "I was actually kind of shocked that he gave in that easy," Evans recounts. "He didn't ask me any questions whatsoever," like, Why do I have to come down now?, the kind of thing Evans had come to expect from criminals. She thought Williams might be trying to appear cooperative so as to avoid looking suspicious. "But to me *that* looked suspicious," she says.[16]

Williams drove himself down to the station behind a police car at around 6:30 P.M. His purple-pink Chevy pickup bore bumper stickers like SEX IS LIKE PIZZA. WHEN IT'S GOOD, IT'S VERY GOOD. WHEN IT'S BAD, IT'S STILL

PRETTY GOOD! (Those stickers, which Evans noticed later, would reinforce her belief that he was Michelle's killer; they were another sign of his over-the-top, creepy attitude toward sex.) Williams did not realize that he was a suspect. But he wondered: What did they need to get cleared up at the station that they couldn't get cleared up there at the scene? He figured they probably wanted to hear more about Michelle, his 911 call, and his observations in her apartment. "He didn't seem threatened at that time," his mother remembers. "He felt comfortable" going down.[17]

Williams told his parents that he'd meet them at the restaurant for dinner afterward. It wouldn't take long, the police said. About an hour. "They said that he was voluntarily going to the police station to give a statement and give whatever information he could that would help them out," Rhea Williams recounts. "And we ended up going to the restaurant and waiting and waiting and waiting."[18]

Meanwhile Billy Bosko had also gone down to the station to provide a statement and elimination prints. He phoned his home in Pittsburgh probably between 7 and 8 P.M.; Williams was then in another room waiting to speak to Evans and Halverson. "Something really bad happened," Billy told his mom between sobs. Michelle had been murdered. She had been laying in a pool of blood when he found her, he cried. "You have to come and get me. . . . I can't do this by myself."[19]

After she hung up the phone, a badly shaken Pat Bosko informed her other son, eleven-year-old Michael, and her thirteen-year-old daughter, Sarah, that Michelle was dead. Michael became hysterical. Sarah went to her room and "just sat there." She stayed up for two days. "I couldn't eat, I couldn't sleep," she remembers. "It was horrible."[20]

That evening, Michelle's parents returned to their own home in Pittsburgh with their youngest son from his Little League baseball game to find a police car in their driveway. They refused to believe that their daughter was dead. At 9:20 P.M., Detective Halverson phoned Carol Moore, Michelle's mother. She was beside herself. The first person Carol called was her sister Barbara, who collapsed to her knees.[21]

Sitting in the larceny office at the Norfolk Police Operations Center, a one-story brick structure with a blue sign out front, drinking a soda between cigarette breaks, waiting to be interviewed, Danial Williams had never found himself in this kind of situation before. He had no criminal record. By his testimony, he had never been suspected by police of committing a crime. Indeed, he'd never been a troublemaker of any kind. His parents had taught him to trust and respect cops. They were like "second parents," he'd been told. If he had a problem, they were there to help. The father of a good friend had been a policeman; his friend later became a cop himself.[22]

Standing 5'7", with short brown hair, a mustache, a high forehead, and large round eyeglasses, Danial Williams had spent six years in the U.S. Navy. He had enlisted with pride during his senior year of high school in Owosso, Michigan, where he'd graduated 117th in his class of 231 students, with a grade point average of 2.2. In eighth grade, his vocabulary and independent reading had tested at the fifth-grade level; he had flunked second grade. His IQ tested in the low nineties. Williams was sensitive about feeling stupid. His career goals were not ambitious ones. "I don't think he really had any," his mother remembers. "I just pretty much wanted what my parents had," Williams recalls. "You know, a nice family, to be able to have money to get things every once in a while."[23]

Williams had been a Boy Scout and delivered newspapers for years. He'd fished and hunted with his dad, and played football and the cornet. "He was not a good musician," his school band director, Carl Knipe, remembers. Music theory was a struggle for him. "But he was there all the time, and he marched pretty well," Knipe says. He took pride in his marching—one didn't have to tell him to pick up his feet. He was an affectionate and obedient kid with a good heart. "If you asked him to do something, he'd do it," Helen Frezon, his grandmother, recalls. "I'd say he was thoughtful." He had taken to his Uncle Gary, who was blind. While some people kept their distance from Gary, just sat there and stared at him, or even seemed a little fearful, Danny was Gary's right-hand man when around him. He wanted to know how he could help him.[24]

Williams was easygoing and passive, and little seemed to rile him. "He was not one to make a fuss about anything," his aunt Doreen Trevena recalls. Low in self-esteem, he was a suggestible and gullible person who tended to believe what other people told him. It was not like Danial to be contrary or express strong opinions. He was a follower, and had been raised to comply with orders.[25]

Williams's personality left him ill-equipped for what he was about to undergo. Indeed, he was almost a sitting duck. While the mentally handicapped and juveniles may be the most easily led by police to confess to crimes they didn't commit, people with highly suggestible, naïve, and submissive personalities are also particularly vulnerable. They may be more disposed to please their interrogators than to protect themselves. And if interrogated long or forcefully enough, they're apt to tell the police what they want to hear. Even if it isn't true.

Williams was also hesitant to open up to people. Just plain wary in many cases. He hadn't been among the popular kids in school; one didn't see him around girls much. Shy and introverted, he did not communicate easily or well. "A very blank-affect kind of guy," his lead attorney, Danny Shipley, would later find. "No emotion." But he was loyal to his few friends; he would do almost anything for them.[26]

Williams's marriage had been driven by expediency: Nicole needed his navy medical benefits. But Williams loved her and enjoyed caring for her. He had spent several days by her side at the hospital before Michelle's murder. Their relationship was his first serious one with a woman. She was far more experienced, and had a rocky history with men.[27]

Norman Williams, Danial's father, was a private and reticent man. He had dropped out of school after the ninth grade, then worked for General Motors for almost thirty years. Rhea Williams, his mother, had also not earned a high school degree. A large, outspoken, and strong-willed woman with brown hair, she had supplied the unusual spelling for "Danial" in a groggy state after giving birth to him. "I just blurted out letters," she laughs.[28]

Danial Williams loved country and western music and was part of a group that hung out at The Banque. The bar, which sat in a drab shopping area off a main boulevard in Norfolk, was popular with sailors. Mainly navy or ex-military, along with friends and a few women, the group had taken to calling themselves the Banque Crew. They adopted a theme song for their crew: Garth Brooks's "Friends in Low Places."[29]

Williams strove hard to succeed in the navy, which had helped his self-esteem, but his performance was mediocre. It took him too long to complete tasks, he required steady supervision, and punctuality was a problem. He also began to abuse alcohol. The navy consequently placed him in a rehabilitation program. By the time of Moore-Bosko's murder, "I hadn't had a drink in quite a while," he recalls.[30]

.   .   .

After waiting for over an hour while Maureen Evans, Scott Halverson, and other detectives interviewed Billy Bosko and Tamika Taylor ("We wanted to pick Tamika's brain a little bit more about this Danial guy," Evans recalls), Williams entered an interrogation room at the police station at about 8 P.M. The room was typically small and unadorned; it measured only around eight feet by eight feet. It was windowless, save for a tiny window in its only door. A table was pushed up against the right wall. There were three chairs around the table and carpet on the floor. Evans was still carrying her gun—a practice that police are taught to avoid because a suspect could seize the gun and because it might cause a judge to deem the interrogation coercive and thus exclude any confession. Evans directed Williams to take the seat farthest from the door, in the back corner. She sat next to him; Halverson sat closest to the door.[31]

Evans asked Williams if he could read and write. Williams said he could. Evans then directed him to read the first line of a Miranda rights form: "Do you understand that you have the right to remain silent?" Williams read the line and wrote "yes" in the blank below it, also initialing his response at Evans's direction. Evans then read him the remaining six lines on the rights form:

> Do you understand that any statement you make may be used as evidence against you in a court of law?
>
> Do you understand that you have a right to talk to a lawyer and to have the lawyer present during all questioning, if you so desire?
>
> Do you understand that if you cannot afford to hire a lawyer, a lawyer will be appointed to represent you and be present during all questioning, if you so desire?
>
> The above rights have been fully explained to me, and I sign this paper with complete understanding of them.
>
> I further state that I waive these rights and desire to make a statement.
>
> This statement is completely free and voluntary on my part without any threat or promise from anyone.[32]

Williams wrote "yes" in the blank below each line, again initialing his answers. "I was there under the pretenses that they just wanted to get more information," he said later when asked why. And "I had nothing to hide and had done nothing wrong and never thought of asking for a lawyer."[33]

Evans asked Williams if he wanted something to eat. It was important to establish for the record that he had not been deprived of food. No, Williams replied, he wasn't hungry, despite having eaten neither lunch nor dinner that day. His stomach was a little upset, he said. "From the events of the day I had lost my appetite due to the murder that I saw when I saw the body" of Michelle Moore-Bosko three hours earlier, he later testified. How about a soda and cigarettes? Evans asked him. Yes, Williams responded. He drank Pepsis and smoked throughout his interrogation, which to his growing disquiet would continue throughout the night and into the morning, by which time his life had changed irrevocably.[34]

Evans directed Williams to relate the events of the day before, July 7, 1997, and of that day. He and Nicole had visited his parents at the Jamestown campground on July 7, Williams recounted. They had then gone out to dinner at around 8 o'clock and returned to their apartment at about 10. How did he know when they got home? Evans quizzed him. He had looked at his alarm clock, Williams replied. After helping his ill wife with her medication, he would recall later, "I took care of a couple of things, and I was right in bed behind her."[35]

He awoke around 9 A.M., Williams told Evans. After breakfast, he got a haircut, ran some errands, and took his wife to try to visit a friend of hers. They arrived home about 3:30 P.M., he remembered. He wasn't there long before Billy Bosko had banged on his door. According to Evans, Williams said that he only went to the doorway of Michelle's bedroom, and to see whether she was dead.[36]

Evans and Halverson then left the room. Nine minutes later, at 8:24 P.M., when they reentered, Evans asked Williams to go over the events again. Williams repeated his account and remembered seeing blood on Michelle's face. He had talked to her only a couple of times, he told Evans. Michelle was "good-hearted," he added. Asked if he had been in her apartment before, he said that he had, but it was only in the last week that he had started talking to her. They would speak to each other when passing through the common hallway of their building, he recalled. He had last seen and talked to Michelle on Saturday, three days earlier.[37]

Had he had any kind of relationship with her? Evans and Halverson probed. He was not having an affair with her, if that's what they meant, Williams shot back.[38]

Evans got Williams to acknowledge that his wife's medications "knock[ed] her out" when she went to bed. That, Evans knew, would help explain how he could have attacked Michelle when his wife was across the hall. But she did not wonder about the likelihood that a man married only ten days earlier, to a wife dying of cancer, and whose parents were then visiting him from out of town, would commit a rape and murder. She felt she had her man, based on his alleged interest in Michelle. "It all made sense to me," she remembers: His wife was dying, she couldn't satisfy him, he was obsessed with Michelle, and "he was going to have his quest." Williams was "the only suspect at the time—no indication whatsoever that anybody else was involved," she recalls.[39]

Evans then "confronted" (to quote her notes) Williams about the time that he and Nicole had arrived home the night before. Having obtained his baseline account and locked him into it, it was time to become more accusatory and point out flaws in his story. Evans had spoken to Nicole over the phone earlier, and Nicole had told her that they had returned around 8:30, not 10. After Nicole had taken her medication and gone to bed, she had said, Danial had walked into the kitchen to do something and then joined her in bed. Williams could not explain the time discrepancy. That was cause for suspicion to Evans.[40]

Evans also "confronted" Williams about his relationship with Michelle. They were just neighbors and he had only talked to her on occasion, Williams responded. But Tamika Taylor had told Evans that Williams had gone over to Michelle's apartment several times. Taylor had also talked about his "nasty dancing" next to Michelle ("Man, this guy's obsessed beyond explanation," Evans had thought). "Well, that's funny," Evans said to Williams. "I have a witness that says that you've been there more than once." "Yeah, I've been there several times," Williams replied, according to Evans. But only when Taylor or other people were there, he added. Well, according to witnesses, he had been there by himself, Evans said. Maybe once or twice, Williams relented. But he denied going over to Michelle's at all hours of the night. He had mainly visited when his wife was in the hospital, he said. What had they talked about? Evans wanted to know. "He stated that the conversations were about his problems and his wife having cancer and what he was going through mentally and physically," Evans and Halverson recorded in their notes. He denied having any sexual or emotional feelings for Michelle.[41]

Unbeknownst to Williams, Evans was trying to prod him to at least admit being in Michelle's apartment the night of her murder. Then it would be easier to squeeze a confession out of him. "When a guilty suspect places himself far from the scene of the crime, or denies any contact with the victim, it becomes much more difficult for him to eventually tell the truth about commission of the crime," the leading manual on police interrogations, *Criminal Interrogation and Confessions*, observes. "I really had nothing, other than the fact that he was obsessed with her," Evans admits. But "Danial was so hard to get just to that point"—of saying that he was there. "Sometimes when I looked at him, I felt like he was looking through me. He just had a sense about him that I just don't think was all there." At moments, Evans even felt somewhat intimidated by Williams.[42]

Evans said something to him about the knife that had been found on the floor near Michelle's head. But she didn't push it. "I knew I had to back way the hell down, because that's like going after the jugular," she says. "If you try to get somebody to confess to that"—stabbing someone, early in an interrogation— "then you're not going to get anything." An interrogation is like a big card game, Evans reasoned. You've got to very methodically place each card down and hold them close to your face.[43]

At 8:35, Evans asked Williams if he would be willing to take a polygraph. Hoping the test would clear him, Williams said that he would. Evans hoped the exam would induce a confession. That is the primary goal of lie-detector tests administered by police, and they are often powerful prods. Told that this scientific technology has proven their guilt and that no one will believe their claims of innocence anymore, many suspects confess after being tested. Some are even led to believe that they committed the crime because they failed the test.[44]

At 8:45, Evans left the interrogation room to summon Detective Randy Crank, a seasoned officer who would administer the polygraph while representing himself as a neutral party. Detective Halverson, who remained in the room, asked Williams if he had left his apartment after going to bed the night before. No, Williams responded. Had he touched anything in Michelle's apartment when he had followed Billy Bosko over there? At first Williams said no, but then he indicated that he had picked up the white blanket that he and Bosko had draped over Michelle's lower body. He had also touched the door, he said. "In earlier interviews, he stated that he touched nothing in the apart-

ment," Evans and Halverson pointed out in their notes. Williams recalled that
he had hardly ever talked to Michelle. "He stated that he may have knocked on
the door late one night and stepped inside but doesn't remember. Earlier in
the interviews, he stated that he did not go over there late at night," Evans and
Halverson wrote. Halverson also asked Williams if his roommate, Joe Dick,
had a relationship with Michelle. Williams said that he was not aware of one.[45]

At 9 o'clock, Evans and Halverson asked Williams if he would be willing
to submit to a Physical Evidence Recovery Kit (PERK) test, which involved
collecting samples of his blood, pubic hair, and head hair, confiscating his
underwear, and swabbing his penis. Williams said yes. "I knew I had nothing to be afraid of so I agreed to do whatever the police asked of me," he explained later. Evans wondered why a guilty man would give up his blood so
readily.[46]

At 9:45, Evans and Halverson turned Williams over to Detective Crank. After Williams took the polygraph, Crank and Evans informed him that he'd
failed it. "They came back and told me that the machine said that I was lying
throughout the whole thing," Williams recounts. "And in my heart I knew I
wasn't. . . . I was baffled." He had actually passed the test. Suspects who submit to lie-detector tests are often told they failed them even when they passed.
Jon Babineau, a Norfolk-area attorney who has practiced since 1987, and a
former cop, says that he has rarely seen cases in which police tell a suspect that
he or she has passed the test. The police themselves grade it, and "if they want
you to fail, you can fail," Babineau points out. "There's so much that's discre-
tionary." Interpreting the results of polygraphs is inherently dubious, as the
tests only measure physical reactions to questions. They cannot tell whether
someone is lying because there is no reaction that occurs only when people lie
but that never occurs when they are being honest. People who are telling the
truth but who are nervous—and just about anyone being interrogated about
a brutal rape and murder would be nervous—might easily register the same
responses as people who are lying. Indeed, a genuine "lie detector" does not
exist. Because they are subject to such high error rates, polygraph results are
not admissible in most criminal courts in the United States.[47]

Meanwhile, Williams's parents and wife had been waiting for him to join
them at the restaurant. They finally phoned the station. The police "wouldn't
let us talk to him at all," Norman Williams remembers. "They said that he
was giving information to help catch a person. . . . 'He's still answering some

questions. It'd be just a few minutes.'" "So we went ahead and ate," Rhea Williams recounts. "And, of course, after we were done, he still wasn't there. We didn't want to pass him on the road, so we made sure that he was still there, and then we went down to the police station." They asked if their son was under arrest. No, the police replied. But they still wouldn't let them talk to him. What if the Williamses advised their son to ask for a lawyer? Indeed, that's what they say they would have done. "They said, no, he couldn't be seen while he was giving information," Rhea recalls. "But . . . the gentleman said, 'He's being *very* helpful. He's answering a lot of questions for us that are going to help us with our investigation.' And that he should be home very shortly. So, 'Don't worry about it and go home.' Naïve as we were, we went ahead and went home."[48]

At Danial's apartment, Rhea, Norman, and Nicole Williams continued to wait. After several hours, they phoned the station again. Danial was still answering questions, the police said. The Williamses weren't sure what to think. It was an awfully long night.[49]

During a break after being polygraphed, Williams ran into Billy Bosko at the station. "Hey, man, I'm really sorry about this," Williams remarked to Bosko, according to a newspaper article. "If you ever need anyone to talk to, you know, I'm here." "I offered my condolences," Williams recalls.[50]

Two of Billy's shipmates, Chuck Litle and Jeremy Odom, later picked up Billy at the station and took him to their place for the night. But he couldn't sleep. "His whole world was just stomped out in front of him," Litle remembers. "He was gone," his naval supervisor James Godfrey recalls. "There was nothing there. It was too traumatic for him to even really grasp what was going on." Bosko would later remember feeling "an overwhelming emptiness and helplessness. Just rage and sorrow and everything all wrapped up in one."[51]

After the polygraph, police escorted Williams back to the interrogation room, where he submitted to the PERK test. Several minutes later, at 12:08 A.M., Evans and Halverson began interrogating him again. "They just pretty much came at me with both barrels," Williams recounts. "Evans was always trying to get up in my face. As a matter of fact, I got pissed off so bad one time I called her a bitch." He was not being straight with them, Evans charged. She again "confronted" Williams about his feelings for Michelle. "We were hearing from several of the victim's friends that he had affections and obsessions towards the victim," Evans would testify later. "We found out through another witness that he liked to touch the victim in a way that he would brush her hair or touch her shoulder. When I confronted Mr. Williams on that, he laughed it off and said, Well, I like to joke around with people and play jokes on people like brushing their shoulders"; when they would look down to see what he was doing, Williams said, he would "flip the nose." He again denied having a crush on Michelle.[52]

When Williams said that he was worried about Nicole and asked to call her, Evans refused to permit it. "Detective Evans accused me of lying about Nicole's cancer and said she did not even believe Nicole was sick, which made me very angry," Williams recounted afterward.[53]

Evans and Halverson had their own frustrations. At points in this card game, particularly when Williams wasn't saying *anything* to them, they wondered whether they really had their guy. He still hadn't even admitted being interested in Michelle. "You're fighting your gut feeling, you're fighting what you think you know," Evans remembers. "And you just kind of get beat down. . . . You question yourself." That tended to happen at some point in any interrogation, particularly a long one, but she'd never been wrong about her man before, Evans felt.[54]

At 12:30 A.M., after Evans left the room, Halverson asked Williams to recount the day's events again. Around this time Williams told Halverson that he wanted to go home. "I was tired and I wanted to get some rest," he later testified. But Halverson advised him that it would look better if he told them the truth now rather than wait six weeks for the results of the DNA test to come back and find out that he had committed the crime. At 12:55, talking man to man, Halverson induced Williams to admit that he wanted to have sex with Michelle, according to the police notes. "He stated that he was infatuated with her," the notes say.[55]

At 1:50 A.M., Evans spoke with Michelle's friend Erin (soon to be the wife of Chuck Litle), who informed her that during a phone conversation with Michelle several days earlier, Michelle had started whispering. When Litle had asked her why she was whispering, Michelle had replied that the guy who lived across the hall sometimes heard her. He followed her all the time, Michelle told Litle, and sometimes peeked out his door as she entered or left her apartment. Once when she was outside, Litle recalled Michelle saying, he started talking to her and wouldn't let her go.[56]

Eighteen minutes later, Evans apprised Williams that she knew that he had kept Michelle against her will one time in the parking lot of their apartment building. Williams denied it. He may have talked to her, he said. He also denied opening his front door whenever he heard Michelle's front door. He stated that his roommate, Joe Dick, and his wife "never knew about his obsession with Michelle," Evans and Halverson wrote.[57]

Evans had come to think that Williams was unaware that his obsession with Michelle was really an obsession, and that he believed Michelle actually liked him. There were lots of nuts like that. Evans and Halverson suggested to Williams that "maybe she gave you some kind of implication that gave you the go-ahead to have sex with her," Evans recounts. "Or maybe you guys had consensual sex; I don't know, that happens. Sometimes affairs happen. And then something went wrong." Evans asked Williams if he knew about DNA evidence. She gave him a little lecture on it: If he'd had sex with Michelle, she advised him, he'd better tell them right now, because they were going to find out. "Mr. Williams stated that he had not, and that he was not there," Evans and Halverson recorded. "It was then explained to him that maybe there was a possibility that they had decided to have sex and then later decided not to but may have been in the middle of doing the act, and then something had happened for them to stop what they were doing. It was then discussed with Mr. Williams that there may be a possibility of pubic hairs being recovered from the scene. He was then asked several times whether these pubic hairs that were recovered were going to come back as being his." "I do not know," Williams "blurted out," according to Evans and Halverson's notes. "They might be." What did he mean by that? Evans inquired. "He then blurted out again, 'I do not know. I may have sleepwalked, but I don't remember,'" Evans and Halverson wrote. "He was getting mad and he yelled that out," Evans recalls. Taken aback, Evans and Halverson glanced at each other across the table. What was *that* supposed to mean, and where had it come from? Williams seemed to them on the verge of *something*. "This was obviously an admission of some respect, and we weren't going to let it go," Evans remembers.[58]

Williams was by now questioning his memory. He had begun to wonder if maybe he *had* raped and murdered Michelle but had blocked the whole experience out. "I was starting to doubt myself," he recounts. As police interrogators routinely do, Evans had told him repeatedly that he was lying and that she knew he had done the crime. "Frequently a guilty suspect will confess simply because he perceives that the interrogator appears to *know* that he is guilty," *Criminal Interrogation and Confessions* observes. Evans had even claimed that an eyewitness had seen Williams leaving Michelle's apartment. When Williams responded that the witness was either mistaken or lying, Evans said that she believed the witness. Williams didn't think police would conjure up a witness out of thin air, though, in fact, they often do. "I guess that started playing in my mind too," Williams remembers. "It's like, 'Okay, maybe I was so tired that I didn't know what I was doing, and I went over there, and then she [the witness] saw me coming out.'" And now he was so exhausted that it was hard to think clearly. Sleep deprivation heightens suggestibility in interrogations. But each time Williams put his head down on the table, Evans or Halverson told him to pick it back up.[59]

Williams recalls that one of his interrogators proposed that he could have suppressed the crime from his memory. Blacked out, perhaps, or even been sleepwalking when he attacked Michelle (Evans strongly denies suggesting that Williams sleepwalked). It's not unusual for police to suggest amnesia, then add that they're there to help get the truth out. They often point to the use of alcohol or drugs or a possible mental problem to account for their suspect's alleged lapse in memory. It's usually easier to convince a suspect who has abused alcohol or drugs that he blocked the experience out than it is to convince someone who hasn't. In one infamous false-confession case, police persuaded eighteen-year-old Peter Reilly that he had killed his own mother by slashing her throat and body—almost beheading her—and then blocked the gruesome act from his memory.[60]

Evans had attacked Williams's own memory to the point that he no longer trusted it. But he was still resistant to offering a confession because of his uncertainty. At 3:22 A.M., Evans and Halverson left the interrogation room again, bringing Williams another Pepsi and cigarettes. He declined their offer of food, although it had been eighteen hours since he'd last had anything to eat. His stomach was still queasy.

When Williams's inquisitors reappeared, he told them that he had always wanted to have sex with Michelle, according to their notes, "but he didn't think Michelle wanted to, so he never pushed the issue, and he stated that he would never forcibly do so." Evans reminded him that his pubic hairs might well be found at the scene. "He once again stated that he did not know if they were going to be there or not," Evans and Halverson wrote. At around

4:35 A.M., after Halverson had left the room, Evans tried to appeal to Williams's conscience, a standard interrogation tactic. Did he have any remorse or feel sorry that "Michelle was no longer with us"? "It was at this time that Mr. Williams became upset and started to cry somewhat," Evans recounted. She was finally getting to his heart and his feelings, she thought. She had finally broken him down. His body language told her that something was going on inside him, and that he was getting ready to confess. But then he seemed to quickly gather himself. Could he have a minute alone to go over his thoughts? he asked Evans. Evans said okay and left the room.[61]

Some of Evans's male colleagues at the station had meanwhile been wondering if Williams would *ever* confess to a female. Or at least to Evans. They decided to bring another man into the room, one they believed could push Williams over the edge. Also a homicide detective, this man had been working his regular night shift at the time. He'd interviewed Tamika Taylor and heard all about Williams's obsession with Michelle.[62]

Evans was not happy about the move. After all, it had been her case, she'd been plugging away at it for about twelve hours, she'd been working on Williams for a long time, and he seemed to her on the brink of confessing. And now she had to step back, which was not something she was used to doing. But she also thought that Williams had some serious issues with women ("what he did to this girl, there was a lot of rage there," she perceived), so if it took another man, that's what it took. "I'm not real selfish like a lot of detectives are, to the extent of, 'No, he's mine, and I'm going to keep going at him until he gives me a confession,'" Evans says. "They would never, ever let me go in to do their interrogations."[63]

The man who was about to enter the room was around forty years old, of medium height and stocky, with graying hair, dark eyebrows, swarthy pock-marked skin, and a bulbous nose. He was attractive in a rugged sort of way; his voice was husky. One might have easily mistaken him for a New York homicide detective. Some colleagues called him Sipowicz after the detective on the television show *NYPD Blue*. Rough around the edges, with a temper, he was not liked by everyone. "Many people can do without him," one former Norfolk cop says. "If you're not on board with him, he doesn't want anything to do with you." He could be arrogant and self-righteous; he intimidated some of his younger colleagues. He liked to drink and joke around, and he wasn't shy about telling sexist jokes in front of women, but he could also be quiet and soft-spoken. He was street smart but not intellectual; his grammar wasn't always the best. He didn't trust the media. A veteran cop, he'd been in homicide around ten years and on the police force eight years longer. He had a lot of CIs, or confidential informants, who are often pivotal to solving murders. He had worked security at The Banque.[64]

He was good at what he was about to do. He'd done it for many years and learned plenty from his experiences. He had attended at least two homicide schools that included training in interrogations; he'd read manuals on how to conduct them. In other criminal cases, he'd been able to extract confessions from suspects when his colleagues had failed. "He's very tough," Jon Babineau says. "You hear that from lots of clients. . . . He employs those police tactics of in-your-face in a very effective way to get you to break." He was passionate about his work and quite proud of his rate of clearing cases. "He really takes all his cases personally," Babineau notes.[65]

But some attorneys, including prosecutors, who were familiar with Detective Robert Glenn Ford's interrogation techniques found him overly manipulative, overbearing, over-the-top. They put little past him. "He gets his man," the lawyer B. Thomas Reed says. Ford was known for being especially aggressive with suspects and threatening them physically without actually assaulting them. He also had a reputation for putting words into suspects' mouths, for laying out his scenario of the crime—providing all the details—then relentlessly pressuring them to regurgitate those details. "That is Ford's MO," Reed says. "To tell people what Ford thinks happened." Over a number of hours, Ford will "tell them enough about the case so that when it's time for them to give a [taped] statement" at the end of the interrogation, Reed says, "it seems as though they are originating these facts that only the people involved in the murder would know. Well, over the course of ten hours, I could educate you on any murder, and if I get you to the point of making a statement, your statement is going to include what I have told you about the murder." ("I don't tell them anything," Ford would testify.) And it was not unusual for Ford to tell suspects that they could go home that night if they confessed, and that their jail sentence would be light.[66]

One respected former prosecutor who handled lots of murders in Norfolk and who had considerable contact with Ford describes him as "shady." "You don't feel comfortable with everything you're dealing with when you're dealing with him," he says cautiously when asked to explain. He also found Ford "a little pushy and manipulative," behavior that he thought masked Ford's insecurities. Another former prosecutor remembers naïvely accepting everything that the police told and gave her in her early days in the Norfolk commonwealth attorney's office. Then she started to see things differently; it became clear that police operated "just this side of the law," and that some officers were "willing to fudge things" and enter "gray areas." She became cautious when dealing with them and questioned their reports. One of these officers was Ford. "You always look at his cases a little more closely," she says. Ford had earlier been on the police department's vice and narcotics squad. "I don't think anyone ever believed him" there, she says, including a judge who presided over many of his cases. However, a former reporter for the local *Virginian-Pilot* newspaper who investigated controversial cases in the early 1990s says that Ford's name is not one of those that kept coming up as a source of the problems. "Glenn kept his head down and did his job," he recalls.[67]

Ford had extracted false confessions from some of his suspects in the past. In a messy case in 1990, he and two other detectives had elicited false statements from three teenagers who had been charged in the murder of Norfolk bar owner Jeffrey Kampsen. The teenagers, who were no angels (one would later get ten years for burglary and attempted grand larceny), had confessed to being at the scene of the killing, but had not been. "I can't lie any longer," one had declared toward the end of his interrogation in the early morning hours. "I wasn't there. I was home watching TV"—a claim he had made at the start. Ford and the other detectives had been transferred to uniformed duties as a result. William P. Robinson, Jr., the attorney for one of the teenagers, a fifteen-year-old boy, said that his client "was promised things. He was fatigued. He was scared to death. He was told he could go home if he told the police what was going on." Ford also induced false confessions from suspects in 1994 and 1997. One wonders how many others he elicited ("more than his share," Williams's attorney Danny Shipley surmises). "When a defendant tells me that 'Ford made me confess to something I didn't do,' I believe it," says Reed, who considers himself a friend of Ford's. "Because I've heard it so many times."[68]

Ford would later state, however, that in over twenty years on the police force he had never heard of a false confession. He was not likely to doubt that any confessions he obtained were true, except, perhaps, some of their details.[69]

At 4:51 A.M., Ford entered the interrogation room with Detective Halverson. After about twenty minutes of "listening," Ford put his chair directly in front of Williams. He wasn't messing around. He asked Williams what had *really* happened that night at Michelle's apartment and how things with her had escalated. Williams again acknowledged having sexual fantasies about Michelle but denied being in her apartment that night. Ford accused him of lying. He knew that Williams had been in Michelle's apartment and had had something to do with her death, he proclaimed. "At times, Detective Ford got right in my face and yelled at me," Williams would recount. "He repeatedly poked me in my chest and told me that he knew I killed Michelle." (Halverson later denied under oath that Ford touched Williams.) Ford let Williams know that he was facing capital murder charges. But if he cooperated and confessed, Ford said, he'd help him get a lesser charge. It was a veiled promise of leniency (one that Halverson also denied occurred). "He put his hand up high on the wall next to me, showing me where capital murder charges were, and then lowered his hand and showed me where the lesser charge was that he could help me with if I confessed," Williams recalled.[70]

At around 5:40 A.M., with the sun about to come up, Williams requested a five-minute break. That was fine, Ford responded, but when he came back into the room, he needed to hear the truth from Williams. According to Halverson, Williams looked Ford in the eye and said, "I will give you the truth." Ford extended his hand, and Williams shook it. Ford and Halverson then exited the room and brought Williams, whose nerves were already shot, a cup of coffee. "He's ready to confess," they advised Evans.[71]

Ten minutes later, when Ford and Halverson were back in the room, Ford asked Williams "if he had something to tell us," Halverson testified later. "And that's when he started to admit having something to do with Michelle's death."[72] It had taken Ford only an hour to wrest a confession from Williams, who was worn to a shadow and feeling defeated.

Although in an interview seven years later Williams would remember Ford as being less aggressive than Evans, when asked just months after the interrogation why he confessed, he testified: "Detective Ford started getting into my face and I was getting scared because I didn't know what he was going to do, and he started . . . saying that I was the one who had done it and just to tell the truth and it would be better off for me. . . . To me it felt like that they weren't going to let me go, that they had the person that they wanted to charge with the crime." And "I was confused, upset. I really didn't know right from wrong at that time. . . . I was tired. I wasn't feeling well." In an affidavit in 2005, Williams stated that he was unsure why he confessed, but he recalled: "I felt helpless and finally could not take it anymore . . . so I told him what he wanted to hear. . . . I made the details up. I knew that what I was telling Detective Ford was not the truth, but I just wanted the questioning to end." Asked later why she thought Ford was able to extract a confession from Williams so quickly, Evans responded with a chuckle, "I'm not going to comment too much on that," then added, "I'm sure it has a lot to do with Ford's style. . . . There may have been some intimidation."[73]

He had forced himself on Michelle, Williams told Ford. He had walked across the hall to her front door wearing only his white underwear ("Where did I come up with *that*?" he wondered years later. "I must have been tired." Or thinking about sleepwalking). But his bare footprints had not been found in Michelle's apartment. His wife was then asleep, Williams said. Michelle had been hesitant to open her door, but he had persuaded her to unlock it and turn the doorknob. He had then barged in and pushed her to the bedroom, he said. What was she wearing? Ford asked him. A black T-shirt, Williams responded, since that's what she had on when he saw her dead body twelve hours earlier. She was screaming but he was unable to close her mouth, he said. He didn't remember whether he hit her. He did not ejaculate, he stated, although sperm would later be found on the white blanket and in Michelle's vagina. Michelle was still "hollering and screaming when he left," he told Ford. That would have been impossible given the causes of her death. Did he use any weapons? Ford asked him. No, Williams replied. And he did not choke her. But the autopsy, of course, would show that she had been stabbed and strangled.[74]

Michelle had hit him a couple of times, and he had hit her a couple of times, Williams then offered. But he couldn't remember where. "Maybe in the head," he said, perhaps to account for the blood he had seen on her face. Afterward, he went home and didn't say anything to anybody about what he had done.[75]

Why did he do it? Ford asked him. "He stated that everything was building up for not having sex for a couple of months to the frustrations and because Michelle was a pretty girl," Halverson and Evans wrote in their notes.[76] One can imagine Ford suggesting such motives to Williams. To make a confession easier for a suspect to accept (and more persuasive to jurors and judges), police often suggest possible justifications—called "themes" in their police manuals—to suspects.

At 6 A.M., Ford and Halverson left the interrogation room. They were apparently struck by the meager outfit Williams had recalled wearing when he went over to Michelle's apartment, because when they reentered six minutes later they asked him again what he had on. White briefs, and he was in his bare feet, he stated. "Get out! Get out!" Michelle had yelled as he pushed her to the bedroom, he said; he then "tossed her to the floor, and she was resisting," Halverson and Evans recorded afterward. "He stated he held her arms up over her head and laid on top of her and stuck his penis in her. She kept saying no." Williams now said that he hit her a couple of times with his fist on the side of her head. He couldn't remember whether he hit her with any objects. But he then stated that he hit her once on the head with a hard-soled shoe that he picked up off the floor. Evans had earlier suggested to him that he might have hit her with an object that he found in her bedroom—like a shoe—after she had decided not to have sex with him anymore. "We put a lot of these things into his head," Evans acknowledges. "He admits to things that me and Scott basically made up." Indeed, Michelle had suffered no injuries to her head. Williams told Ford that he didn't think at all about what he'd done until Billy Bosko appeared at his door the next afternoon. "Then he got real scared," Evans and Halverson wrote.[77]

At around 6:24 A.M., Evans bought a chicken hoagie for Williams. But he only ate half of it. It just made his stomach more upset.[78]

Evans then paged a stenographer: it was time to take a taped statement from Williams. That would be more persuasive to a jury than a written confession or simply police notes on his interrogation. After the taking of this taped statement, Halverson and Evans would have their handwritten notes of the interrogation typed up, cleaned up to their advantage in the process, then perhaps cleaned up some more; later those handwritten notes might be thrown away so that defense attorneys could not use them as a basis for challenging what had transpired in the interrogation room. That was standard operating procedure for Norfolk detectives, according to the lawyer B. Thomas Reed.[79]

At 7 A.M., Ford and Halverson turned on two tape recorders. After ordering the spent and muddled Williams to state his full name, date of birth, Social

Security number, and other personal information, and to confirm his earlier waiving of his Miranda rights, Ford instructed him to "tell me in your own words what you know" about Michelle Moore-Bosko's murder and rape, starting from the beginning.[80]

He had gone over to her apartment at around 11:30 or 11:45 P.M., Williams said. After he had pushed his way in and forced her to the bedroom floor, he recounted, she had hit him a couple of times on his chest and struggled to get him off her while angrily screaming at him to get away from her. He had hit her three times with his hand, he now said. Then "I grabbed a flat, hard shoe and I struck her with it once." He could not tell Ford the color of the shoe. What made him stop raping her? Ford asked. "I got scared and I started panicking because I could get in trouble for it," Williams replied. He did not recall seeing any blood, though there was, in fact, plenty at the scene. He again said that Michelle was still alive and screaming when he left her apartment. "She couldn't have been hollering and screaming when you left," Ford pointed out. "Yes, she was," Williams insisted. "She just wanted me to leave, get out of there." After raping her, "I got up and I left and I went back to my place," he said, locking Michelle's front door on the way out. He then climbed back into bed with his dying wife.[81]

"What made you go over to Michelle's house?" Ford asked. "I was feeling sexually alone," Williams responded. He had gone over to her place at "all different times of the evening . . . two, maybe three times," he said. That night, he had been trying to live out his sexual fantasy about her, he agreed with Ford. But he had not intended to rape her: "I went there to see if I could get laid and not do anything else."[82]

Ford asked Williams what his thoughts had been when he had gone over to her apartment with Billy Bosko the next day. "I couldn't believe when I saw that she was laying on the floor dead," Williams replied. "I became really scared and I just wanted to go and hide. I didn't want to face what I had done."[83]

At 7:15, after turning off the tape recorders, Ford and Halverson left the interrogation room again. Williams then laid down on the floor. Twenty-five minutes later, Evans checked up on him. He was asleep, she wrote in her notes. "Actually, I was just resting," Williams recounts. "I *wanted* to go to sleep, because I was tired." Williams told Evans he was cold, so she brought him a blue windbreaker.[84]

Later that morning, Evans peered through the small window in the door of the room to inspect Williams again. He was now lying on the floor looking up at the ceiling, laughing hysterically, she recalls. She stood there at the door and watched him for a minute. "I just went, 'Jesus Christ,'" Evans recounts. "It gave me the heebie-jeebies."[85]

At 8:07, Evans obtained an arrest warrant for murder, followed by another warrant for rape. Around the same time, Halverson phoned Jack Moore, Michelle's father, and notified him of Williams's confession and arrest.[86] They had Michelle's killer, Halverson told Moore in all likelihood, after what must have been an excruciating night for the Moores.

Police also notified Nicole Williams. She dropped to the floor and cried upon getting the news. After Norman Williams took the phone, the police asked him to come down to the station to get his son Danial's pickup truck, keys, and other possessions. "They wouldn't answer questions after I went to pick up his truck," Norman recounts. Nor would they allow Nicole or his parents to talk to Danial. His processing would take a while, the police explained.[87]

The Williamses were thunderstruck. He *couldn't* have done it, Nicole exclaimed—after all, she had slept with him the night of the murder. Rhea and Norman Williams weren't sure what to think. They wanted to believe that their son was innocent, of course, and committing a vicious murder and rape would have been way out of character for him. But they wondered why he would confess if he didn't do it. Maybe he'd been drinking the night of the crime. "At first, you just didn't know," Rhea recalls. In the military, "they train you to do certain things," Norman reflected. For long afterward, Rhea and Norman Williams would be perplexed by their son's confession.[88]

Meanwhile, that morning's edition of the *Virginian-Pilot* had come out with a short article stating that "a woman's body was found Tuesday afternoon in a home near Norfolk Naval Air Station. Police are investigating it as a possible homicide." Williams's arrest would be noted briefly in the next morning's edition.[89]

At 8:20 A.M., Evans spoke over the phone with Dr. Elizabeth Kinnison, who was set to conduct the autopsy. Evans gave Kinnison some "very brief facts" on Moore-Bosko's murder, including that Williams had confessed to it. Evans then quickly headed over to the district office of the chief medical examiner for the autopsy. There, standing over Michelle's body, conversing with Kinnison, she noticed "quite a few discrepancies" between Kinnison's findings and Williams's statements to her. She observed Kinnison removing the black Crown Royal T-shirt from Moore-Bosko's body, which had arrived at the office in a labeled pouch and been refrigerated (making it difficult to determine the time of her death). There was still black fingerprint powder on Moore-Bosko's pelvis and legs; her hands were enclosed in paper bags to prevent the loss of any hairs or fibers (none were found there). "There were several tears in the shirt that may have been done by a sharp knife or sharp object," Evans recorded in her notes. Kinnison pointed out the three deep stab wounds to Michelle's chest, which, she said, could well have been inflicted by the bent steak knife found at the scene. Williams, of course, had said nothing about stabbing Michelle. Kinnison also noted the superficial stab wound and the knifepoint abrasions on Michelle's chest. What the heck were those all about? Evans asked her. Kinnison said she didn't know. Kinnison also pointed out the signs of strangulation. They too raised Evans's eyebrows, since Williams had denied choking Michelle.[90]

There were at least two competing explanations for these and the many other discrepancies Evans observed: either Williams had been lying about what he had done to Michelle, or he had not been at the crime scene and didn't know how she had died. Evans chose the first explanation. When a confession doesn't fit the crime facts, she thought, it meant the perpetrator was either lying, forgot the details, or got confused. "Innocent people don't confess to crimes they didn't commit," she says.[91]

What Evans did not know, and what most people who would become involved in this case did not know, is that false confessions occur regularly in the United States and are among the leading causes of miscarriages of justice. Some 15–20 percent of cases in which innocent prisoners have been exonerated by DNA evidence involved a false admission or confession. In capital cases, false confessions are the most common cause of miscarriages due to police prior to trial. Law enforcement officers, who are legally permitted to lie to suspects and do so routinely, employ powerful interrogation techniques designed to undermine a suspect's self-confidence, overcome his expected denials, and convince him that police have indisputable evidence against him. That evidence may include not only witnesses but blood, semen, hair, fingerprints, or the like. By referring repeatedly and with great outward confidence to this alleged storehouse of evidence against him in response to each claim of innocence, they attempt to persuade a suspect that the case against him is air-tight, that voicing further denials would be pointless, and that his situation is hopeless. Innocent suspects often become increasingly distressed, confused, and disoriented (more so than guilty ones). Some become flat-out desperate. Frequently police also try to convince suspects that they will be treated more leniently if they confess. Although direct offers of leniency and threats are un-constitutional, they are made nevertheless or expressed indirectly but no less effectively. Held in isolation in a small interrogation room for hours, often at night, and deprived of sleep—while his interrogators take turns and breaks—a suspect may easily come to believe that the only way to escape the room and avoid whatever punishment police are threatening is to give in and voice a confession. Some suspects, like Williams, come to believe that they might ac-tually have committed the crime. Too often, police—convinced that their sus-pect is guilty from the start—give little or no thought to the possibility that the confession they elicited could be false.[92]

The many discrepancies Evans noticed between Williams's statements and the physical evidence should have triggered doubts in her mind about Williams's guilt. Such discrepancies are a strong indication of a possible false confession. With their glaring major inaccuracies, Williams's statements should have been considered a sign of innocence or simply unreliable.[93]

Dr. Kinnison also assumed that police had Michelle's killer. Nothing about the autopsy results were inconsistent with one assailant, she later testified. "I would have expected that I would have said something" to Evans if she thought there'd been more than one, Kinnison said.[94]

At 9:25 A.M., the stenographer gave Detective Halverson the transcript of Williams's confession. Halverson again found Williams on the floor of the in-terrogation room, clothed in the blue windbreaker. Williams asked Halverson to read the transcript to him. At Halverson's direction, he initialed the top and bottom of each page, then signed the last page at 9:28. Halverson said later that he had been "awake and alert."[95]

Halverson then received a page from a Sergeant Hamlin of the homicide squad. Hamlin had talked to Evans over the phone from the medical exam-iner's office, and Evans had related findings from the autopsy, including the pattern of bruises on Michelle's neck. Was he right- or left-handed? Halverson asked Williams. Right, Williams responded. Did he grab or hold the victim's neck in any way? Maybe while she was screaming, Williams said. Which hand had he used? Or had he used both hands? Probably his right hand, Williams replied. Or maybe both. He wasn't sure.[96]

After 11 A.M., upon returning from the autopsy, Evans was back in the room with Williams. She was tired too. And she was angry. That asshole lied to me, she was steaming. "My emotions started getting the better of me," she remembers. Michelle's horrible death "started getting to me." So, "when I went in there, I was not nice. . . . Because I was at the breaking point of, 'Dude, you've got to stop messing with my time here. Because I need to go home and get some sleep, and you're going to jail, and we need to get the truth out.'" Evans's voice dripped with sarcasm. "Danial, guess where I've been?" "Where?" "I've been at the autopsy. And guess what? She didn't die of somebody hitting her in the head with the shoe. And I'm sure you're shocked by that." Had he done anything else to Michelle? No, Williams replied. "Let's think back to the knife that I told you about that was in the room," Evans directed him. What did he think might have happened with that knife? Williams didn't know. Well, Michelle had died of stab wounds, Evans informed him. "They started feeding me information about what had happened to her," Williams remembers. "I didn't know the specifics on how she died. That's when they started . . . letting me know that . . . she had been strangled and stabbed in the chest . . . and about how many times." Evans didn't tell Williams exactly how many stab wounds Michelle had received, but she demonstrated on her chest where Michelle had been stabbed.[97]

Evans was contaminating her suspect. When an interrogator feeds a suspect the facts of the case, such as the method of committing a murder, it may no longer be possible to confirm the veracity of his confession.

"I asked him flat out, 'Did you stab the victim?'" Evans later testified. "And he stated he did not because there was nothing that he could have stabbed her with." If he did, he could not remember doing so, Williams added. "I said that because I wanted Detective Evans to leave me alone," he recounted later. Evans suggested to him that it was possible Michelle kept a knife in her bedroom out of fear, since her husband was away at sea. When she again asked him if he stabbed her, Williams sat back in his chair and appeared to be on the brink of tears. "Yes," he moaned. "How many times did you stab her?" Evans asked. "Three," Williams responded, according to Evans (four, says Williams, who had been reluctant to hazard a guess). "I was like, Wow, that was easy," Evans recounts. "I mean, it was that quick. . . . I knew right there that that was the piece that I needed. Because I think that other crap"—about him beating her with his fist and the shoe—"wouldn't have flown."[98]

Where had the knife come from? Evans inquired. Michelle was coming at him with it, Williams replied, and he had taken it from her. When Evans wouldn't believe that and again advanced the theory that Michelle had kept a knife in the bedroom for protection, Williams offered that "the knife was lay-ing right there beside them on the floor" when he was on top of Michelle. "He stated he then took his penis out of Michelle Bosko, and that's when he saw the knife, and he grabbed the knife and stabbed her in the chest area . . . to try to get Michelle to stop screaming," Evans and Halverson wrote in their notes. "He stated he then got up and dropped the knife and ran out the door because Michelle was still screaming and hollering."[99]

After providing Williams with another Pepsi and more cigarettes, Evans took another taped statement from him. In this second statement, run-ning only three minutes, Williams denied hitting Michelle with a shoe. As he was raping her, "I started to look around for something that I could use to keep her quiet," he said. "I was putting my hands over her mouth, push-ing her mouth closed, trying anything to keep her quiet. I started really pan-icking, pulled my penis out, and I started looking around for something, and I saw a knife. I picked it up, and I stabbed her about three times." Williams, of course, could not describe the knife. And he said nothing about the knife-point abrasions on Michelle's chest. Evans didn't ask him what had caused them. "It was one of those questions in my mind that wasn't answered," she says.[100]

That morning, a haggard and lost Billy Bosko returned to the police station to retrieve the two bags that he had taken with him during his naval cruise and then deposited inside the front door of his apartment upon arriving home. When the police informed him that Williams had confessed to his wife's mur-der and rape, Bosko was livid. "I walked in to get my bags and I saw Williams and I made a start to go after him, but I ended up being restrained, so to speak, by the police," he remembered. They'd like to give Williams to him, but couldn't, they said.[101]

When Billy's mother, Pat Bosko, and her husband arrived at the Norfolk naval base later that morning to take Billy home to Pittsburgh, they were escorted to the captain's quarters of his ship. Someone then went to get Billy. "As soon as he saw me, he just fell in my arms and just started sobbing," Pat recalls. He "literally just fell apart in my arms." In the car on the way back to Pittsburgh, Billy hardly said anything for the first several hours. When he finally spoke, he wailed, "Every time I open my eyes I just keep seeing Michelle! I just keep seeing Michelle." He wept, but without really letting go.[102]

Shortly after noon, Danial Williams tried to phone his wife, but there was no answer. Rhea, Norman, and Nicole Williams had gone out to the Jamestown campground, where Rhea and Norman had been staying until the murder. Williams was then transported to the Norfolk City Jail.[103]

Three days later, Michelle Moore-Bosko was buried in Pittsburgh. Seeing her dead body—her hair stringy, her face caked with makeup, her eyes closed, her lips in a frown—in a casket was unbearable for the Moores. At the final good-byes, Carol Moore broke down. She would later describe the visitation and funeral services as "totally devastating." The Moores' pain, enormous as it was, would grow even greater in the years ahead. "Honestly, you really can't imagine how hard this is," an in-law remarked seven years later. "There's nothing that helps."[104]

Dressed in his naval uniform, Billy stuck close to his own family at the funeral. He didn't want to be alone. As Sarah Bosko, Billy's sister, peered at Michelle's body, which was clothed in a dark purple outfit, she thought to herself, "She should be in something brighter." She'd been such a cheerful person, and it just didn't seem fitting.[105]

Relations between the Moores and the Boskos would soon become strained. It was difficult to see each other. Unhappy that Michelle had followed Billy to Norfolk, Carol and Jack Moore considered him partially responsible for her death.[106]

Williams's friends were shocked by his arrest. He just didn't seem like the type of person who could do something like that. When Derek Tice first saw him in a jail jumpsuit behind the Plexiglas, "it was like a nightmare," he recalls. Surreal. There was *no way*, Rick Pauley thought: "I knew him well enough to know that he wouldn't have done anything like this. . . . He was just too nice of a person."[107]

Williams's relatives up in Michigan were stupefied, heartbroken, sick to their stomachs. This wasn't the kid they knew either. He didn't seem remotely capable of killing someone. It was hard to even conceive of it. The whole thing didn't make any sense, his grandmother Helen Frezon pondered. What were the police doing? Danial's uncle Jerry Frezon wanted to believe that Danny was innocent ("I have to think of a totally different person that would have done it," he says), but he didn't know where to go with the thing. "Where there's smoke, there's fire," he suspected. And, short of torture, it was hard for him to fathom somebody confessing to something they didn't do. That wasn't an easy matter for other relatives either.[108]

Danial's parents were not eager to talk about the case or all that forthcoming about their own views. "Norman specifically didn't really want anyone to know about it," his sister-in-law Doreen Trevena remembers. It was none of your business, he'd say. Underneath, his emotions were running high. So were Rhea's. They were meanwhile losing friends and acquaintances. Danial's arrest and confession were covered in their local newspaper; the article suggested he was guilty of premeditated murder. His picture was splashed on the front page. Rhea and Norman began to get a lot of "daggered looks" from people who thought they'd raised a bad kid. Some folks they'd associated with for years gradually withdrew from them. Rhea and Norman would each later suffer heart attacks that they believed were caused in part by stress over Danial's case.[109]

3

"I Did Not Kill Michelle"

Norman and Rhea Williams could not afford to hire an attorney to represent their son, so the court appointed Danny Shipley. A likeable man of forty-seven years with gray and white hair, a fairly broad face, glasses, and a southern accent, Shipley was a graduate of William & Mary law school not far from Norfolk. He liked to jokingly introduce himself to people with the line, "Hi, I'm Dan Shipley, famous trial lawyer." He was inclined to speak frankly; one generally knew where he was coming from. "I'm not going to mince words," he says. Two years earlier, he had handled a grueling and controversial case with his good friend James Broccoletti, the lead attorney, in which their client, Derek Barnabei, had been given the death penalty for killing and raping another "cute little white girl" in Norfolk. The victim had been a year younger than Michelle Moore-Bosko. Shipley had cried for hours after the sentence was handed down (though he thought his guy was probably guilty of the murder). "So I'm scared to death" of losing another client, he remembers. "When I saw Michelle Bosko, I saw this other girl."[1]

Danial Williams first met Shipley at his arraignment. After the hearing, outside the courtroom, Shipley had some blunt words for his parents. "Dan Shipley came right out of there and he said, 'You know, your son did it,'" Rhea Williams recounts. She felt like she'd been stabbed herself. "What's the sense of going on here if that's what you're telling us?" she thought. Shipley disputes her account. "I wouldn't have said that," he responds. "Because I don't make that decision, period. I may have told her, 'You've got a big problem here,'" given her son's confession. (Norman Williams remembers Shipley's comment was along the lines of, "Your boy really don't have a chance.") Shipley had not spoken to Danial about the crime yet. An upset Nicole Williams tried to tell Shipley that Danial had spent the entire night of the murder in bed with her. But Derek Barnabei's death sentence was on Shipley's mind; he remarked on the case to Rhea and Norman.[2]

Shipley and his co-counsel, Bob Frank, a short, burly, balding former prosecutor with a low-key personality who smiles easily and plays his cards close to his chest, did think Williams was guilty, even as they realized that he could have been easily manipulated by the "notorious" Detective Glenn Ford. "It's very difficult even for lawyers to understand why you falsely confess," Shipley acknowledges. Many attorneys know little about false confessions and, like laypeople, are skeptical that people give them, especially to heinous crimes. Shipley and Frank did not doubt that Williams was interested in Michelle. "I think it stemmed from the fact that he was probably not a very socially successful person with girls," Shipley says. When you have "this mousy little guy and this real cute girl across the hall, it's just sort of a normal thing."[3]

But whether he did it or didn't do it, Shipley and Frank felt, their overriding goal had to be to save his life. "That's how you evaluate victories on this side," Frank asserts. "It's not necessarily winning the case. In a capital case, keeping somebody out of the death chamber can be a victory." The American Bar Association Guidelines for the performance of attorneys in death penalty cases argue that avoiding execution is, in many cases, the only realistic objective, and that capital attorneys should explore with their clients the possibility of achieving a plea agreement at every stage. When the prosecution's evidence of guilt is strong and there is little chance of negotiating a plea to a lesser charge, the guidelines state, "a guilty plea in exchange for life imprisonment is the best available outcome."[4]

Shipley and Frank feared that the death penalty was a real possibility. They knew that the commonwealth attorney's office didn't have a case without Williams's confession. There was no physical evidence linking him to the crime. All the prosecutors could show was that he had allegedly expressed interest in Michelle and had the opportunity; that was hardly enough to convict him of murder and rape. But his confession was plenty. Shipley and Frank knew what a jury would think when they heard it. In Virginia "they're very conservative jurors," Shipley had found. "And juries here do not understand false confessions. . . . Believe me, in Virginia it's very hard to convince a jury that you confessed to a murder that you didn't do." As in most places, false-confession defenses tend to fail in Virginia.[5]

What's more, Virginia is good at executing people. It has executed more people than any other state, and since the death penalty was reinstated in the United States in 1976 it's been second only to Texas in the number of executions carried out. Prisoners also move from sentencing to execution faster in Virginia than in any other state. And death sentences are rarely reversed there. Indeed, Virginia has the lowest rate of reversal of any state in the country. One study found that when reviewing direct appeals of capital verdicts, the Virginia Supreme Court found error requiring a new trial or a lesser sentence only 10 percent of the time; on average, state supreme courts nationwide found error 41 percent of the time. The Fourth U.S. Circuit Court of Appeals, which serves Virginia and four other states, is the most restrictive in the country in providing relief in death penalty cases. "It's the worst place that you can get a death penalty," Shipley says. "Even in Texas you've probably got a better chance of getting a reversal."[6]

When Shipley and Frank considered that Williams's confession was to killing and raping a pretty, young, newly married white navy wife in a quintessential navy town, Williams's plight looked even worse. "That's a pretty sympathetic case for the commonwealth," Frank observes. Jurors would be outraged by the crime, he knew. They'd be shown horrible photos of Michelle lying spread-eagled on her bedroom floor. Shipley had recently seen how jurors respond in that type of situation. "I'm saying [to Williams], 'You've got a big problem here, whether you did it or not,'" Shipley recounts. "'I've been through this before.'" As for the discrepancies between Williams's confession and the physical evidence, the jury would probably overlook them "because they're so outraged at the nature of the offense," Frank believed.[7]

Though still disoriented and questioning his memory, Williams was now proclaiming his innocence. When his parents visited him at the Norfolk City Jail the day after his arraignment, he kept telling them that he didn't do it. His parents asked him about his confession. "Danial said that he confessed because the police kept badgering him and telling him that he did it," Rhea Williams remembered. So "he finally just said something. And he said, 'I don't even know what I said.'" After the visit, Nicole Williams didn't look good, so Rhea and Norman Williams took her to the hospital. Stress and anxiety were the diagnosis.[8]

Rhea and Norman left town a few days later. They were surprised that no police officers came by Danial's apartment to search for evidence (such as bloodstained clothes, towels, or carpet) before they left. But why would they need more evidence? A confession was gold. "It's the most overwhelming piece of evidence in any case," the prosecutor D. J. Hansen, who would later be brought into this case, says. "Everybody lives for a confession. . . . That's the best evidence that a prosecutor presents."[9] Shared by many judges and defense attorneys, that sentiment pervades the criminal justice system.

Williams's friend Derek Tice took Nicole (who was undergoing chemotherapy) to visit Danial in jail almost weekly after his arrest. Williams also told Nicole and Tice that he didn't do it, and that the police had bullied him into confessing.[10]

Shipley didn't ask Williams if he'd committed the crime. "Quite frankly, sometimes you really don't even want to know whether they're guilty or not, because it handicaps you in how you present the case," he explains. If they went to trial, how could he put Williams on the stand to deny involvement if Williams had already told him he was guilty? Defense lawyers have other good reasons not to ask their clients if they did it. For one, trust may suffer; a client might wonder if his attorney will really fight for him if he tells him that he's guilty. But questioning Williams about the case would have helped Shipley investigate whether he'd actually committed the crime. It was not until September— two months after his arrest—that Shipley and Frank first asked Williams what he knew about Michelle's murder and rape. Williams told them that he didn't have anything to do with it. Then why had he confessed? Because the police wore him down. "Almost from the beginning, he was saying, 'The confession isn't true, I wasn't there,'" Frank recounts. Shipley and Frank did not ask Williams about what had transpired during his interrogation until their September visit either.[11]

Around this time they gave Williams a copy of his confession. He jotted little notes on it as he read and reread it. "I got pencil marks all over it," he says. It now really started "sinking in" that he'd been hoodwinked by the police. "After I got locked up and everything was done, I started going back and trying to rationalize things," Williams recounts. "And it's like, 'Hold on.' I didn't have no defensive marks on me. . . . There was stuff underneath her fingernails, and they never checked me for any defensive wounds of any kind. . . . Once I was able to start going through my statement and seeing what I said, I knew there was something wrong. And I just really couldn't tie it all together." Then, "I guess everything fell into place, and I was like, 'Those motherfuckers were lying to me. . . . There's no way in heck that I would be doing that kind of stuff.'"[12]

Shipley and Frank (particularly Frank) began to call Williams "Denial"—to his face, to his parents, and to other attorneys, one of whom then used the nickname in a hearing. To them it was a clever play on 'Danial (which they misspelled "Daniel"). "I said, 'Daniel, your name is perfect,'" Shipley remembers. That irritated Williams, who figured his attorneys were trying to provoke him to admit his guilt. His parents didn't think much of the nickname either.[13]

Frank and Shipley found Williams hard to talk to and unforthcoming. "He just wouldn't really talk about anything," Frank recounts. "He'd just say, 'I wasn't there.' . . . He basically was sticking his head in the sand, and he didn't want to talk realistically about anything. . . . We really couldn't get anywhere else with him. And we're trying to impress upon him what he faced. And Danny in particular, having had somebody just immediately before that receive a death sentence, was trying to convey that to him. That it was a very real possibility." But "he didn't want to hear what we were trying to say to him." Sometimes it was difficult to even get Williams to speak. On occasion Shipley and Frank would think that they were getting somewhere with him, only to be met with that blank expression on his face when they were through. "Or he'd ask you a question after it was all over that indicated he obviously didn't understand what you were telling him," Frank remembers. His often vacant look, his thick glasses that magnified his eyes, and his overall demeanor would suggest to Shipley and Frank that there was "something weird going on." Moreover, he seemed exceptionally depressed, which is not surprising given his personal nightmare combined with his wife's cancer. He felt guilty that he was not there to care for Nicole, who would die on November 2, four months after his arrest. He was prohibited from attending her funeral, "which tore me up inside," he recalled. "I now felt totally alone."[14]

Clients are sometimes difficult in reaction to their lawyers' behavior, or to simply bad lawyering, and Williams found dealing with his attorneys like talking to a brick wall at times. "I had a hard time communicating with them," he recounts. "I'm telling them that I didn't do it, you know. And Bob, he would keep telling me, 'Well, I was a prosecutor for so many years. And when people confess, they've done it.' . . . That's what I was getting from him."[15]

In November, Shipley and Frank filed a routine and fairly generic motion to suppress Williams's confession. "Various promises or inducements were made to defendant that he would receive certain benefits if he confessed," they argued. Further, "his attempts to end his interrogation were ignored" and "his will was overborne by virtue of lengthy interrogation and deprivation of sleep." Such motions are rarely granted—the history of false confessions leading to wrongful convictions is replete with denied suppression motions—but to Shipley and Frank it was about Williams's only hope. Yet Williams was reluctant to testify at a hearing on it. "He didn't want to take the stand to say how he had been treated" by the police, Frank remembers. His insecurity and difficulty expressing himself seemed to be why. Without his testimony, however, the chance of getting his confession thrown out would have gone from slim to none. Frank and Shipley ultimately persuaded Williams to take the stand, but their motion was, predictably, refused.[16]

At the suppression hearing, Shipley largely just went through the paces. He never even raised the possibility that Williams's confession to police was false, nor did he point out any of the blatant discrepancies between it and the physical evidence. He did not prepare Williams much for his own testimony either. His questioning focused on obligatory matters: the sequence of the interrogation, the interrogation room and seating arrangements, whether Williams had been offered food and drink, when he had last slept and ate, whether he had told police he wanted to go home, and whether police had made him any promises or threats.[17]

Not long after the hearing, the lead prosecutor of Williams, Valerie Bowen, offered Shipley and Frank a plea bargain. If Williams would plead guilty to capital murder and rape—and accept a sentence of life in prison with no possibility of parole—the commonwealth would not seek the death penalty. Shipley and Frank wanted Williams to take the deal and advised him to do so. But they told him that he didn't need to make a decision right away, to think about it. "I said, 'There's a good chance they're going to execute you,'" Shipley recalls. His confession would be "hard to get around." The deal could save his life.[18]

Williams was reluctant. "I told them that I did not want to plead guilty because I did not kill Michelle," he recounts.[19]

So Shipley and Frank turned to Williams's parents. Maybe they could persuade him to take the deal. Three months after the suppression hearing, Frank wrote them a letter urging that they come to Norfolk for a meeting with their son at the jail. "Danial seems unwilling to accept the fact that [the] Commonwealth has a very good case against him for capital murder," Frank wrote. "Unfortunately, under current Virginia Law a life sentence on capital murder literally does mean for the rest of your life. However, our view is that life in prison is far superior to being executed. Danial does not seem to be able to understand the advice that we have been giving him and it is our hope that we can meet with you and explain to you why this is a reasonable offer and why he should accept the offer. . . . Together we can perhaps bring Danial to his senses with regard to whether or not he should pursue a trial." Four days earlier, Frank had requested a psychological evaluation of Williams to determine his competency to stand trial and sanity at the time of the crime since "extensive discussions with defendant have left counsel to believe that he may not fully understand the gravity of the situation with which he is faced." He did not seem able to "rationally evaluate" their advice, Frank told the court.[20]

Rhea and Norman Williams eventually came to Norfolk for a meeting at the jail, "which is unusual," Frank notes; it required special arrangements with the jail. They were far from excited about making the trip. They didn't fly, and Norman disliked talking about the case even with Danial's attorneys; when Shipley and Frank flew out to Michigan to interview family members for a background investigation, "Dad walked in and said hello and went to another part of the house and that was it," Frank recounts. At the jail, Frank and Shipley went through their reasoning on why Danial should take the plea—his confession, the fact that jurors wouldn't believe it was false, Tamika Taylor's claims of his interest in Michelle, the low rate of reversals of death penalties in Virginia, and so on. "They wanted us to try to get Danial to accept the plea agreement, to rationalize and say that, 'Danial, if you did do this, then just admit it and let's get on with it,'" Rhea Williams remembers. Shipley "told us that Danial was guilty and that with all of the evidence against Danial he should plead guilty." Frank kept saying that their son was in denial.[21]

The Williamses, who believed their son, were unenthusiastic about a plea. At some point Norman asked Shipley or Frank, rather pointedly, "If that was your kid, would you have him sign it?" "He couldn't answer me," Norman recalls. "I don't know if he was just trying to get it over with or what." Rhea and

Norman eventually told Danial's lawyers that they couldn't tell him what to do because he was an adult.[22]

Shipley and Frank would on one occasion try another tack with Danial: What would you rather have happen? they asked him. To have your family watch you get executed and then have to bury you? Or to at least be alive where they can still visit you?[23]

Plea bargaining, which is the way the overwhelming majority of criminal cases in the United States are settled, has often been criticized. The process is hidden from public view, and it places more power in the hands of prosecutors, who have many incentives to cut a deal: they can handle more cases quickly, achieve a higher conviction rate, obtain information on other suspects, and save money. Defense attorneys also have incentives to bargain: private attorneys can often make more money by handling many cases and pleading them out (especially when they charge flat fees for their services); public defenders are motivated by their huge caseloads; many lawyers feel pressure from prosecutors, judges, and court clerks to process cases quickly, and their relations with these people tend to be important to them (though Shipley says, "I've never felt any pressure to plead cases out"); and, not least importantly, they may fear a harsher sentence at trial. Defendants who are convicted at trial usually receive worse punishments than those who take pleas. "Threat is an essential part of all plea bargaining: take the deal or you'll do worse after conviction," the law professor Samuel Gross writes. "There is, undeniably, a coercive aspect to this bargain." The greatest threat is the death penalty.[24]

Shipley and Frank were paid by the state of Virginia 125 dollars per hour for in-court work and 100 dollars per hour for out-of-court work on Williams's case in 1997. Those rates, which were later raised to $150 per hour, are far lower than what they would have charged a client who had retained them directly in a capital case (though relatively few attorneys in capital murder cases are privately retained). But Williams's case gave them work and there was no cap on their total income from it. Hence, it is unlikely that they would have sought a plea to move on to more lucrative cases. Indeed, one court-appointed attorney in the area was suspected of taking a case to trial for the money.[25]

With plea bargaining, there is also the particular problem of innocent defendants pleading guilty to avoid risking a harsher sentence. These pleas offend one's sense of justice. A 2004 American Bar Association study found that innocent indigent defendants are often pressured by their lawyers to plead guilty without even understanding their legal rights. Too often, when such defendants meet their lawyer for the first time, the lawyer has already assumed their guilt and begun negotiating a plea. Since prosecutors are particularly eager to bargain when their case is weak, the greatest pressure to accept a plea is often marshaled against defendants who might be innocent. And while guilty pleas must be entered voluntarily—it is against the law in the United States for an attorney to coerce his or her client into accepting a plea bargain—the choice of pleading guilty to avoid the death penalty isn't really much of a choice at all. Moreover, after a defendant has entered a guilty plea, the search for exonerating evidence usually stops, and the standards for posttrial reviews of such cases are higher than for those involving trial convictions. It is even harder for someone who has pled guilty to prove their innocence with DNA evidence.[26]

The system was failing Williams. Many defense attorneys will go to the limit to defend clients who confess to crimes but whom the attorneys believe are innocent, even in capital cases. One of the basic duties of defense lawyers is, of course, to prevent innocent people from being convicted. And the quality of the attorney is pivotal in reliably determining guilt or innocence. On top of virtually presuming Williams's guilt from the start based on his confession, Shipley and Frank did not even investigate his claims of innocence. "There was absolutely no pretrial investigation of the facts," says one attorney who is familiar with Williams's case. Shipley and Frank did request money for the appointment of an investigator to determine whether someone else could have committed the crime. But that was because Nicole and Danial had told them that there had been similar assaults on women in the area at the time. A young woman named Melissa Morse had been blindsided and assaulted with a baseball bat or the like in the same block two weeks before Michelle's murder; her attacker had mistaken her for somebody else. That angry mob that had appeared outside Billy Bosko's patio door demanding the head of Tamika Taylor's friend Omar Ballard had thought that Ballard was Morse's assailant; Ballard and Taylor had denied it. Eleven days after Michelle's murder, a girl had been raped a mile away. The court granted Shipley and Frank's request for money for an investigator, but they never even hired one.[27]

The American Bar Association advises that attorneys in death penalty cases "fully investigate the relevant facts" starting "immediately upon counsel's entry into the case" and "before entering into plea discussions." Early investigation "is a necessity," the ABA argues. The attorneys "must promptly obtain the investigative resources necessary" and "independently investigate the circumstances of the crime, and all evidence—whether testimonial, forensic, or otherwise—purporting to inculpate the client. To assume the accuracy of whatever information the client may initially offer or the prosecutor may choose or be compelled to disclose is to render ineffective assistance of counsel." A thorough investigation of guilt should be conducted "regardless of any admission or statement by the client" and "regardless of overwhelming evidence of guilt," the ABA says. The defense attorney "should not expect client to accept plea bargain unless opinion is founded on experience and leg work investigating the case." Yet substantial investigations by defense attorneys are rare.[28]

Shipley and Frank also requested money for the appointment of a DNA expert, but the judge told them to wait until the DNA test results were in. They then never refiled their motion. They also failed to take a statement from Nicole Williams, although she was their client's alibi witness and they were aware that she had cancer. "There was a lot of things that [Shipley] could have done that he didn't do," says the attorney who is familiar with Williams's case.[29]

Shipley and Frank filed all the standard motions on Williams's behalf, but more zealous advocates might have done more to contest what was an obviously flawed confession. Had the case gone to trial—and that's what Williams wanted—Shipley and Frank might not have been in a position to present a strong defense.

However, most attorneys don't have the time or resources to investigate criminal charges independently. They must thus advise their clients based mainly on information supplied by the prosecution and on their own legal experience. Errors by attorneys are often products of systemic problems, and even if Shipley and Frank had chosen to hire an investigator, all the court had provided to pay him and all they had requested was $1,000.[30] Not a drop in the bucket, but Williams deserved better.

. . .

Meanwhile, back in Pittsburgh on emergency leave from the navy, Billy Bosko was incapacitated. "He couldn't even function," his mother, Pat Bosko, recalls. He had no desire to live. "The brother that I had no longer existed," his sister, Sarah, remembers. "He just seemed like a vegetable." His mother and sister had to tell Billy to change clothes, to shower, and to eat. "It was like having a baby," his mother says. He couldn't sleep. He lost twenty pounds in a month. "Every time I tried to eat, it would come right back up," he recounted later. "I was very, very paranoid, very jumpy." At the smallest suspicious noise at night, he would quickly spring up "ready to do battle."[31]

He still wasn't letting his emotions go; he would weep without really crying. Even after Michelle's burial, he didn't let himself go. "I was just so worried that once he did, I didn't want him to be by himself," his mother recalls.[32]

Billy's commanding officer phoned him in Pittsburgh: the navy wanted him to move on and resume his duties. At first Pat refused to let the officer speak to her son because she thought that Billy was in no condition to talk to anybody. She tried explaining this to the officer, and although he was sympathetic, "he really was adamant: he had to come back," Pat recounts. "And I said, 'Look, somebody better keep an eye on this kid. Because when he gets there, I'm telling you right now, he's got no reason to go on in his mind.'"[33]

Compounding the Bosko family's nightmare, Pat and her husband received an eviction notice from their landlord eight days after Michelle's murder. They were given fifteen days to get out. They had lived in the place for virtually Sarah's entire life. "I just simply forgot completely about the rent," Pat says.[34]

In August, the month after the murder, Billy returned to Norfolk. "He was still a wreck," a friend recalls. It was unbearable to be on his ship again. If he hadn't been off on that cruise, Billy ruminated, Michelle would still be alive. And there were too many memories. He had to get out of Norfolk—living there made everything far worse. He couldn't perform his duties. With help from a senator's office, he was honorably discharged from the navy.[35]

In September, Billy went back to Pittsburgh, where he shared a room with his sister. Sarah had a fish tank, and the light for the tank had to be kept on at all times, as darkness unnerved him. In the middle of one night, after Billy had finally fallen asleep, Sarah woke up and looked over to check on him. He was lying there with his covers off, in a cold sweat. After going to the bathroom,

Sarah noticed that he was sitting up and hugging himself. "Sarah, why did this happen?" he cried. She didn't know what to say—she was barely a teenager. On other nights, Billy would ask his sister to stay up and talk to him until he could fall asleep. "I miss her so much," Billy would say, then start weeping again. "I was losing my brother," Sarah remembers. In November, Billy suffered a breakdown. He announced that he wanted to die. He vomited and cried uncontrollably, collapsing to the ground. He was prescribed two medications for anxiety attacks.[36]

The pain of Michelle's parents was no less excruciating in their own home in Pittsburgh. When Carol Moore cried, which was often, her youngest son, Michael, would become upset or angry, while her other son, John, would grow quiet and head off to his bedroom. Jack and Carol Moore had first told Michael that his sister had died in a car accident, but he learned the truth from a neighbor kid a few months later. The Moores entered counseling, and Jack and Carol joined a support group for victims of violent crimes. But they did not find this help particularly effective.[37]

That fall, Assistant Commonwealth's Attorney Valerie Bowen and Maureen Evans, the first lead detective on the case, brought Joe Dick, Danial Williams's roommate, into the Naval Criminal Investigative Service (NCIS) office in Norfolk for questioning. Evans had recently been hired by NCIS and had come back from North Carolina, her duty station, for the interview. Dick had to know something about Michelle's murder, Bowen and Evans figured. "You can't be best friends with Danial and him not tell you that he did this," Evans said to Dick. But Williams hadn't told Dick anything. Dick informed Bowen and Evans that he had no direct knowledge of the crime.[38]

Bowen and Evans also wanted to know about Williams's "behavioral problems," Dick remembers. Had Williams beat him up? No, Dick responded. "We monkeyed around," Dick recalls telling them, "but that's about as far as that went." Someone in the navy had reported that Dick had worn his shirtsleeves down for a while. One of Dick's petty officers had ordered him to keep them down. But Bowen and Evans "thought something might have happened between me and Williams, and he might have bruised me or something," Dick recounts, and that he was covering up his injuries. "I could tell that Danial had some kind of hook on him," Evans says.[39]

Although she didn't suspect that Dick had any involvement in Michelle's murder, Evans asked him where he'd been that night. On duty on his ship, the USS *Saipan*, Dick told her.[40]

Dick wouldn't look at Evans and Bowen as he spoke to them. He seemed extremely shy to Evans, and "easily intimidated and easily controlled." If she hadn't known otherwise, Evans might have thought that he was from some small town or rural area, perhaps in the Midwest, one of those backward kids who were not used to socializing with a lot of other people. She wondered what might have happened in his childhood.[41]

At one point, Dick appeared to Evans to be on the brink of divulging something about what he knew. Evans felt she could tell when somebody was getting ready to spill. "We were talking about him knowing something, and then he brought up the fact that Danial may get out of jail," Evans recounts. "And I said, 'Danial's not getting out of jail, Joe.' . . . It was very obvious to me that he was going to tell me something and he was very afraid of Danial getting out of jail and hurting him." But then Bowen, who wanted Dick to answer her questions, interjected something and the conversation went elsewhere. Evans later thought the case could have been broken at that point had they pushed Dick.[42]

That December, police and prosecutors received a shocker: the Virginia Division of Forensic Science's Central Laboratory in Richmond reported that Williams's DNA did not match the sperm, blood, or other genetic material recovered from the crime scene. Police and prosecutors had considered the case open and shut. "We assumed naturally that the DNA was going to come back to him," Bowen would recall. "We thought we had the one and only perpetrator." Years later Bowen could still vividly remember the day she received the phone call informing her that it wasn't Williams's DNA at the scene, "and how shocked I was." Upset, she contacted Evans, who was then at the massive law enforcement training academy in Glynco, Georgia. "I got a phone call, which was kind of weird, because we stayed in dorms and we weren't very easily contacted at that point," Evans recounts. "She's basically—I won't say frantic, but she's like, 'What the hell's going on?'" Evans advised Bowen to press Dick. The focus of their investigation, she said, should now be on him.[43]

There were several possible explanations for the stunning DNA results. One was that Williams had done the crime but had not left any DNA. But someone's sperm had been found in Michelle, and it wasn't Williams's, or her husband's. Another line of reasoning was thus that Williams had raped and stabbed Michelle, as he said, but that another person had been with him, somebody who had left the unidentified DNA. An alternative interpretation of events was, of course, that Williams was innocent and hadn't been there at all. But police and prosecutors rejected this notion out of hand: hadn't he given them a detailed confession? If Detective Glenn Ford wondered about Williams's statement at all, he would not have wanted it known that he had elicited another false confession. "You're going to be inclined to believe that it's true, absent some bizarre circumstances," the prosecutor D.J. Hansen says.[44]

Many prosecutors are reluctant to acknowledge that people falsely confess to crimes, particularly atrocious ones. Asked how often he believes that false confessions occur, Hansen replied, "Rare, if ever. And certainly not here" in this case. Sailors like Williams had been put under tremendous stress in boot camp and in wartime footings on ships, Hansen argued. They knew how to deal with pressure. Why would they then buckle in an interrogation room if they were innocent? "I just don't buy it," Hansen says. "People confess because they are guilty," he would tell jurors. "They want to get something off their chest. It's as simple as that." In Cook County, Illinois, in 2003, however, the state's attorney's office acknowledged that false confessions were a problem. It held training sessions designed to help prosecutors recognize them. "Innocent people do confess to horrible crimes they didn't commit," Robert Milan, the chief deputy state's attorney, stated. "When we were coming up, no one taught us that. Why? Because we didn't believe it."[45]

But police and prosecutors in Norfolk assumed that the negative DNA results meant that somebody had been with Williams.[46] Somebody, perhaps, that he was protecting.

When Williams heard that his DNA didn't match the evidence, he realized that he had an opening. A big one. "It blows a hole in my statement," he told his attorneys, he recalls, and "it blows a hole in the prosecution's theory." But "they still didn't want to run with that. They were saying that even though it does help, if we went for a jury trial, the jury would be able to see my statement and they could come to a conclusion [that] maybe while I was raping her I didn't get off, or I used a condom." It wasn't necessarily a winner, Shipley felt. While a DNA match can certainly convict someone, he reasoned, the absence of a match will not always get him off. Yet it was powerful evidence of innocence that, presented effectively, could have been persuasive to jurors. "It's like they didn't want to go with anything that I suggested," Williams remembers.[47]

He didn't understand what was going on: the DNA test had proven his innocence, but prosecutors had not dropped the charges, and his own attorneys didn't seem to be fighting for him. This was not the legal system that he'd been taught in school.[48]

NCIS and Bowen brought Dick in for questioning again. He had lied to them about the case, they charged. "I was very confused and distraught because I knew I had told them the truth," Dick remembers. He spoke to his immediate supervisor in the navy, First Class Petty Officer Michael Ziegler, the *Saipan*'s sailor of the year in 1998. He believed that Ziegler had assigned him to be on duty on the *Saipan* at the time of the murder. Ziegler asked Dick, who was increasingly frightened by the whole situation, whether he knew anything about the murder. "Joe looked me straight in the eye and swore that he had nothing to do with the crime and knew nothing about it," Ziegler recalls.[49]

Ziegler figured that it was easy enough to determine whether Dick had been on duty. He took a look at some duty records along with his desk calendar. Dick's duty section had indeed been scheduled to be on duty at the time of the crime, Ziegler found. He double-checked his calendar to make sure he hadn't made a mistake. Dick would not have been allowed to leave the ship without permission; the ship's exits were guarded. And his duty lasted for twenty-four hours, from 7:30 in the morning to 7:30 the following morning. Several roll calls, documented in muster reports, were made during shifts, and Ziegler did not recall ever being notified that Dick had missed a roll call, which, he said, would have been a memorable event. Nor would Ziegler recall Dick ever requesting permission to leave the ship while on duty. And Ziegler remembered that he had ordered Dick to sleep on the *Saipan* that month because Dick had had trouble getting to work on time. He did not recall any time when Dick disobeyed that order. "There's no doubt in my mind he was on duty that night," Ziegler would later testify.[50]

On the morning of January 12, 1998, a Monday, the *Saipan*'s security office notified Ziegler that Norfolk police wanted to talk to Dick. After he located him, Ziegler told Dick that he needed to get in his dress blues for the interview. "In typical Joe fashion, he went to berthing and disappeared for a while," Ziegler would recount. Upon tracking Dick down, Ziegler noticed that he was nervous (and that he had on the wrong color of socks for his dress blues, which was vintage Dick). An NCIS agent drove Dick down to the NCIS office to talk to the police. Before he left, Ziegler advised him to just tell them the truth.[51]

It was the last time that Ziegler would see Dick.

4

The Roommate

Joseph Jesse Dick Jr. was an odd young man who evoked pathos. Lanky at 6'1" and 160 pounds, with wavy light-brown hair, a long but not thin face, a light mustache, and dark-rimmed glasses, he had been raised in a working-class neighborhood in Baltimore. His mother, Patricia (Trish) Dick, a polite, giving, and sensitive woman with salt-and-pepper hair who speaks with a native Baltimore accent and who manifested a palpable sense of sadness mixed with love for her son when interviewed for this book, is a secretary for a textile company. A devout Catholic, she was active in her church in Baltimore and regularly led her congregation in song and prayer. Her kids came first in her life; she was always hugging and kissing Joe and his younger sister, Michele, and telling them that she loved them. She tended to be bubbly and jovial. Joseph Jesse Dick Sr., Joe's father, was a sergeant first-class in the Maryland Army National Guard. A hunter and outdoorsman who had dropped out of high school, he is a big man with glasses and formerly blondish hair that has turned white, and a practicing Catholic himself, though not as devout as his wife. He is prone to exclaiming "Judith priest," "Jesus priest," or just plain "Jesus Christ." He has a strong personality and can be dogmatic, rigid, and difficult. A cynical person, "I don't trust anybody," he says. "I don't trust my mother. And she's dead."[1]

The son of an alcoholic father, Joe Dick Sr. was hard on little Joe. He would sometimes beat him with a belt. He called it an "ass whopping." Joe Jr., who looked up to and feared his father, says he got it "only when I deserved it." ("My mom gave it to me when I deserved it" too, he adds; she used a paddle.)

"I'd try to bullshit him, and he would know when I'm bullshitting him," Joe Jr. recounts. "I had a hard time trying to pull the wool over my dad's eyes. That's when he was hard on me," or when Joe would fail to complete his chores. His dad treated Joe as if he were in the army, one of Joe's teachers remembers. Joe dared not become angry or disagree with his father lest he get a beating. He would deny to a probation and parole officer that he'd been abused, however. He had a "so-so" relationship with his father and was a "momma's boy," he told the officer. "We didn't have much of a rapport to begin with," his dad recalls. "Because I was out of town and out at work a lot." Joe did not develop into the son he'd hoped for, one relative says. He wished Joe were sharper and tougher. He paid more attention to his daughter. "I think little Joe was constantly competing for his father's attention or okay," the relative says. But big Joe would take his son fishing and down to the land they owned in West Virginia, where they'd camp and maintain the property. Joe Sr. also helped his son advance in the Boy Scouts, which was a struggle. "I became frustrated when Joe failed to understand simple instructions or made mistakes when completing simple tasks," Joe Sr. recalls. "I wished that Joe could perform at the same level as the other boys in his troop."[2]

Extremely withdrawn, introverted, and lacking social skills, Joe had a hard time making friends as a boy. He had few, if any, perhaps one or two. "Joe was always kind of like a loner," his mother remembers. "Always on the outside looking in. . . . He was never one of the in-crowd." Though his voice boomed at times, he tended to be so quiet in class that you might not even know he was there. He was a timid kid, unusually fearful of adults and loud noises (even shouts of other children behind him), which made him cringe; as a young child he had been afraid of "everything," his mother said. He feared confrontations. But he got along well with his cousins and seemed happy around them. And in machine shop at his vocational high school, most of the other kids liked him, although the school was over 90 percent black and he was white.[3]

Joe was not the sharpest kid around. His mind worked slowly; long pauses often preceded his speech. One had to pull things out of him. His second-grade teacher judged his difficulty expressing himself and his verbal-mental limitations "severe." He had problems processing more complex ideas. "And when it came out it always came out on the kid level instead of on a more intellectual level," his aunt Theresa Bankard-Sharpe recalls. "He was more simple, more basic. I don't think he had a lot of critical thinking." Once, while talking to Joe when he was twenty-two, Bankard-Sharpe felt like she was talking to a twelve-year-old. "My wife and I used to argue constantly, because I always used to say he was slow," his father reminisces. "And she would get mad at me and say, 'He's not slow. There's nothing wrong with him.'" But his sixth-grade teacher would remember him as "a simplistic young man with limited ability." Some suspected he had a learning disability. He was unable to contribute much of substance to family conversations; it was as if he were hearing a different conversation. He had a hard time comprehending jokes. His grades fluctuated; he regularly failed to complete assignments and daydreamed in class, fiddling with and breaking his glasses. He had to be pushed constantly, but even when he strove mightily his performance was usually subpar.[4]

Joe's attention span was limited. Twenty minutes was really all he had, his grandfather would say. A fidgety and helter-skelter kid, he was prescribed Ritalin for attention deficit disorder. His pediatrician kept increasing the dosage. "I came home from work and found out that he was taking the highest dosage of any child that was on that," his father remembers. "And I just went ballistic. I grabbed him, jumped in the car, we went up to the doctor's, and I said, 'You're taking him off this right now. You understand me? *Right now*.'"[5]

When Joe was three years old, he and his father were swinging one day on a large swing set. Do you want to see how high daddy can go? his father, who weighed 200 pounds, asked him. Yeah, little Joe replied. So his dad started sailing way up and back. Little Joe was laughing. "Then I went up and I came back one time and he wasn't there," his dad recounts. "And that fast—boom—I hit him." Joe had run behind his dad and gotten nailed in the forehead. "When he turned around, his eyes were in the bottom of his head, and he—boom—fell over," his dad recalls. In tears, big Joe carried his son into the house and put him to bed instead of taking him to a doctor. For years afterward, he and Patricia would be troubled by the possibility that the accident had damaged their son's brain. A psychiatrist who later evaluated Dick found it likely that he had suffered frontal lobe damage that affected his mental functioning.[6]

Joe was extraordinarily gullible and naïve. He believed anything that anyone told him. If somebody said the sky was bright green, he'd buy it until he went outside. He was easily manipulated, partly because his grasp of reality depended inordinately on outside influences (he seemed "disconnected from reality" to one classmate). As a child, he had been persuaded to trade an expensive toy for a Twinkie. His peers later coaxed him to claim that he owned an imaginary device for masturbating after saying they all owned one. It wasn't hard to fool him into thinking you were his friend. Even more than Danial Williams, Joe was a follower. If he was walking with a group of guys, he would be in the back, behind everyone else, loping characteristically along with long, bouncy, awkward strides on his toes. And if the group threw rocks at a window, he would be the last one to turn and run—he'd still be looking at the shattered window.[7]

Immature, Joe was held back in the fifth grade because he wasn't emotionally ready to advance; he got along better with younger kids. He loved playing with Lego, matchbox cars, and toy trucks, tanks, and soldiers. Even after going through boot camp in the navy, he thought nothing of playing with toy cars.[8]

He tended to be oblivious to the consequences of his actions. His first part-time job was mowing the lawn at his church. One day, when he was a sophomore in high school, he reached down to clear the grass along the edge of the mower without turning the mower off. The blade sliced off the index and middle fingers of his right hand at the knuckles. "I didn't think it would do that," he said afterward, though he'd been forewarned. "He proudly showed me his hand with parts of his fingers missing," his uncle Al Bankard recalls. "He was not at all embarrassed by it."[9]

When Joe was young his parents had him evaluated by the Kennedy Krieger Institute in Baltimore for children with developmental disabilities. At the institute's recommendation, he saw a speech therapist for a couple of years and had his tongue clipped. The institute also advised that he undergo a complete assessment for disabilities, but his father took offense to the idea and vetoed it.[10]

Joe Dick was teased mercilessly by his peers. They recognized his limitations. Kids called him Dickhead and other choice names. His teachers could tell by his body language and facial expressions that the teasing upset him; he'd wring his hands and shift his weight uncomfortably from one foot to the other. But sometimes he'd laugh, or say something like, "Well, you don't know how to plan a search-and-rescue mission." He didn't always realize when kids were taunting him. Uncoordinated, he was the kind of kid other boys picked last when selecting players for sports teams. Stuck in the outfield in Little League, he'd lose interest, then start digging in the grass or messing around. He usually sat by himself on the team bench.[11]

But he was eager to please people. If someone needed his help, he'd usually be there. At school, "he would go out of his way to help you," one teacher remembers. An ultra-affectionate boy, "he was always hugging everybody," his aunt Theresa Bankard-Sharpe recounts. "Just a very loving family member," even as a teenager, when his displays of affection seemed out of synch with his age. When he went to say goodbye to his grandmother before entering the navy at age nineteen, he embraced her effusively and kissed her. "I'll never forget that," she says.[12]

Joe attended church regularly and was an altar boy for eight years. He also did volunteer work for his school and church. But he could be dishonest; he sometimes lied to his teachers. His dad felt he often didn't get the truth from him. "I could walk in the kitchen and he'd have his hand in the cookie jar," Joe Sr. recounts. "And I'd say, 'Joe, what are you taking the cookies for?' And he'd say, 'I don't know what you're talking about.'"[13]

Joe trained to be a machinist in high school, but he wanted to follow in his father's footsteps in the military and enlisted in the navy early his senior year. (His first choice had been the army, but his father had worried that he wouldn't succeed in the army and actually convinced him that the army wouldn't be able to cope with two people named Joe Dick.) Some people were surprised, even shocked, when Joe was accepted by the navy. And he did not perform well there. He required "intense supervision" and "very specific step-by-step instructions," his supervisor, Michael Ziegler, recalls. "Joe tried very hard, but simply did not have the wherewithal to perform basic tasks." He had to repeat training schools. Assigned to repaint the fluorescent outlines of hatch doors on the *Saipan*, he splattered paint everywhere, including the ceiling. He received numerous reprimands for tardiness, and failed to maintain his uniform; Ziegler routinely sent him back to the berthing area to get his dress in order. His personal hygiene was lousy. When an officer spoke to him about it, Dick explained that he didn't like to take showers in front of other guys. Ziegler, too, wondered how Dick got into the navy. Upon reviewing his scores on entrance exams, he discovered that Dick had barely passed.[14]

Dick remained largely a solitary figure in the navy. People made fun of him there too. As a gauge calibration technician, he enjoyed recalibrating dials for hours on end by himself. On a Mediterranean cruise, Danial Williams had to practically drag him off their ship to get him out and about. It was hard to get him out of their apartment as well. "He really didn't want to have a social life," Williams perceived. Eric Wilson, another sailor, who felt sorry for Dick, also tried to get him out to meet some people, but that didn't work out. A clinical psychologist who would interview Dick wrote: "According to Mr. Dick, his degree of social withdrawal resulted in a very simple lifestyle. He basically worked his shift on the ship and then spent his evenings watching television or constructing airplane models. He had only a few friends, and no girlfriends. He did not go to other social activities typical of persons his age and background, such as movies, clubs, church events, or parties." The psychologist suggested that Dick suffered from "schizoid personality disorder," characterized by detachment from social relationships, choice of solitary pursuits, and restricted emotional expression around people. So did a psychiatrist who later evaluated him. To some people, Dick seemed off in his own world, "weird," even "kind of creepy," and not all there. He occasionally frequented The Banque bar, but he was not part of the Banque Crew nor a big drinker.[15]

Dick recalls learning about Williams's arrest for the murder and rape of Michelle Moore-Bosko on the local television news at noon on board the *Saipan* at the Norfolk Naval Shipyard. "I couldn't believe it," he recounts. "The man's married, and now he's arrested for doing something stupid." Williams didn't seem capable of it to Dick (he told Michael Ziegler that Williams was innocent), but he wasn't sure what to believe. Dick says that he was at work on board the *Saipan* the day of the murder from 7 A.M. until 4 P.M. After showering, he remembers, he ate at the chow hall at the shipyard since the galley on the *Saipan* was closed owing to work being done on the ship. He then returned to the *Saipan* because Ziegler had ordered him to sleep on board, which he says he did. Unfortunately, the *Saipan*'s muster reports, which could have verified Dick's presence on the ship (more than the duty assignment records Ziegler found), were discarded by the navy six months later.[16]

After Williams was arrested, Dick continued to live in their apartment with Williams's dying wife, Nicole, until she was evicted because of her husband's arrest. Dick was smitten with her. "He was crazy about Mrs. Williams," one person says.[17]

·   ·   ·

On January 12, 1998, six months after Michelle Moore-Bosko's murder, and after the Naval Criminal Investigative Service agent drove Dick over to the NCIS office, Detective Glenn Ford and his partner, Detective Brian Wray, asked Dick to accompany them to the Norfolk Police Operations Center to answer some questions. Dick readily complied. The three arrived at the station at 10:10 A.M.[18]

Like Danial Williams, Dick had never been interrogated by police before. He too had no juvenile or adult criminal record, nor had he suffered any brushes with the law.[19] He was putty in Ford's hands. Indeed, it would be hard to find someone less equipped to handle a high-pressure police interrogation, save for a mentally disabled person or a juvenile.

After placing Dick in an interrogation room, Ford, who was now the lead investigator in the Moore-Bosko case, wheeled around and walked out, only to reenter the room with Wray about ten minutes later. "Prior to embarking upon the actual interrogation, it is advisable to allow the suspect to sit in the interview room alone for about five minutes," the leading manual on police interrogations, *Criminal Interrogation and Confessions*, recommends. "A guilty suspect will rapidly try to review everything that is going to be said, and this preparation will cause him to become insecure. Additional doubts and concerns will arise in the suspect's mind and thereby further disorganize efforts at deception." Ford put a Miranda rights form in front of Dick and asked him to read the first line. After Dick read it, Ford read him the remaining six lines on the form. In capital letters, Dick wrote "YES" in the blank below each line. It is unlikely that he fully understood what he was doing.[20]

Wray and Ford made an imposing pair. Tall and stocky, Wray was a big man, built like a football player, with a thick neck and brown hair, around thirty years old. In that little room, his size alone would have been intimidating. And then there was Ford with his rough, loud voice and aggressive, threatening interrogation style. Wray's main roles were to take notes on the interrogation, observe Dick, and to be able to confirm in court, if necessary, that Ford did not abuse or threaten Dick, make him any promises, or otherwise act in a way that might cause a judge to suppress any confession Dick gave. Most of the time, "Wray just sat across from me at the table quiet as a mouse," Dick remembers.[21]

Ford informed Dick that they were conducting an investigation into the murder and rape of Michelle Moore-Bosko and asked him where he had been at the time. Dick replied that he believed that he had been on duty on the *Saipan* that night and for the whole week afterward. He had left his apartment on that Sunday, the day before the crime, with his uniforms and other belongings and never returned from his ship during the week, he said. "He denied his involvement as soon as we started talking to him," Wray later testified.[22]

How long had he known Danial Williams? Ford asked him. Since February 1996, Dick responded. What had Williams's own duty status been the week of the murder? He had been on emergency leave that whole week because of his wife's cancer, Dick replied.[23]

Ford asked Dick if he had known Michelle Moore-Bosko. Yes, Dick stated, but the first time that he had ever seen her was two days before her murder, in the common hallway of their apartment building with a bag of groceries. He had seen her again that night when she took out her trash. Had he ever been in her apartment? Ford probed, although in his own mind he already knew the answer. No, Dick replied.[24]

Ford wanted to know if Williams had ever intimidated Dick and tried to make him do things he didn't want to do. Sometimes it is easier for police to get a suspect to confess to a crime if they play down the suspect's responsibility for it. Williams did indeed intimidate him, Dick responded, and many times he did whatever Williams told him to do. Williams had even threatened to beat him up on occasion and perhaps even did once, Dick stated. But he did not give Ford the confession he sought.[25]

After asking Dick how long he had known Nicole Williams, Ford announced that he knew that Dick had not been on duty when the murder took place. Only ten minutes had passed since Dick had waived his Miranda rights, but to Ford, who had no evidence of Dick's involvement, it was time to express certainty in his guilt. "A fundamental principle of interrogation . . . is that the more often a guilty suspect denies involvement in a crime, the less likely he will be to tell the truth," *Criminal Interrogation and Confessions* argues. Better to cut him off quickly.[26]

Dick then told Ford that he thought he might have worked either the day before or the day after the murder, but that "he wasn't sure." His will was already weakening. Ford admonished Dick that he needed to tell them the whole truth about what really happened that night: *Was* he in the victim's apartment with Danial Williams? Again Dick denied any involvement, and indeed denied even being with Williams that night.[27]

Dick recounted that on the Saturday evening two days before the murder, Williams had gone across the hall to Moore-Bosko's apartment at about 10 P.M. with his CD case. This was the same night that Tamika Taylor later testified that Williams had arrived later than that and departed at 4 A.M. after dancing in a disturbing sexual manner. Dick informed Ford that Williams had returned home around 2 A.M. He had woken him up, Dick said.[28]

Ford and Dick then went "back and forth," Dick recounts, with Ford repeatedly proclaiming his guilt, Dick denying any involvement, and Ford angrily charging that he was lying. "I was telling them that I wasn't there, and that there was no way I could have done it," Dick recalls. "And that I was on board the USS *Saipan* at the time. . . . And Ford kept yelling at me, telling me that he knew I was there." The police had confirmed that he had not been on his ship, Ford told Dick, though Ford would never even contact Michael Ziegler about Dick's whereabouts. (The prosecutor D.J. Hansen would say later that police determined that Dick had been on duty the day Michelle's body was found, not the night before when she was killed.) The more Dick denied involvement, the angrier Ford seemed to get. Wray, who also warned Dick to stop lying, would later state under oath that "we never raised our voice," although he acknowledged that "Ford's voice changed" when telling Dick that they knew he had been involved. Wray also admitted that this claim was "not true."[29]

Ford let Dick know that Williams had given them a confession, without revealing that Williams had not mentioned Dick in it. Williams had already told them what Dick had done, Ford was implying. Ford also advised Dick that they had DNA evidence proving his guilt. Wray later acknowledged that they had no such evidence. But "you got to make him see that you have something," Ford would testify. Dick did not inquire about the nature of this alleged DNA evidence.[30]

Would he be willing to take a lie-detector test? Ford asked Dick. Yes, Dick said, "because I had nothing to hide," he wrote later. He hoped the test results would get him the hell out of that room. Ford, of course, sought to induce a confession. As it had been with Williams, this game was rigged: the police would tell Dick that he had failed the test regardless of the result (though Dick thought he "knocked Ford back on his ass" by agreeing to take the test—"he didn't like that"). Ford phoned Detective Randy Crank at his home and asked him to come in to administer the polygraph. Ford placed Dick in the exam room with Crank at around noon. According to Wray and Ford's notes, after Crank finished with the test, he informed them that "he could not clear Joseph Dick and say that he passed the polygraph. He stated that there were indications on the test that led him to believe that Joseph was lying about something, especially when it came to the question about if he ever put his penis in the victim's vagina or sexually assaulted her."[31]

Dick had actually passed the test. "How I ever passed that thing I'll never know," Dick recalls. "Because I was *nervous like hell*. And I've got bad nerves to start out with." Ford informed Dick back in the interrogation room that the results "were not good," however, "and that he was lying," Wray and Ford wrote afterward. In Dick's retelling, Ford declared that he had failed the test so spectacularly that he almost broke the polygraph machine. "I was confused and extremely upset because I had told the truth," Dick recounts. Ford refused to show him the results of the test or explain them to him. "By that time [in the interrogation], I'm pissed off," Dick remembers. "I'm worn down mentally. I'm frustrated. And I want to knock Ford upside the head real bad. But for some reason I don't. I just keep myself under control. Because that would make me look bad."[32]

When Dick continued to profess his innocence, the temperature in that tiny room rose even further. What little he knew about the crime he had learned from the news, Dick tried to tell Ford. He had never even been in Michelle's apartment, Dick pleaded once more. That just provoked more angry yelling from Ford.[33]

Around this time, Ford let Dick know that he would beat him with rubber hoses if he could. "I took that as a threat," Dick says. Wray and Ford did not include that threat in their record of the interrogation. Ford advised Dick that he could get the death penalty: Did he want to die? "Detective Ford told me the only way I could avoid the death penalty was to tell him the truth," Dick recounts. "I tried repeatedly to explain that I was telling the truth," but to no avail.[34]

Like Williams, Dick had begun to question his memory of the night of the murder. When Ford informed him that he had flunked the polygraph badly, he wondered if he might actually have participated in the crime and then somehow blocked it from his memory. "You probably blacked out and don't remember," he recalls Ford or Wray telling him. Ford's claims that they had evidence of his participation also shook Dick's confidence in his memory.

"Every time they keep telling me that they know I was there, and they can prove I was there, and they've got evidence and all, it just keeps telling me, 'Okay, maybe I *was* there,'" he recounts. Perhaps he hadn't been on the *Saipan* at the time after all. Ford's refusals to even entertain his claims of innocence also undermined Dick's self-confidence, which was minimal to begin with.[35]

That is the usual sort of scenario that unfolds when police convince innocent suspects that they may be guilty: they keep hammering away about purported evidence, refuse to take no for an answer, express absolute certainty in the suspect's guilt, claim that his alibi is contradicted by the facts, and suggest a possible reason for his alleged amnesia. Minimizing the legal consequences of the crime can also make it easier for a suspect to believe he committed it. The interrogator thinks he is lying about not remembering and suggests amnesia to help overcome his resistance to confessing; the suspect can then no longer be sure that he didn't do it. By the time he voices a confession, his confidence in his memory has been shattered. He may conclude that the only way he can comprehend his criminal act is by relying on the evidence laid out by the police and on details that are public knowledge. Or he may desperately make up the details or simply guess about them. He will typically express certainty in neither his guilt nor his innocence; his language will be tentative: "I could have," "I probably did," and so on. Peter Reilly, the eighteen-year-old who police convinced that he'd brutally murdered his own mother, told his polygraph examiner, "I would say you're right, but I don't remember doing the things that happened. That's just it. I believe I did it now." Persuaded by police that he had tortured, raped, and killed a neighbor, a Florida man named Tom Sawyer remarked resignedly, "I guess all the evidence is in. I guess I must have done it."[36]

Dick's grasp on events was plenty murky. Typical of persuaded false confessors, he was confused and had not formed an actual memory of his involvement. So tenuous, so shaky was his belief in his guilt that he could later tell a probation and parole officer that he "forgot about the entire incident" and "did not think about the crime he had committed" until his interrogation by Ford, now six months after Michelle's murder.[37]

Dick's relatives were not surprised when told later that police had led him to believe that he had committed a crime that he had not, in fact, committed.

"It wouldn't take much to persuade him," his aunt Theresa Bankard-Sharpe commented. "Joe can be easily persuaded by anybody who is intellectually superior to him. . . . 'If they keep telling me I did it, I must have done it.'" His uncle Tom Bankard, a retired army officer, said he could have taken somebody like Joe and gotten whatever he wanted out of him. He could have nailed him to the cross even better than Ford.[38]

At around 2 p.m., Ford asked Dick if he had spoken to Nicole Williams about the crime since Danial's arrest. Dick replied that she had told him that a black man had been arrested for committing a rape in the area and had admitted it. Dick thought this might have been the rape and killing of Michelle. Had he ever been attracted to Nicole? Ford quizzed him. Yes, Dick acknowledged, but he would never try anything with her because she was married. How about Michelle? Had he been attracted to her? No, not in any way, Dick responded. Again, he stated that he had been on the *Saipan* at the time of her murder and for that entire week. How did he get to the ship? Ford wanted to know. A Yellow Cab, Dick explained.[39]

At 2:10 p.m. Ford shoved a photo of Michelle's dead body in front of him. Though the move may have been intended to stir Dick's conscience, *Criminal Interrogation and Confessions* cautions, "A suspect should not be confronted with photographs that gruesomely display a victim's wounds or injuries." Such photos might not only inhibit him from confessing by reminding him of the seriousness of his crime, but "may reveal incriminating information about the nature of the crime that only the guilty suspect would know," the manual points out. "Withholding such information is critical to help corroborate the details of a confession the suspect does offer."[40] In other words, Ford was contaminating his suspect.

When he saw the photo, Ford keenly eyeballing his reaction, Dick almost started to cry, "because of how old she is, and how she died," he recounts. And, years later, "every time I think about it I start breaking down and crying. I try and put it in the back of my head and forget about it. . . . I still shed a tear every now and then." According to Wray and Ford's notes, the first thing Dick said to them after seeing the photo was that the white blanket on Michelle came from his apartment. How did it get over there? Ford inquired. When Williams had gone over to her apartment two nights earlier with his CD case, he had taken it with him, saying that he was cold, Dick responded. (Billy

Bosko would later testify that he wasn't sure whose blanket it was, but that "it could have been Michelle's.")[41]

A minute or two later, Ford warned Dick that he was "in some serious trouble," and that if he wanted them to prove their case against him, they certainly would. After Ford left the interrogation room, Wray admonished Dick that he needed to tell them the truth about what had happened that night. They knew that he had been there and could prove it, Wray likewise claimed. Wray appealed to Dick's conscience, urging him to get it all off his chest and come clean about what had really happened. Dick had been wondering the last six months when they were going to come to talk to him, as everything had been building up inside him, Wray purported to know. "Just tell the truth," Wray exhorted him. Dick said that he would.[42]

He then began to give Wray a confession. When we asked him why years later, Dick explained that after hours of Ford yelling at him, "I figured that he would shut up if I told him anything he wanted to hear. I was tired and frustrated and I just wanted him off my back. . . . I just gave in . . . because I knew DNA would clear me." He did not realize that he could end the interrogation by asking for a lawyer, he felt his predicament was hopeless, and "I could no longer stand the pressure." And after hours of Ford's lies, "I was able to believe that I had committed the rape and murder," Dick says. He felt guilty about it.[43]

Since Dick had no memory of his involvement, he simply "made up the details" that he gave Ford and Wray based on what he thought might have happened, or just repeated back to them what they told him about the crime. Plus he'd heard details that friends of Williams had picked up from court hearings and newspaper articles.[44]

He and Williams had gone across the hall to Michelle's apartment that night, Dick told Wray. When Danial knocked on her door, she let them in. "Once inside the house," Dick said, "they joked around and were just bullshitting around in the living room when Daniel [sic] started making some advances towards Michelle," Wray and Ford wrote. But "Michelle pushed him away and appeared not to take well to his advances." Williams then knocked her to the floor, pinned her shoulders down, "pulled her pants or shorts off"—Dick, of course, didn't know whether she was wearing pants or shorts—removed her panties, "and started jerking off," Dick offered. Williams then raped Michelle on the floor. He also committed oral sodomy on her, Dick told Wray.[45]

All of this took place in Michelle's living room, according to Dick's account. But, of course, Michelle's body would be found the next day lying prostrate on the floor of her bedroom.

What was he doing this whole time? Wray asked Dick. "He stated that he was just sitting there watching, and he was not involved in any way," Wray and Ford wrote. Asked what else Williams did to Michelle, Dick said that he forced her to give him a blow job. "He stated that then Daniel [sic] Williams put the blanket under the victim and did the same process all over again, raping her repeatedly." But Williams's DNA had not been found on the blanket or in Michelle. Dick told Wray that he got tired of watching all of this and ran out of Michelle's apartment.[46]

Wray then left the interrogation room. About twenty minutes later, a little after 3 P.M., Dick agreed to give police a sample of his blood ("I said, 'Yeah, no problem,'" he remembers). After a paramedic drew Dick's blood, Wray and Ford directed Dick to repeat what he had just told Wray. They needed to "clear up some points," they claimed. After he and Williams had done their "joking around and bullshitting" with Michelle and Williams had repeatedly sexually assaulted her, Dick reiterated, he bolted out of her apartment.[47]

Ford rebuked Dick that he needed to tell them the *whole* truth, not just part of the truth. DNA analysis would prove that his own penis had been inside of Michelle. What did he think about that? "I think you are right," Dick replied.[48]

Ford wanted to know what Williams had said to him before they went over to Michelle's apartment. That he needed to get out of their own apartment and was spending too much time in it, Dick responded. Once inside Michelle's apartment, Dick stated in this version of events, they all three listened to some music while sitting on the living room floor. Williams then began rubbing Michelle's breasts and vagina. "She let him do it for a while," Dick stated. After she started resisting and Williams pinned her to the floor, Dick said, Williams asked him to hold her shoulders down, so he did while Williams performed oral sex on her. Williams then told him to do the same thing with her. Did he put his penis anywhere? Ford asked. Yeah, in her vagina, Dick replied. He also put it in her mouth, he said. But Michelle tried to bite it, so he took it out and slapped her a couple of times. If she did it again, he warned her, he would slap her even harder the next time. While this was going on, Williams was raping her, according to Dick's story; they then switched places.

Dick would later tell a clinical psychologist that he'd never had a girlfriend nor any sexual contact with anyone.[49]

What was the victim doing this whole time? Ford asked him. She was fighting and trying to get up, Dick replied. After he was finished, Dick said, he got up and told Williams that he wanted to leave. But Williams wanted him to stay. They argued for around five minutes about it, Dick told Ford. Michelle was crying. Then she got up off the floor, went into the kitchen, and grabbed a knife, Dick said. He and Williams were still arguing when she went to get the knife. What kind of knife was it? Ford queried him. He didn't know, Dick responded, just that it was a kitchen knife, and that it was sharp; not a butter knife. "How was I to know that the murder weapon was a steak knife?" Dick wrote later. He suspected that Michelle had been stabbed, however—that's why he brought a knife into the picture. "It's not hard for somebody with any brains to look at the news, to put two and two together and come up with four, and then look at the photos that they show you in the interrogation room, and realize, 'Oh, okay. This was done with a knife,'" he says. "It don't take no idiot to figure that out."[50]

Michelle went after Williams with the knife, Dick continued. Williams grabbed her hand, and Dick took the knife out of her hand and put it down. What did Michelle do then? Ford asked. She broke down and started crying again, Dick responded.[51]

Ford scolded Dick that he was still not telling them the whole truth. He needed to tell them what he really did with the knife.

He and Williams knew they had to kill her, Dick then offered. When he grabbed the knife from Michelle, he stabbed her twice. Or maybe more, he said later. Then he dropped the knife. Where did he stab her? Ford inquired. He didn't know, Dick replied. He couldn't remember.[52]

All of this was still unfolding in Michelle's living room, according to Dick's account. But the living room would be found in neat condition the next day, with no sign of a struggle or an assault.

After he dropped the knife, Dick went on, Michelle came at him, so he grabbed her, and then Williams, who had picked up the knife off the floor, stabbed her twice himself in the chest as he held her. Michelle then fell to the ground. Dick said that he threw the white blanket over her legs—the one that, in reality, Billy Bosko and Williams had draped over her the next day. Dick then left her apartment as Williams remained behind, he stated.[53]

Why did he do it? Ford asked Dick. He didn't know, Dick replied. But he thought that it was an "accident"; he didn't mean to do it.[54]

One wonders if Ford or Wray suggested to Dick that it could have been an accident. It is, of course, easier to get someone to admit to an accident than to a murder. Then you go on from there. "Now that I've told you the truth, can I go home?" Dick asked at one point, since it had only been an accident.[55]

At 3:55 P.M., before leaving the room, Ford and Wray advised Dick that they needed to take a taped statement from him. That wouldn't be a problem, Dick responded. Wray later testified that they taped Dick "when he had finished telling us all the details of what had happened." How did they know those details were true? Dick's attorney at the time, Michael Fasanaro, asked Wray. "Because of the crime scene, the stuff we knew about the crime scene, about the victim and how she was found, how she was killed," Wray replied.[56] But Dick had said nothing about strangling Michelle, nor anything about the five knife pricks on her chest. And Ford and Wray were aware that both she and the knife had been found in her bedroom, not her living room. Indeed, far from being true, those details should have raised doubts in Ford's and Wray's minds about whether Dick had actually been there.

At 4:15, Wray asked Dick if he needed anything to eat. Tuna fish would be fine, Dick replied, so Wray brought him a can of tuna fish and some crackers. Wray knew that Dick would be headed straight to the rough Norfolk City Jail after he gave them a taped statement, and then later in all likelihood to prison. As he snacked on the tuna fish and crackers, it is doubtful that Dick had much of an idea what was in store for him. He still didn't see far down the road.

After reentering the interrogation room, Ford apprised Dick that they needed to "clear up" some more things. Where did all this start? Ford asked. In the living room, Dick responded, and that's where they raped her. "He stated that he did not remember where they ended up, if it was in the bedroom or dining room or what room they were in when it finally ended," Wray and Ford wrote in their notes. That should have been a red flag. It would be hard to forget, and why would Dick fudge it? Could they have ended up in the bedroom? Ford probed. They could have, Dick replied, but he wasn't sure. "He did not remember what color shorts or panties that the victim had on that night" either, Wray and Ford recorded. When he ran out of the apartment, Dick said, Williams wanted to have sex with Michelle again. They had both stabbed her by this point, according to his account. Did he think Michelle was dead when he left? Ford pressed him. He thought she was going to die or that she had already died, he replied. Asked what he did the next day, Dick said that he went to work as usual.[57]

At 5:18, after a lieutenant removed Dick's navy shirt, leaving him in his undershirt, Ford and Wray brought out two tape recorders. In his taped confession, an absurd story worthy of a cheap pornographic novel, Dick said that he had ejaculated in Michelle's mouth. But no semen had been found there. When Williams grabbed Michelle's arm after she had come at him with the knife, Dick stated in this version of events, she dropped it. "I went, picked it up and accidentally stabbed her twice," Dick said. "I didn't realize what I was doing at the time." He believed that they were still in the living room when Williams stabbed her "about two to three times" and she collapsed on the floor. "You don't recall which room she was in when she fell?" Ford asked, incredulously. "It could have been either in the dining room or in the living room," Dick replied. "Do you know how she would have ended up in another room in the house?" Ford queried him. "Dan could—probably placed the body in another room in the house," Dick responded. After he left, "Dan stayed behind to clean up or whatever he was going to do, and he got back to the apartment late." They never talked about what they had done, Dick said.[58]

Ford and Wray then gave an audiotape of Dick's confession to a stenographer to transcribe. It was important to get Dick to sign his statement as soon as possible, before he had a chance to reconsider and retract it. "Many good cases have been lost because an investigator assumed that the next morning, or a few hours later, would be time enough to have a confession written and signed, only to find that, in the meantime, the offender had changed his mind about admitting guilt," *Criminal Interrogation and Confessions* points out. "It is a safe practice, therefore, to lose no more time than is absolutely necessary in obtaining some kind of signed statement." At 7 P.M., Ford reentered the interrogation room with the transcript. He instructed Dick to read it and correct any mistakes. If he made changes, it would be harder for him to later deny reading the document before signing it and to claim that his confession was coerced. Police are trained to insert errors in suspects' statements and to prompt them to correct them. Dick duly made several corrections, initialing them at Ford's direction. The prosecutor Valerie Bowen would draw attention to those corrections during Dick's preliminary hearing the following month.

As Bowen also pointed out, Dick initialed the top and bottom of each page, again at Ford's behest. He signed the statement at 7:12 P.M.[59]

After he submitted to a PERK test and paperwork was completed, Dick was transported to the Norfolk City Jail. In a stupor, he was charged with capital murder and rape and held without bail.[60]

Shortly after 5 P.M. on Thursday, January 15, three days after Dick's confession and the day after his arrest was reported in the local *Virginian-Pilot* newspaper, his mother arrived home from work to the sound of her phone ringing. The commander of the USS *Saipan* was on the line. Joe had asked him to call his parents, he said. Her son had been arrested for capital murder and rape, the commander informed Patricia Dick. "I was just in shock," she remembers. "I got off the phone and I started shaking. I started getting hysterical. I just was in total shock." The commander emphasized the word *capital*. Joe had been arrested for murder? Patricia had asked him in amazement. No, for *capital* murder, the commander had responded. Patricia didn't know what the word meant in this context. She wasn't aware that it meant her son was facing a possible death sentence. But she wrote the word down, as she knew that it was important.[61]

Patricia had always worried that Joe would get involved with drugs; if somebody said to him, "Try this, you'll like it," he would be dumb enough to try it, she had feared. But she never, *ever* imagined him committing a murder and rape. He simply wasn't that kind of kid. "At first, I just couldn't believe he did it," she recalls. "Because I knew him, and I just could not picture him doing anything like that." One summer in Baltimore when he was in high school, there had been a lot of rats in their neighborhood, so they had put rat poison underneath some steps. On a Saturday when her husband was working, Patricia noticed a rat on one of the steps. It was still alive but on its last legs. "Oh, just take a shovel and bang it on the head," a neighbor urged her. Little Joe then piped up, in a puffed-up macho voice (one he often used in interviews for this book), "I can do that." He grabbed a shovel and headed valiantly over to the rat. But he couldn't get himself to hit it. "This is a *rat*," Patricia recounts. "He can't take the shovel and hit the rat over the head. . . . And if he couldn't kill a rat, how can he kill a human being? I really don't think it was in him." Unless he had gotten involved with the wrong crowd, she ruminated, or he had been in the wrong place at the wrong time. "But it's not something on his own that he would ever do," she thought. "It's just not him."[62]

It wouldn't be long, however, before his mother would conclude that Joe had been too ashamed to call home.[63]

After getting off the phone with the *Saipan*'s commander, Patricia called her husband at work. He wasn't in, so she left a message, saying it was an emergency. When he phoned back, she told him what had happened. His head spinning, Joe Sr. anxiously rushed home. "[Joe's] mom and dad were totally crushed, humiliated, and embarrassed and took it very bad," Patricia's brother Al Bankard wrote later.[64]

Joe phoned his parents shortly, probably within the next twenty-four hours. After his mother spoke to him, she handed the phone to his father. "He's yelling at me over the phone: 'Dad, I didn't do it! I didn't do it. I didn't do it,'" Joe Dick Sr. recounts. It was the first thing Joe said to his father. He sounded adamant; at least outwardly, it wasn't the voice of someone who was still confused. Most people who become persuaded by police that they committed a crime they did not commit do not hold their belief for long; once out of the interrogation room, they usually begin to reconsider the information they were given and then recant. And after mulling things over in jail, Joe had come to believe he was innocent. "I know you didn't do it, Joe," his dad reassured him over the phone. He knew he wouldn't ever do something like this. "And we'll help you in every way possible that we can—whatever it takes to get you out of this." Joe mentioned to his father, rather obtusely, that he had told the cops something. "What do you mean?" his dad asked. "I just told them what they wanted to hear," Joe replied. Alarming as those words were to Joe Sr. (and he felt his hair standing on end), he believed his son's denials, he says. He knew that the police could get Joe to sign anything. But he also thought: if by some chance my son *was* a party to this, then he deserves whatever he gets.[65]

During this conversation or their next one at the Norfolk City Jail, Joe told his parents that he'd been on the *Saipan* the night of the murder. His dad wondered: why would he be on the ship when he was paying for an apartment in order to be *off* it? Joe did not tell his parents that he'd been confined to the *Saipan* because of his tardiness. Indeed, he never told them. That cut to a troubling matter for them: Joe's accounts often shifted over time. "Patricia would say his story is always changing, and she didn't know what to believe," her brother Al remembers. When Patricia learned later that Joe had indeed been assigned to duty on the *Saipan* the night of the murder, she was angry. It was "mind-boggling" to her that her son had an alibi but nobody checked it out.[66]

Against her husband's wishes, Patricia told her relatives about Joe's plight. Out of embarrassment, she didn't offer specifics, just that he was in serious trouble and might be facing the death penalty. When Patricia visited her mother one night, Catherine Bankard knew something was wrong the minute her daughter walked in the door. It was the anguished expression on Patricia's face. "She sat down at the table and just started crying," Bankard recounts. "She was brokenhearted, and kept crying and sobbing." "What's wrong?" her mother asked. It was about little Joe, Patricia said, but "I just can't tell you. It's really bad." Her mother couldn't imagine what Joe might have done, but when she asked, half seriously, after a series of inquiries that ratcheted up the possibilities, if he had *murdered* somebody, Patricia "looked at me and just went all to pieces," she recalls.[67]

Bankard's own heart was breaking. Joe had been her first grandchild; she had always felt a deep love for him. And she had felt sorry for him—it was just something about the boy. She couldn't fathom him killing anyone either. "I never knew Joe to do anything bad, criminal, reckless, damaging, or anything like that," she remembers.[68]

Patricia phoned her sister, Theresa, early one morning. "She didn't want me to hear it from anybody else," Theresa Bankard-Sharpe recounts. "And, of course, she was crying and very upset." Theresa told Patricia that she couldn't believe that little Joe would have done anything. He wasn't a violent person; there wasn't a mean bone in his body. In tears, Patricia asked her brother Al and his wife to pray for Joe. The crime would have been "so out of character" for him, the coordinator of altar servers at Joe's church reflected.[69]

Apart from disbelief, one thought was present in the reactions of virtually everyone who knew Joe Dick: If by some possibility he *did* do it, then it had to have been a result of peer pressure or a desire to belong.

When Petty Officer Michael Ziegler learned that Joe had confessed to Michelle Moore-Bosko's murder and rape, he was astonished. There was no way Joe could have done it, he told his supervisor, because Joe should have been on duty at the time. "I was concerned that Joe had been railroaded,"

Ziegler remembers. He recognized as well as anybody that it wouldn't be hard to get Joe to confess to something he didn't do.[70]

Ziegler and his supervisor approached their lieutenant commander, who said that he'd look into it. But two or three days later, the commander reported that Joe had signed a written confession, and that since the muster reports for July of 1997 were no longer available, they had no proof that Joe had been on the *Saipan*. It was a civilian matter, he said, and there was nothing that the command could do.[71]

Ziegler did not pursue it. He had followed his chain of authority and accepted the command's position. But he expected to hear from the police, a prosecutor, or a defense attorney. "As Joe's immediate supervisor, I would be the most obvious person to contact," he reasoned. To Ziegler's surprise, however, no one contacted him: "It baffled me."[72]

5

"Everybody Had Me Believing That I Was Guilty"

The Saturday after getting the call from the *Saipan*'s commander about Joe's arrest, Patricia and Joe Dick Sr. drove down to Norfolk from Baltimore to visit their son and try to find out what in the world was going on. They had an emotional meeting at the jail. "I'll tell you the truth, I can't remember what we talked about," his father recounts. "Because we just didn't know *what to do.*" After their time with Joe was up, his parents were standing around in the lobby of the jail wondering where to go from there; they didn't know anybody in Norfolk. A short, elderly man, apparently a bondsman, approached them. "Maybe I can help you," he said. The man introduced himself and asked what they were looking for. They needed a lawyer for their son, the Dicks told him. The man gave them the names of a couple of attorneys. After Joe Sr. told him that they couldn't afford the really high-priced guys, the man handed them the card of one Michael F. Fasanaro Jr. He's very reasonable and very good, the man said. Try him. "He said he was the best person to get," Patricia Dick remembers.[1]

When they got back to their room at the Navy Lodge, Patricia phoned Fasanaro's office. He wasn't in, so she left a message in his voice mailbox.

A workaholic who handled lots of court-appointed cases (and apparently used a runner to get more, an acceptable practice as long as the runner does not get an undisclosed kickback), Michael Fasanaro was then in his early sixties. He was from Brooklyn, New York, and still had the accent. He had earned both his undergraduate and law degrees from St. John's University, and had spent more than twenty years in the navy as a Judge Advocate General (JAG) officer, or military attorney, as well as a judge; he'd been the commanding officer of the Norfolk Naval Legal Service Office. He was a respected, experienced attorney with an office way up on the twenty-fourth floor of the Wachovia Bank building aside the Elizabeth River in Norfolk, just across the street from the Norfolk Circuit Court. Just as Danny Shipley, Danial Williams's lead attorney, had recently lost a client to a death sentence, so, to his horrible surprise, had Fasanaro; Mario Murphy had been executed only four months earlier. Fasanaro was not about to lose another client. "Having had it happen once, you sure as hell don't want it to happen twice," another Norfolk defense attorney who is familiar with the Murphy case comments. A fairly big man with glasses, short whitish hair, and a neatly trimmed beard, Fasanaro is combative, direct, and brusque. He often speaks with a sense of certainty, using words and phrases such as *absolutely, no doubt, categorically, of course, 100 percent, 1000 percent,* and so on. He was reluctant to be interviewed for this book, but then consented to a phone interview. And after being informed that Dick and his parents had been interviewed, he agreed to talk in person.[2]

Early on that Sunday morning, Fasanaro came into his office to pick up some files before he made a jail run, and he listened to Patricia Dick's voice mail message. She and her husband were in Norfolk and wanted to retain him to represent their son, who had been charged with capital murder, the message said. Patricia had forgotten to say where they were staying. Since Fasanaro was going to the jail anyway, he decided to visit Joe. According to his notes on their meeting, parts of which he read during his personal interview for this book, but whose meaning was sometimes ambiguous in the rendition, Dick told Fasanaro that he had had no idea why he was a suspect at first. He'd been on his ship at the time of the murder, Dick informed Fasanaro. But he had told police that he'd held Moore-Bosko down during the assault, he said; he didn't recall telling them that he'd raped her. He also told Fasanaro—and here the ambiguity was striking and significant—either that he *said* to police that he had been present during the murder or that he *had* been present. The former is more likely, but according to Fasanaro, Dick "went back and forth a little bit on that first day. . . . He told me both things."[3]

Dick strongly denies that. "I told him that I didn't do it, I wasn't there," he recounts, and that he had given his statement to the cops just so that "I could get 'em off my back."[4]

Later, to help justify his handling of the case, Fasanaro would frequently give what Dick's father calls "his canned speech"—to the Dicks, in his two interviews for this book, and to other people—that Dick *never once* denied his guilt to him in their "thirty" or "eighty" meetings (the number would vary). "That was constant," Joe Dick Sr. recalls. "And I thought to myself, 'What am I talking to? A broken record? And why did I pay this guy?'" (Fasanaro stated several times in his interviews for this book that Dick never denied his guilt to him, before consulting his notes and realizing that that was untrue.)[5]

After visiting Joe at the jail, Fasanaro phoned Patricia and Joe Dick Sr. at the Navy Lodge that Sunday morning and invited them to come over to his office. According to Patricia, "he said he thought it would be a good case to take, because Joe had been an altar boy, and then [in] the Boy Scouts, and he'd never been in trouble with the law. . . . He thought he could get him off was the impression I got." Of course, Fasanaro had not seen a copy of Dick's confession yet; he only knew that Dick had given police a statement. Whatever hope he had evaporated after reading Joe's actual words. "It was a very bad case," he thought. "A death case clearly was in front of me."[6]

Fasanaro told the Dicks that he'd like to represent their son. It would cost $22,500. The $500 was for an investigator, the Dicks believe, but they don't know if Fasanaro actually hired one.[7]

According to a prominent capital defense attorney, Fasanaro's fee was not sufficient to mount an adequate defense in a capital case. And the Dicks understood that Fasanaro would get the money regardless of whether or not Joe's case went to trial. The American Bar Association considers such flat fees "improper" in capital cases and strongly disapproves of them. The reason: the defense lawyer may limit the amount of time he spends on the case in order to maximize the return on his fee. Put another way, he may do only what is minimally necessary to get the money.[8] But perhaps Fasanaro calculated that the Dicks couldn't afford to pay more and hoped the court would provide him additional money if he needed it. Or he may already have been thinking about a plea.

At that first meeting with the Dicks, Fasanaro remembers, Joe Sr. acted "convinced that his son was involved." He "sat across in my office here, right in front of me, and said to me, 'My son killed the girl. There's no question about it. . . . I have no doubt my son was involved in this murder. Not a bit of doubt.' . . . And I remember saying to him, 'You know your son. I don't know him. But why do you say he did it?' He said, '. . . He's a follower. He's following a bunch of guys to do something crazy.'"[9]

Joe Sr. never felt comfortable with Fasanaro nor particularly cared for him. He didn't like his demeanor, didn't like the way he talked down to Patricia and him at times (Fasanaro claimed that he was very good at reading people, including jurors, and told Joe Sr. that he could tell by his face that he was un-comfortable with him). Joe Sr. never knew whether Fasanaro was giving him and Patricia the truth. "But I didn't know where else to go!" he exclaims. "My dad's always thought Fasanaro was telling him a bunch of bullshit," Joe Jr. says.[10]

Fasanaro met with Joe Jr. at the jail again on January 24, 1998, about a week after their first meeting. In Fasanaro's retelling, which again involved reading aloud parts of his notes, after he informed Dick that his naval command had reported that there was no record of him being on duty on July 7, 1997, the day of Moore-Bosko's murder, Dick responded that he could have been on duty on July 6, but he still thought it was July 7. Asked by Fasanaro why he mentioned a knife in his confession, Dick said because someone at The Banque had told him that a knife had been used. At another meeting on January 31, Fasanaro recounts, Dick again asserted that he wasn't there, that he was inno-cent, and that his fingerprints wouldn't be found in the victim's apartment.[11]

According to Dick's memory of these meetings, Fasanaro accused him of lying. "He had done gotten a copy of [my] statement. Done gotten a copy of the police notes. And he'd done read through it. He said, 'Look, I know you were there. I know you did it. . . . In order for you to know this much about it, you had to have been there.' That's basically what he's telling me. . . . Which is the same thing the cops are basically saying." Fasanaro went over Dick's state-ment with him (he would give Dick a copy in early February), as Dick con-tinued to proclaim his innocence. Dick and Fasanaro, a forceful man, "went back and forth for about two or three weeks over this," Dick recounts. "He stopped by about once a week. . . . I'm getting pissed off at him. I want to fire his ass. But I don't know of any other attorney that would take the case." Dick allows that he might not have shown his anger to Fasanaro; indeed, he some-times just passively consented to whatever Fasanaro proposed.[12]

In a sense, Dick's conversations with Fasanaro don't sound that far off from what took place in the interrogation room: in both cases, a dominant person-ality was attempting to erode the will of a weaker one. Though Fasanaro was presumably doing it without all of the yelling and threats, Dick did not stand much more of a chance against him than he did against Ford.

Dick still harbored some doubts about his innocence, and Fasanaro fed them. Eventually, Dick wrote later, "he had me believing that I actually committed the crimes that I was accused of." Dick would come to hate Fasanaro. "*Please excuse my language here*, but this is what I think about Michael Fasanaro, Jr. [He] is nothing but a money-hungry, power-seeking, motherfucking son of a bitch," Dick wrote us. "He lied to me and he lied to my parents." The $22,500 they paid him went "down the drain for *nothing*."[13] Of course, it's not unusual for defendants to speak disparagingly of their lawyers.

Fasanaro, who acknowledges going back and forth with Dick about his guilt for several weeks, denies that he ever accused Dick of lying. "That's not my style. That would be absolutely incorrect. My style would be more along the lines that, 'Joe, if that's what you want to testify to at a trial, it's your trial, and you have to testify . . . as you see fit. Here, however, are the facts as I see them. Here, however, is the evidence that I have in front of me based upon the statements you made and the testimony and the evidence that the police have gathered.'" What, exactly, would be his defense? Fasanaro asked Dick. And why did he give police the details that he gave them?[14] More to the point, perhaps, Fasanaro was not inclined by training or experience to mount a false-confession defense.

Further, "I was convinced in my mind that he had done it," Fasanaro admits. "Fasanaro said he couldn't get past Joe's confession," Patricia Dick recalls. If he ever wondered whether it was false (and a psychological evaluation of Dick that he requested raised that possibility), it is unlikely that he wondered for long. Asked how often he believes that false confessions occur and how serious a problem, if any, they constitute in the criminal justice system, Fasanaro replied that they were "puffed up" and that he had "not run into many." In his phone interview, before he consulted his notes on his meetings with Dick, Fasanaro said that after he had talked to Dick there was "no question" about his guilt. "There wasn't a doubt in anybody's mind, including Joseph Dick's."[15]

But whether Dick's confession was true or false, Fasanaro was well aware that the chance of getting it suppressed was slim, and that if it was admitted into court, Joe had a huge problem. "I mean, generally speaking, I felt that we were in deep trouble," he recalls.[16]

Fasanaro's relationship with his client was awkward for quite a while. Fasanaro found it hard to establish a rapport with Dick; he wondered what was going on inside Dick's head. Early on, "I thought I was talking to the wall," Fasanaro remembers. Dick was "kind of a blank" and "wouldn't necessarily answer the questions. Never looked me in the eye." Sort of like Danial Williams, whose attorneys also wouldn't believe his claims of innocence. Shooting the breeze about professional football helped, Fasanaro found.[17]

One Saturday two or three months after Dick's arrest, his mother received an extraordinarily upsetting phone call from Fasanaro. "I don't really want to say anything over the phone, because you don't know about phones," he told her, but "without a doubt, Joe was involved in every aspect of the case." Patricia Dick was devastated. Fasanaro sounded so certain about it. Well, now we know, was Joe Sr.'s reaction. (He remembers Fasanaro also telling them that Danial Williams's underwear had been found at the crime scene, which was untrue.) "I was kind of like, 'Oh, my God. What am I going to do?'" Patricia recalls. "'If he's a hundred percent certain, if he's telling me that Joe absolutely was part of it, then I guess I have to grapple with this and try to accept it the best I can.' . . . It took a long time, but I think I finally came to terms with, 'Well, maybe something happened, and somehow he was part of it.'" She later wrote Fasanaro that Joe "got in with a wrong crowd and didn't have the maturity or the ability or the guts (having been beaten by Mr. Williams on at least one occasion) to go his own separate way because he always wanted to belong, and so bowed to group peer pressure."[18]

Coming from their son's own attorney, a veteran and recommended one at that, and voiced with such certainty, Fasanaro's claim that Joe had participated in Michelle Moore-Bosko's murder and rape had considerable influence on the Dicks. Well, just save my son's life, Joe Sr. thought. Fasanaro, who had earlier advised the Dicks that there was no record of their son being on his ship that night, began telling them that the best they could hope for would be life behind bars; later, he would raise the possibility of fifteen to twenty years.[19]

Patricia, in particular, took her cue from Fasanaro. If he said Joe was guilty, then he must be guilty. Patricia was a little like Joe in that respect: if someone kept telling her the same thing over and over again, she had a tendency to believe it. "Joe gets it from me—his gullibility and his dumbness," she says. (At family gatherings before all this happened, when she was still cheerful, it sometimes took her a while to get the jokes: "Do you want me to draw you a picture?" her brother Al would kid her.) Her sister, Theresa Bankard-Sharpe, kept trying to tell Patricia that there was no way Joe could have done it—he didn't even have the intellectual ability to plan something like this. "Patricia kept telling me, 'You don't know the facts,'" Bankard-Sharpe recalls.[20] Those "facts," of course, came largely from Fasanaro.

To think that her son was a murderer and a rapist was devastating to Patricia's self-esteem. She, of course, took pride in her two kids and had always tried to do her best for them. What had she done wrong? And, of all the nephews and nieces in her family, why was it *her* son? Her sister was surprised that Patricia didn't suffer a nervous breakdown. Joe Sr. didn't want anybody to know anything about what his son had done. He was mortified by it. "He just shut himself off," Bankard-Sharpe remembers. "He didn't want to answer the door, or answer the phone." He wouldn't speak about Joe to anyone. (Later, when a television show on this case came out and one of his co-workers at the National Guard said something about it in front of everybody, Joe Sr. denied that the Joe Dick in the show was his son. "He left home, don't want nothing to do with me," he told another co-worker when asked if he'd heard from Joe lately.) Although Patricia needed to get her feelings out, she soon began shying away from people too; she had little contact with any of her relatives. Her relations with her siblings became strained. She felt ostracized, as if she were a disgrace to her family or a bad mother, and, indeed, some relatives looked askance at her. Well, somebody has to take responsibility for this, her brother Al told her. Co-workers and friends distanced themselves from her. Their stares made her feel worse: what were they thinking? "She didn't think anybody would have anything to do with her anymore," her sister recounts. "She had this persecuted aura about her. You couldn't look at her cross-eyed or she'd start crying. And any comment about it, she took it to heart." She sunk into a depression and eventually retreated into her own shell.[21]

Joe Jr. wasn't very communicative either, at least with his parents. "He didn't tell us hardly anything," his mother remembers. "It was kind of like you had to know what question to ask." One question his parents didn't want to ask him was, Did you *do* it? They knew that phone calls from the jail were monitored. Their conversations during visits were also overheard, they worried (of course, they'd have to virtually shout out the question above the din). And they were scared of the answer they'd get: in different ways, it could hurt both Joe and them. But Joe never told them he did it. Perhaps the closest he came was during a conversation with his dad at the Virginia Beach jail after he'd been transferred from Norfolk. They were talking through the small hole in the Plexiglas between them; it was hard to understand each other amid the clamor around them. "Why did you do this?" his father asked Joe. He meant, Why did you give police a confession? But he wasn't sure Joe recognized that. "He had this funny grin on his face," his father recounts. "And he said, 'Even I don't know why I did it.'"[22]

Fasanaro sent Joe's parents a copy of his confession. To read Joe's own words was crushing; the statement disgusted his parents and strengthened their belief in his guilt. "I would read a line or two at a time, and then I'd have to stop," Patricia recalls. "I couldn't sit down and read the whole thing through. . . . The language my son used I felt was appalling. I couldn't handle it."[23]

But as Joe's case progressed, his parents would come to feel utterly confused: Had their son been pressured into participating in an abominable rape and murder? Or had he been duped by police?

On February 13, 1998, a month after Joe Dick's confession, a preliminary hearing was held on his case in General District Court in Norfolk. A preliminary hearing is intended to determine if there is probable cause to believe that the person accused of the offense committed it. The hearing also provides an opportunity for the defendant to tell his story and for his attorney to contest the prosecution's evidence. In this hearing, however, Michael Fasanaro asked the commonwealth's witness, Detective Brian Wray, fairly standard and softball questions for the most part: Dick signed the Miranda rights form, correct? What transpired between then and when he gave his taped statement? What time did he deny his involvement? Was the defendant given an opportunity to eat or drink? How many times did he eat or drink? What about bathroom breaks? Did Wray or Glenn Ford ever raise their voices? Did they ever touch or threaten the defendant? Did he ever request to consult with an attorney? Fasanaro did not raise the possibility that Dick's statement might be false, and he failed to point out a single discrepancy between it and the physical evidence (except indirectly, when he asked Wray how he knew that the details Dick gave them were true). But Fasanaro recalls, "We had a full-blown preliminary hearing where I questioned the detective at great length."[24]

Judge Ray W. Dezern found probable cause to believe that Dick murdered and raped Michelle Moore-Bosko and sent the charges to the grand jury, which indicted him in early March. Dezern also found Dick "a danger to the community" and ordered him held without bond.[25]

The same month, Fasanaro requested a psychological evaluation of his client. Conducted by Dr. Evan Nelson, a clinical psychologist, the assessment was based primarily on an interview Nelson did with Dick at the Norfolk City Jail on April 13. Nelson reported that Dick's demeanor was "odd, but not bizarre. He stared intensely and rarely blinked. He spoke at a normal rate of speech, but his voice approached a monotone and the range of emotions he exhibited was highly constrictive. For almost the entire two hours of interviews he sat with his arms crossed in the same position, without fidgeting or adjusting himself. He was overly intense and at the same time emotionally distant." But his "ideas were rational and nothing about his thought processes or manner of expressing himself suggested psychosis, severe depression, or any other acute mental illness. He denied being suicidal or homicidal at this time. He did report some mild symptoms of dysphoria at the jail, but they were not out of proportion to his legal situation. Mr. Dick described himself as a 'loner,' and talked about how he had learned to sleep through the days at the jail and stay up at night in order to minimize his contact with the other inmates." Nelson suggested that Dick's lack of a criminal record before his arrest for Moore-Bosko's murder and rape was explained by his social isolation.[26]

Dick tried to tell Nelson that he was innocent and that he'd been on board his ship at the time of the crime. "I know what my statement says," he told Nelson. "I wasn't there, but it's like I knew what happened." When Nelson asked him if it was possible that he committed the crime but did not remember it, however, Dick said yes.[27]

Nelson deemed Dick competent to stand trial and noted that he had apparently paid close attention during his preliminary hearing. But Dick was unaware of the rights he would lose if he pled guilty. He defined a plea agreement this way: "Plead guilty to a certain extent, and get your time reduced." "Mr. Dick does not have an acute mental illness of the sort which would impair his capacity to rationally understand his legal proceeding or effectively assist his attorney in his own defense," Nelson concluded. But "Mr. Dick has a peculiar interpersonal style that will likely be awkward for defense counsel. His mixture of intense eye contact and strong body posture, with emotional

flatness, may at times seem incongruent. He . . . will seem odd interperson-
ally, but his mental abilities with regard to competency to stand trial are relatively good."[28]

Meanwhile, Dick's life had become "pure hell," as he would later tell a corrections officer. Not only was he behind bars for the first time, for a terrible
crime he was not sure whether he committed, but he was in every way ill-
equipped to navigate relations with other inmates (and with four men to a
cell, eliminating contact was impossible). Other inmates in Dick's cellblock
made fun of him. "He seems to be very scared," his mother wrote Fasanaro in
June. "He got caught in the middle of a fight, I believe." During a meeting in
March, Fasanaro noticed that the frame of Dick's glasses was broken. Assistant Commonwealth's Attorney D.J. Hansen understood that he had been
beaten up after getting caught cheating at cards. "He showed up at a hearing
with one lens," Hansen remembers. The former Norfolk detective Maureen
Evans heard that Dick was getting abused in jail. "Joe at first permitted himself to be sexually abused in order to protect himself from physical injury by
stronger inmates," a psychiatrist who later interviewed him wrote. When Dick
phoned his parents one night and his father noticed that the phone line
sounded different than it had in the past, he explained that he was in another
part of the jail—in solitary confinement. What the hell did you do to get into
solitary confinement? his dad asked him. Dick replied that a guard had observed him in what the guard thought was a sexual position with another inmate in the cell. "*Jesus Christ*, boy. What the hell *else* can you do?" his father
rebuked him.[29]

Fasanaro presented Dick with his legal options: take his case to trial; try to
get a plea bargain by cooperating with the prosecutors, testifying against
Williams, and pleading guilty; or simply plead guilty before a judge without a
deal. Most people charged with felonies (up to 95 percent) enter guilty pleas,
although fewer do in murder cases specifically. Fasanaro counseled Dick to
cooperate; he was "hell bent" on pleading Dick out, another attorney perceived. Mario Murphy's execution was fresh in Fasanaro's mind. Fasanaro let
Dick know what had happened to Murphy. If they went to trial, he feared, the
chance that Dick would get convicted was quite high. He knew that secretaries
and others in the commonwealth attorney's office and the clerk's office at the
Norfolk Circuit Court (where his wife worked) had been brought to tears by
the crime scene photographs. What would a jury think? "I was going to do

everything in my human power" to keep Dick from getting executed, Fasanaro remembers. He felt that he could not responsibly put Dick on the witness stand: "Joe would have been ripped up one side and down the other." He advised Dick that he would not be a strong witness.[30]

But Dick says that he wanted to go to trial. "I told him from the start I wanted to take this to court, and he didn't listen," Dick recalls.[31]

While it is easy to imagine Fasanaro overpowering Dick's arguments and quickly persuading him to favor a deal, Fasanaro was too eager to seek a plea. The death penalty was a real consideration, but so were his client's wishes and proclamations of innocence. Though Fasanaro claims that he investigated Dick's alibi "from top to bottom" and that a warrant officer on the *Saipan* whom he contacted reported that Dick hadn't been on duty at the time, Fasanaro never contacted Dick's immediate supervisor, Petty Officer Michael Ziegler. Nor did he approach Ziegler's own superior. "I was prepared to inform whomever questioned me that I had determined that Joe was scheduled to be on duty on the night/morning of the crime and that he had fulfilled his duty," Ziegler writes. Fasanaro didn't ask whether the *Saipan*'s muster reports were available either, Ziegler says. In reality, Fasanaro did little, if any, investigation. He is not known for being a strong investigator; his high-volume practice does not allow it. And although it would have been readily apparent to Fasanaro that Dick was a suggestible young man who could have been easily influenced by police, he did not arrange for detailed psychological testing of Dick, which would have helped him build a case for a false confession. Nor did he contact a false-confession expert.[32]

A thorough investigation would have allowed Fasanaro to say to Dick, in effect: We've got the following evidence in support of your innocence. But if we lose, we may not be in a good position to ask for mercy, and you could get the death penalty. Then Dick could have made an informed decision about whether to go to trial or take a plea. But, convinced that Dick was guilty, skeptical that he could attack his confession successfully at trial, and determined to avoid the death penalty, Fasanaro was focused simply on negotiating a plea and getting Dick to accept it. Asked if he would have done anything differently had he believed Dick was innocent, Fasanaro responded, "I would have said to him, 'In my opinion, the case is a bad case. I think you'll be convicted based upon the evidence that we have, and [regardless of] whether you have steadfastly told me you're innocent.' I'll never tell a man who tells me he's innocent that he should plead guilty. . . . I would not have shied away from trying Joe Dick's case."[33]

Fasanaro filed a standard motion to suppress Dick's confession, but, again, he said nothing about discrepancies with the physical evidence. Filed on April 6, and subsequently rejected, the motion argued: "During the hours of 10:26 A.M. and 5:07 P.M., defendant was yelled at repeatedly and on occasion called a liar as he steadfastly denied his involvement in this matter. Defendant was worn down by the constant questioning and yelling and was mentally and physically exhausted, causing him to 'do anything he could' to stop the questioning and, as a result, confessed to a crime he did not commit." Did not commit? Asked later whether Dick would have had to have told him he was innocent in order to make this argument, Fasanaro replied, "Not necessarily, no," and he again gave his canned speech that Dick never once denied his involvement to him.[34]

Meanwhile, Danial Williams's lead attorney, Danny Shipley, had seen an article in the *Virginian-Pilot* on Dick's arrest and had driven over to the jail to talk to his client. "I said, 'Have you lost your fucking mind?'" Shipley recounts. "I said, 'Man, why didn't you tell me about this guy? We could have used this. We could have bargained with this.'" Shipley and his co-counsel, Bob Frank, were aware, of course, that if Williams would roll over on Dick, he could probably get a better sentence and be a free man later in life. "Mr. Shipley, how could I tell you about him?" Williams responded. "I didn't do it. I wasn't there." "He still wouldn't help us," Frank marvels.[35]

Williams had been stunned to hear of Dick's arrest. "What the heck did he do?" he wondered. He sent Dick some notes at the Norfolk jail when they were both on the seventh floor. Why did he think the police had charged him? "Did the police say anything about me when they where [sic] talking with you?" Williams also wanted to know. "What are they tring [sic] to pin on you? I need to know please. The police may be in the wrong. . . . Anything you can tell me may help me also get out."[36]

Shipley and Frank gave Williams a copy of Dick's confession. Williams read it intently, marking it up, as he had his own statement. It was a bizarre experience for him. The inconsistencies, of course, were colossal: for one, Williams had not said anything about Dick in his confession. Reading Dick's account, it became even clearer to Williams that he'd been hoodwinked by police.[37]

.   .   .

Sitting behind bars, under the influence of Michael Fasanaro, Detective Glenn Ford, and the prosecution, and largely isolated from anyone who could evaluate their claims critically, Joe Dick's fragile belief in his guilt hardened. The evidence was clear, it was undeniable, they told him—he had to have been there. Dick became convinced that he had participated in Michelle Moore-Bosko's murder and rape and had blocked his involvement from his memory. "Eventually, after a point in time, you say, 'Okay, yeah, I was there,'" he remembers. "From them constantly telling you that. . . . Everybody had me believing that I was guilty." *Everybody* included his parents. And on some level it might have been easier to tell himself that he was guilty than to acknowledge that he would probably be spending the rest of his life in prison because he had confessed to something he hadn't done. But Dick's belief in his guilt fluctuated with the influence of others. At times he was "convinced of his innocence, but could not assert it because of the overwhelming pressure applied by the detectives, the prosecutors, his attorney, and his parents," the psychiatrist who later interviewed him wrote. He still did not have any actual memories of his involvement. He would tell a corrections officer in July of 1999—a year and a half after his arrest—that he did not think he had been "in his right mind" the night of the crime and that he went along with it "in order to fit in. . . . He stated he cries some nights because his conscience affects him," the officer wrote.[38]

"Nut-so," Fasanaro calls Dick's claim that he had been falsely persuaded of his guilt. Asked whether he personally ever suggested to Dick that he might have blocked his involvement from his memory, Fasanaro replied, "I'm not a psychiatrist." But a month after Dr. Evan Nelson's psychological evaluation raised the possibility that Dick suffered from a disorder involving memory loss, Fasanaro investigated the admissibility of testimony on recollections induced through hypnosis.[39] One suspects that Fasanaro believed that hypnosis might unlock Dick's memories of his participation.

Dick's account does sound plenty wild. But although persuaded confessors are the rarest kind of false confessor—most incriminate themselves simply to escape the interrogation room or to receive some implied benefit—and although Dick remained convinced of his guilt for an unusually long time, his experience is not as strange as it might seem.

Paul Ingram was a veteran police officer high up in the county sheriff's office and a fundamentalist Christian in Olympia, Washington, with a strong need to be liked, a propensity for following orders, and, like Dick, an extremely suggestible personality. In 1988 he confessed to raping his two daughters for years, despite initially having no memory of it. His daughters had claimed to have recovered memories of their abuse. "My girls know me," Ingram told two interrogators. "They wouldn't lie about something like this." During the five months Ingram was interrogated, when police, a psychologist, and a pastor (who assured Ingram that God would only allow true memories to come into his head) encouraged him to visualize his acts, his confessions grew increasingly fantastic and detailed. He remembered presiding over gang rapes of his daughters by his poker buddies (who were also cops), raping two of his sons, and participating in bizarre satanic rituals, among other things. He even recalled the time of day (two in the afternoon) when one cop abused one of his daughters. He cried and prayed feverishly during his interrogations ("O Jesus, o Jesus, o Jesus. . . . Merciful Jesus, help me"), and seemed proud of himself when he came up with new memories. "Boy, it's almost like I'm making it up, but I'm not," he told an interrogator early on. Later, he related, "My memory is becoming clearer as I go through all this. It's getting clearer as more things come out." Even more than Joe Dick, Ingram was isolated from everyone except those who appeared certain of his guilt, and thus he was particularly vulnerable to suggestion.[40]

But after Ingram had pled guilty to six counts of third-degree rape, his interrogations ceased, the psychologist and pastor stopped visiting him, and he began having doubts about his memories. His confidence in his guilt crumbled within a month; he soon recanted his confessions. But he was sentenced to twenty years in prison (he was released after serving more than fourteen). Despite an extensive police investigation, no physical evidence was ever found to support his confessions, and his daughters proved to be unreliable witnesses. Both claimed to be covered with scars from satanic torture, but court-ordered examinations found no such scars. And while both alleged that their father had impregnated them, they had frequently claimed to be virgins, and one said her fetus was aborted at a clinic that did not exist.[41]

In 1995, police in Goshen, Indiana, convinced Edgar Garrett that he had clubbed his sixteen-year-old daughter to death. The evidence was overwhelming, they told him, suggesting that he had suffered an alcohol-induced blackout the morning of his daughter's disappearance. "I'm going to help you remember this shit so we can be done," one detective said. "Remember you're talking to a drunk. You're talking to a guy that's had blackouts himself. Okay? I know how them damn things work." Garrett's admissions were tentative and conjectural (for example, "I must have just left her there. And I must have went home"), and he periodically wondered if he was confessing to a crime that he hadn't committed. By the end of his fourteen-hour interrogation, however, he had signed four increasingly detailed statements on how he had murdered his daughter (who had actually been stabbed to death). But he recanted soon after his interrogation, and a jury later acquitted him.[42]

After Peter Reilly discovered his mother's mutilated body on the floor of their cottage in Connecticut one evening in 1973, police interrogated him for eight hours the next day. They suggested that he had killed his mother in a rage and then blanked the crime from his mind. His polygraph examiner claimed that the test showed that his denials were lies. God, maybe he had actually done the unthinkable and murdered his own mother, Reilly thought. "We got to keep drilling at it" to find out, he told his examiner. "I've *always* had a question in my mind if I was mentally right." After his polygraph session was over, Reilly declared, "It really looks like I did it." He apologized to the police for causing them trouble: "You're really busting your ass trying to help me right now and I really appreciate it." Although Reilly realized after he'd been jailed that he'd been duped, he was convicted of manslaughter. But the judge later ruled that "a grave injustice" had occurred and the state dropped the case.[43]

Human memory is quite malleable, beliefs even more so. Plenty of studies have demonstrated how memories and beliefs can be planted or changed through deception, pressure, and suggestion—techniques that are all used in police interrogations in more powerful ways. Researchers have planted the following false memories or beliefs in people: that they had been the victim of a vicious animal attack; that they had been hospitalized overnight; that they had nearly drowned and been saved by a lifeguard; and that they had witnessed demonic possession as a child. Researchers have even planted false narrative memories of the day after a person's birth. In some of these studies, people remembered details (even sensory ones) and expressed emotions about the false events. In those cases where they didn't have concrete recollections and thus lacked the subjective feeling of memory, their perceptions are best termed beliefs rather than memories.[44] That would be true for both Danial Williams and Joe Dick.

Some researchers have posited three stages through which false memories are formed: the person is persuaded that the false event is plausible; he or she is convinced that the false event occurred; through guided imagination, visualization, or manipulation, the person is led to remember actual details, and experiences the event as if it were a real memory. "A 'know' feeling today can become a 'remember' feeling tomorrow," three researchers have written.[45] False beliefs can also become memories when they are reinforced over time.

Many outlandish "repressed memories" have been "recovered" through therapy, hypnosis, guided visualization, dream analysis, and other methods. A nurse's aide in Wisconsin became convinced during therapy that she had repressed memories of eating babies, being raped, having sex with animals, and being forced to watch the murder of her eight-year-old friend. Her memories were all false, as were the overwhelming majority of recovered memories of childhood sexual abuse during the 1980s and 1990s, the heydays of the recovered-memory phenomenon.[46]

Strong beliefs are particularly resistant to change. Most people who are innocent of a murder and rape would be inclined to believe in their innocence firmly, at least until they are challenged. But researchers have discovered that when people are given insufficient time to consider another person's points and formulate counterarguments, they are more susceptible to persuasion, and police are trained to interrupt suspects' denials and barrage them with accusations. What's more, repeated assertions are seen as more valid. Imagining an event can also increase its plausibility, since it becomes easier to picture it, and police interrogators will sometimes urge suspects to envision how they could have committed the crime. The products of a suspect's imagination can then easily become confused with reality. For quite a few people, the authority of police officers enhances their powers of persuasion, as does outside agreement with their claims, even the agreement of a bogus witness.[47]

Although based in part on common tactics of personal influence, the methods that police employ in the interrogation room are particularly potent, given the extreme imbalance in power there and the suspect's confinement. They tend to reduce a person's will and affect their cognitive functioning far more than everyday tactics of persuasion do. The considerable physical and emotional stress felt by suspects undergoing interrogations (particularly for capital crimes), their anxiety and confusion, the time constraints placed on their decision making, and their fatigue can severely disrupt their cognitive processing. They are rendered less capable of retrieving other information, carefully analyzing what they can access, evaluating critically what the police are telling them, and detecting lies. Police interrogation tactics are designed to impair the ability of suspects to recognize false claims. Stress and anxiety engage cognitive resources that could otherwise be applied to their predicament, hindering the ability of suspects to utilize stored information. The distractions and time constraints they face owing to the onslaught of accusations, denunciations, and questions also hamper their memory retrieval and disrupt their critical thinking. Moreover, their social isolation often induces emotional distress, which compromises their cognitive functioning as well. Fear of long-term consequences or short-term bodily harm at the hands of threatening interrogators can also undermine a suspect's ability to think rationally. And when a person's cognitive functioning is impaired, they are particularly inclined to rely on the opinions of others when evaluating a claim, and more likely to be affected by the credibility of the communicator, his confidence in his claims, and the sheer number of claims he makes. People's confidence in their memories varies, of course, as does their ability to evaluate information, and neither Joe Dick nor Danial Williams were sure of their abilities or mentally sharp.[48]

Police also physically restrict access to information in the interrogation room. Family and friends are kept out, as are attorneys, unless the suspect invokes his right to counsel.

The result is that police can persuade innocent people that they might have committed the most appalling acts.

In March of 1998, two months after Joe Dick's confession, the Virginia Division of Forensic Science gave prosecutors and police some more unexpected news: the forensic scientist Robert Scanlon reported that Dick's DNA did not match the sperm, blood, or other genetic material recovered from the crime scene. Two suspects had now confessed to Michelle Moore-Bosko's murder and rape, but there was no physical evidence linking either of them to the crime. Valerie Bowen, the lead prosecutor on the case, who had been staggered when she had learned three months earlier that Williams's DNA did not yield a match, had assumed that the recovered DNA would now be identified as Dick's. "Because DNA does not lie," Bowen said later. "Obviously it belongs to somebody and we know it doesn't belong to Williams. And so now we think obviously it's got to belong to Dick."[49] One can imagine the depths of her distress and bewilderment now.

But rather than deducing that they had the wrong man, prosecutors and police again came to a different conclusion: an accomplice of Williams and Dick was still out there. "We know somebody else is involved and we have to go on," Bowen recalled. Go on to find the elusive third killer. "Obviously we knew we didn't have our hands around the whole case," the prosecutor D.J. Hansen, who would be brought directly into it in a matter of weeks, remembers.[50] Had the prosecutors deemed Dick's and Williams's confessions unreliable (and many prosecutors would not have, particularly when the defendants' own attorneys believe their clients are guilty), they might have acted differently.

When Patricia Dick informed her sister, Theresa Bankard-Sharpe, that Joe's DNA didn't match the evidence, her sister was dumbfounded that Patricia still thought he was guilty. "I looked at her and said, 'Patricia, listen to what you just said. How can you think your son did it if there's no evidence?'" Bankard-Sharpe recounts. "I think she was so brainwashed" by Michael Fasanaro, who claims that he was "not too surprised" that Dick's DNA didn't match since Williams's hadn't either. Theresa and two of her brothers would soon begin digging up articles in the *Virginian-Pilot* on the case, trying to discern what was going on, what, exactly, Joe had been charged with, and any signs of his innocence. One of those brothers, Dick's uncle Al Bankard, was jolted by what he read. "It was unbelievable," he remembers. "Everything in the paper pointed to Joe as being one of the people." Based on the *Pilot*'s articles, Al began to think that Joe was actually guilty, despite the DNA results. "At least he did the right thing," Al remarked to Theresa. "At least he admitted it and owned up to it."[51]

Police set out to track down the presumed third killer. The case was beginning to take on characteristics of a wild-goose chase. Though aware that police agents are prohibited from contacting defendants represented by counsel, Detective Glenn Ford arranged to have an informer placed in Dick's cell at the Norfolk City Jail. The snitch, Timothy W. Gurley, had been jailed on arson charges. Ford told Gurley he would get him immunity on those charges. Ford hoped Dick would reveal to Gurley the identity of the third assailant—and anybody else who had been involved—and other details about Moore-Bosko's murder and rape. Ford paid Gurley in cash for the information he relayed to him—"not a lot," Gurley later testified, around "fifty dollars." Dick, who be-lieved Gurley was a friend who wanted to help him, was asking for Gurley's advice on how to talk to women, including Nicole Williams ("I said, 'Look, you know, it's not a very good situation,'" Gurley recalled), and Gurley en-couraged him to write letters to Nicole and tell her about anyone else who had participated. At first Gurley was not aware that Nicole was dead, but once he learned that she'd died, he didn't inform Dick. "He had me convinced that she was still alive," Dick remembers, indeed that she was "doing okay" and was "excited to hear from me," according to one of Dick's letters to Nicole. Gurley assured Dick that he could get the letters out of the jail for him. But he then turned them over to Ford.[52]

In his letters to Nicole, Dick expressed his love for her and said that he missed her. "When I'm out of this place you and I will go some where peace-ful and quiet," he wrote. "That is a promise that I will keep to you and you have my word. . . . I know that you love me." As for the crime and his confes-sion, "I didn't have a choice since one detective was breathing down my back," Dick said. He believed that he was being "set up. . . . I also just found out that Dan [Williams] is lying through his teeth. You are going to have to give me some more clues as to the other guy. I think I know who but I can not be sure at this point in time. . . . Nicole you know I hope that Dan had planned this from the beginning."[53] Whether Dick actually believed that Williams had planned the crime—or whether he was trying to steal Nicole from her husband—is anybody's guess.

6

Number Three

The informer, Tim Gurley, also induced Joe Dick to write a letter to Gurley's brother Jerry, asking him to "*beat the dog shit out of*" a sailor named Eric. This Eric had short blond hair, stood 6' tall, and weighed 155 pounds, Dick wrote Jerry. He hung out at The Banque bar and was stationed aboard the USS *Shreveport*. He was "beleived [sic] to own a four door, blue, Toyota Corolla" and "beleived [sic] to have a girlfriend," Dick wrote. "If you are asked who sent you say 'Dan sent me to beat you up.'" In one of his letters to Nicole Williams, Dick wrote: "Jerry is going to ask you a question. If the name is wrong give him the right name. This will cost $500. If you can please pay him and I will reimburst [sic] you when everything is said and done. This is important, don't talk to the police if they ask about anything. This is for your safety. Trust him as you are trusting me."[1]

What had Eric done to arouse Dick's animosity? Gone after Nicole, Dick believed. He worried that Eric might win her hand.

Based on Dick's description of Eric, the police tracked him down. Detective Glenn Ford spoke to David Dickerson, a special agent with the Naval Criminal Investigative Service. Ford provided him with the information that Dick had related. "We had the name of Eric that was on a certain ship, that went to The Banque, that wore a white cowboy hat, had a big buckle," Ford later testified. Dickerson pulled the records of everybody named Eric who had recently been on the USS *Shreveport*. Though none of them drove a blue Toyota; there were two Erics still aboard the ship. Dickerson met with them on April 8, 1998, three months after Dick's arrest.[2]

Dickerson spoke with Eric Wilson at around 8:30 A.M. Wilson had just gotten off watch. He'd been up since 3 A.M., but he was in a good mood; he'd only
had to work half a day. He had returned from a six-month Mediterranean
cruise about a week earlier and would be going home to Texas for a visit in a
few days. He already had his plane ticket. He met with Dickerson in the master-
at-arms's office on the *Shreveport*. Did he know anybody on the *Saipan*? Dickerson inquired. "At that point he asked me, 'Is this about Dan?'" Dickerson
later testified (Dan meaning Danial Williams). Yes, Dickerson replied. In response to other questions, Wilson told Dickerson that he knew both Williams
and Dick, drove a Chevy Cavalier, liked country and western music, and hung
out at The Banque bar.[3]

Wilson's answers piqued Detective Ford's interest. He advised Dickerson
that he'd like to talk to Wilson himself. Dickerson then drove Wilson down to
the Norfolk Police Operations Center, arriving at 10:10 A.M. "It was weird,"
Wilson would recount. "I didn't know what to think. I thought I was just
gonna go tell them what I knew and . . . that I was probably gonna be home
soon."[4]

Like Williams and Dick, Wilson had never been interrogated by police before nor had any brushes with the law. He too had been raised to trust people
behind a badge, to respect and obey authority. In his Baptist church in a small
town in south Texas where he'd been raised, there had been policemen among
the parishioners, and there were special days when cops were honored. He
knew many by their first names. "Police are there to help you," he'd been
taught. "Do everything you can, everything possible to help them out." It was
his duty, he felt.[5]

Of course, obedience to authority, taken to an extreme, has led some people
to commit horrific acts. War crimes, for instance. Mass murder. And mass
suicide. A famous experiment years ago by Stanley Milgram at Yale University
showed how people could be led by an experimenter in a gray technician's
coat to inflict seemingly painful and even deadly electric shocks on other
people who made mistakes on a memory task; more than 80 percent continued to deliver the shocks even after the apparent recipient (a confederate of
the experimenter) had fallen ominously silent. In the cases of Williams and
Dick, authority figures had been able to persuade them to come down to the
police station for an interview without an attorney present, convince them
that they might have committed a vile rape and murder, and get them to con-

fess to it. In the military, Williams, Dick, and Wilson had been trained to un-flinchingly follow the orders of their superiors. One follow-up study to the Milgram experiment found that the longer the subject's military experience, the greater his obedience. And neither Williams, Dick, nor Wilson had advanced beyond high school: less educated people are more obedient to authority figures.[6] While committing mass murder or following an experimenter's instructions to inflict pain on others are worlds apart from falsely confessing to a murder, the compliance with authority that is expected in our culture and central to military life played a big part in the behaviors of Williams, Dick, and Wilson.

Twenty-one years old, with strawberry-blond hair, fair skin, blue eyes, a light mustache, and a strong build (though he had been pudgy into his teens), Wilson had led a protected life. "Kind of a backwards, woodsy type of kid," his later attorney, Greg McCormack, says. He loved camping, hiking, and nature. He too was naïve, gullible, and susceptible to being manipulated. Mild-mannered, he was easy to get along with, with lots of good will and a tender heart. (McCormack would be struck by how "*totally* different" Wilson was from his average client who'd done any heavy prison time. "Very clean-cut kid. Extraordinarily polite. . . . I was just impressed by him in many, many respects.") Wilson tended to think the best of people until given reason to believe otherwise. "He was always willing to help people," his friend John Schwertlech recalls. "If he could help you, he would. Even if he couldn't help you, he'd try. It wasn't him to stand by and see an injustice and let it go." In high school, he'd helped keep another boy from committing suicide. If a girl was having a problem with her boyfriend at a party (and this happened on at least one occasion), he'd get her away from the guy and give her a ride home. "Eric was brought up as an old-school gentleman," Matt Sisk, another friend, remembers. "That is the one thing his father pushed most on. Respect everybody. Eric was always, 'Yes, ma'am. No, ma'am.'"[7]

His parents were devout Christians and active in their Baptist church. His dad, Bill, a former boilermaker in the power-plant industry who now owned a business filling vending machines, was a deacon; musically talented, he led the church choir. He was calm and collected unless set off. "Then his blood pressure would rise and he would fly off a bit," Shannon Sisk, Matt's mother, recalls. Eric's mother, Lurames (Ramey), was a soft-spoken, self-controlled, and motherly woman with reddish-brown hair who had taught second grade for eighteen years; Eric had attended the elementary school where she taught. Eric was a faithful presence at his family's church and active in its youth program. "Religion is, and always has been, a big part in my life," he writes. "Religon [sic] is one of those topics that I could write a book on. . . . I have studied every Religon [sic] that I can get my hands on." "He was very adamant about going to church with his family," Shannon Sisk remembers. "And he frequently went on his own." He later got interested in Wiccanism, which according to one study was the fastest-growing religion in the United States in the 1990s; its rituals and beliefs revolve around nature worship. Wilson's attorney, McCormack, who believes that a bent knife is a symbol of Druidism and that the knife that killed Michelle Moore-Bosko did not get bent during the stabbings—and who says that it was of great concern to him during Wilson's case—would later black out with a felt-tip pen Wilson's account to us of his interest in Wiccanism in a letter.[8]

Wilson's upbringing was a disciplined one. He did what he was told. "I was raised in a very strict Southern Baptist home with everything that this entailes [sic]," he wrote us. "I was very sheltered." "It's 'Eric, do this' and 'Do this now,'" McCormack says. "And I think he went through life being treated like that," including in the navy. His parents didn't want him talking back to them or to his teachers, or, of course, to get into any trouble, which he didn't to speak of. "I think a large part of it is he doesn't like the attention focused on himself," his mother says. "And so he's not going to do anything that's going to make people stop and stare at him."[9]

Wilson didn't like to have his picture taken; he wasn't fond of the way he looked in photos. "Eric was not what I would call a forceful personality," his father recalls. "He was kind of timid and quiet." He suffered from mild social anxiety and claustrophobia, and hated being pushed into a corner and feeling trapped. He would be far more likely to agree with people than to argue with them.[10]

Wilson enjoyed role-playing games, such as Dungeons & Dragons, whose action takes place in players' imaginations. He might "game" a couple of nights a week, particularly on weekends. He also practiced karate, which firmed up his body and increased his self-confidence. But if pitted against a weaker opponent—including a girl—he'd usually back off.[11]

In high school, where he was an average student, Wilson discovered girls and attended keggers. Partial to cowboy boots, he began wearing Wrangler jeans and cultivated a deep Texas drawl. He was selective about his friends; he remembers himself as a loner who was not accepted by his peers. "He wanted true friends," John Schwertlech recounts. "He reiterated that many times. He wanted real friends. Friends he could count on, who would always be there. And that's the kind of friend he wanted to be too."[12]

Wilson joined the navy right out of high school in 1995. Serving his country in the military was important to him; he talked about it regularly. He wanted to prove himself and be out on his own. He once remarked how peaceful it was out in the ocean on a ship.[13]

Upon arriving at the Norfolk Police Operations Center, Wilson was placed in an interrogation room in the detective division. A few minutes after he sat down in a chair in a corner, at around 10:20 A.M., Detectives Glenn Ford and Steve Hoggard entered the room. Hoggard, who had been a policeman for about seventeen years, but not in homicide (he investigated burglaries), was assisting Ford. A light-brown-haired man of medium build, he had been brought into the case only about thirty minutes earlier and had quickly read some material on it. Immediately after entering, Ford directed Wilson to sit in a different chair in another corner of the room—the one farthest from the door, between the table and a wall—so Wilson did. "I was pinned in, blocked in," Wilson remembered. (Later during the interrogation, "if I tried to sit in a different chair, Detective Ford would ask me to sit back in the chair he instructed me to sit in.") Ford sat in the chair closest to the door, Hoggard between him and Wilson.[14]

After getting personal information from Wilson, Ford read him his Miranda rights to remain silent and have a lawyer present. Wilson waived them; he felt he had nothing to conceal. In fact, he didn't even realize that he was giving up his rights—he didn't know that he was a suspect. "It never dawned on him that police could question him all [day] and that he should have a lawyer," Dartha Dickinson, a close friend of his family, comments. "In his wildest dream, Eric had no idea what could happen. How they could twist things." Echoes his former pastor Don Higginbotham, "It would never even enter his mind that they would be manipulating him."[15]

Although disastrous, Wilson's decision to waive his Miranda rights—and Williams's and Dick's decisions to do so—are not surprising. In serious criminal cases, more than 80 percent (perhaps as many as 96 percent) of suspects waive their rights and make some sort of statement to police. "To remain silent in a police interview room in the face of determined questioning by an officer with legitimate authority to carry on this activity requires an abnormal exercise of will," as one police expert has written. Innocent suspects are more likely to relinquish their rights than guilty ones. A study by one of the authors found that suspects with felony records were almost four times more likely to invoke their rights than were those without criminal records, and almost three times more likely to invoke them than suspects with misdemeanor records. Many suspects, of course, worry that if they exercise their rights, it will suggest that they are guilty. And innocent ones often think that talking to the police bears no great risk: justice will prevail. "My state of mind was that I hadn't done anything wrong and I felt that only a criminal really needed an attorney, and this was all going to come out in the wash," said Peter Reilly, the eighteen-year-old who falsely confessed to killing his mother. It is only when the interrogation unfolds that suspects grasp their jeopardy. By this time, many erroneously believe that it is too late to invoke their rights or have forgotten about them altogether; few people invoke them after waiving them. Other suspects may not fully understand the significance of their rights, or fear angering their interrogators or being jailed if they remain silent. Talking, some perceive, offers the best chance to exculpate themselves.[16]

Police have developed a host of strategies for eliciting waivers of Miranda rights. They often downplay their import by presenting them in a simple, perfunctory, or hasty manner, as if reading them is an unimportant but necessary bureaucratic ritual—like filling out bureaucratic forms without really studying them—a mere formality, and that they are indifferent to the suspect's response (though nothing could be further from the truth). Developing a rapport with a suspect before presenting his rights can help set the desired tone. Police may also read the warnings without asking the suspect whether he understands them or wants to invoke them, then launch straight into the interrogation. Or they may claim that waiving them will allow him to clear things up, to tell his side of the story, which, they might suggest, will have important consequences for him. If he says, "Maybe I should get a lawyer"—which is not enough to require police to stop questioning him—they might respond, "Maybe you should. But why would you need a lawyer if you didn't do it?" Police commonly suggest it is in the suspect's interest to talk and that they can help him only if he does. The system will treat him more leniently, they might intimate, if he waives his rights; if he doesn't, he will next be facing some ruthless prosecutor. Presented effectively, the Miranda warnings can even make the interrogator appear sympathetic to the suspect.[17]

Then, if a suspect elects to invoke his right to be silent, police might try to change his mind, perhaps by implying that they'll have to rely on incriminating information provided by someone else. Or they may leave him alone in the interrogation room for a while in the hope that he will have second thoughts. If he initiates further conversation with them, courts have ruled, police can attempt once again to persuade him to waive his rights. Some police try to interrogate suspects "outside Miranda" by claiming that they want to talk to them "off the record" and that their statements can't be used against them. But while statements elicited through such trickery can't be used in the state's direct case at trial, they can be employed to impeach the defendant's credibility if he testifies and to develop other evidence.[18]

The Miranda warnings, then, although they did constitute an improvement over no warnings at all when they were mandated by the U.S. Supreme Court in 1966, fail to provide adequate protection against coercive interrogations and unreliable confessions. Too often, they are "merely a 'speed bump' in the interrogation process," as two scholars have written. When courts deem that interrogators gave the warnings properly, scrutiny of their interrogation practices often suffers and it is hard for defense attorneys to establish that a confession was coerced or involuntary.[19]

Ford showed Wilson a photo of Danial Williams and asked if he knew him. Yes, Wilson replied, he had met him at Williams's apartment. How long had he known him? Ford asked. Since only about two weeks before the murder, Wilson said. He had met him through Nicole Williams, whom he had met at The Banque. Did he know Joseph Dick? Ford inquired, displaying a photo of Dick too. Yes, Wilson said, as the Williamses' roommate. Did he know the victim, Michelle Moore-Bosko? No, Wilson responded, he had never even met her, or been in her apartment. Ford asked Wilson if he ever wore a white cowboy hat. He used to, Wilson said. What did he know about the case? That Danial Williams had been arrested for the murder and rape of his neighbor, Wilson replied, but that he couldn't have done it because Nicole had told him that he had been with her that whole night.[20]

Wilson agreed to take a polygraph test. After providing him with a soda and cigarettes, Ford and Hoggard left the interrogation room at 10:33 A.M. Upon reentering an hour later, Ford asked Wilson how he had found out that Williams had been arrested. He had been at Nicole's place a few days later and she had told him, Wilson responded. Asked how much time he had spent at the Williamses' apartment, Wilson said that he'd been there a few times, on and off. Where had he been at the time of the murder? Probably at sea on his ship, Wilson replied. That's why he hadn't found out about the murder until a few days later.[21]

At 11:40 Ford and Hoggard left the room again. Around this time, Wilson tried to go to the bathroom, only to be grabbed by another officer in the hallway and pushed back into the room. To his disquiet, he noticed that the officer locked the door. "That's when I finally started to realize something was going on," he said later. (Ford and Hoggard's notes state that the door was not locked for another seven hours.)[22]

After Wilson took the polygraph test, police placed him in another room, where he was given a submarine sandwich as Ford and Hoggard awaited the results. While waiting, Ford received a call from Special Agent Dickerson of NCIS, who told him that Wilson's ship, the USS *Shreveport*, had not been under way at the time of the homicide. Rather, it had been in port.[23]

Wilson later testified that he didn't know where he was at the time of the crime. In an interview two years after his testimony, he recalled that he had been at his apartment getting ready to leave for a three-day cruise. He was on board his ship by about 5:30 A.M. the following morning, he said, which would be several hours after the murder. The navy refused to release its records on his whereabouts because the U.S. military was in a wartime situation or on alert status then. "We could not develop an alibi for him," Greg McCormack remembers.[24]

At 1:37 P.M., back in the interrogation room, Ford put the screws to Wilson. "We confronted him about several issues about the homicide," Hoggard testified later. He had flunked the polygraph, Ford told him, predictably (though a polygraph examiner McCormack later hired said that the results were inconclusive). According to Hoggard, this was one of only two occasions on which Ford raised his voice during the interrogation; McCormack wrote that Wilson was "yelled and screamed at throughout." Ford's announcement of the polygraph results shook Wilson. "If it says that you did it, that you're guilty, well, maybe I really am lying and don't realize it," he thought to himself, which raised other unsettling questions in his mind. He had not been under way at the time, Ford declared. They knew that he had raped the victim, though they didn't think that he'd killed her. (Why Ford did not pressure Wilson to admit to the murder, after doing so with Williams and Dick, is not clear, though he may have been focused on accounting for the rapist's unidentified DNA.) To Wilson's continued denials, Ford snapped that he was lying and that they could prove it. Ford was his usual overbearing self. He was "very aggressive, very threatening, very angry . . . very loud," Wilson testified. Standing over him in the corner of that tiny room, Ford played on Wilson's obvious discomfort and his claustrophobia. He pinned Wilson's arms down to the chair at the wrists while barking at him several inches from his face. He hit or tapped Wilson in the forehead with his fingers—"he did that for some time," Wilson testified—only stopping when he accidentally poked him in the eye. Ford and Hoggard would both claim later, however, that he never touched Wilson, and Hoggard recalled that it was "probably one of the most relaxed interviews I've been involved in in eighteen years."[25]

Ford let Wilson know that Dick had put out a hit on him from jail and was saying that he had been involved. He tossed him Dick's letter soliciting the hit. Wilson, who had cared for Nicole Williams as she fought her losing battle with cancer, was unaware that Dick had been jealous of him, and thought Dick's letter might have something to do with the murder. "If this guy is willing to do this, wow, there must be something there to make him hate me that much," Wilson mused. Dick was saying some real bad things about him, Ford warned Wilson, so bad that he didn't even want to know what they were. If he didn't tell them what happened, Ford threatened, they would have to go by Dick's account.[26]

Ford showed Wilson a photograph of Michelle Moore-Bosko when she was still alive. Have you ever seen this girl before? he asked. No, Wilson replied. "Oh, *that's right*," Ford spat, sarcastically, "because the last time you saw her she looked like *this*." And he thrust a photo of Michelle's bloodied, half-naked body in front of Wilson. "It was pretty gruesome," Wilson recalled. "I was stunned. I'd never seen anything like that. It was unbearable. You know, one minute you're looking at the picture of this girl in a field, and the next they're shoving a picture of a girl laying dead on the hardwood floor."[27]

Ford went after Wilson for about an hour, as Wilson repeatedly pleaded that he didn't do it, that he'd never been in the victim's apartment, never even met her, never met her husband either, and didn't know about her murder until he got off his cruise. At 2:41 P.M., with a show of disgust, one he'd made in interrogations many times before, Ford stormed out of the room.[28]

Ford was not about to entertain Wilson's denials. Police interrogations are based on a presumption of guilt. They do not interrogate innocent people, police typically claim. They are inclined to believe that a suspect is being deceptive, studies have found. All suspects lie, police say. "You can tell if a suspect is lying by whether he is moving his lips," one detective remarked dryly. But police are no better than anybody else at ascertaining truth and deception. People in general are poor at it; they tend to perform at no better than chance level, though they often act confident even about incorrect judgments. Police are even more confident in their judgments. In one experiment, students were better than police at distinguishing true from false confessions, and police were more likely to judge confessors guilty. Studies have also found that neither police training nor experience increase the accuracy of judgments; rather, they make police more prone to deem suspects guilty and confessions true (one study found that training actually decreased accuracy of judgments). One problem with much police training is that it advocates using visual cues—such as posture, gaze, grooming gestures, and other hand movements—to detect deception, though such cues are not actually indicative of truth or lying.[29]

A supposition of guilt then leads interrogators to behave in self-fulfilling ways: they exert more pressure on suspects to confess while discounting reasonable denials. In one study, interrogators who presumed guilt appeared to interpret plausible claims of innocence "as proof of a guilty person's resistance—and redoubled their efforts to elicit a confession."[30] All of this is consistent with research findings in psychology that, after people form an impression, they look for information that verifies the impression.

What evidence did Ford have for Wilson's guilt before interrogating him? None. Though Wilson appeared to match the description of the Eric that Joe Dick had provided, nowhere in Dick's letter or his writings to Nicole Williams before Wilson's interrogation does it say anything about Eric participating in the murder or rape. Yet Ford would testify that, in Dick's letter soliciting the hit on Eric, "basically he says that he was worried about Eric Wilson and Danial Williams getting together and testifying against him."[31] That is untrue.

Wilson liked Detective Hoggard, who was playing, to use a cliché, the good cop. He "just seemed like a nice guy," Wilson recalls. In the interrogation room after Ford had departed, only to listen from outside the door, "we talked about his family, my family," Hoggard recounted. Hoggard knew that talking about a suspect's family, like playing to their conscience, can sometimes make them uncomfortable and help prompt a confession. "We talked about a number of things not related to the homicide itself," Hoggard remembered. "We talked about him being in the navy. . . . I had mentioned the hobbies I liked and asked him what kind of hobbies he had, and during this time he mentioned that he liked sports and at one time was interested in karate." They also talked about Wilson's friends. "I asked him if he liked to party, if he went out drinking in the bars," Hoggard testified. According to Hoggard, Wilson said that he had had to stop doing karate because he had suffered blackouts. "He said that he had a problem with blackouts because when he would be fighting against someone in the karate matches, he would black out and when he would come to, the person he was fighting would be beat up real bad; he had hurt the person. So he had to give up the karate." Hoggard also testified that Wilson "stated he had had a problem in the navy with the blackouts and that he had been drinking with friends and had blacked out in the past and when he had come to, his friend had advised him that he had beaten a female he was with at the time and tried to forcibly have sex with her. So for that reason he didn't drink much anymore."[32]

Wilson would dispute Hoggard's account. Though he had discussed hurting a karate opponent once and failing to remember it, "I quit martial arts because I didn't have time anymore to take it," he testified. "In fact, *blackout* would be a bad word for" what he experienced. "It is when you get into a fight and you just don't see anything, you act on pure instinct but you are still in control of what you do. . . . And about assaulting the young lady, that is not true, either. . . . I never said that. What I did say was when Detective Ford asked me if I ever told Joe Dick . . . that I assaulted a woman and I said no, the closest thing that I'd ever told Joe Dick to anything even resembling that was the time that we were at a party and a young lady went back into the bathroom with her boyfriend and came out and she had a black eye and was holding her tailbone. And I went up to her and I asked her if he had hit her, and she started crying and said yes, that he had hit her. And then me and several of the other guys at the party threw him out of the room." When Hoggard testified that Wilson had told him he had blacked out and tried to rape a woman, "he was lying," Wilson said. Wilson acknowledged experiencing blackouts, beginning in junior high school, though they sounded more like episodes of ab-sentmindedness. "It is like when . . . you are driving and then all of a sudden you just realize that you just passed up your exit three exits ago and you don't really remember what you were doing." McCormack says that he investigated Hoggard's allegation of sexual assault and found it without merit.[33]

After spending about fifteen minutes alone with Wilson, Hoggard left the interrogation room and apprised Ford of what Wilson had said. As soon as Ford reentered with Hoggard a few minutes later, Wilson asked to speak with Hoggard alone again. "He didn't want Investigator Ford in the room," Hoggard recounted.[34]

"Things were beginning to make sense," Wilson told Hoggard. "He said that he often had a dream in which he had a glimpse of a female . . . thrashing her head back and forth," Hoggard testified, "and it was a violent dream, and he wasn't sure what it was about." Hoggard asked Wilson to describe the dream further. What was the nature of the violence? "It only smelled violent," Wilson said, according to Hoggard's notes. He didn't actually see anything violent in it, just a female thrashing her head back and forth. Was there anybody else in the dream? Hoggard asked—like Williams and Dick, he was undoubtedly thinking. He didn't know, Wilson responded. But the female was in distress. Wilson would later grant that he described a dream to Hoggard, but said that "it was a dream of a memory of one of my ex-girlfriends shaking her head back and forth." Only after Ford came back into the room and "prodded me on making it a violent dream" did he do so, he testified.[35]

Hoggard wanted more out of Wilson on the dream, something incrim-inating that would stand up in court. Does this look like the female in your dream? he asked as he showed Wilson a photo of Michelle Moore-Bosko eat-ing a pretzel. Yes, it did, Wilson replied.[36]

At 3:48 p.m., Hoggard left the room and advised Ford that Wilson had "just identified the photograph of Michelle." Of course, Ford had already shown Wilson photos of her. When Ford quickly came back into the room, Hoggard instructed Wilson to sit back, relax, close his eyes, and tell him what he was seeing in the dream. How many people were in the room? Ford queried Wil-son. There were three, weren't there, beside yourself? Ford suggested, accord-ing to Wilson. Yes, Wilson agreed. "At that point he began speaking really slowly and he said that he saw two unknown people sitting on a couch which was white in color," Hoggard testified. Asked later how he came up with the color white, Wilson recalled that Ford told him, " 'Close your eyes and try and picture a couch.' I said, 'Okay.' So I closed my eyes and the first couch that came into my mind was a white couch with black stars on it. So I told him that that's what I saw. And then Detective Ford said, 'Okay. Was this the couch that you saw?' And he handed me a photo of what I know now to be Mr. and Mrs. Bosko's apartment with a black-and-white striped couch. And I told him, No, that was not the couch I saw. He said, 'That's a bad picture. Let me show you another one.' And he showed me that picture, and I looked at him again, and I told him, no, that that was not the couch that I saw."[37]

One of the people in his dream was throwing the girl to the floor, Wilson told Ford. The girl was shaking her head back and forth on the floor. Was the girl Michelle Moore-Bosko? Ford asked him. Yes, Wilson replied, in obvious pain. "At that time he opened his eyes and he was emotional," Hoggard recounted. "He was crying. He wasn't sobbing but there was tears in his eyes." Which person in the dream was Dan Williams? Ford inquired, again leading Wilson in the direction he sought. The one on the right, Wilson responded. He could see him, and Williams had thrown Michelle to the floor; the other person was still on the couch. Asked who this other person was, Wilson said that he couldn't make him out.[38]

Ford was looking at crime scene photos as Wilson was describing his dream. After Wilson said the couch was white, Ford showed Hoggard one of the photos that included the black-and-white striped couch. Despite Wilson's denials that that was the couch in his dream, black-and-white was close enough to white for Ford. How did he know what the inside of the victim's house looked like if he had never been inside it? Ford grilled Wilson, who was still crying. He needed to tell them what *really* happened and cut the dream shit, Ford added, in so many words. (This was the other occasion on which Ford raised his voice, Hoggard said later.)[39]

His mind in a fog, Wilson was horror-struck by the possibility that he really *had* committed the crime. It was a way to make sense of what the detectives were telling him, the results of the lie-detector test, and Ford's certainty, expressed over and over again, that he had been there. "Eventually it just grates on you," Wilson recounts, speaking of the barrage of accusations. "And you finally say, 'Well, you know what? These guys are supposed to be the good guys. Maybe they're right. Maybe I did do it. Maybe there's something that is wrong with me, so that I don't remember doing it.' And at that point you just start to tell them what they want to hear." And Wilson desperately wanted to be free of Ford. "I was just wanting to do anything to just get him away from me, so I agreed to everything he said. . . . I would have done anything—anything at all—to get Detective Ford out of my face."[40]

He had indeed been there, Wilson now stated. He had gone over to Michelle's apartment with Williams and Dick—neither of whom, of course, had mentioned him in their own confessions. Michelle had opened her door and said hi to Williams, Wilson said. After letting the three of them into her apartment, she had sat on the couch with Williams and Dick. As far as he could remember, Wilson stated, he was standing against the wall. Eventually, Williams threw Michelle to the ground. They were wrestling around and appeared to be having fun, Wilson told Ford. Williams invited him to join in, so he pinned Michelle down; he thought they were still just having fun.[41]

All of a sudden, as Williams was straddling her, Michelle exclaimed, "Wait a minute," Wilson said. What did she have on? Ford inquired. A black T-shirt, Wilson replied; he couldn't remember what else she was wearing. But Wilson knew about her black T-shirt because of the photo of her dead body that Ford had shown him. What was Joe Dick doing at this time? Ford asked. He couldn't recall, Wilson responded. He was then going to the kitchen to have a drink. When he came back into the living room, he went on, Williams was taking Michelle's clothes off and Dick was by her head. Asked later why he gave this account, Wilson testified, "I was trying to get Detective Ford away from me." As for getting a drink in the kitchen, "I just made something up."[42]

Wilson told Ford that he admonished Williams and Dick that that was enough. Either Williams or Dick (he couldn't remember which one) then urged him to join in, but he didn't. Williams had spread Michelle's legs, he stated; her pants were still on (Wilson didn't know that she was wearing shorts). Dick was holding her arm down. Asked with some sarcasm by the prosecutor Valerie Bowen later if Ford and Hoggard had written this account down for him to recite, Wilson said no and added, "But every time I said something, they would say, no, that didn't happen, or didn't it happen more like this? Or don't you mean it was a little closer to this? Or something of that nature, every time I said something they didn't want to hear."[43]

What was he doing now? Ford asked Wilson. Setting down the glass in the kitchen, he offered. Williams was taking Michelle's pants off. Then, Williams got up off the floor, walked over to him, punched him, and said, "Fuck you," according to Wilson's account. The next day, when he woke up, Wilson said, he noticed a fresh scratch on his right hand. Michelle may have scratched him, he told the detectives, who noticed a scar on his hand as they were talking to him.[44]

At Dick's urging, he held Michelle down, Wilson continued. Her right hand broke free, and that's when she scratched his own right hand, he thought. Williams was then raping her. Michelle looked up at him and pleaded with him to help her, Wilson stated. He just made this part up too, he testified later: "I had to make up something to fill in the gaps of what they said and those are the things that I came up with."[45]

Did he have sex with the victim? Ford wanted to know. He didn't remember doing so, Wilson replied. (Whether, in his muddled state, he wasn't sure, or whether he was trying to cover himself, or both, is not obvious.) He got disgusted and left the apartment, Wilson said. When did you leave? Ford quizzed him. Before Joe Dick took his turn? Dick was starting to rape her, Wilson stated. "The police moved me to say that I wasn't there for the murder, and it was up to me to come up with a way of how I left," he recalled later. "So the leaving was the police's idea; how was mine."[46]

Ford showed Wilson a photo of Michelle and her husband, Billy. Is this the same girl this was happening to? Yes, said Wilson, who was now in complete agony.[47]

Ford and Hoggard then left the room. About a half hour later, after receiving a soda, Wilson asked Hoggard if he could get some fresh air, so Hoggard took him out to the parking lot behind the station, where Wilson smoked a cigarette and engaged in small talk with Hoggard, including about the weather. It would help him relax, Hoggard hoped. Between drags on his cigarette, Wilson gazed at Hoggard and remarked, "I think I need to talk to a lawyer." "Okay," Hoggard responded. But, minutes later, Hoggard escorted him back to the room as if nothing had been said, and Ford directed him to go over events again.[48]

Wilson tried to tell Ford in this round that everything had happened in Michelle's living room, rather than her bedroom where her body had been found, but Ford retorted that that wasn't true. It had moved to the bedroom before he'd raped her, Ford declared. Okay, Wilson replied, they could have ended up in the bedroom. But he wasn't sure. "The whole thing disgusted him so much that he left and went to Cheetah's Bar and started drinking," Wilson told the detectives. He later explained: "I tried to think of the most reasonable thing that someone would do after they had just done something like that . . . and the only thing I could think about was someone going and getting drunk."[49]

Ford scoffed that Wilson wasn't telling them the whole truth. He knew that Wilson had had sex with the victim too, Ford claimed. At that point, Wilson reached into his pocket, pulled out a can of chewing tobacco, stuffed some of the tobacco into his mouth, and stated, "We are going to start getting down to the truth," according to Hoggard, though Wilson would deny it.[50]

In Wilson's next version of events, he took a turn with Michelle. Did he ejaculate in her? Hoggard asked him. He didn't know, Wilson replied; he thought so, but he wasn't sure. When he finished, he said, he realized what had taken place, so he urged Williams and Dick to stop, telling them that "that was enough." He then left. Was the victim still alive? Ford asked him. Yes, Wilson replied firmly. He was adamant about it. The next night, he came back and spoke with Nicole Williams, who informed him that Dan had been arrested for murder, Wilson said.[51]

Ford and Hoggard then left the room again. They reentered at 7:05 P.M. to take the all-important taped statement from Wilson. After several retellings under their guidance, his confession had grown more detailed, richer, more consistent, and more incriminating. "A carefully crafted recitation of what the police officers wanted to hear," Wilson's lawyer, Greg McCormack, called it.[52]

Listening to the tape of Wilson's confession, which ran fifteen minutes, one hears him speaking slowly and deliberately, tentatively at times, though for the most part he doesn't sound all that unsure of what he's saying. His voice is often strong and steady, as if he's taking some pride in being able to recapitulate what he's already told Ford. "That's an affirmative," he responds in military style a couple of times to Ford's questions. The tape, one can readily envision, would be convincing to jurors. "The tape's a killer," McCormack comments.[53]

Some parts were particularly devastating. "I grabbed Michelle by either the shoulders or the upper arm—I can't remember exactly—and I was looking down," Wilson stated. "She was shaking her head left and right, saying, 'No.'" Williams was about to rape her. "I didn't know what to do," Wilson said in a tone that sounded genuine. "I was real confused." Also in a convincing tone—

and this is perhaps the most damaging part of the tape—he told Ford, "I remember specifically her looking up at me afterwards, after I had finished, and asking me to help her." When he spoke of seeing the whites in Williams's and Dick's knuckles, he again sounded believable. "What we had just did had clicked, and I was angry," Wilson said. "I was angry at myself. I was angry at them. . . . I said, 'No, fuck this. This is wrong.'" He then left and went to the bar: "I was basically trying to drown the memories of what had happened. I went home, tried to get a good night sleep. Didn't work too good."[54]

Wilson would later comment: "I never thought I could confess to something I didn't do. I never thought I could until I went through it. By the end of the interrogation your head's so messed up that you'll say absolutely anything just to get the man away from you. . . . They keep yelling at you and telling you to just say it and it'll all stop. And eventually you do." As for why he confessed to the rape but not the murder, the police simply didn't question him about the murder or tell him anything about it. "If they had provided the information, I would have confessed to killing her, too," he said.[55]

Although Wilson was not aware of all the ramifications of what he had just done, he knew that he was in big trouble. As Ford and Hoggard were gathering up their two tape recorders and getting ready to leave the interrogation room, he glanced across the table at Ford and remarked, "I'm fucked."[56]

Fifteen minutes later, Wilson knocked on the door of the room and asked to be taken outside for some fresh air again. This time, there was no small talk out there. Shortly after 8 P.M., Ford directed Wilson to read the transcript of his statement and correct any mistakes. Wilson made two corrections, which Hoggard later pointed out at his trial. "If the whole thing was a lie, why would you bother to correct a typo?" the prosecutor Valerie Bowen asked Wilson. Because they had told him to, he replied. "I did everything they asked."[57]

Wilson was then placed in a small cell in the back of the police station. There, alone with his thoughts, and scared to death, it dawned on him that he'd been bamboozled. "That's when it started to hit me: What did I just do?" he recounts. "I didn't do this. I couldn't have done this." But "once that seed of doubt is placed in your mind, it's really hard to get rid of," he says. "Even if you know the truth, it's still there: maybe I did, and I don't remember it for some reason."[58]

.   .   .

NUMBER THREE   115

Wilson was charged with capital murder and rape and driven to the Norfolk City Jail. "I was just walking around with my head in the clouds, wondering what was going on, what's gonna happen next," he recounted later. "I didn't really know what to think or what to do." How should he handle himself with the other inmates? He largely stayed to himself—"just sat there and watched TV and tried not to think of what was going on."[59]

His incarceration would get tougher. "He spent some hard time in Norfolk," Greg McCormack remembers. "I think Eric had a very rough experience." That's almost predictable for a young, blond, white kid new to the system. Sometimes he had to fight just "to get these guys to leave me alone, cause there's always some knucklehead that's gonna try you," he recalled. One inmate threatened to rape him. After being moved into a dormitory at the jail, almost everything he possessed was stolen, including his jumpsuit. New to jail culture, he told a guard about it. Other inmates then called him a snitch. He was moved into a three-man pod with two black inmates (one a Black Panther, he says, the other a 5 Percenter, which usually meant "someone who hates all whites"). He learned prison norms from the Panther, but the 5 Percenter threatened him almost daily. When the situation became intolerable, Wilson called the man into his cell; the 5 Percenter decided the hell with it and backed down. Wilson was in a pod early on with Omar Ballard, the young man Michelle Moore-Bosko had befriended through Tamika Taylor. Ballard was also a 5 Percenter. He was in for several crimes, including rape. Wilson didn't care for him.[60]

Within a span of twenty-four hours, Wilson would later suffer a broken nose and a realigned jaw in separate altercations with other inmates. "I could not open my mouth without pain and my face had swollen badly at the jaw hinge," he recounts. "For the next three months I had to pull my jaw open so that I could move it enough to eat." Wilson had heard stories about prison. "I was thinking this is the start of a very, very long time, and I was actually starting to wonder if I was going to live through it."[61]

7

Three More

Two days after confessing to the rape of Michelle Moore-Bosko, Eric Wilson nervously phoned his parents from the Norfolk jail. His father took the call. It was about ten in the morning in Texas. "At first, when I answered the phone, he was real hesitant, like he didn't really know how to tell me," his father remembers. "Dad," Eric said. "I'm in a lot of trouble and I need some help." "Well, what's wrong?" his father asked. "You're supposed to be on your way home." "Well, I've been arrested," Eric said. "Arrested?" his dad replied with a start. "Yeah, for murder and rape of this girl," Eric told him. "I don't remember a whole lot after that," his father recounts. "I think everybody kind of just went into shock. But I tried to get as much information about where he was and everything as I could before they cut us off." Bill Wilson was trying hard to keep his emotions in check in order to think clearly.[1]

He needed a lawyer, Eric told his dad. He felt ashamed, like he'd let his parents down; he would feel guilty for years about the agony his arrest caused them. Wilson didn't tell his parents that he was innocent, nor did he say that he was guilty. Just that he'd been arrested and needed a lawyer.[2]

His parents weren't sure what to think. Their son hardly seemed capable of raping and murdering anyone, but maybe something outside the pale had happened; perhaps alcohol or drugs had been involved. And once his parents learned about Eric's confession, it was hard to know what to make of it. If he didn't do it, then why did he say that he did? "We were real confused," Bill Wilson remembers. "It was just crushing for both of them," their friend Dartha Dickinson recalls. "How do you describe when your family's been ripped apart at the seams?" Eric's mother, Ramey Wilson, would later testify. "Nothing that we've ever been through would have ever prepared us for this." But no matter what, Ramey told her friend Shannon Sisk, they would stand by Eric.[3]

After getting off the phone with Eric, his father made some calls to Norfolk. He spoke to the Naval Legal Service Office, which referred him to Greg McCormack. A short, balding, paunchy man, McCormack was then in his mid-forties. He had earned his law degree at Western New England College and represented mainly people in the military, including those facing sexual assault, rape, or drug charges. He was a former army JAG officer who advertised himself as an aggressive attorney, and indeed he was. Hardworking, hard-charging, short-tempered, and combative—he would throw himself into this case and butt heads with prosecutors, police, and even Dick's attorney, Michael Fasanaro, an old friend—McCormack was not part of the old-boy legal circle in Norfolk.

McCormack sent another attorney from his law firm over to the jail to see Wilson, then visited Wilson himself. Asked later whether Wilson told him that he was innocent, or whether he was still confused about what might have taken place, McCormack cited attorney-client confidentiality, then stated, "Eric's position throughout the case was that he was not guilty of this offense. There was never any waffling." Recalls Ramey Wilson, "Immediately afterwards, he was telling his attorney and telling everyone else, 'I didn't do this.'" Eric phoned his parents several times over that weekend. But on McCormack's advice, he did not discuss the case with them, since calls from the jail were recorded. "For nearly a whole year, everything was totally avoided on the telephone," his father remembers.[4]

McCormack soon got a copy of Wilson's confession. He, of course, recognized immediately that his client had a gargantuan problem. He wondered if the prosecutors had any evidence tying Wilson directly to Moore-Bosko's murder. The death penalty was uppermost in McCormack's mind. "I very firmly told his family that if he was convicted of capital murder, he would get the death penalty, in my opinion, in Virginia," McCormack remembers. There was no doubt in McCormack's mind. He, of course, didn't know whether Wilson was guilty or innocent. He'd learned long ago to take what his client told him with a grain of salt, to wait and see how things come down, and he only had a small part of the picture here. "He kept telling Eric, 'If you did it, I'm going to fight just as hard for you, but I have to fight a different way,'" Ramey Wilson recounts. "He said it didn't matter" if he was guilty or innocent, Eric recalls. It was Assistant Commonwealth's Attorney D.J. Hansen's perception that McCormack expected Wilson's DNA to come back positive.[5]

But McCormack was mindful of the possibility that Wilson had given police a false confession, even a persuaded one. Was there evidence corroborating his statement? "You look at that very carefully," McCormack says. But that was awfully hard to do without access to information. "I really got jerked around on this case on evidence," McCormack recalls. In Virginia, during pretrial discovery, when prosecutors are required to turn over exculpatory information to the defense, the latter often gets little. Virginia law doesn't require prosecutors to relinquish much, and while many open up their files to defense attorneys, others provide the minimum information required. "Trial by ambush" is frequently the result. Infuriatingly, the prosecutor Valerie Bowen often failed even to respond to McCormack's requests for materials. "I'm throwing these motions at them," he remembers. They didn't have anything exculpatory, the prosecution would say (until Judge Charles E. Poston eventually ruled, in effect, "Let me see what you have and I'll decide if you have anything exculpatory," then ordered that a stack of documents two or three inches thick be turned over to Wilson's defense.) McCormack was astonished when the prosecution professed unawareness of any videotape of the crime scene. "I pushed [Bowen's] button," McCormack recounts. "I said, 'I don't want to listen to this bullshit. There's a damn videotape there. I want the videotape.' Then they come back, 'Okay, we found that there is a videotape . . . but we're not giving it to you.'" At that point, "I went ballistic on her." It took McCormack a while to get Williams's and Dick's statements, to see the crime scene photographs (a month or two on those), "and to get a handle on exactly what we were dealing with." Two and a half months after Wilson's arrest, on the basis of the "bare-bones information" that he had on the case, McCormack told a judge that, short of Wilson's confession, evidence for his guilt was "nonexistent."[6]

McCormack took a close look at Billy Bosko. Perhaps he had had a hand in his wife's murder. McCormack filed writs for Bosko's insurance policies, but he found nothing on him.[7]

In May, McCormack filed a motion to suppress Wilson's confession. His client had been "repeatedly called a liar," "lied to by investigators," and fed details of the crime, McCormack argued. "In a desperate attempt to stop the interrogation," McCormack wrote, he had confessed to rape. To no one's surprise, the motion and a subsequent one were denied.[8]

Not long after filing the first motion, McCormack met with Valerie Bowen and D.J. Hansen in the commonwealth attorney's offices in Norfolk. Hansen had been brought into the case after Wilson had been arrested "because it just kept getting worse," Bowen recalled. (Hansen says that he was enlisted mainly because of his experience prosecuting DNA cases.) A graduate of William & Mary law school originally from New Jersey, Damien J. Hansen was then in his mid-to-late thirties. He was a former navy JAG officer and a conservative law-and-order Republican who'd once had a minor brush with the law himself. "Somebody with his background should have a little bit more sympathy for defendants," one attorney comments. "Instead, it's like he's gone a hundred and eighty degrees to the other side—completely pro-prosecution. If you're charged, you must be guilty." A private, guarded, and unmarried man, Hansen is well groomed, somewhat hippy at the waist, with dark brown hair receding at the temples, glasses, and a deep voice. He's skilled and smooth in the courtroom—far more than Bowen (who would later abandon her career to become a librarian), and smarter—one of the better prosecutors in his office; he would subsequently be promoted to deputy commonwealth's attorney in nearby Chesapeake. A driven man, Hansen is serious about his work, and tenacious. "A gung-ho prosecutor," one former colleague calls him. He would become emotionally invested in this case.[9]

He can be slippery. In response to questions in an interview for this book, he often claimed that he didn't understand them or didn't remember, or simply refused comment. "I wouldn't trust him now as far as I could throw him," one lawyer says. Jennifer Stanton, a defense attorney who would later be involved in this case, lost considerable respect for him through her dealings with him. "He made some blatantly false representations to the judge on the record," Stanton remembers. And "we had to fight for *every single piece of paper* on this case. . . . It was just insane." But "sometimes he can come across as a straight shooter—usually it's a case that he really just doesn't care about."[10]

Hansen is a true believer. "He sees things in black and white," one former prosecutor observes. "When he enters the courtroom, he's convinced he's on the right side of the law." Another recalls, "He was so sure of his own way of handling things." Publicly, Hansen exhibits a sense of certainty about this case;

he's convinced that Wilson, Williams, and Dick are all guilty, he says. Many people have found him arrogant and condescending. He has "an exclusive opinion of himself," one ex-prosecutor comments: "'I am better than all the rest of you.'" "A real arrogant ass," another lawyer calls him, more bluntly.[11]

After being brought into the case, Hansen did most of the heavy preparation. "I handled the motions," he says.[12]

At McCormack's meeting with Bowen and Hansen in the commonwealth attorney's offices, they had an informal discussion about a possible plea bargain. McCormack was interested: given the stakes, he wasn't eager to roll the dice with a jury. "Plea agreements were foremost in my mind all the way through this thing," he recalls. The prosecutors offered Wilson double life terms for murder and rape, though nothing was formally on the table. When McCormack apprised Wilson of the offer, he turned it down. Over that summer, when different terms were thrown about, Wilson's position stayed firm. "His words, very clearly, were, 'I'd rather be executed than spend the rest of my life in prison,'" McCormack recounts. "Repetitively he would tell me that: 'I would rather be executed than spend the rest of my life in prison.'"[13]

All too vividly, Wilson could see it happening. "I woke up every morning visualizing myself in the electric chair," he remembers. Were he to receive a long prison sentence, Wilson decided, he would end his life by his own hand.[14]

On the afternoon of April 27, 1998, some three weeks after Wilson's confession, a meeting was held in an interrogation room at the Norfolk Police Operations Center that included Joe Dick; his attorney, Michael Fasanaro; Valerie Bowen; and Detectives Glenn Ford and Brian Wray. Bowen and the police were, of course, well aware that neither Dick nor Danial Williams had said anything about Wilson in their confessions. They wanted to talk to them about that. Williams was not cooperating, so they had brought in Dick. The prosecution had come to Fasanaro after Dick's DNA had failed to provide a match and proposed a deal: They would not seek the death penalty if Dick would agree to be interviewed and testify against Williams and Wilson. Fasanaro had counseled his client to cooperate and persuaded Dick's parents to encourage their son to do so. Dick had eventually relented: he didn't want to die. "Fasanaro kept telling me to cooperate with them," Dick remembers. "And like a dummy, I just listened to him." He didn't think he had any other choice if he wanted to avoid getting hammered with a death sentence. And "I did not want to upset my parents more than they already were."[15]

Before the meeting, Fasanaro, who knew that Dick could help himself considerably if he would roll over on Wilson, had told Dick that the police knew that Wilson had been involved. He should tell them what Wilson had done, Fasanaro advised Dick.[16]

Detective Ford opened the meeting by telling Dick that he needed to give them the truth about anyone else who had participated in the murder. Ford, whom Dick still feared, showed Dick some letters that Dick had written in jail, probably those to Nicole Williams and informant Timothy Gurley's brother that mentioned Eric. Dick was surprised to see his letters in Ford's hands. Fasanaro let Dick know that Ford and Wray had information about him talking to someone in jail—Tim Gurley would be that someone—about a third assailant named Eric. "We confronted Joe Dick with the fact that somebody else had to be involved, and he was very reluctant to admit it," D.J. Hansen recounted later. "We sensed this reluctance in Joe Dick, for some reason, that he would not implicate other people."[17]

Ten minutes into the meeting, Fasanaro requested to speak with Dick alone. After Ford, Wray, and Bowen left the room, Fasanaro and his client talked for six minutes. There is no record of what was said, but Dick recalls that Fasanaro again urged him to cooperate and counseled him that he would get the death penalty if he did not. By the time the others reentered the room, Dick was ready to talk. "Joseph Dick agreed to tell us the truth about the number of people who were present the night Michelle Bosko was murdered," Wray and Ford wrote in their notes.[18]

Dick now said that Wilson was there. He, Williams, and Wilson had barged into Michelle's apartment after she had answered her door, Dick stated. Williams and Wilson had then forced her into her bedroom. In this latest rendition, there was no "joking around and bullshitting," fondling Michelle, or listening to music with her before attacking her, and the assault took place in her bedroom rather than her living room. Wilson raped her first, Dick said. He put his own hand over Michelle's mouth and Williams held her down as Wilson raped her, Dick stated. After Williams took his turn, Wilson went to get a knife, held it to Michelle's throat, and forced her to give Dick a blow job. He did not ejaculate, Dick said, contradicting his earlier account.[19]

Who stabbed her? Ford asked him. Williams did, about three times, Dick replied. He and Wilson didn't stab her. What made them decide to get a knife and kill her? Ford probed. After raping her, Dick responded, Williams had said, "Oh, shit, we're in a lot of trouble now," then asked Wilson for the knife. When Michelle was dead, according to Dick's story, Wilson had "pulled them out of the room" and said that they were going to dump her body somewhere. Wilson and Williams had then carried Michelle into the living room, but the sound of a car in the parking lot spooked them, so they took her back into the bedroom. After returning to Williams's apartment, Dick said, they agreed to keep their mouths shut.[20]

The detectives asked Dick if he knew whether Williams or Wilson had raped anybody in the past. "He stated that Chief Teller had told him that Daniel [sic] had raped two other people in Great Lakes," Wray and Ford wrote.[21] Whoever Chief Teller was, Williams, of course, had no prior criminal record.

Did anybody hit Michelle? Ford asked Dick. Wilson hit her in the face once, and Williams twice, including on her mouth, Dick responded, which contradicted the autopsy. Ford, Wray, Bowen, and Fasanaro then left the room. When they reentered fifteen minutes later, perhaps after weighing the veracity of Dick's account, Dick told them that he too stabbed Michelle, "two to three times." So did Wilson, "two more times." Either Williams or Wilson—he couldn't remember which one—had said they had to kill her. Wilson put the knife on the floor after stabbing her, Dick said. He thought he saw the knife at Williams's apartment afterward, but he wasn't sure. If he remembered correctly, Wilson was cleaning the knife there. After the stabbings, Dick continued, "he was told at that point to go to the living room to check and see if anyone was coming," Ford and Wray wrote in their notes. "He stated that he checked out the living room and looked out the window, and everything appeared to be clear." But after being frightened by the car in the parking lot, they decided to "move the body later to a wooded area by way of Eric's car." So at around 2:30 A.M., they returned to Michelle's apartment, Dick said. But, to their chagrin, the front door was locked. Apparently, they had locked it on their way out without thinking, Dick surmised.[22]

Not surprisingly, the detectives and Bowen wanted Dick to take a polygraph on his account. Fasanaro consented to have him tested the next day. "In private he assured me he was telling the truth and would pass the polygraph," Fasanaro wrote Dick's parents three days later.[23]

But the test was, as Fasanaro puts it, "a disaster." Dick failed, with a score of −19. Back in the interrogation room, he, of course, heard from Ford on his failure. "Mr. Dick stated that he was afraid for his life"—getting the death penalty—"and that he would tell us the truth," the detectives recorded. He offered them another story. He later testified that it was a lie—as he did about most everything he told the police. In this tale, he was the one who had grabbed the knife from the kitchen. And Wilson did not stab Michelle, at least "to his knowledge from what he could remember."[24]

Dick agreed to take a polygraph on this account too, "because he stated now that he was telling the truth," Wray and Ford wrote. This time—bingo—he scored +7.[25]

But Dick's credibility was not in good shape. After Fasanaro apprised his parents of developments, an angry Patricia Dick lit into her son. "Your father and I are stunned," she wrote him on May 3. "We just don't know what to say. We had heard from Mr. Fasanaro that he had a deal worked out with the prosecutors and all you had to do was pass a lie detector test—that he had finally gotten the whole story. You would not die. . . . Then we got that letter from Mr. Fasanaro saying it was all off and everything was back to square one—because you LIED AGAIN.

"Joe, what is going on? Do you have such a low value on life? Do you understand what you are putting your attorney and your parents thru? Your attorney had *saved your life*—your father and I wouldn't have to watch you die and bury you—and you blew it. *You* threw it all away.

"What kind of a game are you playing? Do you want to die? . . . You have no idea the pain you are putting your father and me thru. And what about your attorney? You are shitting in his face also. . . .

"Do you know what the truth is? Do you know how to tell the truth? Do you know how to be a man and stand on your own two feet and accept responsibility for what you have done and to say that you were wrong and are sorry?"[26]

Patricia Dick wrote Fasanaro the following month that she hoped Joe would listen to them and tell the truth, but that she thought he feared what might happen to him if he named other accomplices.[27]

On April 30, Fasanaro recounts, he met with Dick at the Virginia Beach jail. Parts of Dick's story changed again. In his desire to satisfy the prosecutors, please Fasanaro, or assuage his guilty conscience over the crime, Dick now took more responsibility for events. "I'm going to tell you the truth," he said, according to Fasanaro's notes, which Fasanaro read during an interview. "I really have to tell you the truth. Danny and I spoke about going over, and we spoke about raping her. We forced her into the back. Danny raped her first, and then I did it." She did not give him a blow job, Dick told Fasanaro. And he didn't think Wilson raped her. But he thought that Wilson held her down. "And I went to get the knife to threaten her to keep her quiet," Dick said. "It was my idea." He stabbed her first, followed by Wilson and Williams. "I was told to check the parking lot from the living room. I heard a noise, but I didn't see anybody," Dick stated. It was Wilson's idea to move Michelle's body, he reiterated.[28]

Dick's credibility with the prosecution and police eroded further when they read one of his stranger letters to Nicole Williams. The letter reads as if it was composed by a mind that had slipped off the edge. "This is what I want you to say," Dick instructed Nicole. "(1) Invited over for a card game. (2) Dan aswers [sic] the door on [sic] his underwear. (3) Go to the bedroom. (4) Eric has Michelle's hands pinned and Dan rapes her. (5) Eric tries to force me to rape her. (6) Eric goes in the kitchen for a knife. (7) Eric holds knife to Michelle's throat and threaten's [sic] to kill her. (8) Dan panicks [sic] and repeatedly stabbs [sic] her. (9) Dan and Eric move the body into the living room and leave when they hear a car in the parking lot. (10) Dan threatens me with the knife when back in our apartment. (11) Eric leaves."[29]

Dick added a few sentences later, "I'm going to tell you something and I'm being straight up with you. If my DNA is found to be positive all that happened was Michelle was forced by knife point to give me a blow job. I don't want you to get all pissed off at me for this but this is what happened." Dick also directed Nicole to memorize his eleven points: "After you are done, rip this letter up."[30]

When Danny Shipley got wind of Eric Wilson's arrest, he went over to the jail to have another talk with his client Danial Williams. Guess what happened? Shipley said. Eric Wilson had confessed and named him. Didn't we just have this conversation? Shipley reminded Williams, referring to their talk after Dick's arrest. Why hadn't he told them about Wilson? If he had named him, Shipley pointed out, they could have used it to bargain for a better sentence. Better than life without any possibility of parole—Shipley could see twenty years. If there's more that you can tell us, they want it, Shipley stressed. They wanted it badly. "Mr. Shipley, like I told you, I didn't do it," Williams responded. "I wasn't there. How could I have told you about these guys?" Shipley was disbelieving. "At that point in time, I'm thinking, 'Look, you've confessed, another guy's confessed that you've done it along with him,'" Shipley recounts. "I'm thinking that he has actually *done* it, and he's just in denial. And I keep calling him Denial Williams." Shipley complained to another attorney about Williams's lack of cooperation.[31]

When Shipley gave him a copy of Wilson's confession, Williams, of course, noticed the glaring discrepancies with both Dick's confession and his own statement. There were just too many of them, he thought. None of it added up. "What the heck are they doing?" he wondered. "Are they going on a fishing expedition?"[32]

In June, two months after Eric Wilson's arrest, the Virginia Division of Forensic Science's Central Laboratory in Richmond threw the police and prosecution another curveball: Wilson's DNA did not match the DNA recovered from the crime scene. Three young men had now confessed in some detail to raping Michelle Moore-Bosko, two to murdering her, but there was still no physical evidence linking *any* of them to the crime. "It was just really strange," D.J. Hansen recalls. With Wilson's confession, "we thought we had the case wrapped up. Because it was just so logical. I mean, it wasn't like Joe Dick was pulling somebody out of thin air. We could tie Wilson to the both of them. We figured Joe Dick wouldn't cover twice about it. Little did we know." They still didn't have their arms around the case, Hansen deduced. But as frustrating as that was, it was almost like Michelle was telling them, You don't have everybody yet. "We knew that there was some other person that was out there who had not been caught," Hansen recounts.[33]

Valerie Bowen had a more immediate concern. "Personally, I'm thinking, How am I going to call her parents and her husband and tell them that we don't have a match?" she remembered. She'd already phoned them after the DNA reports had come back negative on Williams and Dick. It hadn't been easy. Calls like that took some deep breaths. "It was just horrific to have to call them every time and say another person was involved in this and we still don't have a DNA match," Bowen recalled. With each confession, Carol and Jack Moore's agony had grown: their daughter had been gang-raped and gang-murdered, it now appeared. No man would confess to such a horrible crime if he hadn't committed it, Carol believed. "I know I sure wouldn't," she says. And how could they provide those kinds of details about the murder if they hadn't been there? Maybe the reason their DNA didn't match was that the cops just did an abysmal job with the crime scene. "I mean, they didn't even have Michelle's fingerprints in there," Carol notes—only Michelle's and Billy's footprints were identified, though that in itself is not indicative of poor police work—"so how good of a job could they have done?" Michelle's suffering had been even greater than her parents had imagined. And "they just could not fathom that somebody who had done this would try to cover up for somebody else," Hansen remembered. They were "quite distressed and distraught . . . and there was an urgency on the part of the police that we need to find out who else is involved." That one—or even more—of their daughter's killers was still out there tormented the Moores. Carol felt that Williams, Dick, Wilson and whoever else had ravaged her daughter "shouldn't even be in jail. They should be raped and stabbed to death."[34]

Billy Bosko was still living his own hell—medicated, fighting a losing battle with insomnia, paranoid at times, struggling without success to keep it all together. His mother, Pat, would take the phone calls from Norfolk about the arrests and then the negative DNA results, and then give Billy the news. This was tough on her too; she never knew what to expect, though she knew that Billy would be upset, and maybe even lose it, no matter how she told him. At first Pat also wondered why the DNA wasn't matching and thought something wasn't right. "But you don't have to be Einstein to figure out they used condoms," she would conclude. Innocent people don't confess, she and Billy also staunchly believed. Michelle's murder was the worst thing that could possibly happen to begin with, Billy would say, "but instead of being able to have a little bit of closure that justice will be done—they have the guy that did this— it just kept going on and on. . . . It was just absolutely horrible." And knowing that they'd be getting another phone call from police later—Pat was almost afraid to answer the phone. It didn't help Billy's mental state that he had to return to Norfolk to testify at Wilson's preliminary hearing in June. Meanwhile, Pat's marriage to Billy's adoptive father was unraveling. They separated that summer and later divorced. "I just didn't have the time or energy, really, to put into my marriage" after Michelle's murder, Pat recounts. "Because I was more concerned with trying to get Billy to find a way to go on."[35]

But Billy had confidence in the police's investigation. And he had enormous regard for Detective Glenn Ford. "Without his tenacity, his determination to get to the bottom of this and get the folks who did this, I don't believe it ever would have been done," Bosko said several years later. "I believe he was the single most important person in this entire case. He's my hero, so to speak." "Ford ran this case to death," D.J. Hansen echoes. "I mean, he worked this case. He wanted to solve it as much as anybody else. And if there were more people involved, he wanted to get them." He was on a crusade, another attorney perceived. His ego was tied up with the case. Ford was not only going to nab Michelle's killers but "he was going to get all the credit for it," the lawyer Jennifer Stanton says.[36]

When Eric Wilson learned that his DNA didn't match the evidence, he thought that he'd be exonerated and released from jail. So did his parents. But the prosecutors didn't hesitate—they were going to go forward. When Greg McCormack phoned Wilson's parents eight months later to report that other DNA analyses on cigarette butts found in Michelle's apartment also excluded Eric, Ramey Wilson passed out on the phone. "I dropped [like] a sack of potatoes," she recalls. Wilson's fingerprints, as well as Dick's and Williams's, were not found in the apartment either.[37]

On June 14, a Sunday, Michael Fasanaro received a phone call from Joe Dick asking to meet. Fasanaro drove over to the Virginia Beach jail that evening. There, Dick dropped a bombshell on his attorney. At least six people had participated in Michelle Moore-Bosko's murder and rape, he now claimed. The number of attackers had doubled. Some hadn't been expected to be there, Dick told Fasanaro. One of them was named George, he said. He thought George's last name was Carr. He could identify George, he said. But he couldn't identify all of Michelle's attackers. "I'm not sure who had the knife first," Dick now told Fasanaro, according to Fasanaro's notes. "I stabbed her after Danny and George. . . . She was barely moving by the time it got to me." Dick couldn't remember the order in which they stabbed Michelle after that. Wilson had already left, he said. Why did Wilson leave? Fasanaro asked. "No one noticed," Dick responded. Fasanaro asked Dick why he stabbed her. "I was told to do it or else I'm next," Dick replied. Whose DNA would be found at the scene? Fasanaro inquired. Maybe George's or one of the others', Dick responded. Though he did rape her, Dick said, he didn't ejaculate.[38]

Fasanaro arranged for Dick to give his account to Detectives Ford and Wray. "As usual, I followed my lawyer's advice and cooperated with the police," Dick remembers. The detectives pulled Dick out of the Virginia Beach jail on the morning of June 16 and brought him up to the police station in Norfolk. Wray, Ford, and the prosecutors were by now acutely aware that Dick couldn't be trusted to tell them the truth; Valerie Bowen would testify later that at times Dick appeared to be telling them what he thought would please them, "which created numerous problems for us," as did his inconsistencies. Ford thought Dick simply didn't have all his marbles. Fasanaro also had his doubts about him. The case "drove me nuts," Fasanaro remarked later ("I think it drove everybody nuts," he added). "Because it was very hard to pin down all of the parties. . . . Every time I go [visit him], he's adding somebody else to the equation." That was "the most distressful thing." Fasanaro complained to Dick's parents about Dick's shifting stories. How could he get Joe to tell him the truth? He wasn't sure what to make of Dick's changes. Was his client just full of shit and making stuff up? Why wasn't his DNA at the scene? But Fasanaro was sure that Dick was guilty, and in one interview for this book he would dismiss Dick's inconsistencies as "meaningless" and predictable for a criminal defendant. "Has he always been a liar?" Fasanaro asked Dick's parents, in effect, during one of their meetings in his office in Norfolk. "Well, he's never, ever told me the truth," Joe Sr. briskly responded. Fasanaro exhorted Dick's parents to get him to tell prosecutors and police the truth.[39]

That led to a wrenching session at the jail. "I broke down and cried," Joe Sr. recounts. "Because we were sitting there, and as I'm looking at my son, I'm looking at this guy—I don't know if he's been duped, I don't know what the hell's going on. . . . And I pleaded with him: 'Please tell the truth. Whatever the truth is, just *please tell the truth.*'" Joe Sr. then asked himself, "What am I crying about? Look at him."[40]

But their doubts about his veracity and stability aside, police and prosecutors *needed* Dick.[41] And there was that pressure to ferret out the other killers.

At the Police Operations Center, at about 10:15 A.M., Ford began by directing Dick to tell them about the other attackers. He knew that more people had been involved, Ford stated. Dick said that there were three others, hence six in all. The only one of the three others that he knew was named George, he told Ford. His last name was Clark (rather than Carr), Dick now said that he thought. ("I don't really know where the name George Clark came from,"

Dick wrote us later. "I guess that I was put under so much stress and pressure that the name just popped into my head," though he may have met a George Clark at a bar.) George was a white male, Dick apprised Ford. He did not know the names of the other two assailants.[42]

George and Danial Williams had planned the crime, Dick stated. He had put his hand over the peephole in Michelle's front door and they all forced their way in when she answered the door, Dick said. After they had raped her, and one of the two guys whose names he didn't know made her give him a blow job, he got the knife from the kitchen. Williams stabbed her first, followed by George and himself. Had Wilson, in fact, left by then? Ford wanted to know. Had Dick been telling them the truth about that? Yes, Dick replied, as far as he could remember, Wilson had left. But he wasn't sure.[43]

Ford and Wray, of course, wanted to hear more about George. The only thing he knew about him, Dick said, was that he had earlier been in the navy. Also, that he "supposedly worked for some company" at the time of the murder; Dick thought the company "might have been involved in computers." George and Williams appeared to be good friends, Dick told Ford. He had seen George at The Banque bar with Williams. But he didn't know where George lived. If shown a picture of George, would he be able to identify him? Ford asked. Yes, Dick replied. Would he also be able to identify the two other guys? Dick said that he wasn't sure.[44]

That afternoon, Ford and Wray had Dick assist a police sketch artist develop a composite of George. The drawing that resulted was of a man with glasses, short hair, a square chin, a long nose, and a full brush of a mustache; his gaze was direct and steady, and a little unnerving. At 5:30 P.M., Wray drove over to the Norfolk naval base's pass office to find out if there was anybody on the parking pass list by the name of George Clark.[45]

Ford and Wray met with Dick again the next day. Did he know anybody who might know George? they asked him. Dick said that a woman named Melissa had been at The Banque one night when he was there with George and Williams. Williams met Melissa at The Banque a lot, Dick related. What did Melissa look like? Ford inquired. She was about 5'10" tall and weighed 120 to 130 pounds, Dick responded. She had either brownish or blond hair, and was twenty-five or twenty-six years old. Her husband was in the navy, Dick said. But he didn't know her husband's name. Pressed more about George, Dick stated that he thought George had been on the USS *George Washington*, and that George may have worn a wedding ring. But he wasn't sure about the ring either.[46]

The following day, June 18, a Thursday, Ford and Wray learned that a Melissa Wharton had visited Danial Williams at the Norfolk City Jail in 1997 after his arrest. After they tracked her down in Florida, Wray gave her a call. According to Wray's notes on their conversation, he told Wharton that he was conducting an investigation into "the Daniel [sic] Williams' [sic] murder case," which he said was "coming up to trial," and that he was calling to inquire about someone named George who she may have known. Wharton, who along with her husband at the time of the murder, Leland "Dusty" Wharton, had been members of the Banque Crew, told Wray that she did not know any- body named George. Wray then asked her if she knew anybody who had been friends with Williams, according to Wray's notes. She gave him the name of Derek Tice, Wray wrote (though Wharton maintains that Wray brought up Tice first). Tice had been "pretty close friends" with Williams and had lived in the Norfolk area at the time of the murder, Wharton told Wray; indeed, she and her husband had lived with him. Then, when she had moved down to Florida in late 1997 with her boyfriend, Robert Mattingly, Tice had also moved down, she recounted. Like George, Tice had earlier been in the navy, Wray learned. Wharton told Wray that she would have Tice call him.[47]

Wray then gave the Naval Criminal Investigative Service Tice's name. Lo and behold, a Derek Tice had been in the navy on the USS *George Washington*. Eyeing a photo of this Derek Tice in a cruise book of the ship, the detectives found it "very close" to the police sketch of George. There were, indeed, some clear similarities—the glasses, the presence of a mustache, the hairline, the square chin—though they were not as striking as prosecutors and Michael Fasanaro would later claim. Bowen and Hansen both contended that the sketch and Tice's photo were "exactly" alike—the resemblance was "uncanny," Hansen testified—and Fasanaro, in touting Dick's cooperation, argued that "the sketch was incredible—hit the person right on the button." Actually, the person in the sketch looked in some ways more like Danial Williams.[48]

Ford and Wray then headed down to the Virginia Beach jail again. A little after 6 P.M., in an interview room in the booking area, they asked Dick to look at pages 488 through 495 of the *George Washington*'s cruise book. Did he see George in there? Yes, he did, Dick told the detectives after about five minutes of scanning photos. On page 492. "As soon as he got there, he pointed to him and said, 'That's him,'" Ford later testified. Tice was George. "There was no doubt in his mind," Dick said, according to the detectives.[49]

Tice would later theorize that Dick named him partly because Dick had been jealous of his friendship with Nicole Williams when Danial was in jail and she was battling cancer. "I know he was a little ticked off about that, because he wanted to step in and be the support for her," Tice remembers. "But she turned away from him and came to me for everything." Tice would tell a probation and parole officer that Dick hated him. But Dick recalls, "I didn't think he had a relationship with Nicole. . . . I mean, deep down, I liked her myself and all. But it wasn't to get back at anybody. It's just that Ford wanted names, so I just gave him names." Why did he offer Tice's name? "He was the last person I saw," Dick says. "He came over asking about Nicole and Danial and all. And he was giving me his business card or something. And that's the last thing I can remember." But Tice had left for Florida two months before Dick's arrest. Asked if he was thinking of Tice when he spoke of George Clark, Dick said that he wasn't sure.[50]

8

Tice

Derek Tice had arrived home at his trailer in Florida at about 6:45 P.M. on June 18, 1998, minutes after Joe Dick had named him. Tice worked at Justice Boat Transports, building stanchions to brace boats in trailers, and he'd walked the couple of blocks home. It had been hot and sticky, typical for Florida in June. His trailer, a standard single-wide that he rented with his girlfriend, Lea Carlile, sat in a small wooded trailer park in Bithlo, a tiny town that was part of Orlando. Construction was the main source of jobs there, and he'd been promised one when he came to town seven months earlier. But that job hadn't materialized.

Tice had traveled to Bithlo with three friends from Norfolk. He'd been out of work, and he wanted to get away from some things, like the local party scene. He and his drinking buddies, the Banque Crew, had been spending a lot of time at the bar. His drinking had been getting out of hand. He had been going to The Banque almost every night. "Tuesday through Sunday," he recalls with a chuckle. "Every time it was open, I was there." And on Mondays, when it was closed, "I was drinking at home."[1]

Tice had been drinking to dull the pain from a broken marriage. It had been tearing him up inside. Three years before coming to Florida, his wife, a tall and husky former bodybuilder and military policewoman, had asked him for a divorce. It hadn't been smooth sailing in their marriage before then; she'd controlled him, disparaged him in public, racked up a healthy credit card debt, and had an affair while living at his parents' house when he was off on a naval cruise. Then there'd been several other affairs, along with the use of crystal meth that didn't make her any easier to deal with. He was often at sea, and she resented his absences and lack of support. But he'd tried desperately to hold their marriage together—"for my daughter's sake," he would say. Katerina was an infant. He didn't want to lose her. He was prepared to do anything to stay with her. (Tears would well up in his eyes when talking about her years later.) But his wife was not interested in salvaging their marriage. That was clear. Six months later, Holly, then twenty-two, was gone. She left with their daughter when Tice was out to sea.[2]

So he'd started drinking to excess. It helped to be around his friends too. Somebody he could talk to about his divorce, or who could get his mind off it for a while.

When Tice arrived at his trailer after work that evening, Lea informed him that a Detective Wray from the Norfolk Police Department wanted to talk to him. His friend Melissa Wharton, who lived in a trailer across the street in the same park, had given Lea Wray's number after he'd phoned her. Tice suspected the detective was calling about an old unpaid speeding ticket. Since he'd received the ticket several years earlier, he figured he could wait until after dinner to respond.[3]

At about 9 P.M., after cleaning up the kitchen, Tice phoned Wray. He reached Wray's voice mailbox, so he left his name and number. Within minutes, Wray called back. He told Tice that he was calling about "the Danial Williams murder case" and that he had a few questions he'd like to ask him about Williams. Williams was about to go on trial and he was just calling to tie up loose ends, Wray said. What did Tice know about the case? Typically polite and deferential ("Yes, sir" and "No, sir" would punctuate his end of the conversation), Tice replied that he'd be happy to answer any questions that he could, but that he didn't know much. He was aware that Williams had been arrested and had confessed but that he now claimed he was innocent, Tice told Wray. But other than that, all he really knew about the case was what he'd seen in the news. Wray thanked Tice for his help and asked him if he would please verify his phone number, address, Social Security number, and birth date. Tice thought the information was for a court summons for Williams's trial, so he readily complied.[4]

Wray then casually told Tice that his partner was not in at the moment and asked Tice if he would be at home the rest of the evening if they had any more questions for him. Tice said he would be. In reality, Wray's partner was very much in, and Wray knew they would not have any more questions for Tice. But he wanted Tice to remain at home.[5]

Tice glanced at a clock. It was now 9:30. After telling Lea about Wray's call, he watched TV while waiting for the detective or his partner to phone again. By 11 P.M. the phone had not rung, so Tice and Lea climbed into the shower in preparation for bed.

At around 11:30, while still in the bathroom, Lea told Tice that she thought she heard someone outside. It was probably only an animal running through the trailer park, Tice said. Perhaps a stray cat, a dog, or a squirrel. "Don't worry about it. It's nothing," he assured her.[6]

Then the phone rang again. Tara, Lea's twelve-year-old daughter from an earlier marriage, picked it up since her mother and Tice were still drying themselves off in the bathroom. A detective wanted to speak to him, Tara informed Tice. He thought it was Wray again, or perhaps his partner. Tell him I'll be right there, he told Tara.[7]

He then wrapped his towel around his waist and walked out into the living room to pick up the phone. Is this Derek Tice? the detective asked him. Yes, Tice replied. The detective said that he was with the Orange County Sheriff's Department and asked Tice to step out onto the front porch to answer some questions. Tice said he would, but that it would take a moment, as he'd just gotten out of the shower and needed to put on some clothes.[8]

Lea had had an argument earlier that day with Melissa Wharton's boyfriend, Robert Mattingly, over a phone bill. Lea and Tice had lived in Wharton and Mattingly's trailer during the preceding month of May. Sixteen dollars was in dispute. "I thought he was being petty and called the police," Tice recalls.[9]

Meanwhile Lea was nervously trying to put her pajamas on. Why had the police now come to visit Derek, and at this late hour? she wondered.[10]

Tice went into his bedroom and slipped into a pair of black Wrangler shorts. Bearded, with brown hair, hazel eyes, and glasses, slightly bucktoothed, weighing around 158 pounds and standing 5'9", Tice then stepped out onto the porch, still wet from the shower, naked from the waist up and barefoot. Several tattoos, including a "war band," a medical symbol, and a cow's skull, decorated his upper arms. About ten feet from the trailer was a small building. In the darkness, he could see the detective standing next to it. "Put your hands on your head. You're under arrest," the detective commanded

Tice. "And then I looked around, and there were guys coming from every angle and every side, around trees, around the other trailers and everything," Tice recounts. "All of them wearing a bulletproof vest with POLICE on it and SHERIFF and all that. And shotguns and nine-millimeters—all pointing at me." There were around a dozen of them, most dressed in black or dark blue. "They had a whole SWAT team out there surrounding the trailer," Melissa Wharton remembers. They had parked out on the main road fifty yards away and crept into the park.[11]

Tice had never been arrested before. "All this for sixteen dollars?" he marveled. "I was like, 'Rob must have said something really wild to get them to come in here like this for sixteen dollars.'" But Tice did what he was told to do—he wasn't about to risk getting shot.[12]

The detective asked Tice who else was in the trailer and then had Lea bring Tice a shirt, a pair of shoes, and his ID. What about socks? Lea asked. "No, we don't have time for that," the detective replied. The police slid a yellow Lori Morgan concert T-shirt over Tice, who was handcuffed, and helped him put on his shoes, a pair of brown hiking boots.[13]

In shock, Lea had no idea what Derek could have done. She kept asking the police what he was being arrested for. The detective claimed he didn't know, only that there was a warrant for his arrest from Virginia. Tice would be able to phone her in a couple of hours to let her know, the detective said. Lea would have nightmares of the SWAT team running around inside her trailer, out of control, throwing their weight around, for months afterward.[14]

Wray, it turned out, had obtained two arrest warrants right after speaking with Tice over the phone. Shortly before midnight, the Norfolk homicide office paged Wray at his home to notify him that Tice was in custody.[15]

Tice's thoughts now returned to the unpaid speeding ticket in Virginia. He told Lea not to worry about him, that everything would be okay. But on the way to the police car, he was given some startling news: the detective told him that he hadn't wanted to say anything in front of his girlfriend, but that he was being arrested for capital murder and rape.

Tice was dumbstruck. "I went straight into shock at that point," he recounts. "I was flabbergasted. I just lost all thought and everything. I was just numb."[16]

But he quickly put the pieces together: he was being arrested for the murder and rape of Michelle Moore-Bosko.

Placed in the back seat of the police car, Tice was asked to confirm his name, age, and Social Security number again, along with his height and weight. His answers came haltingly. His mind was now barely working at all. "I could not think straight," he would recall.[17]

Derek Elliott Tice was then twenty-eight years old, and although his life had not been free of troubles, no one who knew him could have foreseen his predicament now. Raised in North Carolina, he had no criminal record. He was calm, quiet, and respectful, even a bit docile. Two of his later attorneys would be struck by his meekness and passivity. When confronted aggressively, he would retreat into a shell rather than strike back. "Derek Tice's overall behavior and demeanor on evaluation and by history stand in marked contrast to the charges against him," David Keenan, a clinical psychologist who evaluated him, would write in January 2000. "He is generally polite and courteous, often using 'sir' or 'ma'am' when answering questions. . . . Except for these very serious charges, I am aware of no history of violence in Mr. Tice's history." Tice appreciated good humor and could be funny; as an adult he remained boyish—"a child at heart," he says. His caring manner and ability to listen allowed him to form friendships with females readily. With his friends, "I was always the counselor," he says. His father, a short, stocky, levelheaded man with receding dark hair, dark eyebrows, and glasses, was an electrical engineer, his mother a secretary in the nursing and early childhood development department at a community college, where she also taught keyboarding and office etiquette. A thoughtful woman, she'd worked in sewing factories for three decades before then. Both of Tice's parents had grown up in a small southern textile town.[18]

Tice had been raised Catholic his first twelve years and regularly attended mass and confession. After his family became Methodists, he was active in his church youth group and helped out often with church functions. "It was nothing for me to be at the church," he remembers.[19]

He possessed considerable intelligence. His IQ would test between 148 and 164—"in the superior to genius range," the analyst who conducted the test noted. He was articulate and measured in his speech. But Tice had been, at best, an average student in school. He'd been held back in the third and eighth grades (and almost the ninth). He had problems spelling and had attended classes for the learning disabled from second to eighth grades. In high school, he graduated 92nd of 156 students, with a grade point average of only around 2. "He just didn't apply himself," his mother, Rachel Tice, recalls.[20]

Some emotional turmoil he was suffering hindered his schoolwork. His older brother, Robert, had had cancer in his ear as an infant and had received cancer treatments for many years, leaving him only 4'11" with a blemished appearance. Derek was resentful of all the attention Robert received from his parents and other relatives, though he stuck up for him when other kids made fun of him. He came to believe that he had been a "replacement" for Robert, who had not been expected to live. Stumbling in school was one way of "lashing out" at his parents and forcing their attention.[21]

There were other ways. He skipped school, started smoking at age eight, stole his parents' cigarettes, and took money from them for video games. Once he poured lighter fluid in his family's toilet and set it ablaze. His litany of misbehavior included "really anything minor that I could do to get the attention that I felt that I needed or wanted," he says.[22]

His father, Larry Tice, was an often silent figure in his life. "He really didn't do a lot of family things," Derek recounts. "Every once in a while we'd go out bowling as a family, or go to a [car] race, or something like that. But other than that, he really didn't do anything with us kids. He really wasn't involved in our upbringing. . . . Dad never really said anything until we did something wrong and he was disciplining us." Derek felt his dad didn't really want him around. It was an erroneous impression, but his pain was real.[23]

He was closer to his mother. "She was always going to my baseball games when I was little, making sure that we went to first communion and . . . church," he remembers. "If we had something going on at school, she made sure that she was there. So she was a real big support."[24]

After graduating from high school, Derek volunteered with the rescue squad in Clayton, North Carolina, for two years. He'd been taken by the television series *Emergency*, then found he had a knack for the work. His coworkers would remember him as conscientious and devoted, willing to do whatever needed to be done. "He really had a heart to serve the community and wanted to do that," one of his crew leaders recalled. His goal was to be a paramedic and a pediatric trauma nurse. "He would do anything for you," agree two of his former friends.[25]

But his father felt Derek was spending too much time running with the rescue squad and pressed him to get a job that would pay his bills. The pressure and angst about his life in general got to him. He fell into a depression and contemplated suicide. "It just escalated to the point of, 'Maybe suicide would be best,'" he recounts. "You know, I'd get out from underneath Dad and he wouldn't have to worry about me anymore." He saw a psychiatrist about his depression.[26]

Tice enlisted in the U.S. Navy that same year of 1992, at age twenty-two, mainly to get paramedical training. His family had a tradition of military service; he visited his high school several times decked out in his uniform. But his naval career soon hit the skids. He went AWOL for nine days to take care of his wife, Holly, and his daughter, who were sick. "I didn't want to leave both of them there with somebody watching them that I didn't know," he says. "So I took it upon myself to stay and take care of my family." Holly had already talked about leaving him. He called his ship about his wife's and daughter's illnesses, but not quickly enough for his command. His deteriorating marriage led to another bout with depression and a sense that nothing really mattered. He stole a Swiss army knife and a wristwatch from two fellow sailors and fell asleep on fire watch. "With everything that was going on with Holly, I wasn't getting a whole lot of sleep," he remembers. In October 1995, Tice was given an other than honorable discharge from the navy for misconduct.[27]

He moved back in with his parents in Clayton for a year and worked at a Food Lion grocery store. Then it was back to Norfolk and working at another Food Lion, followed by a commission sales job. The money was poor, so Tice took another job as a night driver for a pharmaceutical delivery company, which he held until shortly before moving to Florida.

Only seven months after arriving, however, his hope of gaining a fresh start had been shattered.

As the police were driving Derek Tice to the Orlando City Jail, his girlfriend was tearfully phoning his parents. She woke them up around midnight. It was a hard call for Lea Carlile to make. She had to begin by introducing herself to Rachel Tice, as they had not spoken before; Lea and Derek had only been involved for several months. Her voice cracking, Lea informed Rachel that Derek had been arrested but that the police wouldn't tell her why. "The conversation wasn't long, but she was very upset," Rachel recounts. "She was crying, and it was just very hard for her to tell me that Derek had been arrested." Lea said that she would call Rachel back when she found out more.[28]

Michelle Moore-Bosko and
Billy Bosko. They were married
in Norfolk in April 1997.
COURTESY OF ERIN LITLE

Danial Williams, Michelle
and Billy's neighbor, upon
graduating from high school.
COURTESY OF RHEA WILLIAMS

Eric Wilson in his naval
uniform, seven months
before he was arrested.
COURTESY OF RAMEY WILSON

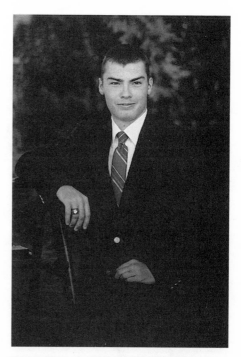

Joseph Dick upon graduating from high school. COURTESY OF PATRICIA DICK

Derek Tice upon graduating from high school. COURTESY OF RACHEL TICE

The Banque bar, the watering hole of the so-called Banque Crew, in Norfolk.
PHOTOGRAPH BY TOM WELLS

Michelle and Billy's apartment building, as seen from the parking lot. Their apartment was on the ground floor, on the left side. PHOTOGRAPH BY TOM WELLS

The common hallway on the ground floor of Michelle and Billy's apartment building. Their unit was on one side of the hallway; Danial Williams's unit was on the other. PHOTOGRAPH BY TOM WELLS

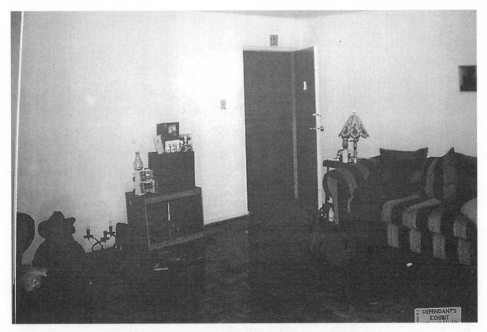

Michelle and Billy's living room at the time of the police investigation.
NORFOLK CIRCUIT COURT RECORDS

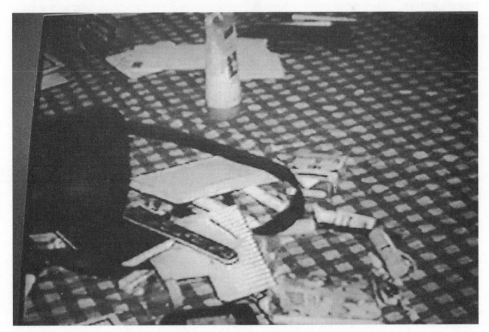

Michelle's purse, with its contents spilled out, on the dining room table.
NORFOLK CIRCUIT COURT RECORDS

Michelle's bedroom after her body was discovered there.

NORFOLK CIRCUIT COURT RECORDS

Michelle's bed, looking somewhat disheveled, after her body was discovered next to it.

NORFOLK CIRCUIT COURT RECORDS

The murder weapon, a serrated steak knife, now bent, lying partially underneath a chest of drawers in the bedroom. NORFOLK CIRCUIT COURT RECORDS

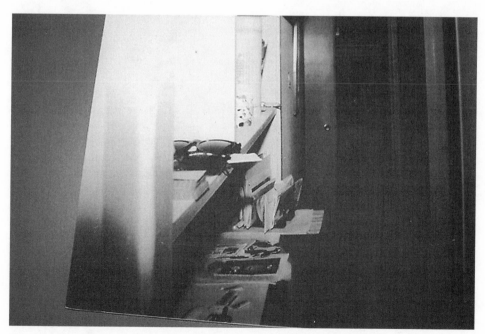

The narrow hallway inside Michelle and Billy's apartment, with papers and other material protruding off the shelves. Police and prosecutors claimed that eight men carried a struggling Michelle down the hallway before raping and stabbing her in her bedroom on the right, and then exited out the same hallway. NORFOLK CIRCUIT COURT RECORDS

Omar Ballard's prison ID, 2005.
COURTESY OF OMAR BALLARD

Sussex I State Prison in Waverly, Virginia, where Derek Tice was held, before being moved to Sussex II in 2006. PHOTOGRAPH BY TOM WELLS

At about 1 A.M., Derek phoned Lea from the jail. He'd been charged as a fugitive from justice for capital murder and rape in Dan Williams's case, he told her. Lea's head was exploding. She was silent for what seemed an eternity. Tice tried to assure her that he had had nothing to do with it, but Lea hadn't known Derek that long: Could he have done it? No way, she thought. "I knew he didn't do it," she remembers. But "my family freaked out and asked me how I could put my daughter in such danger. And I said, 'She's not in any danger. . . . He hasn't done anything wrong.'"[29]

Lea urged Derek not to talk to the police until he had a lawyer. "*Please*," she advised him repeatedly. "*Don't talk to anyone until you get a lawyer.*" Derek said he wouldn't.[30]

After she got off the phone, Lea continued weeping. Shortly, Derek phoned again to tell her that he couldn't reach his parents. It turned out he was so discombobulated that he'd forgotten he had to dial their area code. It thus fell to Lea to tell his mother why he had been arrested. Lea phoned Rachel Tice again at about 1:30 A.M. She was still finding it difficult to talk. "Fugitive from Virginia, capital murder and rape," she managed to say (though she couldn't understand how Derek could be considered a fugitive when he hadn't even known the police were after him). Rachel was extraordinarily upset. "She was very, very tore up about it," Lea remembers. It hurt Lea to have to tell her.[31]

Tossing this horrible news around in her head, unable to sleep for the rest of the night, like Lea, Rachel couldn't imagine Derek killing or raping anybody. "To me it's totally out of his character," she says. When he was a kid, Derek had conducted an experiment with fruit flies, and she told him that he had to get rid of the flies when the experiment was over. "He was very adamant that we don't kill them," Rachel remembers. "So I just can't see it. He's not going to kill an insect—why would he kill a human? Plus, he had worked with the rescue squad, and that's *saving* lives, that's not killing. So, to me, I just couldn't understand what was going on."[32]

If he was going to kill anybody, Rachel ruminated, he would have killed his ex-wife, Holly. Yet the thought did cross her mind: Maybe he'd been drinking and something happened.[33]

Larry Tice was also in a state of disbelief. It was like the whole thing wasn't really happening. It just wasn't real. He didn't think Derek could have done anything like this either, but he didn't have any information.[34]

Cold and tired but unable to sleep at the jail, Derek finally reached his parents a few hours later. "Well, did you do it?" Rachel asked him, point-blank. "*No!*" Derek emphatically replied. That was good enough for Rachel.[35]

The next morning, Tice was escorted to a small room with a table and two chairs. A man in street clothes was sitting in one of the chairs. There was a folder on the table in front of him. A detective, the man introduced himself to Tice and directed him to have a seat. He was there to tell him about extradition to Virginia, the detective said. Tice had been charged with murdering and raping Michelle Moore-Bosko, the detective told him. Did he do the crime? No, Tice replied. Well, then it would be in his interest not to contest extradition and to fight the charges in Virginia, the detective advised him. If he didn't do it, then he had nothing to worry about.[36]

Tice spent a surreal week in the Orlando jail. He remained numb, in a stupor, almost like he'd been anesthetized. Wearing a bright-orange jail jumpsuit, "I was walking, talking, and eating on autopilot," he wrote later. Everything was out of his control. Stuck in a holding cell for three days, he was then packed with about two dozen other inmates in a room in the main cellblock. He felt "scared and alone, not knowing what was going on or why I was there." He kept to himself.[37]

He didn't know who he could trust. Nobody, most likely, he decided. "You don't have any friends in there," he says. If he talked to one inmate, members of a rival gang might think he was in with him. And he feared getting raped. The double bunks were only two feet apart. He was afraid to close his eyes. "You really couldn't get any sleep, because you were trying to keep an eye out on your stuff and your person," he recalls. Then it was up at 6 A.M.[38]

On his last day in the jail, Lea and her daughter, Tara, were able to visit him for fifteen minutes. They had to stand—there was no sitting—and shout above the racket through small holes in a wall. To see each other, they were forced to peer through a Plexiglas circle about the size of a person's face. "It was horrible," Lea recounts. "You're trying to yell louder than the person next to you so you can hear." And seeing Derek in jail clothes was unbearable.[39]

The next day, June 25, a Thursday, Tice was woken up shortly before 5 A.M. and instructed to gather his stuff. A guard handed him his street clothes—the T-shirt, shorts, and hiking boots he had been wearing when carted off to jail. He was then led out of the cellblock and into an empty visiting area, where guards removed his handcuffs and directed him to quickly change clothes. After cuffing him again, they took him downstairs to a hallway off the jail's parking garage. Two men dressed in suits and several guards were waiting for him there.[40]

The plainclothesmen were Detectives Glenn Ford and Brian Wray. Ford did most of the talking. They were from Norfolk, from the homicide squad there, Ford informed Tice. "We've come to take you back and ask you some questions." Ford then went into an office, picked up Tice's driver's license, and signed some papers. After replacing the jail's handcuffs with his own, he and Wray marched Tice out the door toward a rental car. "We're going to walk out there to the car, we're going to put you in the back seat, and we're going to go to the airport," Ford told Tice in a clipped tone of voice. "Don't give us any trouble."[41]

How was he going to cause any trouble? Tice was thinking. His hands were cuffed, and both Ford and Wray had guns. He wasn't going to do anything stupid. Ford's comment "was rhetorical," he thought.[42]

Tice was relieved to be moved. He thought that everything would be cleared up after he got to Virginia. He knew that the police wouldn't believe him at first, and he expected to be locked up again for a time. But the truth would come out and his nightmare would end.[43]

Ford and Wray were not in the best of moods. They had driven over to the police booking station earlier that morning expecting to pick up Tice there. But he had not been transported from the jail as planned. They were behind schedule, they complained to Tice, and might not make their flight. And now they didn't know the way to the airport. Did Tice know how to get there? No, Tice replied, he did not know that much about Orlando. Behind the wheel, Ford chose the route. But as Tice listened to him and Wray talk between themselves, including about their bets at the dog track the previous evening, he noticed a sign that indicated they were going the wrong way and told them about it. Ford thanked him, got off the freeway, turned around, and zoomed back on.[44]

At the airport ticket counter, Ford and Wray were annoyed to learn that they would not be able to make their 7 A.M. flight and would have to wait three hours for the next flight. They then escorted Tice over to the food court and ordered bacon sandwiches, hash browns, and Pepsi for breakfast. "Here's the deal," Tice remembers Ford telling him, in so many words. "I'm going to take the handcuffs off you, and how you act determines if they stay off or we put 'em back on. If you act right, they'll stay off. But the first time you start acting up, we're going to put everything on you. I've got shackles and waist restraints—the whole nine yards. And we're going to put it on you if you misbehave."[45]

They didn't have to worry, Tice responded. He was not going to be a problem. He again thought, I'd have to be pretty dumb to try anything. The airport had security, Ford and Wray had their guns, and he didn't really know anybody in Orlando. Where would he go?

After finishing their breakfasts, Tice and Ford were still hungry, so they each ordered another serving. Ford and Wray acted solicitous of Tice. Was he comfortable? Did he have what he needed? "They were real polite and everything," Tice recounts. It was almost like they were his friends. "It makes the trip go easier," Ford later commented. "You don't have problems with people. . . . It just sets a rapport."[46]

Before eating breakfast, Tice said grace. It was not his custom. But "after I got arrested, it was like, 'I'm going to call on everything I can do to get help,'" he says with some amusement in retrospect. "So I really started saying grace and praying and everything. I started going back to the religion and calling on God." Ford observed Tice as he said grace. He was looking for clues to the man. He knew that Tice had never been interrogated by police. How should he handle him?[47]

Ford then phoned the police headquarters in Norfolk to tell them about the delay, also calling his wife. Meanwhile Tice and Wray had a smoke. Tice watched a bird that was trapped inside the building, feeling sorry for it.

At the gate for their flight, Ford sat on one side of Tice, Wray on the other. Not long after Ford put his feet up on a chair, he fell asleep; Wray dozed off as well. Wray woke up once to check on Tice, who was observing the unloading of a plane. After boarding their flight, Ford fell asleep again.[48]

During a layover in Charlotte, Ford picked up a thick brown accordion folder and asked Tice if he knew what it was. No, Tice replied, though he suspected it contained the extra restraints Ford had mentioned. It was the Moore-Bosko case folder, Ford announced, and since taking on the case it had become his life.[49] But his dedication aside, Ford had long since missed the forest for the trees.

That wasn't unheard-of for detectives trying to solve brutal, high-profile crimes. The pressures on police to solve these crimes, which are usually murders, often without witnesses, can be substantial and mount as a case drags on and becomes more sensational, as this one did. The pressures come from the victim's relatives, the public, prosecutors, and the police themselves. A detective's rate of clearing his cases is important, as is the speed at which he solves them. In homicide, which is the most prestigious unit of most police departments, "the laws of natural selection apply: A cop who puts down enough cases stays, a cop who doesn't is gone," David Simon writes in *Homicide: A Year on the Killing Streets*. A detective's clearance rate, which is a key ingredient in his promotion reviews, is "the litmus test, the beginning and end of all debate." And homicide detectives compete among themselves. Sometimes the pressures to solve high-profile crimes, those violent crimes that really matter—and the vicious killing of a pretty young navy wife in Norfolk, Virginia, did matter—can lead them to focus on the wrong people and engender other errors. Then there's a good chance they'll convince themselves that they're right.[50]

Tice noticed a label on the case folder. It included the names Danial J. Williams, Joseph J. Dick Jr., and Eric C. Wilson. Living down in Florida, Tice had been unaware that Dick and Wilson had also been arrested for Moore-Bosko's murder and rape. He was astounded by the news. "I just couldn't believe that," he recounts. "I was like, 'Ain't no way they got three people arrested for it and they're coming after me.'" He hadn't even met Dick or Wilson until the month after the murder, he says.[51]

Ford would later testify that he told Tice during their trip up to Norfolk that he wouldn't discuss the case with him, and that he did not do so. "Not a word," he said. Tice remembers differently. At the Charlotte airport, he recounts, when Wray was in the bathroom, Ford asked him if he knew Dick and Wilson. Ford said he did not like Dick. "He thought Dick was an imbecile," Tice recalls—"a little goofy and off his rocker." Tice thought back to when he had met Dick. Yeah, Dick had struck him as weird too. Ford let Tice know that he didn't like Wilson's lawyer either. Wilson was going to get convicted, he lectured Tice. Did he know why? No, Tice responded. Because of his lawyer, Ford said, who was telling him that everything was going to be okay. Wilson was a fool for believing the lawyer; he was going to get Wilson killed. Ford also told Tice that he knew that Tice had taken care of Nicole Williams after Danial had been jailed, and that he knew why. He also knew why Tice had broken his hand the previous fall. (Whatever Ford thought, Tice had punched a wall after learning that Nicole had died alone; he had promised her that she would not die alone.) Had he spoken to his parents? Ford asked Tice. Yes, Tice replied. What had they had to say about all this? They had been surprised about his arrest, Tice responded, but they knew that he didn't do it, and they had urged him to just tell the truth. Which is what he intended to do. That was good, Ford remarked. He knew that he would tell the truth. Did Tice know why he knew? Because he had watched him say grace at breakfast, Ford said. Did Tice know why *else* he knew? "Because you are holding all the cards," Tice replied. "That's right, I am holding all the cards!" Ford smiled. Tice told Ford that he would help in any way he could.[52]

When Wray returned from the restroom, Ford informed him that Tice had said he would tell the truth. "It would be nice if he did," Wray commented.[53]

Tice had to go to the bathroom as well, but he was afraid to say anything. As they waited for their plane, "I was trying to figure out why I had been arrested and how mad [Ford and Wray] would be when they found out that I had been wrongfully accused," he wrote afterward.[54]

On the plane from Charlotte to Norfolk, Tice again sat between Ford and Wray. It was a tight fit, and a stewardess asked Wray if he would like to take another seat. He was a police officer transporting a prisoner, Wray explained. The stewardess looked at Tice, who raised his hands as if they were handcuffed. "Oh, I'm sorry," she said before quickly walking away.[55]

Ford and Wray placed Tice in an interrogation room in Norfolk at 2:15 P.M. The room was dirty and dimly lit (one light was on), not that much brighter than if it were lit by a night-light, Tice would recall. There was reddish carpet on the floor. "It smelled like an unclean Port-A-John," Tice later testified, though Ford said it was cleaned daily. There was a chalkboard on the wall. A plant, or perhaps a fake plant, stood in one corner.[56]

Ford directed Tice to take a seat while pointing to an old straight-back wooden chair that was farthest from the door and in a corner. Tice sat down there. He was wearing only his yellow Lori Morgan T-shirt, black shorts, and hiking boots, without socks. The room was cool, and goose bumps formed on his arms and legs. But Ford did not want him getting comfortable. Wray asked Tice if he wanted something to eat. They could order a pizza or something, Wray offered. No, sir, Tice replied, not right now. He didn't think he could keep anything down. How about a soda and cigarettes? Wray asked. Yes, please, Tice said. A Dr Pepper and Marlboros. Wray and Ford then left the room; Tice noticed that they locked the door on their way out. After Wray returned several minutes later with the soda and cigarettes, he left and locked the door again. That was unsettling to Tice. "I sat in the room alone for only a few minutes more, but it seemed more like hours," he recounted later. His breathing was short, and he tried to calm his nerves, telling himself, "Okay, you have nothing to be afraid of, so just tell them the truth and everything will work out okay."[57]

When the detectives reentered, Ford sat down in the chair next to Tice and put the case folder on the floor by his feet. They had to go through a legal rights form, Ford said breezily, and then Tice could talk to them if he wanted to. With nary a pause, Tice waived his rights, against his girlfriend's advice a week earlier. Ford asked him if he would like to make a statement. "I said yes, because *I had done nothing wrong* and I had *nothing to hide!*" Tice exclaimed later. As an innocent man, he didn't think that he needed a lawyer.[58]

Ford told Tice that Williams, Dick, and Wilson had all confessed and that they needed to talk about what happened to Michelle Moore-Bosko. Ford directed Tice to go ahead and tell them everything he knew about the night of the murder, starting from the beginning. Tice said that he had known nothing of it until he got a page one day from a friend, Theresa Lickey, while at work. When he phoned her back, Lickey had told him that she had seen Williams on the news and that he had been arrested.[59]

Tice had been on the road as a salesman for the store Books, Toys, and Novelties when Lickey had paged him. He had stopped at a pay phone to return her call. At first, when she had told him that Williams had been arrested, he had thought she was joking. "Dan put her up to it," he had suspected. Then, when he realized she was serious, he was incredulous. "There's no way Dan could have done that," he thought.[60]

But when Tice told Ford about Lickey's call, Ford abruptly jumped to his feet, sent his chair flying, slammed his hands down on the table, and angrily demanded in a loud voice, "Okay, stop right there! Don't tell us a bunch of fucking lies!" The metamorphosis from Ford's considerate treatment of Tice and often soft-spoken demeanor during the trip up from Orlando was dramatic. They knew that he had been at the victim's apartment the night of the murder, Ford snapped. They would not have spent all that money to fly down to Orlando and bring him up to Norfolk if all they wanted to hear from him was that he knew nothing about it. Tice, who was startled by Ford's reaction to his account and feared that Ford was going to hit him, tried to tell Ford that he was not lying, that he really didn't know about the murder until Lickey called him. Stop lying and tell the truth! Ford again shouted. He *was* telling the truth, Tice plaintively responded. Ford turned to Wray and snorted, "I knew it was too good to be true. I knew he wouldn't tell us the truth." Once more, Ford demanded that Tice tell them what happened, but Tice repeated his account.[61]

If he did not stop lying, Ford warned Tice, he would get the maximum sen- tence when he went to trial. Did he know what the max was? No, Tice replied. "For capital murder the max is death by lethal injection," Ford said, according to Tice. (Ford would later deny under oath indicating how death was effected, or threatening Tice with the death penalty at all.) "Do you want to die?" Ford asked Tice by Tice's account. No, Tice responded. Well, if he didn't want to die, he needed to tell them the truth, Ford said. I *am* telling you the truth, Tice was thinking. "I don't know what you think is the truth, but I'm telling you what I know!"[62]

Ford apprised Tice that there was a secret witness to the crime who nobody had thought about. This witness would place him at the scene, Ford claimed. He pulled out the police sketch of George that had been done under Joe Dick's guidance. "Where do you think this came from?" he asked Tice. Tice said he didn't know. Who did he think it looked like? "It looks a little like Dan Williams," Tice replied. "I don't think so," Ford retorted. He then pulled out a copy of the page in the USS *George Washington*'s cruise book that included Tice's photo. "It's a dead ringer of you!" Ford proclaimed. "Don't you think? I do." Ford held up the sketch and the photo so Tice could compare them.[63]

Ford told Tice that they had physical evidence tying him to the crime, co- defendants who would testify against him in court, and other witnesses. Those codefendants would say that it had been his idea to rape and murder Michelle Moore-Bosko. Ford also reminded Tice that he had said on the way up from Orlando that he, Ford, was holding all the cards. Don't make him play them, Ford warned Tice. But he would if he had to.[64]

Using a softer touch, Ford also assured Tice that everybody makes mistakes. But he needed to tell them the truth about what really happened.[65]

Ford kept showing Tice a photo of Michelle eating a pretzel. "Sometimes when you show people a picture of somebody, it brings a little bit of emotion out of them," Ford later explained. What you-all did to that girl was wrong, he bellowed at Tice several times. It was brutal and uncalled for. How did Tice think her family felt, or her husband felt when he discovered her dead body on the floor of their apartment? How would Tice feel if she were his wife, his daughter, or his sister? With each question, Ford moved the photo of Michelle closer to Tice's face, until it was only three or four inches away. Tice probably thought that Williams wouldn't rat on him since he'd taken care of his wife after Danial had been jailed, Ford told him. But with Nicole now dead, things had changed, and Williams wasn't as loyal as Tice thought he was.[66]

Tice was beginning to wonder if everyone—Williams, Dick, Wilson, the secret witness, and Ford and Wray—was conspiring against him. He felt his sense of reality slipping. But he continued to deny any involvement in Moore-Bosko's murder and rape, as Ford continued to yell at him ("I may have raised my voice once or twice," Ford later allowed), ordering him to quit lying, insisting that they knew he'd taken part in killing that girl. He again asked Tice if he wanted to die. The more Tice denied involvement, the angrier Ford seemed to get. Around and around they went, with Ford hovering over Tice (though he would deny doing so, and Wray claimed that Ford never once stood up), barking like a drill instructor, thrusting his face in Tice's face ("I wasn't nose to nose," he later testified), flexing his muscles, waving his hands close to Tice (Ford would deny making those last two gestures too), "radiating a threatening manner," in Tice's words. "He didn't want to hear the truth. . . . Every time that I would say that I wasn't there and everything, he would call me a liar and tell me that I was there, that he knew that I was there, and that if I kept telling lies . . . I would go to trial and that I would get the needle. I'd say almost every five minutes it seemed like he was saying, 'You're going to die. You're going to get the needle. We're going to make sure of it.'" Tice worried that he would never be able to see his daughter again.[67]

While questioning Tice, Ford was putting forth his scenario of the rape and murder: You went over to Dan's that night and had a party, didn't you? After Nicole went to bed, the talk turned to sex and women, didn't it? Dan started talking about his neighbor Michelle, didn't he? You-all went over to her apartment, and Dan knocked on the door and covered up the peephole, didn't he? And so on, until Ford had laid out his entire theory of what transpired that night; he went through it several times. "He was giving me like a three-minute scenario of what happened, and then it was like, 'That's the truth, right?'" Tice recounts. "None of his questions were open-ended—you know, 'What happened next?' It was, 'This happened, didn't it? And then this happened.' He just kept going through the entire story." To each question, Tice shook his head or answered, "I don't know. I wasn't there." His responses seemed to enrage Ford even more.[68]

Ford and Wray soon left the room, again locking the door on their way out. When they came back in a few minutes later, Ford once more asked Tice if he wanted to die.[69]

The detectives were in and out of the room throughout Tice's interrogation. Being left alone was just as bad as being badgered, Tice would say later, as he didn't know when Ford and Wray would return and what would happen next. If he had thought that everything was out of his control in the Orlando jail, things were far beyond his control now.[70]

At one point, as Wray and Ford were walking out of the room, Wray stopped, turned around, looked at Tice and declared, "Derek, I know that you're guilty. Do you know how I know? Because when we came to pick you up this morning, you didn't say one word."[71]

At around 3 P.M., Tice asked Ford, "What if I took a polygraph and passed it? Then would you believe me?" "Oh, you are going to take it," Ford assured him, "and don't worry, you are not going to pass it." He could guarantee him that he would fail it, Ford said. Ford then left the room again with Wray; he stuck his head in the door several times to let Tice know they were waiting for the polygraph examiner to arrive. Ford and Wray reentered at 3:35 to take another shot at wresting a confession from Tice, but Tice still denied being at the scene or knowing anything about the crime. "He didn't know what we were talking about," Ford said derisively later.[72]

At 4:03, Ford escorted Tice to the polygraph room. Tice would remain there for over three hours. It seemed to him even smaller than the interrogation room. The polygrapher, Detective Randy Crank, told Tice all about the test, how it would be conducted, and about all the classes he had to take to administer it. It could detect lies well, he said. Tice was nervous about the test; his stomach was not in good shape. Following his breakfast almost ten hours earlier, he had not eaten lunch (though he'd been offered it), only two bags of peanuts on the planes. He'd been drinking Dr Peppers and other caffeinated soft drinks steadily. But he expected the exam to clear him.[73]

Crank finished testing Tice at 5:30. He had failed, Crank informed Tice. He had scored –22, a clear sign of deception. The results showed that he had been at the victim's apartment and taken part in killing and raping her, Crank told

Tice. He was going to get the needle if he continued lying, Crank too warned him. It was one thing to know you're going to die, Crank added, in Tice's recounting, which Crank would dispute, but he personally did not want to know the day he was going to die. By the time of Tice's execution, Crank said, he would probably be retired, but he would come out to the prison just to watch him die.[74]

Crank also told Tice that if he did not want Ford—who could be "a little overbearing"—in the interrogation room, he and Wray would do it, but that Tice should come clean. That way, Crank said, he might be able to save his life.[75]

Tice now realized that he needed an attorney. "Maybe I should get a lawyer," he remarked to Crank. "That would be advisable," Crank replied; they then discussed the issue for a few minutes. "Well, that's what I'll do," Tice recalls saying. "I'll get a lawyer." According to Crank's notes, Tice told him that he had decided "not to say any more; that he might decide to after he talks with a lawyer, or spends some time alone thinking about it." Tice had invoked his right to silence. But Crank apparently did not see it that way, and Tice "*did not* request a lawyer," Crank wrote in his notes. If he had, Crank testified later, "I would have stopped immediately." Tice maintains that he did, however, and expected to be put in a jail cell again until a lawyer could be hired.[76]

According to Crank's notes, Tice was also now questioning his memory. When Crank asked him what part he had in the crime, "he stated it was a long time ago, that he blocks it out, like, 'I'm not sure it really happened or not,'" Crank wrote. "It was like a dream. I asked him who knocked on the door, said he didn't remember. He asked me if he could have some time to think about it. If he decide[s] to tell me could he talk to me and Wray?"[77]

At 7:28 P.M., about fifteen minutes after Crank had escorted him back to the interrogation room, Ford and Wray reentered and "the badgering started up again," Tice recounted. What the heck happened to his request for a lawyer? Tice wondered. "It was like Detective Crank never happened," he would recall. His despair mounted. "I believed that if Ford was not going to respect my right to see a lawyer, he was not going to let me out of the interrogation room until I told him what he wanted to hear," Tice remembered. With a grin on his face, Ford pointed out that Tice had failed the polygraph badly, and reminded him that he had told him that he would fail it. He was a liar and the test proved it, Ford said. He again pulled the photo of Michelle Moore-

Bosko from his case folder. Once more he asked Tice how he thought her family felt, or her husband felt, or how he would feel if she were his wife, daughter, or sister. It made him sick to his stomach just to think about what they had done to her, Ford spat. He knew that it was hard for Tice to look at the photo; he didn't want to look at it, Ford charged, because he knew exactly what had happened that night. After putting the photo down, Ford told Tice that he too knew what had happened, but that Tice needed to tell them *why* it had happened, and that if he continued to lie he would go to trial and each of his three codefendants would get up on the stand, point to him, and testify that he had been there and that it had been his idea. What did he think would happen then? "Well, I'll tell you," Ford went on. "The jury is going to give you the death sentence."[78]

Ford encouraged Tice to get it all off his chest: it was apparent that it was eating away at him. If he confessed, Ford said, he would feel better about himself, and they would do their best to help him. Ford would later deny making Tice any promises of leniency, perhaps because courts have deemed promises and threats coercive and have excluded coerced confessions.[79]

After Tice said that he could not confess because he wasn't there, Ford moved closer and said that he knew it had not really been his idea, that the others had pressured him, but that if he kept his mouth shut he was going to die. At that point Ford stepped back, picked up the photo of Michelle again, and put it about a foot away from Tice's face. When he got to the part about how Tice would feel if she were his daughter, Tice became emotional and covered his eyes with his hands. He was thinking about his own daughter, Katerina, who he had not seen for some time, and worrying that he could never prove his innocence against the testimony of his three codefendants and the secret witness. And he knew that it would be horrendous for his family, particularly his mother, if he were to be executed. Ford stopped yelling and put his hand on Tice's shoulder. "I can see that this is really troubling you," he remarked. When Ford asked Tice again if he had been at Dan Williams's apartment the night of the murder, "there was no response from Mr. Tice," Wray and Ford recorded in their notes.[80]

After Ford showed Tice the photo of Michelle once more and exhorted him to make a statement for her family, Tice started crying. It was too much for him, sitting in that tiny room, with no end in sight to Ford's browbeating—and who knew what he might do to him if he got any madder?—feeling like he'd been had by a conspiracy that he did not understand, believing that it was futile to maintain his denials, and just wanting to go home. "I didn't know which way to go, how to go about it," he recounts. "I was tired. I wasn't really thinking straight." But if he kept his mouth shut, he believed, he was going to die. If he talked, he might be able to clear himself later. "I felt like a caged animal," Tice wrote afterward. "Scared, alone, sick to my stomach. I had a headache, thought that Ford was telling the truth about all three of them going to testify against me, thought the polygraph could be used as evidence, [and I was] afraid that Ford was going to hit me if I did not make a statement. [I] wanted out of that room by hook or crook, felt trapped and that my only way out was to make a false statement. . . . Now I just feel stupid!"[81]

His will broken, and his self-confidence obliterated, Tice began voicing a confession to the rape and murder of a young woman he had never even seen. In a calmer tone of voice, Ford prodded him along: "Let me tell you what we know, and you fill in the blanks," "Let me get you started," and so on, once again providing Tice the details he sought. Most of what Tice offered thus came from Ford himself—he "told me just about everything that is in my statement," Tice says, though both Ford and Wray denied that Ford supplied Tice with any crime facts. Other details came from having attended Dan Williams's preliminary hearing and visiting Williams in jail with Nicole; Williams had told Nicole about documents and photos he'd seen and what his lawyers were saying, and Tice overheard some of these conversations. Plus, he simply concocted parts of his confession.[82]

What Tice did not know as he was desperately trying to gain passage out of that room is that he was digging a deep hole for himself, one from which it would be extraordinarily difficult to extricate himself afterward. A confession is usually a kiss of death for a criminal suspect, even an innocent one. It typically spells guilt for jurors, judicial officials, the public, and the media. A confession tends to dominate all other case evidence, and jurors generally regard one as the most damning of all possible indications of guilt (aside from a suspect's capture while committing a crime). A confession usually overrides even solid evidence of innocence. Mock jury studies have found that confessions have greater impact on jurors than eyewitness and character testimony, and that people don't completely discount confessions even when logic and the law dictate they should. A study by one of the authors of this book shows juries convicting false confessors at a rate of 81 percent.[83]

Moreover, a confessor will be treated more severely at every stage of the judicial process. Prosecutors will probably charge him with the greatest number and types of offenses and be less inclined to plea bargain; it will also be harder for him to make bail. If convicted, he will most likely receive a harsher sentence. And once a suspect gives a false confession to police, it is difficult, if not impossible, for him to prove his innocence; the real perpetrator is rarely apprehended. After obtaining a confession, police typically deem the case solved. Prosecutors and police often refuse to acknowledge a confessor's innocence even after DNA tests have absolved him. And once false confessors are convicted, judicial officials rarely take their protestations of innocence seriously. The system, in short, is deficient at discovering and remedying this type of error.[84]

It had been Williams's idea, Tice agreed with Ford. They had been hanging out at Williams's apartment that night. After Nicole had gone to bed early, Tice said, they had started fantasizing about which women they'd like to have sex with. Tice told Ford that if Williams had been infatuated with Michelle, he'd never mentioned anything to him about it, but under Ford's prompting he switched gears and said that Williams kept "going on and on" about Michelle and saying how he'd like to have her. "He stated that Williams seemed to be getting worked up and wanted to go over there to Michelle's house," Ford later testified. When one member of the group at Williams's apartment asked what kind of panties she wore, another suggested, "Well, let's go over and find out," Tice said. He had wanted to leave and warn Michelle, but didn't.[85]

Ford kept insisting that he knew someone besides Williams, Dick, Wilson, and Tice had been there, someone Tice had brought over to Williams's apartment. "You said that I was holding all the cards," Ford reminded Tice. "But that's not totally true. You are holding the trump card—the name of the other person." If Tice told him the whole story including the name of the fifth assailant, Ford said, he would see to it that he did not get the death penalty.[86]

Tice knew that Wilson had been close to Geoffrey Farris, another ex-sailor; Tice himself had lived with Farris briefly in Norfolk and then in Florida. So he told Ford the other assailant was Farris. "He was the first name that popped into my head," Tice remembers. He reasoned that Farris would be believable to Ford, and that perhaps Ford was even thinking of him.[87]

But Ford pretended to already know about Farris. ("We didn't know nothing about Geoffrey Farris," he subsequently testified.) Someone else was also present, Ford declared. After Tice said that he wasn't sure of this other person's name, Ford snapped that "he needed to tell us the truth about the whole thing and not try to protect somebody who was a friend." Tice replied that they were right and that the other attacker was Rick Pauley, another former roommate and friend. As a member of the Banque Crew who had been in Norfolk at the time of the murder, Pauley too would be believable to Ford, Tice figured.[88]

Implicating his two friends "tore my stomach up," Tice recounted years later. "Because somebody did it to me and I knew how it felt. . . . It just tore me up inside." Tice's voice broke at this point.[89]

Ford ordered Tice to go on and tell them what happened that night. At Ford's behest, Tice went through his story several times, adding more detail with each retelling, changing parts here and there, contradicting himself, partly in an effort to satisfy Ford, and partly because he simply didn't know what had happened. "Things were happening so fast, maybe he was off a little bit," Ford would say later to account for Tice's changes.[90]

They had all six gone across the hall to the victim's apartment, Tice stated. Someone had knocked on her door—he wasn't sure who. Did anyone cover the peephole? Ford asked. He thought Williams did, but, again, he wasn't sure, Tice said. "Who is it?" the victim had asked. "It's Dan, your neighbor, and some friends," Williams had replied. Michelle had told them to "go away," Tice stated. Someone then pried the door open with a claw hammer. (Tice had overheard Williams tell his wife during a visit in jail that his lawyers had asked if a hammer had been used.) But there were no marks on the door or frame. "I was trying to give them everything that would corroborate the evidence they collected, and unknown to me it was a fabrication," Tice laughed later. Ford, who knew that there were no claw-hammer marks on the door, did not ask Tice about the discrepancy. Williams was the first one through the door and the first to grab the victim, Tice continued. He had tried to get Williams away from her, but Williams had gone "ballistic."[91]

Tice said that he wasn't sure which room they assaulted Michelle in. She was trying to scream, but someone had their hand over her mouth. He thought this person was Farris, Tice said. He demonstrated how the attacker covered Michelle's mouth. Who took her clothes off? Ford asked. They were all grabbing her, so he didn't exactly know, Tice responded. Who was holding her down? He was holding one leg, Wilson the other leg, Tice replied; Dick was holding one arm and Pauley the other. He was the second one to rape her, after Williams, Tice said. He ejaculated, he told Ford later on tape. He was not sure who raped her next. Asked if anyone made Michelle give them a blow job (as Dick had earlier told Ford), Tice responded that he thought Farris might have tried to, but "I believe that she bit him and he withdrew from trying that again."[92]

Tice told Ford that he left before Michelle was killed, but Ford would not believe him. The "peak attention" part of the lie-detector test showed he was there, Ford asserted. They could prove he was present and knew exactly how she was killed; telling only part of the truth "wasn't going to be good enough," Ford advised Tice. Tice then said that he had not, in fact, left Michelle's apartment. He had started to but had decided to return to the bedroom. Tice then began crying again and put his hands over his face. Asked what he had done in the bedroom, he groaned, "I can't believe I said this, but when I went back into the room, I looked at Danial and stated, 'Just stab the bitch.'"[93]

Farris then grabbed a knife from the kitchen, Tice said. But, of course, he could not describe the knife. They all took a turn stabbing her, he stated in accord with Ford's theory. They held her upright from behind while each took their turn. When Ford asked him if they attempted to move Michelle's body after they had killed her (as Dick had claimed), Tice said only after it had fallen on Farris's foot. "We rolled her over so that Jeff could leave the apartment with us," he would tell Ford almost comically on tape.[94]

Ford wanted to know if their actions involved a cult or rituals. Had Wilson considered himself a Druid? Yes, Tice replied. Wilson had sought to turn the whole thing into some kind of Druid ceremony, complete with candles and other paraphernalia, he said. But he had opposed the idea because it was "wrong" to involve "outsiders" in such rituals.[95]

Who actually planned it? Ford grilled Tice. "Mr. Tice didn't say anything," Wray and Ford wrote in their notes. They knew that he and Williams had planned it, Ford claimed. He asked Tice if he had "any kind of obsession" with Michelle. No, Tice replied, but to make his story more believable he added that Williams had mentioned her to him once before, and that when he had later seen her passing in the hallway he had thought, "Damn, Danial was right. She is good-looking." She reminded him of the actress Sandra Bullock, he had told the others. By this time, Ford had shown Michelle's photo to Tice several times.[96]

It was 11:39 P.M., near the end of a marathon day, when Ford and Wray turned on their tape recorders. To Ford's mind, Tice's account had gotten "as close to the truth" as he would come. "What we were trying to do is narrow him down to as close as he could get to what exactly happened," Ford later testified. "We were trying to get it just right." Listening to a tape of Tice's confession, one hears a drained young man speaking in a flat, affectless tone of voice—there is no emotion there, except in Ford and Wray's sharp and sometimes angry tones—slowly and deliberately, often tentatively, as if he is trying to recite the same story he has previously laid out and keep the details consistent. Sarah Bosko, Billy's sister, would later be struck by "how unbelievably cold" Tice sounded. Of course, when a suspect recounts a story many times, he will tend to show less emotion and may even seem callous. Tice's voice sounds in many places like that of someone trying to be helpful; twenty-seven *yes, sirs* and *no, sirs* mark his responses during the eighteen minutes the tape recorders were rolling.[97]

Though Tice made numerous damning statements on tape, two stand out, each prompted skillfully by Ford: "'Just go ahead and stab the bitch' I believe is what I said" and "I could see in her eyes that she was pleading for help."[98]

Damning if you don't know what led up to them. Had Tice's entire interrogation been videotaped, viewers could see how Ford had worn down and manipulated Tice, fed him details of the crime, and molded his statement. Unfortunately, only eight states in the United States—Alaska, Illinois, Maine, Minnesota, New Jersey, New Mexico, North Carolina, and Wisconsin—and the District of Columbia require videotaping of police interrogations, and only in certain situations (mainly in felony cases). But miscarriages of justice spawned by false confessions could be reduced in no small degree if police were required to videotape or audiotape interrogations in full. There would then be a record for determining a confession's reliability and voluntariness, and for resolving courtroom disputes about what transpired during the interrogation (as it is, the testimony of police is typically given greater credence than that of defendants). Videotaping would also discourage interrogators from employing the most coercive methods. Most police oppose recording interrogations in their entirety, arguing that many criminals would clam up,

fewer would confess, and it would be expensive. The main reason for their reluctance, however, is that they don't want to open up their methods to greater
scrutiny. Most officers who record interrogations enthusiastically support the
practice. In 2006—spurred by this case and many others—Norfolk Commonwealth Attorney Jack Doyle persuaded Norfolk's police department to
begin videotaping all homicide interrogations.[99]

At 12:08 A.M., after giving his taped confession, Tice consented to have
samples of his head hair, facial hair, pubic hair, saliva, and blood taken. Wray
placed the vial of Tice's blood in a refrigerator. At about 1:30, Ford handed
Tice a transcript of his confession and instructed him to review it and correct
any mistakes. Perhaps purposely, perhaps not, The Banque had been misspelled "Bank," and Tice crossed out the misspelling three times and scrawled
"Banque" and his initials above it. In court, Ford and the prosecutor D.J.
Hansen would both later raise this as evidence that Tice had read his confession
before signing it. (In a subsequent habeas hearing, an attorney for the Virginia
state attorney general's office would also point out Tice's corrections—and
add that Tice didn't correct his words "just go ahead and stab the bitch.") Tice
was then hauled off to jail, where he was held without bail.[100]

Three days later, the local *Virginian-Pilot* newspaper reported that
Williams, Dick, Wilson, and Tice had come calling on Michelle, then "gang-
raped," stabbed, and strangled her. "Prosecutors said the case is one of the sad-
dest they have seen," the article said.[101]

9

"Scrappy"

Richard Dale Pauley Jr. was next. After Derek Tice had named him, Detective Brian Wray had run Pauley down. He was living with his parents in their small three-bedroom home in Norfolk. In the late afternoon of Tuesday, June 30, 1998, two police officers pulled up in front of their house in an unmarked blue car.

Rick Pauley, then twenty-six years old, was a fairly small though athletic and outdoorsy young man with blue eyes, longish brown hair that he sometimes tied in a ponytail, and a beard. He worked for a roofing company that police had visited earlier that day. Though he'd had some problems with alcohol and been arrested for driving under the influence, he was a hard and dependable worker. Raised in Norfolk, he had struggled in school; after dropping out in the tenth grade, he'd joined the army reserve. He was married briefly to Nicole Mathewson, later Nicole Williams, the wife of Danial Williams. Pauley hadn't wanted anything to do with her after their marriage collapsed when he'd caught her with another man. "There's no way I would have been anywhere near [the Williams's] apartment," he points out. He did not know either Joe Dick or Eric Wilson.[1]

Pauley's parents were devout and patriotic Christians. His mother, Judy, taught preschool at a Baptist church; his father, Richard Sr., a retired navy aircraft electrician, worked in customer support for a computer software company.[2]

Pauley was home the afternoon the police came by because his grandfather had died of bone cancer two days earlier and his funeral was the next day; relatives and friends were over at the house for dinner. Pauley was aware that the police wanted to talk to him, as a friend at the roofing company had phoned to say they had stopped by there. Pauley was sitting a bit nervously on the front porch waiting for them to arrive. "He wouldn't move," his mother recalls. A neighbor had phoned to ask if somebody could come over to her place so she could donate money for the funeral, and his mother had asked Ricky to go. No, he wasn't leaving the house, Pauley had said. He wanted to be sure to be there when the police arrived. He thought they just wanted to question him about Tice and Williams and whether he knew anything.[3]

His mother, who felt Ricky couldn't have lived with himself if he'd been involved in the murder and that she would have been able to tell, remarked to him while he was waiting, "Rick, I know you didn't do it. But I have to ask you: Do you have any knowledge of this? Do you know *anything* about it?" No, Rick assured her, he didn't.[4]

Pauley quickly got up off the porch and headed out toward the street to meet the two officers when they arrived. To his astonishment, and the bewilderment of his father, who was watching from the front door, they then turned him around, slapped handcuffs on him, and threw him into their car. "Don't get near us," one officer warned his dad when he ran toward them. The police wouldn't tell the Pauleys why they were apprehending their son. "We'll call you," they said.[5]

In the car on the way to the Police Operations Center, the officers didn't say much of anything to Pauley. But at the station, police filed warrants and informed him that he was under arrest for Michelle Moore-Bosko's murder and rape. Pauley was flabbergasted.[6]

His interrogators, Detectives Pat Dunn and Brian Wray, repeatedly told him that they knew he was guilty, as Pauley adamantly denied it. They had witnesses and all the other evidence they needed to get a conviction, they claimed. The other attackers had confessed and were going to stand up in court and testify that he'd been part of it. When Pauley asked the detectives who these other people were, they wouldn't give him any names. It was in his interest to come clean, they said. That way, they could help him; otherwise, he'd get the electric chair. The detectives kept asking Pauley who else had been involved. He didn't know, since he wasn't there, he responded. "I had nothing to do with it, so there was nothing there for me to tell them," he remembers.

He admitted knowing Williams and Tice, but said that he didn't know the victim and had never been to her apartment. "I was even trying to be as honest with them as I could," he recounts.[7]

Pauley told Dunn and Wray that his parents would probably have telephone records showing that he had been talking to his girlfriend, Susan Braid, in Australia the night of the murder. Pauley had an established routine. He normally talked with Braid online or over the phone in the late evening or early morning because of the time difference between Virginia and Australia. And, indeed, his parents would later produce a Bell Atlantic bill indicating that Pauley had talked to Braid for sixty-two minutes starting at 11:05 P.M. on the night of the murder. They had talked about marriage, their fears, and commitment. The Pauleys' home was six or seven miles from Moore-Bosko's apartment, about a fifteen-minute drive away. Rick was working at the Old Dominion Inn as a maintenance person at the time and normally got home in the early evening. His mother would testify that he arrived home between 6:30 and 7 P.M. on the night of the murder. He was on the computer in their kitchen when she went to bed around 10 o'clock, she recalled. His father testified that he last saw Rick that evening on the phone in Rick's bedroom before he went to bed. Neither parent heard Rick leave the house that night, by their accounts. Rick's driver's license was suspended at the time because of his DUI, and had somebody come to pick him up, their dog would have let them know, his parents say. His father took Rick to work the next morning; his employment records verified his work schedule.[8]

In the interrogation room, Pauley offered to take a lie-detector test. After the test, the police, of course, told him he'd failed it. "I couldn't believe it," Pauley recalls. He also asked for a lawyer, he says. "They said that I wasn't permitted to have a lawyer at that time," that "lawyers couldn't come in there."[9]

With two cops bearing down on him, hammering away at him, raising the specter of his execution, Pauley was frightened. He later told his attorney, Jon Babineau, that he would have said absolutely anything to the detectives to get them to leave him alone—short of confessing. "Since I wasn't involved, I wasn't about to," he remembers.[10]

After four or five hours, Dunn and Wray gave up trying to wrest a confession from Pauley. But they'd gotten him to wondering: If they *knew* he was there, if they had witnesses who knew he was there and other proof, maybe he *had* been there, even though he knew in his mind that he hadn't. Or at least he thought he did. When Pauley was allowed to phone his parents after his interrogation was over, he told his mother that they'd almost convinced him he'd done it.[11]

Fortunately for Pauley, Detective Glenn Ford was then on vacation. "I can tell you if it had been Ford he would have probably confessed," Babineau says. Pauley was "just a quiet, laid-back guy that I could very easily see would have buckled under the pressure."[12]

Pauley was jailed with a half-million-dollar bond on his head, which his employer at the Old Dominion Inn, a Republican activist who spoke highly of him, offered to help pay, though the Pauleys still couldn't swing it. Pauley had to surrender his passport since his girlfriend was in Australia, which wouldn't extradite him if he were facing the death penalty. Jail was rough. "He was scared," his mother remembers. "You could see it in his eyes."[13]

When the Norfolk prosecutors learned later that Pauley was on the phone at his parents' house between 11:05 and 12:07 on the night of the murder, they, of course, had a big problem: what time had the crime taken place? Danial Williams had first told police that he went over to Michelle's apartment at around 11:30 or 11:45. Joe Dick had stated that he and Williams had gone over there around 10 o'clock; he later said he thought that he, Williams, and Eric Wilson had arrived between 7 and 8 o'clock. (Wilson had said he couldn't remember the time, and judging from the police records, Tice had apparently not provided one.) According to both Judy Pauley and Jon Babineau, after the Pauleys' phone bill was presented at a court hearing, prosecutors argued that Michelle could have been attacked after midnight, say at 2 A.M. "D.J. [Hansen] tried to move the times around," Babineau recounts. "'He could have done it and then gone home.' Or, 'Everyone could be off a little bit. Time isn't really all that important.' Or, 'How do we even know he was really on the phone during that period of time and didn't just have the link hooked up and left?'" Hansen would tell jurors that Richard and Judy Pauley provided "a poor alibi" for their son. "They can't account for his whereabouts after ten," he argued. "They really can't." Prosecutors even went so far as to assert that Pauley could have altered the time on the phone record. They also posited different times of involvement for different assailants. "The theory was that they came and went . . . so not everybody was necessarily all there at the same time," Babineau remembers.[14]

·   ·   ·

A week after Pauley's arrest, police took Geoffrey Allen Farris, whom Tice had also implicated, into custody. Twenty-three years old, Farris had been a friend of both Tice and Wilson. He'd moved to Florida with Tice, Melissa Wharton, and Robert Mattingly the previous November, only to return to Norfolk a month later after a dispute with them. Farris also knew Williams and frequented The Banque bar. The tall, slender, and blond Farris was an outwardly self-confident and intelligent young man who in high school in Missouri had scored at the ninety-eighth percentile in both math and science in a national exam, and ninety-seventh in composition. He had listed his tentative career goal as "chemist or physicist." He was a big fan of science fiction—books, movies, television shows, whatever. "If it was sci-fi, he was into it," Tice remembers. According to one of his later attorneys, B. Thomas Reed, he'd never been in trouble with the law before.[15]

Farris was working for a remodeling company in Virginia Beach when Detectives Ford and Wray approached him after he had pulled up to the rear of the building on his bicycle at about 3:30 P.M. The detectives stepped out of their unmarked car, introduced themselves, and asked him if he would be willing to come up to the station to talk to them. "About what?" the startled Farris asked. The murder case involving Danial Williams, they replied. Unaware of what was awaiting him at the station ("part of Glenn Ford's MO is not to tell murder suspects why they are being taken into custody," Reed says), Farris agreed to talk.[16]

After being placed in an interrogation room and waiving his Miranda rights, Farris repeatedly denied any involvement in Michelle Moore-Bosko's murder and rape. Ford let him know what he believed had happened the night of the crime and pressed Farris to adopt his scenario. He also told Farris that the other defendants were talking. No one who came into the homicide office ever told the truth the first time, Ford informed Farris, so he wasn't unusual. ("I guess I'm the first one to tell you the truth the first time," Farris cracked to Wray during a bathroom break.) Farris flunked a lie-detector test. When Ford slapped a photo of Michelle's dead body on the table in front of him, Farris declined to look at it. He knew he wouldn't look at it, Ford commented, because it brought back memories of what he had done. At that point, Farris covered his face with his hands, took a deep breath, and started shaking.[17]

At about ten minutes before 6 P.M., when Ford asserted for the umpteenth time that he knew Farris had been involved, Farris stated, "I'd like an attorney." According to Bruce Wilcox, Farris's later lead attorney, Ford and Wray continued to question him; Wray testified that he didn't ask Farris any more "pertinent" questions (his notes would say "any more questions"). At 6:08, "Mr. Farris asked me if his prints aren't in the house, that means he wasn't there," Ford recounted. "And I just stated that wasn't necessarily true. Then Farris stated to me that if his blood didn't match the DNA, that means we would have to drop the rape charge. And I answered no to that also. Then I stated to Farris that he had asked for a lawyer and we couldn't talk about the case anymore." At 7 P.M., Ford advised Farris that he was under arrest for capital murder and rape.[18]

Between 8:15 and 9:30, except for fifteen minutes he spent back in the interrogation room, Farris was sitting in the adjacent homicide office. Ford and Wray were obtaining personal information from him and typing him up. Toward the end of this period, when Ford was out of the office to get an arrest number, Farris turned to his left toward Wray and remarked, "If I did it, I buried it so deep that I don't remember."[19] He, too, had come to question his memory.

His attorneys would, of course, find this statement worrisome and moved to get it suppressed. Reed considered it a "qualified admission of being there." After Ford returned, Wray apprised him of what Farris had said.[20]

Wilcox and Reed later filed an alibi notice contending that Farris had been on duty on the USS *Shreveport* the day of the crime and "was not permitted to leave for a twenty-four hour period." A subsequent alibi notice maintained that he was at a nightclub at the Norfolk naval station that evening. But Reed considered it quite possible that Farris had actually participated in the attack on Michelle Moore-Bosko—perhaps only inflicting a pin prick or holding her down—and was focused more on avoiding the death penalty than exonerating him. "I've had people go into denial after much more involvement in a crime than Geoffrey," Reed says. "He could easily convince himself, certainly given the passage of time, 'I didn't kill that girl.'"[21]

On July 11, the *Virginian-Pilot* reported the arrest of this sixth man in the presumed gang-rape and murder. The same month, prosecutors formally offered Joe Dick a life sentence in exchange for guilty pleas to capital murder—later dropped to first degree—and rape. On the advice of his attorney,

Michael Fasanaro, Dick accepted the deal. Naïvely, he had hoped to "testify and walk with imunity [sic]."[22]

In late August, Derek Tice, Richard Pauley, and Geoffrey Farris were all eliminated as possible sources of the DNA recovered from the crime scene. Six arrests, and still no match. Their fingerprints were not found at the scene either.[23]

The frustration of police and prosecutors was growing. When was this crazy case going to end? And was something amiss? Asked later whether the DNA results affected his thoughts on whether any of the defendants had really been at the crime scene, however, the prosecutor D.J. Hansen replied, firmly, "Not at all." Maybe they left their DNA in their underwear, he would tell jurors. (Police and prosecutors would also speculate that the assailants might have forced Michelle to perform oral sex on them, ejaculated in a piece of cloth or something, and then taken it with them. Or maybe the crime scene really hadn't been processed fully.) But Allan Zaleski, who was appointed Tice's lead attorney, remembers conversations that he had during downtime in court with Hansen and his co-prosecutor, Valerie Bowen, in which they analyzed the case from all angles, puzzled over it, and were unable to resolve it. In one conversation with Hansen, "we were trying to fit the pieces together, and we just couldn't," Zaleski recounts. Asked about these conversations, Hansen refused to comment, then said he didn't recall them.[24]

With their superior knowledge and control of evidence, and their unique power, prosecutors have an ethical duty to promote the truth, to make an independent evaluation of a defendant's guilt or innocence, and to decline to prosecute those people they believe are innocent. And, indeed, district attorneys rarely prosecute people they deem innocent. When they prosecute the innocent—and that happens commonly—it's usually because they are wedded to a theory of the case and they discount evidence that doesn't fit it, as the Norfolk prosecutors did. (However, one recent study of exonerations of death row inmates alleges that about two-thirds of their wrongful convictions resulted from willful, malicious prosecutions.) Some prosecutors argue that they should leave it up to a jury to judge a defendant. Yet they know far more about a case than does a jury, and jurors can be swayed by nonevidentiary factors—including their trust in the prosecutor.[25]

Prosecutors also have a duty to admit their mistake when evidence shows they charged an innocent person. But most are reluctant to do so in the absence of unimpeachable evidence. Many district attorney's offices emphasize conviction rates, which can affect the career advancement of prosecutors and office budget allocations; in some offices, prosecutors' "batting averages" are even tallied. Prosecutors also fear hurting their credibility, opening a can of worms, and appearing soft on crime or hard on the police (which can harm their relations with police). Many simply have difficulty accepting they got the wrong man or admitting a serious mistake.[26]

If Hansen had credited Pauley's alibi, Tice's entire confession would have been cast open to doubt. That would have undermined Hansen's cases against the other defendants, including Tice. Challenging Ford's theory of the crime would have also had risks for Hansen. After all, he had to work with Ford on other cases, and many cops were not all that fond of Hansen as it was. "He's not very well liked among the police, in part because he's condescending and arrogant," one former prosecutor says.[27]

With the latest DNA results coming back negative, prosecutors and police concluded that a seventh attacker was on the loose, one the others were protecting.[28]

The anguish of Michelle's parents and Billy Bosko was just horrific. Over a half dozen young men, it now appeared, had had their way with Michelle. And when would police finally get to the bottom of this?

On August 25, in General District Court in Norfolk, Joe Dick testified at the preliminary hearing of Rick Pauley and Geoffrey Farris. He was, as Pauley's attorney, Jon Babineau, observed, "at best a bizarre witness" who was "all over the place" with his statements. He was also extraordinarily hazy on details (at his apartment before the murder and rape, "I believe Danial started the conversation off, but after that I vaguely recall what went on," Dick testified). It was an arresting performance that should have suggested to everybody in the room that Dick simply didn't know what had taken place. "I don't know that his credibility amounted for anything," Babineau remembers. "He just seemed to be making up so much. And he essentially said whatever you wanted him to say." Listening to Dick's testimony, Babineau thought that he was "a lot smarter than he's leading us all to believe," however. He asked if Dick had ever been treated for a psychiatric disorder. Dick said no.[29]

Wearing an orange jumpsuit, with his attorney, Michael Fasanaro, in the courtroom, Dick now claimed that Pauley and Farris had participated in the murder and rape along with himself, Williams, Wilson, and Tice. He had last told police that six people had been there but that he didn't know two of them and was not sure if he would be able to identify them. Dick still did not know their names, he told D.J. Hansen; he identified these "two other gentlemen" by pointing to them in the courtroom. He subsequently apprised Babineau that, "right now," he did know their names, however, as Hansen had given them to him before testifying. He had never met or seen them before that night, Dick testified. Pauley and Farris did not even know each other. But Fasanaro had told Dick that they had participated and counseled him to testify against them.[30]

"Was anyone else with you?" Hansen asked Dick. "Nobody else to my recollection," Dick responded. "Could there have been somebody else?" Hansen pressed him. "Possibly," Dick replied. Was it possible there was another person and he just didn't remember him? Babineau asked. "Possibly," Dick said again. Could there have been as many as two others? No, Dick replied. Only one other, perhaps. "Is that person white or black?" Babineau asked. "White," Dick said. "Did he have a name?" Babineau inquired. "I have never seen him before, so I wouldn't know his name," Dick responded. When Babineau demanded to know whether there was a seventh person or not, Dick stopped equivocating and said there was. "Was he tall, short, fat?" Babineau probed. "I couldn't tell you," Dick responded. "Fat, skinny?" "Couldn't tell you." Dick also couldn't tell Babineau what this person was wearing, or whether he participated in the discussion at Dick's apartment beforehand ("He might have. He might not have"). And Dick couldn't remember anything that anybody, except Williams, had said that night, including himself. At least "not off the top of my head."[31]

Dick acknowledged that this was the first time he had said there was a seventh assailant. He denied that anybody had suggested to him that it was important that he place Pauley and Farris at the scene.[32]

According to Dick's latest story, Williams had wanted to see what color of panties Michelle wore and to have sex with her, so they had all agreed to go across the hall to her apartment. What did Farris say to express his agreement? his attorney B. Thomas Reed quizzed Dick. "I recall him saying yes," Dick replied, simply. Several people knocked on Michelle's door; Dick couldn't say who they were. After Michelle told them to go away, they went out to the parking lot to have a smoke and discuss the situation, Dick stated. He couldn't remember what they talked about, except that "Williams said that he wanted to go back and get this done tonight."[33]

They returned fifteen or twenty minutes later, Dick testified. Who knocked this time? Babineau asked him. It "could have been any of us," Dick responded. When Michelle opened her door, they forced their way in; all seven of them were pushing against the door, Dick stated. They carried her into her bedroom, he said, though he could not accurately describe the route to the room. Nor could he recall where they placed her there. All six then raped her, he testified, in "no particular order." He denied putting his penis in her mouth, which he had earlier told police more than once that he had done. "I got names mixed up," he would say later.[34]

Everyone stabbed Michelle except perhaps Wilson, Dick stated. But as far as actually seeing all that, "there were so many hands involved, I wouldn't know whose they belonged to." Who got the knife from the kitchen? Reed asked Dick. "It could have been any one of us," Dick replied. "Could it have been you?" "It could have been," Dick said. He stabbed Michelle last, after Farris had handed him the knife. He then dropped the knife on the floor, he testified. They all went back to his apartment afterward, but "I don't know what went on at that point," he said, since "I was out having a smoke." But he later overheard some talk about going out to the bar the next evening.[35]

In late September, Detective Glenn Ford had Derek Tice moved from the Norfolk City Jail to the Hampton Roads Regional Jail to be placed in a cell with Garey Kelly. Kelly was an informer. "We were trying to discover who the number seventh man was," Ford later testified. He informed D.J. Hansen of the move. Kelly was an unsavory figure: an ex-girlfriend would say later that she was terrified of him and that he had beaten her up.[36]

One Sunday in mid-October, Kelly told Ford two days later, he overheard Tice and Eric Wilson talking about Michelle's murder. They were sitting on a bench, Kelly said. He took off his Walkman to listen, as his curiosity had been aroused. "They were discussing the statements that were made by different [defendants]," Kelly testified. Wilson complained that Tice had told police that he had been the third person to stab Michelle, Kelly recounted. "Eric said,

'You know that wasn't true. I don't know why you said something like that.'"
Kelly claimed that he overheard Wilson say that he went fourth. "They were
talking about who did what, who stabbed her when," Kelly recalled. According
to Hansen, who met with Kelly, Wilson and Tice also discussed "who had
whose hand on which part of her body as they were carrying her back to the
bedroom."[37]

Tice was aware that Kelly was a snitch. "The first time that they pulled him
out to take him to the police department, he came back later that night and
told me that he had been to the police department," Tice remembers. Tice and
Wilson had been talking at a table and Kelly was about five feet away and only
heard snippets of their conversation. "Me and Wilson talked about Ford's interrogation techniques, what pictures . . . we were shown by Ford, and questions that he asked," Tice recounts. "But we never really talked about what we
said." Wilson confirms that.[38]

Greg McCormack, Wilson's attorney, was alarmed by Kelly's testimony.
"He's putting a knife in my guy's hand," McCormack underscores. "He's
killing Eric is what he's doing. That's death penalty. . . . We went after that big
time." McCormack paid a visit on Kelly in jail. Whatever he said to him
worked, as Kelly recanted his testimony in a sworn deposition. It turned out
that the police had pressured him to testify to get time off his prison sentence.
Ford had known he was lying, according to Kelly. After McCormack waved
Kelly's recantation in their faces, prosecutors elected not to call him to testify
in Wilson's later trial. "That probably saved Eric's life," McCormack argues.[39]

Though jurors tend to distrust criminals who become state witnesses, prosecutors regularly use information and testimony from snitches who want a
better deal—typically a more lenient sentence or reduced charges—and who
have an incentive to tell them what they want to hear. Snitches are notorious
for prevaricating. Using them is "a dirty business," one judge commented.
"You have to be tremendously careful that you don't give them ideas," said
Stephen Trott, a former prosecutor who is an expert on the use of informants.
"Criminals are likely to say and do almost anything to get what they want,
especially when what they want is to get out of trouble with the law. This
willingness to do anything includes not only truthfully spilling the beans
on friends and relatives, but also lying, committing perjury, manufacturing evidence, soliciting others to corroborate their lies with more lies, and

double-crossing anyone with whom they come into contact, including—and especially—the prosecutor. . . . A 'reliable informer' one day may turn into a consummate prevaricator the next." Manufacturing confessions is a specialty of jailhouse snitches. One who claims that another prisoner confessed to him is "the most dangerous informer of all," Trott writes. "The snitch now stands ready to testify in return for some consideration in his own case. Sometimes these snitches tell the truth, but more often they invent testimony and stray details out of the air."[40]

Many wrongful convictions—around 15 to 20 percent of them—have been fostered by snitches' perjury, and that includes perjury shaped by police. Sometimes, in their drive to obtain convictions, police and prosecutors fail to question the reliability of informants sufficiently; some prosecutors have even used testimony that they knew was false. In a scandal in 1990, the Los Angeles County District Attorney's office was found to have used perjured testimony by snitches for years; much of the perjury was "egregious," a grand jury reported. Some of the snitches had been encouraged by police to become informants and to fabricate confessions.[41]

Garey Kelly also passed on to Ford the names of other possible accomplices that, he said, he got from Tice. Tice told him that Robert Mattingly had been involved, he claimed. Mattingly had also been a member of the Banque Crew. That summer after Tice's arrest, Melissa Wharton recounts, two Norfolk detectives had come to see her in Florida wanting to talk to Mattingly, her boyfriend. After Wharton refused to give the detectives much of anything, including a phone number where Mattingly could be reached, "they came down on me," she recalls. The detectives, who she believes were Glenn Ford and Brian Wray, "were telling me that I was obstructing justice, and everything else, by not giving them any information on him." The encounter brought her to tears.[42]

Police took Tom Hendricks, another member of the Banque Crew, in for questioning. Lea Carlile, Tice's girlfriend, who had since moved to Virginia from Florida to be near Tice, then went down to the police station with Hendricks's wife to find out what was going on. Upon learning that Lea was there, Ford wanted to talk to her too, so he and another officer escorted her into an office. There, Ford acted as if she knew something and wasn't telling. It was as if she was a criminal herself. Why was she still with Derek? he asked her. "I was like, 'What do you mean, why am I still there with Derek?'" Lea recounts. "And they said, 'Well, he's guilty. I can't believe you're staying with a guilty man. He raped and murdered this eighteen-year-old girl. . . .' And telling me I was crazy for being with him. And I told him, 'I love him. And I don't think he did this.' 'Well, if you'd seen the evidence that we have against him.' I said, 'Well, show me the evidence.' 'We can't do that, because it's an ongoing investigation.'" Ford wanted to know what Derek had told Lea about the crime. He hadn't told her anything, Lea replied, because he wasn't involved. Ford also asked her about Derek's other friends.[43]

By now, Ford had come to suspect almost any member of the Banque Crew. Soon his list of suspects would grow to around a dozen, including the six in jail. "He was just basically throwing out the net," the Norfolk attorney Jennifer Stanton recalls. "He would just walk up to somebody and say, 'We think you're involved. Give us your DNA.' I mean, that was really about what it amounted to." Mattingly gave police epithelial and hair samples in late September; five days later, another suspect, Jay Wagner, turned over a blood sample.[44]

Tice, who was smarter than Ford, was aware that it was not hard to lead Ford on. During a phone conversation with the mother-in-law of a friend of his and Rick Pauley's, he observed, with no ill intent, "All I have to do is name him and he's in jail with us." "Of course, the wife [of the friend] and the mother-in-law went ballistic," Judy Pauley recalls.[45]

Meanwhile, Lea had been wondering why the police wouldn't let Derek out of jail since he was obviously innocent and she felt that they'd had enough time to recognize their mistake. Then one day she received a copy of his confession in the mail from his attorney, Allan Zaleski. Derek had told her reluctantly some time after his arrest that he had given police a "statement," but she didn't know that his statement was actually a confession. Upon reading it, she felt like throwing up. Lea didn't believe that Derek's confession was true— "I'm reading fiction here," she thought—but she was appalled nevertheless. Derek's predicament, she now realized, was even worse than she'd thought. And what in the world had he been thinking when he had talked to the police without a lawyer present?[46]

Danny Shipley, Danial Williams's attorney, was also jolted by Tice's statement. Still another guy had incriminated his client. "It was like a wave coming in the ocean," Shipley recalls. "Every time you'd pick yourself up, here comes another wave." To Shipley, Tice's confession was another reason to believe that Williams had done it, and another reason to try to plead him out.[47]

Eric Wilson was driven to tears by it. "Mama, they're trying to kill me for something I didn't do!" he cried to his mother over the phone after learning of Tice's account.[48]

That October the commonwealth attorney's office in Norfolk offered Derek Tice a plea bargain. He would be allowed to plead guilty to first-degree murder and rape rather than capital murder and rape—thereby avoiding the death penalty—in exchange for testifying "truthfully" against all codefendants and identifying the seventh perpetrator "and any other participants." What was "truthful" would, of course, be determined by the commonwealth. Tice was also required to give a full statement to Ford about the crime and pass a lie-detector test on it. Judge Charles E. Poston would impose his sentence.[49]

Allan Zaleski, who met regularly for morning coffee with Poston and several other Norfolk attorneys, including Shipley, liked the deal. He knew how tough it would be to exonerate Tice. "If you can get a guy off that has made a written confession, you're pretty good," he chuckles. And if Tice would incriminate the other guys, Zaleski thought, he could get him a sentence in years rather than life. Zaleski was aware that the prosecutors needed Tice. "I figured the more Tice could testify against the other guys, the better his sentence would be," he recalls. "He would identify three other people, maybe—nail those people. And I could tell the judge that, because of what he did, these other people were brought to justice. And I was very hopeful I'd get a sentence in the bottom range" of the sentencing guidelines, perhaps something like twenty-eight years.[50]

Zaleski believed that Tice was guilty. He couldn't understand why Tice would confess if he wasn't. "Here I've got a man who is very intelligent, charged with a very, very serious crime, and confesses supposedly to something he didn't do," he remembers. "Can I explain that? I mean, the only explanation is he *did* do it." But Zaleski was perplexed by the case. He wondered why Shipley's guy, "Denial" Williams, wasn't fingering other people despite considerable motivation to do so. Prosecutors were claiming that Michelle's attackers had formed a pact not to rat on each other, but Zaleski couldn't imagine such a pact holding up, especially with Ford on top of them. It simply wouldn't survive. "In our business, the biggest problem you have is your co-defendants," he points out.[51]

But Zaleski wasn't judging Tice's guilt or innocence. "That's not my focus, it's not what I'm about," he says. His main concern was pretty simple: "There's a confession. There's a problem." An enormous one. Tice's confession dwarfed in significance what Tice was telling him now, Zaleski reasoned, or even the discrepancies between it and the physical evidence, which Zaleski wasn't paying a lot of attention to. The confession also overshadowed the absence of Tice's DNA at the scene. Sure, a jury might wonder about the missing DNA, "but do you want to roll the dice on that?"[52]

But other attorneys have, some successfully. In 1997, a jury in Alaska acquitted Richard Bingham of first-degree murder and sexual assault. Bingham's confession contradicted the crime facts, and the semen found on the victim's body was not his. Eight years earlier, a jury in Minnesota acquitted Betty Burns of attempted murder although she had also given police a confession, later proven false. The jury even denounced her interrogation and asked that she be compensated monetarily for her ordeal.[53]

When Zaleski discussed the plea offer with his client, Tice didn't protest his innocence or ask why he should plead guilty to something he didn't do. He'd never been at all demonstrative with Zaleski, never expressed strong reactions to anything—indeed, he'd never seemed particularly forthcoming to Zaleski—and "he was interested in it kind of like a business transaction," Zaleski remembers: Was it in his interest? Zaleski persuaded Lea Carlile to help get Tice on board. If Tice went to trial he'd get the death sentence, Zaleski advised her, so "if Derek wanted to live this was his only chance." Lea wasn't excited about the deal, but she hardly wanted Derek to die; she told him that he really needed to think about it. Garey Kelly, the jailhouse snitch and Tice's cellmate, also urged Tice to take the deal.[54]

Tice, who was depressed and blamed himself for his plight ("I knew I wasn't there," he recalls, "but I let Detective Ford manipulate me into confessing"), agonized over the offer in his jail cell daily. The death penalty weighed like a ton of bricks on him. He couldn't get it out of his mind. Other inmates told him he'd *get* it. His mother urged him repeatedly not to plead guilty to something he didn't do, which she felt was a stupid idea, but he would reply, "But I could get the death penalty. And I don't want to die."[55]

Tice decided to take the deal. "I'll cooperate with them as much as I can, and give them as much information as I can, and hopefully I can get a lesser sentence," he thought.[56]

Larry and Rachel Tice would come to believe that Zaleski was largely just going through the motions on their son's case. Just cutting a deal. Whenever Rachel asked him to do something, to look into something—like a possible alibi, for instance—"basically I was put off," she remembers. "Nothing was ever done."[57]

At 3:40 P.M. on the afternoon of October 27, Tice met with Glenn Ford, Brian Wray, D.J. Hansen, and Valerie Bowen in an interrogation room at the Norfolk police station. He was there to be "debriefed" as required by his plea agreement. Zaleski was also present. The meeting was a strange one. "I'll never understand [it]," Zaleski says.[58]

Ford began by directing Tice to tell them the truth about what happened and to "get it all out in the open" so they could move forward with the case. Who was the seventh person? He was someone he knew as Scrappy, Tice responded. He did not know his real name. Scrappy was a friend of a guy named Danny Joe, Tice offered.[59]

Scrappy was someone Tice had met at The Banque once. He was actually a friend of Melissa Wharton. Tice did not know him, but by naming him he hoped to satisfy his plea agreement and save his life. And he figured that the police would never find someone he knew only as Scrappy.[60]

Ford asked Tice if John (C.J.) Danser had also been involved in the crime. Danser, Ford had apparently learned, had been a member of the Banque Crew too. He and Tice had been roommates at one point and cooks together on the USS *George Washington*. No, Tice said, Danser had not been involved. He thought Danser, who had been living with his parents in Warminster, Pennsylvania, at the time of the murder, had been in Norfolk in late July or August of 1997, but not in early July when the murder occurred, Tice said. But Ford pretended to know that Danser had been at the crime scene. He asked Tice if Robert Mattingly or Robert Wilson, another former roommate, had been present too. No, Tice responded, the only person who had participated besides the six already in custody was Scrappy.[61]

Scrappy had been at Danial Williams's apartment when he arrived that night, Tice told Ford. What did Scrappy look like? Ford inquired. He was about his own height, weighed 130 to 140 pounds, was skinny, with short black hair, Tice replied. Scrappy was in the navy at the time and was not a member of the Banque Crew, he said.[62]

Ford asked Tice if Eric Wilson (who was unrelated to Robert Wilson) had participated in the stabbing, as Tice had stated in his first confession in June. Tice now said that Wilson had left before the killing. When Ford scoffed at that, Tice reversed course and said that Wilson had, in fact, stabbed Michelle.[63]

Ford lectured Tice that he didn't believe him about Scrappy—if that was even this person's name. Tice was protecting someone else, Ford charged. He had lived with the case for over a year, he pointed out, and Scrappy had never come up before. After Tice denied lying, Ford and Wray narrowed their eyes and asked him to tell them "a little bit more" about Scrappy. Where did he work? What kind of car did he drive? Tice's answers didn't satisfy the detectives.[64]

At 4:05 p.m., Ford, Wray, Hansen, Bowen, and Zaleski left the interrogation room, leaving Tice alone there. Zaleski confided to Ford, "I know that he's making it up. It's not true." Zaleski then went back into the room to speak with his client, just the two of them. He was in a difficult position. He wanted the plea agreement, but he also wanted Tice to tell the truth. To tell everything, for god's sake. What the hell difference would it make now that they had a deal? If Tice also wanted the agreement, if he did not want to face the death penalty again, with a taped confession staring him in the face, Zaleski counseled him, he had to tell the truth. "I didn't do it," Tice said. Remember what I told you earlier? "But I'm trying to satisfy them because I want the deal."[65]

Zaleski was dumbfounded. This was one of the weirdest experiences he'd had with a client in his life. "Well, it doesn't work that way," he advised Tice. "You've got to tell the truth. If you aren't telling the truth about it, and the truth is you weren't there, let's all go home." There was no point in even being there. Zaleski counseled Tice that if he made another statement and later recanted, they'd have to suppress two statements.[66]

At 4:20, Zaleski emerged from the room feeling unsettled and a bit annoyed. His deal was in jeopardy. It looked like he might now have to try the case, and he could even lose his client (though he thought that unlikely because of Tice's background). He told Ford and Wray that he could not even get Tice to admit to being at the crime scene.[67]

Ford and Wray then spoke to Tice by themselves, with Zaleski's consent. Fifteen minutes later, they exited the room "because Mr. Tice stated that he wanted to talk to his lawyer first, before telling us the truth," they wrote in their notes. Tice recalls trying to tell Ford and Wray, at either this point or another one, that he had not been at the scene of the crime, "but they did not want to hear it."[68]

Zaleski then went back into the room to speak with Tice alone again. There is no record of what was said, but Tice was prepared to make another statement. "I'm like, 'All right. As long as it keeps me on their good side, that's what I'll do,'" he remembers.[69]

When Ford and Wray reentered a few minutes later, they demanded that Tice tell them the truth this time. According to their notes, after they asked Tice whether Scrappy had really been there and ordered him to tell them who *had* been there, Tice said that Scrappy had not been present after all. He wanted to tell them the truth, the whole truth, Tice stated, but he did not want his attorney or the prosecutors present.[70]

At 5 o'clock, after the detectives apprised Zaleski, Hansen, and Bowen of what Tice had said, Zaleski spoke with his client alone again. Tice told Zaleski that he would give Ford and Wray the truth and that Zaleski could go ahead and go home. Zaleski was by now getting fed up with the whole thing. "Take him back to the jail," he said to Ford. "I'm leaving. This is the end of this. Nothing's going to happen." The deal was dead, he thought. Plus, it was getting to be time for dinner "and I'm ready to go home. I've had enough of this."[71]

"Do you mind if I question him while you're gone?" Ford asked Zaleski. "I don't care," Zaleski replied. "If you want to stick with him and go through this, it's fine with me." Zaleski then left along with Hansen and Bowen. Zaleski gave Ford his home phone number before departing.[72]

Zaleski's departure was questionable for a criminal defense attorney, particularly one whose client is still maintaining his innocence. It was especially curious since Zaleski himself had counseled Tice at their first meeting, in a smelly lockup outside General District Court in Norfolk on June 26, not to talk to the police anymore outside his presence.[73]

At 5:20, Ford and Wray were back in the room with Tice, free to conduct their business however they saw fit. Tice would spend the next eight or nine hours at the station. "Tice stated immediately to these investigators when asked to tell the truth that CJ [John Danser] was the seventh person and not Scrappy," they wrote in their notes. "He stated that he did not tell us this earlier and also in his first confession to the police because CJ and him were real close friends." Asked on tape a few hours later what changed his mind, Tice pointedly replied, "Looking at the death penalty." When we asked him for this book why he offered Ford Danser's name, Tice said because Ford had already placed Danser at the scene. Tice was still feeling bad about naming Rick Pauley and Geoffrey Farris in June, and incriminating Danser compounded his guilt ("If I could talk to them, I would ask their forgiveness," he said later). But he desperately wanted to live.[74]

Tice stated that they had all gathered at Williams's apartment "because CJ was back in town and they were having a party for him." A birthday party. July 7 was Danser's birthday. During their party, Tice said, after Farris and Tice had started talking about "a set of novels that we had both read" including one entitled *The Color of Her Panties*, Danser had suggested that they go see what color of panties Michelle wore. After discussing the matter further, they decided that they were going to rape and kill her, according to Tice's story. None of them had been drinking or using drugs, he said, though this was a beer-drinking group.[75]

After knocking on Michelle's door, Tice went on, Williams announced that they were having a party for C.J. (Tice later amended this to say that Danser "piped up" to tell Michelle "that it was his birthday"). She opened the door a little after "a few minutes of coaxing. . . . I believe she opened up the door to wish CJ a happy birthday." Tice acknowledged that his earlier statement about using a claw hammer was untrue. "She was reluctant to open up the door, but Dan kept talking to her about a party," Tice said. "We were having a party, would like to invite her, would like to introduce her to everyone that was at the party so she would feel more comfortable." After they had her on her bed, Danser tried to take off her shirt "but never got it all the way off," Tice stated, since he'd learned from the autopsy report that Michelle had been found wearing a T-shirt. After everyone had raped her, he continued, Danser urged that they grab a knife from the kitchen. He believed that Danser was the one who then went and got the knife, though he had last told police that Farris had. Were any words exchanged between them as they passed the knife around? Ford asked. "Just that it's your turn, you know, you need to stab her," Tice replied simply. She was on the floor rather than upright when they stabbed her, he now said. Other details had also changed from his first confession.[76]

Around ten or eleven o'clock, Ford phoned Zaleski at his home. He'd broken, Ford exulted. He'd identified the seventh assailant and given them another statement. And they were going to bust Danser within hours. "Man, you are *good*," Zaleski told Ford.[77]

By 2:30 A.M. that morning, police in blue-collar Warminster, just north of Philadelphia, were staking out Danser's home. They arrested him without incident an hour or two later. The sleepy, twenty-five-year-old Danser was astounded that they had come after him. "He absolutely could not believe that he was being charged with this thing," Jennifer Stanton, his appointed attorney, recalls.[78]

At 6'1" tall, with a boxer's nose that bore a scar from an iguana bite, dark hair, a mustache, and a closely trimmed beard, John Elmer Danser was a tough and self-assured young man. He fancied himself a gift to women. He wasn't about to be pushed around by anybody, though he could be quite polite when he wanted to. In the navy, he had been written up for assault, unauthorized absences, "provoking speech," "consistently unsatisfactory appearance," poor personal hygiene, and poor self-control. Hence he had not been recommended for reenlistment. After getting out in 1996, he had attended a trade school for heating and air-conditioning workers and become a service technician. In Norfolk he had known Danial Williams as well as Tice, but not the other defendants. "I have no idea who [those] gentlemen are," he would testify.[79]

After spending a week in jail in Warminster, Danser was picked up by Detectives Ford and Wray early on the morning of November 4 and extradited by plane to Norfolk. In an interrogation room there, when Ford advised him that they needed to go through his legal rights, Danser declared that he knew his rights because he used to read people theirs when he was with the military police. But Danser waived his. He admitted having been in Norfolk in July of 1997, the month of Michelle's murder, but said he did not remember the exact dates; he had come to see his friend Dusty Wharton, who, it turned out, had just gone out to sea. He had stayed at the Econo Lodge across from The Banque and then at another motel, he recounted. He had just been fired by Lindsey Mechanical Services; he thought his last day had been July 10. Danser told Ford that he had definitely been in Pennsylvania on July 7 and 8, when the murder and rape had occurred, as July 7 was his birthday and he remembered what he had done that evening. Some friends had taken him out to a bar in Philadelphia. "He stated that he knew nothing about why he was being charged with Capital Murder and Rape because he did not have anything to do with it and wasn't there," Wray and Ford noted.[80]

Danser had an airtight alibi. His attorneys would later unearth daily time sheets and work orders of Lindsey Mechanical Services establishing that Danser had worked in Warminster until 6:30 P.M. on July 7 and reported for work at 7:30 A.M. on July 8. His attorneys also produced an ATM receipt showing that he had used his Core States Bank card at 8:42 P.M. on July 7 in Philadelphia, before he went to the bar. It's about a five-and-a-half-hour drive from Philadelphia to Norfolk, around six from Warminster; there is no record of Danser flying. In order for him to have participated in Moore-Bosko's rape and murder, Danser would have had to have done his part around 2 A.M., then driven quickly back to Warminster and reported immediately to work; he could not have joined in any premurder birthday party for him or discussion about Michelle and her panties at Williams's apartment. But Valerie Bowen would later claim that he could have gotten to Norfolk in time, and in court her co-prosecutor D.J. Hansen would argue that the time sheets and Danser's credit card were hearsay documents. At a sidebar, Judge Charles E. Poston asked Hansen, "You don't really believe this man was there, do you?" Hansen replied, "The commonwealth takes the position that he was there." Poston rolled his eyes in annoyance. He didn't see how Danser could have been.[81]

But back in the interrogation room, Ford told Danser that they knew he had not been in Pennsylvania the night of the murder. In fact, he had been in Norfolk. They knew all about his involvement. Danser responded that he could not tell them what they wanted to hear because he didn't know anything about it. He repeatedly tried to tell the detectives that he had gone out to the bar in Philadelphia.[82]

At 1:24 P.M., after Detective Randy Crank had given Danser a polygraph and Ford had predictably announced that he'd failed it, Danser asked for a lawyer. "He became very emotional stating that he didn't do it and if he did he would be the first to turn himself in," Wray and Ford wrote. Ford advised Danser that "if he wanted to talk we would talk to him, but we could not at this point because he wanted a lawyer." Wray added that they would have to send him to jail; the next day, Wray said, he could see his lawyer. At that point

Danser told the detectives that he did want to talk to them without a lawyer, "but he wanted to be treated like a human, and not be accused and treated like a liar," Wray and Ford recorded. When Ford pulled out a photo of Michelle when she was still alive, Danser said that he'd never seen her before. Wray tried to phone Lindsey Mechanical Services to check Danser's last day of employment, but the company had apparently gone out of business.[83]

Ford wanted to know how Danser had paid for his motel rooms in Norfolk that July. His Discover credit card, Danser replied. He had used it to pay for everything. Several weeks later D.J. Hansen would tell Jennifer Stanton that police called the motels, but that there was no record of Danser having stayed in them. Stanton subpoenaed his credit card and other records, however, and found that Danser had, in fact, stayed where he said he did, when he said he did. "Hansen just totally lied to me about it," Stanton recalls. Police had actually contacted the motels and confirmed Danser's account, she found out. But they did not obtain his work and ATM records. "They didn't want to know that *anybody* in this case was telling the truth if it was any different from their theory of the case," Stanton says. "So they never bothered."[84]

The detectives asked Danser how he had found out about the crime. Tice had told him that Williams had been arrested for murder when he was in Norfolk in July, Danser recounted. Tice had said that he'd heard that a black man had actually committed it.[85]

Tice had heard some rumors. From Victoria Wilson, Tice's roommate, and her sister, Rachel, who would at some point claim to have seen the black man running from the apartment complex. (Whether the police heard these rumors is unknown, but Victoria Wilson would not have been a reliable source: she was manic-depressive with a history of alcohol and drug abuse.)[86]

At 3:25 P.M., Ford showed Danser a photo of Michelle's dead body and asked if he remembered her looking like that after he'd raped and murdered her. After Danser again denied any involvement, Ford left the room. Wray then asked Danser what he would do when his DNA was found to match the evidence. "I don't know," Danser replied. He reiterated that he'd been in Pennsylvania on his birthday and said that his mother could verify that. He had come to Norfolk on the same day his mother was hired for her job at a printing company, he recalled.[87]

Wray then picked up the phone and called Danser's parents. According to his notes, Danser's mother asked if her son had a lawyer. It was up to him to decide if he wanted a lawyer or not, Wray told her. Danser's father said that he recalled his son being at a neighborhood picnic on July 4, 1997 (actually, it was July 5, and he'd gotten drunk and belligerent). His son was also in town on July 7, he remembered, as John went out that night and the next day his boss accused him of having alcohol on his breath. Wray left a message with someone at his mother's company, but didn't get a response.[88]

At 4:30 Ford took another shot at Danser. But he wasn't budging. At 6 o'clock both Ford and Wray tried it again, but no luck. He knew nothing about it, Danser declared once more. The detectives then gave up. They had Tice's account. Danser was then carted off to jail and held on a half-million-dollar bond.[89]

Jennifer Stanton, a middle-aged woman with long reddish-blond hair, freckles, a blunt way of speaking, and a bulldog approach to investigating her important cases, and her co-counsel, David Bouchard, would subsequently drive up to Pennsylvania to see what they had. They interviewed Danser's family, neighbors, co-workers, employer, and the lady whose air conditioner Danser had repaired until 6:30 P.M. on July 7. They timed the drive to Norfolk (seven hours for them). And they subpoenaed "everything." Stanton was so convinced that Danser was innocent that, although she was not required to provide any of her alibi evidence to the commonwealth until ten days prior to trial, she and Bouchard presented their entire alibi defense to D.J. Hansen and Valerie Bowen. "I can't believe that they wanted to kill this guy!" Stanton exclaims. "They were asking for the death penalty, and they knew that he wasn't even there."[90]

After listening to Stanton's alibi case, which he found strong, Hansen went up to Pennsylvania that weekend to investigate it personally because he had "family business" nearby anyway. "I talked to the people that they had talked to, and I came back and I presented my conclusions to the commonwealth attorney," Chuck Griffith, he recounts. "And we discussed it. And we decided that the case was going to go forward." The attorneys Danny Shipley, Bob Frank, and Allan Zaleski all later heard that Griffith directed Hansen to prosecute Danser, despite the alibi evidence. "Hansen concluded that Danser couldn't have done it," Zaleski says. "That's the word I had." But "Griffith said, 'You've got a statement from a guy. You've got a case.'" Zaleski adds, "You know, you hear all this stuff about, 'I'll only prosecute those who I think are guilty.' 'I only prosecute those people I'm *told* to prosecute.' There's a difference."[91]

Prosecutors have an ethical obligation to decline to prosecute those they believe are innocent even if their supervisor tells them to do so. Of course, that can take courage, and even a willingness to lose their job. Had Hansen gone to Griffith, whose office increased the number of capital murder prosecutions from his predecessor's, and told him that he couldn't go forward with the case, Griffith might have said that he had to step aside. Hansen denies that Griffith overruled him on the case, but he refused further comment on his discussion with Griffith. He also refused to say whether he had any doubts about Danser's guilt—or Pauley's or Farris's, for that matter—but he insisted, "I'm not going to prosecute anybody that I think is innocent." Stanton doesn't believe it: "I think he knows damn well my guy wasn't there. But he doesn't have the balls to admit it. . . . They will not admit publicly that they charged the wrong men." She adds, "I'm confident that there are prosecutors out there who would be the first to say, 'We made a huge mistake on this.' But not D.J." [92]

On November 5, 1998, the day after Danser's interrogation, police brought Derek Tice back to the station from jail. His lawyer, Allan Zaleski, was not present. "At that point I've got a deal," Zaleski explains. "The commonwealth's happy. I've got a cooperating witness. And he's going to plead. And everything's great." But not for Detective Glenn Ford. He informed Tice that Danser had been arrested because of his October 27 statement, but that there were "some points that needed to be cleared up." He asked Tice some questions that he should have asked him in October—before busting Danser—ones that would have helped him determine whether Danser had really been in Norfolk at the time of the murder: Where had Danser stayed? How long had he stayed? Where had Tice seen him? Tice responded that he had met Danser at his and Dusty Wharton's apartment, that Danser had stayed at the Econo Lodge, and that he had been in Norfolk for only a day or so before returning to Norfolk the first week of August. [93]

But Ford wasn't buying it. Danser's motel and credit card records showed that he had come to Norfolk around July 24, not at the time of the murder, Ford informed Tice. "Ford told me that my plea was in trouble because Danser had an airtight alibi," Tice remembered. Faced with this news, Tice backpedaled and said that Danser had not, in fact, been there. He had named him "because he fit," he told Ford. Tice reminded Ford that he had told him in October that he thought Danser hadn't come down until late July, but that

Ford had not believed him. Everyone was mad at him for lying, Ford advised Tice, but he could still save his plea agreement if he told them the truth about the seventh person. The commonwealth wanted to use him as a witness rather than Dick, because Tice was more credible and stable, Ford said. When Tice claimed that the seventh assailant had been at Williams's house when he arrived that night and that he didn't know his name, Ford was incredulous.[94]

After a thirteen-minute break, Ford told Tice that all they wanted from him was the truth, and, indeed, that it was all they had ever wanted. Tice replied that he would tell them the truth: the seventh assailant was a black man. Asked to describe this black man, Tice said he stood 5'9" or 5'10" and had a somewhat muscular build. He thought that he was in the navy; Williams was the only one who knew him, Tice offered.[95]

Why had he never told them about this black male before? Ford grilled Tice. Because they were all scared of him, Tice responded. But Ford was still disbelieving. After all, the six defendants were all white, and they hung out with other white guys. Joe Dick, who like Tice knew that a black man had assaulted a woman not far from the apartment complex shortly before the murder, had tried to tell Ford months earlier that a black man had participated, but Ford had not believed him either.[96]

Okay, Tice said, he would tell them the truth now. The other person wasn't really a black man. In fact, he didn't know who this person was, because "I wasn't there." One can imagine Ford's exasperation. When Tice told him about hearing that a black man had been seen running from the apartment complex the night of the murder, Ford sniffed at that too, and Tice noticed that the other detective in the room, one D.R. Norrell, who was taking notes, did not write down what he said.[97]

On December 28, a preliminary hearing was held on John Danser's case. His lawyer, Jennifer Stanton, was not aware that Tice had recanted his earlier statements about Danser's involvement. The commonwealth had not turned over to her Ford's notes on his November 5 interview of Tice, though they were exculpatory evidence. She would not get those notes for over a year, and they would come not from Hansen but from Tice's attorney at the time, James Broccoletti, who had requested them. According to Hansen, police had not transcribed them until then and thus he didn't have them or even know about them earlier. Irate, Stanton investigated the possibility of filing a lawsuit against the commonwealth attorney's office and the Norfolk police. But she learned that, in Virginia, her chances were poor. Actually, they would be poor anywhere in the country: prosecutors have virtual immunity from civil suits, except over their actions when investigating a case. The main issue, Stanton recalls, was when Hansen learned about Tice's recantation. She had an investigator ask Hansen about it. But Hansen's answer, which Stanton calls "a lie," seemed to eliminate any hope of a successful suit.[98]

At the preliminary hearing, Tice did another about-face. He testified that he had, in fact, participated in Michelle Moore-Bosko's murder and rape along with Williams, Dick, Wilson, Pauley, Farris, and Danser. Testifying, he recounts, was "torture. I wanted to tell the truth, but at the same time I knew if I did and told the actual truth—that neither of us knew anything about the crime—that I'd get hammered with the death penalty. And I really wanted to keep that off the table." Tice stated that he saw Danser stab Michelle. Other details were still changing. Stanton pointed out how implausible it was that although Danser had had no contact with Tice for well over a year—"didn't know where he lived, didn't have a phone number, nothing"—Danser then "automatically shows up from some other state in Dan Williams's house to agree to go across the hallway and commit rape and murder. I think that is inherently . . . unbelievable." Under Stanton's cross-examination, Tice revealed that Ford had told him in November that Danser had not been involved. But Judge Ray W. Dezern Jr. ruled that there was probable cause to believe that Danser was guilty of both murder and rape.[99]

Two months later, in February 1999, Danser was eliminated as a possible source of the DNA found at the crime scene. So were two of Ford's other suspects, Robert Mattingly and Jay Wagner. Seven young men were now behind bars for what appeared to be one of the biggest gang-rape murders in Norfolk history, but there was still no DNA match. The unease of police and prosecutors continued to grow. A year and a half after Michelle's slaying, they still didn't have everybody. At least one other killer was still on the loose, they believed; doing what, nobody knew. Police "are looking into several other leads," Valerie Bowen told Judge Poston that month.[100]

They should have been reviewing the evidence, and carefully. They had a crime scene that was inconsistent with a gang attack. In Michelle's freshly cleaned living room, nothing had been in disarray after the murder. Next to the front door, a small table that prevented the door from opening fully still held a drinking glass and lamp—an unlikely scene had seven men rushed in. There were, of course, no defensive or restraint injuries on Michelle, though the confessors had said that she had put up a fight, and the blood underneath her fingernails indicated she was willing to fight (maybe she couldn't or didn't resist, Hansen would counter). Her stab wounds, they knew, were all within a small area, and the three major ones had the same depth and entry angle. "To say that eight people, or five people, or even two people could have done that—it's like a snowball in hell for everybody to follow the exact same parameter," one longtime medical examiner who has analyzed the evidence comments. Michelle's vaginal injuries were also consistent with one attacker.[101]

Those papers that had been found protruding off a shelf into the hallway did not square with a gang attack. If eight people had carried a struggling, terror-stricken young woman down that narrow hallway, which barely fit two people and was partly blocked by a chair next to the dining room table, and then exited up the same hallway, it's a good bet that some of those papers would have been dislodged. ("If those papers fell, somebody could have easily just picked them up and stacked them right back there," Hansen argues.) There were also no marks on the hallway walls, and photos there were undisturbed. There were no signs of a gang attack in Michelle's tiny bedroom either, where the space available for the assault was further constricted by the furniture to about seven feet by seven feet. Besides the nightstand and the objects on it that were still in place, a carefully balanced full-length mirror remained standing only a foot or two from Michelle. Nothing had been overturned or broken in the bedroom. And, of course, only Michelle's and Billy's prints had been found there; had eight excited young men raped her on that polished parquet floor, somebody would have left a fingerprint. And the more attackers involved, the greater the chance that physical evidence would be left and that objects would be askew. The odds of property being stolen would also go up, as would those of neighbors reporting suspicious noise or activity. But neither occurred.[102]

On top of all that, the defendants simply didn't all mesh well together, or even know everybody else. Eric Wilson's friend John Schwertlech comments with some amusement, "Eric does not hang out in a group of eight people."[103]

To say the least, the police and prosecution's theory of the case strained belief. "They just never stopped to say, 'Wait a minute. It just is not making sense
anymore,' in my opinion," Jennifer Stanton says. "They just never waved the
bullshit flag and said, 'Something's wrong here. Something's *really* wrong
here.'" But Valerie Bowen would claim that there was "a lot of corroborating
evidence" in support of the defendants' confessions. "I can't even go into all
of [it] now, it would just take too long," she said. And D.J. Hansen asserts,
"Everything fits together. . . . It just all makes so much sense when you look
back on it."[104]

10

"Guess Who Did That?"

In January 1999, Danial Williams finally succumbed to pressure from his attorneys and pled guilty to capital murder and rape. He would receive two life terms in prison without the possibility of parole. He entered his plea reluctantly. Danny Shipley and Robert Frank had advised him that, if he went to trial, which was scheduled for February, he would get convicted and probably receive the death penalty. "There's a good chance you're going to get it," Shipley had told him. On top of his confession, which was devastating by itself, both Joseph Dick and Derek Tice would testify against him, they pointed out. It was a no-win situation, Shipley felt: "I said, 'You know, you're not going to win this case. Not with a confession, and not with two guys testifying against you.'" That combination was a losing hand every time. "They pushed me really hard to take the plea," Williams recounts. "I pretty much gave up." He thought about requesting new attorneys, "but it had dragged on long enough, and I just wanted to get it over with."[1]

The deal required Williams to sign a stipulation of facts on the crime. It was intended to keep him on the reservation if he was called to testify at trials of other defendants (though the agreement did not require him to testify—D.J. Hansen had tried to throw that condition in after the deal had already been struck, but Shipley had excoriated him in chambers, and Hansen had backed down). In the stipulation, Williams endorsed the police and prosecution's theory of the case. Joe Dick, Eric Wilson, Derek Tice, Richard Pauley, Geoffrey Farris, John Danser, and himself—all seven of whom were members of the Banque Crew, he agreed—had gathered in his apartment that evening, where he had brought up his fascination with Michelle. "Williams was obsessed with sexual desires toward Michelle Bosko, and made numerous attempts to ingratiate himself with her," the stipulation read. "His most frequent ruse to gain entry into her apartment and talk to her was to use her telephone." The Friday night before her murder, he had used that pretense to join the small party at her apartment where he had danced alone to some of his own CDs "in a sexually suggestive manner, undulating himself on the wall, the floor, furniture, and behind Michelle," he stated. The evening of the attack, after all seven of them had raped her, they each took a turn stabbing her, the stipulation read. They pledged not to tell on each other, which was why Williams had not named anybody else in his earlier confession. Asked later why he signed the stipulation, Williams said he had no choice to get his deal of life in prison. "The attorney says, 'They're not going to change it. Just sign it,'" he remembers.[2]

In a required postplea interview in an interrogation room at the police station with Detectives Glenn Ford and Brian Wray, D.J. Hansen, and Bob Frank on February 9, Williams tried to tell the detectives and Hansen what they wanted to hear. He had gone over to Michelle's to see not only what kind of underwear she wore but also their color, he said, absurdly. Once they'd all raped her, everybody but Wilson stabbed her, he now stated—because he had talked to Wilson in jail, Ford suggested, but in reality because he had read Wilson's confession in which Wilson had said that he left before the stabbing. "When asked if anyone else was there, Mr. Williams stated that he didn't know," Wray and Ford wrote in their notes. "When asked if Robert Mattingly was there that night, he stated that he did not know." Williams seemed stingy on details to the detectives. He "appeared to be real evasive about the facts of the case and appeared to be telling these investigators just what was on the agreed stipulation that he had signed during his guilty plea," they wrote. "When asked once again was there anyone else there and present when this happened that was involved, Mr. Williams stated he didn't know." At that point, Frank asked Ford, Wray, and Hansen to leave the room so that he could speak with his client alone. But he was unable to get Williams to provide any other information, so he told the detectives the interview was over.[3]

Williams had already strayed from the stipulation, and Hansen promptly moved to get him back in line. In the interview, Williams "retracted a material

statement contained in the stipulation" by saying that Wilson did not participate in the murder, Hansen argued in a motion on February 26. He had
thereby breached his plea agreement. Hansen thus asked the court to revoke
it. The death penalty would again be in play.[4]

That month, a remorseful Joe Dick, who continued to think that he had actually participated in the crime, drafted a letter of apology to "the Bosko/Moore
family." "I've given this alot [sic] of thought and I've made my mind up to do
this," he wrote on February 19. "I would like to take the time and apologize for
what I did to your daughter, Michelle. I'm sorry that I took part in the crime.
All I ask is for your forgiveness. I know what I did was wrong and I'm trying
to correct an error that I made by testifying against those who are also involved. I know that I would give my life just to bring Michele [sic] back to life.
I'm also sorry about all the pain and hard times that you are going through.
You might not think that my apology is genuine, but . . . it is. Every time I
think about what I have done, I get frustrated. I hope and pray that you find
it in your heart to forgive me. I would like you to know that I was raised
better. . . . I don't know what was going through my head. . . . If I could bring
her back, I would do it in a heartbeat. Thank you for taking the time to listen
to me."[5]

On February 22, the Michelle Moore-Bosko case changed dramatically. Or it
would have in a system better at correcting its mistakes. That day, shortly after noon, Delvie Stover, the mother of Michelle's friend Tamika Taylor, walked
into the Norfolk Police Operations Center and handed police a stunning letter. Addressed to "Karen and Kamonte and family," the letter was angry, ob-
scene, and more than a little threatening. The author was upset that Karen
Stover, who was married to Kamonte Stover, one of Taylor's brothers, hadn't
written him. "You wanted to know how I really felt about you and I told you,"
he wrote. "You never even wrote back to say fuck you or nothing. . . . Hatred
in my heart is thick. Ain't no forgiving you or nobody else. . . . Nobody know[s]
what I'm going through so don't try and understand me."[6]

The author of the letter let Karen Stover know what he was capable of doing to her. "You remember that night I went to Mommie's house and the next
morning Michelle got killed. Guess who did that. *Me*, ha, ha. It wasn't the first
time. I'm good ain't I. I don't give a fuck about nobody. If I was out I would

have killed that bitch down the street from you too. . . . Tell the police, tell the FBI. Tell anybody who gives a fuck. Not me. You thought you knew me. You don't Karen. Trust me. Yall [sic] don't. Nobody knows me. I'm untouchable Karen. And I'm coming." The author's prose then turned pornographic; he claimed that Karen wanted him.[7]

Then he made his threat more specific. "I'm going to give you one week to write me and send some nasty pictures of yourself or money or I'm going to put *you* in checkmate," he warned Karen. He wanted "pictures of you in panties and bras and a nasty letter and money or you'll be with Michelle in hell." "Baw bitch, you dead," he added, for emphasis, at the bottom. The letter was signed "Two face 'Ab.'"[8]

Its author was Omar Abdul Ballard, Tamika Taylor's friend who had gotten to know Michelle through Taylor. Ballard had lived with Kamonte and Karen Stover in Norfolk earlier. Known to his friends as Ab or Abdul, he had found Karen attractive ("I love her very much, even to this day," he wrote in 2005). Karen had looked at Ballard as something of a little brother. Ballard had written her a letter earlier in which it seemed to Karen that he was trying to tell her that he loved her. She had shown it to Kamonte. She had not responded because she and Kamonte had planned to visit Ballard the following weekend. Then Karen had received Ballard's threatening letter, which she and Kamonte had read together. She had taken it over to Delvie, Kamonte's mother, and his sister, Tamika, about two days later. Karen, Delvie, and Tamika had all been unsettled by it. "I was upset," Karen testified later.[9]

They had reason to be nervous about Ballard. Two weeks before Michelle's murder, as the lynch mob that had pursued Ballard that day had believed, he had assaulted a female named Melissa Morse in the same block. Ballard, who was then nineteen years old, had scurried over to Taylor's place, where he'd basically been living, following the assault, and Taylor had then brought him over to Michelle's, saying he was a friend. Michelle's husband, Billy Bosko, had refused to turn Ballard over to the mob when it had shown up outside their patio door demanding "the nigger." Billy didn't see how Ballard could have just assaulted someone when he'd spent the last hour or two sitting right there, rather quietly and politely, in the apartment. "I wasn't going to watch this guy get beat up or worse for something that I didn't think he'd done," Billy said later. He and Michelle had even told the police that Ballard didn't do it, Ballard says. The arrest warrant for Ballard for assaulting Morse had been issued the same evening that Danial Williams was being interrogated for Michelle's murder.[10]

It was shortly after Billy and Michelle had shielded him from the mob that Ballard had become friendly with Michelle. They spoke at the apartment's pool. Michelle then let Ballard into her apartment for visits several times in the evening when Billy was out to sea, according to Ballard: "We drank together, laughed and talked." He was either high or drunk when he dropped by, he recalls. Michelle felt comfortable around Ballard; he wasn't an intimidating person. And he was good-looking and could be engaging and entertaining. "She thought he was a friend," Taylor said later. Taylor also testified that Ballard would stop by Michelle's apartment at around 5:30 "every morning," ostensibly to see if Taylor was there. Taylor wondered about his real motives. Michelle wouldn't hesitate to let him in, Taylor said. Ballard had even come by Michelle's apartment at about 5:30 the morning before she was murdered, Taylor testified. But Ballard calls Taylor's testimony "ridiculous," saying he was typically asleep at that hour.[11]

According to Ballard, he had a consensual sexual relationship with Michelle. They had sex "a few times," he says. "Nothing major, like love." That is unlikely. "I don't believe that whatsoever," Michelle's close friend Erin Litle comments. "Michelle wasn't like that. When she was with somebody, she was with somebody."[12] What's more, Michelle and Billy had only recently married, and Billy was everything to his new wife.

Ballard had pled guilty to malicious wounding for the attack on Melissa Morse and received a five-year suspended sentence conditional upon serving a year in the Norfolk City Jail. D.J. Hansen, who had prosecuted him, had not made any connection between the assault and Michelle's murder. Ballard had been banned from the apartment complex because of the attack, but that hadn't stopped him from visiting Taylor or Michelle.[13]

The night of Michelle's murder, after saying goodnight to her outside their apartments, Taylor had had a frightening dream about Michelle. Her mother, Delvie, had had one too. Hers had involved Ballard. He had been trying to climb up onto a bed to get to Karen Stover. Delvie had told Karen about it the next day. (Taylor and her mother would later call their dreams "visions.") After Taylor learned of Michelle's death, she spoke to Ballard—he had spent the night of the murder at Taylor's place—and he had not acted surprised or upset by it. When Karen saw him walking toward her house that day and asked him if he had been at Michelle's the night before, Ballard said that he'd stopped by to see if Tamika was there. Told that Michelle had been killed, he did not seem surprised to Karen either. Rather, his face looked oddly blank.[14]

Then, ten days later, Ballard raped a fourteen-year-old girl. He assaulted Virginia Owens between 10 and 11 P.M. about a mile from Michelle's apartment. He had followed her as she had walked home from a McDonalds restaurant, said he had a gun behind his back, and stolen her pocket change. He had then pulled her behind a building. When she had refused to pull her pants down, Ballard had punched her and threatened to kill her. When she had started to scream, he'd choked her. "Stop yelling, bitch, or I'll kill you," he had snapped. Ballard then penetrated her. When the crying Owens told him it hurt and tried to wrestle away, Ballard choked her even harder. "You're probably prejudiced too," he taunted her. "Have you ever done it before? You probably like to mess around with those little white boys." Ballard punched her several more times when she begged him to let her go. But Owens was finally able to break free, and a nearby resident saw her running hysterically down the street with only a shirt on, screaming for help. She was treated for a broken nose and contusions and underwent surgery for tears to her vagina.[15]

A week later, Virginia Owens's sister noticed a man at a nearby shopping center who matched Virginia's description of her attacker. She called Virginia, who came to the shopping center and identified Ballard. He was wearing the same green army camouflage pants, dark blue-and-white shirt, and dog collar he had been wearing when he had assaulted her. Police then arrested him. "He acted like he didn't know what was going on," a police spokesman said. He later admitted raping Owens. He was found guilty of rape, malicious wounding, and robbery, and sentenced to forty-one years in prison.[16] He had written his letter to Karen Stover from the Augusta County Correctional Center in northwestern Virginia.

Tamika Taylor had suspected that Ballard had had something to do with Michelle's death, in part because of his early-morning visits to Michelle's apartment, and his arrest for raping Virginia Owens had fed her suspicions. Tamika's mother, Delvie, had told Karen Stover after Ballard's arrest that she believed he'd had something to do with Michelle's killing too. Her dream about Ballard climbing onto a bed to get to Karen, Delvie said, must have been about Michelle.[17]

According to a legal affidavit she later signed, Taylor had asked police several times to check out Ballard, starting shortly after Michelle's murder. She had spoken to more than one person about it, she says—if those people included prosecutors, they did not inform defense lawyers—and well before he had written his letter to Karen. "I really thought the police should see if Omar had been involved in Michelle's murder," she remembers. Her mother had shown her Ballard's letter to Karen right before she had taken it to the police. "The letter confirmed what I had suspected about Omar being involved all along," Taylor recounts. But Taylor didn't believe that Ballard had acted alone: she thought that Danial Williams, Joe Dick, Eric Wilson, and Derek Tice had been with him, as they had all confessed.[18]

Despite Taylor's requests to police, Ballard's assaults on Melissa Morse and Virginia Owens, his close proximity to Michelle, and their friendly relationship, police had not investigated him. They had a confession from Danial Williams and had not questioned it. Ballard had been shocked that the police had not come after him.[19] Not until evidence of his involvement had been handed to them on a silver platter by Delvie Stover did they consider Ballard a suspect in Michelle's killing. But by now, of course, they had developed a multiple-perpetrator theory of the crime and they weren't about to give it up. They had gone too far down the wrong road to admit their mistakes and acknowledge that they had put seven innocent young men behind bars. And with some creative modifications to their theory, they could even convince themselves that Ballard had conspired with the others.

Ballard's history of violence against women could be traced back to his childhood. His mother was a prostitute and drug addict who had effectively abandoned him. He held that against her. He had "bad feelings against women" because of it, he told police. "There was no question in my mind that Ballard had some real serious issues with women," recalls Jennifer Stanton, John Danser's attorney, who represented Ballard in the Melissa Morse case. "He would go hot and cold. . . . As long as you're telling him what he wants to hear, you're his best friend. And then if you tell him something he doesn't want to hear, it's psycho killer. It's literally a distinct Jekyll-and-Hyde thing with him." Once, when Ballard's mother came up in a conversation with Stanton, he tensed visibly and appeared close to going off.[20]

When Ballard was a toddler, his mother was never around, so the state put him in a foster home. He was two years old at the time. Then he was shunted to another foster home. He last saw his mother when he was ten or eleven. He never even met his father, who was white.[21]

Ballard was raised by adoptive parents in a rough area in New Jersey. "The neighborhood we lived in was chaos," he remembers. "Shootings, drug selling, police, sex, money, murders, fights—every day. . . . I fell victim to all of this. . . . All I knew and ever loved was the life of crime." He dealt narcotics and guns, took drugs, drank daily, beat people with bats, shot at them, and robbed them. "That's what made me happy," he says. "Nothing else could compare to the life of crime."[22]

His adoptive parents, Betty and Bobby Shuler, were black. Bobby Shuler was a janitor at Rutgers University, Betty a nurse. Ballard had several adoptive siblings. He later told a probation and parole officer that his life with the Shulers was happy, that all his material needs were met, and that they gave him ample love, support, and guidance. He described his family as middle class. "Emotionally, though, things were off balance," he recalls. "Knowing that this family isn't yours, and feeling out of place, is kind of hard. I never felt wanted or loved. Hence my rebelliousness. . . . There was abuse and drugs throughout my home."[23]

Ballard fought in school. His head was cracked open twice and his mouth busted up. He had an explosive temper; it didn't take much to set him off. "My anger was out of control," he remembers. He saw a psychiatrist after trying to jump out of a school window.[24]

Ballard dropped out of school after the tenth or eleventh grade and moved to Virginia. Tamika Taylor had been raised in the same Jersey neighborhood, he'd known her since they were children, even lived with her for a few months, and he traveled to Virginia to be with her there too. In Norfolk, he ran the streets with her brother Kamonte, smoking pot, drinking, selling drugs. He drank or got high "every night." Police cited him for being drunk in public twice.[25]

On February 24, 1999, two days after Delvie Stover gave police Ballard's letter to Karen Stover, John Danser's attorney, Jennifer Stanton, told Judge Charles E.

Poston that she'd just learned there were now nine defendants and possibly even ten. "Judge, I don't think it's going to stop, I mean, at the rate we're going," she commented at a hearing on Danser's case. "The potential tenth person, and probably the most important of the group," Stanton told Poston she had learned, was "a gentleman by the name of Abdul." A letter by him "clearly confessing to the crime" had been turned over to police or prosecutors by a prosecution witness, Stanton informed Poston. "We asked Mr. Hansen about that before the Judge came out on the bench. He says he's not aware of anything and refuses to give us anything." "If he's not aware of it, how can he give it?" Poston replied. "Well, Judge, the problem is that I know that he *is* aware of it," Stanton said. "He doesn't have it, but it's got to be in their possession or in the possession of one of their agents. And we want a copy of it because this Abdul person is not naming anyone other than himself as being involved in this crime."[26]

Poston peered down from the bench at Hansen. "Do you know anything about Abdul?" he asked. "Do I have anything?" Hansen replied, evasively. "No, Your Honor." Asked again whether he knew anything about him, Hansen equivocated, then declared, "I am not in receipt of any evidence." He was "just being real namby-pamby," Stanton recounts, and his co-prosecutor Valerie Bowen "as much as yanked him into his chair and stood up and corrected him." "There is an ongoing investigation as to a letter that we understand has been received," Bowen advised Poston. "We have not seen the letter, but the police are investigating it right now. I anticipate that the letter probably will be turned over once we see it." A peeved Judge Poston, who felt that he had already made it abundantly clear to the prosecutors that they needed to turn over everything they had and that he wasn't about to waste time arguing about such things, ordered that they provide him copies of "any letters dealing with Abdul."[27]

Hansen and Bowen were not eager to give Ballard's letter to defense attorneys. "They weren't going to turn it over," Stanton remembers. "And it's totally exculpatory evidence." Hansen denies withholding. "I mean, I wasn't going to go to a trial without turning that over," he says. After Poston's order, Hansen gave Ballard's letter to the judge for inspection to determine if it contained exculpatory information. On March 15, Poston directed that it be released.[28]

Suppressing exculpatory evidence is the most common and most dangerous form of prosecutorial misconduct. It makes a fair legal contest impossible. Yet prosecutors are typically not held accountable for it; few are hauled before disciplinary committees or punished by their superiors, and criminal prosecution of them is almost unthinkable. (When Greg McCormack, Eric Wilson's attorney, asked Judge Poston on March 4 to sanction prosecutors for allegedly withholding police notes of interviews with Dick and Tice in which they said that Wilson had left before Michelle's murder, Poston called the request "frivolous" and denied it.) When prosecutors withhold exculpatory evidence—and most understandably are disinclined to reveal information that could harm their case—usually no one ever finds out. And when sanctioned, prosecutors usually receive only a slap on the wrist, even for flagrant misconduct, including that leading to a wrongful conviction. To get a conviction overturned because prosecutors withheld exculpatory evidence, the defense has the difficult task of showing that the evidence likely would have led to a different result. According to the courts, the prosecutors' good or bad faith is irrelevant. Nonetheless, several hundred murder convictions have been thrown out because prosecutors concealed evidence suggesting innocence or presented false evidence. None of these prosecutors was barred from practicing law; rather, many enjoyed career advancements. One became a congressman.[29]

When Hansen saw Ballard's letter to Karen Stover, he, of course, knew that it transformed the case. It would hardly help his prosecution of the other defendants. But he didn't believe that Ballard killed Michelle by himself, he recalls. Nor, in his retelling, was he surprised by the letter. At that point, "I was prepared to deal with just about anything," he says. He figured that Ballard simply wasn't telling the whole truth. He knew what kind of guy Ballard was, and that both Dick and Tice had tried to tell Detective Ford earlier that a black guy had been with them, but that Ford hadn't wanted to hear it. Nor had their own lawyers. Everybody had thought that they were "just trying to pin it on some random black guy," Hansen recounts. "And then when this letter came through, it just changed everything." Hansen theorized that Ballard didn't want to share responsibility for the crime with white people, particularly since he was in prison where he associated with a black organization, and that he wanted to wear the murder as a badge.[30]

But would his DNA match? Hansen learned that Ballard's blood was not in the state's DNA databank as required by his felony convictions (there was a backlog), so the prosecution called the Virginia Division of Forensic Science and requested that they insert his profile.[31]

On March 2, at about 1 P.M., Detectives Ford and David Peterson paid a visit to Ballard at the Augusta Correctional Center in Craigsville, some 220 miles from Norfolk. Ballard was pulled from a recreation yard and escorted to a small room. They were there to talk to him about the homicide of Michelle Moore-Bosko, Ford informed him. What did he know about it? Nothing, Ballard snorted. Well, they had a letter that he had written saying he had done it. Ballard denied writing the letter. When Ford said that they had lifted his fingerprints off it, Ballard scoffed that somebody else might have written the letter after getting the paper out of his cell. Ford whipped out some photos of the other defendants and asked Ballard if he knew them. No, Ballard replied. Well, they had some unidentified DNA and were going to compare it with his DNA, Ford said. Go ahead and do it, Ballard retorted. It wouldn't match. When they found out it didn't match, Ballard added, they should come back and apologize and take him to the prison canteen and let him buy anything he wanted. Okay, Ford said with a smile. He would do that. But if his DNA matched, he had to tell them the truth. Ballard said he would, but that he had nothing more to say now. It "was a very short meeting," Ford remembered.[32]

Two days later, Ford and Peterson returned to Augusta. On their drive up, they stopped at the forensic laboratory in Richmond to pick up the DNA results.

They finally had a hit.

Ballard's DNA matched the semen found on the white blanket in Michelle's bedroom. The odds were infinitesimal that anybody else had caused the stain: the semen was 21 billion times more likely to have originated with Ballard than with an unknown white person, and 4.6 billion times more likely to have come from him than from an unknown black person. And the sperm found in Michelle's vagina was 23 million times more likely to have been Ballard's than an unknown white person's, and 20 million times more likely to have been his than an unknown black person's. The blood found underneath Michelle's fingernails was consistent with a mixture of Ballard's and Michelle's DNA.[33]

The logical conclusion—or the logical conclusion for anyone without an investment in the seven prior arrests—was that they finally had their guy, that the seven young men in jail were innocent. Ballard had never even met six of the seven. He had seen Williams, whom he'd heard was stalking Michelle, at the small party at her apartment several nights before her murder. "The crazy guy stopped over for a minute," Ballard later told police. They had not spoken at the party. "I left after he came in," Williams recalls. "He just gave me this weird feeling." When Eric Wilson had been jailed and found himself in the same pod with Ballard, he had not even known who Ballard was.[34] And none of the confessors had mentioned Ballard in their statements.

But, as farfetched as it might seem, police and prosecutors sought to get Ballard to place the other defendants at the scene with him. To confess and then incriminate everybody.

When Ford and Peterson arrived at the Augusta Correctional Center at 2:30 P.M. on March 4, Ford apprised Ballard that they were there to talk about the Moore-Bosko homicide again and that they had some DNA results to show him. Ford then handed Ballard the certificate of analysis. Ballard looked it over. Okay, he would talk, he said, only minutes into the interrogation, unlike Williams, Dick, Wilson, and Tice, from whom Ford had needed hours to wrest confessions. Ballard said that he had gone over to Karen and Kamonte Stover's house around 11:30 the night of the murder, then walked over to Michelle's between midnight and 1 A.M. He had intended to go to Tamika's but had decided to stop by Michelle's place first. He hadn't known whether Michelle's husband was home or not, he said. He had knocked on her door, and Michelle had let him in. He had been drunk and high, he remembered. Michelle had told him that he was welcome to drinks in the refrigerator and to use the phone, so he grabbed a beer, and Michelle walked back to her bedroom. After she returned to the living room, they talked for thirty to forty-five minutes, he said. They then had consensual sex on the bed and maybe on the floor of the bedroom, he claimed. He had had sex with her once before, he stated.[35]

Ford told Ballard that they could prove he had raped Michelle, but Ballard denied raping her. Ford suggested that Ballard didn't want to admit to it because it would get him a capital murder charge. No, he wasn't worried about that, Ballard responded. Would robbery get him capital murder? Yes, Ford replied. Well, he had taken thirty-five dollars from her purse, Ballard said.[36]

Ballard wanted to die. He'd already had enough in his short life. "I was ready to receive the death penalty," he remembers. He would tell Lyn Simmons, his appointed attorney, that he preferred execution to life behind bars. "I don't even have anyone to write me in prison," he lamented. "I don't even have anyone to help me with my canteen. . . . I have nothing to live for. No family supporting me. No kids, no nothing. I'm not to be missed. . . . I don't care about anything or anyone no more."[37]

After he and Michelle had sex, Ballard went on, he killed her. He didn't remember how, he told Ford. He took the money from her purse on the dining room table before leaving—"to get drunk, I guess, or to get some weed or something." He was the first defendant to say anything about taking money. How could he remember stealing thirty-five dollars but not how he'd killed her? Ford asked him. He needed to think for a few minutes, Ballard replied. After falling silent for a time, he recalled that he had stabbed her three or four times in the chest with a knife that he had grabbed from the kitchen. He had been on his way out of the apartment after having sex with her but had changed his mind and returned to the bedroom. "She was in a daze when I came back in the room with the knife," he said. Michelle was either getting up off the bed or was already up when he stabbed her the first time, he remembered. After she fell to the floor, he stabbed her about two or three more times—"I'm not quite sure" how many. Asked what made him kill her, "he stated that sometimes he just flips, he'll just be flipping, and that sometimes he feels like snapping," Peterson and Ford wrote in their notes. "When I was leaving, I don't know, I guess something just ticked in my head," Ballard said later on tape. "I guess I was just drunk and thinking about my mother." He accurately described the steak knife that had been found on the floor of Michelle's bedroom; he was the first confessor to do that too. He never hit Michelle, he recounted. He thought he dropped the knife before leaving; Michelle was moaning when he departed. He then spent the night at Tamika Taylor's place. He remembered police questioning Tamika about the case the next day.[38]

When the detectives asked Ballard whether anyone was with him, he said no, that he had done it by himself. Ford, who didn't want to hear that, laughed in his face. "He thought that to be very humorous," Ballard recalls. That incensed Ballard. Ford tried several times to get Ballard to embrace his scenario of the crime. He knew that the other guys had been with him, Ford claimed— they had told him. He couldn't have done it by himself. Why was he protecting those assholes? "Ford asked me a series of leading questions in an attempt to get the version of the crime that he wanted," Ballard stated in an affidavit later. "For example, Ford would tell me some detail about the killing of Michelle and then ask me a question, encouraging me to use the detail he had just provided in my answer. I repeatedly told Ford that I committed the crime alone, but Ford wanted me to say that the other defendants had been involved." "Detective Ford is scum," Ballard wrote Paul A. Dowling, the executive producer of the television series *Medical Detectives* and *Forensic Files*. "He will not give up until you say what he wants you to say." He "puts words in people's mouths" and "won't stop until you agree. And that's what the four white guys are guilty of, 'agreeing.'"[39]

When Ford asked Ballard why he hadn't come forward when the seven other defendants were being arrested, Ballard said he didn't know. "Are you sorry now for what happened to Michelle?" Detective Peterson inquired. "I mean, yes, I guess," Ballard responded. "I don't know." Was there anything he wished to add? Ford asked Ballard at the end of his taped statement. "No, just them four people that opened their mouths is stupid," he retorted.[40]

The same day, in Norfolk, prosecutors withdrew their motion to revoke Danial Williams's plea agreement. With their case against Williams and the other defendants undercut by Ballard's DNA match, it was best to preserve any and all incriminating testimony, including Williams's plea debriefing.[41]

On March 8, Ford obtained arrest warrants for Ballard. Three days later, police brought Ballard to the Norfolk Police Operations Center for another interview. "We wanted to confront him one more time" about raping Michelle, Ford testified later. And it was better to do it in an interrogation room than at the prison, where inmates and staff were walking around. Ballard nonchalantly remarked to Ford that he figured they'd be talking again. If they gave him a pack of M&Ms, Ballard said, he'd tell them the truth. After Ford fetched Ballard his M&Ms and a Pepsi, and following some sparring back and forth ("Come on, you raped her, right?"), Ballard admitted raping Michelle. He wrote us that he only did so "because of my impatience with him [Ford]. . . . A *lot* of things that I said was to get the detectives off my back. I was upset that they weren't believing me, so I said what they wanted to hear." He was getting the death penalty anyway. He denies raping Michelle, though the injuries she sustained to her genital area indicated she was raped. When Ford asked him whether she fought him, Ballard replied, "Not really. I mean, I'm strong, you know what I'm saying. . . . She was just telling me to get off." As he was rising to leave after raping her on the bed, he recounted, Michelle cried, "Why did you do it?" He then "snapped," wheeled around, grabbed her neck, and started choking her. After they fell to the floor, he continued strangling her, then hustled into the kitchen to get the knife. "I just blanked," he told Ford. "I figured she was going to tell, so I was like, 'Fuck it.'" When he returned, as Michelle was slowly getting up off the floor, he stabbed her several times. He again denied that anybody had been with him. "Sure did," he responded this time when asked if he felt any remorse. And he had not, in fact, had sex with her before, he said.[42]

It is hard to read the transcripts of Ballard's confessions to police—the way he laid the crime out in response to Ford and Peterson's questions, their choice of questions, and the plausibility of his account—without concluding that Ford now realized that Ballard had committed the crime alone. And, if that's true, everything Ford did afterward to keep the other seven defendants behind bars was to cover himself and keep what he knew was a bad case together. Or—and this is quite possible, perhaps even likely—Ford managed to suppress any doubts he held about the case and convince himself that Ballard was a good liar. He later testified, with some emphasis, that he believed all eight defendants were guilty.[43] And, in a sense, with so much invested in the case, what else could he believe?

Ballard's subsequent accounts of the night of the murder offer more insight into his state of mind than do his statements to police. At Karen and Kamonte Stover's house before walking over to Michelle's, he recounts, he had felt some sexual tension with Karen, whose husband, Kamonte, was off at some church event. He had left for Tamika Taylor's place in a restless and disturbed state. He felt something bad was about to happen. He didn't want it to happen, but it was going to happen anyway. A feeling had been building up inside him, and he felt it powerfully that night. It went back to his childhood. "My frame of mind that night was that I had become angry and frustrated with life and had a sense that there was nowhere I belonged," he recalls. His anger and resentments had reached the boiling point. He didn't even have his own apartment; he had been shuttling back and forth, still like an unwanted child, between Tamika's and the Stovers'.[44]

At Michelle's apartment, he and Michelle had talked and he'd phoned some girlfriend in New Jersey, he remembers. Michelle, he thought, was unaware that he was a pressure cooker about to explode, because he was acting normally. She was wearing only a T-shirt and underwear, he says. As he approached the front door to leave after they had sex in the bedroom, he blew. He grabbed a knife from the kitchen, returned to the bedroom, and sat down in a chair next to Michelle, who was on the bed crying. He had to kill her, he told her. "You don't have to do this," she pleaded. "I'm not going to tell anybody." But he couldn't really hear her; he was in his own world. He stood up, threw her on the floor, and choked and stabbed her. During the first stab, he was feeling anger, he recalls; with the second one, he felt shock. Then he stabbed her two more times. He can't remember why he inflicted the five knife pricks in her chest, he says.[45]

Why did he kill her? "Not to sound like a savage or an animalistic person, but the only logical explanation . . . is mental and emotional unstability," Ballard told us. "I wasn't in my right mind." He wrote Paul Dowling, "I just blacked out. I don't know what happened. One minute I was normal, the next I was gone, like I wasn't in control of myself, but could still see clearly what I was doing." Before leaving he "snapped back" and washed up in the bathroom sink, he recounts. He knew that the police would be looking for a murder weapon, but he had to leave the knife behind because he was headed to Tamika's. He tossed the Newport cigarette he was smoking in the toilet and wiped the doorknobs and the phone with his shirt to erase any fingerprints. At Tamika's, he slept on the couch.[46]

Larry McCann, a businesslike man with graying hair parted at the side, large-framed glasses, and long ears, is a former Virginia State Police officer and an expert on crime scene investigation who was hired in 2005 by lawyers representing Williams, Dick, and Tice. The attorneys asked him to analyze case materials, determine the number of assailants involved in Michelle's rape and murder, and reconstruct the crime. Here are McCann's conclusions, in a nutshell: Omar Ballard was the sole perpetrator. His motive for visiting Michelle that night was sexual, as he did not bring a weapon or steal valuables. Michelle was in the kitchen preparing some food (McCann knew that a frying pan had been left on the stove and an eggshell on the floor) when something Ballard did provoked her to scratch him and flee into her bedroom. Ballard, wielding a knife from the kitchen, gave chase, grabbed and pulled the right back side of her T-shirt near the shoulder—causing some of the abrasions on her neck and throat—which made her lose her footing on the polished parquet floor and fall backwards. "Offender then used a combination of choking and slight knife jabs to control victim," McCann wrote. Hence the pricks on her chest. Ballard next raped Michelle. But he was not angry with her, as he did not beat her. He stabbed her to death to keep her from reporting the assault. He had not stabbed anyone before, however, and thus the initial stab wound was only ½" deep. After wiping his penis and the blood Michelle had coughed onto him on a nearby blanket, Ballard left the bedroom. As an afterthought, he stopped at the dining room table, pulled out a chair, and went through Michelle's purse.[47]

Whatever the particulars of the assault, Ballard is remorseful about it today. "I'm sickened by what I've done to such an undeserving person," he told us. It still vexed Ballard when we corresponded with him in 2004 that the truth had not come out about the case and that no one in the legal system seemed to believe that he had committed the crime alone or to want to hear the truth. "Everything about this case is a lie," he said. He wrote Paul Dowling, "It bothers me everyday that the truth is being hiden [sic] and innocent men are in prison. This is hell and they don't deserve this."[48]

According to D.J. Hansen, he wasn't any more taken aback by Ballard's confessions to police than he was by Ballard's letter to Karen Stover. "I was just completely ready for that," he says. "That just did not surprise me at all. . . . So many things had happened at that point that nothing was going to surprise me." But while it was a relief to finally have a DNA match, it would, of course, not be easy to reconcile Ballard's statements with the prior confessions, or to fit Ballard with the other guys at all. Yet police and prosecutors found a way. Hansen would argue that the autopsy report and the other physical evidence, including the prostrate position of Michelle's body and the neatness of her apartment, were far more consistent with a gang attack than a single perpetrator. Eight men could have swept her up and carried her to the bedroom without disturbing the apartment more easily than one, he would maintain, and even Ballard, "as powerful and as strong of a person that he is" (actually, he was on the slender side and weighed 150 pounds), couldn't have held her down, raped, strangled, and stabbed her by himself. According to Valerie Bowen, seven assailants restrained her while one got the knife, knocked over the garbage can in the kitchen—spilling the eggshell on the floor—and then set the can back up. The knife pricks were also more consistent "with a bunch of scared nervous sailors" who lost their nerve than "somebody as vicious as Omar Ballard," Hansen contended. "If Omar Ballard was going to do this by himself, a couple of stab wounds would have done the trick," Bowen would tell jurors. As for Ballard's exclusive DNA match, the others might not have climaxed, among other possibilities, although in an interview Hansen could not recall another case of a gang rape where only one attacker left his DNA. And the reason the others never mentioned Ballard was fear. "He was a criminal, I mean, and he was tough," Bowen said. Hansen would even argue that Ballard's statement that "them four people that opened their mouths is stupid" was evidence of their involvement: "Why would Omar Ballard say something like that unless he knew . . . that others participated in this with him?"[49]

On March 13, 1999, two days after Ballard gave his second confession to police, the local *Virginian-Pilot* newspaper reported the arrest of this eighth suspect in the case. "By charging Ballard, investigators have a suspect who, unlike his co-defendants, has a violent criminal history involving attacks on women," the article observed. "Something about this case is inherently wrong," Jennifer Stanton commented. "The prosecution has changed its theory of the crime on more than a few occasions. I fear their theory may change a few times more before we're done." (Yet Stanton believed that Williams, Dick, Wilson, and Tice all stabbed Michelle after egging Ballard on and holding her down so that he could rape her. "I think that they would have thought it was probably really funny and cute to see a black man rape a white woman," she says.) A week later, the *Pilot* reported Ballard's DNA match. "This new evidence confirms what we suspected all along: The statements by the other defendants are lies," another defense attorney told a reporter.[50]

11

"I Would Have Told Them
I Handed Oswald the Gun"

Greg McCormack, Eric Wilson's attorney, had been interested in Omar Ballard for some time. In the summer of 1998, a year after Michelle Moore-Bosko's murder, Tamika Taylor had told a private investigator whom McCormack had hired that he needed to take a look at Ballard. It was apparent to McCormack, who also spoke with Taylor, that she no longer cared for her former longtime friend. Taylor also carried the burden of having put Michelle into contact with Ballard. Now, by March of 1999, McCormack had finally "tracked the son of a bitch down." But how to approach a guy like Ballard? After mulling it over, McCormack decided to simply send him a letter. On March 5, after McCormack's investigator had learned of Ballard's letter to Karen Stover confessing to Michelle's murder, McCormack's co-counsel, Russell Woodlief, wrote Ballard at the Augusta Correctional Center, where, lo and behold, he was doing time for rape. "I represent an individual who has been accused of crimes involving a Mrs. Michelle Bosko," Woodlief informed Ballard. "It has come to my attention that you may know something of this situation. I would be very eager to speak with you about this matter."[1]

Ballard not only knew the matter intimately, but he knew what to do when somebody wanted something from him. "Matter of fact I know the whole situation," he wrote Woodlief. "*Only I* hold information, that I can live or die with." But he had a few questions for Woodlief and McCormack before he went any further: "If your client is innocent, why is he locked up? Why would he make any statements? Why would he mention anything about the case, when, if he knows nothing? . . . How does he know Michelle Bosko anyway?" And, most importantly, "Why should I tell *you* anything? What has your client done for me since I been locked up? Nothing at all."[2] That last part encapsulated Ballard's attitude at the time.

If Wilson wanted to get out of jail so bad, Ballard told Woodlief, he needed to send him three hundred dollars "as soon as you read this." Then he would tell Woodlief and McCormack everything he knew. "This is a money thing now, it's business, because some stupid people put themselves in this matter," Ballard wrote, rather memorably. If the lawyers showed his letter to the police or failed to send him the money, he warned, he wouldn't tell them anything at all. "It's your call. . . . What's $300 for your freedom? What's $300 when you dead?" In his interview with Detectives Ford and Peterson on March 11, the day after writing this letter, Ballard told them about Woodlief's letter and his response, but claimed that he hadn't asked the lawyers for any money, and indeed that he wasn't looking for any money from the case. Based on his remarks about the two letters, Norfolk police had officials at Augusta go through Ballard's belongings, and they intercepted Ballard's letter to Woodlief before he had a chance to mail it. D.J. Hansen would argue later that Ballard solicited a bribe to testify falsely in Wilson's trial.[3]

When Danny Shipley, Danial Williams's attorney, learned of Ballard's talk of stupid people confessing to something they didn't do, his statements taking sole responsibility for the crime, his lack of connection with the other defendants, and, most significantly, his DNA hit, he decided it was a new ballgame. He now had something to work with, and something big. And, was "Denial" actually innocent? That was an unnerving thought, especially for an attorney who'd just pled his client out to life in prison without the possibility of parole. But Shipley became convinced of Williams's innocence. Now all those negative DNA results before Ballard made sense. Shipley and his co-counsel, Bob Frank, advised Williams that they could file a motion to withdraw his guilty plea based on the newly discovered evidence of Ballard's guilt. "I really wanted to get this plea withdrawn and try this case," Shipley remembers. The picture had changed substantially, he and Frank counseled Williams. "We said, 'You've got a much better shot than you had before,'" Shipley recounts. But such motions were seldom granted, Shipley and Frank pointed out, and if his was,

Williams would again be facing the threat of the death penalty. "There was a lot of ambivalence there, at least on my part," Frank recalls.[4]

Shipley and Frank gave Williams a copy of Ballard's letter to Karen Stover. "What's this?" Williams asked them. "Go ahead and read it," they urged him, interested in seeing his reaction. "I'm skimming over it," Williams recounts. "And it's like, 'You know, this don't make no sense to me.'" Then, "I see Michelle's name. And it's like, 'What? *He did it? He confessed in a letter?*' And I was like, 'Hey, you need to get rid of this plea agreement. Talk to him.'" But "I had a hard time convincing them even to put the motion in." Frank, at least, said "that it wasn't a good idea." So "I actually had to turn around and tell them, 'Get it into court. I want to drop it.'"[5]

On April 14, Frank filed a motion to withdraw Williams's plea. It had been "improvidently entered," he argued, "particularly in light of recent exculpatory revelations." In a brief in support of the motion, Frank stated that Williams had pled to ensure that he wouldn't get the death penalty. Nowhere did Frank say that Williams was actually innocent. And at a hearing on April 28, Frank's ambivalence came through and he made a fervorless, perfunctory pitch to get the plea set aside. He still feared losing Williams, still thought he was guilty, and his heart didn't seem in it. Asked if there would be any testimony, Frank replied, "The court may wish to hear from Mr. Williams." "That's up to you," Judge Charles E. Poston pointed out. "It's your case." "We won't put him on then," Frank said. He hadn't prepared Williams to testify.[6]

Assistant Commonwealth's Attorney Valerie Bowen made a more impassioned plea for denying the motion. Williams was "not uneducated," he'd acknowledged his guilt, he'd signed a thorough stipulation of facts, three other defendants had implicated him, he'd "stalked" Michelle, and "there isn't anything particularly new in the case that this defendant wasn't aware of or should have been aware of," she contended, implying that he should have known all about Ballard. And setting aside his plea would "open a can of worms" since if Williams received the death penalty he could argue in a habeas petition challenging the legality of his imprisonment that his lawyers had been ineffective. Before Judge Poston gave Williams his two life terms at the end of the hearing, which was attended by Michelle's sobbing mother supported by her father, Bowen went on to say that what Williams had done to a fellow sailor's wife was "cowardly." He "obviously couldn't do this by himself.

He had to go in there with a number of other people." And "he's shown no remorse whatsoever." (It is difficult for an innocent person to show remorse, but this typically does not help his sentence.) Rather, Williams had now changed his story "to suit his particular needs and desires."[7]

Poston, a white-haired, square-jawed, even-tempered, and approachable fifty-three-year-old who was half of a Norfolk power couple (his wife was chairperson of the Norfolk school board and would soon be elected president of the Virginia Bar Association), rejected Williams's motion. Too little, too late, he ruled, in essence. Williams's plea had been "voluntarily and intelligently made," he'd signed the stipulation and sworn that it was true, and "I don't see this new evidence as a defense to his case in light of the statements he's made" and the stipulation. Moreover, Williams's fear of the death penalty was not sufficient grounds for withdrawing his plea, Poston said, and "he has never asserted his innocence before this court." Poston believed that Williams was, in fact, guilty. The young man had confessed more than once and had had plenty of time to reconsider his initial confession away from the interrogation room. When Frank told Poston, "I accept your denial," his mixed emotions, perhaps even satisfaction with the ruling, were poles apart from his client's dashed hopes.[8]

According to Michael Fasanaro, when he learned of Ballard's confessions he immediately told his client Joe Dick all about them and their ramifications— "I went through everything with him"—and advised him that he didn't have to enter his guilty plea as planned. In Fasanaro's recounting, Dick replied, "Mike, I was involved in this crime. I have to plead guilty." But Dick emphatically calls Fasanaro's account *"bullshit"* and says that he now wanted to go to trial but that Fasanaro persuaded his parents that it would be best to enter his plea—"that's just a categorical untruth," Fasanaro responds—and that they talked him into it. Ballard or no Ballard, he would still probably be sentenced to death if he went to trial, Fasanaro counseled Dick. Fasanaro told Patricia Dick that Joe didn't want to put her through the emotional rigors of a trial and wished to spare her and Joe Sr. the public embarrassment. Fasanaro claims that he immediately notified Dick's parents of Ballard's confessions, but they say he never contacted them and that they did not learn about Ballard until later. He was not surprised by Ballard's DNA hit, Fasanaro commented to a reporter. He believed that Ballard was the black man Dick had earlier mentioned to police.[9]

With Fasanaro, his parents, the prosecutors, and the police all leaning on him to plead guilty, Dick entered his plea on April 21. "I am pleading guilty because I am in fact guilty of these charges," Dick indicated on an advice form; he could have taken an Alford plea declaring that he was pleading guilty simply because he did not want to risk a trial. When asked by D.J. Hansen in court two months later why he pled guilty, Dick replied, "Because I have a conscience. My conscience was bothering me and it was the right thing to do." Fasanaro told a reporter who asked him about Dick's plea that on top of Dick's confessions, two co-defendants were prepared to testify against him, but, in reality, none were now. The evidence against Dick was "overwhelming," Fasanaro remarked to the reporter. (Asked later what evidence he was referring to, Fasanaro said he didn't remember making the remark.) Although prosecutors said nothing about Ballard in their summary of the case, Fasanaro failed to point that out.[10]

Many people were taken aback by Dick's plea. His aunt Theresa Bankard-Sharpe was heartsick over it. She couldn't understand why he'd plead guilty to something he didn't do ("a bad lawyer," she would conclude). Greg McCormack, Eric Wilson's attorney, was "absolutely shocked." There was "no physical evidence that supports Joe Dick's statement," he told a journalist. "I definitely have a problem with what's going on." (Fasanaro responds that McCormack "perhaps doesn't know his ass from his elbow either.") One problem, McCormack knew, one that worried him, was that Dick might now be called to testify against Wilson at his trial. Dick's agreement required him to "cooperate fully" with police and prosecutors and to "testify truthfully against any co-defendants, if needed" (though Dick did not realize that meant he had to testify in court). Fasanaro told a reporter that he didn't expect prosecutors to call Dick to the stand since he'd given so many conflicting accounts, and D.J. Hansen would tell McCormack that he wouldn't be putting Dick up there. But McCormack didn't place great stock in either remark. And what would Dick say in the witness box? Two pugnacious men, McCormack and Fasanaro had words outside the courtroom after Dick pled. "He berated me in public about pleading him guilty," Fasanaro recounts. Fasanaro accused McCormack of telling somebody else that he would personally write Dick's habeas petition against Fasanaro for ineffective assistance of counsel ("totally ludicrous!" McCormack replied). Fasanaro also warned McCormack that, by taking Wilson's case to trial, he was just walking his client into a death sentence. Dick declined to talk to McCormack, despite McCormack's entreaties to Fasanaro to arrange an interview. "He was trying to get to my client, and I didn't appreciate that," Fasanaro recalls.[11]

When a reporter asked her about Dick's plea, Valerie Bowen responded, "Not a lot of innocent people confess and plead guilty." She's right, but they're not as rare as one might think. And, typically, they plea to avoid the death penalty. Some incriminate themselves on the stand like Dick and Derek Tice. After a frightened and worn-down twenty-two-year-old named Chris Ochoa falsely confessed to a 1988 murder and rape to avoid the death penalty, he pled guilty and testified graphically for the prosecution at his co-defendant's trial (sickening the victim's mother, who fled the courtroom). Like Fasanaro, Ochoa's attorney believed that his client was guilty and persuaded his mother to get him to take the plea, which Ochoa did after the stress landed his mother in the hospital. The soft-spoken Ochoa even stuck to his lie in an interview with police ten years later because he feared hurting his chances of gaining parole. He was freed after serving twelve years behind bars, however, when an Innocence Project exonerated him. He later went to law school and became an attorney.[12]

Following his plea, Dick fingered Ballard. It was expected of him. He could now even identify Ballard since Detective Ford had shown him photos of Ballard. The account Dick offered—"the whole story," Bowen would call it—was another fantastic one. But he believed it to be true—or he came to believe it after concocting and telling it. It racked his conscience, he says. The way Jennifer Stanton, John Danser's attorney, heard the tale in a meeting with Dick and Fasanaro in May, and the way Dick subsequently laid it out in court, after Michelle had told them to go away, Dick and the others had come upon Ballard as he was traipsing through her parking lot. He didn't know Ballard at the time, Dick said. Nor had he seen Tice, Danser, Richard Pauley, or Geoffrey Farris before—"as the case progressed I learned their names through my attorney," he testified. After they'd told Ballard of Michelle's rebuff, Ballard had boasted that he could get them inside. All eight had then gone up to her front door. "As far as we knew, it was just to see what color her panties were," Dick said, and to listen to some music with Michelle. Ballard warned them that if they ever said anything about his presence, "we were next," Dick testified. Ballard had knocked and identified himself, and Michelle had opened her door. They had all then charged in, raped her ("I'm not sure of the order,"

Dick stated), and stabbed her (except for Wilson, Dick thought, though he wasn't sure of that either) with a knife that he first saw in Wilson's hand. One of them may have sat down on the living room floor and listened to some CDs before leaving, Dick stated. He also told Stanton that little subplot he had offered police and Bowen during their meeting at the Norfolk police station a year earlier about intending to dispose of Michelle's body, only to return to her apartment to pick it up and find her front door locked. "It would have happened that way," Stanton thought. "Just so stupid, and very Three Stooges." Stanton, too, figured that Ballard was the black guy Dick had mentioned earlier.[13]

Dick now calls this account "a bunch of baloney. That never happened. That's something I was telling the cops so I could get them off my back. Because every time I made a new statement to them, even though Fasanaro was present and all, it's like they're still on my back." He adds, "Everything I told Ford's a bunch of bullshit. With the exception of me denying it."[14]

When Allan Zaleski, Tice's attorney, heard about Ballard, he didn't know what to make of the whole thing. "Well, this is getting to be a very strange situation," he ruminated. "I mean, we're set to plead guilty on the fifteenth of April and I don't know what to do about this new information," he told a journalist. Zaleski already had a deal, and Tice had not only incriminated himself in open court but confessed to the cops several times. If Tice backed out now, Zaleski worried, he'd probably get convicted, possibly even executed. Zaleski still wanted the deal, but he also wanted to find out more about Ballard, so he filed for a continuance of Tice's case until the afternoon of May 7.[15]

Tice thought that Ballard's confessions and DNA match meant that the police would stop harassing him and that he'd be released. Or, barring that—and he'd gotten more cynical about the legal system—at least a jury would realize that he was innocent. Whatever happened, he wasn't going to prolong the charade of professing involvement in a crime that he didn't commit. "I couldn't keep up with the many lies that I was telling," he recalled. "I couldn't remember who I told what to or the order of how we went into the [bed]room or what the room looked like. I couldn't remember any of the details. I can't possibly get up there and lie anymore and be believable. There's no way. . . . I'm tired of lying and whatever happens, happens." In a statement Zaleski put together that was filed on the morning of May 7, Tice said that he was aware that if he got convicted he would receive either life in prison or the death penalty, and that he had orally agreed to the plea agreement, but that he had weighed his options very carefully and had decided to try his case against his attorney's advice. The reason—and this Tice wrote on two blank lines at the bottom of the statement in longhand—was "that I was not there and that I lied to Ford when I made my statements . . . due to the fact that I was scared out of my right frame of mind." "I thought your client was smart," Valerie Bowen remarked dryly to Zaleski when Tice withdrew his plea.[16]

Zaleski felt that he had no choice but to step aside. He'd gone too far with the plea and vouching for Tice's statements to try the case. "I felt I was too much committed down that road to effectively represent him [and say] that 'No, he didn't do it, he wasn't there,'" Zaleski recounts. He told Rachel Tice that he'd be a better witness for her son than a lawyer now.[17]

Meanwhile Omar Ballard had been insisting to his attorney, Lyn Simmons, a willowy, attractive, and self-assured black woman from Norfolk who had previously been a prosecutor and would become one again, that he had committed the crime alone. But how could that be? Simmons wondered. The others had confessed, and she'd read their confessions and other material on the case. Plus she was friendly with both Valerie Bowen and D.J. Hansen and had spoken with them about the case. "I didn't think Omar Ballard was the only one involved," Simmons remembers. "The crime scene pictures—you know, it just didn't seem that it was a one-person deal." Simmons thought Michelle's bedroom looked "pretty disheveled." She was aware that people sometimes confess falsely to crimes, but they were usually people with fairly low IQs, she reasoned, and "I didn't think these guys were the kinds of people who would confess to something as serious as this if they had *no* involvement." Moreover, Simmons knew that Ballard had failed a polygraph on one of his statements to police that he'd committed the crime by himself. Dick's story about Ballard meeting up with the others in Michelle's parking lot and getting them inside made sense to Simmons; when interviewed for this book, she firmly believed it. "I thought the parking lot scenario was really what happened," she recounts. "It just seemed the only real plausible explanation. . . . To me, it fits all the facts. It fits everything." She believed that Ballard was taking sole responsibility for the crime because he didn't want to be labeled a snitch in a maximum-security prison.[18]

When his own lawyer wouldn't believe him, then added insult to injury by talking down to him, Ballard's indignation swelled. He thought Simmons and her co-counsel, Cathy Krinick, were stereotyping him as ignorant, depraved, a liar. "My lawyers thought I was a reprobate," he recounts. "Everything I said was ignored to some degree. When I told them that I did it alone, they repudiated what I was saying. So what was I to do but stop talking and listen to them?"[19]

But Ballard refused to consider a plea agreement. "He wanted to try the case, and if they gave him the death penalty, that would be fine," Simmons remembers. He'd worked it all out with himself and was unbending. One didn't tell Omar what to do. Simmons, who felt a life sentence was a win, told Ballard that she'd be destroyed emotionally if they went to trial and he received death. "This case really wrecked me," she recalls.[20]

When police phoned the Boskos in Pittsburgh to report that Ballard had been arrested for Michelle's murder and rape and that his DNA matched the evidence, Pat Bosko took her son Billy away from the house for a few hours. She knew how upset he was going to be when she gave him the news, and she didn't want him around his two younger siblings. Telling him about Ballard was one of the hardest things she'd ever had to do. "I was just absolutely enraged," Billy would recall. He'd faced down a lynch mob outside his apartment to protect Ballard after Ballard had assaulted Melissa Morse, and two weeks later the scumbag kills his wife? "I flipped out when I got the word," Bosko recounted. "I started throwing stuff and breaking stuff. I couldn't believe it." Although he was glad that there was finally a DNA match, Billy didn't believe that Ballard had acted alone either. Not for a minute. He was certain that all eight defendants were guilty. He wanted them to suffer horrible fates, just as Michelle did. God forgives, but he didn't. "I was so angry that Ballard had decided that he was going to say he acted alone," Billy's sister, Sarah, remembers. "That angers me so much."[21]

In most capital cases in which a miscarriage of justice is uncovered, the real perpetrator confesses, often when incarcerated for another crime, as Ballard was.[22] And Ballard was virtually shouting out his guilt to anyone who talked to him. In the infamous Central Park jogger case, five teenage boys who falsely confessed to attacking a female jogger and who were subsequently convicted were freed from prison after a serial rapist, Matias Reyes, said that he was solely responsible and his DNA alone was found to match semen recovered from the scene. Like Ballard, Reyes did not know the other defendants, who had not mentioned him in their confessions. And, as in this case, there were major discrepancies between the confessions, which contradicted the crime facts. After other exculpatory evidence surfaced, the Manhattan District Attorney's office joined a defense motion to vacate the boys' convictions. But D.J. Hansen and Valerie Bowen weren't about to back off. Whatever they really thought about the veracity of Ballard's confessions, it would not help their reputations to admit to prosecuting seven innocent people, and now putting two of them away for life.

In other cases, however, innocent people have been released from prison when the exonerating evidence was less compelling. Scores of men wrongfully convicted of rape have been freed after DNA recovered from the victim was found to match someone else. But frequently when DNA analysis has excluded a defendant, prosecutors have pooh-poohed its value, changed their theories of the crimes to fit the test results, or, if the case went to trial, argued that the test results would not have affected the verdict. Prosecutors have often used a double standard: if DNA testing establishes guilt it is solid evidence, but if it establishes innocence it is dubious, particularly if there is other alleged evidence of guilt. And after obtaining a conviction, the natural tendency of prosecutors is to feel that justice has been done. But an evolution is unfolding across the country: driven in part by public dismay over wrongful convictions—which DNA testing has shown to occur far more frequently than most people had imagined—prosecutors and legislators who were once resistant to postconviction DNA testing increasingly view it as a legal safeguard.[23]

Actually, Hansen and Bowen did back off to a degree, but only because they were forced to. After doing a U-turn and choosing to go to trial, Tice refused to testify against Pauley, Farris, and Danser. With Dick's credibility worn thin, the commonwealth no longer had a case against those three, and in mid-May it "nol-prossed" their cases (meaning, it discontinued them but reserved the right to recharge them later). In a holding area before the hearing, Pauley and Farris were not even sure of each other's identity. Such was the nature of the conspiracy. Pauley and Farris had been jailed for over ten months, Danser for almost seven. They had been offered the option of pleading straight up to rape only, which would have precluded any chance of getting hit with a capital murder charge again, but had turned it down. Prosecutors rarely reinstate charges after they have been nol-prossed; Jennifer Stanton found the prospect of Danser being recharged "laughable." She dared prosecutors to take

Danser's case to trial. Though she wanted him out of jail, "if my client was not looking at the death penalty, I would have loved to have taken that case to trial and broken it off in their ass," she recalls. "I mean, it was *just that insane*."[24]

Pauley, Farris, and Danser emerged from jail with a sense of immense relief. They had been scared to death about their fates, grown weary of waiting for trial dates that seemed to be continually postponed, and wanted to put their nightmares as far behind them as they could. Indeed, they wished to forget that the whole thing had ever happened. They'd also become leery of the legal system. "It made me rather suspicious of the police department, that's for sure," Pauley remembers. "I still don't understand how all this could have ever happened, how they could do this to you—you know, they didn't even have any evidence or anything." Pauley moved to Australia to be with his girlfriend that July.[25]

The nol-prossing outraged the Boskos and Michelle's parents. Billy Bosko entertained the thought of hunting down Pauley, Farris, and Danser himself. Sarah Bosko was incensed that Tice had decided to let them walk. Years later, Carol Moore still wanted them rounded up.[26]

Michael Fasanaro was disappointed too. "I felt that they were involved in the murder," he remembers. "Joe insisted they were involved." Fasanaro had "no doubt" that all eight defendants were guilty. "I mean, I have no question about this case," he says.[27]

Despite the nol-prossing, Hansen and Bowen would prosecute Wilson and Tice under the theory that Pauley, Farris, and Danser had participated in the murder and rape.

Eric Wilson's trial was held in Norfolk Circuit Court, Judge Charles Poston presiding. On the left side of the courtroom, facing Poston, sat Wilson's nervous parents and brother, who had traveled 1,600 miles from Texas. On the right side were Michelle's bereft mother and father, who had come from Pittsburgh, along with Billy Bosko's mother and sister. It was a tragic case, Poston thought as he surveyed the room from the bench. Good, solid citizens on both sides, equally stricken with grief.[28]

Two days before the trial opened on Wednesday, June 16, prosecutors reduced Wilson's murder charge from capital to first degree. He would no longer be facing the death penalty. But life in the penitentiary—which Greg McCormack advised Wilson that he'd get if convicted—struck him as worse.

He'd been in jail for over a year, hated it of course, and here he was stuck in an isolation cell at the Norfolk jail for his trial, no one really to talk to, no television, radio, or books, his nerves about as raw as they'd ever been. "Wow, this could be the rest of my life," Wilson thought. "And I never even met this woman. And I never even seen this woman. And I could be spending the rest of my life just like this sitting on my bunk—four walls and a sink." There was no way in hell that he was going to let that happen. The reduction of the murder charge came as a huge relief to McCormack. At least he couldn't lose Eric.[29]

After opening statements, Valerie Bowen led Billy Bosko through a re-counting of his relationship with Michelle, a description of their apartment, his plans to meet her at the pier following his naval cruise, and his discovery of her dead body upon his return. The prim and proper Bowen, a slender, angular woman with short blond hair who had graduated from the University of Richmond's law school, did not have an easy way in the courtroom, particularly in the early going in trials. She tended to have rough starts. "She's not the best lawyer," the attorney James Broccoletti comments. "I don't think she makes a great presentation," though she could be humorous and engaging outside court. She didn't carry the same self-confidence and aura of certitude that D.J. Hansen did when he entered the courtroom; there was more gray in her world. In his cross-examination of Bosko, McCormack underscored the orderly state of Michelle's apartment—no sign of a gang attack there—and pointed the finger at Omar Ballard, who, he suggested, Michelle would have allowed in.[30]

After Investigator Wayne Bryan laid out the crime scene for the prosecution and Dr. Elizabeth Kinnison described the autopsy results, Bowen called Tamika Taylor to the stand. Taylor's hair was dyed bright blue one day during the trial and pink another; she was "dressed like a hooker straight off the street," McCormack recalls. Bowen had Taylor inform jurors of Danial Williams's purported obsession with Michelle and the lascivious way that he allegedly looked at her.[31]

Then the prosecution's essential witness—his orange jail jumpsuit drooping on his gangly frame, his wrists handcuffed, his "memory" refreshed by a two-hour meeting that he'd had with the prosecutors and Detectives Ford and Wray two days earlier (and another meeting the week before—he'd talked to prosecutors and police "countless" times by now)—shuffled over to the witness box. Joseph Dick was a striking witness. Something didn't seem right about him, and it was hard to take your eyes off him. He appeared to McCormack to be "a basket case," as if "his brain was fried on something" or physically damaged. "There's something *seriously, seriously* wrong with this guy," McCormack thought. "He is *not* all there." "He looked like a whipped puppy," William Wilson, Eric's father, recalls. Asked by Hansen if he knew Wilson, Dick said yes. But at the time of the murder, he hadn't known Wilson's last name, Dick stated. "We were pretty good in the way of friends," though, he claimed. The evening of Michelle's murder, as he was cooking dinner, Dick said, Wilson arrived at his apartment to visit Williams's ill wife, Nicole. Nicole wasn't home, so Dick invited Wilson to stay for dinner. After dinner, Wilson left, then returned after Danial and Nicole had arrived and Nicole had gone to bed. Tice, Pauley, Farris, and Danser had shown up minutes later. After he and the others had failed to get into Michelle's apartment and then run into Ballard in the parking lot, Dick testified, they'd all rushed in on her and raped her. Though he didn't believe that Wilson stabbed Michelle, Dick said that he saw Wilson holding the knife to her throat while Williams was forcing her to give him a blow job.[32]

Wilson had known that Dick was going to implicate him, but it was disturbing to hear Dick's actual words. "I just couldn't believe that he would lie like that," Wilson recounts. When it came his turn to examine Dick, McCormack didn't waste any time slicing him up. "Mr. Dick, you would agree you are a liar, correct?" was his first question. "Yes," Dick replied. Dick acknowledged giving false accounts of the crime numerous times and lying in court. "Because Joseph Dick does not want to die, correct?" McCormack stated. "Yes," Dick responded. But "I'm doing this because I want to do it," he insisted, not because he was trying to satisfy his plea agreement. Dick agreed with McCormack that he was avoiding the death penalty by testifying, however, and, indeed, that he was putting himself in a better position to ask for less than life at his sentencing. (Ford had told Dick that he would try to get him a better sentence if he testified, Dick remembers.) It was McCormack's perception that Dick really believed his account of the crime, and Dick now says that he testified against Wilson because "through Michael Fasanaro and Glenn Ford I was led to believe that I was guilty." When he gave the same description of the crime to a corrections officer the following month, he expressed remorse. In his cross-examination of Dick, McCormack ridiculed Dick's account and his conflicting statements. "Dick made a horrible witness," McCormack recalls. "I chewed his butt in that court. He had, in my mind, zero—zero—credibility."[33]

Prosecutors next called Detective Steve Hoggard. The mild-mannered officer recounted Wilson's interrogation and confession of a year earlier in some detail. When Hansen played the tape recording of the confession, jurors were riveted. In his cross of Hoggard, McCormack tried to suggest that what Wilson had actually given police was a coerced persuaded false confession in the form of a dream.[34]

To try to keep Wilson's lead interrogator, Detective Ford, off the stand, Mc-Cormack had a former homicide detective outside court ready to testify on false confessions if Ford testified. "Every time Ford is in the hallway, my guy is right there," McCormack remembers. "And he knew who the hell he was." (McCormack and Ford did not care for each other. At a pretrial hearing, Mc-Cormack had asked Ford, "You deny telling [the informant] Garey Kelly I am an asshole?" "No, sir, I don't deny that," Ford responded with a smile. "I said you were an asshole, sir.") Ford did not take the stand.[35]

The defense's first witness was Omar Ballard. But when McCormack asked him if he knew Michelle Moore-Bosko, Ballard took the fifth on the advice of Lyn Simmons. He was excused.

Judge Poston then informed the jury of a defense exhibit showing that only Ballard's DNA had been found in Michelle and at the crime scene. Wilson's had not, the jurors learned. But "the absence of DNA evidence may or may not be indicative of whether a particular person was present at a crime scene," Poston advised them. Poston also ruled that three documents in which Ballard confessed to the crime—his statements to police on March 4 and 11 and his letter to Karen Stover—along with his intercepted letter to Russell Woodlief demanding three hundred dollars to talk about the murder were admissible as evidence.[36]

McCormack next called Wilson. It was important that the jury hear Wilson say unequivocally that he was innocent, McCormack felt. "I was utterly terrified," Wilson recounts. "My entire life was going to be decided right then, by people I didn't know. And the only glimpse they have of me is what they see right there." After Wilson discussed his background and family in a steady voice, McCormack abruptly asked him: "Did you rape Michelle Moore-Bosko?" "No, sir, I did not," Wilson replied. "Did you in any manner participate in her murder?" "No, sir, I did not." Wilson described his interrogation and Ford's intimidating style. Then once more: "Eric Cameron Wilson, are you guilty of these charges?" "No, sir, I'm not."[37]

Wilson calmly held his ground under Valerie Bowen's cross-examination, which was often groping and didn't go well for her. Her voice quivered at times. When she asked Wilson with a dose of sarcasm if Ford had physically tortured him into giving his account, Wilson shot back, "Describe torture." He challenged Hoggard's retelling of the interrogation. "What I told him was true," Wilson said of his alleged problem with blackouts. "What he said to the jury was not." Wilson declared that he would have confessed to killing Michelle in addition to raping her if Ford and Hoggard had told him how she was murdered. "If they had told me that I killed JFK, I would have told them I handed Oswald the gun," he said. (To Carol Moore—who had been led to believe by Joe Dick's stories that Wilson "wanted to take my daughter out and do satanic rituals on her"—that statement "didn't make any sense.") "What about the part where you described that the victim was yelling, 'Stop, stop,' and that she looked up to you as if to ask for help?" Bowen asked. "What about it?" Wilson replied. By the time Bowen had finished her cross-examination of Wilson, she was plainly upset.[38]

Outside the courthouse later, McCormack and Woodlief told the Wilsons that they thought Eric was going to walk. He had presented himself well: straightforward, accurate, no wavering, good eye contact. But in her closing argument, Bowen zeroed in on his confession. "Innocent people do not confess," she stressed. "This confession, ladies and gentlemen, says it all."[39] Wilson's trial had lasted all of three days.

After the jurors had deliberated for a short time, Poston dismissed them for the weekend. They resumed deliberations on Monday morning. With a worried look on his face, McCormack told Ramey Wilson, Eric's mother, "That jury is sitting back there playing that tape, and playing that tape, and playing that tape." That's precisely what it was doing. If all the jurors had was a transcript of Eric's confession, McCormack thought, Eric's chances would be a lot better.[40]

At 11:10 A.M. on Monday, the jurors filed back into the courtroom. "It took every ounce of energy and control I had just to keep my composure when they walked in," Wilson recounts. "I was afraid to stand up, my knees were shaking so bad." Not guilty of murder, guilty of rape, Poston announced. A drained and shell-shocked Wilson put his head in his hands. His confession, he knew, though his brain was barely functioning, had done him in. "There were points in the confession—how he felt and how he was angry—that we felt showed that there was genuine emotion," the jury's foreman revealed afterward. "He wasn't making that up."[41] So persuasive was Wilson's confession that it had overridden a potent triad of exculpatory evidence: DNA, the absence of any other physical indications of his involvement, and Ballard's own confessions (jurors didn't get to hear the police tapes of those).

The commonwealth called Billy Bosko and Carol Moore to the stand before jurors recommended Wilson's sentence. "It is hard to even do my daily routine," Moore testified. "My two boys, I can't even give my whole self to them. It is not fair. We go to the cemetery to bring her [Michelle] flowers and balloons every week. And I can't even function at work." When Michelle had cracked the door to her apartment, Bowen argued, "the bums rushed in. And this defendant was one of them." Wilson "obviously made the wrong decision," McCormack said in a plea for leniency.[42]

To the surprise of most observers, the divided jury recommended a prison sentence of only eight and a half years. "I think the sentence may have been some kind of compromise," Bowen commented. Outraged, Carol Moore banged her fist on a bench after the jury departed. "What the hell was this jury thinking?" Billy Bosko, who demanded to speak to Poston, fumed. But McCormack and Wilson breathed a sigh of relief; in fact, McCormack was thrilled. In his mind, he'd won the case.[43]

On September 8, at Joe Dick's sentencing hearing, Patricia Dick read a statement asking for mercy for her son. She had seen the Moores' and Boskos' victim impact statements, she testified (Pat Bosko wanted the "eight monsters" who she believed had killed Michelle to be tortured and put to death), and could "totally understand their feelings." But Joe was, at root, a "good person," she pleaded. Because of his naïveté and gullibility, "he became friends with the wrong person"—Danial Williams—"and was easily led to make egregious errors in judgment because he wanted to belong," she stated. "I apologize to the members of Michelle Bosko's family for my son's participation in this crime." Patricia still thought Joe was guilty.[44]

Michael Fasanaro spoke next. "I don't usually give long arguments . . . but this is a case that I think requires me to emphasize everything that I possibly can on behalf of Joseph Dick," said the lawyer who had urged his innocent client to take a plea and helped persuade him of his guilt. "Joseph Dick, from day one when he was questioned by the authorities, admitted his guilt," Fasanaro claimed, although Dick had repeatedly professed his innocence to him. At first Dick had implicated only himself and Williams because "he was the type of individual who simply would not share the blame with other people," Fasanaro argued. He had gone through a lot as a kid, been "teased and ridiculed . . . and you can understand why." But Joe had "a heart of gold," Fasanaro said. With Moore-Bosko's murder, he had "wanted to be a part of a group, but when this group got out of hand he found himself in the midst of it." Since his arrest, however, Joe had been "the only person who has not attempted to duck his responsibility," Fasanaro stated. He had made himself available to police "time and time again," "never once shirking his role"; he had gone "the last mile." Over a year earlier, he had even told police about a black man's involvement, and "boy, that has borne out to be the truth." He had testified in court and "stands willing to testify in any other case," Fasanaro assured Judge Poston. And unlike Williams and Tice, he had not attempted to withdraw his plea. Although there was "no question about his involvement" and "we don't excuse it," Fasanaro said, and though Dick "deserves incarceration for a lengthy period of time," fifteen to twenty years would be appropriate. Later, Dick wondered why Fasanaro didn't present the DNA evidence of his innocence and Ballard's letter to Karen Stover. But according to Fasanaro, other people "told me that's the best closing argument anyone had ever heard. . . . Judge Poston told everybody it should have been on TV."[45]

After Valerie Bowen argued for two life sentences, Dick himself spoke. "I would like to apologize to the family for what I did, and I know I shouldn't have done it," he said. "I have got no idea what went through my mind that night, and my soul, Your Honor. I cried and cried because of what I have done. Sometimes I have sleepless nights and I keep thinking back to what I should have done that night and I know I was raised better than this and I have accepted the responsibilities for my actions and I ask that you judge me fairly and look at me for who I am as a person and not as an animal, Your Honor." Fasanaro had counseled Dick to offer an apology. But, Dick wrote us, "I apologized to Michelle's family *because I was led to believe that I was guilty* and I thought that it was the right thing to do."[46]

Dick's apology devastated his parents. In his entire life, his son had never once apologized for anything, Joe Sr. reflected, never said he was sorry. So when he apologized for killing and raping Michelle, it was crushing. "That flipped me out," Joe Sr. recounts. "You might as well have just stuck a pistol in my head and put me out. Because that just killed me. . . . When I heard that, it was all I could take."[47]

Then Judge Poston, who felt there was no "credible mitigation" for Dick's involvement in "a vicious, premeditated rape-murder," addressed Dick. "I don't understand how either one of you got into this situation," he said, also referring to Wilson, whose own sentencing hearing would follow that afternoon. For both the murder and rape charges, Poston decreed, "it is the judgment of the court that you shall serve the remainder of your life in the penitentiary."[48]

Those were harsh words to Dick's parents. The door had, for all intents and purposes, already clanged shut. The Dicks would never forget that moment. As her only son was being escorted in restraints out of the courtroom, Patricia appeared to Joe Sr. like she was on the verge of collapse. And with newspeople surely outside, "the only thought that I had in my mind is, 'I've got to get her out of here,'" Joe Sr. recalls. "And 'I want to get as far away from this place as I possibly can. . . . And I damn sure want to get away from Fasanaro.' Well, Fasanaro was closing his brief up. We made it about two-thirds of the way down the hall, and there was this guy, this couple," who approached them. The man had followed them, almost running to catch them before they left. "My prayers are with you," he said, softly.[49]

Who the hell is this guy? Joe Sr. was wondering. Patricia knew who he was: Eric Wilson's father. "Mrs. Dick?" Ramey Wilson had said after they stood up to leave the hearing. "I'm Eric Wilson's mother. I'm very sorry." The Dicks looked to the Wilsons as if they really didn't know what to think anymore. "Your son didn't do this," William Wilson told them. "My son didn't do this. Something is terribly wrong here." Virtually in tears, Joe Sr. thanked him—he was too distraught to say more.[50]

Fasanaro caught up with the Dicks before they got outside the circuit court building. Joe could have received the death penalty, he reminded them. They'd saved his life. And since they'd gotten the murder charge reduced to first degree from capital, Joe would be eligible for geriatric parole, starting at age sixty. In their car later, Joe Sr. told Patricia that the judge's words "the remainder of your life" didn't sound anything like an early release. And if Joe did get out, he added, they'd both be dead by then anyway. Patricia wrote

Fasanaro several weeks later that she'd been under the impression that Joe's sentence would fall within the sentencing guidelines, which ranged from twenty-five to forty-one years. It was Fasanaro who'd given her that impression. Joe "was part of a crime, yes; punishment should be given," Patricia said. But the judge had given no consideration to his cooperation or his basic goodness. "He got in with a wrong crowd and didn't have the maturity or the ability or the guts . . . to go his own separate way," she wrote.[51]

That afternoon, Carol Moore testified at Eric Wilson's sentencing hearing. "The fact that the jury found you not guilty of the murder, even though you were there when our daughter was murdered, is beyond our understanding," she declared. "Why did you choose to run instead of helping her?" Moore called her daughter's attackers "a pack of animals" and said that her family's anger would "never go away. We only hope to have some satisfaction knowing you will suffer in the way our daughter did while you were taking your turn with her." Moore wanted Wilson to die, "basically."[52]

A few days later, Billy Bosko, who continued to suffer from insomnia and paranoia (he had three locks on his door and kept a loaded pistol), filed court papers blaming his former landlord for Michelle's murder. The owners and managers of their apartment complex had promised, but failed to provide, sufficient security, his lawyers contended. Bosko asked for more than $19 million in damages.[53]

12

"You Got Nothing to Say, Right?"

Derek Tice went on trial in February of 2000. At the request of his newly appointed lead counsel, James Broccoletti, a highly capable and likable criminal defense attorney in his late forties with a squarish, bespectacled face and neatly cut brown hair beginning to gray at the sides, the trial was held in Arlington, Virginia. There had been too much publicity over the case in Norfolk. Again, Judge Charles E. Poston presided. Tice's mother and father sat each day on the left side of the courtroom (they evoked compassion in the jury foreman, Randall McFarlane), along with Lea Tice, Tice's girlfriend whom he had married behind bars the previous March. It was a horrible time for Lea. The three-day trial brought back with a vengeance all of the pain, anger, and anxiety she had felt over Derek's ordeal. "I couldn't eat hardly anything but soup that whole week," she recounts. "I spent many a time in the ladies room throwing up during that trial. It was just a lot of stress. Because there were a lot of emotions again; everything was right there." The Moores and the Boskos again sat on the right side of the room. Carol Moore sobbed frequently. McFarlane expected to carry to his grave his memory of her weeping at his elbow as he was examining those awful autopsy photos of her daughter.[1]

Derek Tice was scared but optimistic. So, pretty much, was his father. The engineer in Larry Tice analyzed the case—no physical evidence, Omar Ballard's confessions and DNA match—and told him they shouldn't even be at trial. But, like his son, he was getting cynical about the criminal justice system in Virginia. It smelled. During the trial, which seemed to him to resemble a "weird chess game" focused entirely on winning, he would get the sense that

Judge Poston was on the same side as the prosecutors and police. And Assistant Commonwealth's Attorney Valerie Bowen seemed out to get Derek because his withdrawal of his plea had forced her to let Rick Pauley, Geoffrey Farris, and John Danser go. But Larry knew it was important to keep his composure in the courtroom.[2]

Broccoletti was worried too. He recognized that it would be hard to overcome Derek's confession, which he'd not attempted to suppress because he thought he'd lose that battle while revealing part of his trial strategy. Broccoletti also knew that in Arlington juries usually gave defendants convicted of capital murder the death penalty. And although he went back and forth on Tice's culpability in his own mind, Broccoletti tended to think he was representing an innocent man. That added in no small measure to the pressure he felt.[3]

In his opening statement, the prosecutor D.J. Hansen told jurors how Tice had openly admitted his guilt to police, "laid out the whole chilling scene," and told his accomplices that they couldn't leave Michelle alive. In his own opening, Broccoletti stressed the unreliability of Tice's confession and the absence of any scientific evidence against him. Ballard, Broccoletti asserted, had done it by himself, as shown by the DNA tests.[4]

The pitiable Joe Dick was again the prosecution's key witness. Jeffrey Russell, Broccoletti's co-counsel, a perceptive and guarded sole practitioner with a relaxed but uninspiring manner in the courtroom, found Dick's appearance and demeanor on the stand a bit startling. "He was just tremendously gaunt, and emotionless," Russell recounts. "He was kind of fixed in his eye contact— nothing could describe it as normal at all." When his glassy eyes weren't trained on somebody (usually his examiner), "they were darting all over the place," like Groucho Marx, Broccoletti remembers. To Broccoletti, it seemed as if nobody was really at home. Dick struck Russell as tortured. But Russell didn't know if Dick was tortured because he'd participated in an abominable gang-rape and murder or because he'd "made a deal with the devil to save his life" and thus was in the horrific position of being forced to implicate himself in a crime he didn't commit.[5]

In his jail jumpsuit, Dick told essentially the same story that he'd offered at Wilson's trial. He had seen Tice rape and stab Michelle, he claimed. When Hansen asked him why he was testifying, Dick responded, "Because I'm trying to set things straight. I'm doing this because I want to do it, not because I have to." He'd been coached, but he also still believed that he was guilty. "It didn't cross my mind that I was lying," he said years later.[6]

"Mr. Dick, you are an honest man?" was Broccoletti's first question to him. "No, I'm not," Dick acknowledged. He couldn't even begin to tell the jury how many times he had lied in the past, he admitted. He denied that his plea agreement required him to testify. Broccoletti pointed out countless inconsistencies and falsehoods in Dick's prior statements, but he did not present any evidence that Dick was actually on duty the night of Michelle's murder. He had talked to Dick's attorney, Michael Fasanaro, who had said that Dick had no alibi. While the jurors didn't particularly trust Dick, many thought his hangdog look and expressed desire to set things straight reflected genuine remorse. "His testimony was very effective with some of the jurors," foreman Randall McFarlane remembered.[7]

The next morning, prosecutors called Glenn Ford. The detective recounted Tice's confession at length; Hansen then played the tape recording of it. It was a long and difficult eighteen minutes for Tice and his two attorneys. Jurors were glued to the tape. Under cross-examination, Ford denied threatening Tice with the death penalty or saying that he would try to help him if he confessed.[8]

Police perjury—"testilying"—occurs far more frequently than people are led to believe. "Judges, prosecutors, defense lawyers, and repeat offenders all know that police officers lie under oath," as one law professor writes. They lie with particular frequency in suppression hearings. Some acquire reputations for dishonesty within their own departments. Police, of course, want convictions, they want to win, and they don't want confessions or other evidence thrown out or discredited because of their investigative methods. Professional witnesses, they learn to describe their interrogation techniques in ways that square with the law. They also know that jurors are more likely to believe them than defendants, and that they can get away with lying in court. It is unusual for police to be prosecuted for perjury, or, indeed, to be punished at all. And while judges and prosecutors will talk about police perjury in private, they're less inclined to do so publicly. Both regularly ignore it.[9]

Russell then called Jerry Sellers of the Virginia Division of Forensic Science. Sellers had examined evidence collected from the crime scene and determined what was suitable for DNA analysis. After a dull examination by Russell that probably went nowhere with jurors, Hansen prompted Sellers to tell them that it was possible to have sexual intercourse with someone and not leave any evidence of it. Robert Scanlon, a forensic scientist who conducted the DNA analyses, then educated jurors on DNA testing in detail; he revealed that none of the defendants except Ballard were sources of DNA recovered from the scene. Tice had been excluded. Scanlon spoke of the infinitesimal odds that anyone other than Ballard had caused the stain on the white blanket in Michelle's bedroom or deposited the sperm found in her vagina. But the point—critical as it was to the defense—was diluted by all the numbing detail (the fault was Russell's, not the witness's).[10] The defense did not call any independent experts on DNA analysis or forensic pathology to point out flaws in the prosecution's multiperpetrator theory.

Ballard himself was the next defense witness. Broccoletti had been surprised when Ballard's attorney, Lyn Simmons, had apprised him earlier that Ballard would not be invoking the fifth. He thought she'd given him bad advice. Broccoletti suspected that Simmons had "some secret deal" with the prosecutors, one that would save Ballard's life. "It all was too weird to let that man testify when his case was still pending," Broccoletti mused, unaware that Ballard was doing so against his lawyer's advice. Ballard's testimony worried Broccoletti; Simmons had declined to let him interview Ballard. And his testimony—his "availability," under rules of evidence—could jeopardize admission of his confessions to police. Most rules of evidence—and this reflects a distrust of criminal defense evidence, specifically statements offered to exculpate a defendant—strictly limit the ability of defendants to introduce evidence that a third party confessed to the crime. One exception allows it to be introduced if the third party is unavailable at the time of the trial.[11]

When Ballard stepped into the witness box, two or three muscular deputies flanked him. Handcuffed and bulked up himself (he now "looked like a linebacker for the Washington Redskins," Broccoletti recalled), he exuded anger and defiance. He was a dangerous and violent young man fully capable of committing murder and rape, Broccoletti hoped jurors noticed. In an unusual move, Simmons sat in the box with him. "Mr. Ballard, did you kill Michelle Moore-Bosko?" Broccoletti asked him right off the bat. "No, I didn't," Ballard responded. As for his statements to police that he did it alone, "I wasn't under oath then. I'm under oath now. And I had nothing to do with it," he proclaimed. Asked if he could explain how his DNA ended up at the crime scene and in Michelle, Ballard said no. His testimony reflected his position to Simmons at the time. Also, "my trial was still pending, and I didn't want to say nothing or do nothing . . . that would jeopardize myself," Ballard later recounted. He professed to be telling the truth on the stand now. "He was totally without any credibility," Randall McFarlane, the jury's foreman, remembered. Judge Poston refused to admit into evidence his confessions to police ("he has already testified as to these statements") or his letter to Karen Stover, or to allow Broccoletti to question Ballard about the letter. Poston had earlier rejected a defense motion to admit documents on Ballard's other assaults on women.[12]

Russell then called Robert Morgan, a neighbor of John Danser in Pennsylvania. The defense hoped to cast doubt on Dick's testimony by showing that Danser hadn't been involved in the crime. As far as he could remember, Morgan stated, Danser's vehicles were home on the evening of Michelle's murder and the following morning.[13] It's unlikely that had much impact on jurors.

The defense next called Wayne Kennedy, a former Norfolk homicide detective who had visited the crime scene for the defense and taken measurements of the rooms and photographs. Kennedy attested to the narrowness of the apartment's hallway and the small dimensions of the bedroom, which did not accord well with a gang attack. Poston, who had earlier rejected a defense motion to permit the display of a full-scale wooden model of the bedroom and hallway in the courtroom, refused to admit photographs of Broccoletti and Russell standing in the hallway. He also refused to allow Kennedy to testify before the jury on police interrogation techniques and false confessions. Poston believed that jurors could understand on their own that people sometimes give false statements.[14]

Tice himself did not take the stand. In mock cross-examinations, he had not stood up well. He had not been forceful enough, and too meek, Broccoletti thought. To be effective, Tice needed to be able to tell jurors with conviction that he was innocent, and to respond strongly, even aggressively, under cross-examination. And what would prosecutors do with his other statements to police if he testified? His credibility could be shattered.[15]

In her closing argument, after an awkward start that included an out-of-the-blue mention of Michelle's resemblance to the actress Sandra Bullock, Valerie Bowen spoke of Danial Williams's "thing for Michelle," his black CD case that he left in her apartment the night of her murder (the one whose ownership prosecutors actually never determined), and how the physical evidence was more consistent with a gang attack than a single assailant. "If Omar Ballard was going to do this by himself, a couple of stab wounds would have done the trick," Bowen stated. Dick testified because he had a conscience, she argued—"he has nothing to gain by coming here and testifying." To believe that Ballard was the sole perpetrator, "you have to totally discount Joe Dick's testimony," she told the jurors, to think that Dick confessed on the stand "when he wasn't there. And that makes no sense at all. . . . Joe Dick wasn't here making up a story about an offense that he didn't participate in." Bowen contended that the absence of Tice's DNA didn't mean he was innocent; after all, they hadn't found Dick's DNA either. Most compelling, Tice had confessed in chilling detail. "Do you think if you weren't there . . . that you would say you looked into your victim's eyes and saw that she was pleading for help?" Bowen asked the jurors. She dramatically replayed two snippets of Tice's taped confession, including the incalculably damaging " 'Just go ahead and stab the bitch,' I believe is what I said."[16]

Russell followed by reminding jurors that "not an iota of DNA" matched Derek Tice, "not a nanogram." The close grouping of the three fatal stab wounds, the uniformity of their angle and depth, the lack of bruises on Michelle's body, Ballard's DNA hit—they all showed that Ballard was the sole perpetrator, Russell asserted. Broccoletti then spoke of the pristine condition of Michelle's apartment, those papers sticking out in the hallway, that DNA evidence ("Do you believe Bob Scanlon, or do you believe Joe Dick?"), the contradictions between Dick's and Tice's confessions, their blatant inaccuracies, and Dick's guilty plea to avoid the death penalty (but "now he has convinced himself of it"). Broccoletti laid out a disturbing scenario of how Ballard killed Michelle.[17]

Jurors deliberated for over six hours over two days before reaching a verdict: "We, the jury, find the defendant guilty of capital murder of Michelle Moore-Bosko. We, the jury, find the defendant guilty of rape of Michelle Moore-Bosko." Tice was flabbergasted; he looked down at the table in front of him and shook his head. "It is hard to put into words how I felt when the verdicts were announced," he would recount. "Take every sad or depressive and hurtful feeling that you have had in your life and press them into one nanosecond, and that is only one-hundredth of the way I felt at that time. I wanted to crawl into a corner and die." His parents were sickened and in utter disbelief; Larry Tice felt like he'd been "hit with a Mack truck." What was wrong with these people? Had they sat over there with their eyes and ears closed? It took every ounce of self-discipline that Larry and Rachel Tice could muster not to say anything. Lea Tice, Derek's wife, wept silently. So did Carol Moore, though of course her thoughts were for her daughter; she believed that Derek Tice was "guilty as guilty can be," and so were all eight of them. His growing cynicism aside, Larry Tice had thought that the system would exonerate an innocent person. *What had happened?*[18]

Some of the jurors had puzzled over the orderly state of Michelle's apartment, the absence of any physical evidence tying Tice to the crime, and his lack of a criminal record, among other things. But Tice's confession "just washed everything else away," Randall McFarlane recalled later. "That was the supernova circumstance of the entire trial. It overwhelmed everything else." On a gut level, some jurors were highly skeptical of the whole notion that anybody would falsely confess to a murder and rape. Tice's calm recounting of the crime on tape made McFarlane think of Hannah Arendt's "banality of evil." Tice had no advocates for his innocence on the jury. McFarlane, a banking lawyer, had "no doubt" about his guilt given his confession. Tice was ashamed and wanted to get it off his chest, McFarlane thought.[19]

The presentencing testimony was wrenching. Billy Bosko wept on the stand. "I don't trust anyone anymore," he lamented. "I don't have anything." Carol Moore also broke down. "I don't want to get out of bed," she said. Jurors cried too; the trial was an extraordinarily emotional experience for them. Tice's former rescue squad co-workers in North Carolina, his high school counselor there, and his band director testified to his character, politeness, and dedication. McFarlane was impressed by his rescue work, but other jurors "rightly viewed that a bit sourly, in terms of learning how to save people's lives and then going out and killing someone," McFarlane remembered. Dr. Paul Mansheim, who had conducted a court-ordered psychological evaluation of Tice, predicted that he would not be a danger to others in prison and would adjust well. That made an impression on jurors. "He is a very special man, very kind, caring, loving," Lea Tice said. "I never met anybody like him before." He had never been violent to her, she stated, and "I know in my heart and my mind that he is innocent." "Do you love your son, Mrs. Tice?" Broccoletti asked Rachel Tice at the conclusion of her testimony. "There is not a day that I don't thank God for him," she replied. "If a mother doesn't love her child, she is not a human."[20]

But D.J. Hansen argued that what Tice had done was outrageously and wantonly vile and that he remained a serious danger to society. One of those two conditions was required for imposition of the death penalty. "Imagine the look in her eyes when she heard them say, 'Get the knife,'" Hansen urged the jurors. It "was not an easy death for Michelle." She had been "tortured." Tice had medical training, Hansen pointed out, but he had used his training "to ensure her death, to make sure that they did it right" by telling the others to stab her rather than simply strangle her. "How perverse, how wanton, how depraved." And Michelle had been "robbed of her dignity even in death," as "pictures of her privates" were "now forever part of the public record—forever—and perfect strangers have to look at them because of what this man and his cohorts did." Hansen asked for Tice's execution.[21]

But the emotionally exhausted jury fairly quickly agreed on double life behind bars. "Some of us thought that a life in prison might be worse punishment than if he had a lethal injection tomorrow," one juror said afterward. Tice's favorable background saved him; jurors did not think he was a future threat. McFarlane felt his involvement in the murder and rape was "an unfathomable anomaly in his life."[22]

"I hope he suffers every day in jail," Billy Bosko commented. "I hope he lives a long time." At his sentencing hearing later, Tice offered his sympathies to the Moores and Boskos.[23]

On March 22, Omar Ballard reversed course again and pled guilty to Michelle's murder and rape. In return, he too received two life sentences without parole. He had decided his life was worth living after all, even in prison. "I felt the only way to escape the death penalty was to plead guilty," he later testified. "Well, you finally convicted one guilty guy in this case," Danny Shipley, Danial Williams's attorney, commented with a wry smile to Valerie Bowen after Ballard's plea. Bowen was miffed.[24]

In a debriefing required for his plea agreement, Ballard and Lyn Simmons had met earlier with Detectives Glenn Ford and David Peterson at the Norfolk police station. According to Ballard's later testimony, which Ford disputed, after Ford advised him that he needed to tell them the truth about the crime to get his deal and asked him what the truth was, Ballard responded that it was what he had been telling him all along: he had done it by himself. Ford laughed, Ballard recounted, and assured him that he'd never get his plea agreement if he kept lying. Ford said that he knew Ballard had met up with Williams, Dick, Wilson, and Tice in the parking lot of Michelle's apartment and then led them inside. "He put this story out there for me," Ballard testified. There was no mention of Pauley, Farris, or Danser. After leaving the room for a few minutes, in Ballard's retelling, Ford returned and asked Ballard if he was ready to tell the truth. Yeah, Ballard replied, he had done it by himself. "Well, I guess you don't want your plea agreement," Ford stated. In Ford's version of the debriefing, after he asked Ballard what he had to say, Ballard launched straight into the parking lot story.[25]

However long it took, Ballard eventually told Ford what he wanted to hear. Ballard was sick of nobody believing him, still infuriated by it, and telling the truth seemed to be "all in vain." And he wanted away from Ford for good. "He laid out that scene for me a number of times"—attacking Michelle with the others, though bumping into them in the parking lot was a new wrinkle—"so to get him off of my back, I agreed with him," Ballard says. He figured that neither Ford nor Simmons would accept the truth. And "at the time, I had no one's best interest at heart," except his own. "I'm sure if he had gone through the debriefing and said, 'I did it by myself,' they wouldn't have taken" his plea, James Broccoletti comments.[26]

According to Ford's notes on the debriefing, Ballard stated that when he met up with Williams, Dick, Wilson, and Tice in the parking lot, he bummed a cigarette and they told him that Michelle had refused to let them into her apartment. Ballard said that he could get them inside because he was a friend, he told Ford. He then knocked on her door, and when she opened it "they all rushed in" and raped and stabbed her. "Ballard stated that this was the truth and that the others never told on him because he had told them that he would come back and get them," Ford wrote. "Ballard stated that he had not told this story because he was already in prison and a member of the 5 Percent [nation] and didn't want anyone to know that he had been involved in a crime with white boys." But Ballard later called the tale "totally false" in a legal affidavit. "Nothing in that story was the truth," he testified. But "I just went with [it] because that was the only thing I felt I could do to escape the death penalty."[27]

Under Simmons's counsel, Ballard agreed to take a lie-detector test on the story. "I didn't want to, but I listened to her, being that she was my lawyer and was supposed to have my best interest at heart," Ballard writes. He failed the test. According to both Simmons and Ballard, police then tested him again. He needed to tell them what *really* happened, Ford snapped, in Simmons's recounting. But he failed to pass the second test too.[28]

Imagine the situation: for their different reasons, the police and Ballard's attorney were both trying to validate a story that was malarkey, despite Ballard's repeated assertions that it was bunk and its lack of common sense. Even Carol Moore wondered how a bunch of navy guys got hooked up and plotted a murder and rape with a career criminal like Ballard. It was "the one thing that never made sense, I think, for the family," Carol's brother-in-law says.[29]

Meanwhile, Williams, Dick, and Tice were all in tough straits behind bars. Williams had crawled into a shell. He didn't want to talk about his case with anyone. He'd tell other inmates that he still had an appeal in and couldn't discuss it, though he lost his appeal in July 2000. For his relatives, getting a letter or phone call out of him was like pulling teeth. His aunt Doreen Trevena sent him some letters and cards, but it took him a long time to respond. And she was disappointed in what she finally got from him, given all his free time. His letters were generic notes that said "something about not doing anything." His ex-lawyers never heard one word from him after his sentencing—"no letters, no requests for help, no nothing," Danny Shipley recalls. That surprised them. He didn't seem interested in helping himself. It was as if he wanted to cut himself off from everybody. Did that mean he was guilty? some relatives wondered. "He never has talked openly to us about his case," his mother, Rhea Williams, said in 2003. During prison visits—and no one came to see him but his family every few months—he just wasn't himself. Too quiet. When his grandmother, Helen Frezon, visited, he'd answer her questions but she'd have to lead the conversation. His parents' visits were painful for them. They had plenty of time to think on the long drive from Michigan, and seeing Danial behind prison walls broke their hearts. Norman Williams teared up when talking about it in an interview.[30]

Danial blamed himself for his plight. Like many people who confess to crimes they didn't commit, he was embarrassed about it. And he had always been prone to feeling dumb. "I guess I just really didn't want anybody really to know what had happened," Williams says. "You know, it's due to my stupidity that I'm in here. It was just really due to my stupidity that I confessed to a crime that I didn't commit. And I just don't really like talking about it."[31]

Williams was spending a lot of time watching television and playing cards; he had a job sweeping floors. He dealt with his life in prison "one day at a time," he said. His predicament seemed hopeless to him. After losing his appeal, "none of my lawyers told me that there was anything else I could do to try to overturn my conviction," he recalls.[32]

Joe Dick remained a solitary, detached, and sad figure behind bars. He spent most of his time in voluntary lockdown—"in my bunk sleeping it away" or "laying back watching TV." He also did some reading on military history. He had no close friends and tried to keep to himself. After initially being housed in a penitentiary with the highest level of security that held inmates who'd displayed disruptive, assaultive, or predatory behavior, Dick had ended up in a tough prison only one security level lower. Other inmates continued to take advantage of him there; he acceded to their demands in order to survive. "I have not recieved [sic] any flak from the other inmates but the silence will not last for long," he wrote in 2003. He struck one person who visited him as quite depressed and having clearly suffered through "a rough time." His parents, of course, came to see him, though his dad hated the visits. "I have this attitude that I'm sitting someplace where I shouldn't be," Joe Sr. says. And being under the thumb of guards enraged him. His son had mixed emotions about the visits. "I don't trust my family any farther than I could throw them," he would say, since most of his relatives, and that included his folks, thought he was guilty. "You are the only other person who believes that I am innocent besides myself," he wrote one Michael Black, who contacted him about his case.[33]

Dick had finally come to realize that he'd been duped by police, prosecutors, and his own lawyer. After receiving documents from his case file from Michael Fasanaro in mid-2000 for his own rudimentary legal efforts, he concluded that he couldn't have committed the crime. The conflicting confessions, the autopsy report, the total lack of any physical evidence against him, Ballard's letter to Karen Stover and confessions to police, and, most importantly, the DNA tests—they all pointed to his innocence. "I know that the

DNA evidence tells me that I am not supposed to be in prison but because of some legal reason I was given two life sentences," he told Michael Black. He hoped to "get back in court." Dick wanted to petition for a governor's pardon, but could not afford an attorney: "All I have is DNA."[34]

Derek Tice was having his own struggles: migraine headaches that sometimes caused vomiting, other health problems, stolen possessions, lying snitches, ignored complaints about prison conditions, "racist black captains," and guards who threatened to have him beaten or worse. "If it was up to me, Tice, you would be dead already," a female guard warned him. At one point, Tice would not leave his cell for fear of an orchestrated beating. And he had to endure taunts that he was "a fag"; if he fought in response, the guards could put him in the hole. His clashes with the authorities were incited largely by his complaints over conditions and his father's own protests and crusade to exonerate his son. Larry Tice was writing jail and prison officials, the Virginia Department of Corrections, Norfolk's police chief and mayor, the state Department of Health, national news media—ABC, CBS, NBC, PBS, you name it—members of Congress, the ACLU, the FBI, everybody he could think of. He wrote an article on the case (and two subsequent pieces) for *Justice: Denied*, a magazine on wrongful convictions. His crusade had provoked Billy Bosko, now working as a prison guard, to send him an angry e-mail: "Tice. . . . This is a warning. Do not for a moment disregard this, for it is the only one you shall recieve [sic]. If you or any of your supporters so much as type my name or that of my wife again I will own whatever meager possesions [sic] your so called family posses [sic]. I have contacted my lawyer and have instructed him to proceed at once at my word. . . . First and Last warning." It was like something out of a bad made-for-TV movie. Detective Brian Wray would write Larry: "Have you ever considered publishing accurate information?" Larry, who had begun to think that the whole justice system was just flat-out corrupt, vowed to fight "until Derek is free, or I'm in my grave."[35]

Larry's crusade had brought him and Derek closer together. They had not connected well when Derek was a boy. But after Derek had been jailed his father had written him a letter in which he had told him that he loved him and was behind him one hundred percent. "That kind of opened up the doors for our relationship to grow into what it is now," Derek remembers.[36]

But Derek and his wife were growing apart. Lea had been nearly destroyed by Derek's conviction. She had believed that he would eventually get himself out of the jam he had put himself in by talking to police without a lawyer present and giving them a statement. But now it looked like he would never be getting out. When she'd visit him at the prison, she'd suffer "horrible anxiety." She wanted to help him so bad, to cheer him up, to smile, to say that everything would work out, but she just couldn't do it. In the prison parking lot, she'd have panic attacks where she could hardly breathe; she'd throw up or get the dry heaves. She had to take her driver's license out of her purse to bring inside as identification, and "I don't know how many of my driver's licenses I lost in that parking lot," she recalls. Sometimes, she couldn't even get herself to go in. On top of all that, she'd met another man.[37]

At Sussex I State Prison, a fairly new high-security prison consisting of low-lying gray concrete buildings in Waverly, Virginia, Tice got along well with other inmates despite his troubles with guards. He made a point of showing them respect—he'd wait off to the side when they were using the phones or taking showers, for example—minded his own business, but helped people out when they asked for something without requiring anything in return. "I get a lot of respect that way," he says. "I try and help anybody and everybody out that I can." And he'd listen when people wanted to talk about their problems, then offer advice. Most of all, he just tried to be himself. He had always thought that only guilty people went to prison, but he soon learned otherwise. That was an eye-opener. Indeed, in all likelihood, thousands of innocent people are idling away in U.S. prisons. The main reasons: mistaken eyewitness identifications, unreliable and even fraudulent forensic science, false confessions, official misconduct, dishonest informants, and bad lawyers.[38]

When interviewed for this book, Tice acted upbeat and smiled frequently. Sitting in a cheap plastic chair in the visiting room at Sussex I, tattooed inmates and their visitors all around him, he had a twinkle in his eyes at times. "I look at the best of everything," he says. "I guess I'm one of the few people that always sees the silver lining." But he'd get depressed, such as over the holidays or after his conviction, of course; some days, he didn't want to do anything but lie on his bed in a semicomatose state and listen to the radio. And he wasn't the only one—there was lots of depression in there. Other days, he'd feel like he could "walk through walls."[39]

Asked in a phone interview how he now looked at the choice he had made, in his own mind, between confessing in an effort to save his life and facing the death penalty, he responded, "Now, being behind the bars and facing that realization of spending life in prison, I don't know if I would have taken the same course." Asked whether it was possible to carve out a decent life in prison, he replied, after a long pause, "Not here in Virginia."[40]

Eric Wilson, who had been convicted of rape only, had ended up at the Haynesville Correctional Center, a medium-security facility and "going home camp" where most inmates tried to stay out of trouble. It wasn't bad, at least compared to the Norfolk City Jail. "You get used to it," Wilson said. But it was stressful nonetheless. "You're always on a heightened sense of alert," Wilson recounts. "Which is in and of itself very taxing on your nerves. And with everyone being that taxed, you can imagine the tempers." It made Wilson mad when he thought about why he was locked up. He'd hear these stories about people getting released after many years behind bars because of exculpatory DNA evidence, and here he sat despite such evidence. He tried not to think about it, though, or about his release date of September 2005, or about his false confession, which he too felt had been a dumb move. "I know that that is the source of all of my problems, but I don't see a point in beating myself up over it," he says.[41]

Upon getting out, Wilson planned to return to Texas and live with his parents, maybe do something with his hands. His dreams were no longer big ones. "Hopefully find a good woman and get married," he wrote us from prison. "Then buy some land on which to become compleetly [sic] self suficient [sic] in order to deal with as few people as possible." He knew that he would have to register as a sex offender and that his conviction would be publicized: how would he explain everything to people? And he realized that he'd have to report in to the authorities regularly; otherwise, he could go back to prison. "I'm going to be embarrassed with this for the rest of my life," he said.[42]

Like the Tices, Wilson and his parents had lost faith in the legal system. "My belief in the system has been shot," Wilson said. It turned out that everything he'd been taught as a kid had been wrong. Often, the police seemed more corrupt than the people they were putting away. He'd become far more suspicious of people in general. His mother had also grown more skeptical. She was no longer inclined to defend the police or to believe what she saw on

TV. Or to press her second-grade students to just admit that they did it—they might just tell her what she wanted to hear.[43]

Omar Ballard went into prison like gangbusters. "I slipped into the 'tough guy' group," he recalls. "I always looked for a fight or ran my mouth because I felt that I had to prove myself as no coward." That "led me to numerous run-ins with the staff and a[n] isolated area of the prison 90 percent of the times. I was unreasonable, when a little reason would have soothed the problem. I shut down emotionally and felt everyone around me had an agenda. I judged people so quickly most times that when I was proven wrong, I was thrown for a loop. But time and dissatisfaction [sic] made me grow up." He acted as a mentor to some of the younger inmates and grew interested in radical politics, reading Howard Zinn and Noam Chomsky.[44]

Still, Ballard's background and revulsion at taking orders from anyone limited his transformation. When a lawyer visited him at Wallen's Ridge State Prison in early 2005—the same facility in which Dick resided, though they had no real contact—an officer told the lawyer that Ballard had "a reputation" at the prison and was one of the inmates they had to watch. Ballard had recently lost his temper with a guard and was in segregation because he'd allegedly put out a hit on another prisoner. During the visit, Ballard was shackled and wearing a harness that extended out the door so that a guard could tell if he moved from his chair. If he misbehaved again, the lawyer was told, they'd reel him in.[45]

Four months after Tice's sentencing, his attorney, James Broccoletti, appealed his conviction. Broccoletti contended that Judge Charles E. Poston had incorrectly instructed the jury when he had stated that they could find Tice guilty of capital murder even if they determined that "someone acting in concert with him" had killed Michelle Moore-Bosko. Poston had earlier denied a defense motion to set aside the guilty verdict that made the same argument. Poston's instruction to the jury ran contrary to Virginia law, Broccoletti maintained, which stipulated that only the "immediate perpetrator" could be convicted of capital murder. The instruction was "obviously incorrect," Broccoletti wrote. Poston had also erred, he argued, in refusing to admit Ballard's confessions to police, letter to Karen Stover, and prior criminal record.[46]

Eight months later, in June of 2001, The Learning Channel broadcast a television program on this case. "Eight Men Out," which was part of the *Medical Detectives* series and would be aired many times, suggested that the confessions of Williams, Dick, Wilson, and Tice were false. The program rankled Assistant Commonwealth's Attorney Valerie Bowen, who was interviewed for it. She phoned a producer after the show aired and accused him of sandbagging her. "You told me this was a DNA story and a murder mystery story," she complained. Bowen tripped over numerous questions in her interview and seemed ignorant or forgetful of many details of the case. But her stumbling was not shown in the program. "If I wanted to get her, I could have gotten her," Paul Dowling, the executive producer of the show, says. "I actually made her look pretty good, I thought."[47]

The show also incensed the Boskos and the Moores. Billy Bosko, who was interviewed for it at his trailer in Pennsylvania, didn't care for the press in the first place and felt burned; he thought the program had not told the whole story. Carol Moore's brother-in-law would call it a "terroristic show" that was "unbelievably biased in favor of the murderers." But Billy had appeared to enjoy being on camera and to give the interview crew what they needed. "He was Mr. B-Roll," Dowling recalls.[48]

Paul Ferrara, the respected director of the Virginia Division of Forensic Science, declined a request for an interview for the show. "Paul is not going to go on camera with you and say this was a gang rape," a colleague of Ferrara's told Dowling.[49]

Patricia Dick's brother Al Bankard found himself mesmerized by the program. Having read earlier about the discontinuation of several cases, recantations of confessions, and Ballard's admissions, he had started to wonder anew whether his nephew Joe was really guilty. He had written a letter to Judge Poston asking for leniency before Joe's sentencing in which he'd acknowledged Joe's guilt. He couldn't ignore Joe's confessions and his sister's own beliefs. But Al was stopped dead in his tracks by the program. Joe now maintained his innocence, it indicated, showing an excerpt of a letter he had written Dowling in which he had declared that he wasn't involved. The show convinced Al that Joe was indeed innocent. He detested this Valerie Bowen. "I had the urge to do something really violent to her," he recalls. A church deacon, he felt his old Marine Corps mentality coming back.[50]

During the first commercial break, Bankard phoned his other sister, Theresa, who quickly switched channels to watch the show. Tears were soon streaming down her face. After the program was over, she cried to Al over the phone, "Oh, my God, I told you he was innocent!" They had to do something for Joe.[51]

Al called Patricia, though their mother had urged him not to, as she knew how brutally frank he could be (*tactless* would be another way to put it) and how sensitive Pat was about Joe's case. Had she seen it? Al asked his sister. No, Patricia said, and she didn't care to. Well, were she and her husband going to do anything to get Joe off? He's innocent, Al told her. Patricia said she'd look into it. "It was like a brush-off," Al remembers. He dropped off a copy of the program at Patricia's office; she made him leave it in the reception area rather than take it to her desk. Later, Al really came at Patricia with both barrels, "blasted" her, saying that it was time to quit feeling sorry for herself and entreating her to do something for Joe. She had a duty before God to do what was right, Al exhorted her. Patricia responded that Joe was guilty and getting what he deserved, then cried about how members of their family were talking about her behind her back. It was quite a blowout.[52]

When they finally watched the show, Patricia and Joe Sr. were troubled and perplexed, but not entirely convinced. Michael Fasanaro, their son's attorney, had told them that Joe had identified everybody involved in Michelle's murder and rape, but they now learned that Derek Tice had named Rick Pauley, Geoffrey Farris, and John Danser. And hearing about Omar Ballard and his confessions staggered them. But who was one to believe? Patricia phoned Fasanaro: Had he seen the show? No, but he'd heard about it, Fasanaro replied, in Joe Sr.'s retelling. (Fasanaro recalls that he "happened to switch channels one night and saw it on television.") Well, what did he think about it? Joe Sr. asked. Fasanaro launched into his canned rap about Joe never once denying his guilt to him. Asked later about his reaction to Joe's letter to the show's producer, Paul Dowling, recanting his confession, Fasanaro replied, "If the guy lied to me thirty times, then he's a big fool." What about this guy Ballard saying he did it by himself? Joe Sr. asked Fasanaro. Well, he'd since repudiated that position, Fasanaro pointed out, referring to Ballard's statement for his plea agreement.[53]

Dick's letter to Dowling was a curious one, befitting its author. Besides professing his innocence, Dick wrote (and this part was not included in the program), "I did not know that Mrs. Bosko had been murdered until two defendants came out of the bedroom with a knife and blood on them. I then panicked, and scared to death, I ran home." When Dowling asked Dick who these two defendants were, he said they were Pauley and Farris. "They are now on the street," Dick wrote. "Both of these people were present when the rape and murder happened. The blood was on there [sic] hands because they participated in the stabbing of Mrs. Bosko. They both knew the system and did not make any statement." That's nutty stuff, but Dowling figured that Dick was implicating Pauley and Farris because "these two assholes got off. We're the assholes that are in. These guys were smarter than us and got off, and I'm going to place them at the scene." When we asked Dick for this book why he told Dowling that Pauley and Farris were there, he said that he didn't know. "I might have still had some doubt at that time and maybe I was angry but *I am really not sure why I said that,*" he wrote us.[54]

"Eight Men Out" made the defendants minor celebrities in prison. "I saw your show last night," a guard remarked to Derek Tice.[55] Larry Tice mailed copies of the program everywhere.

In May 2002, the Virginia Court of Appeals reversed Derek Tice's conviction. "We agree that the [trial] court erred by giving an instruction that allowed the jury to find Tice guilty of capital murder without finding that he was an active or immediate killer of the victim," the court ruled. The instruction "was not an accurate statement of the law." The Court of Appeals also ruled that Judge Poston erred in prohibiting Tice's counsel from questioning Ballard about his letter to Karen Stover, since "the contents of the letter pointed directly to the guilt of a third party and was a factual question for the jury to decide." The court consequently remanded Tice's case back to the commonwealth for a new trial.[56]

Tice's retrial opened on January 27, 2003, this time in Alexandria. Tice was no longer facing the death penalty since jurors had rejected it at his first trial; he could not incur double jeopardy. Again, the two camps quickly distinguished themselves: Michelle's parents, Carol and Jack Moore, would often cluster with Glenn Ford, Brian Wray, and prosecutors when court wasn't in session, sometimes joined by Billy Bosko and his new wife, Amy, along with his mother and sister. It was the first time that Billy and the Moores had spoken since Michelle's murder over five years earlier. If the unease in that relationship wasn't enough for Billy, Amy tended to get upset at the mere mention of Michelle and felt threatened by her even in death. (At Billy's request, his mother had removed a photo of Michelle from her living room "because it just bothered [Amy] too much.")[57] The Tice camp was smaller, and partly for that reason again evoked compassion.

Before trial opened, Judge Poston had rejected a defense motion to allow an expert witness on false confessions to testify. Though one might be needed in a case involving a mentally retarded person or a juvenile, Poston ruled, an expert wasn't needed here since jurors could "understand that confessions can be coerced."[58]

Assistant Commonwealth's Attorney Derek Wagner, a younger man with blond hair and a pointed nose who had been a prosecutor for about five years, gave the prosecution's opening statement. In a deliberate and unanimated voice, though Carol Moore would cry and dab at her eyes as he spoke, he told the jurors that Michelle had been savagely gang-raped and stabbed to death, and that they would "hear the defendant's voice on a tape recorder as he confesses to these crimes." In the defense's opening, Jeffrey Russell argued that Tice had falsely confessed to avoid facing the death penalty and that his statement was "filled with errors." Omar Ballard, Russell said, was the real killer.[59]

A well-groomed and broad-shouldered Billy Bosko, wearing an olive-green suit coat and glasses, again testified for the prosecution and described the horror of discovering his wife's dead body upon returning from his cruise. Tamika Taylor followed him to the stand and told her overblown tale of Danial Williams shadowing Michelle. When recalling Michelle's failure to emerge from her apartment the morning after she was murdered, Taylor wept. During Investigator Wayne Bryan's testimony, the prosecutors played the police videotape of the crime scene for the jury—"This is Ms. Bosko on the floor."[60]

On the stand the next morning, Dr. Elizabeth Kinnison, the forensic pathologist who had conducted the autopsy, was noncommittal about whether Michelle's injuries had been inflicted by one or multiple perpetrators. Either scenario was "possible," she said, circumspectly. An outside expert witness in forensic pathology would have done better for Tice, but again the defense would not call one.[61]

Then Joe Dick once more made his way to the witness box. Dressed in a drab-green jumpsuit, sporting oversized glasses and a light mustache, with pale olive skin, Dick glanced nervously about the courtroom to his right as he walked to the stand. Tice's attorneys were on edge: What was the guy going to say now? They suspected that he would implicate Tice and everybody else—why else would the prosecutors call him?—but "I didn't know what he was going to do," James Broccoletti remembers. "He's such an unusual person—erratic." Broccoletti and Russell had paid a visit to Dick in jail two days earlier, a Sunday. "I can either do it the commonwealth's way and die in prison, or I can tell the truth and try and set the record straight," Dick had told them. "Well, what do you mean by that?" they had asked him. "We just want you to tell the truth." "I wasn't there," Dick responded. "Why did you say that you were there at the last trial?" Broccoletti inquired. "Because I had to in order to get my deal," Dick said. He repeatedly proclaimed that he was innocent but had testified for the commonwealth to get his plea agreement. Broccoletti and Russell tried to persuade him that his most advantageous course now was to tell the truth, that it might ultimately be to his benefit down the road. "Eight Men Out" had generated a lot of interest in the case, they informed him. He would gain nothing from perpetuating a lie at this stage of the game; nobody would help him. "Well, I'm sure that Ford's going to come talk to you tonight," Broccoletti said. "That's okay," Dick replied, in his feigned macho voice. "Let him come talk to me, and I'll tell him the same thing I'm telling you—that I wasn't there." He had made up his mind to tell the truth. "We were left with the impression that he might come in and say that he wasn't involved," Russell recalls. But Dick seemed conflicted. "I thought he appeared to be confused and perplexed as to what to do," Russell says. "And still kind of tortured."[62]

Dick had a lot to say to his visitors about Michael Fasanaro. He complained that his former attorney had "sold him down the river, and never did anything for him," Broccoletti recounts. And his parents had paid Fasanaro all that money. Fasanaro "never would believe him," Dick told Broccoletti. "He never would listen to him. He never would come to see him. Never would file any motions for him. Never fought for him. Never believed *in* him." Dick said "a lot of negative things." He also related that he was studying European military history and that once this whole thing got straight he wanted to open a military souvenir store in Maryland. He asked Broccoletti and Russell to send him a tape of "Eight Men Out" as well as Ballard's DNA results and confessions. He was still trying to collect material for his own legal effort.[63]

After the two attorneys left, Broccoletti remarked to Russell, "I don't know what he's going to do. . . . But if Ford does get to him, then we should expect him to testify" against Tice.[64]

Assistant Commonwealth's Attorney D.J. Hansen and Detectives Ford and Wray visited Dick the next evening. They, of course, knew that their case against Tice could be fatally undermined if Dick said that he wasn't there. Their visit was one of a series. At the request of Hansen, who was in regular touch with Fasanaro and had probably learned of Dick's legal endeavors, Ford and Wray had come calling on him in prison several weeks earlier. Their goals: to determine whether Dick would testify for the prosecution and to persuade him to do so, if necessary (though Ford would deny the second part). According to Ford's version of that earlier meeting, Dick had said that Wayne Kennedy, the former Norfolk homicide detective who had testified for Tice at his first trial, had visited him and told him about a so-called Freedom Group. Kennedy had said that the group was "looking to get involved in the case," Dick had stated. Kennedy had told Dick "that if he didn't testify, he stood a chance of getting with this Freedom Group," Dick had recalled, according to Ford. Well, he had already pled guilty, Ford and Wray had reminded Dick; they didn't know where he thought this thing with the Freedom Group was going. Was he now going to claim that he didn't do it? "No, we did it," Dick had replied, according to Ford. "But they told me if I testify, then this Freedom Group won't help me." According to Broccoletti, Wayne Kennedy never even met with Dick.[65]

During the meeting at the prison, Ford and Wray had let Dick know that they felt he deserved better than a double-life term. They had thought that Valerie Bowen was going to give him a break for everything he had done for the commonwealth and ask for less than double life at his sentencing, they had said, and they wished that she hadn't requested double life and didn't like it. In Ford's retelling, they had added that there was nothing they could do about it, however. According to a letter Dick later wrote Ford, Ford had indicated that he would like to retaliate against Bowen for "the shit she pulled" (in Dick's words). "I know how much you want to get her back," Dick wrote. If Ford could help get him released with immunity from reprosecution, "that would be the ultimate revenge against Mrs. Bowen," Dick told Ford.[66]

After Ford and Wray had played Dick for a while during their visit at the prison, Dick had told them, "I'm going to testify," Ford recalled. "Tell Mr.

Hansen I am going to testify." Ford and Wray had then reviewed Dick's testimony at Tice's first trial with him; they had the transcript with them. Dick recounted the same story to them. Before Ford and Wray left, Dick said that he always liked talking to them.[67] Ford still had Dick under his thumb.

After the meeting, Ford had phoned Hansen and informed him that Dick said he would testify. But they wanted to be sure, and to be sure of what he was going to say. They still didn't trust him, and they knew that Broccoletti was going to visit him. Hansen wanted to review his testimony with him again. In all likelihood, he sought to keep Dick's account as consistent with his prior testimony as possible. At Ford, Wray, and Hansen's meeting with Dick at the jail the night before his testimony, Dick declared after Hansen told him the purpose of the meeting, "I need to tell you something," Ford recounted. He was really confused and didn't know which way to go, Dick said. Broccoletti and Russell had visited him and told him that the Freedom Group wouldn't help him if he testified, he stated, in Ford's retelling. (Broccoletti says that he has never heard of a Freedom Group.) Was he going to jump ship and get on that bandwagon? Wray asked Dick. Or was he going to do what he'd done all along—get up there and tell the truth? Dick was silent for a while. When Ford asked him again if he was going to say he didn't do it, Dick replied, No, they did it, according to Ford's account. But he still didn't know what to do.[68]

According to Dick's version of the meeting, Hansen and Ford threatened him. "They frightened me again," he recalls. Hansen warned him that if he didn't testify "truthfully"—that is, the way he had in the past, incriminating both himself and Tice—they could revoke his plea agreement and recharge him with capital murder. He would then be facing the death penalty again. Ford became incensed when Dick spoke of telling the actual truth. Either Ford or Hansen also told Dick that he would try to help him in some way if he testified against Tice, Dick recounts. But they could not promise him anything, as he'd already been sentenced. Ford later acknowledged that Hansen spoke to Dick about his plea agreement and told Dick that he had to testify truthfully, but he denied that anybody threatened to withdraw the agreement or brought up the death penalty. When told Dick's account of his visit in an interview, Hansen refused to comment "on anything I talked about with Joe Dick" or "on anything Joe Dick may or may not have said."[69]

About fifteen minutes into the meeting, Dick stated, "I'm going to testify. I'm going to do what's right," in Ford's retelling. Hansen then went over his testimony with him. He handed Dick either a transcript of his previous testimony or one of his statements to police. "Joe said he remembered everything, and that he would be fine," Ford recounted. But he brought up the Freedom Group again. "When we got up to leave, we said, 'Joe, what are you going to do?'" Ford recalled. "He said, 'I am going to get up there and tell the truth.'"[70]

The next morning, Ford and Wray went to see Dick again, this time at a holding cell at the courthouse in Alexandria. They weren't taking any chances. They spoke to him through the bars. "He said Mr. Broccoletti and Mr. Russell had just left," Ford later testified. (Broccoletti says that he did not visit Dick that morning.) "And I said, 'Well, what are you going to do?'" Ford recounted. "He said Mr. Broccoletti got mad at him . . . 'because I told him I'm getting up there and telling the truth.' He said at that time Mr. Broccoletti said to him, 'What truth are you going to tell today, Joe?' And Joe said 'the honest truth. I was there and so was Derek Tice.'" After leaving, Ford went upstairs and apprised Hansen that Dick said he was ready to go.[71]

Dick felt like his head was in a vice. "I was under a lot of pressure from both sides to do the right thing," he wrote Paul Dowling after Tice's trial. "I cannot make good decisions under pressure." Dick wrote Fasanaro: "I sat in the jail cell waying [sic] my conscience. I finally came to a decision that I would testify for the prosecution." He wasn't about to risk the death penalty again. "That's what it came down to," Dick now says. He didn't know that it would be quite difficult, if not impossible, for the prosecutors to revoke his plea agreement since he'd already been sentenced.[72] Once a defendant is sentenced, there is generally no going back.

On the witness stand, as Dick started to tell his tale of the gang-rape and murder, the tension in the courtroom was palpable. Although Tice's attorneys were ready for this moment, hearing Dick's actual words ("Eric Wilson arrived about fifteen minutes after I got home"—they knew what was coming next) was like getting hit in the stomach. They'd lost that round with the prosecution, and it was a big one. Tice couldn't believe what he was hearing; he had thought that Dick was going to let the cat out of the bag and acknowledge that he wasn't even there. "I wanted to get up and just call him a bald-faced liar," Tice recounts. But "I just had to sit there and take it." When Dick got to the part about everybody raping Michelle, Carol Moore, whose eyes were sunken, was crying once more in her seat. Up in front of her, Dick was sobbing too. He would say later that he was thinking about the photograph of

Michelle's dead body that Ford had shown him during his interrogation, and how Michelle had died. But it was easy to get the impression watching Dick that he was overcome by shame—or tormented by having to confess to something he didn't do. To Derek Tice's mother, Rachel Tice, who was floored when Dick launched into his tale, he seemed on the brink of telling the truth, and to want to tell it, but to catch himself because of the perceived repercussions and so "choked it back inside." For Patricia Bosko, Billy's mother, however, Dick's crying confirmed that the police had it right. He was "so remorseful," Carol Moore thought.[73]

In his cross of Dick, Broccoletti argued that Dick's plea agreement required him to testify. "I've got no idea about that," Dick stated. He wanted to testify, he claimed. Broccoletti pointed out numerous discrepancies between Dick's prior statements and his testimony, and repeatedly asserted that he hadn't even been there. Yes, he was, Dick kept replying. "I know that I was there," he declared at one point. Judge Poston refused to allow into evidence Dick's letter to Dowling maintaining his innocence—Here we go again, Larry and Rachel Tice were thinking—though Broccoletti was able to read from the letter. "As recently as Sunday night, Mr. Dick, you said you weren't there, didn't you?" Broccoletti reminded Dick. "That's true," Dick admitted. He by now was looking quite forlorn. During Hansen's redirect, Dick said that he'd denied involvement to Dowling because he thought it would help him, "but when I was researching various cases looking for a way out, I realized that there's no way out." Dick wrote Fasanaro after the trial was over that he thought he had done "the right thing" by testifying. But he also hoped it would help get him out of prison.[74]

Detective Ford then took the stand. He went through Tice's confession in detail and Hansen played the tape recording of it: "I had one leg. Eric had the other leg. Joe had one arm." Carol Moore cried again. These trials were excruciating for her.[75]

Judge Poston refused to allow Broccoletti to ask Ford in front of the jury whether he had obtained false confessions from suspects in the past. Poston also prohibited Broccoletti from calling to the stand another prison inmate who'd confessed falsely to Ford. These were "extraneous" issues, Poston stated. "Whether he obtained a false confession or not seems to me to be relatively benign, because I suspect that many police officers have done that, because we have all seen people who confess to anything."[76]

In his cross of Ford, who would sometimes smirk at "Mr. Broccoletti" (used derisively), Broccoletti brought out many of the inconsistencies in Tice's confession and asked Ford if they'd concerned him. No, because "the bulk of the story was the same," Ford responded, and "he keeps saying he did it."[77]

After the forensic scientists Jerry Sellers and Robert Scanlon testified for the defense and these jurors too learned that Tice's DNA was not found at the scene but that Ballard's was (one juror was frustrated that Jeffrey Russell did not question Scanlon more forcefully about the improbability of eight people raping a woman and only one of them leaving any DNA), the defense called Omar Ballard. On the chubby side now—"a porker," a local reporter would call him—and no longer mean or threatening in appearance, Ballard had been the recipient of a pretrial visit from Ford and Wray, just as Joe Dick had. Several weeks earlier, at Hansen's request, the two detectives had visited Ballard in prison during the same trip they had taken to see Dick ("same day, same play," Ford said later). They had just shown up unannounced. Ballard had been called out of his cell and taken to a small contact-visit room. He was handcuffed, with a chain linked to his waist, and another link from his waist to his feet, which were shackled. He was again tethered to two guards positioned outside the door. "We were told if anything happened we were not to move, they would take him," Ford recounted.[78]

After Ford casually asked Ballard how he was doing and they joked around a bit (Ballard seemed comfortable with Ford, having talked to him several times by now, and they spoke briefly about a new *Playboy* magazine piece on false confessions that discussed the case), Ford informed Ballard that Tice was going on trial again and that Ballard would be called as a witness. What did he intend to do? "At that time, I was planning to testify truthfully that I committed the crime alone," Ballard later stated in an affidavit. Before Ballard could articulate what he wanted to say, however, Ford told him that the people who were in prison for the crime were guilty and that he didn't want him to get up there and say anything that would get them released. "He then told me the best thing to say is that 'I have nothing to say,'" Ballard remembers. What did he care if Tice got the death sentence or walked?[79]

Ballard was stunned. "I thought I was going to be given the opportunity after so many other different opportunities to finally set the record straight," he later testified. But Ford "kept making sure I wouldn't testify by asking me in answer form, 'So you got nothing to say, right.' It was not a question, it was a statement." It was also a violation of Tice's right to a fair trial; courts have found lesser governmental interference with defense witnesses unconstitutional. Ford and Wray both later denied that Ford encouraged Ballard to have nothing to say, however: "Oh, absolutely not," Wray testified. In Ford's version of the meeting, Ballard told him, "I'm not going to help you keep them in prison. I'm not going to help them get out of prison." He was going to do his time for what he confessed to, and the other guys needed to do theirs, he said, according to Ford. He was "tired of these dweebs riding on my coattail," he complained. Ballard told Ford he would take the fifth. When Ford pointed out that he couldn't take the fifth because he was a convicted killer and that the judge would hold him in contempt of court, Ballard laughed, "What the hell is he going to do to me? I got double life plus forty."[80]

Ballard took Ford's advice about saying nothing "in stride," he recalls. Ford "ain't going to have no say over what I do anyway," he knew. But then James Broccoletti and Jeffrey Russell visited him too. They came calling on him in jail three days before his testimony, a Sunday, the same day they had visited Joe Dick. They had been escorted to a little room. "I don't want to be in here alone with him," Broccoletti had told the guards. "I don't know what he's going to do to me." Broccoletti had not forgotten Ballard's anger at Tice's first trial, and how he had questioned Ballard harshly. "I thought this guy was going to come out and just want to beat the shit out of me," Broccoletti reminisces. "Can't you stay in the room for us?" he asked the guards. "No, we don't stay in the room," the guards replied. "We watch on closed circuit." "I could be *dead* by the time you get down here from that video room," Broccoletti exclaimed, only half jokingly.[81]

After Ballard was led into the room—unrestrained—Broccoletti looked up at a surveillance camera to make sure the guards were watching. But to Broccoletti's surprise, Ballard "was just as happy-go-lucky as you can imagine." "Affable Ab," Broccoletti and Russell would dub him. Broccoletti was suspicious: This was not the same Omar he'd met earlier. What was going on?[82]

Broccoletti also informed Ballard that he was going to be called to testify at Tice's trial and asked him what he was going to do. "I had no idea what this man was going to do or say," Broccoletti later testified. "His case was complete. He had no scruples, obviously." Russell felt Ballard was "quite capable of saying and doing anything to help himself." Of course, at Tice's first trial, he had denied any involvement. Broccoletti wanted to know if Ballard was going

to be unavailable to testify. If so, Broccoletti reasoned again, his prior statements to police could come into evidence. That wouldn't have made Broccoletti unhappy at all. Indeed, he preferred it to Ballard testifying. "I didn't think
it could get any better than the statements that he gave to the police," Broccoletti would recall. And if Ballard was unavailable, he couldn't be cross-examined
by D.J. Hansen and impeached by his other prior statements; his confessions
to police couldn't be cross-examined. "I thought that the statements said all
that they needed to say without taking a chance of having Mr. Ballard say
something that I didn't know or couldn't expect or couldn't control," Broccoletti remembered.[83]

Broccoletti apprised Ballard that he would have to call him to the stand to
establish whether he was going to testify or be unavailable. What was he going
to do then? "I'll tell that judge I ain't saying *shit*," Ballard replied. "Well, I don't
know if you should say that," Broccoletti chuckled. Ballard made it clear that
he was not interested in helping anybody. "I'm comfortable," he told Broccoletti and Russell. "I've got what *I* need." What did he mean? Broccoletti asked
him. "I've got girls writing me letters, sending me nude pictures," Ballard
boasted. "I've got my cell. I've got a warm bed. I've got three meals a day. And
I'm not getting the death penalty." He had his deal and he was done; he acted
surprisingly content with his imprisonment. He even fancied himself a celebrity
because of publicity over the case.[84]

In Ballard's account of the visit, Broccoletti told him that he wanted him to
know "for the record" that no matter what he said on the stand, it would neither help nor harm Derek Tice. "Broccoletti said he would prefer that I not say
anything," Ballard stated in an affidavit, even though "it was clear that Broccoletti knew I was going to testify that Tice was not involved in the murder of
Michelle." Ballard let Broccoletti know that he committed the crime alone.[85]

"I was baffled," Ballard remembers. This was Tice's own attorney encouraging him to be unavailable. Nobody seemed to care about the truth or to want
to hear his account of what happened. Everybody had their own agenda. This
had been going on for years. He was fed up with it. "I wanted to be done with
it," he recalls. Broccoletti and Russell's visit clinched it for Ballard: When
called to the stand, he would say nothing. "I just felt like it was a no win for me
to say anything at all," he recounts.[86]

After Broccoletti and Russell had come calling on Ballard, a male prosecutor (probably either Hansen or Derek Wagner) visited him as well. This

visitor, too, encouraged Ballard to have nothing to say, Ballard stated in an affidavit.[87]

As Ballard was escorted in shackles by two deputies into the courtroom, he glanced at Ford, who looked at him. When asked on the stand if he raped Michelle, Ballard responded, "I have nothing to say." Did he murder her? "I have nothing to say," he grinned. He had "nothing to say to no questions." It was, in reality, a huge blow to a criminal defense based on the argument that Ballard was the sole killer; Ballard could have provided powerful exonerating testimony, harmful cross-examination or not. When Judge Poston pointed out that nothing Ballard could say could hurt him since he'd been convicted and that the defendant felt he could help him by testifying, Ballard retorted again, "I have nothing to say." Poston held him in contempt, ordered him detained until he testified, and urged him to reconsider. "It would be a pity if this person happens to be innocent, or even if he doesn't, because if you have something to say that could help him . . . it would be your duty to do it," Poston lectured him.[88]

Broccoletti then called Detective David Peterson, who had interviewed Ballard with Ford in March of 1999. But because Ballard had not signed his confessions of March 4 and 11, Poston refused to allow them into evidence. Broccoletti's strategy had backfired because of a police omission. (Or had Ford intentionally left Ballard's statements unsigned?) Broccoletti had Peterson read Ballard's confessions to the jury, however, including the parts about nobody being with him. Poston also refused to admit Ballard's letter to Karen Stover because it had not been "properly authenticated." Peterson had claimed that he could not identify Ballard's handwriting—"I'm not a handwriting expert"—though he knew full well the letter was written by Ballard. Broccoletti had assumed that Peterson could authenticate it. Broccoletti and Russell could have authenticated the letter through other means, but they did not do so. In his cross-examination of Peterson, Hansen educated jurors about Ballard's March 2000 statement for his plea agreement in which he implicated Tice, Williams, Dick, and Wilson.[89]

Judge Poston then ordered Ballard brought back into the courtroom. But Ballard reiterated, "I don't have anything to say."[90] He was now a dead end for the defense.

Next Russell called John Danser, who had been pacing nervously outside the courtroom (where he declined a request for an interview for this book without a moment's hesitation) to the stand. Dressed in a black leather jacket, the tall, goateed Danser (he *did* look mean), who believed that his ex-friend Tice was guilty, was accompanied by his attorney, Jennifer Stanton. Poston had ordered Stanton to be there since Danser's case had been nol-prossed rather than dismissed. Russell elicited Danser's well-documented alibi: that he had worked until 6:30 P.M. in Warminster, Pennsylvania, the day of the murder; withdrawn money from an ATM in Philadelphia at 8:42 P.M. that night; then left Philadelphia about 2 A.M. and driven back to Warminster, where he reported to work the next morning at 7:30. Danser denied raping or murdering Michelle, or ever being in Danial Williams's apartment. The defense was trying to raise doubt about Tice's confessions and Dick's testimony since they had both named Danser, but jurors were having difficulty keeping track of how and when each defendant had been implicated, and indeed of the entire sequence of events in the case—"defense counsel was not helpful in making [it] clear," one juror would write afterward—and it's unlikely that Danser's testimony went far with them. Indeed, some may not even have fully understood its relevance. "The defendant didn't even mention [Danser] in his confession" of June 1998, Hansen would inform them.[91]

Broccoletti then called Judy Pauley, mother of Rick Pauley, whom Tice had also named, followed by Richard Pauley Sr. Both parents testified that their son had been home the night of the murder.[92] But jurors tend to be unimpressed by alibis offered by family members, and whether Pauley had been there or not, Tice had certainly implicated himself.

Along with a suit coat and tie, Tice wore a bushy mustache and slightly tinted glasses, neither of which, combined with his masculine appearance, conveyed the gentleness in his personality that made him such an unlikely murderer. He again did not take the stand. Greg McCormack, Wilson's attorney, who had elected to put his client up there and seen Wilson stand up to the pressure well, was "just blown away" by Broccoletti's decision. If Tice had gotten in the witness box and declared that he wasn't involved, and explained why he confessed, "that would have had one hell of an impact upon the jury," McCormack thought. As for the risks of testifying, "what the hell did he have to lose?"[93]

Before the closing arguments would begin on the trial's third day, Tice's attorney Jeffrey Russell remarked outside court that he'd be happy with a hung jury. An acquittal was unlikely, he felt, given Tice's confession. He was a real-ist. Minutes later Detective Ford could be heard nervously tapping his foot in his seat as Poston was giving the jury its instructions ("the defendant is pre-sumed to be innocent," though in reality most everyone in the justice system—police, prosecutors, defense attorneys, judges, and jurors—are inclined to believe that people charged with crimes are guilty).[94] From the row in front of Ford, a person could hear his pant leg rubbing rapidly back and forth against the wood. His tapping would continue throughout closing arguments. He had a lot at stake. Tice was not only his guy, but he hardly wanted to hear later that jurors had acquitted Tice because they thought Ford had wrung a false confession out of him. Ford's reputation would take a hit, and some of his other confessions could also be questioned.

In his closing argument, Hansen quickly choked up. He was telling the ju-rors about how he was there to speak and obtain justice for Michelle and her family, and looking at some photos of her, when he suddenly appeared ready to cry. A cynic might have said that his display of emotion was feigned, but Broccoletti thought otherwise, and Hansen recalls, "I didn't mean for that to happen. . . . I was just arguing, and it just comes out." The physical evidence simply didn't show that Ballard committed this crime by himself, Hansen told the jurors. Michelle "never had a chance to struggle," as she could have against one man, he said, because she had been "swept off her feet" by seven or eight assailants and carried to her bedroom. Those knife pricks on her chest were inflicted by "a bunch of scared, nervous sailors," Hansen argued, not "some-body as vicious as Omar Ballard." And Joe Dick had nothing to gain by testi-fying: "All he wanted to do is get this over with, get it off his chest, to make some sort of amends for what he did. . . . Joe Dick has never, ever testified that he didn't do this." But "what it comes down to in this case, ladies and gentlemen, is the confession given by the defendant," Hansen stressed. "People just do not confess, particularly to something of this magnitude, this heinous, this vi-cious, without having participated in it. It's just not natural, it's just not rea-sonable." At the defense table, Tice was shaking his head.[95]

Russell argued that all the reasons Hansen gave for concluding that the crime was committed by multiple assailants were "more logically" indications of one attacker only, Omar Ballard. DNA, he declared, was "the linchpin" of the case. A verdict of not guilty, Broccoletti told the jurors, was "justice—

justice for the Bosko family, justice for the community, justice for society, and justice for Mr. Tice." They had seen "evil incarnate" when Ballard had appeared before them in chains that morning with his two life sentences, Broccoletti said. Dick had testified "not because it's the right thing to do," Broccoletti stated, but because of his "binding contract" with the commonwealth, his plea agreement; if he didn't testify, he'd be "back to square one, capital murder." Broccoletti once more put forward a riveting scenario of how Ballard murdered Michelle.[96]

The jury deliberated for over an hour before going home for the night, then debated throughout the following day, a Thursday, without reaching a verdict. Like Tice's previous jury, they had some questions about the lack of physical evidence tying him to the crime and the neat condition of Michelle's apartment. They also wondered about how, exactly, Tice had come to be implicated, about Dick's testimony, and about the discrepancies between Dick's and Tice's confessions and with the evidence. Further—and this came up over and over again—they wondered how so many men could have conceivably confessed to such an atrocious crime if they were innocent. Then, on Friday at about 10:45 A.M., the jurors filed into the courtroom with their verdict. One of the female jurors in the front row appeared to have been crying. In his seat among the spectators, Glenn Ford was again nervously tapping his foot; he looked weary, as he had much of the week, with reddish eyes. "We, the jury, find the defendant guilty of the murder of Michelle Moore-Bosko," the court clerk read. "We, the jury, find the defendant guilty of the rape of Michelle Moore-Bosko." The words rang out like the tolling of another death to those who believed that Tice was innocent. But on the other side of the courtroom, people were smiling. "Yes!" Tamika Taylor exclaimed. That was awfully tough for Larry and Rachel Tice to take. "Oh, they were happy," Rachel Tice recounts. "It was like joyous laughter or something." Derek Tice closed his eyes. He was absolutely shocked by the verdict, and quite devastated. But in the days ahead, he would seem more worried about his mother than himself.[97]

After the jurors had been polled and left the courtroom, and as Judge Poston was leaving, there was a bitter exchange between two of the spectators. A woman on the left side of the room, whom Billy Bosko's sister, Sarah, took to be Rachel Tice (actually, she was Larry Tice's sister, Karen), blurted, "This isn't over. This will never be over." "Yes, it is over," Sarah said. The woman glared at Sarah with a cold expression, a reflection of her outrage at the verdicts and the revelry of the other side. "Well, at least mine's alive," she replied. In no time at all, Sarah's face turned bright red, and tears were streaming down her face. Her mother knew from the look on her face that there was going to be trouble. "I'm going to kill you," Sarah snapped, then went after the woman. She couldn't hear anything around her as she started her charge. She fully intended to hurt the woman. But Tamika Taylor grabbed her from behind, and the wispy Amy Bosko, Billy's wife, jumped in front of her. Deputies also intervened, then escorted the Tices from the building while holding the Moores and Boskos behind.[98]

It took jurors only about fifteen minutes to agree on a sentence: life on both counts. They had no other option on capital murder, but could have gone as low as five years on rape. Judge Poston immediately imposed the penalty.[99]

Billy Bosko, to whom "at least mine's alive" confirmed that Tice's parents lacked human decency just like their coward of a son, told a reporter for the *Virginian-Pilot* after Tice's sentencing that he hoped Tice "dies a slow, painful death." But Larry Tice vowed to soldier on for his son and complained that the defense had been "robbed" by Poston's rulings, including his refusal to permit expert testimony on false confessions. "Its [sic] over," Pat Bosko wrote Larry Tice later.[100]

Some attorneys around Norfolk were surprised by the verdict. Dan Shipley, Danial Williams's lawyer, found it remarkable that jurors could convict Tice after knowing what they did about Ballard. But Tice's confession had sunk him a second time. It and Dick's testimony were, "by far, the most important evidence to our jury," one of the jurors wrote afterward.[101]

In May 2003, Tice appealed his conviction. James Broccoletti no longer represented him. "After the second trial was completed, I was literally spent representing Derek," Broccoletti said later. "There was no gas left in the tank." A lawyer from the Public Defender Commission in Richmond handled Tice's appeal.[102] But the Virginia Court of Appeals denied it that December, two days before Christmas. A subsequent appeal with the Virginia Supreme Court was rejected as well.

Larry Tice was also spent. It took him some time to recharge his batteries and get geared back up to fight. "It's taken such a toll on me mentally," he commented two months after Derek's retrial. Every day was a struggle. "The tragedy of Derek's wrongful conviction has devastated our family," Rachel

Tice wrote; sometimes she would just sit and cry. The tragedy did not help Rachel and Larry's marriage; the emotional roller coaster they were on because of Derek's case wore both of them down. But they learned to be more tolerant of each other, and in some ways their marriage grew stronger. Rachel put everything in God's hands and kept going. It helped that Derek was in Virginia and she was away in North Carolina. But Derek was always in her thoughts.[103]

13
Heavy Artillery

After Derek Tice was convicted a second time, Richard Leo, a co-author of this book, asked Peter Neufeld of the Innocence Project in New York if the Innocence Project would take on the cases of Tice, Danial Williams, Joe Dick, and Eric Wilson. "I explained that it really wasn't an Innocence Project case, because they've already done the DNA testing and they're excluded," Neufeld recounts. "And that we take on cases . . . to secure DNA testing where none had been conducted." Neufeld told Leo that the four prisoners needed "top lawyers from the top law firms to pursue the insanity of these convictions." The best way to obtain the attorneys, Neufeld thought, was through George Kendall, a capital defender who had recruited law firms to take on capital cases and other injustices in the past.[1]

Neufeld owed Leo a favor. "There was a deal," Neufeld chuckles. He had asked Leo to do some pro bono consulting on another false confession case when Leo was swamped with other work. Leo said that he'd do it, but that Neufeld had to get lawyers for the Norfolk false confessors in return. Fine, Neufeld said. "I was sold on the case even before Richard asked me to get involved," Neufeld remembers. "I knew about the Norfolk Four. . . . It was one of these obvious miscarriages of justice. But an entrenched criminal justice bureaucracy was not going to bite the bullet. It was plain and simple."[2]

Neufeld was struck by the sheer craziness of the case. It was an atrocity, he thought, and one unique in his experience. He didn't know of any other case in which DNA evidence had excluded so many defendants, yet the state persisted in prosecuting them. He'd found it "extraordinarily rare" for prosecutors to go forward and prosecute even one defendant whose DNA had been excluded (though it is far from unprecedented). "The DNA trumps the confession," he says. "And in 99 percent of those instances, those charges will be dismissed. . . . The way the prosecutor and police conducted themselves here is so off-the-wall, is so unconscionable, and unfathomable, that there really is no precedent for it."[3]

In the spring of 2004, a year after Tice's second conviction, Neufeld approached George Kendall about the case. Kendall is an observant and intelligent-looking man in his mid-fifties, balding, with wavy gray hair, a white beard, light-brown skin, and a slender build. He is outspoken and direct, though typically polite. "There is not a condescending or a pretentious or snobbish bone in that man's body," says one person who knows him. A quick thinker, he digests information readily and speaks rapidly. He often wears an amused grin. Energetic, driven, and tenacious, "he's somebody who's just working all the time, and appears not to have much opportunity or time to eat," says one friend. He tends to have a rumpled look about him. "He's not a dandy of any sort," his friend says. "He doesn't really care too much about those kinds of superficial things. It's all about what he's thinking and what he's doing."[4] He is efficient with his time, and his e-mails are precise; they employ the minimal number of words—and even letters—necessary to convey what he wants to say. One suspects that his correspondents often take on the same style, out of respect and concern for taking up too much of his time.

Kendall is from southeastern Connecticut, where his father was an engineer in a shipyard. He came from a family of Rockefeller Republicans; his twin brother and older sister are both Republicans. "I'm the black sheep, politically," he says. After graduating in philosophy and government from the University of Richmond, Kendall had gone into Volunteers in Service to America (VISTA), where he'd wound up in a prisoner reentry program; he'd helped inmates who were close to being paroled look for jobs and housing. He had gotten to know some of them personally and discovered that they weren't all that different from him. "But all of them had had these horrific sorts of upbringings," he remembers. "You know, their parents were alcoholics. It was like, 'There but by the grace of god goes me.'" He decided to attend Antioch School of Law in Washington, D.C., to do public defender work; the school was a training ground for aiding the disadvantaged.[5]

After earning his law degree, Kendall worked for several years at a firm of Antioch graduates. Meanwhile he heard a talk by Millard Farmer, a well-known capital defender in Georgia, who observed that there were numerous inmates on death rows in prisons in the South who didn't have lawyers. That just can't be true, Kendall thought. But he learned otherwise, and so he started doing capital defense work for the ACLU of Georgia. He later handled capital cases at the NAACP Legal Defense and Educational Fund in New York. Today he is widely respected (one is tempted to say *revered* in death-penalty circles) and employed at Holland & Knight, a huge law firm based in New York, where he does pro bono work. He has spoken widely around the country on capital litigation. In 1997, the *American Lawyer* listed him as one of forty-five lawyers in the public sector in the United States who were making a difference. "He has been one of the leaders in organizing the capital defense bar in the nation for at least the last decade," Neufeld says. Though Kendall hasn't received as much public recognition as many other high-powered attorneys, that doesn't seem to bother him. "George is in this to do good for people who can't help themselves," another attorney says. "And that's *all* he wants out of this. He never wants fame, he never wants to be at the center of attention."[6]

When Neufeld spoke to Kendall about this case, he told him that it was too big for the Innocence Project. "It's three or four guys, and these false confession cases just take a lot of work," Neufeld said. Would Kendall be interested in taking one of the prisoners' cases, and finding some law firms for the others? Kendall replied that he'd see what he could do. "I said to Peter, 'You guys have a full plate, and so do I, but . . . whatever direction these cases go in, I will try to find counsel for them,'" Kendall recalls. In effect, "pass the baton to me, and either we will do this or I'll find somebody else." Neufeld and Kendall discussed strategy and how many law firms they'd need—three, they learned, since Eric Wilson was still represented by Greg McCormack.[7]

That April, Tom Wells and Richard Leo had a conference call with Kendall and Neufeld about the case. Kendall then approached Des Hogan with Hogan & Hartson (no relation, though it didn't hurt to have the name), the immense and politically well-connected law firm based in Washington, D.C. Kendall had worked earlier with Hogan, the white valedictorian of his class at predominantly black Howard University's law school, on a case in Texas involving wrongful drug convictions. Tall and laid-back, with an easy way with people, but forceful when needed, Hogan was the son of a former progressive

Catholic priest; he was once a finalist for the National Lawyers Association's Trial Lawyer of the Year award. Kendall also phoned Don Salzman of Skadden, Arps, Slate, Meagher, & Flom, like Hogan & Hartson a top corporate law firm and indeed one of the largest firms in the world. A handsome, slender, and articulate man from Rochester, New York, with dark hair and a rectangular face, Salzman was Skadden's pro bono counsel in Washington; he had earlier been a public defender in Maryland for some fifteen years. He was the president of the Mid-Atlantic Innocence Project and on the steering committee of the Innocence Commission for Virginia. Another good fit, Kendall thought.[8]

Kendall spoke to Hogan and Salzman about two matters: Norfolk and Guantánamo Bay. He wished to recruit lawyers to represent prisoners at Guantánamo, where many alleged terrorists were being held unconstitutionally. Neither Holland & Knight, Hogan & Hartson, nor Skadden, Arps took up the Guantánamo cases, however: one of Holland's partners had been killed on September 11 ("this is just too close to home," other partners thought), and Hogan & Hartson had recently hired someone from the upper reaches of the Justice Department ("we can't do it, politically"). But Hogan and Salzman were both intrigued with Norfolk. "My initial reaction was, 'This sounds like a classic case of wrongful conviction, *if* the facts are as they'd been presented to George, and as George was presenting them to me,'" Salzman remembers. "But," he adds, "there are a lot of cases that sound that way."[9]

Kendall traveled to Washington to meet with Hogan and Salzman individually, and then with a larger group that included several lawyers from each of their firms. The attorneys decided to look hard at the case, but that the firms would assess it separately and form their own judgments about it. They also discussed who they might represent. "It wasn't like we pulled straws out of a hat, but we sort of just arbitrarily chose a client," Kendall recounts. Hogan took Tice, Skadden Williams, and Holland Dick. "And then off we went, independently doing investigation," Kendall recalls. They reviewed all of the prisoners' confessions, the police's notes on their interrogations, the trial transcripts, and other case materials, and obtained what they could from their clients' previous attorneys.[10]

Some of them wondered if all their clients were really innocent. Even among public-interest-oriented pro bono lawyers, there is a great deal of cynicism about people in prison professing innocence. "Initially, I was skeptical, I think like anyone who looks at a case that involves false confessions," Deborah Boardman, one of Tice's attorneys at Hogan, recalls. "We had to do our due diligence that these were, in fact, cases where there was a very, very strong case of a miscarriage," Kendall remembers. "The law firms we work for are not in the business to get guilty people out of prison. They're in the business of making a lot of money, and to do some pro bono work, and if there are these cases of injustice to . . . do them correctly." The attorneys had to be able to look people squarely in the eye and say that a horrible wrong had occurred (though many lawyers who represent prisoners postconviction do not believe their clients' claims of innocence or are agnostic about them). But it was reassuring to know that the case came from the Innocence Project, and that there was no evidence against their clients aside from their confessions.[11]

That fall, Tom Wells provided the attorneys copies of the documents that he and Richard Leo had collected on the case for this book. Wells also met with the attorneys at Hogan & Hartson's Washington offices to discuss the case. By that point the lawyers had pretty much agreed to represent the three prisoners, "but I don't think we had totally decided," Kendall says. They wanted to pick Wells's brain about the case. At the meeting, which was catered and held around a long, oval, wooden table in the Frank Hogan Room on the firm's top floor (the choice of the room reflected not only the size of the group but the importance Hogan & Hartson attached to the case), Kendall was clear on their options: the only way to "spring these guys" (in his later words) was to mount a campaign for pardons by Virginia's Democratic governor, Mark Warner. "There is no judicial remedy, in fact," Kendall stated. He knew that the innocence statute recently enacted with much fanfare in Virginia that allowed inmates to file petitions for writs of actual innocence based on newly discovered evidence more than twenty-one days after sentencing—the previous limit for petitioning state courts—was actually pretty narrow. Inmates who had pled guilty and whose claims lacked newly discovered biological evidence, for example, were ineligible. That meant that Williams and Dick were out of court. "We didn't have a whole lot of choice," Kendall recalls. "Joe Dick and Dan Williams were literally going to die in prison if we can't somehow get the governor of Virginia to look at this very seriously." In Virginia, Kendall adds, "once you get convicted, the legal remedies available to you are nearly nonexistent." (As of July 2007, no prisoners in Virginia had been found innocent after filing petitions for writs of actual innocence based on non-DNA evidence. The statute "was essentially set up to fail by creating too many obstacles," Kent Willis, the executive director of the ACLU of Virginia, said. A "false hope," a defense attorney called it.)[12]

The lawyers at Hogan & Hartson learned that Tice did have a judicial option, though: to file a petition for a writ of habeas corpus with Virginia challenging the legality of his imprisonment. The statute of limitations on habeas writs had expired for Williams and Dick. Hogan & Hartson had a long history of prosecuting habeas petitions, and when Tice's attorneys began looking for constitutional violations in his case, "it wasn't too hard to find them," Deborah Boardman remembers. To their amazement, they learned from Detective Randy Crank's notes in James Broccoletti's files that Tice had invoked his right to silence during his police interrogation. They also believed, based on Crank's notes, that Tice had requested a lawyer. Yet Broccoletti and his co-counsel, Jeffrey Russell, had not motioned to suppress Tice's confession. "We were surprised that no motion to suppress the confession had been filed, given that the confession was essentially the only evidence against him other than Joseph Dick," Boardman recalls.[13]

As for the clemency campaign, it would have to be custom-made. There was no boilerplate for such campaigns. "You look at your strengths and you look at your weaknesses," Kendall says. "And I think the strength of this was we had four *very* unlikely people to commit something like this. Not that it's impossible, but very unlikely. I mean, these guys are not from central casting. If central casting sent these guys over, you'd say, 'Wrong people.' You know, the military background—these are just true-blue homegrown sort of kids who grew up and wanted to serve their country, and were doing that. And they get pulled into something that is way beyond their ability to deal with it."[14]

But their confessions, not to mention Dick's and Tice's incriminating testimony in court, would not be easy to explain, to the governor or anybody else. Though jurors may harbor some doubts about a defendant's guilt and nonetheless send him to prison, even send him to the gas chamber, to free a prisoner, his attorneys have to demonstrate his absolute innocence. It's a tough task; in some cases, it's almost impossible. The attorneys thus had to research their clients' cases exhaustively and show overwhelming evidence of innocence. "You need to basically look at every single claim that the prosecutors have made in the case about why the guys are guilty, and then demonstrate why that's not accurate," Don Salzman thought. The attorneys had to explain why their clients' confessions simply weren't credible, that there were logical reasons why they shouldn't be accepted, why, in fact, they didn't make any sense.[15]

And confessions or no confessions, it is far easier to convict an innocent person than to exonerate them, in Virginia or any other state. To free an innocent person from prison usually requires superior attorneys who are willing to spend years on the case—nearly eleven on average for the murder and rape cases the Innocence Commission for Virginia examined—and who possess great determination and substantial resources. It also requires the support of others and publicity. Most innocent people languishing in prisons across the country do not have access to that kind of legal help and attention, or anything approaching it. They can't even get to first base. Many log long hours in spartan prison libraries and cells struggling to put together appeals on their own. In one study of capital cases in which convicted defendants were later found innocent, the researchers discovered that in none of the cases was the defendant largely responsible for the exposure of the injustice. "Without exception the defendant needed the help of others," the researchers found. Though there was no typical route of vindication, "it is rare for anyone within the system to play the decisive role in correcting error," they wrote.[16]

Williams, Dick, and Tice had about the best legal assistance imaginable—sharp, experienced attorneys from giant law firms with deep pockets—but there was the additional problem that prosecutors tend to resist postconviction claims of innocence. Indeed, prosecutors often seem more concerned with making a conviction stick than with uncovering the truth. To acknowledge committing serious errors can hurt their reputations and credibility, and even put a halt to their career advancement. Prosecutors also don't like to spend time correcting their mistakes because of their heavy workloads. And closure is important for the victims, they often say. Many have resisted postconviction DNA testing, opposed new hearings, stonewalled about turning over potentially exculpatory evidence after convictions, or even destroyed that evidence, often in the name of finality. Resisting postconviction claims of innocence is the cultural norm in most district attorneys' offices. When prosecutors accede to such claims, it is frequently because it is to their political advantage or to avoid a serious cost.[17]

What's more, governors obviously make political calculations when considering clemency requests. Most don't want to appear "soft on crime." They

know their decisions will be scrutinized, and they are reluctant to question juries' verdicts. If it turns out that a person they pardoned is guilty, it can kill
their political career. Mark Warner had been mentioned often as a possible
presidential candidate in 2008: he had to be careful.

The attorneys reasoned that they would have to put themselves in Warner's
shoes—or, more precisely, in his press office's shoes. How would he explain
pardoning their clients to the public? "You have to write a press release," says
one attorney involved in the campaign. A successful clemency campaign
"boils itself down to a two-page press release that explains overwhelmingly
why this makes the greatest sense in the world."[18]

That press release would have to show not only that their clients were innocent but that there were powerful people who believed in their innocence.
The attorneys would thus have to get influential figures with experience in the
criminal justice system to endorse their petition; they also needed to generate
media coverage of the case. They had to grab Warner's attention, and quickly,
since he would be leaving office in January 2006.[19] In Virginia, governors are
barred from serving consecutive terms.

Kendall was frank with the other lawyers about the tough road ahead
of them. "I told everyone, 'Look, these are very hard,'" he recounts. "'They
shouldn't be as hard as they are. . . . And once you get on this, you're going to
come to believe in your client's innocence. But I want you to just remember that
these things are oftentimes unsuccessful. And so we've got to leave no stone
unturned. We've really got to do this thing right, and maybe it will work.'"[20]

Greg McCormack, who had already filed a clemency petition for Eric Wilson, elected not to join their campaign. After speaking with Kendall several
times over the phone and allowing him to see some of Wilson's case file, Mc-
Cormack told Wilson's mother that "they didn't want to help us at all," Wilson
remembers. "They just wanted to do it so that we would give them all of our
information. So it was very one-sided, according to my lawyer." Perhaps Mc-
Cormack, an independent man, was not eager to share the credit if his client
was pardoned. But he asked the governor's office to put Wilson's petition on
the same time track as Williams's, Dick's, and Tice's request.[21]

Michael Fasanaro, Joe Dick's lawyer, was openly unhappy with the campaign to free his client. When one of the clemency attorneys phoned Fasanaro
about it, "the first thing out of his mouth was, 'What does he want now?'" the
attorney recalls. The attorney found Fasanaro difficult and "not a believer in

this campaign. I know that he's made some disparaging comments to *Night-line*." The attorney told Fasanaro that Dick had made no claim against him and that he was therefore obligated by attorney-client privilege to keep his mouth shut. "I don't know whether he has or not," the attorney says. (He didn't: Fasanaro later told a journalist for a piece on the case in the *New York Times Magazine* that he still believed Dick was guilty. "I've seen nothing to convince me otherwise," he said.) Of course, Dick's exoneration would cast a poor light, to say the least, on Fasanaro's handling of his case, including his prior assertions, both in open court and to Dick himself, that Dick was guilty. It's not unusual for defense attorneys to worry that postconviction reviews of their cases will make them look bad. But Dan Shipley, who had come to believe in his client Danial Williams's innocence and wanted him freed, provided Don Salzman with Williams's case file. "Danny Shipley has been extremely cooperative and open with us," Salzman says.[22]

Omar Ballard also wanted to help. When we told him that we had given his prison address to one of the attorneys, Ballard replied, "I wouldn't mind talking to the lawyers, as long as they listen to me, and not try to come up with thier [sic] own scenario on what took place. I won't lie, as a matter of fact, I'll be overjoyed to inform the world that these guys had absolutely nothing to do with the crime. I think it's good that some people . . . are interested in the truth and would allow me the time to release the truth." Ballard met with Tice's attorneys, including Deborah Boardman, who found him introspective, open, and honest. He had nothing to hide, Ballard told her. But when he first provided his account of the murder to one of the attorneys, it was obviously hard for him to do. He seemed to be feeling a lot of emotion inside; he initially had a hard time even looking the attorney in the eye. But Boardman's visits "solidified my belief that he did this alone," she remembers. Ballard provided the attorneys with a key affidavit in which he took sole responsibility for the crime. "None of the other individuals who were charged with raping or killing Michelle were there or involved in any way," he wrote. "They are all innocent."[23]

The petition for a writ of habeas corpus that Hogan & Hartson's lawyers filed in September 2005 argued that Derek Tice's due-process rights were violated when Detective Glenn Ford encouraged Ballard not to testify at Tice's second trial. Tice's rights were also violated, the attorneys maintained, when Ford and

D.J. Hansen threatened to withdraw Joe Dick's plea agreement unless he testified for the prosecution (the attorneys later withdrew this claim, however,
based on evidence that the state planned to present). They argued further that
the commonwealth violated Tice's rights by withholding from the defense exculpatory evidence: that Tamika Taylor had advised police early on to investigate Ballard. And Tice had been deprived of his right to effective assistance of
counsel, they contended. James Broccoletti and Jeffrey Russell had a duty to
present exculpatory evidence, but they had suggested to Ballard that he say
nothing at Tice's retrial. "What trial counsel should have done—and had an
obligation to do—was to vigorously *encourage* Ballard to testify truthfully on
Mr. Tice's behalf," the attorneys wrote. In addition, Broccoletti and Russell
had failed to get Ballard's letter to Karen Stover admitted into evidence. And
they had not moved to suppress Tice's confession despite his invocation of his
right to silence, his request for an attorney, and Ford's overbearing of his will.
"Any reasonable defense counsel would have moved to suppress the confession," the attorneys wrote. Finally, they argued that Broccoletti and Russell
should have offered expert testimony to debunk the prosecution's multiple-
assailant theory of the crime.[24]

Some two weeks later, Eric Wilson was released from prison. He had served
almost seven and a half years of his eight-and-a-half-year sentence. Upon his
release, the state of Virginia handed him all of twenty-five dollars and a bus
ticket to anywhere he wanted in Virginia. No wonder so many inmates find
themselves back in prison after getting out: about 29 percent of Virginia's inmates are reincarcerated within thirty-six months of their release (national
recidivism rates are even higher). Fortunately for Wilson, he had family in
Texas. But life outside prison was a struggle; his rape conviction plagued him.
"It's been very hard," he told us in February 2007; for a long time, things were
"pretty black." Every year on his birthday, he had to suffer the utter humil-
iation of registering as a sex offender. On the Texas Department of Public
Safety's web site, his postprison mug shots, description, and address—complete
with a link to a map—were available to the public. He applied for an appren-
tice electrician's license, but was denied because of his sex conviction. His appeal was denied too. Then he lost a job as an electrician's helper owing to a
random license check, which found that he had no license, so he went on un-
employment. After hiring a lawyer, he petitioned the licensing and regulatory

board and was finally granted a license. But he worried about how his sex conviction would affect him next.[25]

In November 2005, the attorneys for Williams, Dick, and Tice held a press
conference at a law firm in Richmond, Virginia, the state capital, announcing
their campaign for pardons. Placards bearing large photos of the three prisoners in their naval uniforms and facts about their cases were lined up behind
the lectern; another poster boasted Ballard's photo and a quote from his letter
to Karen Stover. After George Kendall, Don Salzman, and Deborah Boardman
spoke, Larry McCann, the expert on crime scene investigation they had hired,
told the journalists on hand that his analysis of the case led him to conclude
that "there was only one person in that apartment with Michelle when she
was killed." "Some mistakes are irreversible. This is not one of them," McCann
wrote two weeks later in an opinion piece in the *Washington Post*. Richard
Ofshe, a prominent expert on false confessions the attorneys had also hired,
declared that he'd "never seen a case as horrible, as egregious, and as clear-cut
as these cases. . . . These confessions are an illusion." The parents of the three
petitioners gave short emotional statements on behalf of their sons. "We miss
Derek more than words could ever express," said Rachel Tice, who had driven
up to Richmond from North Carolina with her husband early that morning.
"There has not been a day gone by in the past seven years when I have not
been brought to the edge of tears thinking of how my loving and compas-
sionate son is trapped in a wretched prison cell." "Please, sir, do what is right,
do what is just," she implored Governor Warner, on the brink of breaking
down again. "Please release my son from prison. He is innocent, and we want
him home." Members of the audience were tearing up too.[26]

After suffering many dark days since their sons' arrests, the parents were
in high spirits after the press conference. Rhea Williams, Danial Williams's
mother, thought the whole event—the big boardroom, lawyers, media, and
cameras all over the place—looked like something out of *L.A. Law*. She wondered if they might next be on *Good Morning America*, it was that impressive.
She and her husband began making plans for Danial's return over dinner the
next evening, only to realize that they were getting way ahead of themselves.
Derek Tice was "on cloud nine" after seeing two TV news reports on the conference; his mother was in one, his father was in the other.[27]

In the clemency petition, a thick and well-documented request that was "a mind-boggling indictment of the criminal justice system," in the view of the *Virginian-Pilot* newspaper, the attorneys wrote that they had "no doubt" that Williams, Dick, and Tice were innocent. Justice for them was "long overdue," the petition argued. It included reports from McCann, Ofshe, and Dr. Werner Spitz, a well-known forensic pathologist, whose study of the case had also led him to believe that Michelle was killed by one person only. It was "extraordinarily unlikely" that more than one inflicted her stab wounds, and "even less likely that several people produced these wounds," Spitz wrote. Given the close proximity and common direction and depth of the major ones, Spitz said, the notion that a gang of young men passed a knife around "does not make any sense." And "it is highly unusual to have multiple offenders penetrate a victim without a positive DNA match from multiple suspects." To Patricia Dick, who had come to believe that her son was innocent after meeting with his attorneys, the petition confirmed it.[28]

But Billy Bosko and Carol Moore were angered by the petition. "No one is going to confess to crimes of this magnitude unless they were guilty," Bosko maintained yet again. "And I hope common sense prevails." "There's no way that they're innocent," Moore declared. "No way." Maureen Evans, the former Norfolk homicide detective who had interrogated Williams, was in "complete shock" over the petition and planned to convey her views to the Virginia Parole Board, who would be reviewing it and then prepare a report for Governor Warner. Kevin Hall, a Warner spokesman, said that the governor had received three such petitions before and "we granted their requests for absolute pardons." But there was no time limit on the review.[29]

The *Virginian-Pilot*, whose articles on the case had largely reflected the police's theory of it, stunned many people when it came out in support of the petition. If the first seven young men who were arrested were indeed innocent, as it appeared, a *Pilot* editorial pointed out, "then police, prosecutors, defense attorneys, juries and judges all failed. And they failed multiple times." The credibility of both the Innocence Project and the big law firms representing Williams, Dick, and Tice was one reason to believe the petition's claims, the editorial noted. The lawyers had earlier notified the *Pilot* of their press conference and showed them material on the case, piquing the paper's interest; they'd also held an hour-and-a-half phone conference with the *Pilot*'s editorial board. "To their great credit, they were very well prepared, they asked a lot of hard questions," Kendall remembers. Six weeks later, another *Pilot* editorial called the clemency petition "among the most thorough ever assembled in the state" and exhorted Warner to act before leaving office. No less than the *Washington Post* also urged Warner to consider the petition. It "makes a strong case that Mr. Warner cannot ignore," the *Post* observed. The attorneys' approach to the media was both simple and effective: "We alerted the media that this matter was pending, and if they were interested, then, 'Here are the papers,'" Kendall recounts. "'And if you want to talk to anybody, then let us know. . . . Ask us anything you want.'" They believed strongly in their clients' innocence, the attorneys said, and "if we're wrong, we're going to hear we're wrong pretty quickly."[30]

D.J. Hansen and Derek Wagner, who had prosecuted Tice, felt compelled to respond. Tice "has never testified under oath to his innocence," they pointed out in the *Pilot*. And Dick, whose alibi lacked credibility, they said, "has testified to three separate juries that he and the others are guilty. He stood up to three withering cross-examinations." Williams knew Ballard, they claimed. "It is unfortunate that the facts of this case, as decided by the justice system, are being drowned out by a series of post-trial armchair opinions that have no scientific basis and would not be admissible in a court of law in this commonwealth," they wrote. "These convicts know this. . . . Their petition for pardon is replete with unsubstantiated and vicious attacks on a Norfolk police detective and long-standing members of the Norfolk defense bar. It deserves serious scrutiny of its veracity, not commendation." Hansen and Wagner said that there was "ample evidence to support" the petitioners' confessions: "It's all in the record."[31]

In December, after calling the petitioners' attorneys, *Time* magazine ran a story on the case whose underlying tone was sympathetic to the petition. But Hansen told *Time* that there was nothing new in the request that hadn't already been weighed in the judicial process ("That's just not so," the *Virginian-Pilot* responded). "Justice was done," Hansen proclaimed. The same month, *Nightline* aired a television piece on the case after talking to the attorneys.[32]

In early January 2006, the lawyers released a letter from nine of the jurors in Eric Wilson's trial that urged Warner to "promptly" grant clemency to all four petitioners. After reviewing material that they did not have at the trial, the jurors wrote, "we now firmly believe that Wilson, Dick, Tice, and Williams are all innocent." The lawyers also released an affidavit from one of the jurors in Tice's retrial expressing regret over the jury's verdict and stating, "I am outraged that many people who were entrusted with investigating and finding the truth about this crime apparently went out of their way to cover up the truth, to interfere with witness testimony and to mislead the jury." She, too, urged Warner to swiftly pardon the prisoners. "I feel very badly I helped send this man to prison," she told the *Post*. The attorneys distributed letters they had obtained from former judges and prosecutors advocating clemency as well; several ex–state attorneys general would also come out in support of the petition. "That doesn't come around every day," Kendall observes. "These guys are asked often to do this, and they usually say no." One of the former attorneys general commented, "It's just a bad case that should have been caught in the system and wasn't."[33]

Meanwhile, the petitioners' attorneys were leaning directly on Warner's office. "We pushed him very hard," Kendall remembers. The case was a terrible miscarriage of justice, they told Warner's aides over the phone; he couldn't just leave these guys in prison. But, Kendall recalls, "his thing was . . . 'There's a system here, and we're going to use the system. And what I will do is I will say the parole board has to get after this one.'" But the attorneys were coming in late in the governor's term, Warner's aides pointed out. The lawyers were not unaware that, for political reasons, most pardons are granted at the end of a governor's term.[34]

Warner turned over his office to Virginia's new governor, Tim Kaine, also a Democrat, on January 14, 2006, without coming to a decision. The parole board had not completed its review, letting Warner off the hook.[35]

In August, Derek Tice's lawyers took a videotaped deposition from Detective Glenn Ford for Tice's habeas petition in the executive boardroom of a Marriott hotel in Norfolk. It was not a process Ford cared to undergo. For the most part, he appeared subtly resentful of the proceeding, even scornful of it. He grew increasingly irritated with Des Hogan's questions, which drilled away on his visits with Dick and Ballard ("my buddy," Ford said) before Tice's second trial. Always a tough witness for defense lawyers to examine, he seemed to understand Hogan's agenda and wasn't about to give in.[36]

The next month, a hearing was held on Tice's habeas petition before Judge Everett A. Martin Jr. Ballard once again proclaimed his guilt and recalled how both Ford and James Broccoletti had encouraged him to keep his mouth shut at Tice's retrial. After authenticating Ballard's letter to her, Karen Stover said that she would have been available to do so at Tice's retrial. And Michael Ziegler, Dick's naval supervisor, testified that he had no doubt that Dick was on duty the night of the murder. Broccoletti, Russell, Tice, Crank, Ford, and Wray also took the stand; the detectives' accounts of Tice's interrogation differed from Tice's retelling on numerous points.[37]

Helen F. Fahey, the chair of the parole board, dropped by the hearing. Fahey was formerly the U.S. attorney for the eastern district of Virginia and a tough, hard-nosed prosecutor. "The sentences that they were giving out of [her office] were just off the radar screen," Kendall says. A congressional resolution commending Fahey upon her departure as the U.S. attorney noted that her office "has drawn frequent praise from the Attorney General of the United States"—John Ashcroft—"for its aggressive approach to criminal and civil prosecution." But as the Arlington commonwealth's attorney earlier, Fahey had helped obtain a pardon for a false confessor named David Vasquez. "My view is that she saw that case as an anomaly," one attorney comments. "And that she is very skeptical of a case where there are four false confessions." Fahey and the other members of the parole board were monitoring Tice's petition. The board would not make a recommendation to the governor on clemency until all judicial proceedings were finished, a Kaine spokesman said.[38] That, of course, was not what Williams, Dick, Tice, or their attorneys wanted to hear.

After the hearing on Tice's habeas petition, Judge Martin offered both sides some of his "impressions" to help inform their writing of their posthearing briefs. "First of all, with respect to Mr. Ballard, he's an unadjudicated, self-admitted perjurer," Martin stated. "He's committed more felonies than he can remember. He raped and murdered a woman who had given him sanctuary when an angry mob was after him. I don't think I'd believe a word that monster said." So much for the claim that Ford had interfered with his testimony. And Martin suggested that Ballard's letter to Karen Stover was "cumulative to" his confessions to police. "Seems to me, Ms. Boardman, if you've got any arrow in your quiver, the strongest one is the failure to suppress the confession," Martin said.[39]

Two and a half months later, Martin issued his ruling. James Broccoletti and Jeffrey Russell had been deficient in failing to motion to suppress Tice's confession, Martin determined. Tice had unequivocally invoked his right to silence when questioned by his polygraph examiner, Detective Randy Crank, as indicated by Crank's notes, which Broccoletti must have seen. And a motion to suppress on that basis would probably have succeeded, Martin wrote. Moreover, without his confession, Tice might well have been acquitted. Martin rejected all of the habeas petition's other arguments. It was not a friendly decision overall; Martin even said that there was "physical evidence" against Tice, which was nonexistent.[40] But all it took was agreement with one argument to vacate Tice's convictions. Barring a successful appeal of Martin's decision, Tice would now get a new trial—if prosecutors elected to try him again. His confessions would likely be inadmissible in light of Martin's ruling and Crank's notes. And Dick would no longer be testifying against him since Dick was now asserting his innocence. The commonwealth's case against Tice had apparently evaporated. And if prosecutors didn't retry him, he would be released. Of course, the annulment of his convictions could also provide Kaine cover for granting clemency to all four petitioners.

Tice and his attorneys were elated. The vast majority of habeas petitions are unsuccessful, the chances of success in Virginia are low indeed, and it's especially difficult to win claims, standard as they are, of ineffective assistance of counsel. The attorneys hoped Martin's ruling would budge Kaine on clemency; Danial Williams talked of being home with his family in Michigan by Christmas. "I'm still about three feet above the ground," Larry Tice told a reporter. After all of his dashed hopes in Derek's case, he couldn't believe that they'd actually won something. Carol and Jack Moore, Michelle Moore-Bosko's parents, were "profoundly disappointed" by Martin's ruling, however. "The pain does not go away, not even for a moment," they said. The director of the Institute for Actual Innocence at the University of Richmond law school aptly commented, "If we allowed the emotions of a grieving family to trump accuracy, we would pay a very high price."[41]

The Virginia state attorney general's office indicated that it would appeal Martin's decision and asked that Tice remain in prison while the Virginia Supreme Court considered the case. Two days later, the *Washington Post* came out with another editorial on the case, pointedly titled, "Attention: Tim Kaine: It's time for Virginia's governor to do something about the 'Norfolk 4.'" "They have made what seems a powerful case for their innocence," the *Post* stated. It was "wrong" for Kaine to wait until Tice's legal proceedings were finished to rule on clemency, the editors argued. The petitions "have been pending for more than a year. Given the magnitude of the injustice they claim, it's time Mr. Kaine gave them an answer."[42]

Ten days later, an editorial in the *Virginian-Pilot* argued that Martin's ruling "strengthens the clemency petitions. . . . A host of credible observers, including two former attorneys general, have said profound error appears to have occurred and needs to be set right. . . . Whatever the hold-up at the parole board, it's time to get the process moving."[43]

These editorials would have been unthinkable several years earlier, before the three prestigious law firms took up the case. The *Post* had not covered Moore-Bosko's murder and rape, given its location, and readers of the *Pilot* had been told more than once of a terrifying gang attack, multiple chilling confessions, defense lawyers who had pled their murderous clients out, and incriminating testimony against all eight assailants. Media coverage of the case had shifted dramatically; indeed, it was even possible to get the sense that the law firms were steamrolling their way to victory.

When a Kaine spokesman stated in December that the governor did not, in fact, intend to wait until the conclusion of the state's appeal of Martin's decision to rule on clemency, the attorneys weren't sure what to expect. The same month, Martin refused a request by Tice's lawyers that their client be released from prison while the state appealed. "If I'd spent eight years of a life sentence in prison, and I was looking at retrial on capital murder, I'd be looking toward Mexico," Martin said.[44]

In January 2007, the petitioners' lawyers made their case before the parole board in Richmond. After Don Salzman gave an opening statement, Michael Ziegler testified on Dick's alibi, and Larry McCann and Werner Spitz discussed how the physical evidence was inconsistent with eight attackers. A DNA expert also spoke, as did Chris Ochoa, who told the board how he had falsely confessed to a murder and rape, pled guilty, and then continued to incriminate himself for fear of his life. Frank Stokes, a former FBI agent who was appalled by the case, also addressed the board. The parents of Williams, Dick, and Tice then gave brief statements.[45]

When members of the board questioned the speakers, Helen Fahey was by far the most active among them. She had stated at the outset that she'd been designated to play the devil's advocate, and she played that role well. Many of her questions were pointed. "To her credit, she was very familiar with the record," George Kendall remembers. "I think for sure she'd been in touch with the prosecutors. . . . And virtually every question she asked was a question of testing—to be generous—our case. To be not so generous, it was just a hostile question." The attorneys wondered if Fahey was really just playing a role; she obviously had her doubts about their case. At least one attorney thought she exhibited a degree of skepticism that wasn't grounded in the facts. But she also appeared pleased with their presentation, and "she's a smart lady, and she knows criminal defense," the attorney notes. The lawyers felt their presentation went well. The board told them at the end of the meeting that they wanted to think more about the case and do some additional investigation, and that they'd be in touch.[46]

Whichever way the board went, the attorneys planned to press Governor Kaine to move on their petition, "either up or down," Kendall said. "If it's bad news, it's bad news. If it's good news, it's good news. But let's not let these guys just hang there and twist forever." Kendall suspected that Kaine would indeed decide to wait until Tice's legal proceedings were finished to rule, and if Tice was actually retried, to let the jury decide the case.[47] That would give Kaine cover in either direction.

That September, the attorneys met with Larry Roberts, Kaine's counsel. The meeting lasted six hours, into the early evening. Fahey also attended. Larry McCann, an ex–FBI agent, and a Washington homicide detective spoke; each said they believed that Omar Ballard had been the sole assailant. Dr. Richard Ratner, a psychiatrist who had evaluated Dick at the attorneys' request, also addressed Roberts, as did Barry Scheck of the Innocence Project and several others. The attorneys found Roberts thoughtful, interested, and sincere. "We have them really listening," one commented afterward. They were close to persuading the governor's office on the merits of the case, the attorney perceived, but clemency remained a political issue, and Virginia was a conservative state. Moreover, exceptional political courage was hardly commonplace. How many governors had granted pardons in cases involving four confessions, three jury convictions, and two guilty pleas?[48]

But there was considerable community support for clemency, the attorney mused the day after the meeting, as he was driving home after an all-nighter (his second of the week) and feeling more optimistic than he had for a while. And Kaine didn't have to follow the parole board's recommendation, whatever it turned out to be. The attorney suspected that the board was "very split." And that had been the lawyers' goal: to split it. They'd doubted that they would receive a unanimous vote for clemency from it anyway. The division probably explained why the board hadn't come in with a verdict yet. Now it had apparently stepped out of the way.[49]

Shortly after 9 A.M. on January 11, 2008, the Virginia Supreme Court announced that it had reversed Judge Everett Martin's ruling vacating Derek Tice's conviction. Tice's lawyers at Hogan & Hartson had failed to prove "that there was a reasonable probability of a different result at his criminal trial if the jury had not considered his confession," Justice Barbara Milano Keenan wrote. Tice's trial counsel had not presented any evidence to jurors that Joe Dick, "who had participated in the rapes and murder of Michelle," Keenan wrote, had a motive to fabricate his testimony on Tice's involvement. And while Tice's defense had been based on the theory that Omar Ballard was the sole assailant, Tamika Taylor's testimony that Danial Williams had an obsession with Michelle as well as Dick's testimony undermined that theory. "In short, the record before us does not undermine confidence in the outcome of the proceedings," Keenan stated. The Court also considered whether Tice's trial counsel had been ineffective because they had failed to get Ballard's letter to Karen Stover admitted into evidence. Justice Keenan argued that Ballard did not indicate in the letter whether he had acted alone (though that would have been the logical reading of it). And the letter was "merely cumulative of other evidence of Ballard's commission of the crimes." (Upon reading the letter after Tice's trial, however, one of the jurors said that it would have fed her inclination to acquit Tice and strengthened her belief, which she advanced during jury deliberations, that Ballard was more likely to have acted alone than with seven men he didn't even know.)[50]

Larry and Rachel Tice, Derek's parents, were at the Virginia Supreme Court in Richmond to hear the Court's ruling. The decision came as yet another blow in their long fight to exonerate their son. Larry Tice, who had now sent no fewer than ninety-four letters to Governor Kaine asking for clemency, had been "so positive we were going to win this thing." Derek's lawyers also appeared stunned by the ruling. But another attorney involved in the clemency campaign found the Court's decision "no surprise." The Court hardly ever ruled that defense counsel were ineffective, he points out—it was as unreceptive to claims of ineffectiveness as any state supreme court in the country—and it had only part of the case before it. "It's no wonder that you get these kinds of rulings," he says. The Court's opinion was "a continuation of the tunnel vision that the courts have shown in this case from day one." Plus, the Court had not been obligated to hear the state's appeal of Martin's ruling, and when courts exercise their discretion to hear an appeal, more often than not it means reversal.[51]

Carol and Jack Moore were pleased by the Court's decision. "We are thankful that the Virginia Supreme Court did not allow Derek Tice to escape the consequences of this horrible crime based upon a legal technicality," they told the press. "These men are guilty, and we pray that our family will not have to suffer through any more appeals."[52]

After the Court had announced its ruling, the lawyers for Williams, Dick, and Tice held another press conference in Richmond. Two of the former Virginia attorneys general who had come out in support of clemency and a past president of the Virginia Bar Association urged that Governor Kaine grant clemency. "There should be no innocent people in Virginia's prisons," Richard Cullen, one of the ex–attorneys general, declared. The lawyers and their supporters argued that the Court's decision and the case for clemency were apples and oranges: the Court had before it a narrow legal issue and an incomplete record of the case, while Governor Kaine had in front of him a claim of actual innocence and the full picture. "Today's ruling addresses only one part of the case," Cullen pointed out. Even if the Court was right on the question of law, the attorneys for Williams, Dick, and Tice asserted, that spoke in no way to their clients' guilt or innocence. But they knew that the Court's opinion did not help their clemency request. Far from providing cover for Kaine, the Court had essentially said their clients were guilty.[53]

Yet the attorneys still thought they had a good chance of obtaining pardons. Larry Roberts, Kaine's counsel, had asked for additional information on the case, and his requests had given them more reason for hope. Roberts had also indicated that the governor wanted to get moving on their petition. "I think [Kaine's] going to sit down and decide this sooner rather than later," one attorney predicted the day after the Court's ruling.[54]

The next day, the *Washington Post* came out with yet another editorial in favor of clemency and exhorting Governor Kaine to act soon. There was "overwhelming evidence" that Williams, Dick, Tice, and Wilson were innocent, the *Post* stated. Two days later, the *Virginian-Pilot* ran another editorial advocating clemency as well. "In our system, the governor is the final fail-safe against a breakdown in our courts," the *Pilot* noted. "Kaine has an obligation to set it right."[55]

If Kaine denied their clients pardons—a prospect that was almost too distressing for them to ponder—the attorneys intended to take their case to Virginia's next governor after Kaine left office in 2010. They also planned to file a petition in federal court for a writ of habeas corpus based on absolute innocence. "We're simply going to say, 'Yes, the statute of limitations has run. But when you can show this kind of innocence, and when there's no process left, including clemency, then a court in America has to be open,'" one attorney says. They were prepared to go up to the U.S. Supreme Court, if that's what it took. "Even if there is bitter disappointment—and that's what it will be— if Kaine leaves these guys in there, then that's not going to be the end of this," the attorney says.[56]

Acknowledgments

We wish to thank everybody who agreed to be interviewed for this book. Their help was indispensable. We are also grateful to the following people for providing legal documents, court transcripts, interview transcripts, photographs, tape recordings, or other materials: Deborah Boardman, James Broccoletti, Patricia Dick, Paul Dowling, George Kendall, Erin Litle, Greg McCormack, Don Salzman, Lori Searcy, Larry Tice, Rhea Williams, and Ramey Wilson. Marc Young at the Norfolk Circuit Court took pictures of the case photographs for us at the court. George Schaefer, the clerk of the court, was also helpful.

We thank Deborah Boardman, Donald Connery, Peter Honigsberg, George Kendall, and Don Salzman for reading the manuscript. Connery, Gil Geis, and Carol Tavris provided useful comments on our book proposal, and Jon Gould and Steve Rosenfield patiently answered our questions.

We are grateful to the Open Society Institute for awarding us Soros Justice Senior Fellowships for the researching and writing of this book; Kate Black at the Institute was an impressive force.

Our agent, Judith Riven, has been superb in all departments. Diane Wachtell, our editor at The New Press, and editorial assistant Priyanka Jacob provided invaluable editorial advice. Diane helped shape the book from its early stages and has been a pleasure to work with.

Finally, we wish to thank our wives, Lisa Bryant and Kim Richman, for putting up with our obsessions with the book and offering perceptive advice.

A Note on Sources

The following people were interviewed for this book, many more than once: Jon Babineau, Omar Ballard, Alphonse Bankard, Catherine Bankard, Tom Bankard, Theresa Bankard-Sharpe, Deborah Boardman, Pat Bosko, Sarah Bosko, James Broccoletti, Sharon Combee, Joe Dick, Joe Dick Sr., Patricia Dick, Dartha Dickinson, Paul Dowling, Maureen Evans, Michael Fasanaro, Robert Frank, Helen Frezon, Jerry Frezon, James Godfrey, D.J. Hansen, Don Higginbotham, George Kendall, Carl Knipe, Chuck Litle, Erin Litle, Greg McCormack, Peter Neufeld, Judy Pauley, Richard Pauley Sr., Rick Pauley, John Poyer, Tom Reed, John E. Roger, Jeffrey Russell, Don Salzman, John Schwertlech, Dan Shipley, Lyn Simmons, Matt Sisk, Shannon Sisk, Jennifer Stanton, Derek Tice, Larry Tice, Lea Tice, Rachel Tice, Doreen Trevena, Joel Vanucci, Derek Wagner, Ben Weber, Melissa Wharton, Danial Williams, Norman Williams, Rhea Williams, Eric Wilson, Ramey Wilson, William Wilson, and Allan Zaleski. Other sources requested anonymity.

This book also relies extensively on legal documents, including police notes, reports, recordings, photographs, and other materials; transcripts of trials, hearings, and confessions; letters and memoranda; motions, briefs, affidavits, and notices; court orders; lab analyses; presentence reports, psychological evaluations, school, and military records of the defendants; plea agreements; autopsy and medical examiner reports; attorneys' records; alibi materials; polygraph reports; and warrants and indictments. Most of these documents were obtained at the Norfolk Circuit Court in Virginia. We also consulted numerous secondary sources.

Notes

Legal documents cited in the notes were obtained from the Norfolk Circuit Court's files or from people involved in this case. Those documents obtained from people are noted as "in authors' possession" the first time they are cited in the notes. Shortened titles of secondary sources have been used; full titles and citations for these sources are provided in the bibliography.

1: Discovery

1. Bill Bosko testimony, Eric Wilson trial, June 1999; Erin Litle interview.

2. Bosko interview for "Eight Men Out" television program, 2001.

3. Bosko testimony, first Derek Tice trial, February 2000, and Wilson trial, June 1999.

4. Bosko testimony, first Tice trial, February 2000, and second Tice trial, January 2003; John E. Roger interview.

5. Author visits to apartment building; *Virginian-Pilot*, July 9, 2000; Erin Litle interview; Bosko testimony, Wilson trial (sentencing phase), June 1999.

6. Sarah Bosko interview; Erin Litle interview; Carol Moore testimony, Wilson trial (sentencing phase), June 1999; Joel Vanucci interview; Pat Bosko interview.

7. Bosko testimony, preliminary hearing of Richard Pauley and Geoffrey Farris, August 25, 1998; Bosko testimony, second Tice trial, January 2003; Bosko interview for "Eight Men Out"; police crime scene videotape (in authors' possession).

8. Bosko testimony, Wilson trial, June 1999; police crime scene videotape; Bob Frank interview; Tamika Taylor testimony, second Tice trial, January 2003, and first Tice trial, February 2000.

9. Taylor testimony, first Tice trial, February 2000.

10. Taylor testimony, second Tice trial, January 2003; Omar Ballard to Paul Dowling, March 4, 2003 (in authors' possession); Bosko interview for "Eight Men Out."

11. Taylor testimony, first Tice trial, February 2000, and Wilson trial, June 1999; Greg McCormack examination of Bosko, Wilson trial, June 1999.

12. Taylor testimony, Wilson trial, June 1999; Bosko testimony, first Tice trial, February 2000.

13. Rhea Williams interview; Danial Williams interview.

14. Taylor testimony, second Tice trial, January 2003, Wilson trial, June 1999, and first Tice trial, February 2000.

15. Taylor testimony, Wilson trial, June 1999, first Tice trial, February 2000, and second Tice trial, January 2003.

16. Taylor testimony, second Tice trial, January 2003, and first Tice trial, February 2000.

17. Police crime scene videotape; Erin Litle interview; Vanucci interview; photo of tattoo (Norfolk Circuit Court records).

18. Taylor testimony, Wilson trial, June 1999; Joe Dick interview; D.J. Hansen interview.

19. Bosko interview for "Eight Men Out"; Bosko testimony, first Tice trial, February 2000, and second Tice trial, January 2003; police crime scene videotape.

20. Bosko testimony, Wilson trial, June 1999; Bosko interview for "Eight Men Out."

21. Bosko testimony, Wilson trial, June 1999, and second Tice trial, January 2003; police crime scene videotape.

22. Police crime scene videotape; police crime scene photos of Michelle Moore-Bosko (Norfolk Circuit Court records); Elizabeth Kinnison testimony, Wilson trial, June 1999; Bosko testimony, Wilson preliminary and suppression hearing, June 23, 1998 (in authors' possession); diagram of apartment and items (in authors' possession); Norfolk Police Department Forensic Investigation Report, July 9, 1997 (in authors' possession); Report of Autopsy, July 9, 1997 (in authors' possession).

23. Report of Autopsy, July 9, 1997; Kinnison testimony, Wilson trial, June 1999, and second Tice trial, January 2003; Hansen opening statements, first Tice trial, February 2000, and closing statements, second Tice trial, January 2003; Bowen closing statements, first Tice trial, February 2000; Derek Wagner opening statements, second Tice trial, January 2003.

24. Kinnison testimony, second Tice trial, January 2003; Wayne Bryan testimony, second Tice trial, January 2003; police crime scene videotape.

25. Bosko testimony, Wilson trial, June 1999, and first Tice trial, February 2000; Bosko interview for "Eight Men Out."

26. Rhea and Norman Williams interview; Danial and Rhea Williams affidavits, November 2005, clemency petition; Danial Williams interview.

27. Danial Williams interview.

28. Rhea, Norman, and Danial Williams affidavits, November 2005, clemency petition.

29. Rhea and Norman Williams affidavits, November 2005, clemency petition; Rhea Williams interview.

30. Danial Williams interviews; Bosko interview for "Eight Men Out"; Rhea Williams interview; Rhea Williams affidavit, November 2005, clemency petition; Bosko testimony, Wilson trial, June 1999.

31. Rhea and Norman Williams interview; Bosko testimony, first Tice trial, February 2000, Wilson trial, June 1999, and second Tice trial, January 2003; Bosko interview for "Eight Men Out."

2: The Neighbor

1. Maureen Evans interview.

2. Ibid.

3. Ibid.

4. Ibid.; *Virginian-Pilot*, July 10, 2000.

5. Evans interview.

6. Ibid.; *Virginian-Pilot*, July 10, 2000; Hansen interview for "Eight Men Out."

7. Bryan testimony, second Tice trial, January 2003, first Tice trial, February 2000, and Wilson trial, June 1999; police crime scene videotape.

8. Results of Latent Print Examination, August 14, 1997 (in authors' possession).

9. Physical Evidence Recovery Report, July 8, 1997 (in authors' possession); Virginia Division of Forensic Science Certificate of Analysis, August 15, 1997 (in authors' possession); Bryan testimony, Wilson trial, June 1999.

10. Danial Williams interview.

11. Testimony on Motion to Suppress, November 17, 1997 (Norfolk Circuit Court records, Williams file); Evans interview.

12. Taylor testimony, first Tice trial, February 2000, second Tice trial, January 2003, and Wilson trial, June 1999.

13. *Virginian-Pilot*, July 10, 2000; Evans interview; Taylor declaration, June 2005, clemency petition; "Memorandum in Support of Petition for Absolute Pardon," November 2005, clemency petition.

14. Findley and Scott, "Multiple Dimensions"; Martin, "Police Role," 79.

15. Innocence Commission for Virginia, "Vision for Justice"; Findley and Scott, "Multiple Dimensions"; Fisher, "Just the Facts."

16. Evans interview; Danial Williams affidavit, November 2005, clemency petition.

17. Testimony on Motion to Suppress, November 17, 1997; *Virginian-Pilot*, July 11, 2000; Evans interview; Danial Williams interview; "Memorandum in Support of Petition for Absolute Pardon," November 2005, clemency petition; Rhea Williams interview.

18. Rhea and Norman Williams interview.

19. Evans and Scott Halverson notes, July 1997 (in authors' possession); Pat Bosko interview; Pat Bosko letter to Larry Tice, 2003 (in authors' possession).

20. Sarah Bosko interview.

21. Carol and Jack Moore victim impact statement (in authors' possession); Evans and Halverson notes, July 1997.

22. Danny Shipley interview; testimony on Motion to Suppress, November 17, 1997; Rhea Williams interview; Rhea, Norman, and Chris Williams affidavits, November 2005, clemency petition.

23. Danial Williams's school records (Norfolk Circuit Court records, Williams file); Shipley interview; Doreen Trevena, Carl Knipe, and Dennis Campbell affidavits, November 2005, clemency petition; Trevena interview; Rhea Williams interview; Danial Williams interview.

24. Rhea and Norman Williams interview; Knipe affidavit, November 2005, clemency petition; Knipe interview; Helen Frezon interview; Trevena interview.

25. Rhea Williams interview; Trevena interview; Jerry Frezon interview.

26. Derek Tice interviews; Knipe interview; Knipe and Dennis Campbell affidavits, November 2005, clemency petition; Shipley interview.

27. Frank interview; Danial Williams affidavit, November 2005, clemency petition; David Keenan psychological evaluation of Williams, March 1998, clemency petition; Rick Pauley interview.

28. Trevena interview; Danial Williams school record; Rhea Williams interview.

29. Derek Tice interviews.

30. Danial Williams's navy records, clemency petition; Trevena interview; Danial Williams interview.

31. Evans interview; testimony on Motion to Suppress, November 17, 1997; Danial Williams interview; Inbau et al., *Criminal Interrogation and Confessions*, 83–84.

32. Evans and Halverson notes, July 1997; Norfolk Police Department Legal Rights Advice Form (in authors' possession).

33. Evans and Halverson notes, July 1997; Danial Williams interview; Danial Williams affidavit, November 2005, clemency petition.

34. Testimony on Motion to Suppress, November 17, 1997.

35. Ibid.; Evans and Halverson notes, July 1997; Danial Williams interview.

36. Evans and Halverson notes, July 1997; testimony on Motion to Suppress, November 17, 1997.

37. Evans and Halverson notes, July 1997.

38. Testimony on Motion to Suppress, November 17, 1997.

39. Evans and Halverson notes, July 1997; Evans interview.

40. Evans and Halverson notes, July 1997; testimony on Motion to Suppress, November 17, 1997.

41. Evans and Halverson notes, July 1997; Evans interview; testimony on Motion to Suppress, November 17, 1997.

42. Evans interview; Inbau et al., *Criminal Interrogation and Confessions*, 283.

43. Evans interview.

44. Evans and Halverson notes, July 1997; Danial Williams interview; Lykken, *Tremor in the Blood*, passim.

45. Evans and Halverson notes, July 1997.

46. Ibid.; Danial Williams affidavit, November 2005, clemency petition; *Virginian-Pilot*, July 12, 2000.

47. Danial Williams interviews; Polygraph Report, July 8, 1997, clemency petition; Jon Babineau interview; Lykken, *Tremor in the Blood*.

48. Rhea and Norman Williams interview.

49. Rhea Williams affidavit, November 2005, clemency petition; Rhea and Norman Williams interview.

50. *Virginian-Pilot*, July 11, 2000; Danial Williams interview.

51. Chuck Litle interview; James Godfrey interview; Bill Bosko interview for "Eight Men Out."

52. Evans and Halverson notes, July 1997; Danial Williams interview; Danial Williams affidavit, November 2005, clemency petition; testimony on Motion to Suppress, November 17, 1997.

53. Danial Williams affidavit, November 2005, clemency petition.

54. Evans interview.

55. Evans and Halverson notes, July 1997; testimony on Motion to Suppress, November 17, 1997.

56. Evans and Halverson notes, July 1997; Erin Litle interview.

57. Evans and Halverson notes, July 1997.

58. Evans interview; Danial Williams affidavit, November 2005, clemency petition; testimony on Motion to Suppress, November 17, 1997; Evans and Halverson notes, July 1997.

59. Danial Williams interview; Inbau et al., *Criminal Interrogation and Confessions*, 78–79; Danial Williams affidavit, November 2005, clemency petition; Kassin, "Psychology of Confession Evidence," 226.

60. Danial Williams interview; Danial Williams affidavit, November 2005, clemency petition; Evans interview; Ofshe and Leo, "Decision to Confess Falsely," 1000; Connery, *Guilty Until Proven Innocent*.

61. Evans and Halverson notes, July 1997; Evans interview.

62. Testimony on Motion to Suppress, November 17, 1997; Glenn Ford testimony, second Tice trial, January 2003.

63. Evans interview.

64. Babineau interview; Evans interview; anonymous sources; Jennifer Stanton interview; Ford testimony, first Tice trial, February 2000.

65. Shipley interview; Ford testimony, second Tice trial, January 2003; "Memorandum in Support of Petition for Absolute Pardon," November 2005, clemency petition; Babineau interview; Evans interview.

66. Greg McCormack interview; Jeffrey Russell interview; B. Thomas Reed interview; Ford testimony, Tice habeas hearing, September 2006 (in authors' possession); Frank interview; Stanton interview.

67. Anonymous sources.

68. *Virginian-Pilot*, December 16, 1990, and July 31, 1991; Kenneth Shannon, Leroy Hoggard, and Fred Williams files (Norfolk Circuit Court records); "Memorandum in Support of Petition for Absolute Pardon," November 2005, clemency petition; Shipley interview; Reed interview.

69. Paul Dowling interview; Reed interview.

70. Evans and Halverson notes, July 1997; Ford testimony, Tice habeas hearing, September 2006; Danial Williams affidavit, November 2005, clemency petition; testimony on Motion to Suppress, November 17, 1997.

71. Evans and Halverson notes, July 1997; testimony on Motion to Suppress, November 17, 1997; Evans interview.

72. Testimony on Motion to Suppress, November 17, 1997.

73. Danial Williams interview; testimony on Motion to Suppress, November 17, 1997; Danial Williams affidavit, November 2005, clemency petition; Evans interview.

74. Evans and Halverson notes, July 1997; Danial Williams interview; Virginia Division of Forensic Science Certificate of Analysis, August 15, 1997.

75. Evans and Halverson notes, July 1997.

76. Ibid.

77. Ibid.; Evans interview.

78. Testimony on Motion to Suppress, November 17, 1997.

79. Reed interview.

80. Taped confession of Danial Williams, July 9, 1997, transcript (in authors' possession).

81. Ibid.

82. Ibid.

83. Ibid.

84. Evans and Halverson notes, July 1997; Danial Williams interview.

85. Evans interview.

86. Arrest warrants, July 9, 1997 (Norfolk Circuit Court records, Williams file); Evans and Halverson notes, July 1997.

87. Rhea and Norman Williams interview.

88. Ibid.

89. *Virginian-Pilot*, July 9 and 10, 1997.

90. Evans and Halverson notes, July 1997; Kinnison testimony, first Tice trial, February 2000, and Wilson trial, June 1999; testimony on Motion to Suppress, November 17, 1997; Report of Autopsy, July 9, 1997; Evans interview.

91. Dowling interview of Evans; Evans to Wells, January 2005.

92. Ofshe and Leo, "Social Psychology," 191–207; Garrett, "Judging Innocence"; Bedau and Radelet, "Miscarriages of Justice," 56–58; Leo, "Inside the Interrogation Room," 278.

93. Leo and Ofshe, "Consequences of False Confessions," 438–40.

94. Kinnison testimony, first Tice trial, February 2000; Petition for Appeal, Tice case, May 2003 (in authors' possession).

95. Evans and Halverson notes, July 1997; taped confession of Danial Williams, July 9, 1997, transcript; testimony on Motion to Suppress, November 17, 1997.

96. Evans and Halverson notes, July 1997.

97. Evans interview; testimony on Motion to Suppress, November 17, 1997; Danial Williams interviews; Danial Williams affidavit, November 2005, clemency petition.

98. Testimony on Motion to Suppress, November 17, 1997; Danial Williams affidavit, November 2005, clemency petition; Evans interview; Danial Williams interview; Keenan psychological evaluation of Williams, March 1998, clemency petition.

99. Evans and Halverson notes, July 1997.

100. Supplemental taped statement of Danial Williams, July 9, 1997, transcript (in authors' possession); Evans interview.

101. Bill Bosko interview for "Eight Men Out."

102. Pat Bosko interview.

103. Evans and Halverson notes, July 1997; Rhea Williams interview.

104. Sarah Bosko, "Character Sketch of Michelle Lynn Bosko" (in authors' possession); Sarah Bosko interview; Carol and Jack Moore victim impact statement; phone conversation with Carol Moore and her brother-in-law.

105. Sarah Bosko interview.

106. Ibid.; Pat Bosko interview; Erin Litle interview.

107. Derek Tice interviews; Judy Pauley interview; Rick Pauley interview.

108. Trevena interview; Trevena affidavit, November 2005, clemency petition; Helen Frezon interview; Jerry Frezon interview.

109. Trevena interview and e-mail to Wells; Rhea and Norman Williams interviews.

3: "I Did Not Kill Michelle"

1. Babineau interview; Shipley interviews; anonymous source.

2. Rhea and Norman Williams interview; Shipley interview; "Memorandum in Support of Petition for Absolute Pardon," November 2005, clemency petition.

3. Shipley interview; Frank interview.

4. Frank interview; "American Bar Association Guidelines for the Appointment and Performance of Defense Counsel in Death Penalty Cases" (hereinafter ABA Guidelines), 91, 94, 95.

5. Frank interview; Shipley interviews.

6. Edds, *Expendable Man*, 71, 78–80, 113, 182; www.deathpenaltyinfo.org; Shipley interview.

7. Frank interview; Shipley interview.

8. Rhea Williams affidavit, November 2005, clemency petition; Rhea Williams interview.

9. Rhea and Norman Williams interview; Hansen interview.

10. Derek Tice interviews.

11. Shipley interview; "Memorandum in Support of Petition for Absolute Pardon," November 2005, clemency petition; Danial William affidavit, November 2005, clemency petition; Frank interview; anonymous source.

12. Danial Williams interviews.

13. Shipley interview; Frank interview; Danial Williams interview; Zaleski interview; Babineau interview; Michael Fasanaro interview; Reed cross-examination of Billy Bosko, preliminary hearing of Pauley and Farris, August 25, 1998; Rhea Williams interview.

14. Frank interview; Shipley interview; Rhea Williams interview; Danial Williams affidavit, November 2005, clemency petition.

15. ABA Guidelines, 70; Danial Williams interview.

16. Motion to Suppress, statement and hearing, November 7 and 17, 1997 (Norfolk Circuit Court records, Williams file); Frank interview.

17. Motion to Suppress hearing, November 17, 1997; anonymous source.

18. "Memorandum in Support of Petition for Absolute Pardon," November 2005, clemency petition; Shipley interview; Frank interview; Danial Williams interview.

19. Shipley interview; Danial Williams affidavit, November 2005, clemency petition.

20. Frank to Norman and Rhea Williams, February 17, 1998, clemency petition; motion for competency evaluation, February 13, 1998, and hearing, February 23, 1998 (Norfolk Circuit Court records, Williams file).

21. Frank interview; Shipley interview; Rhea Williams interview; Rhea Williams affidavit, November 2005, clemency petition.

22. Norman Williams interview; Rhea Williams affidavit, November 2005, clemency petition.

23. Danial Williams interview.

24. Hessick and Saujani, "Plea Bargaining"; Cole and Smith, *American System*, 340–51; Shipley interview; Gross, "Risks of Death," 487.

25. Shipley time sheet, 1997 (Norfolk Circuit Court records, Williams file); Stanton interview.

26. Hessick and Saujani, "Plea Bargaining"; ABA report, "*Gideon*'s Broken Promise"; Oh, "Innocence After 'Guilt'"; Alschuler, "Prosecutor's Role," 60.

27. Anonymous source; Transcript of Proceedings, October 27, 1997 (Norfolk Circuit Court records, Williams file); Danial Williams interviews; arrest warrant, July 8, 1997 (in authors' possession); Stanton interview.

28. ABA Guidelines, 5–6, 58, 70, 76, 78, 80–81, 95; Findley and Scott, "Multiple Dimensions," 333.

29. Transcript of Proceedings, October 27, 1997; anonymous source.

30. Samuel Pillsbury op-ed, *Los Angeles Times*, November 28, 1999; ABA Guidelines, 16; anonymous source.

31. Pat Bosko interview; Sarah Bosko interview; Bill Bosko interview for "Eight Men Out."

32. Pat Bosko interview.

33. Godfrey interview; Pat Bosko interview.

34. Pat Bosko interview; Sarah Bosko interview.

35. Chuck Litle interview; Pat Bosko interview; Godfrey interview.

36. Sarah Bosko interview; *Virginian-Pilot*, July 12 and 13, 2000.

37. Carol and Jack Moore victim impact statement.

38. Evans interview; Joe Dick affidavit, no date, clemency petition.

39. Joe Dick interview; Evans interview.

40. Evans e-mail to Wells; *Virginian-Pilot*, July 13, 2000.

41. Evans interview.

42. Ibid.

43. Valerie Bowen interview for "Eight Men Out"; Evans interview; Evans e-mail to Wells.

44. Hansen interview.

45. Ibid.; Hansen closing argument, second Tice trial, January 2003; *Chicago Tribune*, March 30, 2003.

46. Bowen interview for "Eight Men Out."

47. Danial Williams interview; Shipley interview.

48. Danial Williams affidavit, November 2005, clemency petition; Danial Williams interview.

49. Joe Dick affidavit, no date, clemency petition; Michael Ziegler testimony, Tice habeas hearing, September 2006; Ziegler affidavit, October 2005, clemency petition; Tom Bankard affidavit, November 2005, clemency petition.

50. Ziegler testimony, Tice habeas hearing, September 2006; Ziegler affidavit, October 2005, clemency petition.

51. Ibid.

4: The Roommate

1. Patricia and Joe Dick Sr. interview; Theresa Bankard-Sharpe interview; Joan Sikorsky to Fasanaro, June 9, 1999 (Norfolk Circuit Court records, Dick file); Patricia Dick essay, no date (in authors' possession).

2. Anonymous source; Elizabeth Penn affidavit, November 2005, clemency petition; Joe Dick Sr. affidavit, November 2005, clemency petition; Fasanaro interview; Richard Jamison affidavit, November 2005, clemency petition; Joe Dick interview; Sister Francesca affidavit, November 2005, clemency petition; declaration of Dr. Richard A. Ratner, November 2005, clemency petition; Dick's presentence report, July 1999 (in authors' possession); Joe Dick Sr. interview; Alphonse Bankard to "The Honorable," June 25, 1999 (Norfolk Circuit Court records, Dick file).

3. Joe Dick's school records (in authors' possession); Dr. Evan Nelson's psychological evaluation of Dick, May 1, 1998 (in authors' possession); Patricia Dick interview; Penn affidavit, November 2005, clemency petition; Jamison affidavit, November 2005, clemency petition; Dick's presentence report, July 1999; Alphonse Bankard interview; Ben Weber interview.

4. Patricia Dick essay, no date; Bankard-Sharpe interview; Bankard-Sharpe affidavit, November 2005, clemency petition; Patricia and Joe Dick Sr. interview; Sikorsky to Fasanaro, June 9, 1999; Joe Dick Sr. affidavit, November 2005, clemency petition; Michele Campbell affidavit, November 2005, clemency petition; Denise O'Connor affidavit, November 2005, clemency petition.

5. Catherine Bankard interview; Patricia and Joseph Dick Sr. interview.

6. Joe Dick Sr. interview; Ratner declaration, November 2005, clemency petition.

7. Dick's presentence report, July 1999; Campbell affidavit, November 2005, clemency petition; Ratner declaration, November 2005, clemency petition; Jamison affidavit, November 2005, clemency petition; O'Connor affidavit, November 2005, clemency petition; John Poyer interview.

8. Patricia Dick interview; Bankard-Sharpe interview; Bankard to "The Honorable," June 25, 1999.

9. Patricia and Joseph Dick Sr. interview; Al Bankard affidavit, November 2005, clemency petition.

10. Patricia Dick essay, no date; Ratner declaration, November 2005, clemency petition; anonymous source.

11. Poyer interview; Penn affidavit, November 2005, clemency petition; Adams affidavit, November 2005, clemency petition; Jamison affidavit, November 2005, clemency petition; Patricia and Joe Dick Sr. interview; Patricia Dick essay, no date.

12. Poyer interview; Bankard-Sharpe interview; Catherine Bankard interview.

13. Joe Dick interview; Dick's presentence report, July 1999; Joe Dick Sr. interview.

14. Ratner declaration, November 2005, clemency petition; Tom Bankard affidavit, November 2005, clemency petition; Jamison affidavit, November 2005, clemency petition; Fasanaro interview; Ziegler affidavit, October 2005, clemency petition; Dick's presentence report, July 1999; Evans interview.

15. Ziegler affidavit, October 2005, clemency petition; Nelson's psychological evaluation of Dick, May 1, 1998; Danial Williams interview; Eric Wilson interview for "Eight Men Out"; Ratner declaration, November 2005, clemency petition; Melissa Wharton interview; Derek Tice written statement (in authors' possession); Dick's presentence report, July 1999.

16. Joe Dick interview; Ziegler testimony, Tice habeas hearing, September 2006; Dick to Michael Black, no date (in authors' possession); PNCS L.S. Jones Jr. e-mail to Wells, November 12, 2003. Williams also recalls that Dick was on duty the day of the murder and at least the following day (Williams interview).

17. Derek Tice interview; Fasanaro interview.

18. Wray and Ford notes, January 22, 1998 (in authors' possession).

19. Dick's presentence report, July 1999.

20. Wray and Ford notes, January 22, 1998; Inbau et al., *Criminal Interrogation and Confessions*, 216–17; Norfolk Police Department Legal Rights Advice Form, January 12, 1998 (in authors' possession); Joe Dick Sr. affidavit, November 2005, clemency petition.

21. Joe Dick interview.

22. Wray and Ford notes, January 22, 1998; Dick's preliminary hearing, February 13, 1998, transcript (in authors' possession).

23. Wray and Ford notes, January 22, 1998.

24. Ibid.

25. Ibid.

26. Ibid.; Inbau et al., *Criminal Interrogation and Confessions*, 304.

27. Wray and Ford notes, January 22, 1998.

28. Ibid.; Taylor testimony, first Tice trial, February 2000.

29. Joe Dick interviews; Joe Dick affidavit, no date, clemency petition; Ziegler affidavit, October 2005, clemency petition; *Virginian-Pilot*, January 11, 2006; Dick's preliminary hearing, February 13, 1998.

30. Dick's preliminary hearing, February 13, 1998; Ford testimony, second Tice trial, January 2003.

31. Dick to Dowling, April or May 2001 (in authors' possession); Joe Dick affidavit, no date, clemency petition; Joe Dick interview; Wray and Ford notes, January 22, 1998.

32. "Eight Men Out"; Joe Dick interview; Wray and Ford notes, January 22, 1998; Joe Dick affidavit, no date, clemency petition; Dick to Black, no date; Dick to Wells, June 2003.

33. Joe Dick interviews; Wray and Ford notes, January 22, 1998.

34. Dick to Wells, November 2003; Dick to Richard Leo, February 2004; Joe Dick interview; Joe Dick affidavit, no date, clemency petition.

35. Joe Dick interviews; Dick to Wells, December 2003.

36. Ofshe and Leo, "Decision to Confess Falsely," 999–1000, 1107–14; Ofshe and Leo, "Social Psychology," 215–20, 231–38; Davis and O'Donohue, "Road to Perdition," 922–23, 951; Connery, *Guilty Until Proven Innocent*, 69.

37. Joe Dick interview; Dick's presentence report, July 1999.

38. Bankard-Sharpe interview; Tom Bankard interview.

39. Wray and Ford notes, January 22, 1998; Joe Dick affidavit, no date, clemency petition.

40. Wray and Ford notes, January 22, 1998; Inbau et al., *Criminal Interrogation and Confessions*, 82.

41. Joe Dick interview; Wray and Ford notes, January 22, 1998; Bosko testimony, first Tice trial, February 2000.

42. Wray and Ford notes, January 22, 1998.

43. Dick to Wells, November 2003; Joe Dick interview; Joe Dick affidavit, no date, clemency petition.

44. Dick to Wells, January 2004; Joe Dick interview; Nelson's psychological evaluation of Dick, May 1, 1998.

45. Wray and Ford notes, January 22, 1998.

46. Ibid.; Virginia Division of Forensic Science Certificate of Analysis, March 26, 1998 (in authors' possession).

47. Wray and Ford notes, January 22, 1998; Joe Dick interview.

48. Dick's preliminary hearing, February 13, 1998; Wray and Ford notes, January 22, 1998.

49. Wray and Ford notes, January 22, 1998; Nelson's psychological evaluation of Dick, May 1, 1998.

50. Wray and Ford notes, January 22, 1998; Dick to Black, no date; Joe Dick interview.

51. Wray and Ford notes, January 22, 1998.

52. Ibid.

53. Ibid.

54. Ibid.

55. Evans interview. Wray told Evans later about Dick's remark.

56. Wray and Ford notes, January 22, 1998; Dick's preliminary hearing, February 13, 1998.

57. Wray and Ford notes, January 22, 1998.

58. Taped confession of Joe Dick, January 12, 1998, transcript (in authors' possession); Virginia Division of Forensic Science Certificates of Analysis, August 15, 1997, and March 26, 1998.

59. Inbau et al., *Criminal Interrogation and Confessions*, 376; Wray and Ford notes, January 22, 1998; taped confession of Joe Dick, January 12, 1998, transcript; Dick's preliminary hearing, February 13, 1998.

60. Wray and Ford notes, January 22, 1998; arrest warrants, January 12, 1998, 8:54 P.M. and 8:56 P.M. (Norfolk Circuit Court records, Dick file).

61. Dick's sentencing hearing, September 8, 1999, transcript (in authors' possession); *Virginian-Pilot*, January 14, 1998; Patricia Dick interview.

62. Patricia Dick interview.

63. Dick's sentencing hearing, September 8, 1999.

64. Joe Dick Sr. interview; Bankard to "The Honorable," June 25, 1999.

65. Joe Dick Sr. interview; Ofshe and Leo, "Social Psychology," 215, 219; Joe Dick to Wells, December 2003; Joe Dick Sr. affidavit, November 2005, clemency petition.

66. Patricia and Joe Dick Sr. interview; Alphonse Bankard interview; Patricia Dick phone conversation.

67. Joe Dick Sr. interview; Catherine Bankard interview.

68. Catherine Bankard interview.

69. Bankard-Sharpe interview; Bankard to "The Honorable," June 25, 1999; Francis X. Kaspar letter "to whom it may concern," August 10, 1999 (in authors' possession).

70. Ziegler affidavit, October 2005, clemency petition.

71. Ibid.

72. Ibid.; Ziegler testimony, Tice habeas hearing, September 2006.

5: "Everybody Had Me Believing That I Was Guilty"

1. Patricia and Joe Dick Sr. interview.

2. McCormack interview; Fasanaro interviews; anonymous source.

3. Fasanaro interview.

4. Joe Dick interviews.

5. Joe Dick Sr. interview and phone conversation; Fasanaro interviews; Dick's sentencing hearing, September 8, 1999.

6. Patricia Dick interview; Fasanaro interview.

7. Patricia and Joe Dick Sr. interview; Patricia and Joe Dick Sr. affidavits, clemency petition, November 2005.

8. Anonymous source; phone conversation with Patricia and Joe Dick Sr.; ABA Guidelines, 49, 50, 53–54.

9. Fasanaro interview.

10. Joe Dick Sr. interview; Joe Dick interview.

11. Fasanaro interview.

12. Joe Dick interviews; Fasanaro interview; Bowen to Fasanaro, January 26, 1998 (in authors' possession).

13. Joe Dick interviews; Dick to Black, no date; Dick to Wells, December and June 2003.

14. Fasanaro interview.

15. Fasanaro interviews; Patricia Dick interview; Nelson's psychological evaluation of Dick, May 1, 1998.

16. Fasanaro interview.

17. Dick's sentencing hearing, September 8, 1999; Fasanaro interview.

18. Patricia and Joe Dick Sr. interview; Joe Dick Sr. affidavit, November 2005, clemency petition; Patricia Dick to Fasanaro, October 3, 1999 (in authors' possession).

19. Patricia and Joe Dick Sr. interview; Joe Dick to Wells, December 2003.

20. Bankard-Sharpe interview; Patricia Dick interview.

21. Alphonse Bankard interview; Tom Bankard interview; Bankard-Sharpe interview; Joe Dick Sr. interview; anonymous source; Catherine Bankard interview.

22. Patricia and Joe Dick Sr. interview.

23. Patricia Dick interview.

24. Dick's preliminary hearing, February 13, 1998; Fasanaro interview.

25. Dick's preliminary hearing, February 13, 1998; grand jury indictments, March 4, 1998 (Norfolk Circuit Court records, Dick file).

26. Scheduling Order, February 19, 1998 (in authors' possession); Nelson's psychological evaluation of Dick, May 1, 1998.

27. Nelson's psychological evaluation of Dick, May 1, 1998.

28. Ibid.

29. Dick's presentence report, July 1999; Joe Dick interview; Timothy Gurley testimony, pretrial hearing in Eric Wilson's case, January 6, 1999, transcript (Norfolk Circuit Court records, Wilson file); Patricia Dick to Fasanaro, June 14, 1998 (in authors' possession); Fasanaro interview; Hansen interview; Evans interview; Ratner declaration, November 2005, clemency petition; Patricia and Joe Dick Sr. interview.

30. Fasanaro interviews; Cole and Smith, *American System*, 340, 361; McCormack interview; Joe Dick interview.

31. Joe Dick interview.

32. Fasanaro interviews; Ziegler affidavit, October 2005, clemency petition; Berlow, "What Happened in Norfolk?"; anonymous source.

33. Anonymous source; Fasanaro interview.

34. Motion to Suppress, April 6, 1998 (Norfolk Circuit Court records, Dick file); Fasanaro interview.

35. Shipley interviews; Frank interview.

36. Danial Williams interview; Williams notes to Dick, undated (in authors' possession).

37. Danial Williams interview.

38. Joe Dick interviews; Dick to Wells, December 2003; Ratner declaration, November 2005, clemency petition; Dick's presentence report, July 1999.

39. Fasanaro interview; Nelson's psychological evaluation of Dick, May 1, 1998; D. Mills to Fasanaro, June 15, 1998 (in authors' possession).

40. Wright, *Remembering Satan*, passim; Ofshe and Watters, *Making Monsters*, 165–75; Ofshe, "Inadvertent Hypnosis."

41. Ofshe, "Inadvertent Hypnosis," 134; Wright, *Remembering Satan*, 105, 184, 186–88, 196; Leo and Ofshe, "Truth About False Confessions," 336–40; Ofshe and Watters, *Making Monsters*, 172n.

42. Ofshe and Leo, "Social Psychology," 231–34.

43. Connery, *Guilty Until Proven Innocent*.

44. Loftus, "Make-Believe Memories"; Mazzoni, Loftus, and Kirsch, "Changing Beliefs"; Loftus and Bernstein, "Rich False Memories"; Loftus, "Creating False Memories"; Loftus, "Our Changeable Memories."

45. Loftus, "Make-Believe Memories," 871; Mazzoni, Loftus, and Kirsch, "Changing Beliefs," 58.

46. Leo, "Social and Legal Construction," 654–88; Loftus, "Creating False Memories," 70–71.

47. Kenrick, Neuberg, and Cialdini, *Social Psychology*, 153–55, 159, 163, 166–69; Davis and O'Donohue, "Road to Perdition," 931–32, 935–37.

48. Davis and O'Donohue, "Road to Perdition," passim.

49. Virginia Division of Forensic Science Certificate of Analysis, March 26, 1998; Bowen interview for "Eight Men Out."

50. Bowen interview for "Eight Men Out"; Hansen interview.

51. Bankard-Sharpe interview; Fasanaro interview; Tom Bankard interview; Alphonse Bankard interview.

52. Gurley testimony, pretrial hearing in Wilson's case, January 6, 1999; Joe Dick affidavit, no date, clemency petition; Joe Dick interview; Joe Dick to Nicole Williams, April 1, 1998 (in authors' possession).

53. Joe Dick to Nicole Williams, April 1, 1998, and other undated letters (in authors' possession).

6: Number Three

1. Joe Dick to Jerry, no date, and Joe Dick to Nicole Williams, April 1, 1998 (in authors' possession).

2. David Dickerson and Ford testimony, pretrial hearing in Wilson's case, January 6, 1999 (Norfolk Circuit Court records, Wilson file).

3. Eric Wilson interview for "Eight Men Out"; Dickerson testimony, pretrial hearing in Wilson's case, January 6, 1999; Ford and G.S. Hoggard notes on Wilson's interrogation, April 8, 1998 (in authors' possession).

4. Dickerson and Ford testimony, pretrial hearing in Wilson's case, January 6, 1999; Eric Wilson interview for "Eight Men Out."

5. Ramey and William Wilson interview; Don Higginbotham interview; John Schwertlech interview; Eric Wilson interview for "Eight Men Out"; Eric Wilson to Wells, received from McCormack in April 2004.

6. Milgram, "Behavioral Study of Obedience"; Slater, *Opening Skinner's Box*, 48; Kenrick, Neuberg, and Cialdini, *Social Psychology*, 201–7.

7. Matt Sisk interview; Schwertlech interview; McCormack interview; Dickinson interview; Eric Wilson to Wells, received from McCormack in April 2004; William and Ramey Wilson interview.

8. Dickinson interview; Shannon Sisk interview; Ramey Wilson testimony, Wilson trial (sentencing phase), June 1999; Higginbotham interview; Eric Wilson to Wells, received from McCormack in April 2004; *Denver Post*, December 10, 2003; McCormack interview.

9. Eric Wilson to Wells, received from McCormack in April 2004; McCormack interview; Ramey Wilson interview.

10. Ramey and William Wilson interview; Schwertlech interview.

11. Matt Sisk interview; Ramey and William Wilson interview.

12. Matt Sisk interview; Eric Wilson to Wells, received from McCormack in April 2004; Schwertlech interview.

13. Matt Sisk interview; Ramey Wilson interview.

14. Wilson and Hoggard testimony, Wilson trial, June 1999; Ford and Hoggard notes, April 8, 1998; Wilson interview for "Eight Men Out."

15. Hoggard and Wilson testimony, Wilson trial, June 1999; Wilson interview; Dickinson interview; Higginbotham interview.

16. White, *Miranda's Waning Protections*, 76; Leo, "*Miranda* and the Problem of False Confessions," 275; Gudjonsson, *Psychology of Interrogations and Confessions*, 148; Kassin and Norwick, "Why People Waive," 215; Leo, "Impact of *Miranda* Revisited," 654–55; Ofshe and Leo, "Social Psychology," 199; Kassin, "On the Psychology of Confessions," 219; Cloud et al., "Words Without Meaning," 499–507; Leo, "*Miranda's* Irrelevance," 1013–14.

17. White, *Miranda's Waning Protections*, 78–91; Leo, "*Miranda's* Irrelevance," 1014, 1016–19; Leo and White, "Adapting to *Miranda*," 431–47; Simon, *Homicide*, 206, 214, 215.

18. White, *Miranda's Waning Protections*, 91–99; Weisselberg, "Saving *Miranda*," 132–40.

19. Cole and Smith, *American System*, 198; Leo, "*Miranda's* Irrelevance," 1025.

20. Wilson interview for "Eight Men Out"; Hoggard testimony, Wilson trial, June 1999; Ford and Hoggard notes, April 8, 1998; Wilson interview.

21. Ford and Hoggard notes, April 8, 1998.

22. Ibid.; Wilson testimony at his trial, June 1999; Wilson interview for "Eight Men Out."

23. Ford and Hoggard notes, April 8, 1998.

24. Wilson testimony at his trial, June 1999; Wilson interview for "Eight Men Out"; Ramey and William Wilson interview; McCormack interview.

25. Ford and Hoggard notes, April 8, 1998; Hoggard and Wilson testimony, Wilson trial, June 1999; Ramey Wilson e-mail to Wells; Motion to Suppress, May 12, 1998 (Norfolk Circuit Court records, Wilson file); Wilson interview; Wilson interview for "Eight Men Out"; Hoggard testimony, pretrial hearing in Wilson's case, January 6, 1999 (Norfolk Circuit Court records, Wilson file); Dowling interview.

26. Wilson to Wells, received from McCormack in April 2004; Wilson interview; Wilson interview for "Eight Men Out."

27. Wilson testimony at his trial, June 1999; Wilson interview for "Eight Men Out."

28. Wilson testimony at his trial, June 1999; Ford testimony, pretrial hearing in Wilson's case, January 6, 1999; Ford and Hoggard notes, April 8, 1998.

29. Inbau et al., *Criminal Interrogation and Confessions*, 8; Kassin, "On the Psychology of Confessions," 216; Kassin, Meissner, and Norwick, "'I'd Know a False Confession'"; Kassin and Fong, "'I'm Innocent!'"; Meissner and Kassin, "'He's Guilty!'"; Leo, "*Miranda*'s Revenge," 281.

30. Kassin, Goldstein, and Savitsky, "Behavioral Confirmation."

31. Joe Dick letters to Jerry and to Nicole Williams; Ford testimony, pretrial hearing in Wilson's case, January 6, 1999.

32. Wilson interview; Hoggard testimony, Wilson trial, June 1999; Ford testimony, Wilson's preliminary and suppression hearing, June 23, 1998 (in authors' possession).

33. Wilson interview; Wilson testimony at his trial, June 1999; McCormack interview.

34. Hoggard testimony, Wilson trial, June 1999.

35. Ford and Hoggard notes, April 8, 1998; Hoggard testimony, Wilson trial, June 1999; Wilson testimony at his trial, June 1999.

36. Ford and Hoggard notes, April 8, 1998.

37. Hoggard and Wilson testimony, Wilson trial, June 1999; Ford and Hoggard notes, April 8, 1998.

38. Ford and Hoggard notes, April 8, 1998; Hoggard and Wilson testimony, Wilson trial, June 1999.

39. Hoggard testimony, Wilson trial, June 1999; Ford and Hoggard notes, April 8, 1998; Hoggard testimony, pretrial hearing in Wilson's case, January 6, 1999.

40. Wilson interview; Wilson testimony at his trial, June 1999.

41. Ford and Hoggard notes, April 8, 1998; Hoggard testimony, Wilson trial, June 1999.

42. Ford and Hoggard notes, April 8, 1998; Wilson testimony at his trial, June 1999.

43. Ford and Hoggard notes, April 8, 1998; Hoggard and Wilson testimony, Wilson trial, June 1999.

44. Ford and Hoggard notes, April 8, 1998; Hoggard testimony, Wilson trial, June 1999.

45. Ford and Hoggard notes, April 8, 1998; Wilson testimony at his trial, June 1999.

46. Hoggard and Wilson testimony, Wilson trial, June 1999; Ford and Hoggard notes, April 8, 1998; Wilson interview for "Eight Men Out."

47. Ford and Hoggard notes, April 8, 1998.

48. Ibid.; Hoggard testimony, Wilson trial, June 1999; Wilson interview.

49. Wilson and Hoggard testimony, Wilson trial, June 1999; Ford and Hoggard notes, April 8, 1998.

50. Hoggard and Wilson testimony, Wilson trial, June 1999; Ford and Hoggard notes, April 8, 1998.

51. Ford and Hoggard notes, April 8, 1998; Wilson and Hoggard testimony, Wilson trial, June 1999.

52. McCormack and Russell Woodlief, "Motion to Set Aside Verdict," July 20, 1999.

53. Audiotape of Wilson's confession, April 8, 1998 (in authors' possession); McCormack interview.

54. Audiotape and transcript of Wilson's confession, April 8, 1998 (in authors' possession).

55. Wilson interview for "Eight Men Out"; Wilson testimony, Wilson trial, June 1999.

56. Ford testimony, Wilson's preliminary and suppression hearing, June 23, 1998.

57. Ford and Hoggard notes, April 8, 1998; Wilson and Hoggard testimony, Wilson trial, June 1999; transcript of Wilson's confession, April 8, 1998.

58. Wilson interview.

59. Wilson interview for "Eight Men Out."

60. McCormack interview; Wilson interview for "Eight Men Out"; Wilson interview; Wilson to Wells, received from McCormack in April 2004.

61. Wilson to Wells, received from McCormack in April 2004; Wilson interview; Wilson interview for "Eight Men Out."

7: Three More

1. William and Ramey Wilson interview; Wilson to Wells, received from McCormack in April 2004.

2. Wilson to Wells, received from McCormack in April 2004; William and Ramey Wilson interview.

3. Ramey and William Wilson interview; Shannon Sisk interview; Dickinson interview; Ramey Wilson testimony, Wilson trial (sentencing phase), June 1999.

4. McCormack interview; Ramey and William Wilson interview.

5. McCormack interview; McCormack interview for "Eight Men Out"; William and Ramey Wilson interview; Eric Wilson interview; Hansen interview.

6. McCormack interview; Gould, *Innocence Commission*, 185–87; Shipley interview; McCormack to Teich, various letters, 1998 (Norfolk Circuit Court records, Wilson file); Ramey and William Wilson interviews; order signed by Poston, February 17, 1999 (in authors' possession); Wilson's preliminary and suppression hearing, June 23, 1998.

7. McCormack interview; subpoena duces tecums (Norfolk Circuit Court records, Wilson file).

8. Motions to Suppress, May 12 and September 18, 1998 (Norfolk Circuit Court records, Wilson file).

9. McCormack interview; Bowen interview for "Eight Men Out"; Hansen interview; anonymous sources; Zaleski interview; Broccoletti interview.

10. Hansen interview; anonymous source; Stanton interview.

11. Anonymous sources; Hansen interview.

12. Hansen interview.

13. McCormack interview.

14. Wilson to Wells, received from McCormack in April 2004; Ramey Wilson interview.

15. Wray and Ford's notes of April 27, 1998, meeting with Dick (in authors' possession); Fasanaro interview; Patricia and Joseph Dick Sr. interview; Joe Dick interview; Joe Dick affidavit, no date, clemency petition.

16. Joseph Dick affidavit, clemency petition, no date.

17. Wray and Ford notes, April 27, 1998; Ratner declaration, clemency petition, November 2005; Hansen interview for "Eight Men Out."

18. Wray and Ford notes, April 27, 1998; Dick to Wells, January 2004; Dick affidavit, clemency petition, no date.

19. Wray and Ford notes, January 22 and April 27, 1998.

20. Wray and Ford notes, April 27, 1998.

21. Ibid.

22. Ibid.

23. Ibid.; Fasanaro interview.

24. Fasanaro interview; Dick's polygraph results, April 28, 1998 (in authors' posses-

sion); Wray and Ford notes, April 28, 1998 (in authors' possession); Dick testimony, Wilson trial, June 1999.

25. Wray and Ford notes, April 28, 1998.

26. Patricia Dick to Joe Dick, May 3, 1998 (in authors' possession).

27. Patricia Dick to Fasanaro, June 14, 1998 (in authors' possession).

28. Fasanaro interview.

29. Fasanaro interview; Dick to Nicole Williams, no date (in authors' possession).

30. Dick to Nicole Williams, no date.

31. Shipley interviews; Frank interview; Zaleski interview.

32. Williams interview.

33. Virginia Division of Forensic Science Certificate of Analysis, June 10, 1998 (in authors' possession); Hansen interview; Hansen interview for "Eight Men Out."

34. Bowen interview for "Eight Men Out"; phone conversation with Carol Moore and her brother-in-law; Results of Latent Print Examination, August 14, 1997 (in authors' possession); Hansen interview for "Eight Men Out"; Hansen interview. Carol Moore's brother-in-law phoned Tom Wells, with Carol on another line, and did not give his name during the conversation.

35. Billy Bosko interview for "Eight Men Out"; Pat Bosko interview; Sarah Bosko interview.

36. Billy Bosko interview for "Eight Men Out"; Hansen interview; Stanton interview.

37. Eric Wilson interview for "Eight Men Out"; Ramey and William Wilson interview; Virginia Division of Forensic Science Certificate of Analysis, February 18, 1999 (in authors' possession); Norfolk Police Department fingerprint examination report, August 22, 1998 (in authors' possession).

38. Fasanaro interview.

39. Dick to Wells, January 2004; Wray and Ford notes, June 16, 1998 (in authors' possession); Bowen testimony, Dick's sentencing hearing, September 8, 1999; Derek Tice interview; conversation with Fasanaro at Norfolk Circuit Court; Fasanaro interviews; Patricia Dick affidavit, clemency petition, November 2005; Patricia and Joseph Dick Sr. interview.

40. Joe Dick Sr. interview.

41. Hansen interview.

42. Wray and Ford notes, June 16, 1998; Dick to Wells, January 2004 and December 2003; Dick affidavit, clemency petition, no date.

43. Wray and Ford notes, June 16, 1998.

44. Ibid.

45. Ibid.; composite of "George" by R.P. Wensel, June 16, 1998 (in authors' possession).

46. Wray and Ford notes, June 17, 1998 (in authors' possession).

47. Wray and Ford notes, June 18, 1998 (in authors' possession); Melissa Wharton interview.

48. Wray and Ford notes, June 18, 1998; composite of "George" by R.P. Wensel, June 16, 1998; Tice photo in *George Washington* cruise book (in authors' possession); Bowen interview for "Eight Men Out"; Hansen interview for "Eight Men Out"; Hansen closing argument, second Tice trial, January 2003; Fasanaro testimony, Dick's sentencing hearing, September 8, 1999.

49. Wray and Ford notes, June 18, 1998; Ford testimony, first Tice trial, February 2000, and second Tice trial, January 2003.

50. Tice interview; Tice's presentence report, March 2000 (in authors' possession); Dick interview; Dick to Wells, January 2004.

8: Tice

1. Derek Tice interview.

2. Derek Tice interviews; Dr. Charles Broadfield's court-ordered evaluation of Tice, December 1998 (in authors' possession); David Keenan's court-ordered evaluation of Tice, January 2000 (Norfolk Circuit Court records, Tice file); Rachel Tice interview.

3. Lea Tice interview; Derek Tice written accounts (in authors' possession). Derek Tice later wrote several statements for his attorneys on his arrest, flight to Virginia, and first interrogation. They are referred to hereinafter as "Derek Tice written accounts."

4. Derek Tice written account; Wray and Ford notes, June 18, 1998; Ford testimony, first Tice trial, February 2000; Derek Tice interviews.

5. Ford testimony, first Tice trial, February 2000.

6. Derek Tice written account; Derek Tice interview; Lea Tice interview.

7. Derek Tice to Paul Dowling, April 24, 2001 (in authors' possession); Derek Tice interview.

8. Derek Tice written account; Derek Tice interview.

9. Derek Tice interview.

10. Lea Tice interview.

11. Derek Tice interviews; untitled form, July 27, 1998 (Norfolk Circuit Court records, Tice file); Tice's presentence report, March 2000; Wharton interview; Lea Tice interview.

12. Derek Tice interview.

13. Derek Tice interviews; Derek Tice written account.

14. Lea Tice interview.

15. Wray and Ford notes, June 18, 1998; Tice arrest warrants, June 18, 1998 (in authors' possession).

16. Derek Tice interview.

17. Derek Tice written account.

18. Tice's presentence report, March 2000; Broccoletti interview; Zaleski interview; Keenan's evaluation of Tice, January 2000; Wharton interview; Derek Tice interview; Larry Tice interview; Rachel Tice interview.

19. Derek Tice interview.

20. Broadfield to Wells, September 15, 2003; Broadfield's evaluation of Tice, December 1998; Dr. Paul Mansheim's court-ordered evaluation of Tice, January 2000 (in authors' possession); Tice's high school transcript (Norfolk Circuit Court records, Tice file); Rachel Tice interview.

21. Derek Tice interviews; Broadfield's evaluation of Tice, December 1998; Robert Tice affidavit, clemency petition, November 2005.

22. Derek Tice interview; Walter Dalton notes of Tice interview, September 1998 (in authors' possession).

23. Derek Tice interviews.

24. Derek Tice interview.

25. Ibid.; Rebecca Danning, James Barbour, and Dana Pounds testimony, first Tice trial (sentencing phase), February 2000; Pounds affidavit, clemency petition, November 2005; Wharton interview; Rick Pauley interview.

26. Derek Tice interview; Mansheim's evaluation of Tice, January 2000.

27. Mansheim's evaluation of Tice, January 2000; Derek Tice interviews; M.L. Minter testimony, first Tice trial (sentencing phase), February 2000; Keenan's evaluation of Tice, January 2000; Broadfield's evaluation of Tice, December 1998.

28. Lea Tice interview; Rachel Tice interview.

29. Lea Tice interview; Wharton interview.

30. Lea Tice interview.

31. Ibid.; Rachel Tice interview.

32. Rachel Tice interview.

33. Broadfield's evaluation of Tice, December 1998; Rachel Tice interview.

34. Larry Tice interview.

35. Rachel Tice interview.

36. Derek Tice written account; waiver of extradition, June 19, 1998 (in authors' possession).

37. Derek Tice written account; Derek Tice interviews.

38. Derek Tice interview.

39. Lea Tice interview.

40. Derek Tice written account; Derek Tice interview.

41. Derek Tice interview; Ford testimony, second Tice trial, January 2003.

42. Derek Tice interview.

43. Ibid.

44. Derek Tice written account; Derek Tice interview.

45. Ibid.

46. Derek Tice interview; Ford testimony, Tice habeas hearing, September 2006.

47. Derek Tice interview; Ford testimony, second Tice trial, January 2003.

48. Derek Tice written account.

49. Ibid.; Derek Tice interview.

50. Gross, "Risks of Death," 475–79; Simon, *Homicide*, 40–41; Jackall, *Street Stories*, 130; Evans interview.

51. Derek Tice interviews.

52. Ford testimony, first Tice trial, February 2000; Derek Tice interviews; Derek Tice written account; Tice to Dowling, April 24, 2001.

53. Derek Tice written account.

54. Ibid.

55. Ibid.

56. Wray and Ford notes, June 25, 1998 (in authors' possession); Derek Tice affidavit, clemency petition, September 2005; Derek Tice interview; Derek Tice and Ford testimony, Tice habeas hearing, September 2006; diagrams of Interview Room E (Norfolk Circuit Court records, Tice file).

57. Derek Tice written accounts.

58. Wray and Ford notes, June 25, 1998; Derek Tice written account; Ford testimony, first Tice trial, February 2000.

59. Wray and Ford notes, June 25, 1998; Ford testimony, first Tice trial, February 2000; Derek Tice written account.

60. Derek Tice interview.

61. Derek Tice written accounts; Derek Tice testimony, Tice habeas hearing, September 2006; Derek Tice affidavit, clemency petition, September 2005; Ford testimony, first Tice trial, February 2000; Wray and Ford notes, June 25, 1998.

62. Derek Tice written accounts; Ford testimony, second Tice trial, January 2003; Ford and Derek Tice testimony, Tice habeas hearing, September 2006.

63. Derek Tice written accounts.

64. Wray and Ford notes, June 25, 1998; Derek Tice written account.

65. Wray and Ford notes, June 25, 1998.

66. Derek Tice interview; Ford testimony, second Tice trial, January 2003; Tice to Dowling, April 24, 2001; Derek Tice written account; Wray and Ford notes, June 25, 1998.

67. Derek Tice interviews; Ford testimony, first Tice trial, February 2000, and second Tice trial, January 2003; Derek Tice, Ford, and Wray testimony, Tice habeas hearing, September 2006; Derek Tice written accounts.

68. Derek Tice written account; Derek Tice interview; Derek Tice affidavit, clemency petition, September 2005.

69. Derek Tice written account.

70. Derek Tice interview; Broccoletti interview.

71. Derek Tice written account.

72. Derek Tice written accounts; Ford testimony, second Tice trial, January 2003, and first Tice trial, February 2000; Wray and Ford notes, June 25, 1998.

73. Wray and Ford notes, June 25, 1998; Derek Tice interview; Derek Tice written accounts; Larry Tice interview.

74. Tice's polygraph results, June 25, 1998 (in authors' possession); Derek Tice written accounts; Randy Crank testimony, Tice habeas hearing, September 2006.

75. Derek Tice written account.

76. Derek Tice interview; Randy Crank notes, June 25, 1998, exhibits in support of Tice's habeas petition, 2005 (in authors' possession); Crank testimony, Tice habeas hearing, September 2006; Derek Tice affidavit, clemency petition, September 2005.

77. Crank notes, June 25, 1998, exhibits in support of Tice's habeas petition, 2005.

78. Wray and Ford notes, June 25, 1998; Derek Tice written accounts; Derek Tice testimony, Tice habeas hearing, September 2006; Derek Tice affidavit, clemency petition, September 2005.

79. Wray and Ford notes, June 25, 1998; Derek Tice written account; Derek Tice interview; Ford testimony, first Tice trial, February 2000.

80. Derek Tice written accounts; Derek Tice affidavit, clemency petition, September 2005; Wray and Ford notes, June 25, 1998; Derek Tice interview.

81. Wray and Ford notes, June 25, 1998; Derek Tice written account; Derek Tice interview.

82. Tice to Dowling, April 24, 2001; Derek Tice testimony, Tice habeas hearing, September 2006; Derek Tice written account; Derek Tice interviews; Ford and Wray testimony, Tice habeas hearing, September 2006.

83. Leo and Ofshe, "Consequences of False Confessions"; Kassin and Neumann, "On the Power of Confession Evidence"; Kassin and Sukel, "Coerced Confessions"; Drizin and Leo, "Problem of False Confessions."

84. Leo and Ofshe, "Consequences of False Confessions"; Drizin and Leo, "Problem of False Confessions."

85. Wray and Ford notes, June 25, 1998; Ford testimony, first Tice trial, February 2000; Derek Tice written account.

86. Derek Tice interviews; Derek Tice written account.

87. Derek Tice interviews.

88. Ibid.; Ford testimony, first Tice trial, February 2000; Wray and Ford notes, June 25, 1998.

89. Derek Tice interview.

90. Derek Tice written account; Ford testimony, first Tice trial, February 2000.

91. Wray and Ford notes, June 25, 1998; Derek Tice interview; Ford testimony, second Tice trial, January 2003.

92. Wray and Ford notes, June 25, 1998; Ford testimony, second Tice trial, January 2003; taped confession of Derek Tice, June 25, 1998 (in authors' possession).

93. Wray and Ford notes, June 25, 1998.

94. Ibid.; taped confession of Derek Tice, June 25, 1998.

95. Wray and Ford notes, June 25, 1998; Derek Tice interview; taped confession of Derek Tice, June 25, 1998.

96. Wray and Ford notes, June 25, 1998; Derek Tice interviews; taped confession of Derek Tice, June 25, 1998; Ford testimony, first Tice trial, February 2000.

97. Wray and Ford notes, June 25, 1998; Ford testimony, first Tice trial, February 2000; taped confession of Derek Tice, June 25, 1998; Sarah Bosko interview; Kassin, "Psychology of Confession Evidence," 230.

98. Taped confession of Derek Tice, June 25, 1998.

99. Leo and Ofshe, "Consequences of False Confessions"; Sullivan, "Police Experiences"; *Virginian-Pilot*, November 27, 2006.

100. Wray and Ford notes, June 25, 26, 1998 (in authors' possession); consent to conduct search form, June 26, 1998 (in authors' possession); taped confession of Derek Tice, June 25, 1998; Ford testimony, first Tice trial, February 2000, and second Tice trial, January 2003; Hansen closing argument, second Tice trial, January 2003; Stephen McCullough cross-examination of Tice, Tice habeas hearing, September 2006; commitment order, June 26, 1998 (in authors' possession).

101. *Virginian-Pilot*, June 29, 1998.

9: "Scrappy"

1. Judy Pauley and Richard Pauley Sr. interview; Babineau interview; Rick Pauley interview.

2. Judy and Richard Pauley Sr. interview.

3. Ibid.; Rick Pauley interview.

4. Judy Pauley interview.

5. Judy and Richard Pauley Sr. interview; Rick Pauley interview.

6. Rick Pauley interview; arrest warrants, June 30, 1998, 5:19 and 5:20 P.M. (Norfolk Circuit Court records, Pauley file).

7. Rick Pauley interview; Babineau interview.

8. Babineau interview; Bell Atlantic phone bill including EXCEL Telecommunications bill, August 11, 1997 (Norfolk Circuit Court records, Wilson file); Judy and Richard Pauley Sr. interview; Judy and Richard Pauley Sr. testimony at second Tice trial, January 2003.

9. Rick Pauley interview.

10. Ibid.; Babineau interview.

11. Rick Pauley interview; Judy Pauley interview.

12. Wray and Ford notes, June 29, 1998 (in authors' possession); Babineau interview.

13. Babineau interview; Rick Pauley interview; Judy Pauley interview.

14. Judy Pauley interview; Babineau interview; Hansen closing argument, second Tice trial, January 2003.

15. Derek Tice interview; Danial Williams interview; Farris's school records (Norfolk Circuit Court records, Farris file); Reed interview.

16. Wray and Ford notes on Farris interrogation, July 21, 1998 (in authors' possession); Reed interview.

17. Wray and Ford notes, July 21, 1998; Reed interview.

18. Wray and Ford notes, July 21, 1998; Motion to Suppress, December 31, 1998 (Norfolk Circuit Court records, Farris file); Wray and Ford testimony, hearing in Farris case, January 6, 1999 (Norfolk Circuit Court records, Farris file).

19. Wray testimony, hearing in Farris case, January 6, 1999; Wray and Ford notes, July 21, 1998.

20. Memorandum in Support of Motion to Suppress, January 6, 1999 (Norfolk Circuit Court records, Farris file); Reed interview; Wray testimony, hearing in Farris case, January 6, 1999.

21. Notices of Alibi, February 1, May 11, 1999 (Norfolk Circuit Court records, Farris file); Reed interview.

22. *Virginian-Pilot*, July 11, 1998; Bowen to Fasanaro, July 24, 1998 (in authors' possession); Dick to Nicole Williams, no date (in authors' possession).

23. Virginia Division of Forensic Science Certificate of Analysis, August 28, 1998; Norfolk Police Department fingerprint examination report, July 1, 1998 (in authors' possession).

24. Hansen interview; Hansen closing argument, second Tice trial, January 2003; Evans interview; Zaleski interview.

25. Gershman, "Prosecutor's Duty to Truth"; Toobin, "Killer Instincts," 54; *New York Times*, August 2, 2007.

26. Medwed, "Zeal Deal."

27. Anonymous source.

28. Hansen interview; Bowen interview for "Eight Men Out."

29. Preliminary hearing of Pauley and Farris, August 25, 1998; Babineau interview.

30. Preliminary hearing of Pauley and Farris, August 25, 1998; Rick Pauley interview; Joe Dick affidavit, clemency petition, no date.

31. Preliminary hearing of Pauley and Farris, August 25, 1998.

32. Ibid.

33. Ibid.

34. Ibid.; Dick testimony, Wilson trial, June 1999.

35. Preliminary hearing of Pauley and Farris, August 25, 1998.

36. Ford testimony, pretrial hearing in Wilson's case, December 9, 1998 (Norfolk Circuit Court records, Wilson file); Nora Nellis phone conversation on visit with Kelly's ex-girlfriend.

37. Ford and Kelly testimony, pretrial hearing in Wilson's case, December 9, 1998 (Norfolk Circuit Court records, Wilson file); Hansen interview.

38. Derek Tice interview; Wilson to Wells, received from McCormack in April 2004.

39. McCormack interview; McCormack interview for "Eight Men Out."

40. Trott, "Words of Warning," 1383, 1385, 1394; Clemens, "Removing the Market," 186; Toobin, "Killer Instincts," 57.

41. Garrett, "Judging Innocence"; Zimmerman, "From the Jailhouse"; Clemens, "Removing the Market"; Los Angeles County grand jury report on use of informants, June 26, 1990.

42. Kelly testimony, pretrial hearing in Wilson's case, December 9, 1998; Wharton interview.

43. Derek Tice interview; Lea Tice interview.

44. Stanton interview; Virginia Division of Forensic Science Certificate of Analysis, February 18, 1999 (in authors' possession).

45. Judy Pauley interview.

46. Lea Tice interview.

47. Shipley interview.

48. Ramey Wilson interview.

49. Bowen to Zaleski, October 23, 1998 (in authors' possession).

50. Zaleski interview.

51. Ibid.

52. Ibid.

53. Leo and Ofshe, "Consequences of False Confessions," 477.

54. Zaleski interview; Lea Tice interview; Derek Tice interview.

55. Broadfield's psychological evaluation of Tice, December 1998; Derek Tice interview; Derek Tice testimony, Tice habeas hearing, September 2006; Rachel Tice interview.

56. Derek Tice interview.

57. Larry and Rachel Tice interview.

58. Wray and Ford notes, October 29, 1998 (in authors' possession); Bowen to Zaleski, October 23, 1998; Zaleski interview.

59. Wray and Ford notes, October 29, 1998.

60. Derek Tice interview; Broccoletti interview.

61. Wray and Ford notes, October 29, 1998; Derek Tice interviews.

62. Wray and Ford notes, October 29, 1998.

63. Ibid.

64. Ibid.; Zaleski interview.

65. Zaleski interview.

66. Ibid.; Derek Tice interview.

67. Zaleski interview; Wray and Ford notes, October 29, 1998.

68. Wray and Ford notes, October 29, 1998; Derek Tice interview.

69. Derek Tice interview.

70. Wray and Ford notes, October 29, 1998.

71. Ibid.; Derek Tice testimony, Tice habeas hearing, September 2006; Zaleski interview.

72. Zaleski interview.

73. Ibid.

74. Wray and Ford notes, October 29, 1998; taped statement of Derek Tice, October 27, 1998 (in authors' possession); Derek Tice interviews; Berlow, "What Happened in Norfolk?"

75. Wray and Ford notes, October 29, 1998; taped statement of Derek Tice, October 27, 1998.

76. Ibid.; Derek Tice interview.

77. Zaleski interview.

78. Wray and Ford notes, October 29, 1998; Stanton interview.

79. Derek Tice interview; Stanton interview; Danser's military service records (Norfolk Circuit Court records, Danser file); Danser testimony, second Tice trial, January 2003.

80. Wray and Ford notes, November 4, 1998 (in authors' possession).

81. Danser's daily time sheets and work orders, July 7 and 8, 1997 (Norfolk Circuit Court records, Danser file); Danser testimony, second Tice trial, January 2003; Stanton interview; Bowen interview for "Eight Men Out"; Hansen objection during Danser's direct examination, second Tice trial, January 2003; Broccoletti interview; anonymous source.

82. Wray and Ford notes, November 4, 1998.

83. Ibid.

84. Ibid.; Stanton interview.

85. Wray and Ford notes, November 4, 1998.

86. Derek Tice interview; Walter Dalton notes on interview with Victoria Wilson, 1999 (in authors' possession).

87. Wray and Ford notes, November 4, 1998.

88. Ibid.; Robert Morgan testimony, first Tice trial, February 2000.

89. Wray and Ford notes, November 4, 1998; *Virginian-Pilot*, October 29, 1998.

90. Stanton interview.

91. Hansen interview; Shipley interview; Frank interview; Zaleski interview.

92. Gershman, "Prosecutor's Duty to Truth"; Zaleski interview; Hansen interview; Stanton interview.

93. Zaleski interview; Ford and D.R. Norrell notes, November 5, 1998 (in authors' possession).

94. Ford and Norrell notes, November 5, 1998; Derek Tice interview; Tice testimony, Danser's preliminary hearing, December 28, 1998 (in authors' possession).

95. Ford and Norrell notes, November 5, 1998.

96. Ibid.; Dick to Wells, January 2004; Dick testimony, first Tice trial, February 2000; Hansen interview.

97. Ford and Norrell notes, November 5, 1998; Derek Tice interview.

98. Stanton interview; Broccoletti interview; "Motion to Exclude," January 27, 2000 (in authors' possession); Hansen interview; Center for Public Integrity, *Harmful Error*, 43–44.

99. Danser's preliminary hearing, December 28, 1998; Derek Tice interview.

100. Virginia Division of Forensic Science Certificate of Analysis, February 18, 1999; Hansen interview; hearing in Danser's case, February 24, 1999 (in authors' possession).

101. Police crime scene videotape; McCormack and Woodlief, "Motion to Set Aside Verdict," July 20, 1999; Larry McCann, "Crime Scene Analysis and Reconstruction of the July 8, 1997, Sexual Assault and Murder of Michelle Moore-Bosko," November 3,

2005, clemency petition; Hansen interview; *Washington Post*, November 10, 2005; Kinnison testimony, first Tice trial, February 2000.

102. McCann, "Crime Scene Analysis," November 3, 2005, clemency petition; Hansen interview; police crime scene videotape.

103. Schwertlech interview.

104. Stanton interview; Bowen interview for "Eight Men Out"; Hansen interview.

10: "Guess Who Did That?"

1. Shipley interviews; Danial Williams affidavit, clemency petition, November 2005; Danial Williams interview.

2. Stipulation of Facts, January 22, 1999 (in authors' possession); Williams's plea agreement, January 22, 1999, clemency petition; Shipley interview; Williams interview.

3. Wray and Ford notes, February 25, 1999 (in authors' possession); "Memorandum in Support of Petition for Absolute Pardon," November 2005.

4. "Notice and Motion," February 26, 1999 (Norfolk Circuit Court records, Williams file).

5. Joe Dick to the Bosko/Moore family, February 19, 1999 (in authors' possession).

6. Ford testimony, Tice habeas hearing, September 2006; Ballard to Karen and Kamonte and family, no date (in authors' possession).

7. Ballard to Karen and Kamonte and family, no date.

8. Ibid.

9. Declaration of Karen Armstrong Stover, June 2005 (in authors' possession); Ballard to Wells, May 4, 2005; Hansen interview; Stover testimony, Tice habeas hearing, September 2006.

10. Arrest warrant, July 8, 1997 (in authors' possession); Taylor testimony, Wilson trial, June 1999; Bosko interview for "Eight Men Out"; Ballard to Dowling, March 4, 2003 (in authors' possession).

11. Ballard to Dowling, March 4, 2003; Ballard to Wells, July 7 and 26, 2004; Lyn Simmons interview; Taylor testimony, second Tice trial, January 2003, first Tice trial, February 2000, Wilson trial, June 1999.

12. Ballard to Wells, April 13, 2004; Erin Litle interview.

13. Trial and Sentencing Order, February 1998 (in authors' possession); Hansen interview; Bayshore Gardens Management Team to Taylor, June 26, 1997 (Norfolk Circuit Court records, Wilson file); Ballard to Dowling, March 4, 2003.

14. Taylor declaration, clemency petition, June 2005; Stover declaration, June 2005; Lori Searcy phone conversation.

15. Stipulation of Commonwealth's Evidence, no date (in authors' possession).

16. Ibid.; Ballard's taped statement to police, July 25, 1997 (in authors' possession); *Virginian-Pilot* article, no date (Norfolk Circuit Court records, Ballard file); Sentencing Order, March 31, 1998 (in authors' possession).

17. Taylor declaration, clemency petition, June 2005; Stover declaration, June 2005.

18. Taylor declaration, clemency petition, June 2005; phone conversation with Nora Nellis.

19. Deborah Boardman interview.

20. Ballard to Wells, March 29, 2004; Ford and D.M. Peterson notes on Ballard interrogation, March 4, 1999 (in authors' possession); Ballard's taped confession, March 4, 1999, transcript (in authors' possession); Stanton interview.

21. Ballard to Wells, March 29, April 13, 2004.

22. Ballard to Wells, March 29, April 13, 2004, May 4, 2005.

23. Ballard to Wells, May 25, 2004, May 4, 2005; Simmons interview. In her interview, Simmons read parts of a presentence report on Ballard by a probation and parole officer.

24. Simmons interview; Ballard to Wells, June 14, May 25, 2004, May 4, 2005.

25. Taylor testimony, second Tice trial, January 2003; Ballard to Dowling, March 4, 2003; Ballard's taped confession, March 11, 1999, transcript (in authors' possession); "Notice of Intent to Present Evidence of Unabjudicated Conduct," December 10, 1999 (Norfolk Circuit Court records, Ballard file).

26. Transcript of Proceedings, February 24, 1999 (in authors' possession).

27. Ibid.; Stanton interview; anonymous source.

28. Stanton interview; Hansen interview; court order, March 15, 1999 (in authors' possession).

29. Yaroshefsky, "Zealous Advocacy"; Gershman, "Tricks Prosecutors Play"; *Virginian-Pilot*, March 4, 5, 1999; *New York Times*, March 21, 2004; *Chicago Tribune*, January 8, 1999.

30. Hansen interview.

31. Ibid.

32. Ballard's suppression hearing, November 4, 1999, clemency petition; Ballard testimony, Tice habeas hearing, September 2006; Ballard's preliminary hearing, May 5, 1999 (in authors' possession); Ballard affidavit, clemency petition, March 2005.

33. Virginia Division of Forensic Science Certificate of Analysis, May 6, 1999 (in authors' possession).

34. Ballard to Wells, March 29, June 14, 2004; Ballard's taped confession, March 11, 1999; Danial Williams interview.

35. Ballard's preliminary hearing, May 5, 1999; Ballard's suppression hearing, November 4, 1999, clemency petition; Peterson and Ford notes, March 5, 1999 (in authors' possession); Ballard's taped confession, March 4, 1999.

36. Ballard's suppression hearing, November 4, 1999, clemency petition; Peterson and Ford notes, March 5, 1999.

37. Ballard to Wells, March 29, 2004; Simmons interview.

38. Peterson and Ford notes, March 5, 1999; Ballard's taped confession, March 4, 1999.

39. Peterson and Ford notes, March 5, 1999; Ballard to Wells, March 29, 2004; Ballard to Dowling, March 4, 2003; Ballard affidavit, clemency petition, March 2005.

40. Ballard's taped confession, March 4, 1999.

41. Bill Blaine to Charles E. Poston, April 27, 1999 (Norfolk Circuit Court records, Williams file); "Memorandum in Support of Petition for Absolute Pardon," November 10, 2005.

42. Arrest warrants, March 8, 1999 (Norfolk Circuit Court records, Ballard file); Ballard's suppression hearing, November 4, 1999, clemency petition; Ballard's preliminary hearing, May 5, 1999; Peterson and Ford notes, April 20, 1999 (in authors' possession); Ballard to Dowling, March 4, 2003; Ballard to Wells, March 29, 2004; Ballard's taped confession, March 11, 1999.

43. Ford deposition, Tice habeas petition, August 2006, videotape and transcript (in authors' possession).

44. Searcy phone conversation on her visit with Ballard in prison, January 2005; Ballard declaration, clemency petition, March 2005; Ballard to Wells, March 29, 2004.

45. Ballard to Wells, May 4, 2005, March 29, 2004; Searcy phone conversation; Ballard to Dowling, March 4, 2003.

46. Ballard to Wells, March 29, June 14, 2004, May 4, 2005; Ballard to Dowling, March 4, 12, 2003; Searcy phone conversation; Ballard declaration, clemency petition, March 2005.

47. McCann, "Crime Scene Analysis," November 3, 2005, clemency petition.

48. Ballard to Wells, April 13 and July 26, 2004; Ballard to Dowling, March 4, 2003.

49. Hansen interview; Bowen interview for "Eight Men Out"; Hansen closing argument, second Tice trial, January 2003; Bowen closing argument, first Tice trial, February 2000; Hansen interview for "Eight Men Out."

50. *Virginian-Pilot*, March 13, 20, 1999; Stanton interview.

11: "I Would Have Told Them I Handed Oswald the Gun"

1. McCormack interview; Ramey and William Wilson interview; Woodlief to Poston, February 23, 1999 (Norfolk Circuit Court records, Wilson file); Woodlief to Ballard, March 5, 1999 (in authors' possession).

2. Ballard to Woodlief and McCormack, March 10, 1999 (in authors' possession).

3. Ballard to Woodlief and McCormack, March 10, 1999; Peterson and Ford notes, April 20, 1999; Hansen statements on letters, Wilson trial, June 1999; Notice of Intent to Present Evidence of Unadjudicated Conduct, December 10, 1999 (Norfolk Circuit Court records, Ballard file).

4. Shipley interviews; Frank interview.

5. Danial Williams interviews.

6. Motion to Withdraw Guilty Plea, April 14, 1999; Brief in Support of Motion, April 22, 1999; hearing on motion, April 28, 1999 (Norfolk Circuit Court records, Williams file); anonymous sources.

7. Hearing on motion, April 28, 1999; *Virginian-Pilot*, April 29, 1999.

8. *Virginian-Pilot*, May 24, 2001; hearing on motion, April 28, 1999; anonymous source; Shipley interview.

9. Fasanaro interviews; Dick's sentencing hearing, September 8, 1999; Joe Dick interviews; Joe Dick to Wells, November 2003; Joe Dick affidavit, no date, clemency petition; Patricia and Joe Dick Sr. interview; Patricia Dick affidavit, November 2005, clemency petition; *Virginian-Pilot*, March 20, 1999.

10. *Virginian-Pilot*, April 22, 1999; "Advice to Defendants Pleading Guilty," no date (in authors' possession); Dick testimony, Wilson trial, June 1999; Fasanaro interview; McCormack to Fasanaro, April 29, 1999 (in authors' possession).

11. McCormack to Fasanaro, April 29, 1999; Bankard-Sharpe interview; McCormack interview; *Virginian-Pilot*, April 22, 1999; Fasanaro interviews; Dick's plea agreement (Norfolk Circuit Court records, Dick file); Joe Dick affidavit, no date, clemency petition; McCormack to Fasanaro, May 17, June 7, 1999 (in authors' possession).

12. *Virginian-Pilot*, April 22, 1999; Leo and Ofshe, "Consequences of False Confessions," 478–81; *Star-Telegram*, March 7, 2004; Vollen and Eggers, *Surviving Justice*, 13–46.

13. Dick interview; Bowen interview for "Eight Men Out"; Stanton interview; Dick testimony, Wilson trial, June 1999.

14. Dick interview.

15. Zaleski interview; *Virginian-Pilot*, April 14, 1999; Criminal Continuance Order, April 15, 1999 (in authors' possession).

16. Derek Tice interview; Derek Tice testimony, Tice habeas hearing, September

2006; "Statement of Derek Tice," May 7, 1999 (in authors' possession); Larry Tice e-mail to Wells.

17. Zaleski interview; Motion to Withdraw, June 24, 1999 (Norfolk Circuit Court records, Tice file); Rachel Tice interview.

18. Simmons interview.

19. Ballard to Wells, March 29, 2004; May 4, 2005.

20. Simmons interview; Ballard to Wells, April 13, 2004.

21. Pat Bosko interview; Sarah Bosko interview; Billy Bosko interview for "Eight Men Out."

22. Gross, "Risks of Death," 498.

23. New York Times, August 30, 2003; Zacharias, "Role of Prosecutors"; USA Today, January 31, 2006.

24. Virginian-Pilot, May 14, 1999; Rick Pauley e-mail to Wells; Babineau interview; Stanton interview.

25. Virginian-Pilot, May 14, 1999; Rick Pauley interview; Stanton interview.

26. Billy Bosko interview for "Eight Men Out"; Sarah Bosko interview; phone conversation with Carol Moore and her brother-in-law.

27. Fasanaro interviews.

28. Eric Wilson interview; anonymous source.

29. "Notice of Intent to Amend Indictment," June 14, 1999 (Norfolk Circuit Court records, Wilson file); Wilson interview for "Eight Men Out"; Wilson interview; McCormack interview; McCormack interview for "Eight Men Out."

30. Bosko testimony, Wilson trial, June 1999; anonymous sources; Broccoletti interview.

31. Bryan, Kinnison, and Taylor testimony, Wilson trial, June 1999; McCormack interview.

32. Dick testimony, Wilson trial, June 1999; William Wilson interview; McCormack interview.

33. Eric Wilson interview; Dick testimony, Wilson trial, June 1999; Dick to Wells, November and December 2003; McCormack interview; Dick's presentence report, July 1999.

34. Hoggard testimony, Wilson trial, June 1999; McCormack interview.

35. McCormack interview; Ford testimony, pretrial hearing in Wilson's case, December 9, 1998.

36. Poston on defense exhibits, Wilson trial, June 1999.

37. McCormack interview; Eric Wilson interview; Virginian-Pilot, June 19, 1999; Wilson testimony, Wilson trial, June 1999.

38. Wilson testimony, Wilson trial, June 1999; William Wilson interview; phone conversation with Carol Moore and her brother-in-law.

39. William Wilson interview; *Virginian-Pilot*, June 19, 1999.

40. McCormack interview; *Virginian-Pilot*, June 22, 1999.

41. Wilson trial transcript, June 1999; Wilson interview; *Virginian-Pilot*, June 22, 1999; letter of nine Wilson jurors to Governor Mark Warner, January 4, 2006, clemency petition.

42. Carol Moore testimony, Bowen and McCormack arguments, presentencing, Wilson trial, June 1999.

43. *Virginian Pilot*, June 22, 1999, July 15, 2000; McCormack and Wilson interviews for "Eight Men Out"; McCormack interview.

44. Dick's sentencing hearing, September 8, 1999; Pat Bosko's victim impact statement, no date; Patricia Dick interview.

45. Dick's sentencing hearing, September 8, 1999; Dick interview; Fasanaro interview.

46. Dick's sentencing hearing, September 8, 1999; Dick interview; Dick to Wells, November 2003.

47. Patricia and Joe Dick Sr. interview.

48. Sentencing guidelines, Poston notation, September 8, 1999 (Norfolk Circuit Court records, Dick file); Dick's sentencing hearing, September 8, 1999.

49. Patricia and Joe Dick Sr. interview; Ramey Wilson interview.

50. Patricia and Joe Dick Sr. interview; William Wilson interview.

51. Joe Dick Sr. interview; Patricia Dick affidavit, clemency petition, November 2005; Patricia Dick to Fasanaro, October 3, 1999 (in authors' possession).

52. Wilson's sentencing hearing, September 8, 1999.

53. Billy Bosko victim impact statement, May 1999 (in authors' possession); *Virginian-Pilot*, September 15, 1999.

12: "You Got Nothing to Say, Right?"

1. Motion for Change of Venue, October 21, 1999 (in authors' possession); Randall McFarlane interview for "Eight Men Out"; Lea Tice interview.

2. Derek Tice interview; Larry Tice interview; Larry Tice interview for "Eight Men Out."

3. Broccoletti interview; Broccoletti interview for "Eight Men Out."

4. Opening statements, first Tice trial, February 2000.

5. Russell interview; Broccoletti interview.

6. Dick testimony, first Tice trial, February 2000; Dick to Wells, December 2003; Dick interview; Berlow, "What Happened in Norfolk?"

7. Dick testimony, first Tice trial, February 2000; Broccoletti testimony, Tice habeas hearing, September 2006; Broccoletti interview; McFarlane interview for "Eight Men Out."

8. Ford testimony, first Tice trial, February 2000.

9. Cloud, "Dirty Little Secret"; Dorfman, "Proving the Lie"; Slobogin, "Reform"; *Denver Post*, August 26, 2007; Chin and Wells, "'Blue Wall of Silence.'"

10. Jerry Sellers and Robert Scanlon testimony, first Tice trial, February 2000.

11. Broccoletti interview and e-mail to Wells; Simmons interview; Ballard to Wells, March 29, 2004; Findley and Scott, "Multiple Dimensions," 342–46.

12. Broccoletti interview for "Eight Men Out"; Broccoletti and Ballard testimony at Tice habeas hearing, September 2006; Ballard testimony and Poston rulings, first Tice trial, February 2000; Simmons interview; Ballard to Wells, June 14, 2004; McFarlane interview for "Eight Men Out"; memorandum in support of motion to admit Ballard's prior offenses, January 20, 2000 (Norfolk Circuit Court records, Tice file).

13. Robert Morgan testimony, first Tice trial, February 2000.

14. Wayne Kennedy testimony and Poston rulings, first Tice trial, February 2000; defense motion to allow use of model of bedroom, January 2000 (in authors' possession); anonymous source.

15. Broccoletti interview; Broccoletti testimony, Tice habeas hearing, September 2006.

16. Bowen closing argument, first Tice trial, February 2000.

17. Russell and Broccoletti closing arguments, first Tice trial, February 2000.

18. First Tice trial transcript, February 2000; Derek Tice interview; McFarlane interview for "Eight Men Out"; Larry and Rachel Tice interview; Larry Tice interview for "Eight Men Out"; *Virginian-Pilot*, February 12, 2000; phone conversation with Carol Moore and her brother-in-law.

19. McFarlane interview for "Eight Men Out."

20. Presentencing testimony, first Tice trial, February 2000; *Virginian-Pilot*, February 12, 2000; Broccoletti interview for "Eight Men Out"; McFarlane interview for "Eight Men Out."

21. Hansen presentencing argument, first Tice trial, February 2000.

22. *Virginian-Pilot*, February 15, 2000; McFarlane interview for "Eight Men Out."

23. *Virginian-Pilot*, February 15, and June 8, 2000.

24. Ballard's plea agreement, March 22, 2000 (Norfolk Circuit Court records, Ballard file); Ballard testimony, Tice habeas hearing, September 2006; Shipley interviews.

25. Ballard and Ford testimony, Tice habeas hearing, September 2006; Ford deposition, Tice habeas petition, August 2006; Ballard to Wells, March 29, 2004.

26. Ballard to Wells, March 20, 29, 2004, May 4, 2005; Ballard testimony, Tice habeas hearing, September 2006; Broccoletti interview.

27. Ford's notes on Ballard debriefing, March 15, 2000 (in authors' possession); Ballard affidavit, clemency petition, March 2005; Ballard testimony, Tice habeas hearing, September 2006.

28. Ballard to Wells, April 13, June 14, 2004; Broccoletti interview; Simmons interview.

29. Phone conversation with Carol Moore and her brother-in-law.

30. Rhea and Norman Williams interview; Danial Williams interview; Trevena interview and e-mail to Wells; Shipley interview; Rhea Williams to Wells, May 2003; Helen Frezon interview; "The Norfolk Four: A Miscarriage of Justice," film, 2005.

31. Danial Williams interviews; Trevena e-mail to Wells.

32. Rhea Williams interview; Danial Williams interview; Danial Williams affidavit, clemency petition, November 2005.

33. Joe Dick interviews; Alphonse Bankard interview; Ballard to Wells, July 26, August 9, 2004; Joe Dick to Fasanaro, 2003, probably February or March (in authors' possession); anonymous source; Joe Dick Sr. interview; Joe Dick to Michael Black, no date.

34. Joe Dick to Wells, January 2004, August, December 2003, and other letters; Dick interviews; Dick to Black, no date.

35. Larry Tice to Roy W. Cherry and others, August 7, 2000; Larry Tice to Melvin C. High and others, July 19, 2000; Derek Tice to Larry Tice, various letters, May and June 2003 (in authors' possession); Tice, "Sordid Tragedy"; Billy Bosko e-mail to Larry Tice, August 5, 2003; Brian Wray e-mail to Larry Tice, February 21, 2004; Larry Tice interview.

36. Derek Tice interviews.

37. Lea Tice interview; Lea Tice to Derek Tice, October 12, 2000 (in authors' possession).

38. Derek Tice interviews; Gross et al., "Exonerations in the United States"; www.innocenceproject.org.

39. Derek Tice interviews.

40. Derek Tice interview.

41. Eric Wilson to Wells, received from McCormack in April 2004; Eric Wilson interview; Eric Wilson interview for "Eight Men Out."

42. Eric Wilson interview for "Eight Men Out"; Eric Wilson to Wells, received from McCormack in April 2004; Shannon Sisk interview.

43. Eric Wilson interview; Eric Wilson interview for "Eight Men Out"; Ramey Wilson interview.

44. Ballard to Wells, June 14, 2004.

45. Anonymous source; Joe Dick interview.

46. Petition for Appeal, October 17, 2000; Motion to Set Aside Verdict, March 22, 2000 (in authors' possession).

47. Videotape of "Eight Men Out"; Dowling interview; Bowen interview for "Eight Men Out." Later, Bowen would refer to the program when explaining her decision to turn down requests for interviews for this book (Shipley interview).

48. Amy Bosko phone conversation; Sarah Bosko interview; phone conversation with Carol Moore and her brother-in-law; Dowling interview.

49. Dowling interview.

50. Alphonse Bankard interview; Bankard to "The Honorable," June 25, 1999; videotape of "Eight Men Out."

51. Alphonse Bankard interview; Bankard-Sharpe interview.

52. Ibid.

53. Patricia and Joe Dick Sr. interview; Fasanaro interview.

54. Dick to Dowling, April or May, and May 2001 (in authors' possession); Dowling interview; Dick to Wells, December 2003.

55. Derek Tice interview.

56. Virginia Court of Appeals ruling, May 21, 2002 (in authors' possession).

57. Amy Bosko phone conversation; phone conversation with Carol Moore and her brother-in-law; Pat Bosko interview.

58. *Virginian-Pilot*, December 17, 2002.

59. Derek Wagner interview; opening statements, second Tice trial, January 2003.

60. Bosko, Taylor, and Bryan testimony, second Tice trial, January 2003.

61. Kinnison testimony, second Tice trial, January 2003; Tice habeas petition, September 2005.

62. Dick testimony, second Tice trial, January 2003; Broccoletti interview and e-mail to Wells; Russell interview; Dick to Wells, June 2003; Dick interview.

63. Broccoletti interview.

64. Ibid.

65. Ford deposition, Tice habeas petition, August 2006; Broccoletti e-mail to Wells.

66. Ford deposition, Tice habeas petition, August 2006; Dick to Ford, no date (in authors' possession).

67. Ford deposition, Tice habeas petition, August 2006.

68. Ibid.; Broccoletti e-mail to Wells.

69. Dick affidavit, clemency petition, no date; Dick interviews; Dick to Wells, November, December 2003, March 2004; Ratner declaration, clemency petition, November 2005; Ford deposition, Tice habeas petition, August 2006; Hansen interview.

70. Ford deposition, Tice habeas petition, August 2006.

71. Ibid.; Broccoletti e-mail to Wells.

72. Dowling interview; Dick to Fasanaro, 2003, probably February or March; Dick interviews; Dick to Wells, August 2003. In his interview, Dowling read from Dick's letter to him.

73. Dick testimony, second Tice trial, January 2003; Broccoletti interview; Derek Tice interview; Joe Dick interview; Russell interview; Rachel Tice interview; Patricia Bosko interview; phone conversation with Carol Moore and her brother-in-law.

74. Dick testimony and Poston ruling, second Tice trial, January 2003; Larry and Rachel Tice interview; Dick to Fasanaro, 2003, probably February or March.

75. Ford testimony, second Tice trial, January 2003; phone conversation with Carol Moore and her brother-in-law.

76. Poston's rulings, second Tice trial, January 2003.

77. Ford testimony, second Tice trial, January 2003.

78. Sellers and Scanlon testimony, second Tice trial, January 2003; Kathleen Joy Horvath Imel affidavit, clemency petition, December 2005; Matthew Roy remark to Wells at second Tice trial; Ford deposition, Tice habeas petition, August 2006; Ballard testimony, Tice habeas hearing, September 2006.

79. Ford and Wray testimony, Tice habeas hearing, September 2006; Ford deposition, Tice habeas petition, August 2006; Ballard affidavit, clemency petition, March 2005; Ballard testimony, Tice habeas hearing, September 2006; Ballard to Wells, March 29, 2004; Ballard to Dowling, March 4, 2003.

80. Ballard testimony, Tice habeas hearing, September 2006; Ballard to Dowling, March 12, 2003; memorandum in support of Tice's habeas petition, September 14, 2005; Ford and Wray testimony, Tice habeas hearing, September 2006; Ford deposition, Tice habeas petition, August 2006.

81. Ballard and Broccoletti testimony, Tice habeas hearing, September 2006; Broccoletti interview.

82. Broccoletti e-mail to Wells; Broccoletti testimony, Tice habeas hearing, September 2006; Russell interview.

83. Broccoletti testimony, Tice habeas hearing, September 2006; Russell interview.

84. Broccoletti testimony, Tice habeas hearing, September 2006; Broccoletti interview; Russell interview.

85. Ballard testimony, Tice habeas hearing, September 2006; Ballard affidavit, clemency petition, March 2005; Broccoletti interview.

86. Ballard testimony, Tice habeas hearing, September 2006.

87. Ballard affidavit, clemency petition, March 2005.

88. Ford deposition, Tice habeas petition, August 2006; Ballard testimony and Poston comments, second Tice trial, January 2003.

89. Peterson testimony and Poston rulings, second Tice trial, January 2003; Broccoletti testimony, Tice habeas hearing, September 2006; memorandum in support of Tice's habeas petition, September 14, 2005.

90. Ballard testimony, second Tice trial, January 2003.

91. Danser testimony, second Tice trial, January 2003; Stanton interview; Broccoletti testimony, Tice habeas hearing, September 2006; Horvath Imel affidavit, clemency petition, December 2005; Hansen closing argument, second Tice trial, January 2003.

92. Judy and Richard Pauley Sr. testimony, second Tice trial, January 2003.

93. McCormack interview.

94. Russell remark to Wells, second Tice trial; Givelber, "Adversary System," 260, 264.

95. Hansen closing argument, second Tice trial, January 2003; Broccoletti interview; Hansen interview.

96. Russell and Broccoletti's closing arguments, second Tice trial, January 2003.

97. Second Tice trial transcript, January 2003; Horvath Imel affidavit, clemency petition, December 2005; Larry and Rachel Tice interview; Derek Tice interview.

98. Sarah Bosko interview; Larry Tice e-mail to Wells, March 2007.

99. Second Tice trial transcript, January 2003.

100. Billy Bosko e-mail to Larry Tice, August 5, 2003; *Virginian-Pilot*, February 1, 2003; Pat Bosko to Larry Tice, no date (in authors' possession).

101. McCormack interview; Shipley interview; affidavit of Kathleen Joy Horvath Imel, clemency petition, December 2005.

102. Broccoletti testimony, Tice habeas hearing, September 2006; Petition for Appeal, May 2003.

103. Larry and Rachel Tice interview; Larry and Rachel Tice affidavits, clemency petition, November 2005; Larry Tice e-mail to Wells.

13: Heavy Artillery

1. Peter Neufeld interview.
2. Ibid.
3. Ibid.
4. Anonymous sources.
5. George Kendall interview.

6. Kendall interview; Kendall bio on Holland & Knight's website; Neufeld interview; anonymous source.

7. Kendall interview; Neufeld interview.

8. Kendall interview; Des Hogan bio on Hogan & Hartson's website; Blakeslee, *Tulia*, 263; Don Salzman interview; Salzman bio on Skadden's website.

9. Kendall interview; Salzman interview.

10. Kendall interview and e-mail to Wells; Salzman interview; Boardman interview.

11. Boardman interview; Kendall interview; Salzman interview.

12. Kendall interview and phone conversation; Boardman interview; Wells notes on December 2004 meeting with attorneys; Gould, *Innocence Commission*, 162–63, 214–15; *Richmond Times-Dispatch*, July 16, 2007.

13. Boardman interview.

14. Kendall interview.

15. Ibid.; Salzman interview.

16. Innocence Commission for Virginia, "A Vision for Justice"; Bedau and Radelet, "Miscarriages of Justice."

17. Medwed, "Zeal Deal"; Zacharias, "Role of Prosecutors"; *Denver Post*, July 22, 2007.

18. Anonymous source.

19. Kendall interview; Salzman interview.

20. Kendall interview.

21. Ibid.; Kendall e-mail to Wells; Eric Wilson interview.

22. Anonymous source; Berlow, "What Happened in Norfolk?"; Salzman interview.

23. Ballard to Wells, July 26, 2004; Boardman interview; anonymous source; Ballard affidavit, March 2005, clemency petition.

24. Memorandum in support of Tice's habeas petition, September 14, 2005; Boardman interview.

25. Eric Wilson interview; www.vaperforms.virginia.gov/i-recidivism.php; *Denver Post*, July 25, 2007; https://records.txdps.state.tx.us.

26. Videotape of press conference, November 10, 2005 (in authors' possession); Larry Tice phone conversation; Boardman interview; *Washington Post*, November 27, 2005; Searcy phone conversation.

27. Rhea Williams phone conversation; Larry Tice phone conversation.

28. *Virginian-Pilot*, November 23, 2005; "Memorandum in Support of Petition for Absolute Pardon" and exhibits, November 10, 2005 (in authors' possession); Patricia Dick phone conversation.

29. *Virginian-Pilot*, November 12, 2005; *Washington Post*, November 10, 2005; Evans e-mail to Wells, November 15, 2005; *Richmond Times-Dispatch*, November 11, 2005.

30. *Virginian-Pilot*, November 23, 2005, January 6, 2006; Kendall interview; *Washington Post*, January 5, 2006.

31. *Virginian-Pilot*, January 11, 2006.

32. Kendall interview; Bennett, "True Confessions?"; *Virginian-Pilot*, January 6, 2006; *Nightline*, December 27, 2005.

33. Tangela Banks et al. to Governor Warner, January 4, 2006, clemency petition; Horvath Imel affidavit, December 2005, clemency petition; *Washington Post*, January 6, 2006; letters from former judges and prosecutors, December 2005 and January 2006, clemency petition; Kendall interview; *Virginian-Pilot*, January 6, 2006.

34. Kendall interview; Salzman interview.

35. *Washington Post*, January 6, 2006.

36. Videotape and transcript of Ford's deposition, August 8, 2006 (in authors' possession).

37. Tice's habeas hearing, September 11–12, 2006, transcript (in authors' possession).

38. Boardman phone conversation; Kendall interview and e-mail to Wells; House Joint Resolution no. 38, May 8, 2001; *Washington Post*, January 5, 1989; anonymous source; *Virginian-Pilot*, November 30, 2006; AP article, November 29, 2006.

39. Tice's habeas hearing, September 12, 2006.

40. Judge Everett Martin Jr.'s ruling on Tice's habeas petition, November 27, 2006 (in authors' possession).

41. Boardman interview; *Virginian-Pilot*, November 30, December 4, 2006; *Washington Post*, December 1, 2006; Danial Williams phone conversation; AP article, November 29, 2006.

42. *Virginian-Pilot*, November 30, 2006; *Washington Post*, December 1, 2006.

43. *Virginian-Pilot*, December 11, 2006.

44. *Virginian-Pilot*, December 11, 21, 2006.

45. Boardman interview; Kendall interview; Salzman interview; Larry Tice e-mail to Wells.

46. Kendall interview and e-mail to Wells; Salzman interview; anonymous source; Boardman interview.

47. Kendall interview.

48. Salzman interview; anonymous source.

49. Anonymous source.

50. Virginia Supreme Court's ruling, January 11, 2008 (in authors' possession); Martin's ruling, November 27, 2006; Horvath Imel affidavit, clemency petition, December 2005.

51. Larry Tice phone conversation; anonymous source.

52. *Virginian-Pilot*, January 12, 2008.

53. *Richmond Times-Dispatch*, January 12, 2008; anonymous source; press release, January 11, 2008 (in authors' possession); Virginia Supreme Court's ruling, January 11, 2008.

54. Anonymous source.

55. *Washington Post*, January 13, 2008; *Virginian-Pilot*, January 15, 2008.

56. Salzman interview; Boardman interview; anonymous source.

Bibliography

Alschuler, Albert W. "The Prosecutor's Role in Plea Bargaining." *University of Chicago Law Review* 36, no. 50 (1968).

American Bar Association. "American Bar Association Guidelines for the Appointment and Performance of Defense Counsel in Death Penalty Cases." February 2003.

American Bar Association. "*Gideon*'s Broken Promise: America's Continuing Quest for Equal Justice." December 2004.

Bedau, Hugo Adam, and Michael L. Radelet. "Miscarriages of Justice in Potentially Capital Cases." *Stanford Law Review* 40, no. 21 (November 1987).

Bennett, Brian. "True Confessions?" *Time*, December 12, 2005.

Berlow, Alan. "What Happened in Norfolk?" *New York Times Magazine*, August 19, 2007.

Bernhard, Adele. "Effective Assistance of Counsel." In Westervelt and Humphrey, *Wrongly Convicted*.

Berry, Sheila Martin. "'Bad Lawyering': How Defense Attorneys Help Convict the Innocent." *Northern Kentucky University Law Review* 30 (2003).

Blakeslee, Nate. *Tulia: Race, Cocaine, and Corruption in a Small Texas Town*. New York: Public Affairs, 2005.

Center for Public Integrity. *Harmful Error: Investigating America's Local Prosecutors*. Washington, DC: Center for Public Integrity, 2003.

Chin, Gabriel J., and Scott C. Wells. "The 'Blue Wall of Silence' as Evidence of Bias and Motive to Lie: A New Approach to Police Perjury." *University of Pittsburgh Law Review* 59 (Winter 1998).

Clemens, Aaron M. "Removing the Market for Lying Snitches: Reforms to Prevent Unjust Convictions." *Bridgeport Law Review/Quinnipiac Law Review* 23 (2004).

Cloud, Morgan. "The Dirty Little Secret." *Emory Law Journal* 43 (1994).

Cloud, Morgan, George B. Shepherd, Alison Nodvin Barkoff, and Justin V. Shur. "Words Without Meaning: The Constitution, Confessions, and Mentally Retarded Suspects." *University of Chicago Law Review* 69 (Spring 2002).

Cole, George F., and Christopher E. Smith. *The American System of Criminal Justice.* Belmont, CA: Wadsworth, 2001.

Connery, Donald S. *Guilty Until Proven Innocent.* New York: G.P. Putnam's Sons, 1977.

Davies, Sharon. "The Reality of False Confessions—Lessons of the Central Park Jogger Case." *New York University Review of Law and Social Change* 30 (2006).

Davis, Deborah, and William T. O'Donohue. "The Road to Perdition: Extreme Influence Tactics in the Interrogation Room." In *Handbook of Forensic Psychology,* edited by William O'Donahue and Erick Levinsky. San Diego, CA: Academic Press, 2004.

Dorfman, David N. "Proving the Lie: Litigating Police Credibility." *American Journal of Criminal Law* 26 (Summer 1999).

Drizin, Steven A., and Richard A. Leo. "The Problem of False Confessions in the Post-DNA World." *North Carolina Law Review* 82, no. 3 (2004).

Edds, Margaret. *An Expendable Man: The Near-Execution of Earl Washington Jr.* New York: New York University Press, 2003.

Findley, Keith A., and Michael S. Scott. "The Multiple Dimensions of Tunnel Vision in Criminal Cases." *Wisconsin Law Review* 2006, no. 2 (2006).

Fisher, Stanley Z. "Just the Facts, Ma'am: Lying and the Omission of Exculpatory Evidence in Police Reports." *New England Law Review* 28 (Fall 1993).

Garrett, Brandon L. "Judging Innocence." *Columbia Law Review,* January 2008.

Gershman, Bennett L. "Tricks Prosecutors Play." *Trial,* April 1992.

———. "The Prosecutor's Duty to Truth." *Georgetown Journal of Legal Ethics* 14 (Winter 2001).

Givelber, Daniel. "Meaningless Acquittals, Meaningful Convictions: Do We Reliably Acquit the Innocent?" *Rutgers Law Review* 49 (1997).

———. "The Adversary System and Historical Accuracy: Can We Do Better?" In Westervelt and Humphrey, *Wrongly Convicted.*

Gould, Jon B. *The Innocence Commission: Preventing Wrongful Convictions and Restoring the Criminal Justice System.* New York: New York University Press, 2008.

Gross, Samuel R. "The Risks of Death: Why Erroneous Convictions Are Common in Capital Cases." *Buffalo Law Review* 44 (1996).

Gross, Samuel R., Kristen Jacoby, Daniel J. Matheson, Nicholas Montgomery, and Sujata Patil. "Exonerations in the United States 1989 Through 2003." *Journal of Criminal Law and Criminology* 95 (Winter 2005).

Gudjonsson, Gisli H. *The Psychology of Interrogations and Confessions: A Handbook.* Chichester, England: Wiley, 2003.

Harris, George C. "Testimony for Sale: The Law and Ethics of Snitches and Experts." *Pepperdine Law Review* 28 (2000).

Hessick, F. Andrew, III, and Reshma Saujani. "Plea Bargaining and Convicting the Innocent: The Role of the Prosecutor, the Defense Counsel, and the Judge." *BYU Journal of Public Law* 16 (2002).

Humes, Edward. *Mean Justice.* New York: Pocket Books, 1999.

Inbau, Fred E., John E. Reid, Joseph P. Buckley, and Brian C. Jayne. *Criminal Interrogation and Confessions.* 4th ed. Gaithersburg, MD: Aspen Publishers, 2001.

Innocence Commission for Virginia. "A Vision for Justice: Report and Recommendations Regarding Wrongful Convictions in the Commonwealth of Virginia." http://www.icva.us, March 2005.

Jackall, Robert. *Street Stories: The World of Police Detectives.* Cambridge, MA: Harvard University Press, 2005.

Kassin, Saul M. "The Psychology of Confession Evidence." *American Psychologist* 52, no. 3 (March 1997).

————. "On the Psychology of Confessions: Does Innocence Put Innocents at Risk?" *American Psychologist* 60, no. 3 (April 2005).

Kassin, Saul M., and Christina T. Fong. "'I'm Innocent!': Effects of Training on Judgments of Truth and Deception in the Interrogation Room." *Law and Human Behavior* 23, no. 5 (1999).

Kassin, Saul M., Christine C. Goldstein, and Kenneth Savitsky. "Behavioral Confirmation in the Interrogation Room: On the Dangers of Presuming Guilt." *Law and Human Behavior* 27, no. 2 (April 2003).

Kassin, Saul M., Christian A. Meissner, and Rebecca J. Norwick. "'I'd Know a False Confession If I Saw One': A Comparative Study of College Students and Police Investigators." *Law and Human Behavior* 29 (2005).

Kassin, Saul M., and Katherine Neumann. "On the Power of Confession Evidence: An Experimental Test of the Fundamental Difference Hypothesis." *Law and Human Behavior* 21, no. 5 (1997).

Kassin, Saul M., and Rebecca J. Norwick. "Why People Waive Their *Miranda* Rights: The Power of Innocence." *Law and Human Behavior* 28, no. 2 (April 2004).

Kassin, Saul M., and Holly Sukel. "Coerced Confessions and the Jury: An Experimental Test of the 'Harmless Error' Rule." *Law and Human Behavior* 21, no. 1 (1997).

Kenrick, Douglas T., Steven L. Neuberg, and Robert B. Cialdini. *Social Psychology: Unraveling the Mystery.* Boston: Allyn and Bacon, 1999.

Leo, Richard A. "*Miranda*'s Revenge: Police Interrogation as a Confidence Game." *Law and Society Review* 30, no. 2 (1996).

———. "Inside the Interrogation Room." *Journal of Criminal Law and Criminology* 86, no. 2 (Winter 1996).

———. "The Social and Legal Construction of Repressed Memory." *Journal of the American Bar Foundation* 22, no. 3 (Summer 1997).

———. "The Impact of *Miranda* Revisited." In Leo and Thomas, *The Miranda Debate.*

———. "*Miranda* and the Problem of False Confessions." In Leo and Thomas, *The Miranda Debate.*

———. "*Miranda*'s Irrelevance: Questioning the Relevance of *Miranda* in the Twenty-First Century." *Michigan Law Review* 99 (March 2001).

———. *Police Interrogation and American Justice.* Cambridge, MA: Harvard University Press, 2008.

Leo, Richard A., Steven Drizin, Peter Neufeld, Brad Hall, and Amy Vatner. "Bringing Reliability Back in: False Confessions and Legal Safeguards in the Twenty-First Century." *Wisconsin Law Review* 2006, no. 2 (2006).

Leo, Richard A., and Richard J. Ofshe. "The Consequences of False Confessions: Deprivations of Liberty and Miscarriages of Justice in the Age of Psychological Interrogation." *Journal of Criminal Law and Criminology* 88, no. 2 (Winter 1998).

———. "The Truth About False Confessions and Advocacy Scholarship." *Criminal Law Bulletin* 37, no. 4 (2001).

Leo, Richard A., and George C. Thomas III, eds. *The Miranda Debate: Law, Justice, and Policing.* Boston: Northeastern University Press, 1998.

Leo, Richard A., and Welsh S. White. "Adapting to *Miranda*: Modern Interrogators' Strategies for Dealing with the Obstacles Posed by *Miranda*." *Minnesota Law Review* 84 (December 1999).

Loftus, Elizabeth F. "Creating False Memories." *Scientific American* 277, no. 3 (September 1997).

———. "Our Changeable Memories: Legal and Practical Implications." *Nature* 4 (March 2003).

———. "Make-Believe Memories." *American Psychologist*, November 2003.

Loftus, Elizabeth F., and Daniel M. Bernstein. "Rich False Memories: The Royal Road to Success." In *Experimental Cognitive Psychology and Its Applications*, edited by A.F. Healy. Washington, DC: American Psychological Association Press, 2005.

Loftus, Elizabeth, and Katherine Ketcham. *Witness for the Defense: The Accused, the Eyewitness, and the Expert Who Puts Memory on Trial.* New York: St. Martin's, 1991.

Los Angeles County. "Report of the 1989–90 Los Angeles County Grand Jury." June 26, 1990.

Lykken, David T. *A Tremor in the Blood: Uses and Abuses of the Lie Detector*. New York: Plenum, 1998.

Martin, Dianne L. "The Police Role in Wrongful Convictions: An International Comparative Study." In Westervelt and Humphrey, *Wrongly Convicted*.

Mazzoni, Giuliana A.L., Elizabeth F. Loftus, and Irving Kirsch. "Changing Beliefs About Implausible Autobiographical Events: A Little Plausibility Goes a Long Way." *Journal of Experimental Psychology: Applied* 7, no. 1 (2001).

Medwed, Daniel S. "The Zeal Deal: Prosecutorial Resistance to Post-Conviction Claims of Innocence." *Boston University Law Review* 84 (February 2004).

Meissner, Christian A., and Saul M. Kassin. "'He's Guilty!': Investigator Bias in Judgments of Truth and Deception." *Law and Human Behavior* 26, no. 5 (October 2002).

Milgram, Stanley. "Behavioral Study of Obedience." *Journal of Abnormal and Social Psychology* 67, no. 4 (1963).

Ofshe, Richard J. "Inadvertent Hypnosis During Interrogation: False Confession Due to Dissociative State; Mis-Identified Multiple Personality and the Satanic Cult Hypothesis." *International Journal of Clinical and Experimental Hypnosis* 40, no. 3 (1992).

Ofshe, Richard J., and Richard A. Leo. "The Decision to Confess Falsely: Rational Choice and Irrational Action." *Denver University Law Review* 74, no. 4 (1997).

———. "The Social Psychology of Police Interrogation: The Theory and Classification of True and False Confessions." *Studies in Law, Politics and Society* 16 (1997).

Ofshe, Richard, and Ethan Watters. *Making Monsters: False Memories, Psychotherapy, and Sexual Hysteria*. Berkeley, CA: University of California Press, 1996.

Oh, Eunyung Theresa. "Innocence After 'Guilt': Postconviction DNA Relief for Innocents Who Pled Guilty." *Syracuse Law Review* 55 (2004).

Scheck, Barry, Peter Neufeld, and Jim Dwyer. *Actual Innocence: When Justice Goes Wrong and How to Make It Right*. New York: Signet, 2001.

Simon, David. *Homicide: A Year on the Killing Streets*. New York: Ivy Books, 1991.

Slater, Lauren. *Opening Skinner's Box: Great Psychological Experiments of the Twentieth Century*. New York: W.W. Norton, 2004.

Slobogin, Christopher. "Reform: The Police: Testilying: Police Perjury and What to Do About It." *University of Colorado Law Review* 67 (Fall 1996).

Stamper, Norm. *Breaking Rank: A Top Cop's Exposé of the Dark Side of American Policing*. New York: Nation Books, 2005.

Sullivan, Thomas P. "Police Experiences with Recording Custodial Interrogations." Northwestern University School of Law Center on Wrongful Convictions Special Report, no. 1 (Summer 2004).

————. "The Police Experience: Recording Custodial Interrogations." *The Champion* 28 (December 2004).

Taylor, Stuart, Jr. "Innocents in Prison." *Atlantic Online*, August 7, 2007.

Tice, Larry. "A Sordid Tragedy of Coerced Confession—The Derek Tice Injustice Story." *Justice: Denied*, November 2000.

Toobin, Jeffrey. "Killer Instincts." *New Yorker*, January 17, 2005.

Trott, Stephen S. "Words of Warning for Prosecutors Using Criminals as Witnesses." *Hastings Law Journal* 47 (July/August 1996).

Vollen, Lola, and Dave Eggers, eds. *Surviving Justice: America's Wrongfully Convicted and Exonerated*. San Francisco, CA: McSweeney's Books, 2005.

Weisselberg, Charles D. "Saving *Miranda*." *Cornell Law Review* 84, November 1998.

Westervelt, Saundra D., and John A. Humphrey, eds. *Wrongly Convicted: Perspectives on Failed Justice*. New Brunswick, NJ: Rutgers University Press, 2002.

White, Welsh S. "False Confessions and the Constitution: Safeguards Against Untrustworthy Evidence." *Harvard Civil Rights–Civil Liberties Law Review* 32 (1997).

————. *Miranda's Waning Protections: Police Interrogation Practices after Dickerson*. Ann Arbor, MI: University of Michigan Press, 2001.

————. "Confessions in Capital Cases." *University of Illinois Law Review* 2003, no. 4 (2003).

Wright, Lawrence. *Remembering Satan: A Tragic Case of Recovered Memory*. New York: Vintage Books, 1995.

Wydick, Richard C. "The Ethics of Witness Coaching." *Cardozo Law Review* 17 (September 1995).

Yaroshefsky, Ellen. "Zealous Advocacy in a Time of Uncertainty: Understanding Lawyers' Ethics: Wrongful Convictions: It Is Time to Take Prosecution Discipline Seriously." *University of the District of Columbia Law Review* 8 (Fall 2004).

Zacharias, Fred C. "The Role of Prosecutors in Serving Justice After Convictions." *Vanderbilt Law Review* 58 (January 2005).

Zimmerman, Clifford S. "From the Jailhouse to the Courthouse: The Role of Informants in Wrongful Convictions." In Westervelt and Humphrey, *Wrongly Convicted*.

Index

police interrogations (*cont.*)
> innocent suspects they might be guilty,
> 68, 94–95; and downplaying suspects'
> responsibility or minimizing legal
> consequences, 65, 68, 73; and expressing
> certainty in guilt, 65, 68; and false
> confessions, 36–37, 68, 94–95, 107; and
> Miranda rights, 102–4; and motives of
> suspects, 32–33; and presumption of guilt,
> 37, 107; and promises and threats, 150; and
> sleep deprivation, 27 and videotaping,
> 155–56. *See also* Ballard, Omar,
> interrogations and confessions of; Danser,
> John, arrest and interrogation of; Dick, Joe,
> Jr., interrogation of (first); Farris, Geoffrey,
> arrest and interrogation of; memory, and
> police suggestions and manipulations;
> Pauley, Rick, interrogation of; Tice,
> Derek, interrogation of (first); Williams,
> Danial, interrogation of; Wilson, Eric,
> interrogation of

polygraphs: and Ballard, 210, 231; and Danser,
> 177; and Dick, 66–67, 122–23; and Farris,
> 161; and interpreting results, 23; and
> Pauley, 159; and police goals, 22; and Tice,
> 148–49, 151, 154; and Williams, 22, 23;
> and Wilson, 104, 105, 110

Poston, Charles E., 182; and Ballard, 192–93,
> 226, 236, 239, 249; and Danser, 177, 250;
> described, 206; and Dick, 219, 220, 237,
> 245; and false confessions, 226, 240, 245,
> 253; and McCormack, 194; and morning
> coffee, 170; and Tice, 170, 222, 223, 226,
> 236, 239, 240, 245, 249, 251, 252, 253;
> views on case, 206, 213; and Williams, 205,
> 206; and Wilson, 118, 213, 216, 217, 218

prosecutors: and admitting mistakes, 163–64,
> 261; and civil suits, 182; and DNA
> evidence, 212, 255–56; and exculpatory
> evidence, 193–94; and guilt or innocence,
> 163, 180; and postconviction claims of
> innocence, 261; and snitches, 167–68

Ratner, Richard, 272

Reed, B. Thomas: and Farris, 161, 162, 165, 166;
> on Ford, 29, 30, 161; and police notes on
> interrogations, 33

Reilly, Peter, 27, 68, 93, 103

Reyes, Matias, 211

Roberts, Larry, 272, 274

Robinson, William P., Jr., 30

Russell, Jeffrey: described, 223; and Tice's first
> trial, 223, 224, 225, 226, 227; and Tice's
> habeas petition, 260, 264, 269; and Tice's
> second trial, 240, 241–42, 243, 244, 246,
> 247, 248, 249, 250–51, 264

Salzman, Don, 258, 260, 263, 265, 271

Sawyer, Tom, 68

Scanlon, Robert, 95, 225, 227, 246

Scheck, Barry, 272

Schwertlech, John, 100, 102, 183

"Scrappy," 172, 173, 174

Sellers, Jerry, 224, 246

Shipley, Danny, 170; and asking Williams about
> crime, 45; and Ballard, 204, 205, 229; and
> clemency, 263; and communication
> problems with Williams, 18, 46; and Danser,
> 179; and death penalty, 42, 43, 44, 46, 47, 48,
> 49, 80, 185, 205; described, 42; and Dick's
> confession and arrest, 90; on Ford, 30; and
> investigation, 50–51; and pay, 49; and plea
> bargain, 47–49, 124, 169, 185, 204–5; realizes
> Williams is innocent, 204; and suppression
> motion, 47; and Tice's confession, 169; and
> Tice's second trial, 253; and Williams in
> prison, 231; and Williams's arraignment,
> 42–43; and Williams's DNA results, 55;
> and Williams's perceived guilt, 43, 50, 125,
> 169; and Wilson's confession, 124–25

Shuler, Betty, 192

Shuler, Bobby, 192

Simmons, Lyn: and Ballard's claims of sole
> responsibility, 210–11; and death penalty,
> 196–97, 211; described, 210; and plea
> bargain, 211, 229, 230, 231; and Tice's first
> trial, 225–26; and Wilson's trial, 216

Simon, David, 143

Sisk, Matt, 100

Sisk, Shannon, 100, 101, 117

Skadden, Arps, Slate, Meagher, & Flom, 258

snitches, 167–68, 233. *See also* Gurley, Timothy;
> Kelly, Garey

Spitz, Werner, 266, 271

Stanton, Jennifer: and Ballard, 191–92, 192–93;
> and Danser's alibi, 178, 179, 180; and
> Danser's arrest, 176; and Danser's nol-
> prossing, 212–13; and Danser's

Mug shot of Dominic "Donnie Shacks" Montemarano.

Mug shot of Frank Junior "Fingers" Abbandando.

MUGS

Thomas DiBella.

Mug shot of Alphonse "Little Ally
Boy" Persico.

1992. Federal mug shot of Dominick "Little Dom" Cataldo.

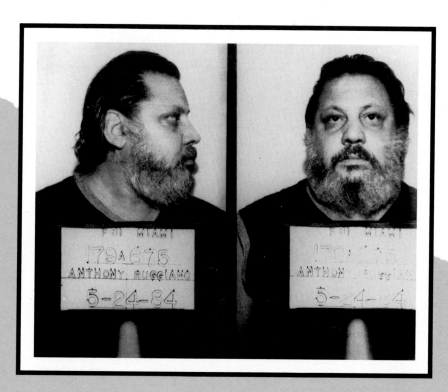

Mug shot of Andrew Ruggiano in 1984 after his capture from being a fugitive since October 1982 from Operation Home Run. Fat Andy was hiding with a motorcycle group to avoid being caught.

SURVEILLANCE

1982. Fat Andy outside Suite 100 talking with a friend.

March 7, 1981. Close-up of Frank Russo at the Diplomat
Hotel in Hollywood, Florida.

SURVEILLANCE

From left to right, undercover agent John "Marino" Bonino, Joe Blaze, Bobby DeSimone, Fat Andy with sunglasses and white shirt, and a friend.

July 1981. In the middle is Junior "Fingers" Abbandando and Bob DeSimone to the right, looking ambivalent about which car to drive.

SURVEILLANCE

July 1981. We are about to leave Suite 100 in the FBI's Cadillac, which was confiscated from a drug operation. From left to right, Joe Dogs, Jack Bonino and Joe Blaze.

1982. Myself and Joe Blaze entering Suite 100.

1982. From left to right, Gerald Alicino and a general contractor who worked on Suite 100.

T.A.

1982. Agro and I embracing. "I don't know if he's showing me affection or if he's feeling me to see if I'm wired." This is in Manhattan, outside of Lanza's restaurant. At this moment, I'm slightly apprehensive. A shot of scotch would probably relax me some.

1981. Agro and back of Joe "Piney" Armone.

Shakedown

South Florida in the mid-1970s reminded me of the Wild West. Everything was there for the taking. The state was growing like a weed, and northerners were pouring in. That meant restaurants and construction sites to be shaken down, money to be shylocked to new entrepreneurs, racetracks to be divvied up, drugs to be dealt, and lots of easy money to be stolen. Whoever had the most muscle took. Between my slugging and Tommy A.'s reputation, we grabbed with both hands.

Crime was just another business, and to get into any other line of work, we figured, was just plain stupid. We never gave a second thought to punching a clock or pension funds or safety nets. We wanted all the money now, and we wanted to spend it all now.

And, believe me, we literally had people begging us to take it from them. One night in 1975, for instance, Bunny and I were sitting in one of our favorite local places, Lord's Restaurant and Lounge in downtown West Palm, when Benny Lord, one of the owners, came over and asked to speak to me for a moment. "I have something of great importance to ask you," he whispered.

"Yeah, Benny, sure. What is it?"

"I'm having a problem with Stanley Gerstenfeld," the restaurateur began. "He comes in here, pushes everyone around, and won't pay his bills. I'd like to talk to you about helping me."

I knew Stanley. He was a local bookmaker and hustler. He was

also a doper and a lush. He'd pop Quaaludes all day long and chase them with vodka. Frankly, I don't know how he did it. If his customers won big, they rarely got paid. If they lost, he'd hound them to death. I'd bet the Preakness once with Stanley, won a big price, and he'd had to run to Freddie Campo to get the money to pay me. So I had no personal beef with him despite his reputation.

"Listen, Benny," I said, "I don't discuss business when I'm out with my wife. Tomorrow I have a big day, so I can't see you then. The problem can keep. Don't misunderstand me now. I'm not passing on it. It's just that the wife and I are celebrating our anniversary, and I really don't have time to take care of you tonight."

"Of course, Joe, I understand. But please don't forget me. Come and talk to me," Lord said as he motioned a waitress for drinks on the house.

"Happy anniversary, Bunny, and you, too, Joe. Many happy returns."

Bunny was crimson as the guy walked away. Our anniversary wasn't for another six months. What, she wanted to know, was that all about?

"I just didn't want to talk to that Jew bastard," I said. "What do I care if Stanley's shaking him down? I'm not a priest for all these people. I'm tired of doing favors for all these fucks and getting nothing in return. Let him go to the cops."

"You're right, honey," Bunny said. "I hope you don't get involved, because I like coming here. This is my favorite spot."

But it wouldn't go away. A few months later I got a call from Benny Lord. "Joe, can you stop over this afternoon? I'd like to talk to you." I told him I'd meet him at his joint at four that afternoon.

"Joe, this Stanley is driving me up a wall," he began. "He won't pay for anything he orders, and everyone here is afraid of him. All the help is threatening to quit because not only is he robbing us, he and his gang never even leave a tip. He sends rounds of drinks to every other customer in the place, and I don't know what to do. Can you help me?"

"Benny, why don't you go to the police?" I couldn't believe I was telling somebody to run to the law. "If I help you, it's like I become your protector. Otherwise it's really none of my business what

Stanley does here. Why should I stick my nose in his business? I wouldn't like it if someone did that to me. Besides, what could I gain if I did it for you? I can't do it as a favor, because I don't do those kinds of favors."

"I threatened to go to the police," Benny Lord said. "Stanley said he'd kill me, and my brothers. It was my decision, with my brothers, to ask your help. And we don't expect you to do this for nothing. We'd certainly want to give you something for your efforts and trouble."

I asked Benny exactly how much he thought my "efforts and trouble" were worth. And I reminded him that I'd have to take any offer to "my people." That made Benny jump. He was always nervous around me, he admitted it himself. Now this protection thing was driving him out of his skin."

"Relax Benny, I'm not here to shake you down. You called me, remember," I reminded him. "Now make your offer. And while you toss it around in your head, remember we are not going to do this for a ham sandwich."

"How about this, Joe?" he proposed. "For the six-month in-season I give you eight hundred a month. Off-season, four hundred a month. And anytime you or anyone in your, er, company comes in, I pick up the tab. If I'm not here, you just sign it. I don't even want to mention about gratuities, as I know you're a man of integrity. Every time you come in the entire staff fights to wait on your table."

"Benny, are you sure you're not patronizing me?" I smiled. "I'll let you know about this by the weekend. In the meantime, play it cool with Stanley." I left.

I drove south to Hallandale that night and told Tommy A. and the crew about the offer. Tommy was down making one of his periodic visits to check up on his territory. He said he had to check Stanley out in New York, because Stanley had been shooting his mouth off about being connected with Henry "Chubby" Buono, who was a made guy with the Genovese Family. It was a Mafia no-no to move in on another *Famiglia*'s joint.

After we got through playing cards we headed over to the Diplomat to catch the show in the Tack Room. There was a good-looking

broad singing there, and Tommy was trying to get her in the sack. He sent her two dozen roses, which sat on top of her piano.

"Do you like the roses, sweetheart?" Tommy asked her during a break. "I sent them from my heart, darling."

"Tommy, I'll sing all night just for you," she said on the way back to the stage.

"I hope she plays the flute for me later. Those fuckin' roses cost ninety-five bucks, and then I had to give the cutie-pie salesgirl a ten-dollar tip for making them special. A buck, five, *minchia*, what is that? Zinc, Joey? She better not have a toothache tonight." Tommy was rocking back and forth in his chair. That thin line of sweat had appeared on his forehead.

Then I remembered something. "Tommy, I forgot to tell you. This guy Stanley is close to Freddie Campo."

Freddie had never collected his end of the Gulfstream fixes from Tommy. As Tommy had suspected, Freddie, the babe-in-the woods bookmaker, unaffiliated with any *Famiglia*, had no pull in New York. And when Freddie had failed when Tommy had practically dared him to come get his money, Tommy, like a shark, lost all respect for Freddie. Not that he had that much to begin with.

"Joey, I don't give a fuck about Freddie," T.A. exploded. "He's shit. In fact, let me go check if I can track down that Chubby Buono now."

When Tommy went to the phone I was left drinking with his crew, Louie Esposito, Buzzy, and the kowtowing Bobby DeSimone.

"Joey, Joey," DeSimone said in his faggy voice. "If we have to, we'll come up to West Palm this weekend and straighten this guy Stanley out. We'll sit him down and let Tommy talk to him. Tommy always makes everybody understand. This restaurant thing looks like a nice earn for us. And if we never have to pay for anything, Christ, I'll drive up with Betty once a week to have dinner."

DeSimone was the freeloader in the crew. He always wore pants with no pockets. A real cheap bastard, he sent his wife Betty out to work while he stayed home. A real two-time loser who talked way too much. As we were sitting there I couldn't help but wonder just what it was that made Tommy Agro feel so "obligated" to Bobby DeSimone.

The music had stopped, and the torch singer headed straight for our table. "Where's Tommy?" she asked. "Did he leave? I wanted to kiss him for the roses."

"No, honey, he didn't leave," I said. "He said he liked you so much that he wanted to get something else for you. He went to the phone to order it, I think. I know he wants to see you after the show." It was a weekday, so there was only one show.

"In fact, here he comes now. Pretend like I didn't tell you anything about the gift. Okay, honey? Please?"

"Okay, Joey, I won't say a word," she said.

"Hi, darling," Tommy said to the broad. "Is Joey behaving or should I break his legs?"

"Oh, no, Tommy, we're just talking. And Joey told me how much you like me. I have some things to do. Can you wait another hour or so for me?"

After Tommy told her he'd wait all night, she left and he turned to me. "*Minchia*, Joey, what did you tell her? She looks like she wants to rape me. But wait, before I forget, let me tell you what Chubby says. I mentioned that guy Stanley's name—I couldn't even remember his last name—but Chubby knew it. And when I told him that Stanley's been bragging that he's close to him, Chubby laughed like hell.

"Chubby says Stanley's a broken suitcase, a beat, and to do anything we want to him. But listen, tell that other Jew, Lord, we want to make it twelve hundred in-season and six hundred off-season, and we still never pay for nothing when we walk in. *Capisci?* Now tell me what you told my baby doll at the piano."

"I told her that you went to buy her a flower so rare that you had to order it over the phone," I said.

"Where the fuck am I going to get a rare flower at this time of night?" T.A. screamed. "You put me in the shitpot, Joey. Now I'll never get her over to my apartment."

"Nah, listen to me Tommy, here's what you do," I said, trying not to bust a gut. "Tell her the flower's at your apartment, and if she wants to know what it is, whisper 'cunnilingus' in her ear."

"Cunna what? What, Joey? What?"

"Cunnilingus, Tommy. Let me write it down for you in case

you forget the word. Now listen to me. Don't blast it out and let everybody hear it, like you're showing off. It's a personal love flower, and she won't appreciate it if you shout it out for everyone to hear.

"So, if she wants to know what you ordered for her, whisper it in her ear, and then kiss her ear. Tell her you've thought of nothing but that since you met her. *Capisci?*"

"Yeah, Joey? She'll like that? If I do it that way?"

"Hey, Tip, would I lie to you?"

I figured it was time to get out of there, and I suggested that the crew leave with me, "so Tommy and his broad can be alone." When I got home and told Bunny the story, she burst out in hysterics and advised me that Tommy was going to kill me.

"I can just see his face when he finds out she wants the blowjob he promised her," I said to Bunny. "Fuck him, I'm not going near him until next week. He's going to need some time to cool down."

I didn't hear from Tommy the following day, and I sure didn't call him. It was Friday, so I took Bunny out to dinner in Palm Beach, and we then went to Lord's for some drinking and dancing. The place was busy, but we got a table with no problem. I had the waitress summon Benny Lord and told Bunny to hit the ladies' room for five minutes.

"That problem you have, Benny? I'll take care of it," I said. "But . . ." and then I gave him Tommy's figures. To make them easier to swallow, I mentioned to him that this meant he was not only protected from Stanley Gerstenfeld but from anyone else who might try to strong-arm him.

"I'll bring the crew around tomorrow or Sunday," I finished. "We'll sit Stanley down, and we'll explain to him about the birds and the bees."

He took the offer on the spot, peeling twelve hundred-dollar bills off a roll and shoving them into my fist. Then I noticed him calling our waitress aside. In a moment she came over and announced, "Mr. Lord says that you're not to pay for anything, Joe. He would like you to sign the check, though, for his own records."

"Fine, honey," I answered. "And just tell Mr. Lord to give me a duplicate copy saying with his compliments."

I didn't trust that Jew. Down the line he could say that I was shaking him down.

Bunny and I were dancing when Stanley came in. He had a slugger with him, a local karate instructor. I'd once used this guy to beat up a client late with his juice payment. Paid him well, too.

The place was packed and everyone was having a good time when suddenly I heard Stanley's voice above the din, yelling something at the bartender about his drink. Then Stanley leaned over and smacked the guy in the mouth. The bartender looked to Lord. Lord looked to me. I couldn't let Stanley get away with this, not in front of all these people. I left the dance floor and walked to the bar.

"Stanley!"

He ignored me.

"Yo! Stanley! Stop hollering like you own the fuckin' joint."

He turned, put his nose up against mine, and shoved me backward. "Who the fuck do you think you are, Joe Dogs?" he asked. "I do own this fuckin' joint."

The place was so quiet now you could hear a pin drop. I had to take a stand. There would be no waiting for T.A. and the crew.

I may have had Stanley by a couple of inches, but he had me by at least twenty pounds. I could feel the entire room staring at the back of my head. I walked up to Stanley and grabbed him by his hair. I smacked his head back and forth, like a broad's, opening a cut in his mouth. Then I gave him the knee in the balls, and when he doubled over I straightened him back out with a left-handed uppercut. I grabbed him by the shirt and dragged him into Benny's office.

As we entered, I noticed the karate instructor trailing behind. "You want to get involved with this?" I asked him. "Then you just come right on in with your friend."

"Fuck, no, Joe, are you crazy?" He smiled. "I don't want my ass washin' up in the 'Glades."

From Benny Lord's office I dialed T.A.'s apartment. Luckily I caught him at home.

"Tip, you know that thing about Stanley? I had to take care of it tonight. It couldn't wait. He got out of hand and I had to smack him around. I wanted you to tell him personally to stay the fuck out of our fucking joint."

I handed the receiver to Stanley.

"Hello, Tom," Stanley said ruefully. Then he listened for three or four minutes. "Okay, Tommy, I promise. I'll never set foot in here again. And, yes, I'll tell Freddie what you said."

"He wants to talk to you," Stanley said, handing me the receiver and starting to leave. I grabbed his arm and motioned for him to wait.

"Yeah, Tom, what's up?" I asked.

"Joey, be careful. And call me tonight when you get home. But don't make it too late." He hung up.

"Stanley," I said, "I'm sorry this had to happen this way. Tommy was going to talk to you tomorrow night, but you forced my hand. Now, be a good boy and stay away from here, because if you don't . . . well, I don't have to tell you."

"Yeah, okay, Joe." We shook hands and left.

Back at the bar I was the hero. Every waitress in the place came up and kissed me when I told Benny Lord that Stanley would never be within a half-mile of his place again.

"See?" I asked Bunny. "See what a nice guy I am?"

She looked at me and made a gesture like she was going to puke.

"Yeah, Tom, I'm home. Stanley left quietly after you talked to him. What did you tell him?" It was later that night.

"I told him I was going to give him some cunnilingus, you dopey fuck," T.A. said. "When I whispered that in her ear, she started to laugh like hell. She says to me, 'Tommy, who told you to say that? Do you know what it means?' So I thought I was going to be a smart guy and impress her, so I told her it's a rare flower.

"She laughed even harder. That's when I knew that fuckin' Joey had got me again. But when she told me what it was, I had to laugh myself. We had a good time, you punchy fuck, but I'll never trust you again."

For a minute I laughed too hard to speak. Finally I said, "I'm glad you had a nice time, Tommy. She seemed like a nice person. And very promiscuous-looking."

"And what does that one mean?" he asked. "Go ahead and tell me another fuckin' lie."

"No, Tom, honest. It means very pretty. You can tell her when you see her that she looks very promiscuous."

In the background Bunny yelled, "Don't believe him, Tommy." So I handed my stool pigeon the phone, and Bunny told Tommy what the word meant. "And if you tell her that, it's like telling her that she looks like a whore." Bunny handed the phone back.

"I was only kidding, Tom. Don't be mad."

"I'm not mad, Joey. She does look like a whore. Maybe I'll tell her that tonight. What's that word—permis-what?"

"Forget it," I said. "Just have some fun with her. Because you'll be tired of her by the end of next week."

"Yeah, you're right, Joe. All those broads fall in love with us because we throw our money away on them. But, hey, Joey, it's a nice life, eh? Now go out and make a score, will you. I have to go in soon."

"Yeah? For how long?"

"For a year. Though I'll probably only do ten months. I want you to run things down here for me while I'm gone."

"But what about Bobby?" I asked. "I thought he was going to do it. I know he expects you to ask him."

"Are you crazy, Joey? I told you I only keep him around as a go-fer. I feel sorry for him, because—Oh, I'll tell you in person sometime."

"Okay, Tip. I'm going to stay home for a couple of days. Call me if you need something." I hung up.

Bunny was glad to hear that. "Wow," she said. "I have you all to myself for the weekend!"

The Cocaine Cowboys

In June of '76 Tommy went in again. He got ten months in the state pen for that extortion bit he'd been running from for years. He left me in charge of his Florida operations. I'd come a long way in four years.

Benny Lord paid his rent. Twelve hundred a month like clockwork. We started collecting in February of 1976 and dropped him down to $600 in May. He sold the place that summer, while Tommy was in prison. With T.A. in the can, I sent his share, as well as whatever else he had coming, to his mother.

Stanley Gerstenfeld never once set foot in Lord's Restaurant and Lounge. In fact, he got married. He married a pretty little redhead, and I went to the reception. I gave the bride a sympathy card with cash in it. It got a laugh from everybody but her. I never did find out the "message" Tommy gave Stanley to send to Freddie. I didn't care to find out, either.

Toward the end of July—just as T.A. was settling into jail time —Little Dom called from New York with big personal news, as well as a piece of work. Florida was filling up with drugs, and this was typical of the kind of schemes Dom always came up with. All he needed was a partner on site with muscle and balls. I was se-

cretly proud that at the age of forty-four, people knew I still had both.

"Joey, I have a friend down there with the Geno. A made guy, Joey. He's like me, only with a different you-know. *Capisci?*"

Congratulations were in order! Dominick, in comparing himself to his friend who was a made member of the Genovese Crime Family was telling me that they'd opened the books up north and Dom had gotten his button. He was a wiseguy.

When they open the books, they open them for every *Famiglia*. Dom was with the Colombos. But that didn't mean the Gambinos weren't swearing in new soldiers.

"Yo, way to go, Dominick. Did Tommy get his?" I asked.

"Joey, I haven't heard. Maybe when he gets out of the joint, eh? But that's not why I called you. I don't give a fuck about that thing. Tommy does, but not me. Anyway, my friend's name is Pete Conte. He's new down there, just moved in, from up here. Go to the Tender Trap in Hollywood, a steak joint. He'll be waiting for you there. See what he wants. And get twenty large up front, because Saratoga's opening up next week and I need some money."

"Hey, Dom, you just told me this guy's a wiseguy, and you want me to ask him for twenty large up front? What are you, wacky?"

"Joey, don't let him know that you know he's a wiseguy. You're not supposed to know. He's got a big problem, and we'll make a lot more than twenty large. Go see him and treat him like a doper. Then get back to me." He hung up.

The Tender Trap was a bleeding-meat joint on U.S. Highway 1. A lot of Colombos, Gambinos, and Genoveses hung out there. Vincente "the Chin" Gigante spent a great deal of time at the place. Gigante would one day succeed Anthony "Fat Tony" Salerno as boss of the Genovese *Famiglia* in New York.

Pete Conte was waiting for me in the lounge. His story was all sob. A local cocaine dealer named Bobbie Kelly had ripped off Pete for $300,000, the down payment on a 200-kilo load of powder. "For six months all I've been getting from him is a hand job," Pete said. He wanted me to either retrieve the money or collect the dope.

"Okay, I want a hundred large as a finder's fee," I said. Pete

stiffened. "And if I get you your dope, I want five keys, too. I want thirty large up front right now. And I'll start tomorrow."

Pete haggled. But he gave me $30,000 that night.

"Bingo jackpot!" I was on the pay phone talking to Dominick, who was ecstatic over the deal. I told him to send his boys down, because there might be some "hard work" involved.

"I'll get you three or four guys," Dominick said. "You just guide them, and they'll take care of everything. But see if the deal can be done without you-know."

He was trying to tell me that he'd prefer if this went down without anyone being killed.

"Hey, Dom, I'll do the best I can. What do you want me to do with this money?"

"Joey, hold it for a week, and then maybe you and Bunny would like to go to Saratoga for a week with me and my wife. I'll whack the money up with you. Did you get that guy Pete's phone number?"

"Yeah, and he wants this done right away," I said. "You better send those guys down."

"Don't worry, Joey," Dominick said. "I'll get you Billy Ray. And Ralphie. You've worked with both of them. And I'll find somebody else. Since I got made I got a million fuckin' worshippers hanging around. I'll call you later." He hung up.

Since Tommy'd gone inside, I was home more. That made Bunny happy. "It seems like old times," she said to me that night. "I hope they keep Tommy in prison forever."

Just Kill Peter, Then Rob Paul

The doper Bobbie Kelly's Hollywood home was set off the street, secluded behind a thick stand of palms, and surrounded by a ten-foot wrought-iron fence. A telephone was attached to the empty guardhouse at the front gate. Billy Ray noticed video cameras nestled into crooks of the trees and atop the fence.

"*Marrone*, this guy is sitting pretty good here." He whistled. Billy Ray and Ralphie had flown in with two other lobs from Dom's crew. I parked the car about a block away from Kelly's front gate. My plan was to just go up and knock on the door. I was going to pretend I was a lawyer. I wanted to get a look at the inside. "Wait here," I told Billy. "Don't try and come in."

"What do you want," a male voice said into the phone receiver. It wasn't really a question, more like a warning.

"I'm a friend, a lawyer for Pete Conte," I said. "I'm alone, and I'd like to discuss a matter with a Mr. Bobbie Kelly." I tried to sound professional.

"Where's your car?" the voice asked.

"I parked it down the street. Do you want me to get it?"

The gate clicked open. I hiked the length of one football field along a hedged-in driveway. It looked like a fisherman's house, with all kinds of nets and fishing poles, buckets, lures—that nautical shit. On the canal side, where I approached, there was a screened-in porch. Three broads in bikinis squatted over a huge oval mirror striped with lines of coke. Behind them, two guys dressed in blue jeans looking stoned.

"I'm looking for Bobbie Kelly," I said through the screen. One of the girls yelled for Bobbie, saying there was a salesman at the door. A third guy then entered the porch carrying a shotgun. When he reached the screen door the other two guys stepped to either side of me. They pulled pistols. The guy with the shotgun opened the door, grabbed my arm, and yanked me inside. *Minchia,* I'm thinking, what the fuck did I walk into here?

"I'm Bobbie Kelly," the thin guy with the scatter gun said. "What can I do for you?" He motioned for the girls to leave. One tried to grab the mirror and take it with her, but Kelly barked, "Leave it. You've had enough for now. Go down by the pool and swim it off."

"Well, Bobbie, I'm here on behalf of Mr. Conte," I brazened out, handing him a card with my "Joseph Russo" identity. "He informs me that you have something of his that he paid for. And he asked me to find out when you either plan to deliver it or return his money."

"Well, Mr. Attorney Russo," he said to me, extending the mirror, "you don't look like no Mafia tough guy to me. Would you like a hit?"

I declined. I don't do that stuff. Especially with rebel junkie motherfuckers pointing shotguns at me. All three of them took a snort. Their eyes looked like glass.

"I happen to know that our friend Pete is in the Mafia," Kelly said. He pronounced it Mayfia. "He's a member of the Genoveesy mob. I know all this because one of his men gave him up. His pal George told me everything. I got George stoned and he even told me that Pete could get killed if his bosses knew he was fucking around with this powder. So he's not going to get it. Or his money."

It occurred to me that the shit they were snorting acted like some kind of truth serum.

"So you tell Pete that he's fucked," Kelly continued. "And if he makes too much noise, I'll get George to drop a dime on him."

This fucking moron, I couldn't believe my ears. But to God's ears from this guy's mouth—he said it.

"Oh, so you really didn't get the stuff," I said. "You just bull-shitted him. I told Pete that I thought it was a lot of baloney. I told Pete that no one as young as you could have a connection in the kitchen in Bogota. I told him. I told him."

I sounded like Gomer Pyle. But I was trying to draw the doper out. They were passing around a quart of Jack Daniel's, and so fucking stoned that if I could have grabbed one of the guns I could have whacked all three of them. But there were also the girls to think about.

"Let me show you something, Attorney Russo," this junkie Kelly said. "And I want you to tell Pete that you saw it."

He shoved me into the house. It was freezing from the air conditioning. In a room off the living room he pointed to stacks and stacks of what I took to be kilos wrapped in thick brown water-proof paper. Kelly ripped one open and showed me the coke.

"Now you can go tell Pete that this young kid does know what he's doing and is no bullshitter. And I want you to give him something for me."

"Yeah, sure," I answered, bracing myself for what I knew was coming.

"This!" he said as he whacked the barrel of the shotgun into my mouth.

I fell back on my ass, my mouth and nose a fountain of blood.

"Now get the fuck out of here and don't come back. Next time I'll kill you." All three of them were laughing as I stumbled to my feet.

Billy wanted to charge back in, guns blazing, when he saw my face. "It's not as bad as it looks," I told him. "I don't think my nose is broken. They were so fuckin' stoned, they didn't know what they were doing. Take me home. I want to change and wash this fucking blood off before I call Dominick."

When we walked into the house, Bunny started to cry. "What happened?"

"Billy hit me," I said.

"Don't believe him, Bunny," Billy jumped in. "He got fresh with a girl, and she did this to him."

"That, I believe." She laughed, relieved that we could joke about it.

Two days later, around 4 A.M., our van pulled up to Bobbie Kelly's guardhouse. It was pitch black outside, and very peaceful.

Billy Ray was the lock expert. He had the wrought-iron gate opened in about a minute. I crept up to the screened porch. Soft music was playing. Inside, Kelly, his two friends, and the three girls were all passed out. All six were naked. Their mirror was piled with cocaine. There must have been at least a pound.

Ralphie stared at the broads' pussies while I glanced around. I put my knife through the screen and ripped it quietly. The sleepers didn't move a muscle. I whispered to Ralphie to go get the van. "We're going to load the stuff quickly and then get out of here."

"Gee, Joe, send one of the other guys," he answered. "I like this here girl."

I didn't believe this! Where did Dominick get this sick bastard?

Billy Ray saw that I was annoyed, winked at me, and volunteered to go fetch the van.

The people lying on that porch were so stoned and out of reality that they didn't bat an eye as we loaded 198 kilos of cocaine into our van. We were very quiet and professional. Dominick had sent good men. Ralphie excluded.

I told the guys to gag and handcuff Bobbie Kelly and dump him in the back of the van. I had some plans for him. He never even woke up.

The thing I think I most admired about wiseguys like Tommy A. and Little Dom was that they would never rob Peter to pay Paul when they could just kill Peter, then rob Paul. We were nothing if

not thorough when it came to filling our pockets. That's why Dominick Cataldo had a Plan B for the rip-off artist Bobbie Kelly.

We'd stashed Kelly in Pete Conte's house in Homestead, south of Miami. Shackled to a cot, fed nothing but bread and water, it took him about a week to lose the shakes and sober up. That's when Little Dom unexpectedly flew in.

Pete met us in the driveway and looked a little shocked to see Dominick Cataldo sitting in my passenger seat. "Dominick, I didn't know you were coming. Joe didn't mention it. Is there anything wrong?"

"Nah, nothing wrong, Pete," Dom said. "Joe must have forgot to mention it. You didn't let that guy Kelly get away, did you?"

Pete hadn't, although he said that Kelly had been a major pain in the ass, screaming like an animal all week while going through withdrawal.

"That's good," I said. "What time is George showing up?"

"He'll be here in a couple of hours," Pete answered. "Do you guys want to tell me what's going on with my man George?"

Neither Dom nor I answered him. Instead, we told Pete to play along with a routine we had planned, and I brought Dominick into the house and introduced him to Bobbie Kelly. When Kelly saw me he started to tremble. That was a good sign. It meant he could remember things. I grabbed him by the hair and smacked him across the mouth with a thirty-eight pistol. I heard the cracking of his front teeth. He writhed in pain.

I lifted his head by the hair and saw a couple of teeth littering the floor. Blood was spurting from the gap in his mouth. I hit him again with the gun butt, on the forehead, just above the eye. Blood was seeping out from there now also.

"Okay," Dom said. "Let me finish him off. I'm going to chop his hands off first. Then his head." Dom was gripping a meat cleaver.

I grabbed Dominick and yelled, "No, Dom, wait. Don't kill the guy. He don't deserve to die."

Pete chimed in. "Yeah, go ahead, kill him. Let Dom go, Joe. I got no use for this scum. He tried to beat me. Let him die."

It was my turn again. "Listen, Pete, hold on. If Bobbie here tells you a piece of information that your guy George told him, will you

let him live? Because Bobbie knows you're a made guy. He told me so."

Pete looked stunned. Then he put two and two together, and it added up to George. Dom and I grinned. Then Dom grabbed the thirty-eight out of my hand and put it flush against Bobbie's forehead. I dove to push the gun away and as I did, Dom pulled the trigger and a loud "bang" echoed off the walls. I should have been an actor.

Dom and I wrestled over the pistol for a while as Bobbie begged for his life. Finally Dom turned to Kelly and said, "I want a ton of grass, you bastard. And I want a promise from you to deliver, or else I'll kill you right now, you cocksucker. And if you promise me now and then don't come through, I'll find you and kill you."

Bobbie naturally agreed to anything. I winked at the guys, who left the room as I uncuffed his ankle from the shackle.

"Bobbie, listen to me," I said. "I'm sorry I banged you on the head, but you had it coming. The only way I can save you from getting killed is for you to tell Pete about George. And you better make good on that promise to that other guy. He's dangerous."

Kelly was sobbing, crying with fright. "Are you sure they won't kill me? You're really not lying?"

"Bobbie, if you don't do what I just told you to do, I'll kill you myself."

Dominick and Pete returned, and Kelly told Pete everything about George. Pete listened without interrupting. When Bobbie was through singing, Pete turned to Dom and me. "What do we do with this guy now?"

Dominick assumed the Godfather role. "Pete, you pay Bobbie the balance of what you owe him, minus what this episode cost you in expenses. Bobbie is now our property. He belongs to me. As far as George goes, he's your business. I just did you a favor here. You clean your own house. *Capisci?*"

As Dom was speaking a car pulled up. George was a little early. Pete made arrangements to pay us our balance due that evening. We'd all meet up at the Tender Trap. Then George walked in, and his eyes nearly popped out of his head when he spotted Bobbie Kelly.

Pete bade us goodbye and put his arm around George. As we walked out I heard him speaking in Italian to George. "Come in, my *compare,* my right-hand man. Sit down. Have a cup of coffee. We have business to discuss."

We weren't out of the driveway before we heard four or five gunshots coming from the house. Bobbie put his head in his hands and started to cry. Dominick patted him on the shoulder. "Don't worry, Bobbie. You're with us now. No one can fuck with you. Not even the Pope."

Later, over cocktails—Kelly couldn't eat because his face was too fucked up—the doper saw the light. "You guys will have to give me a little time to get the grass. My last load got popped by the Coast Guard. You can check it out. But I got about ten kilos of coke left in secret storage at the house. I'm going to give you a key to show my appreciation for not killing me."

Dom and I nodded like he was our new best friend.

Tombstone Territory

Out of the seventy large we received from Pete Conte, Dom handed me $45,000. And he took the five-kilo payment back north to sell in New York. I kept Kelly's peace offering of a kilogram. I kept a couple of ounces, passing it around to the broads. I didn't cut it or anything, and they loved me for it. The rest of the stuff I ounced out for sale. The powder was so good it sold for $2,000 an ounce. I made $60,000 from the kilo. I bought Bunny some jewelry as a present. Naturally that made her suspicious. You just can't please these women.

But every once in a while you have to keep the wife happy. Wiseguys always felt that this was easier to do in groups. That way, the women could keep each other company while we tended to serious business, like playing the ponies. We spent our money until our wallets were empty, especially at the track.

So, flush from the Bobbie Kelly cocaine boost, Little Dom came up with a plan to combine business with pleasure. He called and invited Bunny and me to join him and his wife, Clair, for the Saratoga racing meet in August.

Dom told us to come into New York on Thursday and he'd pick us up at the airport, adding, "Make sure you make it Thursday,

Joey, because there's a horse running Friday and I'm told that it's going to win. *Capisci?*"

Dom and Clair met our flight, and we drove straight to Lake George, where we were all staying in a nice resort. Dominick's sure shot on Friday didn't even finish in the money, and Dom had bet him across the board. He dropped $15,000 and spent the rest of the day bitching about the jockey, threatening to chop off his legs.

We bet with both hands at the Lake George resort for five days. While we were there I met Allie LaMonte, Little Dom's capo in the Colombos. He had a hole in his throat and spoke with a little gargle out of a voice box. Every time one of the horses he bet lost he would rip the tickets in half, look up at the sky, and gargle out, "You Jew bastard." Allie was funny as hell.

On the drive back to the city we took the Taconic State Parkway. Near the Peekskill exit, while Bunny and Clair chatted in the back seat, Dominick nonchalantly pointed to the left and said softly to me, "Joe, there's Boot Hill.

"I think I got eight guys buried there," he added. "There's only one two-story job, though."

Clair must have overheard, because—looking around at the rolling hills and woodland—she asked what two-story buildings we were talking about.

"I was telling Joe that they're supposed to put up a housing project in this area, and they're going to be two stories high," Dom said. "Now shut the fuck up anyway, Clair. You're too nosy. Do you see us asking what you and Bunny are talking about? Pay attention to what Bunny is saying and don't nose in on our conversation."

"Don't talk to me like that, Dominick. I'm your wife, not one of the whores you bed down with. You never hear Joe talk to Bunny that way."

Dominick turned his head slightly to let Clair know he was serious. "Don't start, Clair. Remember your father and your mother. *Capisci?*"

I laughed to myself, knowing what he was threatening. But Bunny had no idea what Dom was saying.

"What has your mother and father got to do with this?" Bunny asked Clair innocently. I looked at Dom, and he was grinning.

"Oh, they got nothing to do with this," Clair explained. "It's just that every time my husband wants to stop arguing, or if I threaten to leave the bastard when he comes home with lipstick all over his shirt and shorts, he tells me he'll kill my mother and father. The lousy bastard."

I couldn't keep it in anymore. Even Bunny and Dom started to laugh.

"He wouldn't do anything like that, would he?" asked Bunny.

"You're fucking-A right he would," winced Clair. "You don't know my husband. That sweet baby-faced fuck. He's a killer, a murderer, and I know I'm going to pay for this."

"You just blew your allowance for the week, big mouth," Dom said to his wife.

"Oh, Dominick, honey, please. I was only kidding," Clair pleaded. "Right, Bunny? I was winking at you, wasn't I? Come on, Dom, you fuck, you know I need my allowance to play cards with the girls. Without it, they won't even let me in the game."

"Okay, if you keep quiet for the rest of the trip home I'll forget about it," Dom said. "But if you open your mouth one more time, it'll be two weeks instead of one without your allowance.

"How do you like the balls on her?" Dom added, turning to me. "She goes to a poker game and plays pot limit."

"Yeah, but I'm a good player," Clair said from the back seat. "I win a lot of times."

"Hey, Clair, what did I say? *Zitto!*"

"Oh, I'm only agreeing with you, my darling Dominick."

We all cracked up laughing, and I heard Clair whisper to Bunny, "I better shut the fuck up."

Bunny held my hand and kissed me the entire flight home. She was showing me how much she appreciated the good time we had had. I think I lost about $25,000 at the races. Dominick must have blown over $100,000. Easy come, easy go. Lake George was beautiful in the summer.

"I Wasn't Made with a Finger"

August '76 came and went, football season started, and I was getting wrecked. Not only were my own customers winning, but the four customers I was booking for Tommy A. were really winning big. This is how Tommy made me his Florida bookmaking partner:

"Joey, let these guys bet into you, and you keep the tabs. We'll split the winnings. But if they win, I'm out. I'm not your partner no more."

So it went, "belonging" to Tommy Agro.

So I got shafted. What's new? October. November. December. I took a major bath. I was tapped. And not only was I losing in football, I was also getting killed at the track. It was a godsend when Dominick called in January of 1977 and told me he'd finally gotten rid of that coke.

"I let it go for three," Dom said. "So fly in and pick up your end before I lose it in the gambling joints."

My end came to $150,000. I flew to New York that morning. Dom picked me up at LaGuardia and we went to one of the lounges and had a drink. Under the table he handed me a paper bag stuffed with the cash. I went to the men's room and filled my

money belt. I wore a jacket and an overcoat, so no one would notice. I'd made arrangements to fly back that night, so I invited Little Dom to dinner to kill four or five hours.

Walking toward his car, Dom said, "Joey, you have to do me a favor. Let's take a ride."

"Sure, Dom. What is it?"

"I have to go to the Taconic Parkway and dig a hole," he said. "I have this motherfucker in the car and I need a hand to put him in a hole. I'll do the digging. I just need a hand getting him out of the trunk. I can't just leave him in the streets, Joey. He was a made guy with the Lucchese Family."

I began backing away from his car. "Dom, you're kidding, right? You don't really have a body in the trunk, do you?"

"Hey, Joe, what the fuck's wrong with you?" he said. "Why would I tell you a story like that?"

Dominick opened the trunk of his car. There was a body all twisted up inside. The hole in the forehead had already formed a bloody scab. I felt sick. I had to get out of there.

"Joey, this guy's been in my trunk for three days now, and he's starting to stink. I need a hand. What do you say?"

He closed his trunk. I walked away. He followed.

"Dominick, I'm going to tell you like T.A. would say it: I wasn't made with a finger. What do you want to do, make another two-story job? Fuck you. Get someone else to help you. I don't want to know where your burial grounds are."

"Yeah, Joey, I guess I can't blame you," he said. "But that's not what I had in mind, honest. I'll get someone else to help me."

"Yeah, and get someone you don't like so you can leave them there, too."

We took a cab to Manhattan, had a nice dinner, a few drinks. Later that night I flew back home. On the plane I began thinking about what T.A. had told me about Dom: *If Dominick knows that you know something about him that could put him in the jackpot, he'll whack you in a second without any grief at all.*

T.A. Gets
His Button

In February of '77, seven months after we'd scared the living shit out of him, Bobbie Kelly called. He had the grass he'd promised Little Dom. He said it was pretty good stuff, and I nodded sagely. To tell you the truth, I wouldn't have known good pot from sawgrass. Dominick and I made arrangements to rent a U-haul under a phony ID. I hired two of my crew to drive it to New York and fly back down. Dominick said he'd settle with me later.

He scored $200,000. Not the greatest price in the world for a ton of pot. Dom owed his Colombo Family compatriot John "Johnny Irish" Matera a piece of his share for some work Irish had done for him. I, of course, had to cut in Tommy, who was getting out soon. I figured half of one hundred large would make him happy.

"Joey, when are you going to come and see me?" It was T.A.'s voice over the phone from New York.

"Hey, Tom! When did you get home? I didn't know you were out. You should have called." It was April 1977.

"Bobby knew I was out. He came to see me. How come you didn't come with him?"

That fucking DeSimone. It would be just like him to have a calendar in his kitchen, marking the days until Tommy was free. Of course he never would have called me to let me know.

"Tommy, why the fuck didn't Bobby call me?" I asked. "But listen. Forget that. Why don't you come down here for a little vacation, and I'll see you then. I have a little surprise for you."

"Fuhgedaboudit, Joey, I'm not coming there. What, are you crazy? You come here."

"All right. Look, Tom, call Dominick. He's got a present for you. Meet with him, then call me back tomorrow and we'll make plans to meet, okay?"

I figured he'd be happy with the $50,000 from the marijuana. I wondered what that skinny fuck Bobby DeSimone had given him. Probably nothing.

Dominick flew down the next day. I picked him up in Miami, and as we were driving to the Castaways Hotel I mentioned that I didn't think two hundred large was the best price going for a ton of pot. Dom explained that Bobbie Kelly had fucked us, sold us shit.

"I'd like to break his fuckin' head," Dominick said. "But seeing how we got it for nothing, forget it. Joe, you had to see Tommy's face when I handed him the fifty grand and told him it was from you. *Minchia*, I thought he was going to have a stroke. He was so fuckin' happy. He told me to tell you that he's flying in tomorrow night and not to tell anyone."

"Good, Dom, that's good," I said. "Did he get his button?"

"Yeah, Joey. He got made with the rest of us, only I didn't know it till now. You are now working for a wiseguy."

I told Dom I had a problem with a guy in Queens. Bobby Anthony, who with his partner Rabbit had done that drug deal with me and T.A. back in '74. He owed me $5,000. I was having a hard time tracking him down. Anthony also owed T.A. some money, but that wasn't my beef. I knew he hung out at a certain bar—even though he was, mysteriously, never there when I called—and I

wondered if Dom could maybe pay him a visit when he returned to New York.

"I know the kid." Dom surprised me. "His real name is Bobby Amelia. Or, was Bobby Amelia. You mean you don't know, Joey? Your friend Tommy had him whacked while he was in the can. Everybody knows it but you, I guess."

"That cocksucker Tommy, he don't tell me nothing," I said. It struck me that Tommy was just crazy enough to still be holding a grudge over the way Bobby Anthony had stood up to him on my front porch three years ago. I didn't mention that to Dom. "Too bad" was all I said. "I liked Bobby Anthony, despite the fact that he was a beat. But do me a favor, Dom. Don't tell Tommy that Bobby Anthony was holding five large of mine. Tommy'll try to bring him back to life for his cut."

Dom paid me my $50,000 and stayed the night. We had a nice time with a couple of hookers. He flew out the next morning as Tommy was flying in. T.A., fresh from the joint, had the run of the Diplomat Hotel. Everyone jumped at his slightest command. He was a wiseguy now. Tommy just wanted his respect, his recognition. That day, over poolside drinks, I thought I'd say something about Bobby Anthony.

"Joey"—he smiled—"would I do a thing like that? Just *zitto! Capisci?* And don't bring it up again. Now what happened with my customers with the football action?"

"Your people won forty-seven large for the season," I said. "I'm in the red. But I guess I'll have to eat that, right?"

"Now you're getting the right idea." Tommy smiled.

He said he was staying a week and he wanted to spend some time with me. He was, he said, very appreciative of the money Dominick had given him. "You did the right thing," he told me. Of course, I didn't mention the money Dom and I had scored off the cocaine while Tommy was in jail.

"Joey, did you hear?" Tommy asked. "I got straightened out."

"Oh yeah?" I said, pretending not to know what Dominick had told me.

"Yeah. They made me, Frankie the Hat—you know him,

right?—and Nicky and Lenny got it, too. You know, Fat Andy's guys."

Frankie the Hat was Frank DeStefano. Nicky Corrazo and Lenny DiMaria were in a crew headed by Andrew "Fat Andy" Ruggiano, based out of Miami. They were all notorious Gambino soldiers.

"Yeah, Joey," Tommy continued, "someday you'll get yours. Just keep doing like you're doing and I'll see that you get it. I mean it. You're my main guy down here. So you do right by me and the Family and I'll do the right thing for you."

"Yeah, sure, Tom. I appreciate it," I said, although I really didn't understand everything that went into "getting made." I did know, however, that getting your button was what every guy working for a Family hoped to achieve someday. And to tell the truth, I saw that it had changed Tommy a little. It seemed to calm him down. Anyway, that's what I thought at the time.

"Joey, you have to expand yourself more," Tommy said.

"Tom, how many more fucking things do you want me to do? I got shylocking going. I got shakedowns. Bookmaking. Drugs. What the fuck is there left? I mean, I'm only one guy. I mean, I got a crew I use, but they're really nothing more than just a bunch of drivers. They never bring anything in, and they don't have the brains or the balls to bring anything down."

Tommy laughed. "Yeah, I know what you mean. But I want to meet your crew someday. Maybe not this trip but next time."

"Yeah, sure, Tom. There's only one guy you'll like. That Don Ritz. He's got a good Italian restaurant on Singer Island."

"Ritz!" T.A. shouted. "What is he, Jewish? You got a fuckin' Jew in your crew? *Minchia!*"

"No, Tommy, Don's Italian. He just shortened his name. I don't even know what his real name is. But he's a good guy. I got mostly greaseballs in my crew. Couple of Irish working for me in bookmaking. But most of the rest are wops."

"Hey, Joey, stop using those words, greaseballs and wops." Tommy was offended. "We're not those things. We're Italians. If my *compare* heard you say that, he'd chop your fuckin' head off. We're Italians, all right? And everyone else is a fuckin' Jew."

Jew, schmoo. What did I know from nationalities. As long as

they earned, they could be Martians for all I cared. Yet most mob guys I knew were always so touchy about who was a true Italian and who wasn't.

Tommy stayed for a week. We spent a lot of time together. He was treating me real good, even though he was upset. He told me that as soon as he'd gotten out of the joint his *compare* had given him a hit to do. He had known the guy's family really well. On the drive to the airport he imparted one last word of advice.

"You see, Joey, in this thing of ours you have to do what you're told. If they know you can get close to someone who trusts you and there's no suspicion, then they choose you to do the job. I couldn't say no. It was an order from the top.

"Just keep your nose clean, Joey," he went on. "Do just like you're doing and you'll get far. Pay attention to what I'm saying, because you came up fast. And any time Jiggs or Little Dom or Johnny Irish or any other crew wants you to do a job, you let me know first. Understand, Joey?"

"Yeah, sure, Tip." I embraced him goodbye. I didn't realize until after he'd gone that it was almost five years to the day since I'd met him.

Gangsters in Love

The '77 football season made up for the last one. I did pretty well and Tommy was happy. But the big news that autumn was Jiggs dying at the racetrack. A heart attack took him as he sat in the grandstand. He was sixty-two. There was no wake or funeral. He'd requested that his body be cremated and the ashes tossed in New York City's East River. That's just what Sophie did.

Earlier in the season, my luck seemed to be turning. I had contracted a drywall job on Hutchinsons Island, three big condominiums. I got the job because they wanted to go non-union and I had connections through Chin Gigante, who was a Genovese capo at the time. He now runs the Family.

I made a deal with the builder: $35,000 per building—above and beyond my drywall fee—would prevent any and all wildcat strikes. There were five of us who split the bread: Chin, Jiggs Forlano, the union delegate, me, and—of course—Tommy Agro.

Once, the builder was a couple of days late with his payment. Three or four gunmen with rifles appeared at the construction site at night and shot the place up. No one was hurt, although they scared the hell out of the night watchman. The builder came run-

ning to me, and I assured him I'd look into the problem and that it
wouldn't happen again. He never missed another payment.

I had my kid brother running the job for me. He was a good guy,
would do anything for me. But I didn't want him to get involved in
my kind of life. I wanted him on the other road, the right road.

The drywall job on Hutchinsons Island was still going strong, so
when I got our next shakedown installment I gave Jiggs's share to
Tommy Farese, the Colombo doper who was part of Johnny Irish's
crew. After Jiggs died, Thomas DiBella, the acting boss of the Colombos, promoted Johnny Irish to capo. Rumor had it that Johnny
put $500,000 in drug money into DiBella's hands. Most of that
money came from Tommy Farese, who got his button from Johnny
Irish in return.

When Jiggs was alive Farese had had to sneak around with the
dope. Jiggs was against drugs personally, but he never enforced any
rules, because Carmine "the Snake" Persico, the former Colombo
head who had since gone to jail, was heavily into the dope trade.
But now that Jiggs was dead, Farese came out into the open and
began to move tens of tons of pot a month and God knows how
much blow.

It was also around this time, late 1977, that I met a young lady and
fell in love. Nena, at thirty-two, was fourteen years younger than
me, and my wife would eventually catch us together in Nena's
apartment about a year later. She must have been tailing me that
day, because she burst in through the door, saw me sitting there
with my pecker blowing in the wind, and that was that. Bunny was
crushed. I had really done it this time. Bunny turned and, with tears
in her eyes, left.

I chased after her. I begged and pleaded for a month. But it was
no use. She told me to get out, and I went to stay at Nena's for a
while.

Don't misunderstand me. Nena, a lovely blonde, was no slouch.
And I cared for her very much. But I just couldn't get Bunny out of
my mind. I'd hurt Bunny so bad. She was miserable, which only

increased my guilt. And now my luck changed terribly. It seemed like everything I touched turned to shit. It was as if I no longer had Bunny as my lucky charm.

I was called before the grand jury investigating racketeering. The "G"—which was what we always called any arm of the federal government—had found out about the Hutchinsons Island payoffs. I didn't know how much they knew, but I realized once they didn't offer me immunity to testify that I was a target. Bob Sailor, my lawyer, had me take the fifth for every question.

To make matters worse, the winter of 1977 was also the season I had a falling-out with the Florida Colombos. I was delivering a cut of a drug deal to Tommy Farese at the Bridge Restaurant in Fort Lauderdale when I ran into Tommy's *compare*, Johnny Irish, in the parking lot. He told me Thomas DiBella just happened to be in Florida checking out his enterprises, and he wanted me to come inside and meet him.

I was hesitant. I didn't want any problems. I got along good with these guys from the Colombo *Famiglia*, and all I wanted to do was stay friends. I knew Johnny didn't care for T.A. that much, and I just felt that he had something else on his mind.

"Come on, Joe, you have to meet him," Irish insisted. "I told him all about you. How you and me and Tommy are all such good pals."

I went into the restaurant to meet Thomas DiBella.

"Tom, this is Joe Dogs," Irish began the introductions. "He's with that fuckin' animal Tommy Agro, but Joe belongs here. He used to be with our people, a long time ago in New York. How he wound up with that fuckin' T.A., I don't know."

"How do you do, Mr. DiBella," I said.

"Tom," Irish continued, "I'm here. You're here. Jog Dogs is here. And T.A. is in New York. See what you can do. Joe Dogs belongs with us. This is one guy I'll straighten out right away."

He meant get me my button.

Things were getting dangerous. I looked from Johnny Irish to Thomas DiBella and said, "Hey, what's the difference as long as we're all friends. It doesn't make any difference what *Famiglia* you're with. We're all friends anyway."

I was trying to fluff it off. I didn't want, or need, any problems with the Gambinos. But the protocol had been violated. You don't cross the line like Johnny Irish had done. He was wrong.

DiBella said, "Keep your nose clean, Joe. I've heard a lot of nice things about you. Let me see what I can do."

That night I cheated on my girlfriend and took my wife out. I missed Bunny. She said she missed me, too, but she'd had too bad a time of it. She would never take me back.

After dropping off Bunny I called Tommy A. and told him what Irish had done. What a mistake! T.A. reached out—as only T.A. can reach out, loud—and left word that Joe Dogs was part of his crew, and no one goes near me without consulting him first.

Now I was on the Colombo Family's shit list. None of them would have anything to do with me. And that really cut my earning power.

Things in Florida were falling apart. A week after Jiggs died, the shylock Jack "Ruby" Stein was discovered mutilated in the trunk of a car. He'd been in Jiggs's crew. In Ruby's breast pocket police found a list of all the juice owed to him from different customers. It led to a lot of investigations and arrests.

Ruby had been safe while Jiggs was alive. That's how strong and well respected Jiggs had been. Now that he was dead, punks felt free to cut Ruby Stein's tongue out. A Lucchese Family soldier was finally picked up and convicted of the murder. He did twelve years. I missed Jiggs.

Tommy and Nena hated each other. In fact, in T.A.'s eyes I lost a little respect for living with Nena.

"Why don't you go home and forget that fucking cunt," Tommy would hound me.

Each time I would explain to him that I'd tried to go home a million times, but Bunny wanted no part of me anymore.

"What the fuck do you want me to do," I screamed at him once. "And don't call Nena a cunt. You don't hear me calling your girlfriends cunts. And you got some nerve, to boot. How come you and Marian are divorced? Practice what you preach, Tip."

He hung up on me.

Unfinished Business

Murdering our own was a fact of life. Nobody liked doing it, but it was the only way to maintain control. Nobody in the Mafia was really scared of anything else: not cops, not jail time, not even a beating. Everybody takes a beating. But, hell, there were some killings I just didn't understand.

On the last day of January 1978, I got a call from Stanley Gerstenfeld. He told me he had to see me. "Joey, you gotta do me a favor."

"Stanley," I said, "I'm not going to loan you a quarter. You're a beat."

"No, Joe, I don't want any money. I have to talk to you. When can I see you?" Stanley sounded very scared. I told him to come around to my house the following afternoon. He thanked me and hung up.

The next day Stanley was a no-show. I waited for him until early evening, finally telling Bunny to relay the message, should he call, that I was pissed off. I went down to Delray Beach to play cards.

The following morning Bunny shook me awake. Stanley was on the phone. I picked up the receiver and told that fucking suitcase how he had ruined my day.

"Joe, please," he said with urgency. "You're the only one who can help me. I have to talk to you. Can I come over now?"

"Sure, Stanley, come on over," I said. "Give me an hour to shower and get dressed. But listen, if you change your mind, call me and tell me. Don't leave me hanging here all day waiting for you."

I waited for two hours. Stanley finally called and said he didn't have to see me after all. "I'm going to the fights in Miami tomorrow," he said. "I'll see you Saturday at the track." He sounded a lot more relieved.

"Hey, Joe," he added before hanging up. "You want to come to the fights with us? I'm going with Robbie and another guy who hangs out with Freddie Campo."

I was throwing a party the next night for my sister's twenty-fifth anniversary, so I declined and hung up. That night I took Bunny to dinner at Papa Gallo's in Palm Beach. During dinner, Freddie Campo walked in, and we invited him to join us.

I mentioned Stanley's phone calls to Freddie. "He sounds like he has a problem," I said. "You know anything about it?"

Freddie gave me a stern look. "Joe, do me a favor and *fatti i fatti tuoi. Capisci?*" Mind my own business. So I didn't ask any more questions. Freddie was right, it was none of my business.

On Friday, February 3, I threw a party for my sister and her husband, Mario. We had about fifteen people over to the house. Everyone was gone by midnight. I helped Bunny clean up the mess and went to bed.

At about three in the morning the phone startled me awake.

"Yeah?" I said groggily.

"Joe, Stanley was shot to death tonight in a parking lot in Miami." Then there was a click.

I recognized the voice as Robbie's. So that's what Stanley wanted to see me about. He had an inkling. Yet they still conned him into going to Miami. Freddie's comment about minding my own business made sense now. Was I ever glad I threw my sister that party, because everyone in town knew I'd smacked Stanley around in Lord's. Poor Stanley, I thought, and went back to sleep.

"He Was Even Ratting On You"

It was two weeks to the day since Stanley Gerstenfeld got whacked in the Miami parking lot, an unusually cold February morning in '78. Bunny shook me awake. "Joe, there's a guy at the door says he has to see you. Looks like a cop."

Cops—the FBI, state dicks, IRS accountants, Alcohol, Tobacco, and Firearm guys, the DEA, even local cherry flashers; they were all plain cops to us—were no more than a nuisance, like taxes (which I never paid anyway), or locusts. They knew what I was up to, most of the stuff anyway. I knew they knew. The trick was to keep them from proving it.

"Tell him you made a mistake," I said. "Tell him you thought I was sleeping, but I'm really not home."

"But, Joe, I already told him you were here. He's going to know I'm lying."

"Tell him! I don't give a fuck what he thinks or knows. Get rid of him. And don't take any papers from him. Tell him to call Bob Sailor."

Sailor was my lawyer. I hopped from bed, dialed his number, and cracked the bedroom door to eavesdrop on Bunny and the cop. Bunny was great. She said she'd made a big mistake, then slammed the front door in the cop's face. He'd tried to hand her a subpoena.

My lawyer accepted the subpoena. We both showed up at the state attorney's office about a week later. Freddie Campo had disappeared. Word was he was visiting a sick aunt in Connecticut. She must have lingered for a while, because I didn't see him back in Florida for several months.

A deputy state attorney by the name of Jack Scarola grilled me. Some of his questions I answered. Some I didn't. I volunteered the information about Stanley's jumpy phone calls. I didn't mention Freddie, although Scarola did. I told Scarola about the middle-of-the-night confirmation of Stanley's death. I said I hadn't recognized the voice on the phone.

Finally I added that I had at least twenty witnesses who would swear I was home all evening the night of Stanley's demise. I was cleared and I left. Stanley Gerstenfeld's murder is still open on the Florida books these fifteen years later.

When Freddie pulled back into town we met at his place. I gave him a play-by-play of the state attorney's questioning.

"Your name came up quite a few times," I said. "Direct from this guy Scarola's mouth. He asked me how I knew you, how long I'd known you. The usual stuff. Wanted to know what you did for a living. Finally I told him that if he wanted to ask questions about me, I'd be glad to cooperate. But if he wanted to know about Fred Campo, then maybe he should be asking Mr. Fred Campo, or this fucking meeting is over."

Freddie was annoyed. "Those cocksuckers ain't got nothing better to do but start trouble."

"But, hey, Freddie, tell me why Stanley's gone," I said. "I mean, he was a pain in the ass, he was a beat artist, but I never thought he did anything bad enough to get killed."

"You don't know the whole story, Joey. He was a fucking rat. My connection in the sheriff's office told me who he was ratting to and what he was saying. Joe"—Freddie paused a beat—"he was even ratting on you."

"On me!" I yelled. "He didn't know a fucking thing about me. If he said anything about me it was either a guess or a fucking outright lie. But, shit, those fucking cops believe anything."

I was pissed. Freddie changed the subject.

The Feds Come Calling

"Come on, Nena, hurry up. We have to drive all the way to the Diplomat to meet Tommy."

"Joe, if it wasn't Diana Ross performing, I wouldn't even go. You know how much I hate that big Mafia friend of yours."

It was New Year's Eve of 1980. Nena and I had been living together in a beautiful apartment in North Palm Beach. I'd decorated it with all new furniture and plush deep-pile rugs. Of course, I'd got all the furnishings on the arm. At least some people still respected me. But I wasn't earning any money. My luck had turned to shit, and my standing in T.A.'s crew had fallen. I was still his top dog, but that was almost by default.

At least I was still earning something—as opposed to the rest of those mopes like Skinny Bobby DeSimone. It had taken me nearly a decade to become the Gambino Family's right hand in South Florida, and I wasn't ready to give up the title. So I'd had a bad run for a year or so. So what? So had Jimmy Carter. Soon I'd be taking my cue from a new president, Ronald Reagan. The 1980s were here, and it was morning in the mob.

Diana Ross was great. Tommy had shown up with two broads, both young and beautiful. Nena behaved herself until the clock

struck 1980. That's when Diana Ross came over to our table and kissed Tommy a Happy New Year.

"You let that nigger kiss you?" Nena asked. She was busting T.A.'s balls.

"Hey, Nena, *zitto!*" Tommy was pissed.

"What did he say, Joe?" she asked.

"He wants you to go over to him, he has something he wants to whisper in your ear." I laughed.

Tommy had quite a few drinks in him, and so did Nena. When she got up and approached him, he turned and hissed.

"Why don't you get your fat ass away from Joe. You have no class. His wife has more class in her pinky than you do in your whole body. Now, Joey, I want to be *solo*. Get her the fuck out of here and call me tomorrow."

We left with Nena bawling.

Nena had attended the American Airlines flight-attendant training school in Dallas. When she graduated, she was stationed in San Francisco. She was there when I had my heart attack, and she took a leave of absence to care for me. Although she was very good to me, we nonetheless had our problems. She wanted me to divorce Bunny and marry her. I couldn't see it. I had given up on Bunny. We were never getting back together. But I didn't want to marry Nena.

After I recovered from the heart attack, Nena got back with American Airlines, this time stationed in Chicago. Things seemed to work out. I missed her, all right, but while she was gone I just busied myself with other broads or my crew. On Sundays I had the entire crew over. I'd cook for them while we watched the football games. Then I'd have a girlfriend come in to clean up the mess.

In January of '80 the FBI went to my landlord and told him that he was renting to a member of the Mafia. My landlord asked me to leave. I rented a brand-new duplex up the street, and the FBI did the same thing. This landlord wasn't so easily intimidated.

Meanwhile, I was back to selling dope. Cocaine. I was hauling consignments by car to a buyer in Arizona. I'd leave on a Friday

night, because those lazy bastards in the FBI didn't work weekends. I guess they thought La Cosa Nostra didn't either.

On one trip, in mid-February, I'd brought a lob from my crew named Aldo DiCuffa with me, more for company than protection. We left Aldo's lovely lady, Valerie, to house-sit my apartment. When we returned, Valerie told us the FBI had been around asking questions.

"Like what?" I wanted to know.

"Oh, the cute one, I think he said his name is Larry, he wanted to know where you and Aldo went," she answered.

I had to wonder how they knew that Aldo had accompanied me. My phone, I figured, must be tapped. And if that was the case, then they'd overheard the recent beef I'd had with T.A., which had turned into a wide-ranging conversation about Mafia mores. Tommy had invested $10,000 in one of my coke deals and the operation went south. My guy had gotten ripped off, and we'd all lost our money. It was an occupational hazard, although Tommy didn't see it quite that way.

"Joey, I don't give a fuck, you're responsible," he'd claimed. "You owe me juice on that ten large until I get it back. It was my *compare*'s money. If I tell him that story about a rip-off, he'd just come after you and hurt you."

"Listen, Tommy," I'd told him. "You go tell that fucking Gallo that he's going to have to try and hurt me, because I'm not paying juice on that ten grand. The guy that got ripped off told me he'll make good. He just needs a little time. So be patient."

That was not a word in Tommy Agro's vocabulary.

"Joey," he said in a low voice, "what are you, sick? If I told him that, he'd have a dozen guys at your house in a few hours. And if a dozen wasn't enough, he'd have two dozen. You fuckin' moron. And listen to this. I told Johnny Irish and Tony Black that I was gonna get you made soon. Very soon, I told them. And you know what they said? They told me I should wait awhile. They didn't think you were ready." Tony Black was a guy who Irish had secured a button for when Irish was promoted to capo.

"First of all, Tip," I replied, "can't I say something about Gallo without you getting all excited? You know I don't mean it. I'm just

getting rid of my frustrations. And secondly, what's wrong with you? Are you so easy to con now? If Johnny Irish thinks it's too early for me to get made, how come he wanted to steal me from you and make me on the spot a couple of years ago?"

"You're right about Irish, Joey," Tommy said. "When I asked him about that conversation he had with you in front of DiBella, he and Tony Black put their tails between their legs and left. They're nothing but punks. But don't say anything else bad about my *compare*. And don't ever mention his name over the phone. Don't worry, you'll get that thing. My *compare*'s standing behind me, so there'll be no blackball. Just don't fuck up. You're almost like me, eh, Joey?"

If my phone was tapped, the FBI had heard all that.

I was awakened, at eight-thirty the morning after I returned from Arizona with Aldo by a knock on my door. I peered through the peephole and spotted two guys. One was tall and skinny, with long hair. The other was stocky, with a mustache, and carrying a briefcase. I was sure they were dopers. I kept quiet, even when the skinny guy began yelling: "Joe! We know you're home. We'd like to talk to you. Don't shoot. We're FBI agents."

This I couldn't imagine. Even dopers didn't dress as sloppy as these guys. The tall, skinny guy bruised his hand on my door for fifteen minutes before both of them left. I got their plate number and called my attorney. He ran a trace on it, and it came back as belonging to someone in Tallahassee. Now I was sure they were dopers from a gang I'd recently had some trouble with. A Genovese Family dealer named Papo Tortora had sold me bad dope, and I'd refused to pay. There had been threats. I called a couple of guys from my crew, and they came rushing over with guns.

We waited. The phone rang.

"Hello," I said into the receiver, disguising my voice like a woman's.

"Good morning, ma'am," a male voice said over the phone. "My name is Larry Doss and I'm an FBI agent. It's imperative I talk with your son. Will you please put Joe on the line?"

I continued with the falsetto. "My son isn't home. Why don't you leave Joseph alone? He's a nice boy. He doesn't harm anyone." My crew was holding their stomachs, trying not to bust a gut.

"Yes, ma'am, I agree with you," the voice continued. "But it's my duty to tell your son something of extreme importance to him."

I took the guy's phone number and told him I'd have Joe call him back. Then I called my attorney with the number and told him to find out where it went.

"That number goes nowhere, Joe," Bob Sailor said when he called back several minutes later. "I can't find anything on it, either in the reverse directory or through my sources. And when I called it myself and asked what residence I was calling, a voice asked me to whom I wanted to speak. When I made up a name, they told me I had the wrong number and hung up."

"Yeah, okay," I told Sailor. "I'll take care of it." I hung up and sent my crew home. Then I called the number myself.

"Is Larry Doss in?"

"Who's calling, please?"

"Tell him it's Joe Dogs."

"Joe, this is Larry Doss! I'm glad your mother passed on my message. She's a nice lady. Is she visiting you?"

"Whoa, slow down," I said to this Larry Doss. "Number one, who are you? And what's the idea of your telling my mother you're an FBI agent? What are you, fuckin' dopey or what? I told Papo that shit was no good, and that's the reason I sent it back. Now, do you want me to take this beef further?"

"Joe," the voice said, "I really don't understand what you're babbling about. I *am* an FBI agent, and I was there this morning with my partner Gunnar Askeland. We knew you were home, but we didn't know your mom was there. When did she get in? We've been on you twenty-four hours a day, but we didn't get a report that she'd arrived. Someone on the late shift must have dozed off."

"Well, listen, Larry, or whatever the fuck your name is," I said. "I called my lawyer and gave him your number. And he didn't come up with any FBI office."

"Joe," the voice replied, "Bob Sailor couldn't find his way home

in the dark. Call information. Get the local FBI number. Ask for Larry Doss or Agent Doss. Remember my voice. I'll be waiting."

That was fair enough. I was kind of hoping it actually was the FBI. Who else would know my lawyer's name? I didn't want any shoot-outs at my house, especially with Papo's gang of dopers. My landlord had told me he didn't give a shit who I was as long as I paid my rent on time. But I wasn't sure if he'd overlook blazing guns.

I dialed the local FBI number, a girl answered, and I asked for Agent Askeland. I was trying a little strategy of my own.

"Hello?" It was a quick, brisk hello.

"Hi, Larry," I said.

"No, this is Gunnar. Who's this? Do you want to speak to Larry Doss?"

"Yeah, put him on," I said.

"Nice try, Joe Dogs," Larry Doss's voice said. Maybe they weren't so dumb after all. Agent Doss repeated that he had something very important to tell me, but he didn't want to speak over the phone. He asked if he and his partner could come by my place.

"No, come alone," I told him. "You don't need your partner. I won't shoot you. Just don't wear a bug. I'm going to frisk you thoroughly, and if you're wearing a wire I'll toss you out on your ass."

Fifteen minutes later a car pulled up in front of my apartment. Sure enough, the tall, skinny guy with the long hair stepped out. He walked in, shook hands, and took a quick glance around. He noticed the rifle and three pistols I had scattered about the apartment.

"You don't need all these guns for me, Joe," Larry Doss said as I was frisking him.

"They aren't for you, Larry. I'm expecting a little problem."

"So where's your mother, Joe?" he asked. "I hope I didn't alarm her this morning?"

I raised my voice to a falsetto. "My mother's in New York, Larry. I haven't seen her for a while."

He smiled, and we got down to business. Agent Doss told me that his sources had told him that Tommy Farese had put out a

contract on me, and it was his solemn duty to inform me and offer protection. Would I help him? Would I cooperate? I declined, telling him that wasn't my cup of tea.

We talked for a good forty-five minutes, and I even put away my guns. Larry Doss seemed like a nice guy, and he conducted himself like a gentleman. Before he left he even promised me he'd pull his surveillance team off. Of course I didn't believe him, although I thought maybe he'd pull them for at least a couple of days.

Agent Larry Doss didn't make any headway with me, although he did convince me of one thing. I wasn't worried about Tommy Farese, but I didn't want the "Eye" down my back. It was time for me to leave the state.

Running to the FBI

On March 1, 1980, I called Nena and told her I was coming to Chicago. I had about $30,000 handy, and a coke dealer in Arizona owed me another $70,000. I gave my daughters all my furniture and loaded up my Lincoln with all the clothes and personal items I could fit. The day after I met with Larry Doss, I drove nonstop to Chicago.

Nena's apartment was small but adequate. And she was ecstatic to see me. "Maybe you could start a business, a legitimate business," she suggested. "The two of us could begin a new life. You can divorce Bunny, and we'll get married. I'd like to have a baby before I'm too old."

That just proved how well she didn't know me. Nena was a good kid, but I didn't want any of the things she wanted. It was a shame, really. I once was a nice guy. But I'd changed so much. Now I was a heel. As if to prove it, I smiled and nodded and went along with her for the time being.

"Yeah, sure, honey, whatever you want. But first let me ask you a favor. You fly to Arizona a lot, right? Let me call my friend Fred in Tucson. He owes me some money and maybe you could pick it up."

She agreed to be my courier, although I had to swear that it wasn't drug money she was picking up.

"I'm a gambler and a shylock," I said in mock indignation. "But you know I don't deal in drugs. I'm ashamed of you for even saying that."

What a woman doesn't know can't hurt her.

I stayed in Chicago for the next few months. *Marrone,* it was cold. I went out and bought a nice cashmere coat, but even that didn't help any. But mostly I missed the action. Nena was gone on runs for days at a time. When she came home we'd fuck and— invariably—argue. It got old.

The phone rang one day while Nena was gone, working a three-legged flight. I picked it up and it was Agent Larry Doss.

"Hey, Larry, why don't you stop breaking my balls," I said. "I got the fuck out of Florida because of you. So why don't you leave me alone?"

"But, Joe, I want to talk to you," he answered. "Can't we meet somewhere. I'll fly anywhere."

I was so lonely in Chicago that I almost took him up on his offer. Almost.

"Larry, you're talking like a fag," I told him. "I'm a Gambino, not an FBI agent. Don't get confused. Why the fuck would I risk meeting and talking to you? Now stop this harassment. Don't call me anymore, or I'll get a lawyer. Leave me the fuck alone." I hung up.

What a pain in the ass, I said to myself, but at least he won't call me anymore.

The phone rang right back. It was Larry Doss offering me his home phone number, in case I ever needed to get a hold of him, "for whatever reason." *Marrone,* the guy was sure a dedicated FBI agent. I wondered if he loved his job that much or if he just really wanted to be part of my crew.

I was getting tired of Chicago. Those midwesterners just aren't my type. I couldn't put my finger on it; they just acted different. They were nice enough people, and maybe that was it. I was used to dealing with snakes and morons. After Nena picked up the $70,000 from Fred in Tucson, and despite the good times I had

with her—and there were a lot—I told her I was thinking about leaving.

I just wasn't ready to settle down. Nena deserved much better than me. I mean, I cared for her a lot, but I don't think I was mature enough to handle the situation. She needed a nine-to-five guy. I slept during those hours.

One morning in late May 1980, Nena and I had an argument. Real bad. She was getting ready for a flight, and I didn't want her to go. I was tired of hanging around that place alone. I missed my friends. I missed my crew. I missed the street.

"If you go on that flight, I'm leaving and you can go fuck yourself," I told her.

"I don't want to leave, Joe, but I'm still on probation," she said. Then she reminded me that the reason she was still on probation was because she had taken the leave to nurse me back to health after my heart attack.

"You remember that, don't you Joe?" she needled me. "I'm not like those other girls you bounced around with. Now I have to go. Kiss me goodbye."

I didn't, and she left. She wasn't out the door before I was on the horn summoning one of my crew.

"Fly to Chicago right away, Ronnie. I want you to drive me back."

Ronnie flew in that day. I had all my stuff loaded into the Lincoln by the time I picked him up at the airport. We left from O'Hare, and drove straight to Singer Island, Florida. I got a room poolside at the Best Western SeaSpray Inn. I paid the desk clerk for a week. I wasn't in the room five minutes when the phone rang.

"Hello?"

"Joe! You just got back, huh? How was your trip?" Agent Larry Doss asked.

"Fuck you," I said and hung up the phone.

Ripping Off
the Eye

Larry called back the next day, and I agreed to meet him on the beach. One thing you have to understand about the mobster life: We were always talking to feds. Nobody ran from them. It was kind of an unwritten rule throughout the *Famiglias*: If the Eye approached, tell them what they want to hear, just don't tell them nothing.

There wasn't a wiseguy worth his button who wasn't polite and blandly accommodating whenever the G came around, from Joe N. Gallo to Tommy Agro to me. Plus, in this case I wanted to see what the feds had to say about the South Florida Colombo crew, the ones who allegedly had a contract out on me. I knew Larry Doss had been bullshitting when he said Tommy Farese wanted me whacked. But it wouldn't hurt to find out exactly what kind of game he was playing.

As we walked along the sand, Agent Doss popped the big question. "Joe, why don't you become my confidential informant? It won't go past me. I'll benefit by it. And I'll pick up all your living expenses."

"Fuhgedaboudit, Larry," I said. "I'm no stool pigeon."

"Think about it, Joe," he pressed. "If you help me, you got carte

blanche. How about right now. Do you need some money? Could you use a thousand?"

I looked at the guy. He wasn't a bad guy. He was just doing his job. Squeezing me. The vibes were right for him. The Colombos were on my ass, T.A. was getting shorter and shorter with me. I wasn't earning. You might say it was a vulnerable time. I asked him to give me a couple of days to think about it. "I'm sure I'll hear from you," I added.

It was good to be back in Florida. I was in my old stomping grounds. I knew all the players, and I knew all the broads. Nena called, crying. But I convinced her that Chicago wasn't the place for me.

"Wait one year, and then we'll get married," I lied to her. "In the meantime, you come down here and see me once a month, because you fly for free, right?"

All I was thinking about was myself. I got a little shylocking going, a little bookmaking. It wasn't all that hard to pick up where I'd left off, although where I'd left off wasn't the greatest place in the world. The heart attack had really slowed me down.

But Nena did come to visit me occasionally. And when she did our routine never varied. We'd go to bed, satisfy our carnal cravings, and then begin to argue. We'd accuse each other of infidelities and then lie to each other and make up.

I didn't tell Nena that I was taking money from the FBI.

The Eye was picking up my hotel tab every week. The telephone bill alone averaged between $200 and $300. I signed for everything at the pool, in the gift shop, at the restaurant, and then I would meet with Agents Larry Doss and Gunnar Askeland and tell them a bunch of things they already knew. I told them nothing about the Gambinos. Well, next to nothing.

I would fly to New York occasionally to see Tommy and pay him the juice on his $32,000 I still had out on the street, and the feds would reimburse all my expenses. I would tell them who I met,

where we ate, what we talked about—to a point. Frankly, most of the time I would have to embellish Tommy's moronic conversations. I didn't lie about anything. I just told them things I didn't think were important. Larry and Gunnar ate it up.

There were times when I gave them solid information. For instance, the latest bars and clubs where T.A. was hanging out. I once informed them that his new in-spot was the Manhattan nightclub Regine's, and sure enough T.A. was visited there by a Brooklyn Agent named Andris "Andy" Kurins. Kurins sent word back to Larry and Gunnar that my info was good. And in exchange for these tidbits I lived and I ate and I drank for free. The FBI didn't even tail me anymore, an added bonus. I had no problems. I was a CI.

Of course, I was going through money fast. I'd returned from Chicago with most of the $70,000 Nena had picked up in Arizona. But that was almost gone. I was paying juice to T.A. every week, almost all of it straight out of my pocket. The people to whom I'd shyed out loans were not paying their interest. But that wasn't T.A.'s problem, as he was quick to remind me. And so soon after the heart attack I didn't feel like breaking heads.

We were in a recession. And the economy affected even the mob.

The '80 football season rolled around, and I got hit real hard from the start. It got to the point where I was doing so bad that I began relying on my FBI money to pay off my customers. I was still having a problem with Papo the doper and his Genovese crew, and at one point Tommy flew in with part of his Brooklyn crew when we thought there was going to be a showdown. We waited with guns. We were going to kill them. But they never showed up.

Tommy left and the FBI picked up his bill. I never told them why he'd been there. The SeaSpray Inn's Top O'Spray lounge and restaurant had been packed every night because a wiseguy was staying there.

By October 1980 I was down to about fifteen large. I'd gotten wrecked booking some NFL preseason exhibitions—I was stupid to list them—and I felt a decided financial pinch.

By November I was barely making ends meet even though the FBI was still picking up my hotel bills. I got pinched for pistol whipping some smart-ass in a bar, and had to lay out $5,500 bail. I held back T.A.'s juice payments for two months.

And by December I was running out of little treats to lead on the FBI. Since I'd refused to give them anything important, I wouldn't see them. I tried to make a deal with the manager of the nearby Colonades Hotel to kick back half of the FBI payments on a suite, but he wouldn't go for it. So when the Eye cut off my hotel expenses completely, I moved in with a broad named Donna, a bartender I knew from DeCaesar's, a nearby ribs joint with delicious food, and I mean delicious.

December came and went, and again I held back Tommy's juice. T.A. was calling all my usual hangouts, desperate to find me, but I was embarrassed. People weren't paying me, and I couldn't pay him. I didn't return any of his messages.

In January 1981, Donna and I moved into a cute little apartment in Riviera Beach. I was still calling Nena and telling her how much I loved her. She arranged for me to meet her in Hawaii, and I was happy, for my luck finally appeared to be changing. I won $35,000 at the Palm Beach Kennel Club—more than enough to pay back Tommy and to throw him a few thousand extra for his troubles. I figured I'd do this when I returned from Hawaii. I never made it there.

The Sting: Operation Home Run

Kicks and Punches and the Clanging of the Pipe

I answered the phone in our apartment on January 19, 1981, a date I'll never forget. Don Ritz, who normally stuttered, sounded even more excited and nervous than usual.

"Joe, he's here! T—, T—, T—, T.A. is looking for you! He's with two guys and he asked for your number but I told him I didn't have it. He took Ronnie out somewhere, probably to get him to talk. And, Joe, you know Ronnie. He'll sell out his own mother."

Ronnie Gerantino, part of my crew, the guy who'd driven me back from Chicago, was all mouth and no balls. I found out later that he'd been working as a confidential informant for Agent Larry Doss for the last couple of years. He was the reason Doss knew I was back in Florida so quick. He was also the guy who'd told Doss

the bullshit about Tommy Farese having a contract out on me. Ronnie had nothing to tell him, so he made up the story.

But even without knowing all that, right then I rued the day I'd hired him. I only kept him around as a go-fer. He was nothing like Don Ritz, or Aldo DiCuffa, or even Tony Micelli, another guy in my crew. If there was one guy in my crew who was going to rat me out, it was Ronnie.

"See if you can get to Ronnie and tell him to keep his mouth shut," I ordered Don Ritz. "I'm leaving tomorrow for Hawaii. And I want to leave with no problems."

Don warned me to "be prepared" before hanging up, and I dialed Larry Doss's number. I told the agent Tommy Agro and two thugs were in town looking for me. I told Larry I didn't know whether I should meet them or not.

"Get out of the apartment if you're afraid," Doss said.

"I'm not afraid, Larry," I lied. "I just want to get the fuck out of here tomorrow and see my girl from Chicago and then see Tommy A. when I get back."

"Joe, I don't understand why you're dodging him," Larry said. "You've been his right hand down here for ten years. Call me if you need me. Call me anytime." And then he hung up.

I hadn't told Larry I had some of Tommy's money shylocked out on the street. And I certainly hadn't told him I was in arrears on my juice payments. He didn't even know that I was going to Hawaii, or about the fact that I'd won thirty-five large at the dog track.

Around noon I answered the phone again. It was that motherfucker Ronnie Gerantino. "Joe, Tommy's here and he wants to see you. He has a couple of guys with him. Here he is."

"Joey," Tommy said, "come over here right away. I have a couple of guys I want you to find some construction work for."

"Why don't you bring them over to my place, Tip? I only live right across the bridge. Ronnie will show you the way."

"Nah," Tommy answered. "Come on over to Don Ritz's Pizzeria. We'll be waiting in the kitchen. And hurry up. I ain't got all fuckin' day. I have to go to Miami. So make it fast."

"I'll be there in a half-hour," I told him before hanging up. "I want to straighten you out anyway, and I have a present for you."

I sat for a few moments in deep thought. There was really nothing to be apprehensive about. I was, after all, a proposed member of the Gambino Crime Family. Tommy was my mentor. Why should I worry about $7,000 or $8,000 in back juice? My paranoia subsided. I convinced myself that all was well. There was, however, no harm in watching my back.

I called Larry Doss and told him I had spoken to T.A., and that everything was going to be all right. "I'm going over now," I added. "I'll be going in through the kitchen door. Just for the hell of it, why don't you and Gunnar try to cover me?"

He agreed, and then I called Nena, who was aware that I owed Tommy juice. "I'm going to see him now. I'll pay him what I owe him, and I'll call you this afternoon. It's only one more day, but I can't wait to see you, honey, I miss you so much. If you don't hear from me today, it means Tommy killed me."

It was a joke. Nena didn't find it so funny.

"Don't talk like that, Joe. If something did happen to you, I wouldn't know how to reach you. I can't see why you can't give me your number—unless you're living with a woman."

"Nena, I've told you, there's no incoming calls to this line. Can't you believe me for once in your life?"

I was a scumbag to the end. She told me to be careful. And she told me she loved me.

I grabbed the cash out of my freezer, where I kept it wrapped in tinfoil. I figured I'd pay T.A. the $8,000 juice, throw him a $5,000 peace pipe, and pay off $15,000 of the principal I owed, leaving me with a $17,000 debt. I left $10,000 in the freezer for the trip to Hawaii.

Singer Island was the fancy part of Riviera Beach, reached by bridge across the Intercoastal Waterway. I was there in fifteen minutes. I wore dress slacks and a silk shirt. The cash was in my back pocket, two stacks of $10,000 and one stack of $8,000.

I parked in the rear of Don Ritz's Pizzeria. As I opened the screen door to the kitchen I saw Tommy A., dressed in an expensive plaid

sportcoat and an open-necked shirt. Tommy was always an extremely sharp dresser. Behind him was a bigger guy, Italian-looking and husky. To Tommy's left—my right—stood another strong-looking Italian guy.

I hadn't noticed the FBI outside. But I knew they'd be there. They were probably just well concealed.

I stuck out my hand to T.A., and moved to embrace him. He grabbed my hand hard and uttered what I seem to recall as "You motherfucker." Out of the corner of my right eye I saw an object that looked like a baseball bat or a pipe coming toward my head.

I sort of felt myself falling, as if it wasn't me, and I remember kicks and punches and the clanging of the pipe and the thrust of both a pipe and a bat and feet and fists to my head, face, and body.

After a while I felt nothing.

"Get Me My Money Right Away"

Two days later I woke up in a dark room. I felt no pain. I could vaguely see. I saw a shadow hovering over me. It was like a blue ghost. Then I saw more blue ghosts. In a moment I could focus. The closest shadow was my daughter Sheryl. Behind her in a row were Bunny, my mother, Molly, and Donna. Eventually even Larry and Gunnar hove into view.

There was also a guy in a black robe. Hey, I know, it's a priest! I wondered why he was praying. Was I in heaven? Doubtful. Was I dying? How did I get here? What the fuck happened? I couldn't think, but I had to think. To remember. In the background I heard everyone crying. Bunny said to the priest, "Let me kiss him good-bye."

Suddenly the phone was ringing somewhere. Far away. No, not far away. In the room. Right next to me. A nurse appeared out of nowhere. "I'm sorry," she said to the huddled group, "but he's passed away."

I shot up to a sitting position. Everyone came rushing over. The

priest said, "God has answered your prayers." I think he said this to my daughter.

The nurse screamed into the phone, "He's alive!" She handed the receiver to me. There was a bandage over my right ear. I pressed the receiver to my left.

"Joey?" The word was harsh, angry.

"Tommy? Tommy! Did you do this to me?"

"Shaddup, you motherfucker. You better get me my money right away!"

I lay there thinking. I don't know how long. Everyone was making a fuss. The priest began praying again. He had beads in his hand.

The doctor walked in and said it was "a miracle."

I stayed in the hospital for five days. Thinking. And crying.

How could my good friend do this to me? We were so close. There wasn't anything in the world I wouldn't have done for Tommy Agro. And he did this for $8,000? After all the money he'd made with me? I couldn't believe it. Me! Joe Dogs! His right hand down in Florida!

I didn't deserve this. Why hadn't he killed me? Why leave me like this, like a vegetable? I cried and cried for four or five days and then checked myself out of the hospital and went to Donna's.

I don't know who took me there. I don't remember much from that time. I stayed at Donna's and started to deteriorate slowly. I lost thirty pounds. I vaguely remember calling Nena. She had gone to Hawaii without me. She said she was glad I was alive.

Donna took good care of me. She was in love with me. I didn't reciprocate. I loved Nena. Or I thought I did. But it was Donna who nursed me back to the point where I could at least get up and walk around the apartment. She did this with ham and cheese sandwiches and canned chicken soup.

My mother dropped in to say goodbye, she was flying back north. And then Larry and Gunnar came by with an offer they were sure I couldn't refuse.

The FBI agents thought they had compromised me, and that was

the reason for the beating. I set them straight, and told them about the back juice. They were angry with me for not having told them before. "Maybe we could have gotten the money from the Bureau," Larry said. It was too late now.

Gunnar said that they had been outside of Don Ritz's, "but we didn't know what was going on until the ambulance arrived. Tommy and his guys must have left through the front door."

It didn't matter. This was my fault. I hadn't been straight with the Eye. Had I told Larry about the juice payments, this would never have happened. I pondered my options. I didn't want to go full-scale with the FBI. What I'd been doing as a confidential informant had been dangerous but peripheral. Now they wanted me to be a part of a wide-ranging operation concentrating on the Gambinos and the Colombos. I needed more time to think.

I called Bunny and pleaded with her to take me back.

"I'll be a good husband," I cried. "Please give me another chance. I can't stay here. Poor Donna loves me, but I can't love her back. Please take me back. I'll never cheat on you again."

"Oh, honey, don't cry," Bunny begged. "After all, I'm only human. But I've made a new life for myself. I'll be glad to take care of you for a while, to help you get back on your feet. I'll put my life on hold. But after you're well, I'll expect you to leave. I still love you in a lot of ways, Joe, but I've fallen in love with somebody else. He was there at my side when I needed him. I hope you understand, Joe."

What a bastard I was. It must have been agonizing for Bunny to tell me these things. I'd hurt her so bad. And here I was doing the same things to Donna and Nena.

"That's okay, Bunny, I'll take care of myself," I told her. "Thanks for being honest, and I wish you the best of everything. Let's always be friends. And I'll always love you."

I was in a lot of pain. In the hospital they'd pumped me with morphine and Darvon, and they'd given me painkillers to take home. But I refused to eat them. I needed all my senses to build up a hate for T.A. and the Gambinos.

The injuries I'd received would scar me for life. My head was the size of a balloon. My nose was busted—not broken, but split open

and crushed. I had a bump on my forehead the size of an orange. My teeth were cracked and broken. My right ear was partially severed. When they found me, it had been dangling from my head. I had broken ribs and swollen balls and cuts and bruises all over my body. I saw double for a full year because of the concussion.

I found out later that Don Ritz's wife, Marilyn, had walked in on the beating. She saw me splayed out on the ground, unconscious, Tommy kneeling over me with a meat cleaver upraised in his hand. One of his goons was holding my right arm extended. Tommy was going to chop off my hand. But Marilyn Ritz's terrified scream sent them scurrying out of the kitchen. She saved my life, and my hand.

Tommy began calling me at Donna's every day, always with the same threatening tone. But I was a vegetable. Finally, seeing no other alternative, I called the FBI.

Getting Even

Larry and Gunnar helped me down the stairs and into a car where their supervisor was waiting. I told the three feds that I was ready to cooperate full-scale with their ongoing La Cosa Nostra investigation.

Gunnar Askeland was dubious. "Joe, you're finished with those guys. You'll never get back in their good graces."

"Oh no? Gunnar, you don't know how wrong you are."

I turned to Doss and said, "Larry, you make those juice payments for me every week, and I'll get Tommy for you. I'll get all three of them."

I knew that to the Eye, Tommy A., his thugs, even me, were just means to an end. Bait, you might say. And that end was the big boys. Gallo. Persico. Castellano.

Gunnar tried to convince Larry that using me was a waste of time. Larry ignored him and had me sign papers stating that I would be willing to record all conversations with any and all organized crime figures. I also signed a piece of paper stating that I would testify to any evidence that I received in the course of an investigation. I told myself I was volunteering to be a cooperating witness. To the rest of the world I'd just become a stoolie.

. . .

Larry called the following day, and we met. It was hard for me to go far, because I couldn't drive. So I hobbled down the block, Larry and Gunnar picked me up, and I began my new job.

Larry wanted me to start taping T.A.'s calls. I told him that would be tough, because Donna would see the recorder, and word of something like that always leaks out. He agreed. Donna was a doll, and she treated me great. And even though I cared for her, I knew it was too late. The FBI gave me a pile of cash, and Larry and Gunnar began taking me around to look for an apartment.

They read the ads for me and drove me to different places. But they wouldn't go in. I went in alone and talked for myself, and I was turned down at two places because I looked like a mook. My head and face were still swollen, I had to cock my head at a forty-five-degree angle to clear the double vision, and my speech was thick and slow. I was also having trouble breathing, as there was a bone chip lodged in my nasal passage.

I wouldn't have rented an apartment to me, either.

The third place we tried was a condo in Lake Worth. I'd come full circle in Florida—out in the boondocks, about six miles south of Palm Beach. I went in, introduced myself, and decided to use a different approach. I told the rental agent I'd been in a terrible car accident and I'd just gotten out of the hospital. My wife and I were splitting up, I said, and I needed a furnished apartment immediately.

An hour later I'd signed a lease on a second-floor one-bedroom apartment for $650 a month. It was the middle of February 1981.

The FBI wanted me to move into my new place that night. But I needed a few days to sneak out on Donna. Two days later, while Donna was at work, I enlisted my daughter Sheryl and her husband to help me move. I felt like a heel. But it was time to start getting even with Tommy Agro.

I couldn't do anything alone, so Sheryl helped me get set up in my new place and did my grocery shopping, and when she heard me talking nice to T.A. over the phone she was sure I had brain damage. She didn't know that the FBI had installed a recorder on the phone in my bedroom. I taped every conversation. I'd let no one but Larry and Gunnar and Sheryl into the apartment.

. . .

Larry and Gunnar would call every morning, asking if the coast was clear. Then they'd come over. Even Sheryl wasn't allowed in unless she called first.

The FBI had given me $1,000 to send as a token to Tommy. This made the motherfucker happy.

In early March, as Sheryl was straightening up, she happened to ask what had happened to all that money I'd won at the dog track. "Holy Christ," I said, the light bulb going off over my head. I'd completely forgotten about the stash of cash in Donna's refrigerator. Then I recalled the money I'd had in my back pocket the day of the beating at Don Ritz's joint.

Tommy must have taken it, I figured, along with the gold watch, diamond ring, and gold chain that had been missing from my unconscious hulk when they discovered me. But I still had Donna's key. And I knew she was at work. "Sheryl, take me to Donna's right away," I said.

On the drive over I told Sheryl about the cash, and she assured me that Donna wasn't the type to take it. But when we arrived at Donna's twenty minutes later, her front door was open and the landlord was standing on the porch.

"Who's going to pay for this mess?" he demanded.

The apartment was empty, and the walls were smeared with black-painted graffiti. "Fuck Joe," and "Hate Joe," and "Love Hate" were written all over. If Donna was the artist, she must have been one angry lady. I went into the kitchen and the refrigerator door was open. It was unplugged. The freezer was empty. The landlord told me Donna had been gone for six days. Someone had taken my money, and I knew it wasn't her. She took only her clothes. The furniture, which was hers, was still there.

"Who's going to pay for this?" he repeated.

"You know what you do, Frank," I told him. "You have the place painted, and in exchange keep the furniture. And if I hear one more word out of your mouth I'll blast *you* all over the walls. *Capisci?*"

I felt some of my old strength returning.

. . .

Don Ritz had opened up a new restaurant in West Palm Beach called Don Luigi's. He was partners with an attorney from Utica, New York. And Don had a problem. A Colombo wiseguy everyone knew as Donald Duck had brought a couple of thugs into Don Luigi's one night and beaten the hell out of Don Ritz with a blackjack. Don called me the next morning.

"Sure," I said, "this is all T.A.'s fault. Now the fucking Colombos are making a move because they think I'm weak. Let me call that *sciallo*." That fucking jackal.

I called Tommy in New York and explained what was going on with Donald Duck and the Colombos. I taped the conversation. I taped every conversation I had, even Don Ritz's, but one.

"Tell Don Ritz to carry a gun and blow their fuckin' heads off if they come back," Tommy said. "Tell your whole crew to carry guns, and not just to make their belts tight."

But my crew was scared, and I didn't blame them. They weren't messing with kids. The Colombos were bad motherfuckers.

The next day, March 5, Larry and Gunnar came over to listen to my tapes. They mentioned that Tommy sounded annoyed and suggested I try to goad him into flying off the handle.

"Antagonize him, Joe," Larry said. "Generate some conversation. You know him. You can make him nuts. Maybe you can get him to say something he'll be sorry for later."

Don Ritz called again with a Colombo update, and at 1:30 A.M. on the morning of March 7, 1981, Tommy called me. I told him that the night before, Johnny Irish, Freddie Campo, Pasquale "Checko Brown" Fusco, and Robbie had all eaten dinner at Don Luigi's. They'd been asking a bunch of questions about me. Wanting to know if I was still attached to T.A. Later that same night, I told Tommy, I'd taken a cab to Joey's Restaurant and Disco in Riviera Beach and run into the same crew.

Freddie Campo, the former free agent, had been cozying up to the Colombos since failing to collect his race-fixing money from Tommy years before. He'd finally seen the wisdom of aligning himself with a *Famiglia*.

"I sent them over a drink, and they didn't even acknowledge it," I reported. "You'd think they'd have sent me one back."

"I wouldn't have sent them my cock," T.A. said.

"Well, Tip, I hate to say it, but you brought this on yourself."

It wasn't hard to trigger Tommy Agro. All you had to do was insinuate that he was at fault for something. I had pulled that trigger.

"Me?" he ranted. "I'm at fault? I got people that will eat the fucking eyes out of your fucking head. You dumb bastard! And they're as loyal as a motherfucker. With balls the size of cows. All I have to do is tell them to load up, be in this place at this time, and they'll walk in and blast everybody. No fuckin' hesitation. No nothin'. And don't look for nothin' beside it. No questions asked. They'll blow you up. You think you got something going? You got nothing going!

"You think I'm easy? You think I'm where I'm at today because I'm easy? What I've done, you haven't dreamt of, my friend. Why do you think people fear me? Because I was a hard-on, you fuckin' moron? You think I got where I was because I was a jerkoff in the street? You're easy, you motherfucker. The most wrongest thing you ever did was fuck me. People fear me, you dumb fuck. You're only alive today, my friend, because Don's wife walked in. Not because we stopped. You wasn't supposed to walk away no more. And I'm gonna even enlighten you more better than that, while you're having these fuckin' hallucinations. I missed you three times. I was there looking for you two other times before this, you dumb motherfucker."

The tape is a classic. Tommy Agro had incriminated himself—the dumb fuck had admitted everything. I stretched out on my bed and smiled as he went on raving for another twenty minutes. He ended his harangue by promising to fly in the following night to let the fuckin' Colombos know who ran Don Ritz's place.

I wanted to play the tape back after he hung up, but I didn't dare touch it. I didn't know too much about tape recorders, and this was one screed I didn't want erased by mistake. I supposed it could wait until morning.

. . .

"Did you hear from Tommy A.?" Larry asked expectantly, brandishing his portable tape recorder. He and Gunnar had arrived at my place around ten-thirty. It was payday. I was doing this for $500 a week plus expenses—or about the amount I used to throw away in tips in one night.

"Oh yeah," I answered nonchalantly. "We talked for a while early this morning. Why don't you give it a listen."

Larry collected the tape while Gunnar pulled out a Form 302, the kind they used to write up their intelligence reports. I handed Larry the two tapes, the one from Don Ritz and the one from the rabid Tommy A. After listening to the first, Larry mentioned that "Don seems kind of scared. I know I'd be if what happened to you and Don happened to me. Wouldn't you, Gunnar?"

Gunnar nodded dutifully. The two FBI agents played as a team. Larry's role was to be in charge, Gunnar's was that of the agreeable yes man. I went along with their charade. It didn't make any difference to me. They were both nice guys who I sensed didn't know too much about organized crime. But they both tried hard, and that counted for something with me.

They put on Agro's tape. I walked into the kitchen and began brewing coffee. After twenty minutes of small talk between me and T.A., Gunnar Askeland turned and said with exasperation, "Joe, does he say anything relevant during this conversation?"

"Yeah, I think so, Gunnar. It gets better about five minutes from now."

You had to see the look on the FBI agents' faces when Tommy began ranting and raving and admitting what he'd done to me. Then he admitted that the beating had been planned for weeks. Larry was so elated he jumped around the apartment like a jackrabbit. Gunnar came over to me and stuck out his hand.

"I'm sorry for doubting you, Joe," he said. "You did a great job."

"We can nail him with this," Larry added. "Premeditated. Conspiracy. He's going to be one sorry wiseguy."

They packed up my tapes and instructed me to call them at home, no matter the time, if and when T.A. reached out for me. After they

left, Sheryl called and asked if I needed anything. I told her Tommy was coming down and I was concerned.

"Don't see him, Dad. He'll hurt you again," Sheryl said. "Is there anything I can do for you?"

"Yeah, honey," I said. "Come on over and clean my apartment."

È Pulito, He's Clean

Tommy called at midnight.

I was now in the habit of pressing the "record" button whenever I picked up the phone. I always made sure there was a fresh tape in the machine. The only person I didn't tape, I wouldn't tape, was Little Dom. It was part of the deal.

"I'm here, Joey, at the Dip. Come and see me tomorrow."

"I'm hurt, Tip," I whimpered. "I'm hurt bad. Please don't hurt me anymore. I didn't do anything wrong. Can't it be over? Can't we start fresh?"

My begging was not a facade. I was really afraid. I dreaded facing him so soon. It had been seven weeks since the beating, and my head was still a mess. The scars from the stitches were still raw.

"Joey, I'm not gonna do nothing to you," Tommy said. "I didn't come here for you. I came here for that Don Ritz thing. I swear on my daughter Kimmy, Joey! I won't do that no more. Believe me, it's all over. I'll never do that again. I really did come here for Don. I've had guys down here for three days now, in case there's a problem."

"You have your guys with you?" I asked.

"Joey, they're not here for you, believe me. Would I tell you they were here if I was gonna hurt you, you dumb fuck?"

"Okay, Tip," I said. "I'll be there around noon, by the pool. It takes me longer to drive now because it's hard for me to see."

I hung up and called Larry. "Don't go anywhere until Gunnar and I see you," he told me. "We'll be there at nine in the morning."

I had problems sleeping that night. I was trying to convince myself that everything was going to be all right. I wasn't doing a very good job. I kept visualizing being beaten with bats and pipes by a mob of guys. I must have fallen asleep sometime around six. The telephone woke me at eight. Larry and Gunnar were on their way.

I made coffee as Larry and Gunnar listened intensely to my conversation with T.A. After it ended, they pleaded with me not to go.

"We can't cover you good at the pool," Gunnar said. "It's the season, and the place will be mobbed. Don't be foolish. You've done enough."

They sure sounded as if they really were concerned for my safety. It didn't matter.

"Look, guys," I explained. "If I don't go to see him, chances are he comes to see me. It would look too suspicious if I don't go. It'll start him to wondering."

Larry and Gunnar wouldn't buy it. They offered to take me to their homes to protect me. I finally convinced them that I had a feel for Tommy's voice, and I knew everything was going to be all right.

But I didn't really.

On the drive down I-95 to the Diplomat I watched Larry and Gunnar through my rearview mirror. I had to steer with my head cocked at an angle in order to see. It took me an hour and a half. I drove like an old lady. The valet parking attendant recognized me and there were no charges. I noticed he charged Larry and Gunnar.

The Olympic-sized pool was packed with tourists. Tommy's cabana was at the south end, near the wading pool. My stomach sunk when the first guys I saw were Paul Principe and Frank Russo, the two sluggers who'd helped Tommy beat me to a pulp. They were staring at me. I slowed down, looking for Tommy.

I became even more nervous when I saw Checko Brown, the

Colombo soldier, talking to Fat Andy Ruggiano, the Gambino capo. Bobby DeSimone was there, fresh from a short prison stretch. I stopped in my tracks and started to tremble. I didn't know whether to run or what. I was frozen to the pavement. Tommy came hurrying over.

"Joey, don't worry, relax. Didn't I tell you we wasn't going to do that no more?"

We embraced.

"What are they doing here?" I asked, motioning to Checko and Fat Andy.

"Everybody at the pool is with me," Tommy said. "Come. Sit down. Take off your shirt. Get some sun."

It was an odd request. Checko was fully dressed. So were Fat Andy and DeSimone. Tommy and the two thugs were in bathing suits. Then I realized. They were expecting a wire. All six stared at me as I pulled off my Ban-Lon.

Everyone seemed to relax a little. We made small talk for about twenty minutes. Though I noticed that the conversation still wasn't going anywhere, as if they were afraid to talk about business.

"Christ, it's hot," I said. "I wish I'd brought a suit."

Everyone in the area heard me, and it loosened things up.

"Tommy, don't you have an extra suit in your room?" Fat Andy asked. "Come on, you're about the same size as Joe Dogs."

I was insulted. Tommy had a good five inches on me.

Anyway, Tommy didn't. But Paulie Principe did. Checko Brown walked me to Paulie's hotel room, and I wondered what the agents were thinking—if they were even still there. I started to get my balls back. I wanted to kill every one of those guys.

Checko found the swimsuit, and I got naked in front of him. Unless the wire was up my ass, they knew I was clean. When we reached the pool the crew looked at me, then to Checko.

"È pulito," Checko said. He's clean. What the fuck? I wondered. Did he think I didn't understand him? I mean, did the fucking moron think I was Japanese or something because my eyes were still swollen?

But everyone came closer to me after that—except Paulie and

Frankie, who remained in the pool. I'd made the right move. Business could now commence.

"Joe Dogs, I was telling Tommy that you said Don Ritz was with you, and to leave him alone," Checko began. "Remember that time I wanted to break his head and you stopped me? Remember?"

"Yeah," I answered.

"Well, I told Tommy that this recent stuff, no way we were involved," Checko said, lying through his teeth.

"Oh, we believe you," Tommy interjected. "Why shouldn't we believe you?"

That was good enough for Checko Brown. He stood, kissed everyone on the cheek, and left.

He wasn't past the pool before Tommy was calling him a "fucking liar."

"Didn't I tell you he'd deny everything," T.A. ranted. He was looking at me, filling me in. "I went to see the Colombo *Famiglia* underboss Gerry Lang yesterday. I told him what that fuckin' pimp Johnny Irish and Checko did to Don Ritz. We had a sit-down. That's why Andy's here. I told Gerry Lang that Don Ritz is with Joe Dogs, Joe Dogs is with me. So that makes Don Ritz with me. Whatever happened between Joe Dogs and me is nobody's fucking business."

"Of course he's a fucking liar," I said. "Did you see his nose start to grow? It was growing like Pinocchio's grew when he told a lie. You know Pinocchio, don't you, Tommy?"

"No, I don't. Who the fuck is he with?"

"Forget it," I said. "I thought you knew him."

Fat Andy was laughing, and said, "Tommy, he's fucking around with you."

"Fucking-A, Joey." Tommy was exasperated. "I'm down here trying to take care of business, and you're fucking around."

Fat Andy changed the subject before things got out of hand. Andy was a big sloppy guy. You'd never think he was a wiseguy. What with the double chins and the bulging eyes and all the polyester. But he was always so quiet that when he spoke he commanded a world of respect.

"Joe, you know what I have in mind?" he asked. "I'd like to start a private club in your area. Do the people up your way like to gamble with cards? You know, blackjack and poker?"

"Yeah. Why?" The people up my way? Christ, the guy lived an hour south of Palm Beach. You'd think he was talking about Alaska.

"Well, Tommy tells me that you and that guy Freddie Campo got a cop on the pad," Fat Andy continued. "And I was thinking maybe he could help get us a private-club charter, a bring-your-own-bottle club. Maybe this cop can kind of make sure that nobody bothers us."

Tommy, Fat Andy, and I discussed the idea for over an hour. T.A. and Fat Andy told me to reach out for the cop and to do it quickly, as they wanted to get started. They both walked me back to Tommy's cabana, where I got dressed and started to leave.

"Joe, why don't you come back down tonight and see the show with us," Fat Andy suggested. "Air Supply is in the big room."

"Yeah, come on back down and we'll talk some more," Tommy agreed.

I told them I'd like to bring along my daughter and her husband. Not only was Sheryl a big Air Supply fan, but I still couldn't see well enough to drive at night. No problem.

On the drive home I didn't see the agents, so I assumed they had left. I decided not to tell them about the swimsuit ploy unless they saw it. Now that Tommy and Fat Andy wanted to start up a club, I wasn't sure where this investigation would go. I didn't mind helping the FBI for a little longer, as long as I was still fucked up physically. But by Tommy coming down and flexing his muscles, I realized I'd be able to go back on the streets with the same respect, if not more. Maybe I could figure out a way to revenge myself on Agro without working with the feds.

But what about those papers I'd signed? Here, I thought, I had a problem. I had many possibilities to consider. Little did I realize at the time that the evidence I'd gathered poolside at the Diplomat would ultimately lead to one of the biggest and most successful undercover operations in the history of organized crime.

"You Should Have Shot Me, Tommy"

The cop on the pad that Tommy and Fat Andy referred to was named William "Boone" Darden. He was the chief of police in Riviera Beach, Florida. Freddie Campo had had Boone on his payroll since God knows when. Boone protected Freddie's bookmaking operation and—for the right price—was usually available with the kind of small-talk, cop-talk information you spent like money.

When I returned to Lake Worth that afternoon, I called Larry Doss. I told him I needed money because I had to go back down south again. I also advised him to bring his pad and pencil. He would definitely want to write up a Form 302. The agents' handwritten Form 302s would later be typed at the FBI office in the event any investigation led to trial. They are considered evidence.

Larry arrived, and I told all. I also insisted that I was comfortable taking my daughter and son-in-law back down for the show. What I needed from him was enough money to pick up the entire tab.

"Let's blind them with greed," I said. He was all for it and handed me $1,000.

"Try to bring me some change," he said on his way out.

When the maitre d' showed us to Tommy's table, everyone stood and embraced. There were Tommy and some Chinese broad, Fat Andy, DeSimone and his wife, Betty, and Joe "Piney" Armone's wife and daughter. Armone, T.A.'s capo, was nowhere to be seen. The thugs Paulie and Frankie arrived just before the show.

We ate. We drank. We listened to Air Supply. And when the check for the evening arrived I wrestled Tommy Agro for it. He threatened to break my jaw. I told him he didn't hit hard enough. That brought a smile to Tommy's face. Out tab came to $470. I gave the waiter $600 and told him to keep the change.

Tommy noticed and gave me a wink. "I see you're back in action," he whispered.

"Hey, Tom, I'm dealing in the babonia," I told him. "You know the money that's in that dope. I'm just starting to get on my feet. But don't say nothing to Fat Andy. *Capisci?*"

"Joey, I don't tell anyone anybody's business. Just be careful and don't get caught, because this club Andy's talking about is going to be a good thing—especially if you can get to the cop. He's an eggplant, isn't he?"

He meant black. "Yeah, but I'm pretty sure he's with us."

After the show, Tony the maitre d' had our table waiting in the Tack Room. We were all talking and having a good time when Tommy suddenly asked me to take a walk.

"Where?" I said, a little apprehensively.

"To my room, Pip. I want to talk to you alone."

My daughter caught the drift of our conversation, came over, and said, "Daddy, Michael and I are really tired. We want to go now."

"Wait ten minutes more, darling," Tommy cut in. "I want to talk to your father for a while."

"I'll be right back," I told Sheryl, leaning over to kiss her cheek. Then Tommy and I excused ourselves and left for his room.

"Does your daughter know about our falling out?" he asked as we walked to his first-floor suite.

"Nah, are you kidding?" I lied. "She never would have come tonight. She thinks the Colombos did this, and you're here to straighten things out."

We arrived at T.A.'s suite and he poured me a Scotch over ice. I wondered whether he'd planned on this meeting, since he had my brand of Scotch sitting on the bar.

"Nah," Tommy said. "That fuckin' petunia I'm with drinks Dewar's White Label. I don't know how any of you can drink that shit. It tastes like medicine."

"It's what you acquire a taste for," I told him. "Some people like black broads. Some people like white. I notice that you're always with dark broads."

"Joey, my broad isn't black. She's a Chink. What, are you color blind? She's red."

"Red is what she ain't, Tommy. But she ain't white either. I suppose that's what all you Sicilians are used to. After all, it's only a short swim to Ethiopia."

"Listen, you fuckin' suitcase, there's something I want to tell you," Tommy said. "But you have to promise me it doesn't go any further than this room. Because if it does, it'll make me look bad, and I'll have a bad taste in my mouth."

"Who would I tell?" I asked, throwing up my arms. "You see how quiet I am. Even to Andy, and he's a capo in our *Famiglia*."

"That's good, Joey," Tommy said. "Because Andy's a goodfellow on Neil's side. You know? The under. Now don't misunderstand me. Fat Andy may be here, but I'm closer to Paulie."

Tommy was referring to a rift that had developed in the Gambino Family between the forces of Boss Paulie Castellano and those allied behind his underboss, Aniello "Neil" Dellacroce. A couple of years later Dellacroce's people, led by John Gotti, would declare war, whacking Big Paulie. I knew all about this intrigue. But for Tommy I played dumb.

"You got me all confused now, Tip," I said. "I thought we were all one big happy Family. So who are we with? And where do I belong? I thought Paulie was the boss and Neil was the underboss.

What are there, two Families in one? Gambino Seniors and Gambino Juniors? I don't know what the fuck you're talking about."

Tommy laughed with me for a moment, but suddenly his face turned serious.

"Joey, I didn't want to hurt you the way I did," he said. "It wasn't my fault. My *compare*, Joe Gallo, made me do it. It wasn't me or the money you owed me. He just used that as an excuse to get to you. I swear, Joey. It wasn't me."

"But why did Gallo want to hurt me?" I asked. "After all the money he made with us on the dope? On the racetrack scam? And what about that beating I gave that guy in Naples for his little fucking bitch?"

"Stop, Joey! Stop right there! I told you once before never to talk like that about my *compare*. That's the reason. That guy you fucked up, the zip with the sister. You fucked him up too much. You weren't supposed to hurt him that bad. That girl, Sophia, left my *compare* over that. It's been eating at him ever since, and he blames you."

I was flabbergasted. This happened to me all because of a cunt! It couldn't be. Tommy had to be lying.

"But what about the proposal that you told me about, the proposal to get me a button?" I asked. "Was that all bullshit? I mean, Gallo had to okay it. You were supposed to be my mentor. And Gallo was your mentor. You even brought me to your capo, Joe Piney. I don't understand.

"That's why I wasn't too worried about the back vig that I owed," I continued. "You knew I'd catch up. For eight months after my heart attack I paid you out of my pocket for guys on the street who weren't paying me. Did you know that? No, you didn't. Because I was too much of a fucking man to come crying to you and get someone else hurt."

"I know, Joey, I know," Tommy mumbled. "What can I say except that my *compare* wanted you *morto!* It's a good thing Don's wife walked in. You would have been either dead or with no right hand."

I said, "You should have shot me, Tommy. You should have killed me. I didn't deserve to be left like this. I've been nothing but

loyal to you for ten years. And look at me. I'm fucked up. I look like a freak. I can't even eat without cocking my head. I don't even feel the liquor I'm drinking. All this because Joe Gallo blames me for his cunt! You wouldn't have done this to Bobby. You feel too sorry for him. That's what you told me, anyway."

The mention of DeSimone's name triggered something in T.A. His face looked like a fist.

"Bobby! Bobby! You know why I feel sorry for Bobby? Because I was the one that whacked both of his brothers. That's why! Remember the guy, Bobby's brother, he worked for you once? The guy that once bought me a watch?"

"Yeah," I said. "Anthony DeSimone." Back in the early '70's I'd gotten Bobby's youngest brother a no-show job on one of my construction sites. I didn't know it at the time, but the Gambinos and the Colombos both had a contract out on Anthony. He ratted some of them out to feds in New York. Tommy now explained to me that he'd lured Anthony DeSimone back to New York under the pretense of a sit-down and whacked him.

"And then a couple years later I had to whack the other one, Tommy," T.A. went on.

"Tommy DeSimone, that fucking nut!" I blurted out. "The real suitcase? The one we met at Bobby's house when we were all playing pinochle, and he started throwing darts at us because he was losing?"

"That's right," T.A. said. "Remember I told you he had a problem with some good people? And he was claiming to be around me? Well, he ended up with a Lucchese crew, Paulie Vario's, and then he whacked a wiseguy in our Family. He whacked Billy Batts. So, Vario and the Luccheses had a sit-down with Neil Dellacroce, and Gallo came to me and told me that I had the contract, because I knew him very well. That fucker John Gotti had me set up to do this. Me and that motherfuckin' Gotti never got along. Batts was part of Gotti's crew, and my *compare* told me Gotti went to the under, to Neil, and said, 'Give this to T.A.' Gotti wanted him nailed as soon as possible. 'Let that bigmouth Agro do it' is how I hear he said it.

"Joey, listen to me, Pippie," he continued. "In this life you do

what you're told. They pick the closest people to whack one another, and if you don't do it it's bye-bye for you. *Capisci?*"

Tommy looked pathetic. We went back to the Tack Room, and Fat Andy gave me his home phone number.

"Call me as soon as you find out about the cop," he said.

But I wasn't paying that much attention. I couldn't take my eyes off Bobby DeSimone. I felt so sorry for the poor bastard.

I had two more Scotches and didn't feel a thing. Fat Andy and T.A. talked as if nothing had ever happened between us. I invited the crew to Don Luigi's the next night for dinner. I would cook. Tommy and Fat Andy wanted to hit Joey's Disco and a few other joints afterward with me and the crew. It was an exercise in muscle flexing.

I decided not to tell the FBI about the conversation in Tommy's room. I wouldn't lie to them. I just wouldn't tell them.

That fuck Gallo is mine, I thought. No one else's but mine.

Poison in the Sauce

"Christ, Larry, I didn't know you and Gunnar worked weekends. Do you get time and a half, or double time?"

I was handing Agent Doss his $400 change from my night at the Dip.

"I have to cook for them tonight," I said, and Larry asked me what kind of cover I needed. None, I told him. We would only be in Don Ritz's. I was safe there.

Tommy showed up at Don Luigi's with Fat Andy and the crew in tow. I looked at DeSimone in a different light now. But Principe and Russo still gave me the creeps. Don Ritz got everyone seated in a private room in the rear of the restaurant, and I headed off to the kitchen to prepare my famous caponata, one of Tommy's favorites. While I was cooking, Don Ritz joined me. He looked nervous.

"Christ, Joe, I can't believe these guys," he stuttered. "They come down here, beat you, leave you for dead, and then they want you to cook for them. I wou—, wou—, wou—, wouldn't do it."

I laughed to myself. Don was a real nice guy. He had a heart of gold and he ran a good restaurant. All he wanted to do in life was make good pizzas.

"Yeah, Don, that's just how they are. I hope they like the capo-

nata, because they didn't like the fettuccine I made. They almost killed me over it."

"I don't know how you can fuck around like that," Don said. "Don't you hate them?"

"Nah. Why should I hate them? By the way, Don, do you have any arsenic? I'm going to kill the whole group."

"Joe, quit fucking around," he said. "I just got this joint. My partner and I stuck a lot of money in here. If you want to whack them, please do it somewhere else."

Don's stuttering became even more pronounced when Bobby DeSimone walked into the kitchen.

"Joey! Joey!" DeSimone said in his fag voice. "I was telling Tommy that you make the best caponata I ever tasted."

"I'm glad you like it, Bobby. But listen, this ain't my joint, so you can't hang around back here. You'll get in the chef's way."

As DeSimone was walking back out, I said loud enough for him to hear, "Don, hand me that shit I wanted to mix into the sauce."

A light bulb went off over Bobby's head. He half turned, looked at me, and continued out.

"Wh—, wh—, why did you say that?" Don asked. "Now he's going to tell them there's poison in the sauce."

"Fuck 'em." I said. "Let them sweat a little."

I spooned the sauce over the perciatelli and told Don to serve it to the crew while I washed up. He brought it out and walked back in smiling three or four minutes later.

"They want you to eat with them," Don said without a stutter. "They're waiting for you before they start."

I walked out of the kitchen with a grin. "C'mon, fellas, dig in."

"After you," Fat Andy insisted. "Here, let me put some on a plate for you, Joe. I mean, after all, you did all the cooking and we want to show our appreciation. Honey? Honey, bring Joe Dogs a nice Scotch. Dewar's, isn't it, Joe?"

Andy filled my dish and told me to dig in while he and the other guys filled their plates. I took a couple of healthy bites and licked my chops. Everyone stared.

"Aren't you guys going to eat?" I asked as I filled my mouth again. They started eating, and the compliments began rolling in.

We got around to discussing Chief Boone Darden and what he could do for the club. Fat Andy and Tommy told me not to let it die. There was, they said, plenty in this for everyone. Tommy gave the waitress a fifty-dollar tip, thanked Don for the drinks, and invited him to go bouncing with us. Don, saying he had to lock up, declined.

We hit a couple of joints and ended up at Joey's Disco. Tommy wanted people to see me with him. The Colombos wouldn't be around anymore. Al Capone got his point across. You can't fuck with the Gambino Family. You can try, but you won't get away with it.

At home that night I lay in bed wondering what to do. I didn't know whether to remain on the Eye's payroll or chase Larry and Gunnar altogether. I definitely wanted to get even with Tommy and Joe Gallo. I didn't care if Tommy had gotten an order from the *consigliere* to kill me. He should have brought it higher, to Neil Dellacroce, or even Paulie Castellano. Gallo was a love-sick old fuck. Castellano would have squashed the contract.

Finally I decided that I couldn't leave the FBI. They'd been good to me. They'd helped me get over the worst part. I'd have to have been a real prick to boot them now. I figured sooner or later it would come down to me pointing my finger at Tommy Agro from the witness box. What the hell, the feds would find me somewhere safe to live.

But what if they couldn't protect me? Guys had gotten whacked in the Witness Protection Program before. I was in limbo. I decided to wait another week before making a decision.

"Your Closest Friend Will Whack You"

Larry and Gunnar came over the next morning. Larry pulled out a Form 302 and told me his West Palm Beach superior had tele-typed a request for more money to their Washington headquarters. They wanted to expand our undercover operation. When I told them about Fat Andy's club idea, and Chief Darden, Larry seemed to get nervous. This was big stuff for two guys operating out of an office in the Florida backwater.

Neither one of them could sit still. Larry, in fact, was running around like a chicken with its head cut off. I liked Larry, and I liked Gunnar. They had become my buddies.

"Joe," Larry said, "if this thing goes all right with headquarters and we start getting into this undercover operation big time, you're going to have to start taping Little Dom Cataldo."

"No, Larry," I told him. "No fucking way. I told you before, and I'll tell you again. Dominick is my friend. I won't record him. Everyone else, yes. But we shook hands on this decision and I want

you to stand by your word. I'll keep mine. Dominick does not go on tape. Not by me, anyway."

"Okay, Joe. That was our agreement. But I think you're making a big mistake. Remember what even Tommy A. said: 'They pick the closest people to whack one another, and if you don't do it it's bye-bye for you.' "

"Dom's not like that," I argued, ruing the day I ever mentioned Tommy's line to the feds. "He's my friend."

"Well, Joe, I believe Tommy A.," Larry said. "But if you're too blind to see, if you can't read the handwriting on the wall, then I feel sorry for you."

What the hell did Agent Larry Doss know? Sure, Dom was a killer. But I didn't want to tape him. I wouldn't tape him. At any rate, I decided to play it by ear for a week or so. But I continued to tape Tommy and about ten days later Larry told me that the Eye had approved money for an undercover sting. The feds wanted me to generate some conversations with Boone Darden.

After a long night of thinking, I came to a decision. I decided to go all the way with the FBI and leave the Mafia for good.

Wired

I'd been working for the feds for two months to the day when I called Police Chief Boone Darden and made my first appointment with him. We set up a meet at Joey's Disco.

I was wearing a Nagra body recorder. It was a rather large, bulky, and out-of-date recorder for an investigation like this. But it was all the West Palm Beach office had. If this was rural Ocala, where they have no organized crime but a lot of horse farmers, then I would have been supplied with the most modern, sophisticated equipment. That was the way the "empty suits" in the Eye worked. They got everything bass-ackward. I was to find out later that both the Manhattan and Brooklyn offices had the same problem. The joke was that the agents on Guam always got the best equipment.

Joey's Disco had a roof deck, and on the afternoon of March 23, 1981, Boone Darden sat up there as if he owned the place. Waitresses hovered about him as he sipped his beer. I extended my hand to shake, and when we clasped, a smile creased his face. I'd palmed three hundred-dollar bills. Talk about coming cheap! Boone took them as if he'd been taking bribes all his life. He probably had.

We made small talk over a couple of dozen clams. Finally I got to the point.

"The boys down south want to get a charter club going up here, Boone. You know, little poker, little blackjack. Bring your own

bottle. Private. But we won't do it unless we're in your good graces. *Capisci?*"

"I understand, Joe. Tell you what, let me think it over for a week. There's an election coming up, you know. City Council. I want to see who's getting in and who's getting out. I don't foresee any problem if one certain friend of mine gets in. And to tell you the truth, this town needs something like that. A little action. And I can help. But give me a week."

"Sure, Boone," I obliged. "You understand that you can earn from this, too. We aren't the type of people who eat alone. You know that, right?"

"Oh yeah, I know," Boone answered. "You're good people, and you and Freddie been friends for a long time. Joe, I'm glad you called. As long as I'm chief I'm sure we can work something out."

After he left I said, for the benefit of the Nagra, "That was Boone Darden." I gave my name, the time, and the date. I had a couple more drinks, paid the check, and left. I saw the agents following me home. Gunnar unhitched the Nagra. Larry took a Form 302. Then they both left.

By April of 1981 the undercover sting was well under way. I had lunch with a Palm Beach county official who offered to help us set up our club. This guy did favors for his friends, and I was now one of them. T.A. was greasing him for a license for an illegal bingo joint, and I was the go-between. He was a typical double-talking politician, and in my opinion the tapes I made of him were worthless. But the FBI liked them. They seemed to get a special hard-on when they thought they could nail a public official.

In the middle of April I took a few days off to visit Nena in Washington, D.C. She had flown there to visit her mom and dad, who worked for a senator. We stayed at her mom's, I cooked several Italian dinners, and her parents seemed to like me.

Back in Florida, I met with Freddie Campo, who was angry with me for approaching Boone without his say-so.

"Boone is with me," Freddie said loudly, and I thought of the

Nagra spinning under my shirt. "He's been with me for a long time. And I'll kill to protect what's mine."

"Okay, Fred, take it easy," I told him. "I meant no harm. He did mention your name, but never said anything about having to get your okay. But look, no problem. I'll tell Fat Andy what you said, and then he'll ask your permission."

After I left Freddie I had to laugh. I couldn't wait to tell Fat Andy. It's too bad I couldn't play him the tape.

The agents met me at my apartment, removed the Nagra, and took down a Form 302.

"You better not tell Fat Andy what Freddie said," Larry warned me after listening to the tape. "We both know Andy will hurt him."

"Fuck him!" I said. "He's standing in our way, so the best way to take care of it is to tell the truth, and whatever happens, happens."

Larry was dubious, but Gunnar agreed. That night I got word to Fat Andy about Freddie.

Throughout the spring of '81 I met every two weeks with Bobby DeSimone to deliver T.A.'s juice payments. Bobby was Tommy's conduit. I was not yet totally back in Tommy's good graces, and if I wanted to talk to T.A., I would have to call Bobby first and tell him to have Agro call me. It was a three-ring circus until sometime in June, when Tommy finally realized that without Joe Dogs he would have nothing going in Florida. Or so I made him think.

At any rate, the day I taped Freddie I met with DeSimone and told him to pass on Freddie's message to Fat Andy.

Bobby must have told the Gambino capo right away, because I got a call that night from Andy instructing me to meet him at the Thunderbird Hotel in North Miami the next night, May first. Larry and Gunnar were nervous. It was the Nagra's—and my—first big test.

"We'll have Miami agents to cover you," Larry instructed. "Your code name will be Bob Jackson. If you have any problem, any at all, try and get to the men's room. An agent will follow you and ask if you're Bob Jackson. If there's a situation, tell him yes. If you're all right, tell him no. *Capisci?*"

"*Capisco,*" I answered. "And, hey, Larry, don't be learning too much Italian. I won't be able to talk about you."

They wired me up, and I drove down I-95 to Miami. Christine Lee's gourmet Chinese restaurant, off the lobby of the Thunderbird, was our meeting spot. I walked in at half past eight. I really didn't feel nervous at all.

Fat Andy was at the bar with Bobby DeSimone and three sluggers from his crew, Joe Blaze, Gerald Alicino, and Frank "Junior" Abbandando. I had a couple of drinks and we all relaxed. After a while, with the music so loud, we moved to a table to eat.

DeSimone, the little big man, was acting like he had a hair up his ass. "Joey, tell Andy what Freddie says to you! Go ahead and tell him, Joey!"

Fat Andy shot a disgusted look at DeSimone.

"Yeah, go ahead, Joe, tell me," he said. "Tell me before Bobby has a stroke."

I related my conversation with Freddie Campo. Fat Andy seemed especially intrigued when I got to the part about Freddie killing to keep what was his.

"I don't fuckin' believe this," Fat Andy finally said. "You mean to tell me that he's telling us that he owns this cop and we have to get *his* permission to talk to this fucking eggplant? Can you believe where this guy's coming from? Okay, Joe, this is what you do: Wait a few days, because I have to go back to New York. Then go to this cocksucker Freddie and tell him I'm coming down to talk to him. Make plans to meet somewhere. Then we'll set him straight."

"But, Andy, he's close to Johnny Irish," I warned. "Johnny's been grooming him."

"I don't give a fuck if he's close to the Pope," he spat out. "I want to hear this cocksucker tell me to my face not to go near *his* cop. Now let's eat. I'm starving."

While we were eating I was so relaxed that I even took my sports jacket off. After dinner I went to the men's room. Joe Blaze followed me in. He had to go, too. I was finished, washing my hands,

when some guy tapped me on the shoulder and said, "Excuse me, but you look like a guy who was my sergeant in the army. His name was Bob Jackson. Is that you, sir?"

I smiled and said, "You know, I was asked that once before. But I'm sorry, it's not me."

Out of nowhere, Joe Blaze piped up with "Yeah, I know the guy he's looking for. Come to think of it, Joe, you do look a lot like him."

Yet again I wondered where the mob gets all their intellectuals.

I had another drink, picked up the tab, and on my way out Fat Andy instructed me to start looking for a site for the club. He was sure, he said, that Boone Darden was going to play ball.

"That Freddie, he's in a lot of trouble," Gunnar said in Italian. We all laughed.

"Where did you learn to speak the Italian?" I asked.

"Larry and I practice it every day. Not bad, huh?"

Actually it wasn't. I definitely was spending too much time with the FBI. Little did I know.

"Joe, the Justice Department prosecutor assigned to our case wants to meet with you," Larry said. "We can have lunch here and talk. What's a good day for you?"

"Sometime next week," I said. "Nena's flying in on May fifth. She's making a service stop."

"Damnit, Joe, I hope she doesn't know what you're doing," he said. "Why does she have to come now?"

"Hey, Larry, I don't mind working with you guys. But my little head don't understand these things. You know what I mean, Sonny Boy?"

They both laughed and left.

Bagging My First Boss

I called Freddie Campo and told him I had to see him. "How about Thursday?" I asked. "Same place and time? *Capisci?*"

"Can't do it," Freddie said. "Not this week or next."

"Hey, Fred, Andy told me to make an appointment with you. What am I supposed to tell him? What, are you a big shot all of a sudden? I need a reason here, Freddie."

"Joe, I got to go to New York with J. from down south here. You know who I mean?" he asked. I did. Johnny Irish. "There's a big important meeting up there. Everybody's going. Everybody in the C. *Famiglia*, right? I'll call you when I get back."

Freddie was trying to impress me with his closeness to the capo Johnny Irish and the Colombo Family. What he didn't realize was that the information he'd given me—after I'd passed it on to the feds—led to the rearrest of the Colombo boss Carmine "the Snake" Persico for parole violation. A warrant was issued on the Snake for attending a Commission meeting at Fred DeChristopher's house on Long Island. Persico ran, but he couldn't hide.

Freddie called on his return, and I asked him how his trip had gone. He didn't want to talk about it and sounded very solemn. Hah!

Operation Home Run

While Freddie was gone, Larry and Gunnar told me that a supervisor from the Eye's Fort Lauderdale office was coming in to oversee our operation. His name was Tony Amoroso, and he gave our sting a name. Operation Home Run. It was an appropriate tag, considering how Agro's sluggers had gotten the whole ball rolling.

Tony came for lunch one day, and I was immediately impressed. He was a good-looking guy, about five eleven and one eighty, and he carried himself with an air that said, Don't fuck with me.

"Tony, it's nice to finally see an Italian." I smiled when I met him. "I thought all the agents were Irish."

"Well, then you'll like me even more after this," Amoroso replied. "Because I'm bringing in an agent from out of state to work with us. He'll be here tomorrow night. Talk to him. Tell him what these guys from New York are like. Be honest with him and, most important, see if you can work with him. I want somebody undercover with you."

I invited everyone back for a veal dinner the next night. The guy Amoroso brought in was an agent named Rossi. He was Italian, all right, but he looked about sixteen years old. He was professional,

and he was anxious, and as we wolfed down our meal I gave him the lay of the land.

"These aren't just kids or bank robbers we're dealing with here," I explained. "They're hardened criminals and killers. If you think for one minute that if they find out you're an FBI agent you're safe, forget it. They'll chop you up and then grind up the parts so no one will ever find you. They'll flush you down the toilet, and your friends here'll be burying an empty casket."

Then I played for Agent Rossi Tommy Agro's infamous "I'll eat your fucking eyes out of your fucking head" tape.

"What's wrong, Agent Rossi, don't you like my veal? You look a little pale. Do you want to lie down?"

Agent Rossi didn't pass the screen test. He'd never be able to hack it. He knew it. We knew it. No hard feelings.

Next up was Agent John "Jack" Bonino out of the Chicago office. He showed up in the beginning of May '81. I prepared veal marsala with a linguine marinara. I also made a nice tomato salad and homemade Italian garlic bread. Larry and Gunnar advised me to drop the flushed-down-the-toilet bit.

"It's unsanitary, Joe," Larry told me. "Tell him instead that they're going to chum him for bait."

John Bonino appeared to be a little more sure of himself, more worldly, than the baby-faced Agent Rossi. He carried himself like he belonged. He ran to over six feet, with a nice trim body. I could see right away that the baby dolls were going to love him.

John seemed to enjoy the meal. He raved over my veal. I warned him about the Gambinos, how they were sure to react when threatened. I explained the dangers of going undercover against the mob. Then I played him Tommy's tape.

After the reel spooled out I looked at John. I was searching for some kind of reaction. There was none.

"You've heard the tape, John," I said. "You see how they are. If you have any questions I'll be glad to answer them the best I know how."

"Well, Joe, there are one or two things I'd like to know," John Bonino said. "If it's not a problem, I'd like to have your recipe for

the veal, and the marinara sauce. I've never tasted better veal marsala."

I looked at Larry and Gunnar and then back to John. "You're going to be just fine," I told him. "We'll get along great."

We finished dinner and shot the shit, and Larry and Gunnar left. John was going to be spending the night at my apartment. John and I drank the same Scotch and smoked the same brand. And to be perfectly honest, he intimidated me a little. Not a lot, but a little, like he had me hoping I'd grow up to be just like him. The ability to act like a wiseguy was in there, you could see that, but you could tell he wasn't programmed for it.

What John possessed wasn't exactly "guts," it was more like "uncommon valor," something the Mafia knew nothing about. It was something I didn't have. Oh sure, I had balls, and I had a feel for the mob. But I always knew their next move. I knew what to expect. Bonino didn't. And that took more courage.

"John, what do you say we go out for a couple drinks? It's never too early to start getting introduced around."

Agent John Bonino and I hit the Yacht Club first, and I introduced him as my partner.

"John and I are starting a private club in Riviera Beach, and I want you to join," I said to anyone we bumped into.

Everyone liked John, especially the ladies. A half-dozen baby dolls must have asked me if the guy was married. My cover story was that he was separated. I didn't know what else to say. John and I had a lot of details to cover. The next day I checked him into the SeaSpray Inn, and the two of us put our heads together about the questions that were bound to arise.

"They'll be curious, John, especially the nobodies," I explained. "The wiseguys won't ask you anything. They'll ask me, though. And then they'll tell some go-fer like Bobby DeSimone to go around my back and casually start up a conversation with you. Our stories better match, and you have to be prepared at all times. The nobodies aren't easy to fool either. Sometimes they're more of a problem

than the wiseguys. And if the nobodies suspect anything, and I mean anything, they'll buzz the wiseguys' ears. *Capisci?*"

"*Hai capito,*" John said.

By mid-June John and I were an item. All the Florida regulars were used to seeing us hang together. We had yet to face the test from New York. One night John and I were sitting in the Top O'Spray lounge when Boone Darden ambled in.

"Give me a couple hundred," I whispered. "And watch this fish."

Boone came over and I introduced the undercover agent as John Marino, an old friend from Chicago. "He's going to be my partner in that club we talked about. Boone, let me buy you a drink."

I tried to slip Boone the hundred-dollar bills. To my surprise he waved them away. "Thanks, Joe, but I can't take the money. You have to check with Freddie first. He don't like me talking to no one but him."

After Boone left, John wondered if he'd spooked the chief.

"Don't think so, John," I said. "We're having a little problem with Freddie. Fat Andy was supposed to straighten him out, but he's been hung up in New York. We're going to have to have a meeting soon, though. It should be all straight by the time you get back from Chicago."

John was scheduled to leave the next day. He was flying back home to pick up his wardrobe, say goodbye to his wife, and establish a phony background—credit, address, former jobs—in case anybody ever got around to checking up on him. He was planning on returning in about two weeks.

"Hurry the fuck back," I told him when we parted.

"Joe, do you always curse like that?" he asked.

"Fuck no!" I responded.

"Johnny Irish Has a Big Problem"

During all our running around I'd met a nice lady, a hairdresser. Believe it or not, our relationship was strictly platonic. She was from Utica, New York, and had been separated from her husband when we first met. But they'd patched things up and were now back together. At any rate, she had introduced me—via telephone—to a friend of hers in Utica named Brooke Johnson. I'd gotten to know Brooke quite well over the phone.

Brooke said she'd like to meet me, and seeing as how I had a little time on my hands with John back in Chicago, I decided to fly up to New York. Surprisingly, even Larry Doss agreed that I owed myself a little "holiday," although he cautioned me that the Eye wasn't going to pick up this tab.

I took a flight to Syracuse. Brooke and my hairdresser friend picked me up and drove me to Utica, and I checked into the Holiday Inn. Ironically, I was to find out later that during my stay I was surveilled by the local feds, who teletyped a bulletin to the West Palm Beach office that a "Joseph 'Joe Dogs' Jannuzzi [sic] has ar-

rived in Utica and we have him under surveillance for a possible drug purchase or sale."

It was a joke. Work with them in Florida, have them try to bust you in New York. I had a tail everywhere I went.

The second night in I called Little Dom, who said he was heading for Lake George, and suggested that I grab my girlfriend and meet him. So Brooke and I, who had hit it off pretty well, drove to the resort hotel in Lake George where Little Dom was staying with his girlfriend Lorraine.

I hadn't seen Dominick for a while, and it was a happy reunion. Brooke raised her eyebrows when Dom pulled out a peanut butter jar filled with cocaine. He drew some lines on a glass table and handed me a straw.

"Nah, Dom, I don't do that stuff. It's bad for your heart, and I have a bum ticker anyway."

So Lorraine snorted some, and Dom snorted some, but Brooke politely declined, explaining that she'd once had a bad experience with the stuff.

"Come on, Joe," Dominick said, looking back and forth between Brooke and me. "The girl probably thinks you're a cop. Here, take a line. Come on."

So I snorted a line. But Brooke still refused. We went to the lounge for a few drinks, and after taking that snort I began to feel nauseated. I excused myself and went to the men's room to up-chuck. When I returned, the girls were gone. Dom said they'd been in the ladies' room for quite a while.

"I bet Lorraine turns her on," he said. But I didn't care one way or the other. It was her nose and her business. To me the stuff was good for one thing: making money.

"Listen, Joe," Dominick said quietly, "I've been meaning to ask you, are you still friendly with that girl Nena, the one whose parents work in Washington?"

I told him we were still friends. "Why?"

"Well, you know I have to go into the can in October." Dom was going in on a weapons charge. "After my kid's wedding. You're coming, aren't you?"

"Yeah. Go on."

"Well, remember you said that Nena's father worked in the Senate Building, for either a senator or a congressman?"

"So?"

"So I was thinking, Joe. Maybe Nena's people got some connections to get me a soft prison, because it's federal time I gotta do."

"Gee, I don't know, Dom. I suppose I can ask."

"Yeah, Joey, ask. And if they can, I'd like to go to Louisville. I think that's the name of the joint. Better yet, Joey, give me a call when you get back down to Florida, and I'll get you the exact name of the prison. It's either Louisville or Allenwood. One of them country clubs. I'll say either number one for Louisville, or number two for Allenwood. Joey, will you remember that?"

"Gee, I don't know, Dom, maybe I should write it down," I said sarcastically. And Dominick told me to go fuck myself before clamming up, because the girls were coming back.

Brooke was talking a mile a minute. She must have taken a hit. Both Dom and Lorraine were laughing at her. While these guys were enjoying their blow I kept wondering if it would be kosher to ask the FBI to do a favor for Dom. They knew how close we were, and I knew Nena's people couldn't help at all. I don't even know where Dom got the idea that they could.

On one of the girls' many trips to the bathroom, Dom leaned across the table and told me a secret. "My friend Johnny Irish has a big problem. He led the FBI from Florida to where the boss was on Long Island. Now the Snake is really pissed off. Johnny's got a big problem, Joey, but don't say nothing to nobody. Fuck him. Just see if you can help me out."

"Who am I going to talk to, Dominick?" I asked. "Irish and his whole crew hate me, thanks to that motherfucker T.A."

Little Dom was saying that Johnny Irish was probably not long for this world. My heart bled.

Brooke and I had a nice time in Lake George. And as we left I told Dom I'd see about that thing. Brooke talked like a jackrabbit all the way back to Utica, and when we got there she fucked like one, too. I really liked her. She was a natural blonde.

The next day my hairdresser friend drove us to the airport, and I kissed both girls goodbye. Then I boarded my plane back to West Palm.

Larry and Gunnar showed up at my apartment early the next morning to ask me if I had a nice time and to tell me how comical it was that the FBI was onto me in Utica.

"They put out on the teletype that you were there to see Joe Falcone," Larry said. Falcone was a button in upstate New York.

"Nah, I didn't go," I told them. "Joe sent word that he wanted to meet with me and invited me to his home. But I knew that I was being watched, and I didn't want to put heat on the guy. I sent word that the next time I'm in town I'd be over."

"You should have gone," Larry said curtly, holding out his empty pad and pen.

"Why, Larry? You told me the Eye wouldn't pay for the trip, anyway. Besides, I was busy with a nice young lady. I wasn't working. But while you got your pad out, write this down. Little Dom told me that Johnny Irish has a problem because you guys pinched the Snake for violating parole. He was consorting, and you know you got him with information that Freddie Campo gave me and that I related to you.

"Remember?" I added with a smirk.

"Where did you see Dominick?" Larry sounded surprised.

I told them about Lake George. And then I asked for a favor.

"It's an unusual favor," I said. "Little Dom's been sentenced. He reports to prison in October, after his son's wedding in August. Dom wants to get into a certain prison. I told him that I'd try. Larry, it will make me look real strong to the whole mob if I can do this. Do you think you can try?"

"Where does he want to go?"

"Either Louisville or Allenwood. They're both federal pens."

"No, really, Joe?" Gunnar said with sarcasm. "We didn't know that."

"Let me talk to Tony Amoroso," Larry said. "It's up to him. I'll

let you know tomorrow. In the meantime, call Dom and ask him which one he prefers. Start generating some calls. Start earning your money."

They both left. And I picked up the phone.

I've Been a Good Boy

"It's number two," said Little Dom. That meant Allenwood.

"I can let you know in a day or so, Dom. I hope I can do something for you."

"I appreciate your trying, Joey," Dominick said and hung up the phone.

Tommy called me that afternoon, wanting to know where I'd been. I figured that this would be as good a time as any to try to get his phone number.

"I went upstate New York."

"How come you didn't get in touch with me?" he asked.

"Because I don't have your phone number. How am I supposed to get in touch with you? I called your manager Bobby's line, and all I got was busy, busy, busy. But I called Little Dom, so I had a nice time with him. He came to Lake George with his girlfriend."

"You should have told Little Dom to reach out for me," Tommy screamed. "He knows how. And Bobby ain't my manager."

"Hey, Tommy, I didn't go to New York to stay on a line making a bunch of phone calls. I went there to have a nice, relaxing time with a young lady. I would have liked to have seen you, and had a nice time with people from my own *Famiglia*. But you're like Ron-

ald Reagan. To get you I got to go through six million channels. *Capisci?*"

"That fuckin' Bobby," T.A. muttered. "His kid is always on the phone. I told him to get two lines."

The thought crossed my mind that maybe now Tommy would kill Bobby, too, going for the DeSimone trifecta.

"Here, take my number," Tommy finally said. "If you have to reach me, call direct. But never talk on my phone. I'll go out and call you back. Do you hear what I said?"

I did. But I wasn't through busting Tommy Agro's horns.

"Maybe you better check with him first," I said. "Or did you do that already?"

"Check with who, Joey?" T.A. said calmly. "What are you talking about? I don't understand what you're saying."

"With Bobby. Maybe you should check with Bobby before giving out your number."

"Hey, Joey, how about I come down there and rip your tongue out of your mouth?" T.A. said before slamming down the phone.

Larry called later that afternoon. His supervisor, Tony Amoroso, had given us the okay. He'd try to get Little Dom into whichever prison he preferred.

"Where does Dominick want to go?" Larry asked.

"To Allenwood."

"That's a real country club, Joe. Mostly for politicians."

"See what you can do, Larry. As T.A. would say, don't let it die. And speaking of that, Tommy called, and finally gave me his home phone number."

"What made him do that?" Larry asked.

"Because I've been a good boy," I said. "He told me I was no longer on probation. I taped the call. You can listen to it."

I was beginning to realize that this job wasn't as easy as it had sounded. In fact, working for the Eye was a nerve-racking experience. Making calls, generating conversations, taping calls, and especially wearing that body recorder to meetings with guys who would sooner whack you than ask your name. It took its toll. Thank God Bonino was joining the operation. I was sure he'd take some of the weight off my shoulders.

Johnny Irish
Is "Gone"

John Bonino returned from Chicago in late June with a lot of luggage. Together we rented him a beautiful apartment on the northern tip of Singer Island, right off Palm Beach. It was on the ninth floor of a lavish condominium. We were now separated by about eighteen miles, but John had done the right thing getting a place close to the mob action. At the time I'd taken my place in the boondocks, I needed to be safe and secure. But now that I was back in the Mafia's good graces I felt abandoned. Yet, I couldn't ask the agents to move me. It was too expensive. Nonetheless, I pouted because John had a nicer pad.

A few days passed as I gave John time to get organized. In the interim I stopped by my hair salon on Singer Island to get a haircut.

I was outside my hairdresser's building, walking to my parking spot, when I spotted the car driving past. Johnny Irish was in the front passenger's seat, Tony Black was sitting behind him, and a knockabout named Skeets was driving. I thought nothing of it at the time.

Later that afternoon John Bonino and I began discussing strategy. The first order of business was getting John some new clothes

and new shoes. He dressed like a cop. I'd been covering for him by telling people that he'd left his wardrobe in Chicago, but now that he was back it was time to drop the Timberland moccasins and Hyde Park Oxford button-downs.

"Fine, Joey, we'll discuss it further tonight. Larry and Gunnar are bringing Tony Amoroso down for some of that fine veal marsala of yours."

"Oh Christ," I said. "I forgot about that. Come on and come shopping with me and we'll talk."

At the supermarket I gave John a few pointers on how to act like a mobster. The don't-fuck-with-me swagger. The jewelry. The moronic stare.

"I don't want to sound pushy," I told him. "It's just that you're a good guy and you're basically here to protect me, and I don't want to get whacked. So if you think I'm overdoing it, tell me, and I'll do it even more. *Capisci?*"

"*Hai capito,*" he answered.

John was smart. He was patient. He paid attention. And most important he took me with a grain of salt. That night I told Tony Amoroso that I'd begun priming the wiseguys for John.

"I've been telling them I have a partner going in with me on the bottle club," I explained. "As far as they know, John's an old babonia partner of mine."

"Huh?" said Amoroso.

"Babonia, drugs," I said. "That's how John supposedly got all this money to invest with me."

"You should have gotten the okay from Tony before you went around with that story," Larry interjected.

"Hey, listen, Larry," I said, a little annoyed. "I talked it over with John. Neither of us could figure a better cover story. All of a sudden John appears with money? It's kind of hard to explain. I just hope the dope story works. Larry, it's John's and my asses hanging out there on the line. Not yours. We need some leeway. We have to make some decisions ourselves. We're out there in the streets! Not you and Gunnar! I mean no disrespect by this, and I don't want you to think that I'm trying to run things. But John's

an agent, he's one of you, and he's capable enough and intelligent enough to make some decisions."

There was a bit of a silence before Tony Amoroso cut the tension. The drug-dealer angle was a good one, okay by him.

"I'm certainly not going to argue with three Eye-talians," Larry said, and we all broke up. The ringing phone quieted us down.

"Hello?" I pushed the "record" button on the nightstand in the bedroom.

"I didn't think you were home. You usually get the phone on the first ring."

It was Dominick. Once I heard his voice I stopped the tape from recording. A mistake.

"Did you find out anything about that thing?" he asked.

"As a matter of fact, Dom, I just got word about twenty minutes ago," I said. "I was going to call you tomorrow. You're going up to where you wanted. Where you said. You know, number two."

"You sure, Joey? You sure?" Little Dom couldn't believe his good fortune. "That's great, buddy. Are you really sure?"

"Yeah, yeah, I'm sure, Dom. You'll get your confirmation in the mail, sometime in July."

"You gave them my address, Joey?" He was always suspicious.

"No, Dom, I didn't give them your address. But I'm sure they already got it. They sentenced you, didn't they?"

"Oh yeah, sure, Joey. I wasn't thinking. You got me all excited. Thanks a million, Joey. I owe you one."

We continued to small-talk, with Dom telling me to expect an invitation in the mail to his son's wedding. Then out of nowhere he asked cryptically, "My friend Johnny, down south there, you know who I mean?"

He meant Johnny Irish. "What about him?"

"He's gone, Joey. Gone."

"Are you kidding me, Dominick?"

"Hey, Joey! Would I kid about something like that? My *compare,* you know, Donny, he told me about six o'clock tonight that he was gone." Dominic "Donny Shacks" Montemarano had taken over Little Dom's crew after Allie LaMonte died in '79.

"Dom, he's got to be mistaken," I said. "I saw him with Tony Black and Skeets driving around Singer Island late this afternoon, about four o'clock."

"Hey, Joe, what the fuck is wrong with you?" Dom said. "I don't give a fuck if you saw him at five-thirty. He's gone. *Capisci?*"

"Look for that prison confirmation." I hung up.

I walked back into the dining room, and Tony immediately mentioned that I looked a little pale.

"That was Dominick Cataldo," I said soberly. "He called to tell me Johnny Irish is dead. He got whacked this afternoon."

Larry jumped in. "I thought you told me you saw Irish with Tony Black this afternoon."

"Yeah, I saw him," I said. "With a guy named Skeets, too. It must have happened after that. Dom told me all about this in Lake George, and I told you. You have it all in that Form 302, if you bothered to write it down."

"I don't imagine that you taped Little Dom?" Gunnar asked. "Did you?"

"Nah, goddamnit, that's why I'm pissed off. I should have taped him, just to let you hear it."

"That's evidence out the window, Joe," Larry said. "You know that, though. Well, I'm not going to preach to you. You know how I've felt about taping Little Dom. We had one argument about it. I don't want another."

Once again, I found myself in the middle of an unsolved murder beef. Like Stanley Gerstenfeld's, nobody was ever indicted for whacking Johnny Irish.

"Did you tell Dom he was going to Allenwood, Joe?" Tony Amoroso asked.

"Yeah, I told him. He was real happy. He must have thanked me a dozen times. He also told me he's sending me an invitation to his son Sammy's wedding August eighth."

"That could be dangerous, Joe," Larry said. "Doesn't Tommy have some kind of affair coming up around then, too?"

"His daughter's wedding. That's the end of July," I told the four agents. "T.A. hinted around that he wanted me up there, but I don't think I'm going to that one. If he sends me an invitation, I'll send a

gift. But I'd like to go to Dominick's. There'll be a bunch of heavy hitters there, and I'm sure that getting him into Allenwood is going to make me a big man with them."

"Why don't you bring John with you?" Tony suggested. "I'd like for him to get to know some of the wiseguys."

"I don't know. It might look strange." The thought of bringing a stranger to a mob wedding didn't thrill me. "I don't think I can take him to the reception, but maybe I can angle a way for him to hang out with me before and after the wedding. John and I can figure out what to tell Agro and Little Dom, I suppose. What do you think, John?"

John, who had been sitting quietly and listening throughout this whole discussion, responded by walking across my living room and picking a daisy out of a vase. One by one he pulled the petals from the flower. "Eenie, meenie, miney, moe . . ." When he'd pulled the last, he said, "That settles it. I go."

"Goddamnit," Larry exclaimed. "I just don't get it with you Eye-talians. Give me another Dewar's."

Over coffee and dessert everyone agreed that John needed new clothes to fit his new role. Larry advised John to follow my leads, but also to use his own judgment in a pinch. "And if Joe gets out of hand," Larry added, "shoot him."

Later that night I met Freddie Campo for drinks. I wanted to see if there would be any discussion about Johnny Irish. But no one mentioned the late Colombo capo. Freddie did, however, tell me that he'd ordered Chief Boone Darden to do whatever he could for our private bottle club.

"Maybe I can buy in for a piece of the action?" he added.

"Fine with me, Fred," I told him. "I'll mention it to Fat Andy. I know he still wants to sit down and talk with you. I'll tell him that you're here trying to help us."

"Good, Joe, good. But listen to me, I told Boone to help you. But he has to get my okay first on anything. *Capisci?*"

"Yeah, okay, Fred."

I left, and as I walked to my car I spoke into my stomach. "I just

had a meeting with that banana-nose Fred Campagnuolo, aka Freddie Campo, in the Howard Johnson's lounge in West Palm Beach, Florida. It is June 29, 1981. This is Joseph Roberto Iannuzzi, Junior, signing off."

I always postscripted the Nagra recordings that way. It aggravated Larry Doss a little. That's why I did it.

Meet My New Partner

The following day was payday for Tommy A. It was also time I began figuring a way to get Agent John Bonino, code-named John Marino, into the middle of things. So I called Bobby DeSimone and told him my car wasn't working.

"It's in the garage, Bobby. I'll mail you the juice."

"But, Joey, Joey, that will take three days and Tommy needs the money now," he whined. "And what if it gets lost in the mail. I don't trust the mail. How about that partner of yours? Can't he drive you here?"

It didn't take a rocket scientist to bait Bobby DeSimone.

"I don't know, Bobby," I said. "I'll ask him. But I hate to take advantage of his good nature."

An hour later I called Bobby back and told him we'd see him at two the next afternoon, July first.

I told John to wait in the car as we pulled up to Bobby DeSimone's house in Hollywood. It would look suspicious if I handed Bobby the money in front of a stranger, new partner or not. "Let Bobby invite you in."

Once inside, I handed over T.A.'s vigorish and gave Bobby a progress report on the club.

"John's rented a building," I told him. "It's a nice place, but it needs some fixing up. There's plenty of parking and everything. It's two stories, so we have the gambling upstairs and the bar downstairs. You'll like it, Bobby. Wait till you see the joint."

"I gotta be honest with you, Joey," Bobby said. "I called Tommy in New York and told him about you and your new partner being all kinds of pals all of a sudden. And he didn't like it too much. He told me to be careful."

"Hey, Bobby, you're the one who asked if John could bring me here," I reminded him. "I didn't ask you. And he don't know from Adam what I'm doing here. He doesn't ask questions."

"How long you known this guy, Joey?" Bobby asked. "We've known you for ten years and you've never even mentioned his name before. All of a sudden, boom, he's everywhere. It don't smell good."

"Look, Bob, I have to eat, all right? I owe that animal in New York a bunch of money and he wants his juice every week. Where the fuck do you think I'm getting this dough? John's indebted to me, he has a lot of bread, and he wants to be close to me. Besides, he's got very good babonia connections. As far as anything else goes, forget it. You and Tommy and Fat Andy don't ever have to meet with him. In fact, why don't you call Fat Andy right now and tell him about your suspicions. And while you're at it, you can tell him to forget about the club.

"Those guys want everything for nothing, and then they want to question my judgment, too? Fuhgedaboudit. I'll do my own thing. I'll pay Tommy off and do whatever the hell I want to do. So long, Bobby. I'll be in touch."

I made it as far as the kitchen door.

"Joey, Joey, wait a minute. Let me at least meet the guy."

"Fuck no!" I exploded. "I don't want you to get diarrhea and shit all over the house after we're gone. Just deliver my messages. I'll tell John to cancel the lease. The poor guy's been sitting out there in the heat all this time. You have no class, Bobby. You should have invited him in."

With that, Bobby went to his front door and yelled for John to come in. He introduced himself. "My friends call me Skinny Bobby, and you have that privilege. I didn't know you were sitting out there. Joe should have invited you in. He's got no class."

Bobby was smiling. Like I said, it didn't take a rocket scientist.

John immediately won Bobby over with his charisma. I was astonished. John didn't come on strong, but he played his role perfectly. When Bobby would ask him a question about, say, something to do with the club, John would inevitably begin his response with "Whatever Joe says, I'm behind him one hundred percent."

On the ride back north I congratulated John and described at least one end of the conversation I was sure was taking place as we drove.

"I can hear Bobby on the phone," I said. "He'll be all excited, saying, 'Tommy! Tommy! I checked him out. He's a nice guy. And Joe didn't even want to introduce me to him. Wanted to keep him in the car.' Et cetera.

"Okay, John, now we've gotten a mope to run with the hook. Next we do nothing and let them come to us."

John and I had bought a lot of nice clothes, but we still needed shoes. On the way home from DeSimone's we stopped in the Bally's at Boca Raton. I purchased three pair, black, brown, and blue. John bought two pair. The shoes were on sale, yet the bill still came to over $900. When we told Amoroso he nearly swallowed his coffee cup.

"Jesus Christ, the pencil pushers in accounting will have heart attacks when they see this bill," he kind of sputtered. "And you say they were on sale? No one in the Bureau spends this much on shoes in a lifetime."

"Fuck 'em if they can't take a joke, Tony," I said. "What do they think, it's easy out there?"

Larry Doss, always on my case about my filthy mouth, could stand it no longer. "Joe, the way you talk is just terrible. And while we're on the subject, you have to stop using the word 'nigger' over

the phone. They're going to be playing those tapes in court, and the prosecutor we drew on this case is a black man. How is it going to look? You'll embarrass him."

Tony Amoroso rode to my defense. "Leave him alone, Larry. If Joe wasn't the way he is, we wouldn't have a case going. He wouldn't know these guys if he was an altar boy."

.

"We'll Blind Them with Greed"

Throughout July of '81 I reached out for Tommy Agro several times. He always called right back. Bobby DeSimone and I were on the phone every day. I made calls to Freddie Campo, as well as to Chief Boone Darden. I was generating a lot of conversation. I was —as I reminded Agent Larry Doss—earning my money. I had to get all the players to start talking to each other. I was on a roll. Now was not the time to stop.

In fact, things were moving faster than I'd expected.

In mid-July John took another ride with me to DeSimone's juice bar. Dumb, gullible Bobby had actually suggested I bring him along. While we were there, Bobby cleared the way for John to meet Fat Andy. We were to gather the following night at the West Palm Howard Johnson's, and from there John was to show the Gambino capo the spot he'd selected for our club. We needed Fat Andy's approval before signing the lease.

The next evening I introduced "John Marino," my old babonia partner, to Fat Andy Ruggiano and his slugger, Joe Blaze. Bobby

beamed at the far end of the booth as John gave Andy the cover story we'd concocted. He told him that the drug business was getting dangerous, what with all the crazy Colombians running around with automatics, and the nightclub business was something he'd always had a hankering for.

"If Joey here can get that police chief for you to watch out for the gambling end upstairs, I'm really just interested in the nightclub side of it," John said. "I have a lot of good ideas, and if you like them, Andy, I'll put one hundred percent effort into it. But I want to hear your opinions, your ideas, too. And if you don't like the place, Joe and I will look elsewhere."

"Let's go see it," Fat Andy grunted.

The site was only a few miles away, and on the drive, with Fat Andy, Bobby, and Joe Blaze following, John asked me how he'd played.

"Everything went fine, John. Fat Andy's a naturally cautious guy. But we got that lob Bobby on our side now. Unbeknownst to him, he's working for us. I'll bet he's singing your praises back there right now."

John wasn't quite convinced. "I don't know, Joe. Andy seemed awful quiet. Do you think maybe he's uncomfortable?"

"Nah, Andy is basically a quiet person," I said. "Not a bigmouth like Agro. But he's sharp. And he's notorious. But if Fat Andy likes you, he'll go to the wall for you. Just keep charming him, John. We'll blind them with greed, the cocksuckers."

Fat Andy was impressed with the size of the building we'd chosen in Riviera Beach, the downscale section of Palm Beach County. We talked in detail about where the bar would be, where we'd put the lockers for club members' bottles, how the tables would be set up. A general contractor I'd worked with stopped by and walked Andy through his recommendations. When we got upstairs, Fat Andy was in blue heaven.

"It's going to be beautiful," he gushed. "Here we can keep the gamblers away from the people downstairs in the lounge. No interference."

"I just hope the gamblers don't get too loud and drive away the drinking crowd," John said.

"Don't worry about that," Joe Blaze piped up. "If anybody gets out of hand I'll just take 'em for a ride."

From the empty site we all drove to the Palm Beach Yacht Club to celebrate. Fat Andy, suddenly a casino designer, held forth about where he wanted the blackjack tables, the roulette wheels, how to set up the poker games. I mentioned to Andy that Boone Darden could smooth the building permits right away, as long as we didn't get any interference from Freddie Campo and his *compare,* Johnny Irish. I wanted to see Fat Andy's reaction. He didn't disappoint.

"Johnny Irish won't be any problem," Fat Andy said. "You'll never have to worry about him anymore." Bobby DeSimone sat there smiling and nodding, so I assumed he knew about the whack, too.

From the Yacht Club we drove to Papa Gallo's Restaurant in Palm Beach for a celebratory dinner. While Andy and I discussed paying off Boone Darden, John schmoozed Bobby and Joe Blaze. We had an exceptionally elegant meal before driving back to the Yacht Club for more cocktails.

Fat Andy was loose, having a good time. He talked about T.A. in a positive light and, when talking to me, referred to Agro as "your friend." If the proposal for my formal indoctrination into La Cosa Nostra went through, Agro would thereafter be addressed as "our friend." Such were the idiosyncrasies of life in the Mafia. They could try to whack you one day and propose you for membership the next.

After the crew left, John and I moved to the bar, and he informed me that DeSimone had interrogated him in what we were both sure Bobby assumed was a subtle manner.

"He wanted to know where I was from, how I met Joe Dogs, on and on," John related. "Finally he said to me, 'John, you are with us now. There is nothing in the world that we can't do. You have the strongest group of people around you. In return for this, you never do anything on your own.' Then Bobby began threatening Freddie Campo, and even Don Ritz. Before he left, he gave me his phone number."

"I wonder what he's got against Don Ritz." Christ, the guy'd never hurt a flea. "It must be something I don't know about. But

the bottom line is, Fat Andy likes you, John. He's not one hundred percent convinced, but as far as first meetings go, yours went well. Tommy's going to be the tough one to convince, though.

"And don't sell Bobby DeSimone short either, John," I continued. "I fuck around and call him a fag and a dummy, but he'll whack you in a minute. Oddly enough, I feel sorry for the guy. Agro's always screaming at him. But Bobby can never be made, because of his two brothers. He's treacherous, but I still feel sorry for him."

I hadn't ever told the Eye about Tommy A. whacking Bobby's brothers. The feds knew they were dead, of course, but I'd piqued John's curiosities with my talk of feeling for Bobby, and he tried to press me on it. I told him it was personal and changed the conversation. There was only so much I was going to report to the FBI.

A Mafia Wedding

Over the next several weeks John was busy overseeing the construction of our bottle club. Boone Darden sent a steady stream of building inspectors around, and we dutifully paid them all off.

I spoke on the phone a lot with both Dominick and Tommy. T.A. I taped. Little Dom I didn't. I was trying to get a feeling from them about bringing John to New York for Sammy Cataldo's wedding. I mentioned to Dom that my new partner was flying in with me, because he had to see his *compare* in New Jersey. "While he's in the city you can meet him, Dom. He's a nice guy. You'll like him."

"That's fine with me, Joey," Dominick said. "But I got to tell you, I don't know if your friend will like it."

"I don't give a damn if T.A. likes it or not," I said. "He doesn't have to meet him anyway. And, Dom, you don't have to meet him either. He's just going to Jersey on business, and we're flying together."

"Calm down, Joey," Dom replied. "I don't care. You're my friend. If he's with you, he's welcome in my house. You know that, so stop talking like an asshole."

· · ·

"Joey, I don't understand. Why didn't you give Bobby the two thousand to bring to me. He's on his way here for my daughter's wedding and I want the dough."

It was the last week in July. Tommy Agro was on the line. The FBI had suggested that I mail T.A. a partial payment of the principal he'd shylocked out to me. They wanted the postal receipt for court and trial purposes. Things were coming to a head.

"Listen, Tip. I asked Bobby to stop by my place to pick it up on his way to New York. He didn't want to. He said it was out of the way. I only live one fucking mile off I-Ninety-five. Maybe he's got a problem. He wanted me to tell John to bring it to him, but I don't want John knowing our business. I mean, you never even met the guy. And I'm busy as a bastard with the club, what with meeting with Freddie and the cop and every fucking friend of theirs who's got a hand out. I mean, Tip, I think I'm going to move into a phone booth."

"What do you mean a phone booth, Joey? What are you talking about?"

"That's where Clark Kent goes all the time."

"Clark Kent? Who's he, Joey? I thought we were talking about Bobby."

"Forget it, Tip." I laughed. "I'll wire the money Western Union. And I mailed back your invitation with a gift for your kid. Sorry I couldn't make the wedding." I hung up.

On August 7 John Bonino and I sat in the Palm Beach County Airport waiting to board our flight to New York.

"So, John, did you call your wife and tell her you were going to New York to meet some of the heavy wiseguys?" I asked.

"No. Why? I don't tell my wife anything about what's going on with us. She don't want to know, anyway."

"Well, I was just thinking, John. I have a strong feeling we're going to get whacked. You know how good my hunches are. I'm usually right on the money, and I have a hunch that this is it. I think you should call her and at least say goodbye."

I searched John's face for some kind of reaction to my put-on. I

saw none. He either knew me too well or had stainless steel balls. Probably a little of both.

We flew first class. To the dismay of the FBI, that is the only way I travel. Somewhere into our first hour and first Scotch I asked John to let me see his return ticket. He handed it to me with a puzzled expression. He frowned even more when I removed his ticket from his folder, replaced it with my return ticket, and put his in my breast pocket.

"What are you doing, Joe? Why the switch?"

"Fuhgedaboudit, John."

"No, really, Joe, you don't do things for no reason. What the fuck did you do that for?"

"Hey, John, you cursed! That's not like you."

We went back and forth for almost an hour. By the time we were preparing to land, John was so uncomfortable I had to give him an explanation.

"Look, John, you have your ticket with my luggage receipts and I have yours, right?"

"Right. So what does that mean?"

"It means," I explained, "that in my suitcase there's a loaded thirty-eight. I wasn't coming to New York without a gun. Just in case. But you're an agent. If they find it, you just tell them who you are. If they find it on my ticket, I'm in big, big trouble. *Capisci?*"

"You cocksucker." John smiled. "I'm going to keep that gun and throw it away. You're not coming back with it."

"All right John, keep cursing. You're beginning to sound like me."

After we landed John remembered that he hadn't brought his FBI credentials along on the trip.

"Don't sweat the small stuff, John. They got phones in New York. Just call headquarters."

As it turned out, we picked up the luggage with no problem.

"Joe! Joe Dogs! Over here!"

It was Dominick's brother-in-law Tito. Dom couldn't make it, so he'd sent Tito to pick us up. I made the introductions and the three

of us proceeded to Little Dom's house. On the way, Tito gushed with gratitude about what I'd done to get Dom into Allenwood Federal Penitentiary. The entire *Famiglia*, he said, was in my debt. It made me feel like a million bucks.

Dominick and John got along great. There was no pressure, as I wasn't working Little Dom. This was a pleasure trip. About eight of us went out for a nice Italian dinner, and Dom and John fought over the check. John won, and it annoyed Dom a bit.

"Joey, you shouldn't let your friend do that," he said. "I'm no cheap fuck, Joey! I'm not like your friend and all the bambinos."

"You mean Gambinos," I answered.

"Call them whatever you want," Dom said. "To me, they're the bambinos. We do all their fucking dirty work. Now come on, let me get you guys set up at the Riviera Hotel. And tell your friend John there that if he puts his hand in his pocket one more time I'm going to chop it off."

While we were at the Casbah having a drink, John mentioned that he had to rent a car to drive to New Jersey. Dominick would hear nothing of it. He offered—no, demanded—that John take his.

"Thanks, Dom," John said. "I'll be careful. I haven't had an accident for a week now."

"I don't care if you demolish it," Dom said with a smile. "I'll get another new one the same day."

John and I dropped Dom at home and went back to the Riviera. I warned John not to do any talking in Little Dom's car, as it could be bugged by another agency. John left, and Dom sent a car to pick me up for his son Sammy's reception. It was being held at a joint called Le Mans, in Brooklyn.

I assumed the FBI was covering the affair, taking pictures and whatnot, so when I got out of the car I turned and waved. Dom and a few of the wiseguys standing with him near the entrance started to laugh.

I said a hello to the guys I knew and Dom introduced me to the rest. I handed Little Dom an envelope with a card and five hundred-dollar bills. And then we all headed for the open bars and buffet. Dom, naturally, had done everything up right. There was every-

thing a hungry and thirsty gangster could possibly want. And then some.

I milled around for a while. There must have been over three hundred guests mingling. Then suddenly, a half-hour into the party, I spotted Tony Black and Checko Brown. Skeets was standing behind them. They saw me and snubbed me. I expected that from those guys.

Dominick ambled by, hugged me, and asked if I was having a nice time.

"Yeah, sure, Dom," I replied. "Except I seen that fuckin' Checko and Tony Black over there, and when they saw me they ignored me."

"Oh yeah?" Dom said. "I'll straighten out those punks right away. Joe, I had to invite them because they're from my *Famiglia*. That fuckin' Johnny Irish gave a button to anybody that made him money. But these guys ain't shit. Come on."

I followed Dom across the dance floor, protesting all the way. "Don't say nothing to them, Dom. Don't ruin a nice party. They don't bother me. And I don't like them anyway."

It didn't matter. We were interrupted on our journey by Donny Shacks, Little Dom's capo.

"Donny, this is my friend Joe Dogs," Dom introduced me. "He's the one I told you about. He's responsible for getting me into Allenwood."

"Joe, all of us really appreciate what you did for Dominick," Donny Shacks said. "If there's anything I can ever do for you, just get in touch."

Dominick, listening to our conversation, decided that there was something his capo could do for me right now. Nodding toward Tony Black and Checko Brown, he said, "See those two punks over there, Donny? They gave Joe a hard time in Florida, and now they're acting like assholes up here. Go straighten them out for me, okay?"

Before I could react, Donny Shacks was huddled with Checko, Tony, and Skeets. I saw him pointing at me as they nodded their heads up and down. They apparently came to some kind of agree-

ment, the huddle broke, and Checko nearly trotted my way. "Joe Dogs!" he yelped, embracing me in a bear hug and kissing both my cheeks.

"I didn't know you were here," Checko continued. "We could have flown in together. That was a wonderful thing you did for Dominick. Come down to Miami once in a while."

Tony Black said basically the same thing, and I was elated. This cleared the way from any interference in our club from down south.

After the reception, Dom and I drove his wife, Clair, home and went on to the Casbah for reception number two. Just the guys. Oh, there were girls, but they weren't wives.

At one point Little Dom left to call home, and when he returned he thanked me profusely for the gift to his son and new daughter-in-law.

"You're welcome, Dom," I said. "The kids can use it. They're just starting out." Just then a sight at the bar caught my eye. "*Marrone,* there's three *melanzanes* over there with two white broads!"

"This *is* New York, Joe," Dom answered. "But I still don't like those fucking eggplants coming around here. It started about two years ago. First there was one. Then another. Before you knew it, the place was overflowing with niggers. The white people were afraid to come in.

"So you know what happened, Joe? One day they found a dead eggplant in the lot next door. Then a couple of days later they found two more. They got the message, the black bastards. But I guess these two don't have Western Union.

"Petey!" Dom yelled to one of his sluggers. "Do me a favor and go and tell those bastards to get the fuck out of here. Them and the two tramps with them. Tell them it's a private party. Tell the bartender I'll chop his arm off if he gives them another drink."

I watched Petey grab another gorilla and saunter toward the bar, his arms waving and his fingers pointing to our table. The black party with the white ladies smiled nervously and left.

"Thanks, Petey. What did you tell them?"

"Aw, nuthin'. Just that if they didn't get the fuck out we was gonna have charcoaled niggers for brunch tomorrow. Big Jake there

insisted they finish their drinks. But for some reason they didn't want to."

Soon after, John walked in. It was about two in the morning. Dom ordered the bartender to fix him a drink, but John demurred and offered to buy the entire party a round.

"No can do, John," I told him. "Dom will take care of it."

John smiled. "Just like Chicago," he said, then turned toward Dominick. "Dominick, I sideswiped a car in Jersey and took off. I don't know if they got your plate number."

"No matter, John," Little Dom replied. "That plate will only come back to some dead guy. As long as you didn't get hurt."

"I'm only kidding." John smiled.

"I know, John," Dom said. "I wasn't made with a finger, you know?"

We kept drinking, the place was packed, and Dom caught me yawning at about four in the morning. So he dragged me into the men's room and shoved a teaspoon half filled with cocaine under my nose. I was in no mood to argue. I snorted the spoon's worth, and it did wake me up.

"Go out there and tell John to come in and take a hit," Dom said. "This is good shit."

"I don't know if he does it, but I'll ask."

Out in the lounge I relayed Dom's request to quick-thinking John.

"Tell him I already snorted a couple grams and I'm coked out," he said. "In fact, I'm going to bed. But I want to say goodnight to Dom first."

I told Dom, who approached John and seemed surprised when the agent handed him an envelope. "Here, Dom," John said. "This is for Sammy and his wife." There were two hundred-dollar bills in the card.

"This isn't necessary, John. You don't even know us," Little Dom protested.

"That's all right, Dom," John said. "Whoever's a friend of Joe's is a friend of mine. *Capisci?*"

What a sweet move that was. John retired to our suite—Dom

had gotten it for us—and Dominick questioned me about him a little. He seemed satisfied with the answers I gave him. But Dom mentioned that word on the street was that Tommy A. was concerned about the new guy I was bringing around.

"Dominick, did John seem nosy or pushy to you?" I protested. "Tell me one thing about him that you didn't like."

"What's not to like, Joe?" Dom answered, shrugging his shoulders. "But that's me. Tommy's paranoid, because of what he did to you. He told me that his kid Bobby DeSimone and even Fat Andy both thought John was all right. But you have to answer to Tommy, not to me."

The party broke up at five in the morning. Not used to the babonia, I was wired to the gills. Not feeling sleepy, I decided to break balls. I grabbed the house phone and dialed our suite.

"John? It's me. Joe. Come down to the lounge! It's an emergency!" I hung up.

A minute later John came barreling into the bar. His hair was mussed, his shirt was unbuttoned, and he was carrying his shoes and socks in his hand.

"John, have a drink," I said.

"What's the emergency, Joe? What's wrong?"

"Nothing. I'm just lonesome. Sit down. Let's talk."

John cursed me up and down. Then he settled onto a stool and ordered coffee with a Scotch chaser. We stayed awake all night, talking, until I was interrupted early in the morning by a call from Tommy Agro. "Come to my house, Joey," T.A. commanded. "And don't bring that guy you call your partner. Come alone."

"He's Going Bye-Bye"

I got to T.A.'s Kew Gardens mansion and was shown into the living room by one of Tommy's geisha girls. Tommy's wife, Marian, was now his ex-wife, and Tommy kept the house stocked with exotic broads. Although I'd only had time for a shower and shave, I felt fairly revived. When T.A. met me we kissed and embraced. Together we moved out to his veranda.

"Here's twelve hundred for four weeks, Tip," I said, handing him his juice. "I know the last week isn't due yet. But I'm here already, so take it."

"Yeah, thanks, Joey," Tommy said. Then he got right to the point. Tommy Agro was not as dumb as he looked. "Listen, who's this guy you brought up here with you?"

"He's a good friend. His name is John Marino. He's from Chicago. And I know him longer than I know you. What's on your mind, Tip?"

"What's on my mind is you're sure he's all right? I mean, you don't have any illusions that you think you can bring a cop in and try to infiltrate us, do you?"

"Look, Tom, in all due respect, I didn't come here to be insulted. I told you who he was. If you'd like to check him out, be my guest.

It would give me great pleasure to get an apology from you. John is my partner for babonia. I earn off the guy. He's indebted to me for something I did for him back in seventy-seven and seventy-eight."

"Oh yeah?" Tommy probed. "And what was it exactly that made you such a big shot with him?"

"Hey, Tip, are you kidding me? What are you, wired? Is this placed bugged? Does Macy's tell Gimbels? You should know better than to ask me something personal like that."

T.A. smiled. He knew I was right. "So this guy's your dope partner, huh? Well, let me tell you something, and I'm only going to tell you once. The boss, Paulie, he's put out the word. No more drugs. He just had three made guys from Neil's side of the *Famiglia* whacked for dealing in that shit. They were all with that cocksucker Gotti's crew.

"So, Pippie, don't make me have to tell you again. No more! Understand? Find some other way to earn. And if that guy John continues to do it, you're going to have to answer for him. So tell him, '*Finito!*' *Capisci?* Don't let me find out different."

"Shit, Tip, and I was just starting to get back on my feet," I said, adopting a conciliatory tone. "Listen, if you want me to chase John, I will. He'll understand. The only thing is, though, we're building the club and he's putting up all of the cash only because he wants to be close to me. He kind of worships me, like the way I kind of did when I first met you. But if you want me to chase him, Tip, I will, because I'm with you."

"Nah, you don't have to chase him," Tommy said. "But don't bring him around me. I don't want to meet him. Fat Andy likes him. That's fine. Put him with Andy. But you belong here. *Capisci?* You aren't going anywhere. But tell that guy if he fucks with drugs, he's going bye-bye and you're the one who's gonna send him off. Are you listening to me, Joey?"

"Yeah, Tip, yeah. John'll do whatever I tell him. Now listen, I don't know if Little Dom told you, and I didn't want to discuss it over the phone, but I got him into Allenwood. He got his confirmation the other day."

"That's very good, Joey," Tommy said in a tone that let me know

he already knew. "Dom's a friend of mine, even though he's over there. I'm glad you could help him out."

We spoke for ten more minutes and then Tommy had his driver take me back to the hotel. I was dead tired now, but we had a flight to catch. John dragged me to the airport, and a couple of Scotches pulled me through. I even made a dinner date with the first class flight attendant. What the hell? You only live once.

A Prison Travel Agent

The FBI was happy with the way things were going. Larry and Gunnar had rented a safe house in West Palm, and we used it to plot our strategy. John was working hard setting up the club, although I never really showed my appreciation to him, because I was beginning to feel that I was in over my head. I didn't want to keep working with the feds, but there was no way to get out of it. I was locked in. I'd made my own bed, and now I had to sleep in it. It was a fitful time.

Fat Andy had finally had his sit-down with Freddie Campo, and he'd made Freddie understand in no uncertain terms that the cop Boone Darden was to cooperate with us in any manner we wanted. The highlights of August and September 1981 were another meeting between Freddie and me and a sit-down I attended with Police Chief Darden. Dominick called constantly, thanking me for his prison assignment.

"I'm having a going-away party October first," Dominick told me. "Why don't you try and fly in?"

I told him I'd see if I could arrange it, but the feds vetoed the idea unless John could tag along. That was impossible. One coincidental trip had been feasible. But a second was out of the question. It

would arouse too much suspicion. I couldn't make Tony Amoroso understand that.

"Tony, this isn't ABSCAM, where you're dealing with a bunch of political fags," I argued. "These are wiseguys. They use real bullets in their guns. We're talking organized crime!"

I embarrassed him and pissed him off, but I didn't care. Most of the shots Tony called were straight and true. This would have been a bad one. Not everyone's perfect. I told Dom I couldn't make it.

On October 1, the night of Dom's party in New York, John and I were in Palm Beach meeting with Bobby DeSimone and my "friend," the Palm Beach county official. We talked about getting an illegal bingo operation going. My friend never committed himself, and DeSimone finally scared him away by mentioning that his kid was doing a stretch for possession. The guy didn't like the word "drugs."

Later that night, as I was unhooking my Nagra, the phone rang.

"Joey, you got my money, you hump?"

I just loved Tommy Agro's sophisticated sense of humor.

"Nah." I laughed. "I'm broke."

"Listen, that's not why I called," Tommy continued. "You know that thing you did for Little Dom?"

"Yeah?"

"Well, I got this friend of mine that I want you to do the same thing for him."

"Who?" I asked.

"Never mind who, Joey. Just do it. Dom's going to call you tomorrow and he'll explain to you. He'll call you from outside, and then you go outside and call him back. *Capisci?* You talk pay phone to pay phone."

"Who is this thing for, Tom?" I was insistent.

"It's someone very close to me," Tommy said. "Dominick will explain everything tomorrow. Don't talk about it now. He'll call by two in the afternoon."

"How come you're not at Dom's party?" I asked.

"I am, I'm here, that's where I'm calling you from," T.A. said.

"Let me go now. But, Joey, make this thing your number-one priority. Do this before you do anything else. It's important."

I had to hurry myself. I was late for an appointment at the Yacht Club with Freddie Campo. I was doing about forty-five, fifty miles per hour in my Lincoln when the Chevrolet ran the stop sign. I smashed into its passenger side. The Chevy flipped up into the air. My Lincoln was like a tank. At the hospital, I was interviewed by a cop and released. I didn't have time to stay in the hospital. It was too bad. I could have made a bundle off that accident.

Freddie was gone by the time I reached the Yacht Club. My daughter Sheryl picked me up and took me home.

The next morning I told Larry about the call from T.A., and he reported it to Amoroso. Later that day Tony himself called, ordering me to tape Dominick.

"You've got to do it, Joe," he said. "He's the one who got himself involved with Agro. We'll just see what they have to say."

I told him I'd do it just to get him off my back. But in truth I had to think about this.

By three o'clock, when I hadn't heard from Dom, I called him myself. I woke him up, and he wouldn't talk over his phone. He wouldn't talk over mine either. He was too hung over, at any rate, and when I told him about my accident we decided to speak the next day. I had to get a portable tape recorder from the Eye.

The following morning Larry arrived with the portable recorder, and I went to the pool area of my complex, where there was a pay phone. There was no one around, so I didn't have any trouble. I'd decided to tape Little Dom.

Dominick told me that the Colombo *Famiglia* boss, Carmine "the Snake" Persico, was currently being held in the MCC, the Manhattan Correctional Center, and he wanted to either remain there or be transferred to the Danbury, Connecticut, prison.

"He wants to stay near New York so he can run the Family," Dom said, referring to Persico throughout our conversation only as the *Serpente*. "He's going to be moved, and he doesn't want to go far. If you do this, Joey, you can write your own ticket."

"I'll see what I can do, Dom, but this one's going to cost you.

Yours was a return favor. I'd done something hard for that politician, and he owed me. But the next one's not free."

"Don't worry about the money, Joey. They got barrels of it. There won't be a problem. Just do it," he said and hung up.

I gave the tape recorder to Larry. He turned it on, and nothing moved. "Shit," he swore. "I forgot about batteries."

The phone rang at nine in the morning. It was October 8.

"I have a collect call from Dominick Cataldo. Will you accept the charges?"

"Yeah, yeah. Dominick! How are you? How is that Allenwood joint?"

Little Dom proceeded to tell me how elated he was to be there. The atmosphere, he said, was pure country club. And the food was delicious. He wanted to know about that favor for the Snake, and I told him I was flying to Washington the next day to see my connection.

I was following FBI Supervisor Tony Amoroso's orders. Tony had himself flown to Washington that afternoon for instructions. Operation Home Run had become the top priority with the FBI's Organized Crime Division. Or, as Amoroso had put it, "We're playing ball in the major leagues now."

On October 20 Dom again called collect.

"It's going to cost your friend forty large," I told him.

"*Minchia*, Joey, that's a lot of bazookas," he said. "I mean, your connection's not getting him out of jail, you know?"

"Hey, Dom, this is what he asked for. You want me to see if I can chop it for you? You're the one who told me that we're playing the game with barrels of money."

"Yeah, Joey, but it ain't my money," he said.

"Dominick, I mean, am I going deaf here or what? You're the one who said, quote, There won't be a problem, unquote. Remember?"

"Yeah, Joe, I know. But I'm in here. I can't tell those cheap fucks what to do. See if you can chop it in half for me. I'd like to be able to tell my friend Donny that this will cost him twenty dollars."

"Yeah, okay, Dom. Call me tomorrow."

"If I can, Joey. I'm in a prison, you know," he said and hung up.

Not ten minutes later Tommy A. called and I related my conversation with Dom.

"Forty thousand dollars!" he screamed. "What is your friend, crazy? How come it cost so much?"

"Tommy, I don't know. You know that Dom's was a favor. This time the guy wants to get paid or he'll move the Snake somewhere up near the Canadian border. Dom told me at first that money was no problem. Now he wants me to chop it in half. Should I do it, or what?"

"Yeah! Chop! Chop it all. That's a lot of money, Joey. They expect it for nothing, like Dom's. That's what he told them, that it wouldn't cost a dime."

"Well, Tommy, they're wrong. I told Dom up front that it was going to cost. And if he said any different, he's a liar."

"Sure he's a liar," T.A. said. "He's sitting in that country club nice and safe and he don't want to know a fucking thing. He got me involved in this, and now he wipes his hands clean. That little fuck."

While Tommy was bitching I came up with a plan. I decided to throw it out without consulting the feds.

"Listen, Tommy, let me be honest with you," I said. "My guy really only wanted twenty-five large. I added the other fifteen large as I figured we should earn from it, since they're not our *Famiglia*. I was going to give you the fifteen to knock my loan down."

"Hey, Joey, I don't want nothin'. The guy, the *Serpente*, is close to me. So see if you could chop it more. See if you could chop it all."

"Okay, Tip, I'm flying there tomorrow. I'll let you know tomorrow night what my friend says."

After I hung up I sat there wondering what I'd gotten myself into. I mean, who needed all this work? Although I did like the idea of the FBI putting something over on the mob.

"Why Choke the Guy?"

November 10, 1981. The Nagra was digging into my ribs. Bobby DeSimone and I were driving south to Fat Andy's hangout, Christine Lee's restaurant in North Miami. The FBI had come up with a plan to have Fat Andy shylock a loan out to John. More evidence, they said. The net was tightening. I was driving south to negotiate the terms.

"You know, Joey, I knew the next day when Johnny Irish got whacked," DeSimone said. "Tommy told me."

Bobby went on and on, incriminating T.A. as the tape recorder rolled under my silk shirt.

Fat Andy was surprised, maybe a little wary, when we showed up without John. Behind him, standing at the bar, I saw Joe Blaze and Gerry Alicino. I explained that John had had to fly to Chicago, where one of his kids had taken sick. They all passed on condolences. It was good to hear that they liked John.

"So how's the club coming?" Fat Andy asked. "Did you get the permit yet?"

The club this, the club that. It was all these guys ever talked about. Soon they would all be peering out from behind bars at Club Fed.

"Not yet," I answered. "But Boone Darden says next week for sure. Now listen, I got a business proposition for you. I told John that I could get him a shylock loan. He needs it for the club. This way, you can earn, too. But I don't want you to choke the guy."

"How much does he need to finish?"

"I think he could do it for twenty-five large," I said.

"You're standing for the guy, ain't you Joe?" Fat Andy asked. "He's with you, right?"

"Yeah, yeah, I trust him with my life," I answered, turning to DeSimone. "No, Bobby, not with my wife. With my life."

"That's all then," Fat Andy said. "As long as you're speaking for him, he can have the loan. I'll only charge him two points a week. Why choke the guy? Then you got to worry about him paying. Two points is enough. When does he want it?"

"As soon as possible."

"How about if we do it around the middle of next month."

"That's fine," I agreed. "I'll tell him. Let's eat now. I'm hungry."

We had dinner and drinks, and on the ride home Bobby talked and talked. I didn't know how anyone could yap so much.

That November I got the okay from Tony Amoroso to move into the same condominium as John on Singer Island. I rented a two-bedroom on the eleventh floor, facing the ocean. John had spurred his fellow agents, saying he needed me close to him for security reasons. Tony also got headquarters to underwrite surgery on my face. My nose was still all fucked up. On the undercover tapes they could barely make out what I was saying. I sounded like a frog. The nose had to be completely rebuilt.

Dominick called collect the day after my meeting with Fat Andy. I was fast becoming a prison travel agent. Besides the demands from Snake Persico's loyalists, there was Tommy's *compare*, the suave Gambino *consigliere* Joe N. Gallo, who wanted his kid moved to a cushier prison. Joe Gallo, Jr., had been popped in New York selling heroin, and he was doing a tough eight-year stretch in Attica, a state-run hellhole in the boondocks of New York. "I want to get him away from the niggers," Gallo, Senior had been heard to say.

"He got no one to protect him up there." The task had fallen to me.

To this day I think about the irony. Gallo's compassion for his son would set into motion a series of events that brought down the entire hierarchy of the nation's strongest Mafia Family. I would indeed get my revenge on Tommy Agro and Joe N. Gallo.

I told Dom I'd managed to chop the $40,000 "travel fee" in half. "It's the best I can do."

"Okay, give me a couple days," Dom said. "I'll get my brother to go to Donnie and get it."

"Just make sure it gets done," I said. "My connection wants his money, and now I got Tommy's *compare* on my ass, you know, for his kid. I don't want that fuckin' animal T.A. to start on me again. So get it to me as soon as possible and I'll give it to my guy."

"Give me three or four days, four tops," said Dom before he hung up.

"I have a collect call to anyone from Dominick. Will you accept?"

"Yeah, operator." It had been five days since we'd last talked. "Yo, Dom, I haven't heard from your brother yet. My guy wants to get moving soon. What's up?"

"You should be hearing any day now, Joey. Don't worry. I won't let you down. How do you feel? How'd the surgery go?"

"Fine, Dom. I hope I hear from your brother soon, because this connection of mine won't do the thing for Tommy's you-know until we get yours done."

"Yeah, look, Joey, I got to run. My brother will be in touch with you soon."

This was feeling more and more like a runaround.

On November 20 Tommy called to say he'd gone to the Gambino underboss Neil Dellacroce to complain about the Colombos and their delaying tactics. He said he didn't like the fact that they were fucking me around on the money. But I knew that he was only afraid that they'd blow the deal for Gallo's kid.

"We had a sit-down with my *compare* and their under, you know, J., plus the little guy's friend." He meant Joe N. Gallo, Colombo underboss Gennaro "Gerry Lang" Langello, and Little Dom's capo, Dominic "Donny Shacks" Montemarano. "You should get the money the first week of December."

I caught T.A. up with club business. We'd finally, I said, gotten the building permits. And then I warned him that if I didn't get the dough soon, my "connection" was threatening to ship "the Snake" to the moon. Tommy swore it was coming.

Oddly, Boone Darden and Freddie Campo had been no help whatsoever in acquiring the various building permits we needed to get the club moving. That big nose Campo must have told his police chief to back off when it came to the building inspectors. They took our bribes, all right, but in fact it was John who got the permits the old-fashioned way. He applied for them and kept squeezing the bureaucracy.

"My *Compare* Wants This for His Kid"

On December 3 I received a cryptic call from Agro. "Joe, fly in right away. I got to talk to you." He hung up.

After a meeting with the agents, I flew first class to New York while Larry and Gunnar sat back in coach. Tommy picked me up at the airport and threw my luggage in his trunk. I was carrying the Nagra in a briefcase I kept with me. It was rigged so that if I pressed a button near the lock it would begin recording. As we drove to the Riviera Hotel Tommy began talking, and I pressed the button.

"That Johnny Irish got whacked because he brought the FBI to the Commission meeting. That's why he got whacked. Persico got put back in the can because of him." Tommy was trying to show me how subtle he could be. It was warning, a hint, a sniff. I didn't answer.

"Anyway, that's not why I brought you here, to talk about Johnny Irish. I needed to see you because my *compare*, Joe, wants this for his kid," he said, thrusting a piece of notebook paper in my face. "Can you read it?"

"I'll look at it when we get to the hotel. It's too dark in the car. Is this your handwriting?"

"No. It's my *compare*'s. You copy it all down, and then I'll throw his away. It's a list of prisons. Where he wants the kid to go. In order. I don't want you to give your connection anything with my *compare*'s handwriting on it. I don't want to take any chances."

We pulled into the hotel valet and the bellhop began hefting my luggage.

"Joe, why don't you give him that to take to the room?" Tommy lifted his chin toward the briefcase.

"I got some important papers in here," I said. "I want to keep them with me at all times."

We headed for the lounge, and Tommy started in with a Gallo sob story. How the *consigliere* was sick at heart that his kid was trapped in Attica with a bunch of niggers. How he needed to get him out of the state pen and into a federal facility. How I just had to do this for the old man.

After a few minutes I excused myself and went to the men's room. In a stall I copied down all the information on the note, waited a few moments, and flushed the toilet. I put the original in my wallet, and the copy in my jacket pocket. When I returned to the lounge I took the copy out of my pocket and asked, "So this is where he wants the kid to go?"

"Yeah," Tommy said. "Where's the one with his handwriting?"

"Oh, I didn't know you wanted it. I flushed it down the toilet. I'm sorry, Tip."

"You did that?" he said. "That's good, Joey. I was going to do the same thing. Let's have another drink here and then head for the Skyway to eat. We'll call Dom's brother Joey and see if they got the twenty thousand yet."

At the restaurant Tommy told me I looked like a businessman walking around with my attaché case. The next day I met with the FBI agents and told them I was comfortable enough in New York, no one was planning on whacking me. They decided to leave while I stayed on. They took the briefcase and the evidence with them.

"What if Tommy asks you what happened to the attaché case?" Gunnar asked before leaving.

"I'll tell the asshole somebody stole it."

I stayed in New York for two more days. I felt good. I felt like partying. I'd gotten something good on Joe N. Gallo. Finally.

Shylock

"Why do we both have to wear Nagras? Can't just one of us wear it?"

It was the week before Christmas 1981. We were at the safe house in West Palm. Me, John, Larry, Gunnar, and Tony Amoroso, planning our trip to Fat Andy's house to pick up John's $25,000 shylock loan.

"It's because if you and John are separated we'll still get all the conversations." Larry looked like shit.

We drove John's Cadillac south. Larry and Gunnar followed at a distance. I felt like breaking balls.

"John, listen to me. I have this feeling in the pit of my stomach that I don't like. I have a strong feeling that something's wrong. I don't think we should go in there wired like this. They're going to search us and whack us. I think this is it, John."

He looked at me seriously, and I thought I had him. Then John stuck out his hand.

"Well, Joe, then let's shake hands now in case we can't later. It was a nightmare working with you, and I hope I don't have to do it again in a new life, if there is one. I don't think we have to worry, though. Larry and Gunnar will be outside taking pictures."

"But, John, while they're out there we'll be inside getting chopped up for bait."

"I don't care, maybe a mermaid will eat me," he said. "Now shut the fuck up. I'm scared to death. Now are you happy?"

Fat Andy met us in his driveway, surrounded by his crew. I introduced John around to some of his sluggers. Sal Reale was a made member of Fat Andy's gang, and Ronnie "Stone" Pearlman was a rich Jew who was only an associate. Junior Abbandando, who was discounted by the manicurist because he had only nine fingers, was there, and, of course, Bobby DeSimone lurked in the background. Gerry Alicino was in the kitchen cooking.

We all went into his dining room. Gerry was making pasta, and Andy told us there was more than enough to go around. We talked about the club, the different prices for building materials, how John already had the trim done upstairs. Finally Fat Andy and Sal asked me to join them in the bedroom. They wanted to ask me some questions about John.

"Joe, how well do you know this guy John?" Sal Reale began. "We're giving him the loan only because of you. You understand that, don't you? Your friend Tommy said that you're tops with him. So that's why we're doing it." Sal was a rich hump with connections all over New York, especially with the cops. He had all these civilian commendations from the NYPD to prove it. I didn't need his shit.

"Well, if Tommy said all those nice things about me, why are we in here?" I asked. "Did you bring me in here to read me the riot act? I feel insulted, Andy. Look, forget about the loan. I can get it somewhere else. You're still a partner, Andy. See you at the club."

I turned for the door and felt a hand on my shoulder. I almost shit in my pants, and I was sure the rivers of sweat pouring off my body were going to short-circuit the Nagra. It was Fat Andy's paw.

"Joe, don't feel insulted," he said. "Sal didn't mean no harm. He just asked you one little question, that's all. Come on, shake hands, and let's all get something to eat. Give Joe the money, Sal. We only got ten thousand now, but we'll have the other fifteen anytime after next week. I forgot to tell these guys that you needed twenty-five. It's my fault, although they usually have that much on them."

Sal and I shook hands and laughed. "*Marrone,* what a hothead," he said as he tried to hand me the ten large.

"Do me a favor," I said. "Give it to John. It'll make him feel respected if you were to hand it to him and make the arrangements with him about the other fifteen large."

"Okay, Joe."

So Sal walked out and gave John the money. They made plans for the delivery of the balance sometime next month.

On the drive home Larry and Gunnar pulled up abreast of our car, and John waved the $10,000 and flashed a big smile. We arrived at the safe house together, and the FBI agents got down to the tedious task of copying down the serial numbers from each shylocked hundred-dollar bill.

I kidded that at least they hadn't paid us in tens and twenties.

"I Put Three or Four in His Head"

Three days before Christmas Robbie called. He wanted to make plans to meet me at DeCaesar's Restaurant in North Palm Beach to straighten out my football bets for the week. I was splitting a book-making sheet, Freddie Campo was my partner, and Robbie was our writer and collector. My customers would call Robbie, give him the code name "Blue," and he'd take down their bets. If the callers gave him the code name "Red," he knew they were Freddie's clients.

Larry had given Robbie's phone number to a dozen or so FBI agents, who would each call in and tape their conversations. Half would bet one team, say, for a hundred apiece, while the other half would bet the other team for the same amount of money. That way the only thing the feds lost was the 10 percent vigorish on the bet.

I invited John along to meet Robbie at DeCaesar's. I couldn't track down Larry or Gunnar, and my Nagra was on the fritz, so we arranged for John to wear his. On the way to the joint, John told me to try and get Robbie to open up and talk about the murder of Stanley Gerstenfeld three years before.

"I'll do what I can, John. He likes to brag about it anyway. He's an egotistical bastard and he might try and impress you."

Robbie was in a good mood when we met, and after paying me my winnings I sprung for drinks all around. As we were eating and talking I brought up the subject of the late Stanley Gerstenfeld.

"You know, Robbie, Stanley had a hunch that something was wrong, because before he went he kept trying to reach me," I began. "In fact he did reach me and wanted to talk to me, but we never got together. I think he knew what was coming."

"He didn't know a fuckin' thing," Robbie said. "When I put the bag over his head, *then* he knew he was going. I put three or four in his head, and one in his heart so he wouldn't bleed all over the car."

"Oh, does that stop the bleeding?" I asked, playing dumb.

"Yeah, Joey. You're putting me on. You know it does."

This entire conversation took place in front of John, who did the right thing by just sitting there nice and quiet and listening. We got the whole thing down on tape.

During the ride back I mentioned to John that deep down Robbie was nothing less than a maniac. "Did you hear him say he wishes he was Italian?"

"More Italians like him we don't need," John answered. "We need nice quiet ones, like Tommy A."

The holidays arrived and John went home to visit his family in Chicago. I spent Christmas with my daughter Sheryl. John returned January 2, 1982, and the two of us headed out to our hangout, the Palm Beach Yacht Club. Our club was finished and looked absolutely beautiful. Upstairs, the blackjack tables had arrived the previous week. We'd ordered cushioned chairs. The rug was a thick plush. Downstairs, there were lounge tables, a dance floor, and a bandstand, all situated around a mahogany bar. Couches lined the wall. Thick drapes covered the windows.

We discussed sending out opening-night invitations. Our goal was the third week of January. We had yet to receive the building inspector's final certificate of ownership.

Fat Andy called two days later. He had John's $15,000. John and I drove to the safe house to be wired, and I began kidding Larry Doss about his haggard appearance.

"When I first met you, Joe," the FBI agent said, "I didn't smoke, I had no gray hairs, and I only drank once in a blue moon. But since this fuckin' investigation started, I drink excessively, my hair's turning silver, I curse like a motherfucking sailor, and I'm keeping Philip Morris in business."

It was the kind of effect I had on people.

Again Fat Andy met us in his driveway. Sal Reale had the money, all right, and he wanted to meet us at a deserted boathouse across the way from the Castaways Hotel on Collins Avenue in Miami Beach. During the drive I went through my usual ritual of trying to scare John. He told me to go fuck myself.

Everything went smoothly. Sal tried to lay some big-man bullshit on us about John being fortunate to get a special two-point juice rate. And he said that if it took John longer than three months to pay back the principal, the vig would jump to three points a week. John, naturally, agreed, and Sal handed him the $15,000. We left, advising Sal that the club would open January 15, in eleven days.

"Do I Look Like an Agent to You?"

Tommy called early on January 11. He was at the Diplomat, and he wanted me pronto. I told him John and I had a meeting with Fat Andy down that way around noon, so we'd both stop by afterward.

"Don't bring that John around me," Agro warned. "I don't want to meet the guy."

I had to give Agro this: He was the only one out of all the wiseguys we were cornering who smelled a rat.

"Okay, Tip, I'll leave him by Andy's."

But then Fat Andy called. He, too, had made plans to meet with T.A. He wanted us at his house an hour earlier for an update on the club.

I arrived at the safe house late. John was already wired. It would take too long to wire me. We decided to go with just John's Nagra. On the trip to Miami I had an idea, and ordered John to pull over at a pay phone.

"Andy, it's Joe Dogs. Listen, there's been an accident on

I-Ninety-five. The traffic's all backed up, and we're going to be late. Maybe forty-five minutes, an hour, I don't know. We ain't moving."

"That's too late, Joe," Andy said. "You know what you do? Come straight to the Dip. I'll be there with your friend. In the Tack Room."

"Okay, Andy, but Tommy doesn't want me to bring John around him. I got the guy in the car with me. What should I do? Leave him sit in the parking lot?"

"Nah! For what? Just tell Tommy I told you to bring him in. Don't worry about it. I don't know why the guy's so worried."

I skipped back to the car. "Let's go. You're finally going to meet Tommy Agro. At the Dip. But first we have to stop for coffee and kill an hour."

John was amazed. "How the hell did you swing that?" he asked.

"Does Macy's tell Gimbels?" I smiled. Later over coffee I told him how I'd done it.

As we entered the Tack Room, Bobby DeSimone grabbed John and pulled him aside. I kept walking to the table where Tommy and Fat Andy were huddled. The ubiquitous Joe Blaze hovered in the background.

"Hey, Tip," I said as I embraced my *compare*.

Tommy was his usual charming self. "Hey, Joey, I thought I told you not to bring that friend of yours around here."

"Tip, Andy told me it was okay! Ask him."

Fat Andy jumped in. "Tommy, I told Joe Dogs to bring John here. Listen, he's a good guy. You should meet him."

Tommy looked back and forth between us. You could almost hear the gears grinding in his head. I was waiting for smoke to billow from his ears. Finally, "Okay, Andy, if you say he's all right, then that's good enough for me. Bobby's talking to him now. When he gets through, I'll meet him."

I looked from Tommy to Bobby and shook my head. They had to be the two worst actors in the world with this limp-dick, too-much-television, good cop/bad cop routine. I mean, here was Bobby over in the corner throwing questions at John, and Bobby was perhaps the dumbest mobster in the world. Well, maybe not the

308 JOE DOGS—The Life & Crimes of a Mobster

dumbest. If Bobby's IQ was somewhere in the low double digits, you could halve that number for Joe Blaze.

"So what's happening with the club?" Tommy growled, breaking my reverie. "Bobby said you were supposed to have an opening, but you cancelled. That's why I'm down here. I was going to come. But I have to be back by next week."

I explained that we were having trouble getting the final clearance for the certificate of ownership, and that the opening would be pushed back a few weeks. I shrugged. Bobby escorted John over to our table.

"Tommy, what a pleasure it is to finally meet you," John began. More than you know, I thought. "I think it would be easier to meet the President, whatzisname?"

"How the fuck do I know the guy's name?" Tommy said. "Nice to meet you."

John took over the conversation. He had them all gawking as the talk ranged from the club to babonia to Caribbean smuggling routes. If that head of the FBI in Washington, William Webster, could have seen John Bonino that day, he would have been proud as hell of his undercover agent. You'd think these fucking gangsters, made guys at that, were talking to Don Johnson. Mobsters are always measuring themselves against images. Other guys. What they see in the movies. Books (for the few that could read). John measured up. They all wanted to think they were just like him. Crazy and handsome and living outside the law. What morons.

"So, like I was telling Joey, I want to fly back for the opening." T.A.'s forehead was watering his eyebrows again. "I told him I don't have my own plane. It costs money, you know."

"Tommy, don't blame Joe. It's all my fault." John was being solid. "I told him to tell you and Andy the date, but I fucked up. But, Tommy, it won't feel like an opening unless you're there. Please fly in when we do it, and I'll give Joe the money to give to you for your expenses."

That clinched John for Tommy, ever the greedy, egotistical fuck. "Thank you, John," he beamed. "See that, Joey. He got class. He's not like you."

We talked for a while and John gave Fat Andy his vig and Andy returned $200, saying he'd overpaid him. "See how honest we are, John." We stayed another half-hour before leaving.

On the drive back I complimented John on the plane-fare move. Very slick.

"Well, why not let the government bring him back," John joked. "How else we going to get him back here?"

Then John told me that Bobby had asked him for some names from his past, so he could check him out. "They're worried I might be an agent, Joe. Do I look like an agent to you?"

"So what did you tell Bobby?" I asked.

"I gave him a couple of names in Chicago and Indiana to check out. But he's not going to check anything. He's full of shit. And if he does, he'll find all my connections, all right. He'll find them in Boot Hill."

The words conjured an image of the body in the trunk of Little Dom Cataldo's car.

Back at the safe house I was introduced to the new undercover agent. His real name was Richard McKeen, but he was going to go by the name of Richard Bennett, or R.B. He was a tall, string-beany mick, with a head of full, frizzy hair. Our new bartender.

"I'm getting a lot of flak from Tommy and Fat Andy about the club not being open," I told Tony Amoroso. "Can't you push those empty suits in Washington, get them to lean on somebody?"

"It's not the agency holding things up." Amoroso sounded annoyed. "It's a judge. We got to get him to sign the wiretap orders. A Title Three. And stop calling the agents empty suits."

"Well, I'm sending out the invitations for a February seventh opening," John cut in. "I can't keep making excuses, Tony. If we don't have a Title Three by then, fuck it, we're opening anyway."

"Yeah!" I said. "How fuckin' long do we have to wait? You guys were in such a hurry before. For what? To sit with our thumbs up our asses? I did that in the army."

By now Larry had come to the conclusion that I was a hopeless

case. "Hey, R.B.," he said. "I hope you enjoy working with Joe Dogs. He's been driving me up a wall. Look at the wrinkles in my face and the gray hair. I even smoke now."

"You do look different since the last time I seen ya." R.B. kind of reminded me of a woodchuck. There were dead ones all over the roads in South Florida. "In fact, you look better."

"Atta boy, R.B.," I said. "Listen, I know a gardener who will cut your hair and straighten it out for you. I'll take care of you, R.B. You look like a fag. But after I'm through with you, you'll be one of the boys."

R.B. didn't say anything.

"So what did Agro say about that twenty large that Dominick is supposed to come up with to keep the Snake in New York?" Tony Amoroso was getting antsy.

"It's not Dominick, it's the Colombos," I said. "And Tommy said I'm supposed to get it in February."

"If we don't get it by February fifteenth, I'll have your pal moved out of that country club."

"Yeah, good." Fuck Dom. "I don't give a fuck. Then maybe the Colombos will finally do something. *Capisci?*"

R.B., sitting in a corner, didn't have a clue as to what we were talking about. John explained to him that I was currently the center of two major investigations for the Eye. The first, Operation Home Run, involved the Gambinos, soldiers like Agro, capos like Fat Andy, and all the way up to the Family's *consigliere,* Mr. Joe N. Gallo himself. The second, John went on, was the Favors Case. That centered on the Colombo Family and went even higher, right up to the head of the *Famiglia,* Carmine "the Snake" Persico.

The new undercover agent, laconic up to this point, allowed some emotion to show on his face. "And Joe Dogs is the key to all this?" he asked, with not a little surprise.

"Who do you think you're working with here, fucko?" I said. "Some gang of West Side micks?"

"Call Tommy tonight and tell him you're flying to Washington

tomorrow," Tony interrupted. "Tell him your connection wants to talk to you about Gallo's kid."

"Oh yeah?" I was skeptical. "Suppose he wants to call me back? Then what? How do I give him a number with a two-oh-two area code?"

"Because you'll be there. Larry made arrangements for you to fly out in the morning. I'm flying up tonight, and I'll pick you up at the airport. From there, after Tommy calls, you fly to New York. I'll tell you tomorrow what to tell Tommy."

"Gesù Cristo!" I said. "How many fucking things do you want me to do? I suppose you want me to wear the Nagra up there, too?"

"No, not this time, Joey," Tony answered. "But this *is* important. The New York office doesn't even know you're doing this, and I can't send Larry or Gunnar. So you're on your own."

I flew to Washington, D.C., the next day, January 12. Tony took me to a hotel and handed me a written sheet of instructions for my conversation with Tommy. He also gave me a portable tape recorder with a half-dozen tapes. I called Agro, gave him my number in the hotel, and had him call me back. When he did, I told him I was having dinner that evening with my Washington prison "connection," and that he should try me back around nine to find out what was going on with Joe Gallo, Jr. The phone rang at nine sharp.

"Tip, let's not take a chance on the phone. Meet me at the Skyway in Queens at nine tomorrow night. I'll grab the shuttle. You're buying dinner. I've got good news for you and your *compare*."

The shuttle landed the next morning and I hailed a cab to the Plaza. Hell, I figured, I may as well stay at the best hotel. The work I was doing for the Eye was dangerous enough to warrant a little luxury. Anyway, the room was only two seventy-five a night. After checking in I took a nap. The phone woke me up. It was Larry Doss.

"How did you know where I was?" I asked suspiciously. "I

didn't tell anybody, and Tony told me the New York office wasn't even aware I was in town."

"Did you really think you could fly to New York without anyone knowing?" Larry asked. "Do you believe we'd do that to you? Listen, Joe, I was just worried about you."

I told the agent I was perfectly capable of taking care of myself. Then I gave him my agenda for the day. Larry made me promise to call him as soon as I returned from my meeting with Tommy A.

"Even if it's after midnight?" I asked.

"Joe, don't any of you Eye-talians unnerstand de Englisha? I said anytime at all, *capisci?* And if you need to reach an agent in an emergency, take this number down. It's the main number in New York. Ask for Andy, and they'll patch you into Agent Andris Kurins. Now go back to sleep."

That night I took a cab to the Skyway. It only cost forty-five bucks. T.A. had already ordered dinner for both of us by the time I arrived. I handed him a slip of paper. "Here's the list my connection told me to give you. He says that within two or three months Gallo's kid will be moved to a federal pen. Hopefully Allenwood. He'll stay there six months, and then he'll be moved somewhere here, to the city, wherever they can find a work-release program. He'll stay there for a year, and then be released altogether. No parole or nothing.

"That's the best my friend could do. These dates and times won't kick in until my friend gets the twenty large, up front. Do you understand this, Tommy?"

"Yeah, that's good, Joey! You know what I'll do? I'll give this to my *compare* and let him decide. He's sick over his kid being in with all them niggers. Now, your guy gave you this paper? This is his handwriting?"

"What, are you wacky, Tom? That's my handwriting. He thinks the same as you. He don't trust no one but me. He's paranoid. Listen, I thought you mentioned Joe Gallo might be here."

"He wanted to come, Joey," Tommy said. "But he's embarrassed because of that thing, you know."

"Oh, you mean a little thing like me getting whacked? Poor guy.

I hate to embarrass him. By the way, Tommy, did you tell Gallo that you told me that it was his idea to make me dead?"

"You crazy, Joey? In fact, he just told me, 'Look at that Joe Dogs, doing all these good things for me after what we almost did to him.' You know, Joey, if this thing happens, you get your thing right away. Your button. You know?"

"Yeah, I hope I get something," I said. "These airplanes and hotels cost a lot of fuckin' money. I don't mind doing it for our *Famiglia*. But the little guy's *Famiglia*! I think the Colombos should come up with the expenses."

We talked for another hour and I caught a cab back to Manhattan. It was midnight when I walked into one of the lounges and ran into one of Tommy's old girlfriends. She was a Penthouse beauty, and she showed me a wonderful time. She told me that Tommy was like Superman in bed. "Faster than a speeding bullet."

I flew back to Florida the next morning and went directly to the safe house, where Larry took a Form 302.

The Opening

The FBI had secured their Title Three. Our opening was set for February 7. I'd been pushing for January 19, the one-year anniversary of the day I was supposed to die. No one else appreciated the irony. John had hired a band and another bartender and a local caterer to lay out hors d'oeuvres. We were slipping into our tuxedos when the phone rang. It was Tony Amoroso.

"Joey, take this address. Meet me there tonight at seven. It's just a few miles west of Fat Andy's house."

"Tony! We're opening tonight at eight! This is all the way down south. What's going on?"

"Just be here, Joe. John can cover for you tonight. So you'll be a few minutes late. And wear a suit and tie. See you then."

What the fuck? I put on a suit and tie and drove south. I arrived at the address around 6:45 P.M. and wound my way through a dozen boxy American-made cars scattered about the driveway and lawn. Safe house, I figured. When I walked in, there were about fifteen agents gathered around a pool table. Tony Amoroso was briefing them. After introductions, Tony turned to me.

"You're just a precaution, Joe, we probably won't even need you. We're going in tonight to bug Fat Andy's house after he leaves for your opening."

The plan was for me and a female agent named Lucy to knock on Fat Andy's door in case he'd left any of his crew behind to guard

the estate. If that was the case, I was to say that my date and I on our way up from Miami had run out of gas, and I needed to borrow twenty dollars to fill up my tank.

"And how many points should I agree to pay on this loan?" I asked Tony, who never seemed to appreciate my humor.

Agents staking out Fat Andy's house called in to say that the Gambino capo was leaving, and fifteen minutes later our federal wagon train rolled.

"No one answers the phone, and we think everyone's gone, but we're not one hundred percent sure." Tony had set up a mini command post in a vacant lot down the street. "So just go up there and knock on the door."

I pulled into Fat Andy's drive and Lucy popped open her purse to show me her thirty-eight. I opened my jacket and showed her mine.

"Joe, you're not supposed to be carrying."

"Honey, when I'm doing agent's work I carry a pistol. *Capisci?* Let's go."

The radio and television were blasting inside, an old Mafia trick. I knocked on the door. I punched the door. I screamed, "It's Joe Dogs," at the top of my lungs. No one was home. We returned to Tony's makeshift command post and I reported that the place was clean.

"Okay, Tony, Lucy here will be back around four in the morning," I said, not letting go of the female agent's hand. "I'll take her back myself."

"Get the fuck out of here, Joe. She ain't one of your bimbos. Come on now, you're already late. Lucy, get in my car."

"Goodbye, darling," I said.

"So long, Joe Dogs," she replied. "And good luck to you, too."

I blasted onto I-95 and sped north at a hundred miles per hour, thinking all the time of an excuse for being late to my own opening. My tux was in the trunk, but my blue suit would have to do. There just wasn't time to change. I looked at the knuckles on my right hand. They were bruised from pounding on Fat Andy's front door.

. . .

We named the joint "Suite 100." I arrived for the opening at nine-thirty, one and a half hours late. The club was packed, wall to wall, the smell of fresh paint and Moroccan leather mixing with booze and sweat. I loved that smell. I made my way through a sea of back pats and cheek pecks until I saw the players, the intellects, sitting at a table in a recessed foyer. Looking grim. They were surrounded by an invisible moat. They'd been waiting for me.

Tommy Agro, Fat Andy Ruggiano, Skinny Bobby DeSimone, and Gerry Alicino stared at me, looking like four bulldogs waiting to be fed.

"So, Joey, where ya been?" Tommy asked. The others stayed silent.

I made a big show of running my left hand over my right fist. John had sidled up beside me.

"Tommy, Tommy, you wouldn't believe what happened. I went to Miami to pick up this baby doll I met on the beach. Tommy, she's gorgeous, twenty-two with a fuckin' body, fuhgedaboudit. You remember, John? Jaclyn's her name. You met her at the Yacht Club two nights ago?"

John nodded.

"So where the fuck is she?" T.A.'s head swiveled. "Bring her in."

"That's why I'm late, Tip. Son of a bitch. Know what happened? I get to her apartment a little late anyway, and we're just getting into my car when her husband pulls in. He starts talking, this and that, yadda-yadda-yadda. Suddenly tears are running down the broad's face. Ruining her mascara. Then this mook jumps onto the hood of my car. So fuck him. I didn't care. I start speeding and he's holding on for dear life.

"So Jaclyn's screaming that I'm gonna kill him. So I slam on the brakes. He falls off. And I got out and hit him. Cut my fuckin' knuckles. She's still screaming bloody murder, so I gave her a boot in the ass, and here I am."

Smiles all around. They bought it. It was their kind of story. I was their kind of guy.

I began mingling. My daughter and son-in-law were there. I

couldn't begin to name all the baby dolls who had come stag. I know I invited at least a dozen myself.

After a few drinks I sat down at Tommy's table and we began talking hush-hush about the favor I was doing for Gallo's kid. Tommy, like the rest of the crew, was drinking heavily. The normally taciturn Fat Andy was even bordering on glib.

"Did Freddie Campo show up?" he asked at one point. "Did you send him an invitation, Joey?"

"Yeah, I sent him one," I answered. "But he sent his right-hand man, the tall guy over there, Lee Lehman, to represent him."

"What is he, a fuckin' Jew?" Fat Andy sneered.

"Nah, he's an Arab, Andy. Nice guy."

"Arab, Jew, they're all the fuckin' same," said the amazing philosopher Fat Andy. "Go tell him we want to talk to him. Better yet, you got an office we could talk to him in?"

Fat Andy and Tommy A. unfolded in unison and headed toward the back room I'd pointed out—Tommy conspicuously ordering Bobby DeSimone to stay put—while I turned in the direction of Lee Lehman.

"What if he doesn't want to come?" I stopped.

Tommy Agro answered. "Then tell him I'll dismember him right here and take him in there chunk by chunk."

Lee Lehman, whose boss had aligned himself with the South Florida Colombos, didn't particularly care for the idea of an office visit to the Gambino delegation.

"Joey, what do they want with me?" he asked weakly. "I haven't done anything. I come here to have a nice time. I don't want to go in there and get hurt."

He's right, I thought. Lee was a nice guy. And he was involved in the simmering Colombo-Gambino dispute over control of South Florida only in the sense that his chicken-shit boss Freddie Campo had sent him here to take the heat.

I gave Lee my personal guarantee that no one would lay a hand on him in my club. It failed to raise Lee's confidence level. It was no secret to anyone what had happened to me at the hands of Tommy Agro. Lee wasn't in the office fifteen seconds before T.A. got right up in his face.

"Where's Freddie? How come he didn't come to my opening? He got an invitation. There's no fuckin' reason that he shouldn't be here."

Tommy's voice increased in volume as he went on.

"That fuckin' Freddie didn't help us with his cop friend. Who the fuck does he think he is? Does he think he owns this territory? Does he think the Colombos do? Where is the cocksucker? He told me to my face not to worry about the cop, who did us absolutely no good. Now where the fuck is he?"

Lee Lehman was ashen. He started to stammer out a reply. "Freddie," Lee said, "just couldn't make it." He meant no disrespect.

"He just couldn't make it," Tommy mimicked him in a high, sing-song voice. "Tell me something, Lee. Can Freddie get us some help in the county sheriff's department? He got an in there?"

Lee answered that Freddie knew no one there.

"Now hold it, Lee," I interrupted. "I promised you that you wouldn't get hurt in here. But if you lie, like you are now, you won't leave this room alive. Now tell them the fuckin' truth."

"Oh yeah." Lee made a big show of scratching his head. "I forgot. He's got a guy in the sheriff's department."

Tommy came around a desk and moved toward Lee. I could sense that he was about to pop him in the face, so I stepped between them. "No, Tommy, no. Don't hurt him. It's the opening. We'll take care of it later."

Tommy backed off. Now it was Fat Andy's turn.

"Listen, whatever the fuck your name is, I don't get as anxious as my friends here." It was the first time I'd ever seen the booze have an effect on the big man. "Freddie sent you here to represent him, so you bring him this message. You tell that cocksucker if he don't want to help us don't try and hurt us. And tell him to take this message wherever the fuck he wants. If he has people to go to, tell him to run to them. Don't walk! Run! Understand?"

"Yes! Yes, sir, Andy. Tommy. Thank you, Joe. Can I leave now?"

"Sure, Lee," Tommy said. "Go have a drink on me and Andy."

Lee left. The three of us talked for a few more minutes before

John knocked on the door and walked in. "Everything all right?" We assured him it was and we all returned to the lounge. As we walked to our table, Tommy passed Lee Lehman holding up a wall.

"Lee, Lee, how are you, old buddy?" he said. "I'm glad to see you're still here."

When we got to our table a pretty broad named Cookie sat on my lap and asked for my phone number.

I gave it to her and chased her.

It was after 2 A.M. by the time people began clearing out. Tommy, showing the effects of the booze, put his arm around John and told him what happened in the office.

"I told Joe to hand Lee a roll of toilet paper so he wouldn't shit his pants all over your brand-new rug." He laughed as we showed him to the door.

The opening had been a success. In more ways than one. Tommy's intimate conversation with John had been a minor miracle and a major breakthrough.

"I just wish we'd had the video already set up," John said. We were hunched over Scotches in the empty lounge. "I know Tony would love to have that scene on tape. Well, soon enough anyway. We're scheduled to wire the room this week."

We opened the club Thursday to Sunday, with live entertainment Friday and Saturday nights. John found the acts. R.B., our kinky-haired undercover nerd, took care of the books as well as tended bar. He was good at both, despite the fact that he had a beer in his hand all the time. But playing a beer-rummy was part of his role. Who would suspect that *this* guy was working for the Eye? R.B. was Larry Doss's protégé. They'd worked some cases together in Philadelphia. And when R.B. was first brought in on Operation Home Run, John and I were considering changing the name to Operation Fuck Up. But all in all, R.B. was all right. He'd give you two fives for a ten.

Aside from R.B., our staff consisted of Gary, our weekend bar-

tender, and Greta and Terry, two foxy-looking waitresses who were friends of the guys in my old crew.

We usually opened the place for business sometime around 11 P.M., and if we had enough customers we'd go straight through till noon. Most nights John and I would both walk in around midnight, just to make an appearance. Then spend the rest of the night and wee hours cruising local joints looking to sign up Suite 100 members.

Aside from the gambling—our blackjack tables came from a local gyp joint the Eye had shut down in Tampa—I suggested to John that we start a little shylock operation on the side. "Just send them to the kitchen" I said, using the mob slang for a shylock's place of business. We had spots for weapons, in case of a stick-up. And we had spots to hide and bury money for the same reason.

The jukebox was loaded with Sinatra records and Italian music. R.B. hectored us for country-western. He spent most of his time fleecing the locals at backgammon while on the job as bartender, and then taking whatever they had left on the golf course. It occurred to me that if you were an FBI agent, golf must be part of your training. I was sure they had courses at Quantico in golfing, fishing, and drinking beer.

At one point I heard rumbles that the guys in my crew wanted to "take care" of R.B. because he was taking all their money. I laid down the law: R.B. was an "untouchable."

"Joey, why don't you get rid of that ugly Irisher bastard?" Don Ritz asked me. "Get an Italian guy in there. One of us."

When Tommy met R.B. he asked me, "Where did you get this stupid-looking fuck? Fat Andy and Skinny Bobby looked at this guy, and they don't know what to think. I'll get you a good Italian guy to tend bar, if you want."

But Tony Amoroso and Larry Doss wouldn't budge. "He stays," they told me in no uncertain terms. So my wiseguy friends were stuck with the hick-looking fed working in their midst.

Little Dom's Contract

"Joey, I'm down here. At the Dip. Bobby's with me. Meet me by the pool. I got to see you about my *compare*'s thing."

It was the second-to-last day of February 1982. T.A. sounded calm.

I phoned Larry Doss, told him Agro was down south. My hunch, I explained, was that T.A. had the money to fix Gallo's kid's prison sentence.

"Well, if he wants to meet you by the pool, you better not wear the Nagra," Larry said. "Call me tonight when you get home, and I'll write out a three-oh-two."

I hung up, but a thought nagged. I knew how important this conversation would be in open court. I decided in the shower that I'd take a chance on the Nagra, poolside or not. When I called back the Eye's offices, neither Larry nor Gunnar were there. John was in Chicago and Tony Amoroso was in Washington, That left only R.B. With some trepidation I called him, and he wired me up.

T.A. and DeSimone were drinking coffee at his cabana when I arrived. Tommy embraced me, and I said hello to Bobby.

"Did you bring the twenty thousand?" I asked.

"No, Joey. It's here, but here's what I want you to do." I smelled

an Agro scam. "My *compare* says the same thing. In fact, it was his idea." Always hiding behind Joe Gallo's skirts. What ever made me think this guy was such a big man?

"Now, Bobby has the money, and he's going to take it and open an escrow account in your name, his name, and John's name. What's his last name anyway?"

"Marino."

"Okay, John Marino. Tell your friend in Washington that the money stays there until the kid is in the third phase of the arrangement. *Capisci?*"

"*Hai capito,*" I answered, ecstatic over how this moron's conversation was going to hang him in court. "Okay, Tip, I'm sure he'll go for that."

"So you just call him up and tell your connection you got the bread," Tommy said. "And everybody's happy."

I stayed there for over an hour with Tommy and Bobby, the Nagra rolling, the two thugs incriminating a lot of people.

"Tommy," I said at one point, "my friend in Washington is having Dominick shipped out any day now to someplace, in his words, 'far away.' There's nothing I can do. He's pissed about not being paid for the Snake staying in New York. He wanted to ship the Snake, too, but I told him it was all Little Dom's fault. That's what you told me to tell him, remember? But I still feel bad. Dominick's my friend."

"You feel bad, Joey? Did you hear that, Bobby? Joey feels bad about his *friend* Little Dom! Do you think I should tell him, Bobby?"

"Yeah, Tommy, I think you should tell him," DeSimone squeaked.

"What? What? Tell me what?"

Tommy started in on one of his slow-voiced rampages. He told me that Little Dom had not only taken credit within his *Famiglia* for his move to the country club, but that he'd also taken credit for the fact the Snake had remained in New York. He'd made it look like he had the connection, not me. Then T.A. stung me with the shocker.

"Little Dom even put a contract out on you, Joey," Tommy said.

"The guy Dom got to whack you came to my people for the okay, and we put a squash on it at a sit-down. So how do you feel about your good friend Little Dom Cataldo now?"

I felt like I was glad that tape was running under my shorts, even though it was breaking my dick. I'd taken to wearing the Nagra in my crotch, because no wiseguy would ever grab you there. I also felt like I should have listened to Larry Doss from the beginning when he urged me to tape Little Dom's calls. I drove home that afternoon shaken. Larry called that night.

"Joey! Joey! How did it go?" Larry was starting to sound more and more like DeSimone every day.

"Okay, Larry. It went good."

"Well, talk to me, so I can write it down."

"Why write it down, Larry? Why not just come over tomorrow and listen to the tape?"

"You wore a Nagra to the pool!" he cried. "Are you crazy?"

"Larry, wait till you hear this one. It's great. We needed this one! I called up that mayonnaise-faced R.B., and he wired me up. I met him at the club."

"See you early tomorrow," Larry said and hung up.

John returned from Chicago in early March, and we set up a plan to lure Police Chief Boone Darden into our net. One night at the club I called Boone and asked him to stop by as John was wiring me up. At ten that night the chief stuck his nose through the door.

"Howya doing, Boone baby?"

"Fine, Joe, fine. I haven't heard from you in a while."

"I know Boone, that's why I called. I got something for you, but let's take a walk in the parking lot where we can be alone."

Outside, I slipped the chief $400 in cash. "This is just in case one of your officers gets overzealous about the gambling upstairs. We open the tables sometime next month. We can't give you no more than a hundred a week until the gambling starts up. Is that okay with you?"

"That's fine, Joe," Boone said. "I know how expensive it is to get a nice place like yours off the ground."

We walked together to Boone's car and I escorted him off. Soon he, too, would be behind bars. A cop in jail has about as much of a social life as a guy with a fistful of fifties in the Women's House of Detention.

The next day John, Bobby, and I drove to Fort Lauderdale to open our escrow account. We did just as Tommy said, putting all three names on the account. T.A. had just buried Bobby along with himself and his *compare* Joe Gallo.

On March 12 Tony Amoroso called from Washington to inform me that Little Dom had just been moved to a tough federal prison in Ashland, Kentucky. I called Tommy A. and relayed the message.

"I expect a call anytime now," I laughed to T.A.

"So you play dumb, that's all," Tommy said. "Make like you don't know nothing. *Capisci?*"

I wasn't off for more than a minute when my phone rang. It was collect, from Dominick. Would I accept?

"Yeah! Dom! How are you? Geez, I haven't heard from you in the longest time."

"They shipped me out, Joey! I'm in fuckin' Kentucky! Your friend should never have did this, Joey. He should have shipped the other guy, not me. I didn't deserve this, Joey. You gotta do something for me quick. There's too many niggers here. I'll die over here, Joey! Please!"

"Hey, Dominick." I was stern. I was taping. "Number one, my friend waited since last November—last year!—and he still hasn't seen a quarter. Your own fuckin' people did this to you, not my friend. You challenged him, and now look where you are. I'm sorry, I can't do anything for you. You gave everyone in my *Famiglia* a bad taste in their mouth for you. *Capisci?*"

Our conversation went on for forty-five minutes. After Dom hung up, I immediately called Tommy to fill him in.

"Good, good, now maybe his people will come up with the ba-

nanas," Tommy gloated. "You didn't tell me nothing. *Capisci,* Joey?"

"Yeah, Tommy," I said. "I never even talked to you." I hung up and laid back in bed and thought about Dominick. So he put a contract out on me, huh? Now he wants a favor? Fuck the motherfucker!

This Joint
Is Kosher

The investigation was now hurtling forward at a frantic pace. On St. Patrick's Day, March 17, 1982, John and I again met with Boone Darden, who asked for an advance. He was in trouble with the Internal Revenue Service and owed $3,000 in back taxes. I told him I didn't think it would be a problem and gave him another $400 in "good faith." He thanked me profusely, sending Larry and Gunnar into convulsions of laughter when they played back the tape.

The following Friday Fat Andy came up to the club trailing his usual witless entourage of DeSimone, Joe Blaze, Fingers Abbandando, and Gerry Alicino. John and I, wired for sound, took them out to Bentley's in North Palm Beach for dinner. From there we all drove to Suite 100.

Despite our best intentions, it was obvious that neither John nor I would last long running a restaurant in the real world. At one point I ordered our weekend bartender, Gary, to buy the house a drink. He complained that John had just sent out three rounds on the house and that at the rate we were going we'd soon be owing our customers money.

I made a face, reminded him who was the boss, and he shrugged

and bought the house again. Everyone toasted me. Ten or fifteen minutes later, John bought the house a drink. When we met the next day in the safe house with Tony, Larry, and Gunnar, R.B. was ordered to tot up the night's receipts.

"Let's see, the place was packed for a good eight hours." R.B. was making a big thing out of it. Drawing it out. "And we brought in a grand total of thirty-two dollars."

"Wow," said Gunnar, "you guys are doing great!"

"Yeah," agreed Larry, "maybe you should hire some more staff."

Tony Amoroso had called us in to inform us that a video camera and bugs were set to be installed in Suite 100's back office the following Monday.

"Make sure Boone Darden gets his three thousand 'advance' in that back room," Tony said. "And anytime any of the wiseguys have something important to discuss, it wouldn't hurt to suggest that they do it in the privacy of your office."

No sooner said than done. Early on the morning of April 3 we videotaped Police Chief Darden taking his payoff. John was there when the chief walked in, pretending he was sweeping the floor. I had just given him instructions on how to hold the broom, straw strands down. R.B. was doing his best to impersonate a guy who knew how to polish glasses.

To activate the video in our office, there was a switch next to the light switch, side by side, as many light switches looked. As I opened the door to the office I would reach in and flick both switches up. After a while it became second nature, like hitting the "record" button on my phone tape.

Boone looked right into the lens, hidden behind a mirror, as I counted out his $3,000.

Our transaction over, I went on to bait him about Freddie's contacts in the Palm Beach County sheriff's department. We went back and forth, long enough for Boone and I to star in a double feature. I was beginning to feel sorry for the dumb bastard.

"How did I look on the screen?" I asked R.B. after Boone had gone. It was R.B.'s duty to monitor the videotaping.

"No doubt about it, Joe," he said. "If they ever make another *Godfather* movie, you'll be able to play the horse's ass."

. . .

By April, I was running out of excuses for the club members who wanted to gamble. The Eye had kept the tables dark for reasons of their own. Personally, I think they were just too lazy to get into that whole area. So whenever the cry went up for gambling I produced a deck of cards.

One night Don Ritz and a friend named Carmine settled in for some high-stakes poker with a bent-nose crew from Utica, friends of Don Ritz. The game started getting a little out of hand.

Don's friends were losing heavily, about $5,000 apiece, and paying off in IOUs. Late in the game, Carmine pulled me aside and asked a favor.

"Mention something to these guys about the money they owe us," he said. "Because if they don't pay us, the word will get around that this joint isn't kosher. We'll give you ten percent for your troubles."

Carmine was right, too. You can't go to a gambling joint and not pay up the markers you owe people. So I stopped the game, bought the table a drink, and politely informed the two Utica gents that they were down about $7,000 each. "Boys, I gotta tell you something before you go any further. Whatever money you lose here, you pay. *Capisci?* This is my joint, and if I get a complaint that this money isn't paid, you will not only still have to pay it all, you will have to answer to me. I'm putting a ten-thousand limit on you two."

The two guys looked at me. This was my first call since I'd been "demoted" by T.A.'s beating. I could tell they were deciding whether to see my bluff. Finally they agreed to the terms. The game stopped after they'd both lost ten large. They promised to get the money to Don Ritz and Carmine within a week. And they did.

It felt good to be respected again.

"Joe, if I didn't know you were working with us in this operation, I'd have believed you," R.B. told me later. "Those two guys were scared shit of what you'd do to them. Good show! But I still think you're a horse's ass."

A Walking
Dead Man

In mid-April Tommy called. "Joey, they're coming up with that."

"With what?"

"With the you-know, the money, you punchy fuck. Little Dom's people. You remember the twenty dollars?"

Obviously Dominick's sudden transfer to Kentucky had shaken Carmine "the Snake" Persico's money tree. "Yeah, good, that's good. It's also about time."

"Well, whatever, Joey, but let me tell you something, my friend," Tommy said, beginning in that patented low growl that would inevitably escalate into an ear-piercing scream. "You better be telling me the truth about this connection of yours. Everything you told the little guy about his you-know, and everything you told me about my *compare*'s you-know, it better be right. Because if I find out that you're making this all up, I'm coming down there to personally yank your tongue out of your mouth. Do you understand me?"

Tommy was screeching now at the top of his lungs. He was indeed so predictable. Although I did wonder from where this sudden distrust in my Washington prison "connection" came.

"Tip, would I lie to you?" I asked, smiling as the tape recorder rolled. "Honest, Tip. Everything I said is legit."

"It better be, Joey. Because I went to the top. Do you know what I'm talking about? Not my *compare*. Not the under. The top!"

"Yeah, I know, Paulie Castellano," I said.

"Don't mention names, you fuckin' moron! My people are going to wind up doing twenty years for all your bullshit. So anyway, fly in the day after tomorrow. You got to meet with the little guy's brother. He's got your bananas. You know who I mean?"

"Yeah, the little guy's brother Joe," I said. "Thanks a million, Tip. My connection will jump around like a jackrabbit he'll be so happy."

"He'll be happy, Joey?" Tommy said sarcastically. "That's good, he'll be happy. Because you tell that fuckin' idiot he fucks up with my *compare*'s kid, I'll make him so fuckin' happy he won't want to live anymore. Do you understand me?"

"Yeah, Tip. Yeah. Don't talk like that over the phone. It might be tapped. I'll see you in a couple of days."

I called Larry Doss and told him I had to go to New York. "Give me a couple of thousand," I added. "For the trip and expenses."

I flew into Kennedy Airport on April 16. Larry and Gunnar were stuck in Washington and couldn't make the trip, so FBI Agent Andris Kurins, who worked out of the Eye's Brooklyn office, met me in the terminal. Kurins and his partner, Joe O'Brien, were building an undercover case against Paul Castellano. Later the two resigned from the Bureau over a dispute involving their best-seller *Boss of Bosses,* detailing the private life of the Gambino Family Godfather. It was a book about a guy whose dick wouldn't work.

Andy Kurins asked me where I wanted to stay, and naturally I told him the Plaza. I had burnt a cigarette hole in the silk shirt I was wearing and Kurins bought me another for $140.

"Don't thank me," he said when I tried to. "Thank your uncle. The shirt was a casualty in the line of duty."

I met Tommy later that night at Regine's. He had arranged for two Penthouse models to join us for dinner. From Regine's I called Joe Cataldo and told him to deliver the twenty large to me at the Plaza the following morning.

"Don't disappoint me, Joe." I told Little Dom's brother. "Because I'm leaving for Washington on the afternoon shuttle to meet

my connection. If I don't show up, he'll ship the Snake out pronto. *Capisci?*"

"Yeah, I'll be there, Joe, don't worry," Little Dom's brother assured me.

"I'm not worried," I said. "Frankly, I don't give a fuck whether you show up or not. This money was supposed to be paid last November."

I had a nice time that night. Tommy picked up the tab at Regine's. Why shouldn't he? He got the money returned to him later. They paid him rent from that place. Twenty cents on each drink sold.

The agents arrived in my hotel room early the next morning to wire me up. Joey Cataldo met me for breakfast, right on time. Dominick's brother was a legitimate guy. He'd been roped into this assignment through the Colombo mob, and I'm glad that the FBI in New York never indicted him. If it had been in Florida, the feds would have thrown the book at him. The Florida prosecutors would indict a guy for stealing a banana from a drunken monkey.

Joey Cataldo was all apologies over coffee and eggs. As far as he knew, it was Dom's capo, Donny Shacks, who was to blame for his brother getting transferred to some sump heap in Kentucky. "That guy Donny shoulda moved quicker on this," he told me.

"Did you count it, Joe?" I asked.

"No, but it should all be there," he answered. "They wouldn't fuck around at this point. The Snake'll kill 'em if he's shipped out."

The bribe money came in two stacks of $10,000. I counted quickly under the table for the benefit of the Nagra. Joe Cataldo and I talked for another half-hour before he left, the agents swooped down to change tapes, and I was off to Lanza's restaurant, in midtown Manhattan, where T.A. and his capo, Joe "Piney" Armone, were waiting for me.

I opened my jacket and flashed the money to Agro, who smiled. Joe Piney said hello to me, and for saying that he got fifteen years in prison. I'll bet he'll never say hello to anyone again for as long as he lives.

Tommy bragged about how Paul Castellano himself, not to mention his underboss, Neil Dellacroce, had gone to bat for me and my alleged connection against the cheapskate Colombos. "C'mon, Joe, who is he, a senator?" Tommy wheedled.

"I can't tell you, Tip. I can't give him up to you no more than I'd give you up to him."

Tommy always had a way of turning his bullying around into some fractured test of loyalty. Today was no exception.

"Good, Joey, good. That's just what I wanted to hear," he said. "If you would have told me I would have been disappointed."

I stayed and chatted for another twenty minutes. I flew back to Florida the next morning. Andy Kurins kept the Nagra and tape. Larry Doss took the $20,000 and marked the serial numbers after he debriefed me.

Two weeks later Tommy woke me up with a phone call. He needed, he said, to see me in New York right away.

"Jesus, Tommy. For what? I was just up there."

"I know, Pip, I know. But I have to talk to you. Get up here right away."

They were onto me. Don't ask me how I knew. I just did. I was, I had been told all my adult life, now a walking dead man. I called Larry, who tried to calm me down. I told him I wouldn't go unless he and Gunnar were right behind me. He argued that there was no way Tony Amoroso would spring for the expense. Hadn't Andris Kurins watched my back just fine last trip? he asked.

It didn't matter. My mind was made up. I wasn't going without the two guys who got me into this whole mess.

The next morning I boarded a flight for New York City. First class, naturally. After takeoff I lit a cigarette, called over the flight attendant, and ordered drinks for the two gentlemen sitting together back in coach.

"They're two FBI agents," I told the stewardess, "and they're following me to New York. Tell them Joe Dogs sends them a drink and ask them to please stop following me."

I looked back a moment later and Larry was shaking his fist at me.

Andy Kurins picked us all up at the airport in a van. They wired me up right away. I was going straight to Lanza's. Then they handed me a little instrument that looked like a miniature transistor radio.

"It's called a T-four," Kurins said. "It's a precision mike that sends back voices to a machine we have here in the van. If you see a problem coming, or if you sense something's wrong, you say the words 'Home Run' and our guys will be on you like white on rice. In seconds, Joe, with guns drawn."

I stuck the T-4 into the front of my cigarette pack. I was admittedly nervous, and the thought of the cavalry being only a "Home Run" away eased my mind.

Inside Lanza's I said hello to T.A. and Piney Armone.

"Joey, how ya doing? You're ten minutes late," Tommy replied.

I hadn't sat down before Tommy decided we should go next door for ice cream. Piney went his own way, Tommy and I headed for the ice cream parlor, and I was hoping this fucking T-4 was working. From my booth I kept one eye on everyone who walked in or out. I was wondering which one of them was going to grab me and whack me. I kept the other eye on Tommy, who had moved to the back of the store and was talking to someone in the shadows.

A waitress brought over ice cream. I thanked her, but I wouldn't touch it. I was sure it was laced with knockout drops. It just sat there and melted.

Tommy came back and sat down. His friend followed. This is it, I thought. I should yell "Home Run" right now! But the guy with Tommy turned out to be an older man, and I calculated hurriedly that I could handle the both of them and still yell "Home Run" should things get out of hand.

Tommy introduced me to his friend "Frank" and asked why I hadn't eaten my ice cream. When I told him I didn't like chocolate, which was actually my favorite, he made me order something else. The closest bin was butterscotch, so I ordered that and watched

carefully as the dessert moved from spoon to bowl to table. No one had touched it. I ate it and didn't gag.

Tommy and I conversed for a while about the same-old, same-old, Gallo's kid this and Gallo's kid that. And though our taped conversation turned out to be a coffin nail in the subsequent prosecution of the Gambino *Famiglia*, there was nothing about it that couldn't have been handled pay phone to pay phone, Florida to New York. They were onto me, all right. And I wondered why I wasn't dead.

After we split up I walked downtown, took out that T-4, and yelled "Home Run" into the receiver as loud as I could without attracting attention. Nothing happened. Those motherfuckers! I stood on a corner and yelled "Home Run" for a fuckin' half-hour before they came driving around and spotted me. My cavalry turned out to be F-Troop.

"How did it go, Joey?" Larry Doss asked.

"Fine, fine, but I'm sure glad you guys taped it in there with this little T-four," I answered. I was in the mood to break some balls.

"Why?" Larry asked.

"Because I forgot to turn the Nagra on. But I don't feel so bad, seeing as how you had all this spy equipment in the van."

Everyone in the van panicked, except Larry Doss, who examined my Nagra. When he saw that I had indeed activated the machine, I sat back and laughed as the New York feds had agita.

The Homestretch

John and I invited Fat Andy and his crew up in late April. Tony Amoroso wanted to get him on videotape. We had been faithfully paying him $500 weekly—or two points—on the $25,000 he shyed out to John, and now we had a business proposition to make him.

After dinner in Palm Beach we all went to the club, and I maneuvered the capo into Suite 100's private office. The videotape began rolling when I switched on the lights.

"Andy, John wanted me to ask you if we could deduct the nine thousand that we put out for you here from the principal we owe?" I began.

"Deduct what from what?" Fat Andy replied. "What nine thousand are you talking about?"

"John's figured his expenses for the upstairs gambling come to something like twenty-seven large. The tables, the carpentry, the rugs, cards, chips, even the thirty-eight hundred we've laid out to Boone Darden. It's all written down in our books. Anyway, since he don't have a piece of the upstairs, he divided that three ways between me, you, and T.A. I talked to Tommy, and he told me to ask you to leave John's juice at two points a week, and to ask you

to deduct your nine-grand share of the expenses from the twenty-five principal he owes."

Trying to get money out of a Gambino is like trying to draw blood from a stone. Fat Andy looked like I had insulted his sainted mother.

"I can't do that," he said finally. "The shyed-out money isn't technically mine, it's Sal's, although I'm the one in charge of it. What I can do, Joe, is make sure John's juice stays at two points. And we'll give him a piece of the upstairs. He deserves it. He works hard, that John. So tell Tommy A. that's what we'll do. And let's go outside now. I need a drink."

Fat Andy headed straight for John to tell him the "good news." And R.B. stopped me before I could join them.

"How'd I look on tape?" I whispered. "Did I look like a horse's ass again?"

"No, Joe," R.B. replied. "You looked good with your suit on. You looked like a jackass this time."

By mid-May Tommy had been convicted of extortion in New York, but he was out pending appeal. He was like a maniac over the phone. He wanted money and he wanted it yesterday. He ordered me to send him the $20,000 the Colombos had forked over to keep Snake Persico imprisoned in New York. Since I couldn't tell him that the FBI had the money, I just refused him outright. I think he threatened to kill me ten times over the next week.

Meanwhile, Tony Amoroso told the undercover team that he felt the feds had gotten all that they were going to get out of Suite 100.

"We'll keep the downstairs bottle club open for a while, but to start in with gambling now is more than it's worth," he said at a meeting at our safe house. Before I could object that the wiseguys were getting suspicious, Amoroso came up with a plan to keep them from squawking.

"Tell Fat Andy and his crew that the FBI has been snooping around asking questions about Suite One Hundred," he said.

And that's just what John and I did at a meeting with Fat Andy and DeSimone at Dano's restaurant in Miami.

"Well then, don't open now, don't take the chance" was the Gambino capo's suggestion. "They'll come in there with axes and chop up the place and plant something there and then you're fucked.

"They might have gotten wind of this through that fucking Freddie," Fat Andy fumed. "That cocksucking rat bastard might have to disappear for good."

John paid Fat Andy four weeks' worth of juice, and then went into a big song and dance about how disgusted he was that our club had run into so many problems.

"I've put close to a hundred grand into that joint, I'm paying five hundred a week juice, and I still owe twenty-five thousand," John raged. "That fucking Freddie has caused me these problems. That fucking *cornuto* prick."

John's outrage was so well done that the thought occurred to me that the FBI agent's acting may have just signed Freddie Campo's death warrant. No matter. We stayed for another forty-five minutes, drinking and eating and bragging about how much money Suite 100 was going to take in once the heat was off.

"Hello?"

"Joey, wake up, you punchy fuck! It's only four o'clock in the morning." It was the lovely voice of Tommy Agro.

"Yeah, Tip. I'm awake. I was waiting for your call."

"Joey, what's your friend doing with my *compare*'s kid? When's it going to happen?"

"In about three weeks. I talked to him today. He said everything is on schedule. Tell your *compare* to tell his kid *niente*, nothing at all with his mouth. *Capisci?* Now let me make love to Lori."

"Who's Lori? Is she nice, Joey? How old is she?"

"Lori, how old are you? Wait, don't tell me, say hello to Tommy."

"Hi, Tommy," my little baby doll purred into the phone. "Oh, thank you. . . . I'm nineteen . . . blond. . . . Oh, I don't know about that. You'd have to ask Joey. . . . Hee-hee."

Lori handed me back the phone.

"You should be ashamed of yourself, Joey. She's too young for you. Send her to me. That's an order, Joey. You hear me, you punchy fuck?"

"You won't like her, Tom. She's white. I'll talk to you tomorrow."

I threw Lori another fuck and sent her home. Told her to come back when she turned twenty.

On June 3 Tony Amoroso ordered me to call Tommy and tell him Gallo's kid would be moved in two weeks. I followed orders.

"That's great, Joey," Tommy said. "I'm on my way to see my *compare* now. I'll tell him. Send me some money, you hump."

That night over drinks at the Yacht Club I asked John when he thought he'd be leaving. We both sensed that after eighteen months Operation Home Run was winding down. It saddened me a little. I was going to miss John. The guy was a true pro, a straight shooter, and he'd become my friend. I know he felt the same way about me. John had taught me something. There was something inside him that all the wiseguys and all the sluggers in the world didn't possess. I wondered if I was going soft.

"I won't be out of here until sometime next month," John said. "We still got seven or eight weeks to break each other's balls. Listen, Joey, who's that girl that's talking to those other two girls, the one that keeps pointing over here? The redhead, the pretty one?"

"She's a ball buster, John. Her name is Annabelle. I don't know her last name. She don't like me. She smashed me once in Lord's restaurant, back when it was open."

"She smacked you? Why?"

"Well, Freddie Campo told me she was rated in the top ten for giving head. So when she came over to our table to have a drink with us, I asked her if every guy's sperm tasted the same. The fuckin' sorehead slapped me and called me a filthy pig. Can you imagine that? The bitch!"

"Yeah, Joe, I see no reason why she should have smacked you for that. She should have shot you. Come on, let's get the fuck out

of here. I'm sick of these joints. Let's go to the club, get a bottle, and go home and drink it."

"Okay," I said. "Whose locker are we going to steal it out of this time?"

"What's the difference, Joey? It's all our booze anyway. R.B. just puts them in lockers in case a liquor inspector comes nosing around. Very few of our members have a bottle in their locker that we didn't give them."

We went to my apartment, talked all night, and finished the booze.

A week later John was in Chicago for a short weekend visit when Bobby DeSimone dropped by the club. He started asking when John planned on paying off Fat Andy's loan.

"I don't know, Bobby, ask him." I said. "If Andy's not worried about it, why should you be? Did Andy tell you to come in here and ask me that?"

"No, I'm asking on my own, Joey. You know we don't know much about John, and the only reason we gave him the loan was because of you."

"Wait a minute, Bobby," I said. "You're saying *we*. Is some of that loan money yours?"

"No, Joey, no. None of it's mine. I just use that term 'we.' I meant to say 'them.' "

"Well, Bobby, you do more talking and worrying than they do. So if you're not part of the 'we' or 'they,' then mind your own business. You're sticking your nose around where it don't belong."

"Yeah, well, I worry about it, Joey," Bobby said. "I hope nothing goes wrong. We—I mean they—can't find out nothing about John's background. He comes back blank."

"That's because he's not like us, Bobby. He's legitimate. I'm the only fucking flaw in his life, and I bet he'd love to get rid of me. Even Tommy trusts him. Tommy's the one who wanted John's name on the escrow account for Gallo's kid, remember? So it looks to me like you're the only one talking."

"I guess you're right, Joey." Bobby was backing off. "I like John

a lot. I just hope nothing is wrong. What do you have on him, Joey, that he's so loyal to you?"

"Good night, Bobby. I don't know who sent you here, and I don't care either. I'll let Tommy know how you're talking."

They definitely knew.

"Kill It"

"Hello?" After picking up the receiver I'd automatically punched the "record" button. The ritual had long since become second nature.

"Joey, go outside and call me right away. I don't trust your fuckin' telephone. I'm home." Tommy Agro hung up.

I reached into a desk drawer and lifted out my portable tape recorder. I opened a fresh tape, inserted new batteries, and wondered if T.A. had ever heard of this invention, the moron.

There was a pay phone just across the street from my condo apartment. It was early in the morning, and there was very little foot traffic. I suctioned the rubber nipple of the recorder onto the back of the receiver and dialed Tommy's number.

"Yeah, Tip. What's up?"

"That thing with my *compare,* kill it."

"What?"

"I said kill it, Joey! Kill it! Don't you understand English? My *compare* is sick over this whole fuckin' thing. I never should have started it. I should have minded my own business. Son of a bitch. He's scared. So kill it."

It was June 10. The Eye was scheduled to move Joe Gallo, Jr., in four days.

"Jesus Christ, Tip, I don't know if I can stop it. He's supposed to go on the fourteenth of this month. You fucking don't know

what you want, and then when it's just about to happen, you call and say 'kill it.' Tommy?"

"I know, Joey. But it ain't me. It's him. He's afraid something is going to happen, that something's wrong. Go get the money out of the escrow account right away. Bobby's calling John right now."

I told Tommy that DeSimone wouldn't find John at home. He was still in Chicago. "He called me last night and said he'll be back in maybe ten days."

"No good, Joey." There was an unfamiliar tone to T.A.'s voice, and it took me a moment to figure it out. Then it hit me. It was desperation. "No good at all. Get in touch with him and tell him to fly back today. He needs to sign out that money. I'll reimburse him for the trip. Better yet, give me his number out there."

"No, Tip, that's all right. I'll call him. He'll fly in if I tell him to. But I'm telling you up front, I don't know if I can stop the kid's move."

"Try, Joey! Try hard! The kid is going crazy in the can. He knows something is up, and he's nervous. Kill it, Joey. Kill it."

I promised Tommy I'd call him back as soon as I knew anything. When I returned to my apartment, I called Tony Amoroso and played him the recorded conversation.

"Something's wrong." I said it softly after the reel had spun out.

John flew back that day. He arrived at the club at midnight, meeting me in the office to go over the next day's scenario.

"Let's bring Bobby back here and make him count the money," John said.

That was a good enough scenario for me. The next morning at eleven Bobby met John and me at Suite 100. We were both wired, naturally. We drove to the bank together. There were no problems. The three of us signed off on the escrow account. We'd even made $181.04 in interest. I was carrying the dough.

We returned to the club, had R.B. mix us three cocktails, and went into the office. I flicked on the videotape. We talked, I handed Bobby the money, and he counted it.

"You know, Junior Abbandando don't like you," Bobby told me out of nowhere.

"Who? Fingers don't like me?"

"That's one of the reasons he don't like you," Bobby said. "All them manicure jokes about him having nine fingers. He thinks you're a smart-ass."

R.B. videotaped us for an hour before Bobby left. R.B. made his regular horse's ass joke. Today it didn't seem so funny. I couldn't help wondering exactly whose neck this noose was tightening around. Mine or theirs.

John didn't go back to Chicago. In fact he threw me a birthday party. On June 14, 1982, I was fifty-one years old and washed up in the mob. It started out at Joey's Disco, but we soon gathered a bunch of people and went bouncing around Palm Beach. The usual crowd showered me with gifts. Unfortunately, they were all the same. I got twelve cigarette lighters.

Tommy called three of the joints we were in. I told him the thing with Gallo's kid had been fixed. I'd killed it. But that didn't seem to make him happy. He kept asking when John was going to pay back Fat Andy's loan. These conversations kept up for the next week. Fat Andy himself never called. He was afraid of talking over the phone.

In early July we sent a juice payment of $3,000 to Fat Andy. We never did pay him back the principal.

Each call from Tommy was more shrill. I was enjoying seeing him sweat. I was also enjoying making him crazy. Or crazier, I should say.

"So anyway, like I said, Tom, I was driving up to the club minding my own business, and two FBI agents stop me. They tell me they want to talk to me about John, and you, and Fat Andy."

"So what did you tell them? What did you tell them?"

"I told them to fuck off, what do you think I told them? I told them that if they wanted to talk to me, they could do it in front of my lawyer."

"Yeah, that's good, that's good, Joey. What did they do? Do you have a good lawyer?"

"They didn't do nothing," I said. "They turned around and left. And yeah, sure, I got a good lawyer. I got sentenced to a month one time and he got me out in thirty days."

"Yeah, yeah, that's good, Joey. Hey, wait a minute, a month is —Stop fuckin' around, you punchy fuck. If I had my hands on your throat right now, I'd choke the shit out of you, you cocksucker! What do they want to know about this fucker John? You and your fuckin' club. I didn't earn a fuckin' quarter from this fuckin' club. You brought this fuckin' guy around for what? Tell me, you motherfucker! For what? Did you hear me, you deaf fuck?"

"Yeah, yeah, I hear you, Tom," I said as I lay back in my bed, a Scotch in one hand, a cigarette in the other, and the phone cradled in the crook of my neck. His tirade brought a smile to my face.

"Tommy, I brought John in to start the club," I told him. "So we all could earn. Don't you remember our conversation a year ago March? When you and Andy told me to start a club? It was your idea, not mine. I just found somebody with money, Tip. *Capisci?*"

"Don't blame me, you motherfucker! Why do they want to talk to him? He's liable to tell the Eye everything he knows."

"What does he know, Tip? He don't know nothin' from me. Did you ever tell him anything?" I was really trying to aggravate him now.

"Did I tell him anything? Is that what you said? Joey, when I get you, you see that tongue of yours, I'm gonna rip it out of your fuckin' mouth and shove it up your ass, you motherfucker! Did you hear me, cocksucker!"

"Yeah, you said you were going to—"

"I know what I said, you rotten bastard. You're going to kill me with all this talk, you motherfucker."

"Tip, take it easy, buddy. Relax, don't get excited. Have a drink. Take an aspirin. Be calm. I don't want you to get sick over this. Let me see John, and I'll call you back, okay? Tip, be calm, buddy. Go lay down."

"Okay, Joey." He was gasping as I hung up.

John was packing to leave when I reached him at his apartment. I invited him up for a drink. He told me he was hoping I'd say that.

We were always there for each other. Don't misunderstand me. We had arguments about what was right and what was wrong. But never anything serious. I was teaching John how to be a hood and he was teaching me how to be an honest, law-abiding citizen, which was a lost cause. He learned. I didn't.

I called Tommy back the next day.

"What did you tell John to do, Joey? And don't start with me again. I'll fuckin' come down there and kill you, you mother-fucker." Today T.A. was half calm and half his normal apoplectic self. I took that as a good sign.

"I told him like this. I said the club is a bust. I told him the Eye and guys from the State Liquor Authority have been around, look-ing to ask him a bunch of questions. I told him to go back to Chicago and leave R.B. down here to sell the place. Only thing though, I told him, he still had to pay his juice every week until Fat Andy got his loan back."

"Yeah, that sounds good, Joey," Tommy said. "What did he say? Can you trust that mick bartender? He looks like a cop. Even Andy and Bobby told me that if he wasn't a friend of John's, they would have made him for a cop all the way."

"Nah, R.B. ain't no cop," I lied. "The guy did eight years in Atlanta. What the fuck's wrong with you guys? Don't you think I check anything? *Marrone!*"

"He was in Atlanta?" Tommy seemed relieved. "Oh good, Joey. You should have told that to me and Andy."

"Well, what's the difference now anyway?" I said. "Everybody will be splitting up after the club is sold. R.B. will be going back to Chicago with John. Anyway, I didn't think I had to prove myself to anyone."

"You don't, Joey," Tommy said. "I didn't mean that. Call me if anything develops."

I reached over to turn off the recorder and found that I'd forgot-ten to put in a tape.

．　．　．

John was off the case, back home in Chicago. The club was closed. I was alone. Tony Amoroso ordered me to leave town with R.B. We skirted the north end of the Everglades and drove to Fort Myers on the west coast, where we hid out for a week. But all we did was play golf and get on each other's nerves. Even when we played golf, we rode in separate carts. The caddy masters never understood. I told them we were playing grudge matches.

I had to get back. Even in Fort Myers I was calling Tommy every day. It's like I was addicted to Agro, which I thought was a good name for a drug. He never even knew I was gone. And when I returned to my condo on Singer Island his was the first number I rang.

"Joey, Bobby's been trying to reach you," he said. "He says you never answer your phone."

"I ain't answering my phone because I think it's the feds trying to reach me," I told him. "What the fuck does that motormouth want? All he talks about is the loan John's got out. Tell him not to call me no more, that fuckin' jerk. He's going to get me pinched."

"Yeah, you're right, " Tommy said. "He does worry about Andy's money a lot. That skinny fuck. Andy's the only one there that's made money from John. That two points a week was good. I'm going to call that skinny cocksucker right now and tell him not to bother you no more."

The Last Whack—Me

The rest of July ran smoothly. Tommy checked in daily, asking about the sale of the club. I told him these things take time. In August I was called to a probation hearing regarding a two-year-old beef where I'd pled to aggravated assault. The prosecutor argued that I'd gotten off easy to begin with, and wanted to extend the probation. The judge ruled in my favor. I had been a good boy, I told him. I was off.

I fell in love again, with a girl named Francie. This was really it.

Around mid-August Tommy called with an urgent message. Carmine "the Snake" Persico had been transferred to somewhere in California, and my "connection" had to get him back to New York. I told Tommy I'd see what I could do, and then forgot about the whole thing while I spent time with Francie.

Finally, a week later, I called T.A. back and told him my "connection" was doing everything he could to get the Snake back to the city, but it might take a little time. Meanwhile, Tony Amoroso was worried for my safety. There were rumors on the street that the Colombo capo Victor "Little Vic" Orena—with whom I'd done B and Es back in the early 1970s—had a source in the Eye. And his

source, so the rumors went, had leaked word that Joe Dogs was cooperating with the feds.

Amoroso ordered Gunnar and Larry to baby-sit me back in Fort Myers while the Eye found me another apartment. I was fuming. I had a date with Francie the day they kidnapped me. But a phone conversation with Tommy, where he threatened to kill me without raising his voice—very unlike Crazy Tommy Agro—convinced me that the feds had the right idea.

The Bureau found me a little one-bedroom place in out-of-the-way Cape Coral, and just in time. On August 16 Larry and Gunnar reported that a couple of Agro's sluggers had been nosing around asking for me at my old Singer Island condo. Agro was looking again to whack me.

Cape Coral had to be the hickest town in western Florida. Five miles up the Caloosahatchee River—and that about says it all— from the "metropolis" of Fort Myers, I was stuck in a town with not one good joint to hang out in. Christ, they even passed off macaroni as pasta. I had no phone, no car, and probably no future. My first day in town I went to the bank and got five hundred quarters, and spent the next five days on the pay phone across the street talking to Francie.

I also had to call the Eye's offices every day to assure Larry I was all right. And then I got to walk around and see the sights. I think I would have rather faced Tommy A. Tony Amoroso had taken my rental car back. He had a plan to shoot the car full of holes and spread some of my blood over the front seat. These guys, I figured, watched too many television shows. Luckily, Tony's plan never got implemented.

When I called the Eye's Palm Beach headquarters on my sixth day in the ghost town, a secretary told me Larry Doss had flown to Washington, D.C., and I was to call him collect immediately. When I reached him he told me to pack four or five days' worth of clothes and fly up to meet him. It was even an ordeal getting to the airport from the spot I was in, and when Larry met me later that night in D.C. I begged him to let me go home.

"You guys aren't gonna leave me in that place?" I whined. "I hate it there. The people are all rednecks."

"Joey, stop your complaining," Larry said. "Once we get you a new car and you meet a few new fiancées you'll grow to love the place."

"Are you kidding?" I asked him. "Fiancées! I asked this broad that lives next door for a ride to the airport. Offered her twenty dollars. She said for that kind of money she'd cook me dinner, too. That's your kind of broad, Larry, not mine. You know, no teeth. You got to get me out of there."

In a Washington hotel they had a big meeting of the minds. Tony Amoroso was there, along with Larry and Gunnar. Agent Andris Kurins had flown down from New York. And a federal prosecutor from Florida, Roma Theus, had come in from Miami. He was the black guy who would prosecute the Operation Home Run case, the same black guy Larry had warned me about embarrassing with my frequent telephone references to "niggers."

They left me in the lounge while they met, which was the wrong place to leave me. Because by the time they were through, I was bombed and in no way able to figure out exactly what they wanted me to do. I had been out of circulation for over a week, and the drinks had a strong effect.

When the agents woke me for breakfast the next morning, Tony explained everything again. The general feeling within the Bureau, he said, was that Operation Home Run was over and that my cover was blown. But no one could be 100 percent sure of that, and Tony had a gut instinct that the investigation could last a little longer. After all, he said, they'd once tried to kill me and taken me back. What was that against a few whispers on the street?

The plan was for me to call Tommy, Tony said, "and act like you just talked to him yesterday. If he starts blowing his top, which we both know he will, then make up some excuse why you haven't called him for a while. Just get it straight in your mind what you're going to tell Agro. This call is important! We have to see what he says, what he sounds like, before we make a decision whether to send you to New York or not."

"Oh, you mean I'm coming back from the dead after the fatal

shoot-out in my car?" I said. "I guess it's a good thing you guys didn't do the trick with my blood. My poor daughters would be heartbroken. They don't even know I'm alive as it is."

"Are you telling me the truth?" Tony asked. "You didn't speak to your kids from Cape Coral?"

"The only person I've talked to is Francie," I said. "And I told her some big fucking lie and she believed it. You told me not to call my kids, Tony. Don't you remember?"

They hooked up the tape recorder to the phone and I dialed Tommy's number. All the agents in my room watched intently.

"Hey, Tip. How you doing, buddy? Listen, Tip, I didn't—Tip? . . . Tommy? . . . Are you there?"

"Joey! You're alive! You're fuckin' alive! I don't believe it." T.A.'s voice was surprisingly calm. I was worried. But I felt better in a moment when he started to scream.

"Where the fuck you been, you cocksucker? You know that you got everybody that knows you thinking you're dead? Did you call your daughter? She's crying. She thinks John killed you. I got a mob of guys. We were going to Chicago to look for John and whack him for whacking you, you dopey fuck."

"My God, Tip, hold your fire," I said. "Why would you think I was dead? And why would you think John would have something to do with it? He's a nice guy. But, shit, my poor daughter. I better call her. I don't know why you would think someone killed me, Tom. Everybody likes me. I'm a nice guy. Ain't I?"

"Yeah, but Joey, this ain't like you," Tommy answered. "You call all the time, then you just disappear. What happened?"

"Oh, Tommy. I'm in love with the cutest little baby doll you ever did see. She wanted to take me to Costa Rica. But I told her first I had business in Washington—that's where I'm calling you from—and that I had to wire you five thousand, and then the two of us would go off to Costa Rica together."

The thought of collecting free money would always, I knew, throw Tommy Agro off any suspicious scent. It didn't fail this time either.

"Oh, you got five thousand for me Joey?" he said.

"Yeah, Tip, but wait, let me finish what I'm saying here. So she's

got her tongue in my ear, telling me to forget about business for a few days, and, well, you know how it is, Tommy. I ended up in Costa Rica. You would have done the same thing. So that's how I got lost."

I smiled and looked up at the admiring agents. Tony flashed me the thumbs-up sign.

"No, Joey, I wouldn't have done the same thing," Tommy said. "We were all set to head for Chicago and whack a few people over there. My *compare* even gave me the okay. Listen, Pip, don't ever do this again. *Capisci?* Now, the little guy's main guy, Mr. *Serpente,* is still out there on the West Coast. What's going on with that thing?"

"That's what I'm doing in Washington," I told Tommy A. "I'll find out this afternoon, sometime before two. Here, take my number and give me a call after that. I'll know everything by then."

Tommy took the number and hung up. The agents took the tape and left. They ordered me to stay put. I'd find out soon what to tell Tommy when he called back.

While they were gone I called my daughter Sheryl, who told me that Bobby DeSimone had been calling her every day and telling her John had had me killed.

"He said they were flying to Chicago to kill John for revenge," Sheryl said. "Gee, Daddy, you almost got that nice guy killed. And he's the best friend you ever had."

I wished then I could tell my daughter that I was working with the FBI, but I just couldn't risk it.

Tommy called right on the dot, at 2:05 P.M.

"Okay, Tom, he could do it," I began. "It'll happen a week from tomorrow. So you can go to the guys and tell them I did it. But you have to call me back and tell me where they want me to ship him."

"Joey, send him to where the little guy was," Tommy said, meaning the Allenwood federal facility in Pennsylvania. "Don't send him back to New York."

"Okay, Allenwood it is," I said. "But just to be sure, call me back at nine tonight and let me know for certain that's what they want."

Tommy indeed called back at nine and complimented me on my thoroughness. "You were right, Joey. Nobody's positively sure where he wants to go. Give me a day on this before we decide."

"Well, Tip, I guess I have no choice. But get somebody to make a decision fast. I want to get back to my girl. It's love this time, Tom. I think I want to get married."

"Good, Joey, I'm glad to hear that. I can't wait to meet her. When you come in, bring her with you."

Exactly twenty-four hours later, at 9 P.M. on August 26, 1982, Tommy Agro called my Washington hotel room. He and the Colombo capo Donny Shacks were partying at the Skyway Lounge. The Snake, they informed me, had decided on Allenwood.

"Joey, these guys thank you from the bottom of their heart," T.A. said. "There ain't a fuckin' thing you can't have in the city. Believe, Joey. They are so happy. Their boss is coming back home!"

Tony had instructed me to try to get some kind of commitment from T.A. about becoming a full-fledged wiseguy. That's why Amoroso was a fed. Never say die, and all that shit. Personally, I thought the idea was ludicrous. These guys planned on whacking me, not handing me a button. The feds may have been blind to the leak in their outfit, but I knew otherwise. Or at least I smelled a rat. I had lived too long with the mob—and thought like them and fought like them and schemed like them—not to realize when my number was up, even if Tony and the other agents thought different. Nonetheless, with everybody so full of gratitude, I figured now was the time to score some brownie points with the people who would soon be protecting me. It couldn't hurt, when they listened to the tape, to see that I was still following orders.

But first I wanted to find out why Tommy had sent his sluggers nosing around my old apartment. I had to give him credit, he thought quick on his feet. He explained that they'd merely been trying to find out why I disappeared, looking for "clues" that John had had me whacked. I pretended to buy it and pressed him about my button.

"Yeah, that's good, Tip. But what about me and this *Serpente*

thing? What about my thing? What do I have to do to get it? Kill a dozen guys? Then I can get it when I'm going to the chair? Is that the way this is gonna work?"

"Joey, Joey, not over the phone," T.A. said. "Don't worry. Right now there's nobody bigger than you. There's no one more respected than you. So don't worry, and don't ask. *Capisci?*"

"Yeah, I'm not asking for nothing financially."

"I know exactly what you're talking about," Tommy said. "Patience, Joey. Patience."

Tony listened to the tape and liked it. A decision had been made. John and I were to be reunited in New York to work undercover. That was fine by me. I wasn't afraid of anything as long as I knew John was watching my back. But first we'd fly back to Florida to give John a chance to make his travel arrangements and then detour through Chicago and say goodbye to his family.

But then our team got stung. Gunnar Askeland quit the FBI. One of his sources told him there was a leak on the streets about Operation Home Run. Gunnar reported it to his supervisor, and when his supervisor ordered him to give up his source's name, Gunnar refused. They lost a good agent. I lost more confidence. Apparently I wasn't alone.

The plan, Tony told me, was on hold. John and I would eventually get to New York, but for now, he said, "Let's move more cautiously."

"Why don't you feel out Tommy," Tony suggested. "See what he thinks about you moving back."

On August 30 I called T.A. from my room at the Hyatt Hotel in West Palm Beach. After guaranteeing him that the Snake was set to be moved within the week, I popped the big question.

"Listen, Tip, I been thinking about moving back to New York. I want to come there with my girlfriend and start a chemical business. She knows all about the business. What do you think?"

"Sure, Joey," he said, a little too eagerly. "I'll be glad to have you here. What kind of business is chemicals? I never heard of that."

"Restaurants use them in the kitchen," I told him. "You know, soap and polish and all that shit. Do you think you could help us get into a couple of joints and hotels?"

"Are you kidding? I'll put you in a hundred places the first week. Will I help you, Joey! You talk like an asshole. Joey, right now you're the biggest guy in New York. You have so much prestige that I don't even have as much as you. You're a five-star general. I'm only a three-star."

Soon we would see. This soldier was moving out.

Still Watching My Back

I drove to Cape Coral the next day to pack up my clothes. When I returned, I called Francie and told her about our new chemical business. "You'll have all the big hotels and restaurants you want," I said. "You'll have a hundred people working for you."

She became all excited and asked how I planned to get all these places and customers. I told her the mayor of New York was a friend of mine. She asked me the mayor's name. I was at a loss for words.

"Don't you know?" I asked her.

"No."

"His name's Carlo Gambino," I said.

She didn't blink an eye.

On September 14 Francie and I flew to New York. I had plans to meet Tommy at the Skyway Lounge in Queens. The FBI didn't like me taking Francie along. In fact they hated it. They thought there might be trouble. But Tommy insisted on meeting her.

After landing, Francie and I checked into the Holiday Inn in Manhattan. Agents Larry Doss and Andris Kurins checked in down

the hall. While Francie was showering I made an excuse to go out, and I walked to their room to get wired. We took a cab to the Skyway that night, and as we exited the taxi I noticed the place was surrounded by agents. Off in a shadowed corner of the parking lot I even saw Kurins and Doss.

The lounge was busy. Agro was sitting at a table with Paulie Principe. Fat Andy was at another table with Sal Reale, Ronnie "Stone" Pearlman, and two or three others from his crew. Not a good sign. The Ravenite Social Club in Manhattan was Fat Andy's usual New York hangout. The Skyway had about seventy-five people in it. Forty of them had to be feds.

After introductions, we sat down and ordered a drink. Tommy was calm, although talking a mile a minute. There was a guy at the table next to us that had to be a fed. No one wore white socks and wingtip shoes to the Skyway Lounge. At one point Francie had to go to the ladies' room. I walked her to the door and three guys walked up to me and asked if I was "Bob Jackson," their old master sergeant from basic training.

If I wasn't so scared I would have laughed out loud.

I walked to the bar for a drink, and the bartender complained that, considering the crowd, he'd never been stiffed so much in his life.

"These fuckin' people aren't tipping tonight," he complained. "That's when I know the joint is crawling with cops."

Christ, I thought, even the bartender knows!

Fat Andy hadn't received his juice from John for close to nine weeks. He was owed $4,500. That definitely was a problem that needed to be solved. If it hadn't been for me taking Francie along, there was no way all those agents would have been present. To this day I feel I was supposed to be killed that night.

When I went to the men's room an hour later, two guys followed me in to ask if I was "Bob Jackson." I told them no and asked how many guys they had covering the joint. "Too many," one of them said.

Francie and I were getting ready to leave when I stopped by Fat Andy's table to tell him John would be back in Florida next week. "Not only to make good on his back juice payments but to settle

up on the principal." I knew he didn't believe me when he patted my stomach, just missing the Nagra stuffed into my pants.

"Gettin' a little fat there, eh, Joey," he said. It wasn't a question.

We left and I knew they were onto me. If all those agents hadn't been there I would have been history. I found out later they even thought Francie was a fed.

Francie and I went into Manhattan for the night and walked through Central Park the next afternoon. It would turn out to be the last time I'd ever walk through my home town. Larry, as disheartened as I was, mentioned that we could still fall back on the blood and bullet-riddled car trick. I declined. I couldn't cause that kind of grief to my family.

When I got back to Florida, Tony closed down the investigation. I was being careful and cautious, taking no calls from New York. Larry moved me out of the Hyatt and holed me up among the hicks of Cape Coral. If it wasn't for Francie's Friday night visits—against all FBI rules—I would have blown my fucking head off.

My agenda was set for the rest of my life. I'd spend the next decade testifying against my old friends, co-workers, and *compares*. Then I could look forward to a change of identity and growing old with grace (I hoped) under the aegis of the Federal Witness Protection Program.

But there was something inside me that still pulled me back to my old way of life. Call it the residue of a bad seed or the love of the easy life. Attribute it to the memories of the thrill I felt being a wiseguy, the power that surged around a mobster like some kind of electrical field. It was this natural force that led me to pick up the phone and dial Tommy Agro's number one last time.

"Tip," I began softly. "You shouldn't have never beaten me. You shouldn't have never fucked me all up."

"What's done is done, Joey. Eh, Joey, did you get followed here the other night? There were agents all over the fucking place." Tommy was speaking calm and slow. I felt like he was only making conversation. Like he already knew the answer. Like he was playing my game back with me, just for old times' sake.

"What do you mean?" I felt weak.

"What do *you* mean what do *I* mean?" T.A. laughed. "I'm telling

you, there were agents all over the fucking place. You brought them down with you. They were even spotted going into my fucking car."

"There was nobody following me," I said halfheartedly, and for a moment I thought he'd hung up.

Then T. A. said slowly and softly, without a lick of heat, "Hey, Joey, let me tell you something here and now. If you're working with those fuckers I'll get you. And if I don't get you, my *Famiglia* will. You better watch your back for the rest of your fucking life, my friend. Because I'll bury you, Pip. I won't miss you next time. And I'll take this promise to the fuckin' grave."

For once Tommy Agro was as good as his word. Based almost solely on my testimony, Tommy Agro was convicted in 1986 on charges of loan-sharking, extortion, and attempted murder. He was sentenced to fifteen years to life, but the verdict was overturned on a technicality. Rather than repeat the ordeal of trial, T.A. pled out and was given twenty years in the Florida State Penitentiary. In 1987 he was granted a medical parole in order to die at home, which he did that June, of brain cancer. I'm still watching my back.

Postscript

I testified in twelve trials over the next ten years, putting away just about everybody I ever worked with. I got my revenge, all right. Some of it sweet, some of it bitter. Thirteen days on the witness stand during the Agro trial was my personal record. But I came close to that with Joe N. Gallo, spending eleven long days pointing my finger at the seventy-four-year-old *consigliere* who dozed through much of his trial—though not my testimony—and who was sentenced to ten years in December of 1987, almost two years to the day that his former boss Paul "Big Paulie" Castellano got whacked. But I felt real bad for Little Dom Cataldo, who got thirty-five years, largely based on what I had to say, and then ended up dying in prison.

And though I became more or less a professional prosecution witness, shuttling between Florida and New York, playing a very serious game, it is the absurd little moments I remember the best. How Tommy A., for instance, who'd been a fugitive for almost a year in Canada, showed up in court in 1986 in a wheelchair, the typical Mafia "sympathy wagon." And how the judge kept yelling at me for smiling at him throughout the whole trial.

Or the way Fat Andy Ruggiano, who had also dodged his indictment and was hiding out with a Miami motorcycle gang, tried to blend in with his new pals by growing a scruffy beard and putting on even more tonnage—so much so that the feds had to handcuff

him in front, as opposed to the traditional rear position, because his arms wouldn't fold backward.

Or Skinny Bobby DeSimone's reaction when agents showed up at his front door with warrants containing my name. "That fuckin' Joey," he raged. "I knew it. I knew it. I told Tommy that it was too fishy that Joey came up with all that money right after the beatin'. I told him it didn't look right. I bet you that John Marino was in on it, too."

The agents nodded, and explained that "John Marino" was actually Agent Jack Bonino.

"And R.B.?" DeSimone asked.

The agents nodded again.

"That fuckin' Joey," DeSimone muttered again. "I'm gonna get a million years in the can for this. I told Tommy we should have killed the motherfucker."

I put them all behind bars. T.A., Skinny Bobby, Little Dom, and Joe N. Gallo. Andrew "Fat Andy" Ruggiano and Ronnie "Stone" Pearlman. Carmine "the Snake" Persico and Dominic "Donny Shacks" Montemarano. Chief Boone Darden and Frank "Fingers" Abbandando. Gerry Alicino, the gentlemanly Joe "Piney" Armone and Sal "the Shylock" Reale.

The jury acquitted Paulie Principe. And Frank Russo, who along with Principe had used my head for batting practice, was indicted but never arrested. The feds eventually dismissed the indictment against him. Out of all the characters I ran with, Freddie Campo came out ahead in that he was never charged in connection with any of our schemes. As far as I know, he is still walking around South Florida. I hear that Freddie's pal Robbie—who told me he put three or four in Stanley Gerstenfeld's head and one in his heart to stop the bleeding—is also still hanging out in South Florida. Apparently, the authorities never went after him—maybe it was just a good story. Who knows?

After we shut down Operation Home Run, Francie and her lovely daughter Danielle came to live with me in Cape Coral. That lasted about a year, or until she got wind of the full scope of the work I'd been doing for the Eye. Who could blame her for being

scared? But to this day I still think about her and still love her. If I knew where she was right now, I'd go running after her.

During the last frenzied days of the undercover operation I received a "Dear John" letter from Nena. How she could have the audacity to do something like that to such a nice, loving, monogamous person such as myself is beyond me. I wish her all the happiness, health, and wealth in the world. She was a fantastic lady.

Case Agent Larry Doss, who received some kind of an in-house FBI award for all his hard labor on Operation Home Run, swore to me that he'd never accept another organized crime assignment again. In fact he said he was so sick of Eye-talians, that he'd stopped eating pizza. Larry's wife divorced him, and he said it was because of the operation. I get blamed for everything.

Agent Gunnar Askeland rejoined the Bureau in 1984, and the feeling here is that the government is fortunate that Gunnar came back. He returned at the time of Skinny Bobby's racketeering trial, and we both got a kick out of the motormouth's courtroom attire. A neck brace. The jury may have gotten a kick out of it, too. But they didn't buy it. After a short stint in the Seattle office, Gunnar was transferred back to West Palm Beach.

The supervising agent of Operation Home Run, Anthony "Tony" Amoroso, retired shortly afterward at the age of fifty. I believe he was annoyed because Judge William Webster gave him the shaft. Tony had applied for the position of FBI legal attaché in Rome and walked around all day listening to Italian tapes and practicing the language. He was led to believe that the post was his up until the last minute, when a non-Italian guy got the job. Tony's wife divorced him, also because of the long investigation. *Marrone,* that's two they're blaming on me.

Agent Richard "R.B." McKeen was transferred from the West Palm Beach office down the road to Fort Lauderdale, where he vowed to memorize every word of the song "Ninety-nine Bottles of Beer on the Wall." The last time I saw him he was dancing to "The Beer Barrel Polka." R.B. didn't get a divorce. He was never married, to my knowledge.

After more than a year of dangerous undercover work, Agent

John "Jack" Bonino returned to his family in Chicago. He had infiltrated the mob using intelligence, charisma, and courage, befriending both a capo as well as a strong, if not maniacal, soldier in the Gambino Crime Family, which had embraced him as one of their own. The $25,000 juice loan he received from Fat Andy was the largest ever received by an undercover operative from La Cosa Nostra.

John received an award from FBI headquarters that in no way truly reflected the danger in which he had placed himself. He did an outstanding job and made me feel safe and secure throughout our investigation. John continues to specialize in organized crime out of the Chicago area. Sarah Bonino, the toughest of all wives, did not divorce her husband.

I have been asked by several people, mostly feds, if, knowing what I know now, I'd ever do it again. It's a tough question. Some nights, after sitting in that witness stand putting my old pals away, I went back to my room and cried. It was never my intention to break everybody, to fuck everything up.

I got into the whole thing for one reason. I wanted revenge on Tommy Agro. Burned with it. Later, when I found out all the circumstances surrounding the beating I got, I wanted Gallo, too. So the answer to that question—Would I do it all over again?—is no. Under the same set of circumstances, I wouldn't have worked with the feds, I wouldn't have turned on all my friends.

I would have just grabbed a gun, killed that fuckin' T.A. myself, and been done with it.

You live and learn. *Capisci?*

Acknowledgments

I never thought I'd write a book, much less a list of acknowledgments. I mean, fuhgedaboudit. Where do you start? There are people in life you can't live without. How do you tell them? I guess you just do. So, first of all, I'd like to thank Bunny and my four children for respecting me, for sticking by me, and for giving me the support and encouragement that allowed me to come through—in one piece —the ordeals of the past ten years.

My thanks and appreciation also go out to Special Agent John Bonino of the Federal Bureau of Investigation. Working undercover, hand in hand with someone in difficult and dangerous situations, allows you take the measure of a man. I know of no one who measured up as John did during Operation "Home Run." Here I must also mention Robin Marie Stienbach Bonino, recently killed in an automobile accident. I know you're in heaven, Robin, and my prayers go out to you and your parents, John and Sarah.

I'd also like to thank my best female friend, Loretta, for helping me with the typing of the first ten chapters of this book. Loretta's husband Bob deserves my gratitude for his understanding and friendship. (For that, Bob, I won't accept any payment for the fishing tackle and angling secrets I taught you in Florida.)

My sincerest thanks also goes out to two dear friends, Ruggero Miti and Nicoletta Jacabacci, of Rome, Italy's RAI television network. Their technical assistance and support was invaluable.

I would be remiss without making mention of the several lovely ladies who nourished me with their kindness and friendship during my wild ride through the Mafia and beyond. Jewel Mason, Janet Scavone, Libby Proctor, Stephanie Lamy, Linda Carter, Cindra Ridge, and Tina Windsor, I thank you. And Bridgid from Naples, I'll never forget you.

I would like to extend my devoted thanks to Michael Korda of Simon & Schuster, who gave me the opportunity to get started on a new life and (I hope) career. God bless you, Michael. Also, thanks to Nick Pileggi for jumpstarting that career by introducing me to Sterling Lord and his wonderful staff, especially Jody Lee and Jacob Hoye. All three showed extreme patience in the face of my ignorance of the literary world.

Thanks also to Bob Drury and Carolyn Beauchamp for their friendship, knowledge, and expertise. (Without Drury, this book would have contained a lot more four-letter words.)

Much thought and gratitude goes to the following FBI agents who helped me with dates, esoteric information, and plain old facts: Supervising Agent Anthony "Tony" Amoroso, Case Agent Larry Doss and Assistant Case Agent Gunnar Askeland of Operation "Home Run"; Agents Al Sadowski, Richard "Dickie" Gentelcore, Dennis "Tricks" Tierney and Don Dowd of the FBI's Florida office; Bruce Mouw, Supervising Agent of Operation "Castaway" in Brooklyn, and Agents Kenny Brown, Charlie Beaudion, Richard Tofani and Ralph "Ralphie" Hilborn, who all worked under the supervision of Agent Christopher Mattiace who deserves special thanks during the Manhattan phase of Operation "Starquest." And, of course, I thank the prosecutors who put the bad guys away, including Roma Theus, Aaron Marcu, Peter Lieb, Laura Ward and Peter Outerbridge.